2ND EDITION

Cultural Anthropology

UNDERSTANDING OURSELVES & OTHERS

Richley H. Crapo received his Ph.D., with an emphasis in cultural and linguistic anthropology, from the University of Utah in 1970. He is currently a professor of anthropology at Utah State University where he has taught the introductory course for over 19 years. **Cultural Anthropology: Understanding Ourselves and Others, 2nd Edition**, was conceived and developed in his classroom. Beginning as handouts that his students used as supplements, it grew over a period of ten years into an integrated text that has been rewritten, class-tested, reviewed and revised into its present form—a coherent, comprehensive and interesting introduction to anthropological understanding of all cultures, including our own.

To Sharon:
With love and gratitude.

Cover photo of Masai children of Kenya, East Africa
by Marc and Evelyn Bernheim—Woodfin Camp

2ND EDITION

Cultural
Anthropology

UNDERSTANDING OURSELVES & OTHERS

Richley H. Crapo

Utah State University

DPG

The Dushkin Publishing Group, Inc.

Credits & Acknowledgments

Chapter 1 2 United Nations photo by John Isaac; 5 Napoleon Chagnon; 6 Tom McHugh—Photo Researchers; 16 The Granger Collection; The Bettmann Archive, Inc.; 17 The Bettmann Archive, Inc.; The Bettmann Archive, Inc.; The Bettmann Archive, Inc.

Chapter 2 22 American Museum of Natural History; 29 American Museum of Natural History; 33 The Peabody Museum of Salem; 36 Courtesy French Cultural Services; 41 Win McNamee—Sipa Press; 42 Kal Muller—Woodfin Camp

Chapter 3 48 United Nations photo; 54 Lee—Anthro Photo; 57 Dr. F. Rainey—American Museum of Natural History; 60 United Nations photo; 61 © Marc & Evelyne Bernheim—Woodfin Camp; 63 United Nations photo by Ida Pickerell; 64 United Nations photo; 66 Courtesy Sperry—New Holland

Chapter 4 68 United Nations photo by Milton Grant; 71 Owen Franken—Stock, Boston; 75 Irven De Vore—Anthro Photo; 76 Mike Mazzaschi—Stock, Boston; 77 Blair Seitz—Photo Researchers; 79 Oriental Institute, University of Chicago; 80 Leopold Pospisil; United Nations photo by Milton Grant; 82 United Nations photo; 83 United Nations photo by Nagata; 85 Stock, Boston

Chapter 5 88 United Nations photo by J. K. Isaac; 90 UPI/Bettmann; 92 Katz—Anthro Photo; 94 The Bettmann Archive; 95 United Nations photo; 97 Dr. J. F. E. Bloss—Anthro Photo; 99 American Museum of Natural History; 101 Leopold Pospisil; 105 UPI/Bettmann

Chapter 6 110 United Nations photo; 114 Courtesy Embassy of Thailand; 116 United Nations photo; 117 UPI/Bettmann; 118 United Nations photo; 124 Shostak—Anthro Photo; 126 Katrina Thomas—Photo Researchers; 128 George Rodger—Magnum Photos; 130 United Nations photo by John Isaac; 133 Etter—Anthro Photo

Chapter 7 136 Peter Menzel—Photo Researchers; 142 Tom Hollyman—Photo Researchers; 145 © Mark Antman—The Image Works, Inc.

Chapter 8 152 Jim Harrison—Stock, Boston; 155 Robert A. Isaacs—Photo Researchers; 158 United Nations photo by John Isaac; 159 Sid Schuler—Anthro Photo; 166 © Don Steffen—Photo Researchers; 170 Leopold Pospisil; 173 Katz—Anthro Photo

Chapter 9 178 United Nations photo by John Isaac; 181 George Holton—Photo Researchers; 187 American Museum of Natural History; 189 Rene Burri—Magnum; Keystone Press Agency, Inc.; 192 H. Terrace—Anthro Photo; 194 The Gorilla Foundation

Chapter 10 208 Brian Spykerman; 210 James Holland—Black Star; 214 American Museum of Natural History; Brian Spykerman; 218 Kit Porter; 221 Brian Spykerman; 224 Courtesy Australian News and Information Bureau; 225 American Museum of Natural History; 227 American Museum of Natural History

Chapter 11 239 Marc & Evelyne Bernheim—Woodfin Camp; 240 Konner—Anthro Photo; 242 American Philosophical Association; Smithsonian Institution; 244 Courtesy Embassy of Indonesia; 248 Photo Researchers; 249 UPI/Bettmann; 253 Napoleon Chagnon; 254 M. Shostak—Anthro Photo; M. R. Harrington—Museum of the American Indian; 256 United Nations photo; 261 Grunnitus—Monkmeyer

Chapter 12 272 Napoleon Chagnon; 274 United Nations photo by Margot Granitsas; 278 American Museum of Natural History; Marc & Evelyne Bernheim—Woodfin Camp; Robert Azzi—Woodfin Camp; 279 United Nations photo by Y. Levy; 282 DeCost Smith—Museum of the American Indian, Heye Foundation; 288 Leonard Freed—Magnum; 291 American Museum of Natural History; 297 United Nations photo

Chapter 13 300 United Nations photo by Antoinette Jongen; 303 The Granger Collection; 309 United Nations photo; 310 United Nations photo by Ida Pickerell; 311 United Nations photo by Shaw McCutcheon; 314 United Nations photo by Claudio Edinger

Chapter 14 321 United Nations photos; Pamela Carley Petersen; 323 Arthur Tress—Photo Researchers; 331 UPI/Bettmann; 334 UPI/Bettmann; 338 Cheryl Kinne—DPG; 342 United Nations photo by Doranne Jackobson; 345 George Hunter—Canadian Government Film and Video Centre; Shirley Zeiberg—Photo Researchers; 347 Courtesy New York Stock Exchange; 348 Courtesy Florida Division of Tourism; 349 Courtesy Minnesota Office of Tourism; 350 Ulrike Welsch—Photo Researchers

2ND EDITION

Cultural Anthropology

UNDERSTANDING OURSELVES & OTHERS

Printed in the United States of America
Library of Congress Catalog Card Number: 86-73095

International Standard Book Number (ISBN) 0-87967-813-5

First Printing

The Dushkin Publishing Group, Inc., Sluice Dock, Guilford, Connecticut 06437

Preface

Anthropology, like its study, humankind, is a tremendously diverse subject. This diversity at once creates its richness and excitement as well as providing a challenge for anthropologists to present to students a coherent and meaningful introduction. While no text is likely to fulfill the hopes of all teachers, I believe *Cultural Anthropology: Understanding Ourselves and Others*, 2nd Edition, will provide the basic insights into the field which a thoughtful student ought to have as part of a liberal education. These include not only facts and theories but most importantly the anthropological attitude of a commitment to understanding and appreciating cultural diversity.

Content and Organization *Cultural Anthropology: Understanding Ourselves and Others*, 2nd Edition, is an integrated text. I have tried to avoid fragmentation by building systematically from one concept to the next. In the process, I cover the wide range of interests which comprise the field of anthropology.

To accommodate the needs of the majority of instructors in introductory cultural anthropology courses, the chapters of this second edition now focus exclusively on the various aspects of culture. Chapters on biological anthropology and archaeology have been dropped, and new chapters have been added in response to suggestions from users and reviewers of the first edition. The new chapters provide expanded coverage of subsistence, economics, politics, kinship, and marriage and the family. Other chapters have also been substantially rewritten and expanded to accommodate the thoughtful suggestions of these reviewers and those who used the first edition in the classroom.

Part I, The Science of Culture The book begins in chapter 1 with a succinct discussion of the often confusing subject of anthropology itself: the breadth of its content, its history and contemporary forms, its methods, and its ethics. Chapter 2 introduces the concept of culture, including discussions of both ideology

and technology, as well as issues of how different cultures respond to and influence each other.

Part II, Survival and Adaptation Building on these basics, the next three chapters discuss aspects of survival and adaptation to the human physical and social environments. In this section, the infrastructural components of human social life are discussed. Chapter 3 discusses the physical environments in which human societies are found, the concept of adaptation, and how human societies organize their subsistence customs in various environments. Chapter 4 builds upon the concept of subsistence systems and discusses the economic customs of the world's societies. Chapter 5 considers how humans adapt to the practical problems of social life with the various mechanisms that form the political system of each society.

Part III, Society and Social Life The chapters in this section discuss the ways in which social life is elaborated beyond the basic needs of mere coping and survival, by the presence of meaningful systems of relationships between individuals. Chapter 6 outlines the concept of social organization, with a special focus on how the statuses of individuals within societies change as they pass through life. Chapter 7 discusses the human notion of descent and how it is elaborated into various kinship systems. Chapter 8 discusses the customs and varieties of marriage that play a role in every descent and kinship system and surveys the family forms that arise from these marriage customs.

Part IV, Ideology and Symbolism The fourth section of the text moves to the superstructure of culture, the realm of symbolism, communication, and religion, and concludes with a discussion of how the human individual is incorporated into the cultural realm. Chapter 9 begins with a consideration of human learning, the human capacity for endowing things with meaning, and the unique role of language as a system of meaningful symbols with which humans communicate and create their cultural order. Chapter 10 takes an in-depth look at religion, the most abstract and creatively varied use of the human symbolic ability. This chapter not only demonstrates the varieties of human religious ideology, but also points out the ways in which both religious thought and social organization are structured in adaptive ways to the circumstances in which people live. Chapter 11 focuses on the individual's relationship to culture and discusses the cultural shaping of personality, altered states of consciousness and psychological disorders.

Part V, Cultural Change and Diversity The final three chapters approach culture from an evolutionary perspective and emphasize the ways in which cultures change. Chapter 12 examines the process of evolution from small-scale bands to large-scale states. Chapter 13 discusses the contemporary mixture of vanishing nonstate societies, peasant cultures, developing countries, and industrialized societies that characterize the world today. The book ends with a special chapter about the United States, interpreting its technological, economic, social, political, family, and ideological characteristics from the unique point of view that cultural anthropology has to offer.

I have attempted to write clearly and logically, and the vocabulary and the level of writing that I have adopted are appropriate for the serious student. I have found that when one addresses one's students with respect and dignifies them with the assumption that they possess more than a modicum of intelligence, it pays off. Students, like anyone else, live up to or down to one's expectations of them. I believe that after a decade in which the conventional wisdom has been that basic texts should be written down to their audiences, the trend is now to recognize this as a tragic error for our educational system. The classroom is a place of education and the purpose of teachers and students and their texts should be the perpetration of wisdom and intellectual skills.

Learning Aids A variety of learning aids has been systematically incorporated into the text.

Each chapter begins with an *outline* to aid students in recognizing the main concepts and in understanding how they will be organized. To facilitate students' learning of the basic concepts of each chapter, all *terms* are defined in context and *underlined* for easy recognition. Each chapter ends with a list of these terms in the order in which they occur, with page numbers indicating where they are defined. These technical terms are also defined in a *glossary* at the end of the book. Since learning the subject matter of a new field also involves acquiring a new vocabulary, students should be encouraged to use these glossaries as a valuable learning review. By testing their knowledge of the meaning of each term, they can readily determine which parts of each chapter need further study in preparation for tests.

Major concepts are often illustrated by *extended narrative examples* integrated with the text. These provide concrete, down-to-earth examples of the material under discussion. For instance, in chapters that concern cultural anthropology, the extended narratives introduce students to appropriate aspects of cultures using an ethnographic record, from the practical reasons for India's sacred cows to attitudes toward conformity in Germany, Japan, and the United States. A number of these narratives describe aspects of Native American cultures, reflecting current interest in these peoples and my own fieldwork among the Shoshoni. These narrative examples are marked with a bullet (•) in the table of contents and are identified within the text by vertical rules.

All cultures to which students are introduced that might be unfamiliar are located on a map at the beginning of the book and are included in the index. All references cited within the body of the text have been compiled into a single bibliography placed immediately before the index. For teachers using the text, I have prepared an instructor's resource guide: *Teaching and Testing from Cultural Anthropology: Understanding Ourselves and Others*, 2nd Edition.

Acknowledgments I deeply appreciate the help of many people who contributed their knowledge, skill, and time in ways that generally enhanced the quality of this book: Carol J. Loveland, who repeatedly shared her expertise in physical anthropology; Edna H. Berry, who was an invaluable source of demographic data; and Gordon Keller, Pamela J. Riley, Brian Spykerman, Mark Lusk, Deborah Marcus, and John Noxon for the original photographic materials that they made available.

I am also indebted to those who gave constructive criticism and expert advice as reviewers of this book and its revision:

Elvio Angeloni, Pasadena City College;
Jeffery A. Behm, University of Wisconsin;
Purnima M. Bhatt, Hood College;
William B. Brunton, North Dakota State
  University;
Matthew Cooper, McMaster University;
John Cottier, Auburn University;
Mary S. de Grys, Winthrop College;
James Eder, Arizona State University;
Mark S. Fleisher, Washington State
  University;
Robert R. Gradie, University of Connecticut;
Daniel A. Grossman, Cuyahoga Community
  College;
Robert C. Harman, California State
  University, Long Beach;
Donald K. Pollack, SUNY at Buffalo, NY;
Robert A. Randall, University of Houston;
Daniel Schwartz, Pima Community College;
James M. Sebring, University of New
  Mexico;

Jay Sokolovsky, University of Maryland,
  Baltimore;
Dorice M. Tentchoff, Oregon State
  University;
Alaka Wali, University of Maryland;
Linda M. Whiteford, University of South
  Florida;
Scott Whiteford, Michigan State University;
Newell Wright, Valdosta State College.

Special thanks are also due to John Holland, Managing Editor of The Dushkin Publishing Group, for his careful attention to detail and for the high level of competence that he expected of those who worked on this text; to Mary Pat Fisher for her exceptional skill as a developmental editor for the first edition, to M. Marcuss Oslander who skillfully edited the second edition and diplomatically guided me in those difficult decisions about what to revise, to Pamela Carley Petersen for finding the right pictures, and to Bill Ferneau for bringing the publisher and myself together. I wish also to thank Sharon Cannon-Crapo for her patient support of my writing efforts and for her useful criticisms of the manuscript as it evolved.

Richley H. Crapo

Contents in Brief

Table of Contents

Note: Bullet • placed in front of an item indicates an extended narrative example.

11 Culture, Personality and Psychological Process, 239

PART V

Cultural Change and Diversity, 270

12 The Process of Cultural Evolution, 273

This map shows the approximate location of the cultures introduced in this book. You will find page references to these cultures in the index.

Avam Samoyed

Yakut

Chuckchee

Tungus

Ancient Greeks

Ainu

Ancient Hebrews

Ancient Eshnunnans
Iranians

Nepalese

Rwala Sumerians

Lepcha

Nuer

Parsis

Taiwanese

Nayar
Toda

Ifugao

Tsembaga
Etoro

tande

Andamanese

Hanunoo

Sebei   Nandi

Semai

Subanun

Arapesh
Tschambuli
Mundugumor

Mbuti
si Hutu   Kikuyu

Semang

Yapese

Gusii   Wa-Taita

Iatmul

Gururumba

Maasai   Wa-Arusha

Dani

Trobrianders

Nyakyusa

Alorese

Dobuans

Javanese

Keraki

Kung San

Balinese

Marind-anim

Murray Islanders

Big Namba   Samoans

Tanala

Yir Yiront

Tully River People

Hottentot

Lau Fijians

Jigalong People

Maori

Tasmanians

PART I

The Science

Anthropology is a discipline through which we seek to understand human nature and the broad implications of social interaction. It is at once personal yet scientific. Anthropologists study societies at first hand with a humanistic interest in their cultures and customs and use a scientific approach to gather information that they hope will ultimately lead to a greater appreciation and acceptance of the diversity in human societies. Chapter 1 details the historical approaches in anthropology as well as the current methods used by anthropologists. Chapter 2 defines in a multi-dimensional way the basic concept of culture as an institutionalized system of ideas, emotions, and survival strategies passed on from one generation to another.

# of Culture

CHAPTER 1

ANTHROPOLOGY: A UNIQUE APPROACH TO UNDERSTANDING

Fieldwork and participant observation are unique methods of studying cultures employed by anthropologists. As with any discipline, the field of anthropology has evolved. The prescientific view saw all non-Western cultures as degenerated forms of an earlier divine creation. This gave way to cultural evolutionism, empiricism, and eventually to the current period of specialization in which many subfields of anthropology exist studying many different aspects of both ancient and modern societies.

CHAPTER 2

CULTURE

The tendency of humans to share their ideas and emotions about their own natures and to develop survival strategies that they pass on to future generations as customs is the basis of culture. Various subsistence technologies derive from a society's pattern of culture and its adjustment to the environment in which it survives. Cultural relativism is the method of trying to understand another culture within its own context, while both the humanistic and scientific approaches provide information about a culture from two different perspectives.

Many of the sciences and humanities study humankind, but anthropology is a special way of understanding our species. In a sense, it incorporates all other ways of studying human societies. This chapter introduces what anthropology is, how it has evolved as a discipline, how it gathers information about human behavior, and how it tries to keep its work on an ethical basis with respect for all its subjects. The chapter ends with an overview of this textbook, defining its unique approach to the study of anthropology.

1

Anthropology: A Unique Approach To Understanding

FIGURE 1.1 *Anthropology*

This young girl lives in Bamako, the capital of Mali, a country on the southern edge of the Sahara. Anthropology is the holistic study of diverse human societies both of the past and the present.

Anthropology excites me and can be exciting to students too because of the breadth of its approaches to understanding the human condition. Anthropologists want to understand human nature, as do members of several other fields, but anthropology also differs from any other discipline that studies human beings. Classified by subject matter, it is one of the humanities, so anthropologists share some of the interests of philosophers, literary and art critics, translators, and historians. Classified by aspiration, anthropology is a science and shares a great deal with sociology, psychology, political science, economics, linguistics, geography, paleontology, and biology. Wolf (1964) claims that anthropology bridges the gulf between the sciences and the humanities.

3

THE BREADTH OF ANTHROPOLOGY

Anthropology is both a natural science, concerned with the organization and function of matter, and a humanistic discipline, concerned with the organization and function of mind. Its subject matter is man, who is both part of the ecology of nature and an improbable departure from what one might expect to find in the natural realm. He is the animal with culture, that is, an animal equipped with the ability to create and use symbols to devise new, artificial worlds of his own making. Just as the subject matter of anthropology is dual, so the concern of the anthropologist is dual: he must mediate between human biology and ecology on the one hand, and the study of human understanding on the other. Necessarily, he must be both outside observer and participant in the internal dialogues of his informants. By definition, therefore, anthropology is less subject matter than a bond between subject matters, and the anthropologist will forever find himself translating from one realm to another. (p. 13)

Diversity and unity in anthropology. This breadth in the subject matter and goals of anthropology has created an extremely diverse field that brings together specialists whose topics of study might be central to other fields. Consider this diversity: In the past decade, the major American anthropological journals have included articles on the changing role of the family in Iran, the definition of religion, the nutritional implications of cannibalism, the origins of agriculture in Southeast Asia, the political and educational implications of creationist theology in the United States, the problems of Third World economic development, the discovery of three-and-one-half-million-year-old fossil ancestors of the human species in Tanzania, the effects of different foods on the wear patterns of teeth, the relationship of diet to human fertility, and the origins and diversity of human languages. Nevertheless, anthropology manages to unite these diverse topics by taking as its goal a unified understanding of the human condition.

The holistic perspective. One difference between anthropology and other fields in which human beings are the topic of study is that anthropology is broader in its scope. Our purpose is to paint a holistic picture of the human condition, that is, one that shows how different aspects of being human relate to and influence one another. For instance, an anthropologist who is especially interested in human economic life is likely to study how the economic customs of a society influence and are influenced by that society's physical environment, political system, religious customs, family patterns, or even its artistic endeavors. An anthropologist who is concerned with human biology might attempt to demonstrate that different frequencies of fractured vertebrae may result from different hunting practices. An anthropologist studying the language of a Native American society may attempt to determine the location of its ancestral homeland by comparing its words for plants and animals with those of other related languages and by considering the geographical distributions of those specific plants and animals for which the related languages share words.

Breadth in time and space. In addition to being more holistic than other fields, anthropology tends to be broader in scope because anthropologists develop their ideas about what is typical of human beings by comparing a broader range of different human groups before drawing their conclusions. For instance, most of the ideas set forth in a contemporary textbook on abnormal psychology are based on research that has been carried out in Europe or North America in societies whose people differ relatively little in upbringing and life experiences. By contrast, a typical anthropological textbook about the nature of mental illness will include comparisons between peoples as diverse as Ituri Forest pygmies, Canadian Inuit, traditional Chinese villagers, and Swedish city dwellers. Anthropologists want their ideas about human nature to be based on as wide a spectrum of human ways of life as possible. For this reason, anthropologists study people in all parts of the world in both simple and complex societies. Their perspective, in other words, is based on cross-cultural research—research that draws data from many diverse ways of life rather than just one.

Anthropology's scope extends through time as well as space. Anthropologists try to uncover as much as possible about societies of the distant past as well as about life in contem-

FIGURE 1.2 *Ethnographical Anthropologist*

One way an anthropologist gathers information about the culture he or she is studying is to live with and participate in the daily activities of that culture. An important part of the research is the accurate gathering and reporting of the observations made as Napoleon Chagnon is doing on his solar-powered computer.

porary societies. The artifacts and fossil remains of ancient peoples are studied for clues to how people lived in the past and how we became what we are today.

KINDS OF ANTHROPOLOGY

There are four main types of anthropologists: cultural anthropologists, archaeologists, anthropological linguists, and physical anthropologists. Generally speaking, cultural anthropologists are interested in understanding the rules that govern ways of life, or cultures. They study the customs of human societies to discover what leads to the similarities and differences in human ways of life. As a part of their training, cultural anthropologists are usually expected to spend a prolonged period of time—often a year or more—living in a society that practices customs very different from those of their own, participating in that way of life, and recording the customs of that society as accurately as possible.

Cultural anthropologists who continue to specialize in recording the customs of human societies are called ethnographers. Their descriptions of human ways of life are called ethnographies. Other cultural anthropologists

known as ethnologists attempt to unravel the general laws that guide the development of human ways of life. Ethnologists have their own specialties, such as people's economic life, political systems, marriages, family and childrearing practices, art, religious practices and beliefs, or psychological traits. The specializations within this branch of anthropology tend to overlap with the interests of professionals in the other behavioral and social sciences within a university. Yet, cultural anthropology has a distinctive contribution to make: to show how each part of human life, be it language, politics, economics, family life or religion, fits into a way of life as a whole. In a sense, other social and behavioral scientists study the various parts in isolation from one another, while the cultural anthropologist is interested in how these relate to the broader context of human life.

Archaeologists, like cultural anthropologists, are interested in understanding ways of life of peoples who have ceased to exist. While the cultural anthropologist studies ways of life described by researchers who lived among the people to observe their customs, the archaeologist reconstructs the history and the culture of a people from the things they left behind. The fieldwork of the archaeologist involves the

5

FIGURE 1.3 *Archaeologist*

Archaeologists reconstruct the history and culture of a society that no longer exists from materials that are left behind. This archaeologist is carefully brushing debris from a layer of butchered bison bones of a Paleo-Indian bison kill at the Hudson-Meng site near Crawford, Nebraska. A recent controversy has emerged involving pothunters and graverobbers who are taking advantage of the rising values of such artifacts. They plunder archaeological sites with no regard for the painstaking effort made by scientists to preserve the history that is discovered. On the other hand, some native American Indians are protesting the right of archaeologists themselves to disturb the graves of their ancestors, shaking, as Maria Pearson, a Yankton-Sioux activist says, ". . . the very roots of a living soul. . . ."

careful, painstaking excavation of places where people have been. The skills required for the work of excavating a site include surveying, map making, photography, and others necessary for the preservation of information about each object unearthed, including exactly where it was located compared to every other object discovered.

To analyze the materials obtained in an excavation, the archaeologist may use skills similar to those of botanists, zoologists, geologists, physicists, and other laboratory scientists, since the original environment of the site must be reconstructed. The archaeologist at this stage may seek to answer questions such as what plants and animals were being eaten and whether these foods were domestic or wild, what the native plants and animals sug-

gest about the climate of the site, or how the materials left behind may provide clues about the age of the site. After such questions have been answered, the work of the archaeologist becomes much like that of the historian and the cultural anthropologist. The goal at this point becomes the description of a way of life and its history.

ARCHAEOLOGY: THE CONTROLLED DESTRUCTION OF A SITE

An archaeological site is an important historical record of how people lived in the past. Unfortunately, there are many ways in which this information can be lost. Natural processes can take their toll: Wind, rain, ice, lightning-induced fires, or flash floods can destroy an archaeological site, but human influences damage the record of our past at an even greater rate. Archaeological sites may be bulldozed into nonexistence during the construction of a road or building. They may be covered by the lake created by a new dam. The Olmec site of La Venta is now an oil refinery.

More dramatic is the impact of deliberate vandalism. Archaeological sites of tremendous public interest been destroyed with increasing frequency in the United States in recent years. For instance, one of the most impressive prehistoric Native American rock art murals in the United States, a mural created at least 600 years ago in Butler Wash, Utah, has been severely damaged on two occasions by vandals using spray paint to cover the original paintings. Elsewhere, a brisk illegal trade in prehistoric artifacts still flourishes despite the efforts of many governments. For instance, remains of ancient Mayan artifacts not yet examined by professional archaeologists have been hacked apart by looters for sale on an international underground market.

Even the excavation of a prehistoric site by professional archaeologists destroys that site. However, there is an immense difference between the trained archaeological excavator and the "pot-hunter" who removes artifacts from their original location without regard to the information that is lost in doing so. Archaeologists proceed carefully and systematically to record the precise location of every artifact uncovered at a site, noting its relationship to other things around it, both natural and artificial. The archaeologist is as interested in a stain in the soil indicating the remains of an ancient fire pit or posthole as in the artifacts themselves. Grains of pollen in the soil, fragmentary bones of animals, or the charred remains of a fire may reveal much about the foods eaten, the uses of the artifacts, or the age of the material being excavated. An archaeological excavation is preceded by a careful survey of the site and methodical selection of the parts of the site to be excavated to gain the greatest amount of information with the least disturbance of the site. Detailed records are kept of everything done while the work is carried out. Even so, the archaeologist of today is likely to leave significant parts of a site untouched, knowing that techniques developed a decade or so in the future may be used to learn even more about the site if the entire site is not excavated today.

Anthropological linguists are interested in the role of language in human life. They may be concerned with the origins of language, the biological characteristics of human beings that make it possible for them to use language, the ways in which languages change, or how they are used in daily life. Unlike linguists in other fields, anthropological linguists are chiefly concerned not with language for its own sake, but with the relationships between language and the human condition. Like cultural anthropologists or archaeologists, anthropological linguists may devote their efforts to fieldwork. In the field, the anthropological linguist may record the little-known languages of the world, the oral traditions, the music, the poetry, the styles of speaking, or the social and geographical dialects that are characteristic of a people. Other anthropological linguists with more theoretical interests may study the data from many related languages, much as the ethnologist compares descriptions of the customs of different societies.

Physical anthropologists are also sometimes called biological anthropologists. The purpose of their research is to answer a variety of questions concerning the origins of the human species, its evolutionary history, and the current biological variation among the peoples of the world. Some physical anthropolo-

gists study the fossilized skeletal remains of our early human ancestors and their close relatives, with the goal of developing an accurate picture of the evolution of our species. Others have a more specialized interest, such as learning about the diseases from which ancient peoples suffered. Some physical anthropologists specialize in studying how the biological characteristics of contemporary peoples differ from one another and how these differences may have come about. There are even physical anthropologists who devote themselves to the study of the biology and behavior of our close nonhuman relatives, such as the chimpanzees, gorillas, and monkeys, to learn more about the similarities and differences between us.

As diverse as the specialized interests of different anthropologists may be, what unifies them is their common desire to better understand the nature of humans and to relate their research to the broader picture of the human condition. It is this integrating tendency and holistic viewpoint that is characteristic of the anthropological enterprise and differentiates it from other disciplines that study the human condition.

METHODS OF ANTHROPOLOGICAL RESEARCH

As a science, anthropology has its own distinctive research methods. These involve fieldwork and the comparative method. In cultural anthropology, these take the form of participant observation and cross-cultural comparison.

Fieldwork

The essential method of anthropological research that is shared by anthropologists regardless of their specialization is fieldwork—study carried out in the field for firsthand observation. Biological anthropologists may spend time in search of fossil remains of human ancestors or observing primates such as chimpanzees or baboons in the wild to learn about the behavior of species closely related to our own. Archaeologists spend time in the field examining and excavating sites once occupied by human beings. Anthropological linguists work with native speakers of diverse languages to gather data firsthand about these languages and how they are used in real-life situations. Ethnographers spend prolonged periods of time living in isolated non-Western societies, in developing countries, or in a variety of settings such as rural villages, religious communes, or central city slums in Western societies to gather data about the life and customs of those they observe.

Direct observation in natural settings is the common factor in data collection by all kinds of anthropologists. This feature contrasts with the work of other social and behavioral scientists, who have traditionally collected their data in artificial laboratory settings or through indirect data-gathering techniques such as questionnaires or polls. Consider, for example, the differences in approach of a psychological anthropologist and a psychologist or sociologist interested in social psychology. Most research by psychologists who study social psychology is conducted in laboratories. For instance, a psychologist who is interested in human aggression might advertise for volunteer subjects and then have these volunteers administer what they are told are electric shocks to confederates of the researcher, ostensibly to study the effects of punishment on learning but actually to study human willingness to follow aggressive role models and authority figures. Volunteers who were exposed to a staged argument on their way to the laboratory might be compared with those volunteers who were not. Despite the insights thus gained, there are significant limitations on the usefulness of such studies. Subjects are limited to people who volunteer to come to the laboratory to participate in the research. Whether people who volunteer for such activities are typical members of society is always questionable in such research. Furthermore, it is not always clear what a subject's willingness to administer an electric shock in a research setting when told to do so by a psychologist wearing a lab smock reveals about the same person's likelihood of participating in a riot during a blackout, getting into a bar fight, volunteering for military service during a national crisis, or committing homicide.

An anthropologist interested in human aggression would be more likely to carry out research in the social environments in which violence occurs. The research would most probably be carried out over a period of months, while the anthropologist lives among the people being studied, interacting with them in their normal, day-to-day settings and recording fortuitous examples of real aggression as they occur spontaneously. Based on repeated observations over long periods of time, the ethnographer might then suggest some general conclusions about the situations or patterns of interaction that are most likely to trigger aggressive behavior in the particular society being studied.

Participant Observation

Most ethnographic research is also carried out using what is called participant observation. The anthropologist does not study people from afar as a sociologist might, relying on secondary data such as census records or data collected by questionnaires sent to subjects through the mail. Rather, he or she goes to the subjects in the field and remains living among them for a long enough period to earn the trust that people require to behave in the ways they usually do when strangers, tourists, or "outsiders" are not present. Ideally, the ethnographer would like to become skilled enough at following local customs to be accepted as a functioning member of the group, while maintaining sufficient objectivity about the way of life to be able to describe and analyze it fairly and impartially. In practice, complete acceptance as a member of the community being studied is rare. After all, anthropologists are usually born and reared according to customs and values different from those of the peoples they study. Nevertheless, the goal of respect for the local community's standards and customs gives the anthropologist the greatest possible chance of inspiring enough trust in the community members that they will feel comfortable and behave spontaneously even when the anthropologist is present. The goal of observing the normal behavior of people is another reason why anthropologists expect to spend months or even years carrying out their participant observation research. Even if the researcher never comes to be seen as a true insider, his or her prolonged presence can breed sufficient tolerance for the people's behavior to return to the routine normally followed when true "outsiders" are not present.

Anthropological observation is called *participant* observation because it is not limited to passive watching and note taking. Anthropologists try as much as possible to practice local customs to gain a "feel" for the way of life that helps them understand it as the people themselves do. Thus, anthropologists expect to learn the native language of the people they study. This is not merely to become better able to understand what is being said around them, but also to give anthropologists a more accurate perception of the native way of life, since a language is a kind of record and model of a people's understandings of themselves and their environment.

Learning the native language also facilitates the direct questioning of a people about their customs and the meanings of those customs. Direct questioning is an important part of participant observation as opposed to simple observation. Anthropologists carry out their questioning in ways that are systematic enough to uncover hidden and implicit but not normally discussed aspects of ways of life that might otherwise remain undiscovered. Systematic questioning requires asking the same questions of many different informants. This is done partly to verify the accuracy of what the researcher is told—after all, anthropologists are outsiders, and they may be considered fair game to informants who may resent their presence or simply enjoy the humor of deceiving them. Asking the same questions of many informants also ensures that the information obtained is typical of the ideas expressed in the community at large.

THE FIELDWORK EXPERIENCE: A CASE STUDY

At the end of my junior year in college I prepared for my first experience in anthropological fieldwork, the study of the Shoshoni language and its probability of becoming extinct. I remember one piece of advice my mentor gave me as we drove for the first time to the reservation which he had selected for my work: Don't ask directly about how many people or families lived on the reservation because such questions would raise the suspicion that I was really gathering information for the government

for some nefarious purpose. I followed this advice even though it slowed considerably my building of a clear picture of the makeup of the reservation.

At first it seemed that I could not have been more fortunate in a fieldwork location. The Tribal Council had graciously offered me a rent-free ranch house that seemed luxurious. It was supplied with propane lighting, a stove, running cold water, and a propane refrigerator. It was furnished with a couch, desk, and bed. Most important of all, it actually had an indoor toilet!

I was ecstatic. With a little bit of sweeping, the dust-covered linoleum floors could be cleaned, and I would be settled in after I had unpacked the supplies I had brought. Weekly trips to the off-reservation store about twenty miles away would make it possible to conduct fieldwork while living not so differently from my accustomed student life. I unpacked my mechanical typewriter and battery-powered tape recorder and began to get organized.

My first crisis was the discovery that although the house had a mechanically perfect toilet, it was unusable. It seems a child had flushed a rubber ball down the drain. Ordinarily this might have been fixed, but the drainpipe narrowed, somewhere in the front yard, to a size smaller than the ball. Thus, my prized possession was as unfunctional as a fur-lined teacup. Fortunately, there was an old outhouse near the house. Some hardships, I reminded myself, simply had to be accepted. I could cope. I consoled myself with the thought that this would at least make future tales of my fieldwork more colorful, more truly anthropological. But closer inspection of the outhouse brought back vague childhood memories of splinters and lurking black widow spiders. Within a week, I had managed to obtain the key to a nearby building that had an operational bathroom.

There were other minor adjustments. For instance, on awakening the morning after my arrival, I found that the layer of dust I believed I had fought so effectively had returned to the living room floor. Although this was desert country in the middle of the Great Basin, it had not been windy that night, so the amount of dust on the floor was perplexing. I soon realized that keeping the dust level down enough so that I did not leave a clear trail of footprints when I walked across the room was fighting a losing battle. The house I lived in was partially built into the side of a hill. Every night, dirt seemed to seep through one wall from the wainscoting about two feet above the floor and creep inexorably across the room.

Perhaps the mice aided in the earth-moving process. At the end of each day, about half a minute after I turned off the gas lights and retired to bed, I could hear the scurrying feet of what I estimated to be a dozen little rodent companions. Their true number remains a guess, because even though I saw one occasionally peeking from a hallway corner or out from under the wood stacked near the cast-iron heating stove, their speed at disappearing into the nooks and crannies gave only the briefest glimpses and made a valid census impossible. At first, the unaccustomed sounds of the nighttime romps of my co-residents made sleep a little difficult, but within a few days, I became accustomed to their evening visits.

One of my most vivid memories about life in the field is how I discovered the source of my drinking water almost three months after my arrival. For some time, I had been mapping the reservation, its roads, fields, canals, and homes—partly as an unobtrusive way of determining how many people there were and who lived where. One day during this period, I decided to trace the source of the drinking water in my house. The plumbing was simple to follow. It led me only a short distance, across a dirt road to a small concrete reservoir that seemed to be the source of the water. There were several natural hotsprings on the reservation, and this concrete box of maybe six feet in length and four in width appeared to have been merely built around one of the small, cooler, secondary springs that formed at lower elevations from the warmer waters higher up the hill. On impulse I opened the hinged wooden top. Three large frogs jumped in different directions and disappeared into the water. There I was, a young city boy with childhood memories of clear bottled water that was delivered fresh each week to my home just to avoid the chlorine taste of the city purification system. I recall a brief queasy sensation following my discovery of what I had been drinking for the past three months. This was quickly followed by a mental reframing of the situation: I *had* drunk this water for a quarter of the year—and, come to think of it, I had not seemed to suffer any ill effects. I continued to drink from the same tap throughout the rest of my

stay. Perhaps that was the day when I began to *be* an anthropologist instead of just a student of anthropology.

The biggest initial adjustment to life in the field was loneliness. Residents of the reservation had their own work to do and lives to live. Most people were cattle ranchers, and their work kept them busy. They did not just drop everything because a young anthropologist had arrived. At first, I was at a loss to know how to go about meeting people. Residences were dispersed over the reservation. There were no stores to form a place of congregation. However, there was a third class post office, where mail arrived and departed only weekly, a small two-room frame structure where I figured people would drop by occasionally. The reservation had no telephones, there was no television reception in the valley, and only a few houses had self-generated electricity to power even a radio, so I assumed that the mail would be an important source of information about the outside world. I stopped by the post office the next time I found it open. Mail was brought out to the reservation once a week by an automobile referred to as "the stagecoach." People did come by to mail a letter or pick up their own deliveries, but few ever stayed long enough for me to get to know them. The one exception, of course, was the postmaster, Billy Mike, who became my first acquaintance. He expressed friendly interest in why I had come to the reservation, and spent many hours helping me learn the Shoshoni dialect that was spoken locally. Eventually he introduced me to other, older members of the community.

My main task was to develop an accurate description of the roles of Shoshoni and English on the reservation. I wanted to discover the rules that governed which language was likely to be spoken by which persons under various circumstances. Thus, I was interested in whether speakers' choice of language in a given conversation could be predicted by combinations of such things as the age or sex of each speaker, the topic being discussed, or the specific vocabulary items that were necessary for that topic. In essence, I was trying to characterize the degree to which English was displacing Shoshoni as the language of choice in conversations as well as the ways in which the displacement was happening.

The single most difficult barrier that I was forced to grapple with was my own lack of fluency in the Shoshoni language. I had been fortunate in having been able to study the language for two years before starting my fieldwork, but what I had learned was only "book Shoshoni," and once I was on my own on the reservation it quickly became clear to me that I lacked the conversational abilities that would be needed to follow the important but subtle nuances of day-to-day speech among native Shoshoni speakers. Shoshoni is a fascinating language whose verbs are particularly problematic for a native English speaker who is accustomed to the need for remembering only a few variations on the past, present, and future tenses. Shoshoni, by contrast, has some sixteen basic tenses that differ not only according to *when* in time the process is placed but also in the style or quality of the action. For instance, there are two simple past tenses that differ only in whether the activity was completed gradually or suddenly. Thus, the English sentence, "She died," requires in Shoshoni a choice of tense that would depend on whether the cause of death were a lingering illness or a broken neck. A third past tense in Shoshoni is used for activities that were completed only in a location different from where the speaker currently is. It is true, of course, that these distinctions can be made by adding the right words and phrases to the basic English sentence, but unfortunately for the native English speaker, these differences in meaning are grammatically obligatory in Shoshoni and—even worse—they are accomplished with suffixes that are appended to the basic verb. Consider the three Shoshoni sentences, *Ny təkka-nu* ("I ate [a leisurely meal]"), *Ny təkka-hkwa* ("I ate [quickly]") and *Ny təkka-hkooni* ("I ate [while I was over there]"). Present tenses are equally elaborate. There is one suffix for an activity that has just recently begun, another for a process that has been going on for a specific period of time, and a third for one that is happening now but has no definite time of onset. To make matters worse, Shoshoni has another set of verb suffixes that are used to specify various qualities of action, such as the direction in which the subject is traveling relative to the speaker. Thus, *kwətti-hki* ("shoot this way"), *kwətti-hkwa* ("shoot that way"), *kwətti-noo* ("shoot while riding"), *kwətti-nəmi* ("shoot while wandering"), *kwətti-hpənni* ("shoot here and there"), or *kwətti-hkinna* ("shoot repeatedly in the same location") are a few of the many common variations that can be introduced into a Shoshoni conversation by a simple choice of verb suffixes. For some time, I despaired of being able to follow the sense of even the simplest conversations. I had discovered that distinctions that a student could readily notice in a neatly typed text did not linger nearly long enough in the air when spoken. For a long time, I contented myself with collecting single words, preferably nouns.

Still, some facts about language use became apparent quite soon after my arrival. For instance, although almost everyone on the reservation that I met spoke both Shoshoni and English, there was tremendous variation in proficiency in both languages from one speaker to another. This was especially noticeable when persons of different age were compared. The oldest resident was a woman who was said to have reached her hundredth birthday and who claimed to speak no English at all. Others who ranged in age from about 60 to 80 were fluent Shoshoni speakers who typically spoke English as well but with a clear Shoshoni accent and an occasional difficulty with English vocabulary. Middle-aged speakers usually had nearly equal proficiency in both languages, while many of those under 40 appeared to be more at home with English than Shoshoni.

Even before I could follow what was being said, I noticed that conversations in Shoshoni were interspersed with English loan words regardless of the age of the speakers. When the topic dealt with technological issues, such as the repair of a water pump, English words such as *pliers*, *hammer*, or *wire* were common. Many words for recently adopted foods such as coffee, grapes, and oranges were also borrowed from English. Shoshoni has no native obscenities, so when the Shoshoni adopted the use of obscenities along with many other aspects of American culture, English words and phrases were simply borrowed and used within Shoshoni sentences. Here the pattern was noticeably age-related. Older speakers of either sex seemed completely unself-conscious in providing me with native Shoshoni words for body parts and processes. Middle-aged speakers were intellectually aware of the American taboo on the English equivalents and chuckled with good humor about this, but used the Shoshoni words matter-of-factly. Those in their twenties or thirties demonstrated inhibitions and embarrassment about using taboo English words, while younger speakers seemed equally embarrassed by the Shoshoni equivalents.

Situations and topics controlled language choice as well. Several families on the reservation were members of the Mormon religion which is a major Christian denomination throughout much of the Great Basin states. Each week a non-Indian representative of this church came to the reservation to hold worship services. In this setting, the English language predominated even in conversations before and after the meeting between Shoshonis who attended.

During my work with the Indians, I would typically tape record the examples of speech that I intended to analyze later. Simultaneously, I made handwritten notes in an abbreviated style about what was happening. They contained comments on such things as the context of conversations, persons involved, and the topics being discussed as well as any spontaneous insights into linguistic or cultural aspects of the conversations that I felt might help my later analysis. At other times, for instance when I was systematically eliciting ways of saying various things, these notes became careful transcriptions of the complete responses. Each evening at home, I would type my notes to produce a separate, neater collection of fieldnotes.

After ordering and expanding my daily fieldnotes, I would work on transcribing and translating the material I had recorded. Since I was working on a language that was not my native tongue, these two processes were inevitably intertwined. The story lines of the material I had recorded raised cultural as well as linguistic questions that also had to be answered. Why, for instance, was the weasel the animal of choice for preparing both gambling and love magic? Or when the "medicines" prepared for these purposes was "spoken to" did this imply a hearing spirit within the supernatural materials or was the speaking merely a way of manipulating the materials by invoking inanimate and unthinking supernatural forces? I made notes on such questions so that I could follow up on them the following day.

As my work progressed, I began recording conversations and folktales that were part of the oral tradition. At the same time, I was able to cross-check the accuracy of what I had learned. Such practice enabled me eventually to follow the sense of conversations that occurred spontaneously in my presence. So I began to examine the interplay of Shoshoni and English in the natural speech that was happening around me. I started recording not just when and where one of the languages seemed to be preferred over the other and how the words of one language were adopted into the other, but also how speakers might switch from one language to another as topics of their discussion changed. At the same time, as I developed an increasing facility with the native language I started to learn things about reservation life that had not been clear through English alone. For instance, I began to learn that adults, who previously had been careful to avoid suggesting that they accepted the traditional Shoshoni religious beliefs, openly discussed such matters as native curing ceremonies and native mythology when speaking Shoshoni in my presence. I began to learn something of the contemporary Shoshoni ideology, a worldview that incorporates both traditional Shoshoni ideas and those of the American mainstream.

The reservation on which I lived was one of the few places throughout the Great Basin homeland of the Shoshoni that was fortunate to have a practicing Indian doctor, a religious curer called a pohakanta. Willie Blackeye was highly respected and held traditional curing ceremonies about once a month for patients who came to him from throughout Nevada. He claimed that he did not speak English, but I am still not sure whether this was so or if his fostering of this belief was a means of maintaining a certain distance from what those on the reservation called "Anglo culture." But whether it was intended or not, the contrast between the predominant use of English in the setting of Mormon worship services and the dominant role of Shoshoni in Willie Blackeye's curing ceremonies clearly marked the contrast between traditional and nontraditional aspects of Shoshoni religious ideology. Thus, as the Indians shared with me the traditional religious lore of Coyote and the other supernatural animals that populate Shoshoni mythology, English loan words occurred only rarely. Stories about more recent history contained many examples of borrowed words. Finally, English was most common in gossip and tales of recent events.

My exploration of language choice among contemporary Shoshoni exemplifies the holistic and integrative nature of cultural anthropology. Although the central concern of my research was a linguistic topic, I was not primarily interested in the Shoshoni language as a closed system. Instead I sought to uncover the cultural rules that governed when and where one language would more likely be used than another. This forced me to examine how the Shoshoni discussed their environment, their artifacts, and their economic activities. I also had to examine social facts of Shoshoni life, since patterns of language use differed so dramatically by age. Ideology also, could not be ignored, because English had not been uniformly adopted for communicating about all aspects of Shoshoni symbolic life.

Although my personal goal was an academic one—completing the requirements for a degree in anthropology—participant observation research is not a process of detached data gathering and analysis. My work was based on data about the use of language in real life, data that I could only obtain by living with my subjects and interacting with them in their own settings. In part, participant observation includes the goal of becoming as unobtrusive a part of the situation as possible, so that the speaking that is recorded is as unaffected by the presence of the fieldworker as possible. Of course, this is an unattainable goal in any absolute sense. Even a fieldworker who becomes fluent in the native language and resides in the community for a long enough period that people become accustomed to his or her presence remains an outsider in some ways. But this is more important in some contexts than in others. In fact, many of the important insights into the dynamics of a society come as a result of the interplay between the fieldworker and the native participants as the researcher struggles to understand the culture. It is the give and take of participant research that is particularly central to the anthropologist's ability to translate another culture into the idiom and metaphor of his or her own way of life. I too found that I was drawn into the life of the reservation in ways that fulfilled my own goals and served the values of the people I had come to study. In fact, I am fortunate to be able to still maintain some contact with people who touched my life in meaningful ways and broadened my understanding of both the range of diversity within the human condition and of the underlying similarities that make us all one human family.

Ethics in Anthropological Research

Since the subjects of anthropological research are human beings, there are important ethical considerations in doing fieldwork. It is generally agreed that the first loyalties of an anthropological fieldworker must lie with the people being studied. Our work must be carried out and reported in ways that cannot be used to harm the peoples whose lives we are investigating. When an anthropologist lives for extended periods of time with a people to thoroughly absorb the details of their lives and customs, it is almost inevitable that the researcher will become privy to information that might be harmful to the welfare and dignity of the host people were it to become public knowledge. Such knowledge is expected to be held in confidence, and anthropological research is reported only in ways that ensure the anonymity of individual informants and the welfare of the communities studied.

Because anthropological research carried out among living peoples is a matter of skilled observation and inquiry, anthropologists generally have no qualms about informing their subjects about the purposes of their research. There are, of course, situations in which the gathering of specific information about people's behavior would be made more difficult by an explicit indication of what the anthropologist is seeking, either because the informants' knowledge would make them self-conscious—thereby causing them to alter their normal behavior—or because informants may sometimes say what they think the investigator would like to hear. For instance, it would probably be self-defeating to announce one's intention to count how often people violate their own rules of public etiquette, since this would warn them to be on their best behavior whenever they see you coming! Thus, anthropologists may be open about their general topic of interest without compromising their ability to observe the specific behaviors that are relevant to learning about that topic. The real issue here is that anthropologists endeavor not to deceive their subjects or carry out research that serves interests that differ from their own. Clandestine or secret research is frowned on by most anthropologists. When anthropologists are hired or supported by government agencies to study a people's customs, they do so only with the understanding that their research is not intended for purposes that will be harmful to their subjects or that will conflict with the values and goals of those subjects. One way of avoiding conflicts of interest over allegiance to the people studied and to others with differing political aims is a commitment to avoid accepting research assignments that the funding agency requires to be carried out in secrecy.

The anthropologist's second allegiance is to the expansion of a scientifically respectable body of knowledge about the human condition. Thus, anthropologists seek to do everything in their power to collect accurate information and to make it openly available to others in a form that does not violate their informants' rights or dignity. This mandate for open publication of research data is a further barrier to undertaking clandestine research for agencies or employers who would prevent researchers from submitting what they learn about a people to the scientific community at large. Anthropologists believe that their work should be carried out and reported in a way that can be shared with the people being studied as well as with others. It is common practice for anthropologists to see to it that copies of their research reports and publications are made available to the communities they were studying. This openness ensures integrity in the research process and loyalty to the values of the subjects, and it also makes it possible for the fruits of anthropological research to be used by the research subjects for their own benefit.

Cross-Cultural Comparison

The third component of anthropological research is cross-cultural comparison—examination of the varied ways a certain aspect of human life is treated in many different cultures. For instance, an ethnologist who is interested in the general rules that relate to aggression in any society might compare the ethnographic data from a broad range of human societies to determine what social factors are consistent predictors of specific forms of aggression.

Anthropological fieldworkers are especially skilled at providing insights into the relationship of a custom to its broader social context. Their in-depth exposure to a particular way of life allows them to notice in detail how one part of a culture influences another. Yet, to develop truly useful generalizations about the ways in which culture functions, it is necessary to demonstrate that relationships that appear to be valid in one culture will hold true for others under like circumstances. Cross-cultural research is the strategy that anthropologists use for this purpose. By comparing a sufficient number of historically unrelated cultures from different parts of the world, it is possible to determine, for instance, whether warfare is more likely in societies in which there are large differences in wealth between families than in societies in which all families have about the same level of wealth, or whether sexual inequality is more likely in societies where warfare occurs between neighboring peoples who belong to the same culture than in societies where warfare occurs between members of very different cultures.

Currently, the most sophisticated collection of data on many different societies is one which was begun in 1937 by George Peter Murdock and several colleagues (1961). This collection of cross-cultural data is known today as the Human Relations Area Files (HRAF). It now contains over three quarters of a million pages of information on 335 major societal groups, each of which has been coded for the presence or absence of characteristics on a standard list of over 700 cultural and environmental traits. Use of data from the HRAF has made it possible for researchers to determine what cultural traits or environmental factors are the best predictors of the presence or absence of various customs, thereby testing their ideas about the effects of one part of a cultural system on another.

HISTORY OF ANTHROPOLOGY

Although anthropology is a relatively young discipline, it has its roots in earlier attempts to learn about unfamiliar cultures. Even after anthropology became systematized as a science, it evolved through many forms.

The Prescientific Period

Anthropology owes its birth to European expansionism of the fifteenth and sixteenth centuries. Exploration and colonization brought Europeans into contact with many peoples of diverse racial characteristics and ways of life. Government officials who wished to exert political control over native peoples and missionaries who desired to convert them to Christianity both had reason to learn about the peoples they were trying to influence. Missionaries, in particular, were active in recording and studying the languages of native peoples.

As knowledge of other cultures grew during this epoch, ideas about the origins of non-Western peoples were dominated by the European religious view that all people were the product of the divine creation described in the Bible. The world itself—indeed, the entire universe—was generally held to be only a few thousand years old. Irish Archbishop Ussher (1581-1656) had set the date of creation as 4004 B.C. by studying the ages reported in the genealogies of the Book of Genesis. In the European view, cultures had degenerated from the way of life that had originally been established among human beings by God. This degeneration was thought to be especially evident in the ways of life of non-Western peoples who were viewed as savages. European civilization, by virtue of its presumably superior way of life, was obligated to bring order and morality to the rest of the world.

The Evolutionary Period

Out of the contrast Europeans saw between simple and complex societies grew the idea that cultures had evolved from simple beginnings to eventually more complex civilization. During the eighteenth century, as a more secular view of the world became prominent, cultural evolutionism, the idea that cultures had evolved from savagery to civilization, became the dominant view among scholars.

Toward the end of the eighteenth century, scholars began to consider seriously the idea that biological species might also be evolving. In 1735 Carolus Linnaeus had published the *Systema Naturae*, which classified plants and animals into a hierarchical system based on their degree of similarity to one another. Although Linnaeus's purpose had been simply to demonstrate the divine order of God's creation, his systematic categorization of humans

and other living things made it easy to suggest that living forms had achieved their current differences through evolution. The discovery of ancient fossils of extinct animals also contributed to the idea that animals had not been simply created all at one time as fixed forms in a single act of divine creation.

Ideas about human racial differences were also growing more sophisticated during the eighteenth century, and they too were gradually incorporated into an evolutionary view of biology. Linnaeus's classification of living things is still accepted today as essentially correct for most animals. His views, however, about the human races were highly distorted by tales from travelers and adventurers about the presence of bizarre human types in far-flung parts of the world. Linnaeus included in his system categories of headless humans, four-footed humans, and other strange human types that were later recognized as nothing more than inventions of the human imagination. This aspect of Linnaeus's work was corrected by Johann Blumenbach, who is cited by some as the father of physical anthropology.

In 1775 Blumenbach published *On the Natural History of Mankind*, in which he divided the human species into five racial types based on skin color and other physical characteristics. Blumenbach's views about human race were still not entirely secular, but they admitted the possibility of change within the species. According to Blumenbach, the Caucasian represented the form created by God, and other human varieties had developed, he speculated, by degeneration from the original Caucasian type.

In the nineteenth century, the belief became popular that the races differed in their natural abilities. This idea was used to explain the differences in people's way of life. Meanwhile, interest in the concept of biological evolution continued to grow. Geology contributed evidence that the world was millions of years old and this made it easier to imagine that species could evolve from earlier, very different forms. Then in 1859 Charles Darwin published *On the Origin of Species*, in which he set forth the first successful theory of the mechanisms by which evolutionary change occurs. About the same time, the discovery of the first known fossil remains of ancient humans added dramatic support to the appli-

FIGURE 1.4   *Charles Darwin*

Darwin was the first scientist to propose the controversial theory of natural selection or the evolution of a species through change.

FIGURE 1.5   *Edward Burnett Tylor*

Tylor postulated, in the 19th century, that culture evolved uniformly and progressively, thus making possible the idea of progress for all societies.

cability of Darwin's ideas to the human species.

In the nineteenth century, archaeology was also providing support for the idea that ways of life evolved. Excavation of the remains of prehistoric societies was showing that earlier human cultures were simpler than later ones that developed from them. In 1871 Sir Edward Burnett Tylor published *Primitive Culture*, in which he developed a theory of the evolution of religion and discussed the concept of survivals, remnants of earlier social customs and ideas that could be used as evidence for reconstructing the evolutionary past of societies. In 1877 a contemporary of Tylor, Lewis Henry Morgan, published another strong argument for the evolution of cultures, *Ancient Society*, a book that has remained influential to this day. In 1883 Tylor became the first anthropologist to hold a position at a university, to gain respect as a professional scientist, and anthropology as a professional field of study was born.

The Empiricist Period

The American brand of anthropology developed its own distinctive flavor about the beginning of the twentieth century under the leadership of Franz Boas. Originally trained in physics, Boas brought to the field of anthropology a scientific emphasis on empiricism that greatly influenced its history in America. Boas stressed the importance of fieldwork by anthropologists. Since his day it has become the rule for students to spend a period of time studying a non-Western way of life by personally living in the society. Boas taught his students that the careful collection of accurate information about other ways of life was as important as the building of theory. He also vigorously condemned armchair theorizing—the building of grandiose theories based on speculation rather than on research. Boas was, in other words, an empiricist who viewed science as a discipline dedicated to the recording of fact. During his career, Boas published over 700 articles dealing with topics as diverse as changes in the bodily form of descendants of American immigrants, Native American mythology, geography, and the relationships between language and thought.

It was Boas and his students who established anthropology as a field of study in major universities throughout the United States. Boas set the tone of the distinctive form that American anthropology cultivated for half a century. Beyond stressing the importance of fieldwork data collection, Boas and his students strongly rejected the idea that cultures were determined by race or that races differed from one another in their ability to learn any way of life. Well ahead of their time, Boas's students became the most outspoken adversaries of racism in the early twentieth century. Similarly, Boas avoided comparing cultures in ways that carried any implication of ranking them. Instead, he stressed the importance of cultural relativism, the idea that it is invalid to try to evaluate other cultures in terms of Western standards and that each way of life is best understood by its own standards of meaning and value. This idea remains a fundamental concept in anthropology to this day.

During the first half of the twentieth century, interest declined in the development of ideas about cultural evolution. Many of the earlier theories of cultural evolution fell into disrepute because of the tendency of earlier scholars to judge non-Western ways of life to be primitive simply because they failed to use Victorian standards of propriety. During the period dominated by Boas, anthropologists commonly adopted the concept of diffusion—the spread of customs, artifacts, and ideas from one society to another—to organize their ideas about how ways of life influence each other. In the United States, the concept of diffusion led to the idea of culture areas, relatively small geographical regions in which different societies, such as the Plains Indians societies of the United States, had come to share many similar traits through diffusion. The idea of culture areas suited the need of museums to find ways of organizing their displays to show the lifeways of peoples from various parts of the world.

During the period of the first half of the twentieth century while diffusionism was the dominant view in America, European anthropologists were also abandoning their interest in cultural evolution and turning to their own

FIGURE 1.6 *Franz Boas*

The first-hand observation of other cultures and careful collection of data about them was Franz Boas's greatest contribution to modern anthropology.

brand of diffusionism as a means for reconstructing social history. European diffusionists felt that earlier anthropologists had placed too much emphasis on the independent invention of social traits and underrated the role of the diffusion of ideas. They traced the spread of social traits and ideas around the entire world from a small number of centers in which they believed those traits had been originally invented.

The Functionalist Period

In England the diffusionist viewpoint took on its most simplistic form. The British diffusionists contended that all important inventions had occurred but once, in ancient Egypt, and spread from there to other parts of the world. By the 1930s this overly simple view of human history had been replaced by an approach known as functionalism. Functionalists turned away from a concern with history or the origins of customs. Their interests were in the mechanics of society, the way in which it functioned. In their view, a society was able to continue to exist because its customs were adaptive and made it possible for people to cope with their environment and with one another. Therefore, a society's customs can be analyzed by their functions, their contribution to maintaining the unity and survival of the society. The main proponents of this view were Bronislaw Malinowski and Alfred Reginald Radcliffe-Brown. Both Malinowski and Radcliffe-Brown stressed the importance of field work and rejected evolutionism and diffusionism. Malinowski emphasized that societies survive by making it possible for their members to meet seven biological and psychological needs: nutrition, reproduction, bodily comforts, safety, relaxation, movement, and growth. He analyzed the functions of a society's customs by how they helped the individual to meet these needs. Radcliffe-Brown, on the other hand, was concerned with social functions, the mechanisms that operate within society to maintain an orderly social life among its members.

While functionalism was on the rise in England, one branch of American anthropology was becoming more interested in the role of psychology in ways of life. Many of the anthropologists of this tradition were students of Boas who were influenced by his interest in human psychology and worldview. The best known of these anthropologists were Ruth Benedict and Margaret Mead. In 1934, Benedict published *Patterns of Culture*, which is still among the most widely read of American anthropological works. In this book, she argued—like the functionalists—that ways of life are integrated wholes. Unlike the functionalists, however, she found this integration in the unity of a people's mentality and values. Margaret Mead stressed the importance of child-rearing practices on personality development. During the 1930s, students of culture and personality, as this new subfield of anthropology came to be known, were greatly influenced by Freudian views of developmental psychology. Following World War II, their influence declined. The early practitioners of culture and personality studies have been faulted for their tendency to overgeneralize about cultural patterns that are based on impressionistic stereotypes that largely ignored many variations in the behaviors of the peoples they studied.

FIGURE 1.7 *Ruth Benedict*

Benedict was instrumental in establishing the importance of studying cultures and their behavior in comparison to other cultures.

The Period of Specialization

After World War II, the two major earlier interests—the symbolic aspects of culture and the material and social conditions to which human life must adjust—continued to be the major divisions within cultural anthropology, but many specialized subfields have developed within both of these approaches to culture. For instance, the major professional organization for anthropologists in the United States is the American Anthropological Association. Its membership has grown so much that a single, general organization is no longer adequate to meet the professional needs of its members, whose areas of specialized interest have become quite diverse. To accommodate these needs in a way that still fosters the historic goal of maintaining a holistic and integrated perspective for the field as a whole, the association was reorganized in 1984 so that it is now composed of over a dozen smaller subunits that help anthropolpgists coordinate their research and share their findings. Most of

FIGURE 1.8 *Margaret Mead*

Mead is best known for her study of culture and personality. The book Coming of Age in Samoa *is her influential study of adolescent development and behavior.*

these affiliated societies publish their own journals, and their members meet together in smaller groups during the annual convention of the parent association. One example is the Society for Psychological Anthropology whose members have tried to overcome the weaknesses of earlier culture and personality studies by emphasizing the use of statistical comparisons of data from many different societies. Cultural anthropologists who are interested in cross-cultural comparative research belong to the American Ethnological Society. Anthropologists who have extended the viewpoint of their discipline to include the study of contemporary Western, Latin American, and Oriental cultures along with the non-Western cultures that were the historic focus of the field, find a home in the Society for Cultural Anthropology. The Society for Humanistic Anthropology houses members who advocate the use of the same techniques that are used for analyzing written literature and folklore for interpreting other aspects of culture as a sys-

tem of meaningful symbols. Anthropologists who have extended the work of ethnography to include modern film and videotaping technologies as means for recording ways of life, work together within the Society for Visual Anthropology. The National Association for Practicing Anthropologists has been formed to bring together anthropologists who use their skills for solving cultural problems and who are often employed today in settings such as industry, private consulting firms, and government.

In spite of its increasing diversity, anthropology still manages to maintain an overall identity as a unified field through the activities of the parent association. For instance, the major journal of the profession, the *American Anthropologists*, regularly publishes articles, book reviews, and correspondence of general professional interest by members of all of its affiliated organizations. The *American Anthropological Association* also organizes the yearly meetings that bring together members of all of its more specialized affiliates and publishes a monthly newsletter that includes listing of employment opportunities for anthropologists and information about current trends in the profession.

Employment in anthropology. In the past, as many as 85 percent of anthropologists were employed in university settings. Today, this is changing rapidly. New anthropologists increasingly are finding employment in other settings. According to Fillmore (1989), " . . .nonacademic employment is expanding as anthropology Ph.D.s fill career niches once exclusively filled by sociologists, economists, and other social scientists. These latter jobs consist of managing research programs in private firms, government agencies, and nonprofit associations, societies and institutes" (p. 32). During the past decade about half of all new Ph.D.s in anthropology have found their employment outside the traditional university and college setting.

THE GOAL OF THIS BOOK

The goal of this textbook is to share some of the understandings of that broader picture of the human condition that has been built up by the work of many different anthropologists.

To this end, the chapter that follows begins by exploring the nature of culture, the distinctive human component of our life as a social animal. Then human adaptation to physical and social environments is examined in chapters that consider the roles of subsistence activities, economics, and politics in determining many of culture's characteristics. This is followed by material about human social life. The first chapter in this section discusses the nature of social organization and the human life cycle. Others focus particularly on kinship, descent, marriage, and the family. Symbolic and ideological aspects of culture are highlighted in chapters about human communication, religion, and the role of culture in human personality. Finally, cultural change is discussed. The first chapter in this section of the book presents the general principles of cultural change and then outlines the stages of increasingly complex societies that preceded the rise of the world's contemporary nation-states. The next chapter discusses the demise of the world's technologically simple societies and the contemporary plight of the peasant cultures of the developing world. The text ends with a discussion of American culture as seen from an anthropological perspective.

This book is intended to provide an overview of anthropological knowledge rather than method. It is not designed to train students in the techniques they will need to learn if they choose to become anthropologists. The purpose here is to characterize the anthropological view of humankind in a general way that may benefit and enlighten the inquiring student whether or not he or she elects to pursue a professional career in anthropology. The emphasis in this text is therefore on understanding how and why people live their lives in a variety of different ways. This text is devoted primarily to cultural anthropology and its various areas of knowledge. In support of this emphasis, anthropological linguistics is examined in terms of the nature of human communication and the relationship between language and human social life. Archaeology is addressed only in terms of its contribution to our knowledge of the evolution of human social life and the origins of civilization.

SUMMARY   Anthropology is the broadest of the disciplines studying the human condition, for it draws on fields as diverse as philosophy, art, economics, linguistics, and biology for its conclusions. The major fields of anthropology itself are cultural anthropology, archaeology, anthropological linguistics, and physical anthropology. They operate by the same basic anthropological method: fieldwork and comparative studies. In cultural anthropology, these take the form of participant observation and cross-cultural comparison. These fields and methods have evolved from prescientific European interest in the customs of unfamiliar cultures. As a science, anthropology has developed historically through attempts to show that cultural complexity has evolved, to gather data on varying cultures in the field, and to demonstrate that customs and ideas have survival value to a society. Today the two main models for understanding—culture as a symbolic system and culture as an adaptation to the environment—are represented by a number of new specialized subfields in anthropology, including psychological anthropology, ethnomethodology, structural anthropology, symbolic anthropology, neoevolutionism, cultural ecology, Marxist anthropology, and neofunctionalism. While most anthropologists continue their work through universities, applied and practicing anthropologists are bringing their skills to nonacademic settings. Even when working for governmental or commercial employers, anthropologists try to maintain an ethical approach that safeguards the interests of the people they are hired to study. This book draws on the findings of all branches of anthropology, with a focus on cultural anthropology.

**KEY TERMS
AND
CONCEPTS**

holistic 4
cross-cultural research 4
cultural anthropologists 5
cultures 5
ethnographers 5
ethnographies 5
ethnologists 5
archaeologists 5
anthropological linguists 7
physical anthropologists 7
biological anthropologists 7
fieldwork 7
participant observation 8
cross-cultural comparison 14

Human Relations Area Files
  (HRAF) 14
cultural evolutionism 15
Systema Naturae 15
survivals 16
empiricism 16
cultural relativism 17
diffusion 17
culture areas 17
diffusionism 17
functionalism 17
functions 18
culture and personality 18
American Anthropological
  Association 18

**ANNOTATED
READINGS**

Agar, M. H. (1980). *The professional stranger: An informal introduction to ethnography.* New York: Academic Press. A good general overview of field research.

Angeloni, E. (Ed.). (1990). *Annual Editions: Anthropology.* Guilford, CT: Dushkin Publishing Group. An annually revised collection of significant articles on contemporary issues in social and cultural anthropology.

Bohannan, P., & Glazer, M. (Eds.). (1973). *High points in anthropology.* New York: Alfred A. Knopf. A thoughtfully selected collection of the classic writings by the major names in the history of anthropology.

Casagrande, J. B. (Ed.). (1960). *In the company of man: Twenty portraits by anthropologists.* New York: Harper & Row. Discussions of fieldwork experiences by ethnographers.

Chagnon, N. A. (1974). *Studying the Yąnomamö.* New York: Holt, Rinehart and Winston. An in-depth report of the fieldwork experience by one of the top contemporary American ethnographers.

Crane, J., & Angrosino, M. V. (1974). *Field projects in anthropology: A student handbook.* Morristown, NJ: General Learning Press. A short book of projects illustrating various types of research characteristic of anthropological fieldwork.

Harris, M. (1968). *The rise of anthropological theory: A history of theories of culture.* New York: Thomas Y. Crowell. An authoritative and comprehensive history of cultural anthropology by a leading figure in contemporary anthropology.

Must reading for students who have decided to major in anthropology.

Lawless, R., Sutlive, V. H., Jr., & Zamora, M. D. (1983). *Fieldwork: The human experience.* New York: Gordon and Breach, Science Publishers. Aspects of fieldwork explored by 12 anthropologists.

Lowie, R. H. (1937). *The history of ethnological theory.* New York: Holt, Rinehart and Winston. The traditional view of the history of cultural anthropology in a readable style.

Pelto, P. J., & Pelto, G. H. (1978). *Anthropological research: The structure of inquiry* (2nd ed.). New York: Cambridge University Press. A discussion of techniques of anthropological research. Especially important for the anthropology major.

Spindler, G. D. (Ed.). (1970). *Being an anthropologist: Fieldwork in eleven cultures.* New York: Holt, Rinehart and Winston. Thirteen anthropologists discuss how they and their families adjusted to life in a variety of cultures. Especially useful to the anthropology major.

Spradley, J. F. (1980). *Participant observation.* New York: Holt, Rinehart, and Winston. A step-by-step overview of how ethnographic research is conducted.

White, L. A. 1949. *The science of culture: A study of man and civilization.* New York: Farrar, Straus and Giroux. A classic text that argues that culture can be validly interpreted only as a system that is made possible by human biology but that follows its own rules in how it functions and changes.

P̶robably unlike other animals, we humans have a persistent tendency to try to make sense of our existence and to share those understandings with others of our group. We also feel a necessity to alter the environment so that we can survive more comfortably and predictably. These ideas and survival strategies are institutionalized and perpetuated as culture, the subject of this chapter. After analyzing the systematic patterning of beliefs, feelings, and ways of surviving, we must note that these patterns differ from one society to the next, commonly resulting in misunderstandings and mistrust between human groups.

2

Culture

CULTURE

IDEOLOGY
Ideological Communication
Beliefs
Feelings

CULTURAL DIFFERENCES
Intercultural Influences
Intercultural Prejudices
Culture Shock
Cultural Relativism

ANTHROPOLOGICAL APPROACHES TO EXPLAINING CULTURE
Anthropology as Humanistic Interpretation
Anthropology as Scientific Explanation

FIGURE 2.1 *Intercultural Influences*

The dress of these Samoan women, both in style and manner, demonstrate the influence of European culture on their traditional, native garb.

All human groups develop complex systems of ideas, feelings, and survival strategies and pass them from one generation to the next. Anthropologists call the system of ideas, feelings, and survival strategies of a particular human group the culture of that group. Great diversity exists among anthropologists' definitions of culture. Kroeber and Kluckhohn (1952) surveyed 158 definitions of culture by other social and behavioral scientists. They found that the concept of culture always centered on the idea that there is a system to the ideas and feelings that unify a human group and give it an identity as a society. Those who share this way of life may be explicitly aware of some parts of the pattern. Other parts of the pattern of a culture may be implicit in a people's customary behavior without their being conscious of it.

CULTURE

Culture is not biologically predetermined. Instincts, innate reflexes, and other biologically predetermined responses are not a part of culture. Behaviors that are guided by culture are learned, rather than acquired through biological inheritance. Some parts of a culture are taught explicitly. Other parts are learned by direct and indirect observation of the behaviors of others.

In learning the customs of their culture, people are taught that they share some "common understandings" with one another and that others expect them to follow those customs. Our North American culture gives particular meanings to behaviors such as shaking hands and applauding a performance. Our common understanding about the use of these behaviors lets us know when we should perform them. A definite awkwardness or embarrassment is felt by everyone involved if someone does either behavior at the wrong time or place. In this sense, much of a way of life is like a set of rules about how one ought to live. These parts of culture, like the rules of a game, give structure and continuity to the social life of each human group. The predictability that culture lends to a people's behavior gives them security since it allows them to anticipate the behavior of others, including those they are meeting for the first time. Therefore, the parts of culture that are explicitly taught are often thought of as the *proper* ways of behaving.

Participating in a shared and traditional system of customs also gives life a sense of meaningfulness. Thus, the World Series, the Super Bowl, prom night, rock concerts, and sunbathing all have meanings that help the people of the United States conceive of themselves as a society with its own distinctive culture. The customs (and products of those customs) that are acquired culturally have personal meanings for the participants and may be thought of as symbols of the culture, as objects and events whose meanings have been created by their users. Clothing, for example, is chosen not only to protect our bodies from the elements—but also to convey symbolic messages that may be interpreted by others according to the shared meanings of our culture.

IDEOLOGY

Within any culture, there are regularities in how people act, think, feel, and communicate, but people are not conscious of all of them. They may never explicitly state an underlying rule to which they seem to be conforming, yet the regularity in their behavior may be obvious to an outsider. Suppose we observed that members of a certain society always took care to lock the doors and windows of their homes and automobiles when leaving them, that they never left their bicycles unlocked when they entered a store, that they never left valuable items unattended or in open view even at home. We might conclude that these people believe that some of their members are likely to steal, even if they never say so directly. If we were further reporting on our observations, we would include in our description of their culture the implicit rule of maintaining the security of one's own possessions, even if these people do not explicitly refer to such a rule when speaking among themselves.

A culture, then, includes all the rules and regulations that govern a way of life, both conscious, formally stated beliefs and feelings—called an ideology—and unconscious, informal, or implicit beliefs and feelings.

Ideological Communication

Given the regularities that culture produces in all areas of human life, people in every society will probably become conscious of many of their shared feelings and ideas. As people communicate about themselves and their environment, they build a consensus about the nature of humankind and the universe in which it exists, as well as how one should live in one's corner of the universe. Ideological communication is an important way in which people identify themselves as members of a group and declare their allegiance to it. While ideological rituals have the outward form of communication, their predictability precludes any new information from being expressed (Wallace, 1966).

Ideological communication reaffirms those things that give identity to the group. It frequently takes the form of highly ritualized acts, such as a pledge of allegiance to a flag or some other symbol of the group, recitation of articles of faith, or singing of hymns that glorify the doctrines of the group. Ritual affirmations of one's social solidarity with others may, of course, be less formally structured, as in so-called "small talk," the content of which is nonetheless highly predictable. For instance, North Americans recognize that the greeting "How are you?" is not a request for information but simply the opening gambit of a ritual communication of friendship and willingness to interact. The more or less predictable response—"I'm fine, thank you"—is not a measure of one's actual state of health but an affirmation of the same willingness to interact and a declaration that one shares the same cultural code of symbolic behavior. Such ritual reaffirmations of mutuality may be interspersed throughout an entire conversation in stereotyped communications, as in a discussion of the weather.

Beliefs

An ideology has two main interacting components: a subsystem of beliefs and a subsystem of feelings. Beliefs are the means by which people make sense of their experiences; they are the ideas that they hold to be true, factual, or real. By contrast, feelings are a people's inner reactions, emotions, or desires concerning experiences. These two systems interact. Although beliefs are judgments about facts, they are not always the result of rational analysis of experience. Emotions, attitudes, and values—aspects of the feeling system—may determine what people choose to believe. Within limits set by the necessities of survival, persons may choose to believe what is pleasing to believe, what they want to believe, and what they think they ought to believe. On the other hand, once people are convinced of the truth of a new set of beliefs, they may change some of their previous feelings to make it easier to maintain those new beliefs. Recognizing these interactions, we will nonetheless examine beliefs and feelings separately, beginning with beliefs.

Conformity to a belief system.   The beliefs of a culture are the intellectual subsystem of its ideology. They are the consensus of a people about the nature of reality. Beliefs are those things that the members of a culture regard as true: "God exists"; "The sky is blue"; "Geese fly south for the winter"; "Spilling salt causes bad luck." Each culture has its own distinctive patterns of thought about the nature of reality.

As children, we learn that the other members of our society share a system of thoughts, a pattern of thinking about the nature of the world. The knowledge of a society is taught to its children either implicitly or explicitly, as *the proper way* of understanding the world. North Americans grow up under a formal educational system in which mechanical models sometimes are used to demonstrate the plausibility of the idea that the moon is a sphere, the apparent shape of which depends on the relative positions of the sun, the moon, and the earth. By contrast, the Shoshoni Indians of the western United States Great Basin area traditionally founded their explanations of the phases of the moon on the idea that the moon was shaped like a bowl or basket rather than a sphere. The phase of the moon was thought to be simply a matter of which side of the moon was facing the observer: A crescent moon was a side view, and a full moon was the outside convex bottom.

We obtain full acceptance as members of our group by conforming to the ways in which others think. Cultural ideas are imposed on us through rewards for conformity and punishments for deviance. Individuals who violate their culture's rules for proper thinking are likely to experience punishment ranging from a mild reproof or laughter to severe sanctions such as banishment, imprisonment, or death. In the contemporary United States, normal people do not "hear voices." Those who do may find themselves placed in mental hospitals "for their own good" or "for the safety of others." In other times and places those who heard voices have been honored as spiritual teachers. North American school children are rewarded for believing that the moon is a sphere and punished for believing otherwise. During my fieldwork on an isolated Shoshoni reservation in the late 1960s, I discovered that my attempt to describe the moon as a sphere evoked either argument or skeptical looks, and my desire for acceptance soon silenced my expression of deviant views.

Widespread adoption of a system of beliefs gives people a sense of identity as a group. A people's knowledge that they share a set of beliefs gives them a feeling of security and a sense of belonging. As people discuss their beliefs, they may begin to think of their shared ideas as a symbol of their identity as a people. When people become self-conscious of their shared beliefs, especially if they assign a name to their system of beliefs, this part of their ideology may begin to function as an active, driving force in their lives. Such conscious systems are particularly common in complex societies. They are most dramatically illustrated by the named religions and political factions that can command the loyalties of great masses of people.

Types of belief systems. Each society tends to develop two different kinds of belief systems: scientific beliefs and nonscientific beliefs. The former occurs because a certain degree of practical insight into the nature of the world and its workings is necessary for any society to survive. Beliefs about such matters as how to obtain food and shelter or how to set broken bones must be based on pragmatic rather than emotional judgments if they are to be useful. These beliefs that are based on the desire to solve the practical day-to-day problems of living may be referred to as the scientific beliefs of a society.

The second basic type of belief found in every culture grows out of a people's feelings about their existence. These nonscientific beliefs are often formally organized within the framework of religious and artistic philosophies. These philosophies have the important task of portraying the universe and of expressing (sometimes in the guise of descriptions of reality) deeply valued feelings about the world in which people find themselves. Strong emotional commitments may also exist in political or recreational institutions. These, too, are often guided by beliefs that express the members' deeply held feelings.

Feelings

Feelings and beliefs tend to strengthen each other. Our feelings may be the motivation for believing things for which no objective support exists. Beliefs may, in turn, validate our feelings. When we believe that our feelings are the same ones that other people experience

in the same situations, we are more confident in our judgments. Recognizing that our feelings are shared by others also supports our sense of belonging to a definable group.

Three major kinds of feelings find their idealized expression within an ideology: emotions, attitudes, and values.

Emotions.   An emotion is a reaction to experience as pleasant or unpleasant, to varying degrees. As we mature, we learn many subtle variations on the two basic emotional themes of pleasantness and unpleasantness, such as delight, elation, affection, love, mirth, happiness, surprise, or exultation, and contempt, anger, distress, terror, or grief. Which emotions we learn to experience in various circumstances depend on the culture in which we are raised.

Each society trains its members to associate certain emotions with certain situations and to experience each emotion at differing intensities in different settings. For instance, the situations in the dominant North American culture wherein unpleasant feelings such as disgust or fear are considered appropriate are not the same as those in which Navajo culture encourages the same emotions. In Navajo culture, it is appropriate to fear the dead, strangers, witches, and lightning. The dominant North American culture has, at times, considered it normal to fear Communists, homosexuals, spiders, and snakes. What excites or fascinates one people may bore or disgust another.

Cultures differ in how strongly or mildly feelings should be expressed and in which emotional experiences are most commonly emphasized. According to Lévi-Strauss (1950), "The thresholds of excitement, the limits of resistance are different in each culture. The 'impossible' effort, the 'unbearable' pain, the 'unbounded' pleasure are less individual functions than criteria sanctioned by collective approval, and disapproval" (p. xii). Cultural differences in emotional intensity were illustrated by Ruth Benedict, author of one of the most widely read anthropological books ever printed, *Patterns of Culture* (1934). For instance, she cited the late nineteenth-century Kwakiutl culture of Vancouver Island as one in which the expression of strong emotion—especially feelings of extreme self-worth bordering on megalomania—was encouraged. She described their religious ceremonies in the following words:

> In their religious ceremonies the final thing they strove for was ecstasy. The chief dancer, at least at the high point of his performance, should lose normal control of himself and be rapt into another state of existence. He should froth at the mouth, tremble violently and abnormally, do deeds which would be terrible in a normal state. Some dancers were tethered by four ropes held by attendants, so that they might not do irreparable damage in their frenzy. (pp. 175–176)

Benedict contrasted the Kwakiutl with the Zuñi of the early 1900s. The Zuñi, who lived in the southwestern part of the United States, had a culture that encouraged moderation in the expression of all feelings. Zuñi rituals were monotonous in contrast with those of the Kwakiutl. They consisted of long, memorized recitations that had to be performed with word-perfect precision. The Zuñi had no individualized prayers; personal prayers were also memorized and recited word for word. As an illustration of how Zuñi culture required moderation in emotion, Benedict cited the case of a woman whose husband had been involved in a long extramarital affair. She and her family ignored the situation, but after she was exhorted by a white trader to take some action, the wife did so by not washing her husband's clothes. In her words, "Then he knew that I knew that everybody knew, and he stopped going with the girl" (p. 108). No argument, no yelling and crying. Just a mild indication that her wifely status was in question. For a Zuñi husband, this message was strong enough.

For the Dobuans, a people of Melanesia whose culture was studied in the early 1900s by Reo Fortune (1932), the dominant feelings were animosity and a mistrust that bordered on paranoia. These feelings permeated their customs. For instance, even husband and wife would not share food for fear that they might poison each other. All deaths were regarded as murders. In deaths that other people might ascribe to natural causes, black magic was the assumed weapon, with the surviving spouse the most likely suspect as the murderer. Dobuans assumed that their spouses were unfaithful whenever the opportunity existed, so they bribed their children to spy on each other. Benedict (1934) described Dobuan paranoia:

> The formula that corresponds to our thank-you upon receiving a gift is, "If you now poison me, how should I repay you?" (p. 166)

Attitudes.   Our attitudes are statements of our preferences, our likes and dislikes. More generalized than our specific emotional reactions to situations, our attitudes are our general tendencies to seek or avoid types of experiences. Skydiving, for instance, may create conflicting emotions: fear and exhilaration. A general attitude toward high adventure— liking or disliking it— determines which way the scales will tip. Attitudes need not correspond to the pleasantness or unpleasantness of the emotions associated with an activity. Probably in every society individuals are taught to dislike or feel neutral about some situations that lead to pleasant emotions and to like other situations in which they experience unpleasant emotions. Athletes may learn to crave the exercise that their goals demand, even though they dread the pain that attends each workout; soldiers may be taught to seek the very situations of battle that arouse their deepest fears; and the pious may steadfastly insist that they now dislike the bodily pleasures in which they had once indulged.

Values.   The third part of the feeling subsystem of an ideology is values: feelings about what should or should not be, what is good and bad. Values include the moral imperatives in dealing with other humans: "Thou shalt not steal!" "Love thy neighbor as thyself!" They also include feelings about right and wrong that do not directly affect interpersonal relations but may affect one's relationship with nature or the supernatural. For instance, Jewish dietary laws, Mormon rules against drinking alcohol or coffee, and the Blue Laws outlawing sales on Sundays fall into this category.

The values of different cultures can be amazingly diverse, to the extent that what is held to be supremely desirable by the members of one society may be despised by another. That which one people hold dear as a religious or moral obligation of the most sacred kind may be viewed as sacrilegious or immoral by another. When the Samoans were first met by Europeans, women did not cover their breasts in public. Indeed, to do so would have been considered highly improper and immodest by the traditional Samoans. In contemporary European culture, an opposing set of evaluations prevails concerning public exposure of the breast; yet, the European woman is quite unconcerned about exposing the back of her neck in public, an act that would have resulted in strong disapproval in traditional Chinese society.

The Toda of India, who have no word for adultery in their language, consider it highly immoral for a man to begrudge another man his wife's sexual favors, but they have strong rules against being seen eating in public. Among the Dobuan islanders, being happy was not a valued emotional state. Yet, the American Founding Fathers declared the pursuit of happiness to be one of the three fundamental values of society. In the United States today, competitiveness seems fundamental to much of day-to-day life, while the early nineteenth-century Hopi of the southwestern United States carefully taught their children that it was wrong to shame others by excelling over them in competitive situations. The child who finished a race first was expected to take care not to do so the next time around.

Ideal vs. real culture.   It is important to note that culture is a system of *ideals* for behavior. People do not always follow the guidelines of their culture. Sometimes individuals violate cultural ideals about proper communication behavior, as North Americans do when they behave rudely to show their anger at a slight. Sometimes people violate their culture's ideals for personal gain at the expense of others, but most of the time their failure to conform to cultural ideals is not consciously intended. For instance, only about 2 percent of United States drivers make technically legal stops at stop signs, but most do not think of themselves as breaking the law as they make their near-stops and proceed. People also tend to say that dinner is eaten about six o'clock in the evening, unaware that the most common dinner time in the United States is closer to seven o'clock.

In studying culture, one must recognize that there is a difference between what is called ideal culture and real culture. The former refers to the ways in which people describe their way of life; the latter refers to the actual behaviors they engage in as a people.

The disparity between the Zuñis' ideal and real behaviors provides a good example of this distinction. If people's actual behavior did not vary from the ideals embodied in their culture, if all members of a society conformed exactly to one another's expectations, then cultures could never change.

IDEAL AND REAL CULTURE AMONG THE ZUNI

Descriptions of the ideals embodied in a culture's rules for living are not always the same as descriptions of the people's actual behavior. Ruth Benedict's portrayal of the Zuñi of the United States Southwest, and presumably their portrayal of themselves to her, was one of a culture in which emotional excess and individualism were held to a minimum. The Zuñi avoided selecting as leaders people they believed sought the office. They carefully taught their children to avoid competition and conflict. Their ritual life idealized emotional restraint. Benedict (1934) claimed of the Zuñi that "Drunkenness is repulsive to them" (p. 82), that violence was so rare that only a single case of homicide could be remembered in village history, and that "Suicide is too violent an act, even in its most casual forms, for most Pueblos to contemplate. They have no idea what it could be" (p. 117).

These cultural ideals do not give an accurate picture of the realities of Zuñi life. Deviance occurred among the Zuñi as it occurs in all other societies. According to Ruth Bunzel (1952), the Zuñi were often split into factions that disagreed about whether anthropologists should be accepted in the village. There was rivalry along religious lines as well. Li An-Che (1937, p. 69) claimed that "A strife of immense magnitude took place between the Catholic and Protestant elements." Zuñi initiation of children into adult life, like initiations at other pueblos, involved severe whippings (Roth, 1963). Village ceremonies were often marred by drunkenness (Barnouw, 1963). Violence was not nonexistent in Zuñi life, and although Pueblo culture might foster a reticence to discuss it, even suicides did occur (Hoebel, 1949).

Culture provides guidelines that mold people's behavior, but there are conditions under which deviance from the guidelines may be more common than conformity to them. One of these conditions is the effect of contact with other societies and their customs. Was Zuñi life more emotionally constrained before its political and economic subordination within the United States nation-state? This may well have been the case, since contact with more powerful societies can be especially disruptive to the internal harmony of a way of life. Certainly the alcoholism must be understood, at least in part, as a result of disruptive outside influence on Zuñi life. Probably we will never know how much pre-contact Zuñi behavior deviated from Benedict's portrayal, but we should remember that ideal culture and behavior are never identical.

CULTURAL DIFFERENCES

Cultures differ greatly in their ideologies and practical responses to their varying environments. What happens when very different peoples come in contact with each other? In some cases, contact between groups changes one of them, usually the one with less political and economic power. Even when both maintain their integrity, members of differing groups may find it difficult to understand and appreciate each other's ways. In this section, we will look at intercultural influences, intercultural prejudices, ethnocentrism (the attitude that one's own culture is the only proper way of life), and cultural relativity (understanding and appreciating other cultures in relationship to their own unique context).

Intercultural Influences

Contact between cultures can bring tremendous change. This is especially true when the two societies differ greatly in economic and political power. Sometimes the extinction of native populations has been carried out by systematic acts of war. Even in less extreme cases, the transition from the original way of life to a socially dependent status is never without turmoil. Cultural subordination of one way of life by another, even when it occurs peaceably, can be a shattering experience both psychologically and culturally.

Time and time again, anthropologists have described the tragic effects on the world's nonagricultural peoples of contact with the

FIGURE 2.2 *Kwakiutl Potlatch*
The Kwakiutl of the Pacific Northwest coast of the United States staged periodic potlatches as a means of enhancing the status of the host chief. The more he gave away, the greater his status. Here, Lagno speaks for the chief who is giving away these blankets at the Fort Rupert trading station of Hudson's Bay Company.

industrialized nations of the world. Diseases introduced from the more densely populated societies sometimes decimate the local population, in which there is less resistance to the diseases of the civilized world. The awareness that other peoples are more powerful and more blessed with luxuries is a blow to the cultural pride that unifies a society. Often, contact is followed by a rise in the rate of internal conflict and other forms of deviance, such as alcoholism and suicide. For the Kwakiutl, contact with Europeans may have led to exaggerated—and destructive—attempts to display wealth and power.

THE KWAKIUTL POTLATCH: A REACTION TO EUROPEAN CONTACT?

The Kwakiutl, the indigenous population of Vancouver Island and the British Columbia coast, were described by Franz Boas (1967), who visited them first in 1886, and by Ruth Benedict (1934), one of Boas's students. When Boas observed them, the Kwakiutl were a people whose culture encouraged emotional extremes, channeled into fierce competition for status between individuals and groups. According to Benedict, "The object of all Kwakiutl enterprises was to show oneself superior to one's rivals. This will to superiority they exhibited in the most uninhibited fashion. It found expression in uncensored self-glorification and ridicule of all comers" (p. 190).

The expansiveness in the Kwakiutl personality was seen at the great give-away *potlatches*, ceremonial feasts at which gifts were lavishly given to guests as part of a public announcement of an important event in the life of the host, for instance the host's claim to having achieved a higher social status. The most dramatic of the potlatches were those at which the Kwakiutl sought to shame their rivals with demonstrations of the unmatchable superiority of their wealth. Kwakiutl potlatch hosts proved their wealth with lavish gifts of food, blankets, and other valuable property. Gallons of fish oil were poured by "slaves" through the smoke-holes of their longhouses onto the fires to make the fires blaze higher. Blankets were ripped to shreds, and holes were chopped in the bottoms of boats to show the host's disdain for surplus wealth. Sometimes entire villages were burned by a chief and the slaves put to death in the extremes of conspicuous consumption. At potlatch feasts, a chief's retainers sang hymns of praise such as the following one reported by Benedict (p. 190):

> I am the great chief who makes people ashamed.
> I am the great chief who makes people ashamed.
> Our chief brings shame to the faces.
> Our chief brings jealousy to the faces.
> Our chief makes people cover their faces by what he is continually doing in this world,
> Giving again and again oil feasts to all the tribes.

What are we to make of such extremes? To Benedict, the Kwakiutl behavior simply illustrated the diversity of culture, but later anthropologists placed this behavior in better perspective. The Kwakiutl described by Boas and Benedict had long been in contact with the Europeans. Intensive trade for almost forty years before Boas's first visit had greatly affected their culture, and many of the extremes he observed were exaggerations of their earlier customs—exaggerations that arose as attempts to adjust to the effects of European contact. Helen Codere (1950)

points to the core of the problem: Smallpox and other diseases introduced by contact with Europeans decimated the Kwakiutl population, which had fallen to less than a tenth of its original size by the time Boas first met the Kwakiutl. Marvin Harris (1974) believes that this population shrinkage and the loss of many working-age people to employment away from the Kwakiutl villages greatly intensified the competition for labor; at the same time, European wages brought unexpected wealth into the Kwakiutl economy, which was also being flooded with blankets and other trade goods in return for native furs. The native practice, common in many small-scale societies, of holding communal feasts at which food is redistributed by the chiefs to the poor, was modified into celebrations of material wealth by which the chiefs tried unsuccessfully to attract people back to the villages.

Intercultural Prejudices

When cultures meet, people may have little understanding or appreciation of groups whose ideologies and adaptive strategies differ from their own. People grow up under the nurturance of their group and learn to fulfill their needs by living according to their group's culture. As people learn their way of life, they generally identify themselves as members of the group that has cared for their early needs and has taught them the rules for living. Simultaneously, they generally develop positive feelings toward this reference group and its behaviors. Often, the training of children in the ways of the group is communicated expressly by contrasting them with the supposed behaviors of outsiders: "Other parents may let their children come to the table like that, but in our family we wash our hands before eating!" Such expressions teach children the patterns of behavior expected of group members, but they also communicate a disapproval of outsiders.

In complex societies with large populations and many competing groups, prejudices between groups within the society may become a common element of daily experience, varying from good-natured rivalry to direct antipathies. In the United States, we may think of our own state as "God's own country," our politics as the only rational way of doing things, or our religion as the only road to salvation. Even such group symbols as hair length and the kinds of clothing we wear have served as grounds for suspension from school, public demonstrations, and interpersonal violence.

The extreme form of allegiance to one's own group is the feeling that the culture of one's entire society is superior to the ways of life of all other societies. The attitude that one's own culture is the naturally superior one, the standard by which all other cultures should be judged, and that cultures different from one's own are inferior is such a common way of reacting to alien customs that it is given a special name by anthropologists. It is called ethnocentrism, meaning centered in one's *ethnos*, the Greek word for a people or a nation. Ethnocentrism is found in every culture. Everywhere, people allow their judgments about human nature and about the relative merits of different ways of life to be guided by ideas and values that are centered narrowly on the way of life of their own society.

Ethnocentrism serves a society by creating greater feelings of group unity. When individuals speak ethnocentrically, they affirm their loyalty to the ideals of their society and call forth in other persons echoed feelings of agreement about the superiority of their social body. This enhances their sense of identity as bearers of a common culture and as members of the same society. A shared sense of group superiority—especially during its overt communication between group members—can help the members to overlook internal differences and conflicts that could otherwise decrease the ability of the group to undertake effectively coordinated action.

For most of human history, societies have been smaller than the nations of today, and most people have interacted only with members of their own society. Under such circumstances, the role of ethnocentrism in helping a society to survive by motivating its members to support one another in their common goals has probably outweighed its negative aspects. However, ethnocentrism definitely has a darker side. It is a direct barrier to understanding among peoples of diverse customs and values. It enhances enmity between societies and can be a motivation for conflict among

peoples whose lives are guided by different cultures.

Ethnocentrism stands in fundamental conflict with the goals of anthropology: the recognition of the common humanity of all human beings and the understanding of the causes of cultural differences. To many students, much of the appeal of the field of anthropology has been its intriguing discussions of the unending variety of customs grown out of what, from the viewpoint of the uninitiated, may seem like strange and exotic, unexpected, and even startlingly different values. A people's values generally make perfectly good sense when seen and explained in the context of their cultural system as a whole. Yet, from the viewpoint created by the symbolic understandings of another culture, they may be unexpected and seem, therefore, strange or even morally incomprehensible. It is often difficult to make sense out of customs that belong to another cultural tradition on the basis of symbolic meanings that similar acts might have in one's own culture. A negative reaction to customs alien to one's own society is therefore easy for people to adopt. But such ethnocentric reactions to other people's customs must be guarded against by the student of anthropology.

Culture Shock

Attempting to cope with alien customs and values can be difficult and stressful. This in itself encourages ethnocentrism. Anthropologists who engage in fieldwork in a culture that differs from the one they grew up in often experience a period of disorientation or even depression known as culture shock before they become acclimatized to their new environment. Even tourists who travel for only a short time outside their own nations may experience culture shock, and unless they are prepared for its impact, they may simply transform their own distress into a motive for prejudice against their host society.

DOING FIELDWORK AMONG THE YANOMAMO

The difficulties of adjusting to life in an alien culture where language and customs differ greatly from one's own can be tremendous.

Even brief isolation in a foreign culture can be a bewildering experience. Finding oneself in an environment where the symbols of one's own culture fail to provide the secure orientation we all need to maintain a sense of psychological well-being can lead one quickly into the extremely distressing state that anthropologists call culture shock.

Napoleon Chagnon (1968), an anthropologist who conducted his research among the Yąnomamö Indians of Venezuela, has described his initial reaction to that people. The Yąnomamö are an extremely fierce and warlike people who value and cultivate extremes of aggressive behavior unequaled in many parts of the world. Their use of hallucinogenic drugs in their religious rituals adds to their distinctive cultural configuration. Although it is certainly not typical of an anthropologist's first day in the field, Dr. Chagnon's uncommonly frank revelation of his feelings on first exposure to a non-Western culture gives some sense of the psychological effects of radical changes in one's symbolic environment and the ease with which ethnocentric prejudices might arise and preclude even the first steps towards the objective study of other ways of life.

> We arrived at the village, Bisaasi-teri, about 2:00 p.m. and docked the boat along the muddy bank at the terminus of the path used by the Indians to fetch their drinking water. It was hot and muggy, and my clothing was soaked with perspiration. It clung uncomfortably to my body, as it did thereafter for the remainder of the work. The small, biting gnats were out in astronomical numbers, for it was the beginning of the dry season. My face and hands were swollen from the venom of their numerous stings. In just a few moments I was to meet my first Yąnomamö, my first primitive man. What would it be like? . . .
>
> My heart began to pound as we approached the village and heard the buzz of activity within the circular compound. Mr. Barker commented that he was anxious to see if any changes had taken place while he was away and wondered how many of them had died during his absence. I felt into my back pocket to make sure that my notebook was still there and felt personally more secure when I touched it. Otherwise, I would not have known what to do with my hands.
>
> The entrance to the village was covered over with brush and dry palm leaves. We pushed them aside to expose the low opening to the village. The excitement of meeting my first Indians was almost unbearable as I duck-waddled through the low passage into the village clearing.
>
> I looked up and gasped when I saw a dozen burly, naked, filthy, hideous men staring at us down the shafts of their drawn arrows! Immense wads of green tobacco were stuck between their lower teeth and lips making them look even more hideous, and strands of dark-green slime dripped or hung from their noses. We arrived at the village while the men were blowing a hallucinogenic drug up their noses. One of the side effects of the drug is a runny nose. The mucus is always saturated with the green powder and the Indians usually let it run freely from their nostrils. My next discovery was that there were a dozen or so vicious, underfed dogs snapping at my legs, circling me as if I were going to be their next meal. I just stood there holding my notebook, helpless and pathetic. Then the stench of the decaying vegetation and filth struck me and I almost got sick. I was horrified. What sort of a welcome was this for the person who came here to live with you and learn your way of life, to become friends with you? They put their weapons down when they recognized Barker and returned to their chanting, keeping a nervous eye on the village entrances.
>
> We had arrived just after a serious fight. Seven women had been abducted the day before by a neighboring group, and the local men and their guests had just that morning recovered five of them in a brutal club fight that nearly ended in a shooting war. The abductors, angry because they lost five of the seven captives, vowed to raid the Bisaasi-teri. When we arrived and entered the village unexpectedly, the Indians feared that we were the raiders. On several occasions during the next two hours the men in the village jumped to their feet, armed themselves, and waited nervously for the noise outside the village to be identified. My enthusiasm for collecting ethnographic curiosities diminished in proportion to the number of times such an alarm was raised. In fact, I was relieved when Mr. Barker suggested that we sleep across the river for the evening. It would be safer over there.
>
> As we walked down the path to the boat, I pondered the wisdom of having decided to spend a year and a half with this tribe before I had even seen what they were like. I am not ashamed to admit, either, that had there been a diplomatic way out, I would have ended my fieldwork then and there. I did not look forward to the next day when I would be left alone with the Indians; I did not speak a word of their language, and they are decidedly different from what I had imagined them to be. The whole situation was depressing, and I wondered why I ever decided to switch from civil engineering to anthropology in the first place. I had not eaten all day, I was soaking wet from perspiration, the gnats were biting me, and I was covered with red pigment, the result of a dozen or so complete examinations

I had been given by as many burly Indians. These examinations capped an otherwise grim day. The Indians would blow their noses into their hands, flick as much of the mucus off that would separate in a snap of the wrist, wipe the residue into their hair, and then carefully examine my face, arms, legs, hair, and the contents of my pockets. I asked Mr. Barker how to say "Your hands are dirty"; my comments were met by the Indians in the following way: They would "clean" their hands by spitting a quantity of slimy tobacco juice into them, rub them together, and then proceed with the examination.

Mr. Barker and I crossed the river and slung our hammocks. When he pulled his hammock out of a rubber bag, a heavy, disagreeable odor of mildewed cotton came with it. "Even the missionaries are filthy," I thought to myself. Within two weeks, everything I owned smelled the same way, and I lived with that odor for the remainder of the fieldwork. My own habits of personal cleanliness reached such levels that I didn't even mind being examined by the Indians, as I was not much cleaner than they were after I had adjusted to the circumstances.[1]

1. From *Yąnomamö: The Fierce People* (pp. 9–10, 10–12) by Napoleon A. Chagnon, 1983, New York: Holt, Rinehart and Winston, Inc. Copyright 1983 by CBS College Publishing. Reprinted by permission.

Cultural Relativism

The alternative encouraged in anthropology students is <u>cultural relativism</u>, the idea that the significance of an act is best understood by the standards of the actor's own cultural milieu. When we try to understand the meanings of an alien custom in a culturally relativistic way, we search for the meanings that those customs have in the actors' own culture instead of in our own. Relativism is not an idea unique to anthropology. In every culture, people interpret the meaning of a thing depending on the context in which it occurs. In the United States, for instance, most people would not be alarmed by a masked stranger who appeared at their door at night if it were October 31st and that person were holding a Halloween trick-or-treat bag. The symbolic basis of all cultural systems invariably leads to variations in the meanings of things from situation to situation. People who share the same culture learn to take the context of one

FIGURE 2.3 *Cultural Relativism*

A culture's symbolic system of communication, customs, and habits are unique and can best be understood by others in relationship to the situation in which they occur. People from other cultures visiting the United States would probably find it difficult to understand the significance of masked figures going from door to door late in October with a request for treats. Only when they viewed it as a cultural custom of celebrating All Hallow's Eve would they be able to place it in the proper perspective.

another's acts into account when they are trying to communicate. Of course, intergroup prejudices sometimes interfere with people's efforts to understand one another, even within the same culture, and relativism is even less used by people in thinking about the customs of other societies. In contrast to ethnocentrism, cultural relativism is an uncommon way of viewing other cultures.

Nevertheless, anthropologists have come to value cultural relativism as a first step toward understanding other cultures. A relativistic view of other cultures holds all ways of life to be equally valid sources of information about human nature. This does not imply endorsing customs such as infanticide or cannibalism, but merely accepting that they, too, are a part of the human condition that we wish to explain. Relativism, as a research tool, reminds us that even customs that seem inhumane or irrational by our own values must be described and analyzed as objectively as possible if we wish to develop scientifically valid understandings of human behavior. Relativism reminds us that all cultures have customs that seem bizarre or repugnant to outsiders. For instance, both electroconvulsive treatment for depression and the use of machines for measuring heartbeat, blood pressure, and respiration to determine whether a person is lying might well seem inhumane or irrational to people whose cultures do not include these practices.

Cultural relativism is easy to reconcile with the anthropological goal of understanding the human condition in a way that is valid for all humankind. In support of this goal, anthropologists historically have elected to conduct most of their research among less complex non-Western societies. Such societies have cultures that differ greatly from those with which Western anthropologists would have been most familiar. In devoting their efforts to the study of diverse ways of life, anthropologists have hoped to maximize their data about the limits of diversity within and between human cultures. Also, they hoped to preserve for future generations knowledge about ways of life that were rapidly becoming extinct as complex industrialized societies expanded their influence throughout the world.

As a result of working among peoples with ways of life very different from their own, anthropological fieldworkers commonly find that the preconceived notions they bring with them do not help them understand what is going on in the culture they are studying. Cut off from their own people and their accustomed way of life, it is they who must learn to understand the meanings of the symbols of the people they are living with, rather than the other way around. The anthropological imperative is "Respect or fail!" Learning to understand the language and the customs as they are understood by the insiders of the group is often a clear and basic necessity for survival in a foreign culture. It can also be prerequisite to the work of gathering accurate information about a culture or of developing insights about how it might have come to be the way it is and why it functions the way it does. The necessity of interpreting the meaning or value of an act within the culture in which it is found, that is, from a cultural relativistic viewpoint, has been long recognized within anthropology as a fundamental first step in learning to understand a culture as a coherent system of meaningful symbols.

It is not always an easy task to make customs sensible in terms that people who follow a different way of life can comprehend. This is especially true when we try to explain things that we ourselves have always taken for granted. Our experiences are so common in our own culture that we rarely need to talk about them or explain them—even to ourselves. This can pose problems when people of quite different cultural backgrounds attempt to communicate. Toelken (1979) described an experience during his fieldwork among the Navajo that illustrates such a difficulty:

"I had lived with the Navajo family of old Little Wagon for several months before he politely asked me early one morning what kind of noise I was making on my wrist every day. I tried to explain to him that my watch was a means of measuring time, but of course since the Navajos have no word for time as we know it, and because I was still learning the Navajo language, I had no way to explain it to him. My first impulse was to believe that I could simply describe what time was like and why it was important to know it and where I was in relationship to it, but I was brought up abruptly by my realizing that nothing I could say to the old man made any sense to him at all. I pointed out to him how the hands went around a dial that was marked off in equal sections. I then told him that by watching where the hands were I could determine what kinds of things I should be doing. 'Like what?' he asked in Navajo. 'Well, eating. It tells me when to eat.' 'Don't your people eat when they are hungry? We eat when we are hungry if there is food.' 'Well, yes, we eat when we are hungry; that is, no, we eat three times a day, and we are not supposed to eat between times.' 'Why not?' 'Well, it's not healthy.' 'Why is that?' And so on. I tried another tack. I said that this machine told me when I needed to do those things that were necessary in order to make my living (there is no Navajo word for *work* that sets it apart from other useful and normal things a person might do). The old man asked, 'Aren't those things that you do anyway? What is it that this tells you to do that you wouldn't do anyway?' 'Well, it tells me when to go out and look for rocks [there was no Navajo word for uranium at the time], and then my company will know how much to pay me.' 'Do you mean if you lost that machine, you would stop looking for rocks?' 'Well, no, I guess I wouldn't.' Finally, in exasperation, I said that the watch actually was my reference point to some larger ongoing process outdoors, and this seemed to satisfy the old man. But later, when we were outside that afternoon, he stopped me and held me by the elbow and asked, 'Where is it? That which is happening out here?' Beginning to be even more frustrated, I said, 'Well, the sun comes up and goes down, doesn't it?' 'Yes,' he agreed expectantly. 'Well, I guess I can't explain it to you. It's nothing, after all. It's all inside the watch. All it does is just go around and make noise.' 'I thought so,' he said" (pp. 277–278).

ANTHROPOLOGICAL APPROACHES TO EXPLAINING CULTURE

In the previous chapter, we noted that anthropology has characteristics of both the humanities and the sciences. The humanistic aspect of anthropology stems from our desire not only to know other cultures but to understand them as well. Anthropologists with a humanistic orientation approach the study of cultures as translators who try to make the symbols of one culture understandable in terms of those of another. They attempt to portray and interpret the customs, values, worldview, or art of one culture so that they can be appreciated by readers accustomed to a different language and way of viewing life. The scientific approach searches for more mechanistic, cause-and-effect explanations of how particular cultures have developed their distinctive characteristics or of what causes some cultural facts to be universal. The focus is on showing the role culture plays in human survival and adaptation to the environments in which people live.

This dual quality of anthropology, the humanistic desire to understand and appreciate other cultures as systems of meanings and the scientific attempt to explain cultures as

mechanistic systems manifests itself in various ways. For instance, ethnographers distinguish between emic and etic descriptions of cultures, a distinction first made by Pike (1954, p. 8). An emic analysis of a culture, though written for outsiders, is one that portrays a culture and its meaningfulness as the insider understands it. As Frake (1964, p. 112) has pointed out, such a model may incorrectly predict the actual behavior of the people whose culture it describes, and still be valid—so long as the native member of that culture is equally surprised by the error. Goodenough (1956, p. 261) has suggested that the adequacy of an emic model of culture can be tested in two ways: It must not do violence to the native's own feel for the structure of what is described, and it must provide an outsider with whatever knowledge is necessary to talk about the culture or behave in the same way as a native. An etic analysis creates a model of a culture by using cross-culturally valid categories, that is, categories that anthropologists have found to be generally useful for describing all cultures. Such models invariably describe each culture in ways that seem alien to its own participants, but that facilitate comparisons between cultures and the discovery of universal principles in the structure and functioning of cultures. According to Harris (1968, p. 575), "Etic statements are verified when independent observers using similar operations agree that a given event has occurred," and etic models are valid insofar as they accurately predict the behavior of the native participants of a culture.

Anthropology as Humanistic Interpretation

Anthropology is a humanistic discipline in its goal of broadening our understanding of culture as a meaningful system. As Geertz (1973) put it, "the aim of antrhopology is the enlargement of the universe of human discourse" (p. 14). In seeking to understand what other ways of life mean to those who live by them, anthropoligists have much in common with translators of foreign languages. The Talmudic scholar Neusner (1979) described the anthropologist's role as a translator who makes the insider's point of view meaningful to the outsider: "Anthropologists study the character of humanity in all its richness and diversity. What impresses me in their work is their ability to undertake the work of interpretation of what is thrice alien—strange people, speaking a strange language, about things we-know-not-what—and to translate into knowledge accessible to us the character and the conscience of an alien world-view" (p. 17). The humanistic problem of how to understand other cultures has also been likened to translation by Dumont (1978): "Interpretation . . .can refer to three rather different matters: an oral recitation, a reasonable explanation, and a translation from another language. . . .In all three cases, something foreign, strange, separated in time, space or experience is made familiar, present, comprehensible: something requiring representation, explanation or translation is somehow 'brought to understanding'—is interpreted" (p. 14).

The skill at interpreting cultures and demonstrating the significance of seemingly strange customs is probably the central feature of anthropology in the public mind—a skill analogous to that of a translator. On a deeper level, the interpretation of cultures can include the study of patterns within the symbolism, language, and ideology of a culture using analytical styles analogous to those of literary interpretation or art criticism. Anthropologists who specialize in the study of religion, art, folklore, and the influence of culture on human personality are often drawn toward the humanistic or interpretive end of the anthropological spectrum. The major traditions within cultural anthropology that stress the interpretation of culture include structuralism, interpretive anthropology, hermeneutic anthropology, and ethnoscience.

Structuralism. One of the most well known interpretive approaches is structuralism, a branch of anthropological analysis founded by the French anthropologist Claude Lévi-Strauss. The viewpoint of structuralism is that beneath all of the superficial diversity of cultures is an underlying unity that reflects the tendency of the human mind first to think in terms of contrasts and opposites such as black versus white, good versus bad, or female versus male and, second, to resolve the dilemmas that some opposing ideas create. According to Lévi-Strauss, it is the nature of the human mind to construct these logical contrasting categories, because of the inherent dual structure of the human mind. Lévi-

FIGURE 2.4   *Claude Lévi-Strauss*

The founder of structuralism, Lévi-Strauss proposed that the human mind perceives and classifies the world around it in a dualistic fashion. In books such as The Savage Mind *he suggested that this cognitive process was a universal constant and manifests itself in humans in every society in the world.*

Strauss finds evidence of symbolic dualities in all aspects of human culture, from mythology to kinship systems. For instance, he has asserted the existence of a regularity of kinship relationships wherein two of the kinship pairs uncle/nephew, brother/sister, father/son and husband/wife will always be emotionally positive, while the other two will be emotionally negative. The combinations vary from society to society, but the duality of two positive and two negative relations among these four kinship pairs is always maintained. In other words, if the father/son relationship is warm and close, then the husband/wife relationship in the same society will be typically cold and distant.

For a common example of how opposites permeate human thought, consider the duality inherent in the symbols and themes of the Cinderella story. A poor young girl works in the house of a rich old woman. The girl is beautiful but unkempt; her stepsisters are ugly but well cared for. Her stepmother is mean and evil; her fairy godmother is the epitome of goodness. In the story, symbols of nature are transformed into symbols of culture. Several tiny mice become the large and beautiful domestic horses that pull the coach which is a transformed pumpkin. Two rats are transformed into elegantly dressed coachmen. Cinderella herself is transformed into a princess on the night of the ball, temporarily surpassing the superior status of her stepsisters. Her temporary triumph is made permanent after the original midnight time limit through the intervention of a paradoxical object, a slipper made of fragile glass—the only magical item that is strong enough to transcend time and survive past the midnight barrier. Another duality brings the story to a close when the slipper fits only the tiny foot of Cinderella, not the huge feet of her stepsisters.

LEVI-STRAUSS AND THE STUDY OF MYTHS

According to Lévi-Strauss (1955), mythology has no obvious practical function, so it is a perfect testing ground for the claim that the human mind follows a dualistic logic. In his view, if dualistic structures do permeate myth, then they must be present in both mental and physical activity. He argues (1950) that myths are best understood by looking beyond the story line and searching for the pattern of recurring dualities within the stories.

Because structuralism is influenced by the methods of structural linguistics, the search for a myth's underlying structure is accomplished by dividing up the story into the shortest possible sentences, which are then grouped together according to their common semantic elements. Through this process a small number of concepts that permeate the myth can be discovered. These basic concepts can be organized into a pattern that represents the unconscious message of the myth, the function of which was to resolve some basic dilemma in the culture from which it had sprung.

Lévi-Strauss illustrated his method of structural interpretation in a study of the Oedipus myth of ancient Greece. He noted that this myth had four recurring themes: Becoming too emotionally involved with kin, becoming too emotionally distant from kin, denial of an earth origin for humans,

and affirmation of a human earth origin. When Oedipus marries his mother contrary to custom or when Antigone buries her brother against the command of the King, the first theme is illustrated. When Oedipus kills his father or when Eteocles kills his brother, the theme of kinship distancing is illustrated. Monsters in Greek mythology are earth symbols, so when Kadmos kills the dragon or when Oedipus kills the Sphinx they are, in effect, denying that the first humans were created, asexually, from the earth. Oedipus's name which means "swollen-foot," his father's name which means "left-sided," and his grandfather's name which means "lame" all illustrated in some way human incapacity, a trait found throughout the world in myths in which people emerge from the earth. Thus, the names of the Oedipus myth's hero and his ancestors symbolically affirm an earth origin for the human line they represent.

According to Lévi-Strauss, these themes occur in a pattern that symbolically resolves a central dilemma in Greek culture: Greek religion asserted that people were created asexually from the earth in spite of Greek recognition that parent-child ties were always the result of sexual procreation. Greek philosophy provided no satisfactory explanation of how there could be a first human without parents, when all humans are created sexually, but the Oedipus myth says between the lines of its story, "Even though our experience contradicts our religious beliefs about the origins of people, social life itself contains the same contradictions. Our beliefs may be accepted in spite of our inability to logically explain why it contradicts our experience, just as we can accept our social life with its parallel contradictions."

Like Lévi-Strauss, Mary Douglas has tried to clarify the order that underlies human cultural symbolism. She argues (1966) that concepts of something unclean—either hygienically or spiritually—are intimately related to a culture's concepts of orderliness. When people categorize the world of their experience, they impose a symbolic order on it. No system of human thought perfectly mirrors the complex world in which people find themselves, so there are always things that do not seem to fit a particular classification system. Because they do not fit the normal system, they are thought of as opposite or as abnormal, disgusting, unclean, or spiritually polluting.

Douglas (1966) has illustrated her approach to symbolism by examining the food taboos of Leviticus. The ancient Hebrews classified the world of living creatures into the three basic types that corresponded to the three realms described in Genesis, the heavens, the earth, and the waters. Birds flew in the heavens and had feathers. Animals had feet and walked, hopped, or jumped. Fish swam in the waters and had scales and fins. Livings things that did not fit properly into any of the categories that were believed to have been pronounced good by God in the Genesis story were spiritually unclean. Thus, locusts that flew instead of hopping, or sea animals such as the octopus or shellfish that had no scales or fins were "abominations." By mixing the characteristics thought to be appropriate to each category, these creatures seemed to cross the boundaries of creation and to oppose the order that Hebrew culture attributed to God's act of things in their proper forms. Therefore they were classified as taboo foods.

Interpretive anthropology. The anthropological approach that most parallels that of translation is known as interpretive anthropology. Interpretive anthropology attempts to explain how each element of a culture relates meaningfully to its original context. Interpretive anthropologists do not search for general principles that govern human cultures. Instead, they view each culture as a distinct configuration of meanings that must be understood on its own terms. An important proponent of this approach is Clifford Geertz (1973), who has summarized the approach as an attempt to understand "the native's point of view . . .to figure out what the devil they think they are up to" (p. 58). Geertz' (1972) analysis of the cockfight as a cultural obsession in Bali is an example of interpretive anthropology at its best. Cockfights begin in the late afternoon and last until sunset. They are an important occasion for gambling by the owners of the cocks, their relatives, and other spectators. The fight is made particularly interesting by the high stakes in the wagers between the owners of the cocks. By betting so

much that the losses will be painful, the matches become statements about the honor, dignity, prestige, and respect of the owners themselves.

Geertz shows how, in its imagery, the fighting cock is both a powerful symbol of Balinese concepts of masculinity and, simultaneously, of animals, the antithesis of all that is human. Metaphors about cocks abound in Balinese discourse about men, and the word for cock, *sabung*, is used with meanings such as "hero," "warrior," "man of parts," "lady killer," or "tough guy." The owner of each cock identifies with his animal and the masculinity it represents, but this identification also implies that there is a darker, nonhuman side to men's nature—a fact that is also evident in the ritual symbolism of the cockfight. A match between two cocks, each armed with a razor-sharp steel spur, is "a wing-beating, head-thrusting, leg-kicking explosion of animal fury" (p. 8) that may last as long as five minutes and ends with the death of one animal. Each fight is prefaced with rituals and chants, because the deaths that end each fight are regarded as sacrifices to demons that control the natural evils of Balinese life such as illness, crop failure, or volcanic eruptions. Thus, cockfights bring their participants into the realm of "The Powers of Darkness" with which humans must contend for success in life.

Hermeneutic anthropology. One of the most recent developments in anthropological thought is the emphasis on making explicit the process by which the anthropologist comes to understand an alien culture. This approach, called hermeneutic anthropology (from the Greek word for "interpretation") examines the interaction of the fieldworker and the native informant, the give-and-take interplay between observer and the observed. Achieving insight into how members of another culture think and feel about what the fieldworker does and says modifies the anthropologist's own understanding of the culture.

Hermeneutic anthropology is an outgrowth of the ideas of the French philosopher Paul Ricoeur, who emphasized the role of understanding others as a means for self-understanding. Ricoeur's ideas have been incorporated into the anthropological process by Rabinow (1977) who has referred to the mutual attempts of the fieldworker and informant to understand one another as "the dialectic of fieldwork" (p. 39). In writings by hermeneutic anthropologists, the anthropologist is very much in the forefront of the narrative, never an "objective" analyst behind the scenes. The biases of the fieldworker are themselves usually brought to light as he or she grapples with the fieldwork experience in the attempt to make sense out of it. Readers are similarly exposed to the emotional and intellectual dilemmas experienced by the native informants as they too are sometimes forced to come to grips with new ways of perceiving themselves and their own culture because of their work with anthropologists.

Ethnoscience. Linguistic analysis has played a major role in the approach to cultural interpretation called ethnoscience, which has borrowed the methodological rigor of linguistics as a tool for analyzing the symbolic patterns within ways of life. In ethnoscience, or cognitive anthropology as it is sometimes called, the goal is to systematically describe a culture as it is perceived by its own people by uncovering the linguistic categories that informants use to discuss their culture. This is accomplished by skillfully formulating and asking appropriate questions that encourage informants to define the boundaries of each concept and its relationship to other concepts. In so doing, the ethnoscientist makes explicit the hierarchy of categories into which a society subdivides the world of its experience. In effect, ethnoscientists construct a dictionary of the native language and culture.

The systematic approach of ethnoscience results in extremely detailed and accurate descriptions of how people classify those things they talk about. One result of the rigor of this approach is that it tends to focus on rather specific and limited parts of an entire culture. Although, in theory, it might be possible to eventually outline the knowledge of an entire culture by such methods, ethnoscientists have been unable to describe more than a fraction of any single culture. For instance, Goodenough (1956) has suggested methods for systematically describing the kinship system of a society. Conklin (1956) has examined the color categories of the Hanunóo of the Philippines. Frake (1961) has outlined how the Subanun of Mindanao diagnose the various types of diseases recognized in their culture, and (1964) has described the native categories of Subanun "religious behavior."

Anthropology as Scientific Explanation

While much of culture exists in the symbolic realm of ideas—the beliefs and feelings of an ideology—there is also a practical aspect of culture that makes it possible for a people to survive physically. Each culture, as a system of common understandings, serves as a form of social bonding and also as the action plan by which a human society interacts with its natural environment to fulfill its survival needs. Anthropologists whose interests lean toward the scientific goal of explaining and predicting human behavior emphasize the practical influences of social life, human biological and psychological needs, technology, and the environment in their models of how the symbolic or ideological elements of culture arise. Their concern is for isolating the factors that give rise to the diverse cultures of the world and for developing models that show how these factors determine the form that a culture develops. The major traditions among these anthropologists include British structural-functionalism, American functionalism, Marxist anthropology, neofunctionalism, cultural ecology, sociobiology, and cultural materialism.

British structural-functionalism. British anthropologists have long emphasized the importance of social structure, the network of social relations between members of a society, in creating the basic customs of each culture. Their approach, called social anthropology, was founded by Alfred Reginald Radcliffe-Brown (1949), who argued that the social relations between individuals and groups were the most important factors in determining the customs of a society. In the small-scale societies that were most often studied by anthropologists, kinship ties were always crucial determinants of how people were expected to treat one another. Because of the concern of Radcliffe-Brown and his colleagues for how a society's customs functioned to maintain its social structure, the analytical method of social anthropology has been given the name structural-functionalism.

American functionalism.   American anthropology was more influenced by the views of Bronislaw Malinowski (1939), who asserted that cultural customs function primarily to support seven basic human biological and psychological needs that must be dealt with by every society: nutrition, reproduction, bodily comforts, safety, relaxation, movement, and growth. Malinowski's list is probably an incomplete summary of human survival needs, but it can be used to illustrate that cultural variation is constrained by the practical necessities of human survival. A culture can only survive if it responds effectively to its members' survival needs.

As cultural creatures, we human beings do not meet our biological and psychological needs directly. Instead, we fulfill our needs as the culture of our social group prescribes. In no society do people eat every edible plant or animal available to them. People eat only those things their culture defines as "foods," and they exclude from their diets other items of equal nutritional value. For instance, in parts of the Orient dog meat is considered a delicacy, while the Western custom of eating cheese and yogurt is considered disgusting.

Similarly, in no society is the need for reproduction fulfilled by allowing all people to mate indiscriminately. In every society, sexual acts are controlled by cultural rules, such as those determining appropriate partners, when and where sexual acts may occur, and how those acts should actually be performed. For instance, among the Navajo of the southwestern United States, sexual intercourse is forbidden between any persons of known familial relationship, no matter how distant. The pre-Conquest Quechua Indians of the Andes, on the other hand, expected their emperor, the Inca, to mate with his full sister.

The need for bodily comforts is dealt with in each society by forms of housing and clothing. These cultural patterns provide each society with a plan for making minor improvements in the individual's immediate environment, such as changing the temperature or humidity in which a person must work, rest, or sleep.

Each culture also includes plans of action for ensuring greater safety in dangerous situations. These include such guidelines as rules for conduct during a fire, when lost, or when attacked by an animal or by a human enemy.

Human skills in coping with danger vary from culture to culture.

The needs for relaxation, movement, and growth are met in culturally patterned rhythms of work and sleep, exercise and rest, recreation and practical activities. Each society trains its young in the way of life of its people and teaches its members the skills they must acquire at each stage of their lives.

Technological influences on culture. Every culture must include valid ways of coping with the natural environment, the source of energies and raw materials used to fulfill group and individual needs. Tools and the knowledge and skills evolved for fashioning them and extracting resources are called the technology of the culture. In every society, objects are manufactured and used in undertakings ranging from recreation and worship to basic survival. Technology provides ways in which the forces of nature, whether physical or biological, are captured, transformed, and utilized for the preservation of human life and provider of comfort. In fact, a human society might well be described as the organized patterns of human interaction through which the energies of nature are channeled from person to person.

The anthropologist Leslie White (1971) has suggested that those activities that are most related to survival—the provision of food, shelter, and defense—have the biggest influence on how the rest of a cultural system is organized. Regardless of how simple or how complex a society is, its tool kit and technological know-how include the means for solving these problems of nutrition, bodily comfort, and safety. And of these, the nature of a culture is most directly influenced by its subsistence technology—the tools and techniques by which the people obtain their food.

Marxist anthropology.   Marx and Engels were the first students of history to attempt to develop a deterministic theory of social change. Their viewpoint was that all history was the outcome of the conflicting economic interests of the various social classes. Marxist anthropology takes up on this theme and focuses on the role of social conflict, especially economic and political conflict, in determining the conditions under which people live. For instance, a Marxist anthropologist, in explain-

FIGURE 2.5   *Neofunctionalism*

Neofunctionalism states that conflict and its resolution are necessary to maintain stability in a society. The two-party system in U.S. politics usually results in spirited campaigning and ideological conflicts, but usually has elected candidates with fairly moderate views. The Supreme Court decision on abortion in 1989 will likely provide some intense conflicts between candidates in future elections.

ing the slow pace of economic change in a nonindustrialized nation, would likely consider that the lands worked by many rural farmers which is owned by nonresident members of the upper class are one important factor. In such a situation, social policies that might benefit the landless food producers would conflict with the economic interests of the landowners who are likely to have greater influence over governmental policy decisions than are the farm workers. Thus, the Marxist anthropologist would point to the conflicting interests of the producers and owners as a barrier to economic development.

Neofunctionalism. An application of Marx's emphasis on the existence of conflict in social life and its relationship to stability in cultural systems is the hallmark of neofunctionalism. The neofunctionalist might point to the conflicting party ideologies in U.S. politics as a part of the system by which stability is maintained in the United States. In a two-party political system, each party strives to obtain the votes of more than half of the electorate. To have their candidates elected, both parties must actually be somewhere near the center of the political spectrum represented by American voters. The conflict between the two parties and the positions of any two competing candidates are expressed in symbols that portray opposite ends of the political spectrum. Thus, a campaign process that emphasizes conflicting values and political commitments is the means by which the central majority of voters are wooed by politicians who, once elected, are likely to be neither extremely liberal nor extremely conservative in practice. Similarly the recurring conflict between unions and management in the U.S. economy has resulted in a relatively stable economic system in which both employees and employers manage year after year to balance their competing needs for a share of corporate income. Occasionally such conflict ends with the bankruptcy of a corporation and the loss of jobs for employees, but most often the ongoing conflict between owners and workers is simply part of the healthy dynamic of a long-lasting company in which the division of income between workers and owners shifts only slightly from year to year.

Cultural ecology.   In the approach known as cultural ecology, the study of the adjustment of ways of life to different habitats, it is assumed that culture is an adaptive mechanism, and that the survival of customs is influenced by natural selection in the same way that the survival of biological traits is in organic species. Indeed, cultural ecologists such as Andrew Vayda and Roy Rappaport (1968) have attempted to include the interaction of both culture and biology in a single adaptive system.

Rappaport's (1967, 1968) analysis of the

41

FIGURE 2.6 *Tsembaga Maring Pig Ceremony*

The Tsembaga pig ceremony illustrates the concept of culture as part of ecological approach. When the herd of pigs becomes too large to manage, the Tsembaga engage in a ritual slaughter intended to reduce the herds and stabilize the ecological balance between pigs, humans, and their environment.

Tsembaga Maring people of New Guinea has become a classic illustration of the cultural ecological approach. The Tsembaga are tropical forest horticulturalists who grow taro, yams, sweet potatoes, manioc, and raise pigs. The root crops are a daily staple for the Tsembaga diet, but pigs are eaten only in ceremonial events that form part of a longer cycle of warfare and peace between neighboring villages. When the size of the herds are small, pigs are easy to care for. They forage for themselves during the day, and their rooting in the gardens actually aids in the cultivation of the soil.

As the herds grow, however, an increasing proportion of garden crops are expended on feeding pigs. Finally, after a period of about eleven years, the costs of maintaining the herds become so great that the adult pigs begin to be slaughtered in ceremonies that mark the beginning of a period of warfare between neighboring villages. The fighting continues for a period of weeks until one of the villages is routed. Its survivors abandon their homes and seek refuge with their kin in other villages. Meanwhile, the victors slaughter the loser's herds and destroy their gardens and houses.

At the end of each war, the major ceremonial slaughter of pigs occurs, as the winners give thanks to their ancestors for their victory and reward the allies who have helped them with gifts of meat. The size of the herds return to manageable numbers, and a truce remains

in effect between the victors and the vanquished until the herds have once again grown large enough that they must be culled again.

Rappaport believes that the Tsembaga pig ceremonies support the long term balance between the human population and the food supply. Since alliances are more easily formed by villages that can demonstrate their ability to support herds large enough to attract supporters who then will be rewarded during the pig slaughter ceremonies, the Tsembaga are motivated not to cull their herds as a source of protein throughout the year. Since the ceremonial slaughter is an integral part of the warfare process, conflicts between villages happen only periodically in a cycle that prevents human population growth from overtaxing the available land resources and geographically redistributes those who survive while their garden plots return to nature and regenerate themselves.

Sociobiology. Like cultural ecology, sociobiology assumes that natural selection influences human behavior, but the concept of culture is given a less central role in the interpretation of the adaptive process. The emphasis in sociobiology is on the role of natural selection on human genetic predispositions for specific behaviors rather than on the direct impact of natural selection on culture and social behavior. This emphasis has not always been accepted by the more traditional cultural anthropologists whose interests have centered on culture as their major concern, but sociobiology is becoming increasingly accepted as one more tool for better understanding the total human condition and for possibly shedding further light on the relationships between culture and the cultural capacities of the human species.

Cultural materialism. The approach known as cultural materialism also shares cultural ecology's interest in the human relationship with the environment, but adds a hierarchy of technological and social variables to explain the ideological facts of culture. Marvin Harris (1979), the anthropologist who gave cultural materialism its impetus, has summarized the major behavioral categories within which culture is manifest and then proposed that all are ultimately linked to practical responses to the world. The first of these behavioral categories is the mode of production, the technology and practices by which people expand or limit their basic subsistence production in their specific habitat. A culture's mode of production includes its subsistence technology, technological relationships to ecosystems, and work patterns. The second category is the mode of reproduction, the technology and practices by which a people expand, limit, and maintain their population. Discussions of mode of reproduction would touch on matters of demography; mating patterns; fertility, natality, and mortality; nurturance of infants; medical control of demographic patterns; and contraception, abortion, and infanticide. Domestic economy—the organization of reproduction and basic production, exchange, and consumption within the family or household—comes next in Harris's model. This is the realm of family structure, domestic division of labor, domestic socialization, age and sex roles within the family, and domestic discipline. Next comes the category of political economy—the organization of reproduction, production, exchange, and consumption outside the domestic setting. Here one finds the political organization of society, its factions, clubs, associations, and corporations. Here also is nondomestic division of labor, taxation, and tribute, as well as public education, class, caste, urban and rural organization, and the mechanisms of social control and warfare. The final category, according to Harris, is the behavioral superstructure, the realm of art, music, dance, literature, advertising, rituals, sports, games, hobbies, and science.

Each of these behavioral categories has a corresponding component within the system of culture. The last, the behavioral superstructure, is most intimately centered within ideology, the symbolic core of culture, and the furthest removed from the mundane influences of practicality. A link exists, nonetheless. Harris contends that the modes of production and reproduction have a major influence on the characteristics of the domestic and political economy, which in turn influence the behavioral superstructure of a culture. In brief, the means by which a people survive and maintain their population within an environment influence their social customs and even the more purely symbolic parts of human life.

PRACTICAL REASONS FOR DOBUAN PARANOIA

According to Reo Fortune (1932), the Dobuans had a fierce mistrust of one another, a mistrust that bordered on paranoia. Their life was filled with sorcery. Food never grew without magic and neighbors engaged in magical theft of one another's crops; the winds did not blow except by magic; sex occurred only when one was bewitched; and all death was believed to have been caused by sorcery, with the surviving spouse the probable sorcerer. It would have been a mistake, though, to interpret Dobuan ideology as rampant mental illness. When the Dobuan outlook on life, nature, and their fellow Dobuans was seen as a cultural adaptation to their unhappy circumstances, it made a great deal of sense.

The Dobuans lived on islands that were much less productive than those of their Melanesian neighbors. They were rocky, volcanic islands that had only sparse pockets of soil. The Dobuans lived in extremely small villages which never numbered more than about 25 people. They made their living with gardens they cut from the jungle. Their staple food was the yam, but the meagerness of their environment made hunger a constant threat, even though they lived in small and scattered groups. There was never enough food to allay the worry about food, and everyone went hungry for several months before each planting time to make sure there would be enough seed yams. Eating one's seed yams was the ultimate mistake, for not even a person's own family would provide new ones to someone who had proven to be such a failure. Dobuan economic life was characterized by fierce and secretive competitiveness, even within families. Husbands and wives maintained separate gardens and, although they worked together and pooled their food, they did not share seed yams.

The death of a Dobuan created severe economic obligations for the in-laws. During the period of mourning, a surviving husband had to work the gardens of his deceased wife, her parents, and her brothers and sisters, while his own brothers and sisters had the added work of caring for his. After the burial, the kin of the survivor had to make a large payment of food and yams to the relatives of the deceased. At the death of a man, his wife's children were required to cook a mash of bananas and taro, a starchy root plant, and deliver it to the relatives of their father. After the mourning period was over, the children were never again permitted to enter the village of their father or to eat food from his garden.

Is it any wonder that with conditions of economic hardship such as these, the Dobuans were not a trusting people? The Dobuans lived in a world of limited resources, and their concept that one could prosper only at the expense of another was not unrealistic. This unhappy outlook on life was exaggerated by the Dobuans when they tried to gain a symbolic modicum of security in an insecure life. Like peoples the world around, the Dobuans sought security in religion. To the Dobuans, nature was not the kind provider; it was magic alone that assured the growth of crops. Yams, the Dobuans believed, would only grow with the aid of incantations inherited from one's mother's family. When hunger still occurred each year, the Dobuans salvaged the emotional security that religion brings at an awful cost—by attributing their poor harvest to the sorcery of their neighbors. They thus affirmed that their magic did work, and in fact was so powerful that it could be used to steal the yams of others. In simplest terms, the Dobuans traded the fear of possible starvation for a mistrust of their fellow humans.

SUMMARY

Culture consists of the learned ideas and survival strategies that unify members of a particular human group. Group members are conscious that some of their beliefs and feelings are shaped by the ideology of their culture. Cultural ideas also subtly influence us in ways of which we may not be aware but which the study of anthropology may bring to our attention. An obvious manifestation of our culture is our subsistence technology, with foraging, horticulture, pastoralism, traditional agriculture, and industrialized agriculture being the major patterns in existence today. Our subsistence technology tends to shape all other aspects of our culture, including its rules about reproduction, its economic organization, and the ideological patterning of nonsubsistence behaviors. Facing different environments with differing ideas about how one should live, cultures have evolved along different lines. Variations are often so extreme that people from different cultures have a hard time understanding each other's ways. When interpreted ethnocentrically, other cultures seem bizarre. But there is another approach, one long used by anthropologists and promising better understanding among all peoples: cultural relativism, in which we try to make sense of the values and behaviors of other cultures within their contexts, rather than our own. Various orientations have developed within anthropology, each with its own approach to making sense of culture. In general, these can be grouped into two broad camps: the humanistic and the scientific approaches. Humanistic anthropologists interpret the symbols of culture so that their meanings can be understood and appreciated by people of other cultural backgrounds. Scientific anthropologists try to explain how cultures originate and change by considering various aspects of human life that may influence the content of a culture.

KEY TERMS AND CONCEPTS

culture   23
symbol   24
ideology   24
ideological communication   24
beliefs   25
feelings   25
scientific beliefs   26
nonscientific beliefs   26
emotions   26
attitudes   27
values   27
ideal culture   28
real culture   28
ethnocentrism   31
culture shock   31
cultural relativism   33
emic analysis   35
etic analysis   35
structuralism   36

interpretive anthropology   38
hermeneutic anthropology   38
ethnoscience (cognitive anthropology)   39
social anthropology   39
social structure   39
structural-functionalism   39
biological and psychological needs   40
technology   40
Marxist anthropology   40
neofunctionalism   41
cultural ecology   41
sociobiology   42
cultural materialism   43
mode of production   43
mode of reproduction   43
domestic enonomy   43
political economy   43
behavioral superstructure   43

ANNOTATED READINGS

Briggs, J. (1980). Kapluna daughter: Adopted by the Eskimo. In Spradley and D. McCurdy (Eds.), *Conformity and conflict*, 4th edition, pp. 44–62. Boston: Little, Brown & Company. A fascinating account of how conflicting role expectations can be part of the process of gaining insight into a culture.

Geertz, C. (Ed.). (1971). *Myth, symbol, and culture*. New York: W. W. Norton. An important collection of essays on culture as a symbolic system.

Harris, M. (1974). *Cows, pigs, wars and witches: The riddles of culture*. New York: Random House. An exciting popular illustration of the cultural materialist approach to explaining human customs.

Kaplan, D., & Manners, R. A. (1972). *Culture theory*. Englewood Cliffs, NJ: Prentice Hall. A simple and straightforward discussion of the major theoretical orientations of cultural anthropology.

Kroeber, A. L., & Kluckhohn, C. (n.d.). *Culture: A critical review of concepts and definitions*. New York: Random House. A survey of definitions and uses of the word "culture" from the beginning of anthropology to the 1950s.

Lévi-Strauss, C. (1950). *Structural anthropology*. New York: Basic Books. Seventeen articles by the founder of structural anthropology, the application of linguistic techniques to the study of culture.

Rappaport, R. A. (1968). *Pigs for the ancestors: Ritual in the ecology of a New Guinea people*. New Haven: Yale University Press. An excellent illustration of the approach of cultural ecology applied to the analysis of warfare among the Tsembaga Maring of New Guinea.

Ruby J. (Ed.). (1982). *A crack in the mirror: Reflexive perspectives in anthropology*. Philadelphia: University of Pennsylvania Press. A collection of studies by ethnographers who forthrightly discuss the anthropologist's role in reflexive anthropological research.

Sahlins, M. (1976). *Culture and practical reason*. Chicago, IL: University of Chicago Press. A critique of the materialist view of culture as the product of practical activity, in which the author argues for an understanding of culture as a system of meaningful symbols, the structure of which determines people's perceptions of what is and is not practical action.

Wilson, E. O. (1975). *Sociobiology: The new synthesis*. Cambridge, MA: Harvard University Press. A complex and controversial look at social systems from a biological perspective.

Wilson, E. O. (1978). *Human nature*. Cambridge, MA: Harvard University Press. A sociobiological interpretation of the human condition. Controversial but worth reading.

PART II

Survival and

We humans must learn to adapt first to our physical environment, and then to the cultural environment we have constructed if we are to survive as individuals and as societies. Chapter 3 illustrates the diversity of physical environments around the world and the subsistence technologies that have been developed to aid in adaptation. Chapter 4 examines how the values of commodities differ from culture to culture and discusses the development of economic systems. Chapter 5 examines the use of power to maintain an ordered society and to restore order when conflicts arise or rules are broken.

Adaptation

*H*uman societies occupy territories, and their customs must enable them to cope with their environments if they are to survive. In this chapter we will examine the different kinds of environments that are found around the world and discuss the ways in which societies have adjusted to different conditions by using the resources that their environments make available.

3

Environment, Adaptation, and Subsistence

ENVIRONMENTAL DIVERSITY
Cultural and Natural Areas
Natural Environments
Carrying Capacity

BIOLOGICAL AND CULTURAL ADAPTATION

SUBSISTENCE ADAPTATIONS AND THE ENVIRONMENT

Foraging
Optimal Foraging Theory
Food Production
The Trend Toward Food Domestication

FIGURE 3.1 *Subsistence Technologies*

The physical environment of a particular group of people greatly influences the development of its methods of food getting, shelter, defense, and ultimately its culture. This farmer is sowing rice in a field in Sri Lanka.

Oats, peas, beans, and barley grow. and potatoes. and tomatoes. Except in times of drought. or too much rain. or Japanese beetles. How long could you survive if you had to grow all your vegetables in your backyard and hunt for your meat in your neighborhood? If you lived in Alaska. or Arizona. Consider the source of your lunch or dinner if you had no supermarket or McDonalds to supply it. Imagine your life without hamburgers and french fries. Imagine eating mostly rice every day. or sushi. or snake meat. You would probably love it. Humans have learned to adapt to many diverse types of foods.

49

ENVIRONMENTAL DIVERSITY

Human beings are unusual among the many species of animals in having successfully occupied so many different environments. Approximately 5 billion human beings are found in habitats as diverse as arctic regions, deserts, and tropical rainforests. Throughout the world, people have managed to survive challenging physical circumstances, and they have learned to exploit an amazing variety of food resources. To understand the success of the human animal in adapting to a complex natural world, it helps to be aware of the different specific environments in which people are found today.

Cultural and Natural Areas

Alfred Kroeber, an American anthropologist, noted (1939) that the culture areas of native North Americans tended to have boundaries that corresponded with important differences in their natural environments. The correspondence between cultural and natural areas can be understood in several ways. For instance, the diffusion of cultural traits from one society to another is influenced by the environment, and by natural boundaries that inhibit communication, trade, and other forms of interaction between peoples. This is not simply because such boundaries are necessarily physical barriers that are difficult to cross—although they sometimes can be—but more importantly because all aspects of a culture are in varying degrees adaptive responses to the environments in which they are found. This is particularly true of culturally governed customs that pertain to food getting, shelter, and defense technologies. Societies occupying the same or similar natural environments may readily borrow cultural traditions from one another that are relevant to successful adaptation. On the other hand, such adaptive cultural traits are less likely to be of interest to neighboring peoples who occupy different habitats.

Natural Environments

James (1959) has classified the world into eight major types of natural environments that are characterized by important differences in climate, vegetation, and animal life. These dif-ferences are based, in part, on their latitude and proximity to oceans and mountain ranges, each of which plays a role in determining the kinds of problems and resources that are present.

Mixed forests. In temperate climates there are mixed forests, such as those of eastern North America, that are made up of conifers and broadleaf trees. They are often accompanied by rolling plains and open areas in which the fertile soil provides an ideal situation for contemporary agricultural societies. So even though they represent only 7 percent of the earth's land surface, they are occupied today by about 43 percent of the human population. Prior to the development of iron tools, when it was more difficult to cut down the trees, these lands may not have held such a large proportion of the human species.

Scrub forests. Regions between coasts and mountains that have mild, wet winters and hot, dry summers are scrub forests that attract a disproportionate share of human population. These areas, such as much of coastal California, represent only 1 percent of the land, but are home to 5 percent of the earth's human occupants.

Tropical forests. Regions such as the Amazon basin of Brazil that have warm climates, abundant rainfall, plant and animal life are tropical forests. Although they cover only 10 percent of the earth's surface, 28 percent of the human species live in tropical forests.

Since heavy rainfall leaches away important soil nutrients and since tropical forest soils are typically high in acidity, they are not particularly productive as agricultural lands. Gardening techniques that rely on periodic changes in garden sites are common. Domesticated pigs have been usefully exploited as food by some societies that occupy tropical forests, most particularly in Southeast Asia and the Melanesian, Micronesian, and Polynesian islands of the Pacific.

Mountain lands. Highly complex landforms of mountain lands such as the Rocky Mountains or Appalachians of North America include a variety of environments, often within close distances of one another. The major environmental differences relate to (1) climate differences that are influenced by elevation and (2) local differences in rainfall and sunlight within a mountain area. For instance, slopes on the eastern sides of mountains near oceans receive greater rainfall than do the western sides, and northern and southern slopes typically receive different amounts of sunlight. These differences result in numerous different plant and animal communities that occupy specific environments within the entire mountain region. Mountain lands seem to have provided few resources except at elevations below 6,000 feet above sea level to peoples who lacked domesticated foods, but have proven most useful to pastoralists and agricultural peoples; they represent 12 percent of the globe's land area and are occupied by 7 percent of the world's people.

Grasslands. Twenty-six percent of the earth's surface is covered by grasslands, a greater area than any other type of environment. Yet only 10 percent of the human species inhabit grassland areas. There are three basic types of grasslands that differ in climate and in the predominant type of grass: steppes, prairies, and savannas. Steppes, such as the vast treeless stretches of southeastern Europe and Asia, have dry climates and extreme temperature changes during the year. Their grasses are short, hardy varieties that can tolerate their dry environment. Prairies, such as the North American Great Plains, have wetter climates and, consequently, support taller varieties of grass. Savannas, similar to some treeless plains of Florida, are found in tropical areas and are characterized by tall grasses and drought-resistant undergrowth.

Grasslands can be exploited usefully by hunters because of the large game animals, especially foraging herd animals, that occupy them. Pastoralists find them productive since they are equally good environments for domesticated grazing animals such as cattle and sheep. Gardening in these environments is difficult without a plow or machine technology, since the grass-dominated soils are difficult to prepare for planting.

Arid lands. The low annual rainfall in desert arid lands, such as parts of the southwestern United States and Great Basin, results in much of the land being sparsely covered by various plants such as grasses and low-growing desert shrubs that are capable of surviving on limited amounts of water. Isolated fertile pockets with year-round water may occur within arid lands, the only spots in which rainfall gardening is possible. Plant cultivation outside these areas require irrigation, and pastoralism is possible but not as productive as it is in grasslands. So arid lands have typically supported dispersed bands of foragers, whose collecting of wild plants and hunting of animals permits them to live in very small nomadic groups that exploit large territories. Thus, deserts comprise 18 percent of the world's land mass but only 6 percent of its people. Yet they are still not the most sparsely settled of the earth's environments.

Boreal forests. Boreas, the Greek god of the north wind, gives his name to heavily wooded regions, mostly dominated by coniferous trees, the boreal forests. Because the climatic conditions are colder and less favorable for plant domestication than are those of other forested regions, the boreal forests such as the logging and mining areas of northern Ontario have attracted few human inhabitants. They represent 10 percent of the land surface of the world, but only 1 percent of the human species occupies these forests.

Polar lands. Regions of cold climates near the north and south poles, polar lands are made up of ice-zones of permanent snow and ice, tundras, level or undulating treeless plains in the arctic and subarctic regions of North America, Asia and Scandinavia, and taigas, swampy coniferous forests of the northern lands south of the tundras. These are the least densely occupied environments of the world, representing 16 percent of its land area, but containing less than 1 percent of the people of the earth. As the environmental zone that is nearest the poles, the weather of the polar lands may be continually below freezing, and even those areas furthest from the poles have only short growing seasons and, therefore, few plants. Therefore, polar lands do not easily support any of the basic subsistence technologies. Until recently, they have been successfully occupied only by foraging peoples who have emphasized the hunting of both land and sea mammals and fishing.

Carrying Capacity

The different natural environments of the world are not equally accessible to living creatures, including human beings. One measure of the ability of species to survive on the resources available to them in a particular environment is the carrying capacity, that is, the upper limit on population determined by the characteristics of that environment. Population can be limited by such things as the food resources naturally available in an environment, the potential fertility of the soil for food production, climate, and the available water resources. The most crucial factor in determining the upper limit to which population can grow is the vital resource that is least available, since a population cannot be sustained at a level that makes its needs for any single resource greater than is consistently available, no matter how abundant the other resources may be.

Generally speaking, populations tend to stabilize at levels somewhat below the theoretical carrying capacity of their environments. The reason for this is that as populations grow toward the limit set by the available resources, competition between individuals for the resources will increase, so the effort and costs that must be expended to sustain each member of a population grows as well. Eventually, it will become increasingly difficult for the population as a whole to meet its needs and a point of diminishing returns will be reached. Thus, the rate of population growth tends to stabilize gradually somewhere below the level that it could be sustained in theory.

BIOLOGICAL AND CULTURAL ADAPTATION

The adjustment of an organism to a particular environment, adaptation is a two-way process, since it involves both changes in the organism in response to the demands of the environment and changes in the environment brought about by the organism. Adaptations in the organism can include both biological and cultural changes that both facilitate and improve its adjustment to a particular environment.

Living species are composed of individuals who differ from one another in their individual biological traits. Such differences can make it easier or harder for some individuals to survive to the reproductive age when they are able to pass their characteristics on to the next generation. Biological evolution is one of the means by which living species, including human beings, are able to adjust to an environment.

Natural conditions select, or determine, which biological traits are most likely to be weeded out of a species over the generations, as the species adjusts through biological evolution to a particular environment. This process was called natural selection by Charles Darwin (1859) who first systematically described parallels between the natural adaptation of a species and the "artificial" adaptation of breeding stock produced over many generations.

Biological anthropologists would be quick to cite examples of ways in which human beings have adapted to different environments around the world. For instance, the human trunk, head, arms, and legs tend to be longer and thinner in hot dry environments, while rounder and more compact body parts are associated with cold environments. The former traits create greater surface areas from which excess heat can be radiated efficiently from the body through evaporation of sweat. In cold environments where heat loss can endanger life, such traits would be less adaptive than the more compact shapes that make heat retention easier. Adaptive benefits have been suggested for other human differences such as skin color at different latitudes, and variations in average lung capacities at different elevations.

More interesting to cultural anthropologists are the ways in which human beings are able to adjust to their diverse environments by changing their habits, customs, and cultures. Culturally governed changes in behavior make it possible for humans to adjust successfully to new environments much more quickly than biological evolutionary changes. For instance, fashioning animal skins and furs into warm clothing, using dog sledge transportation, and constructing igloos from the icy environment probably do more to explain the ability of Inuit peoples to survive so successfully in the arctic north than does Inuit body stature.

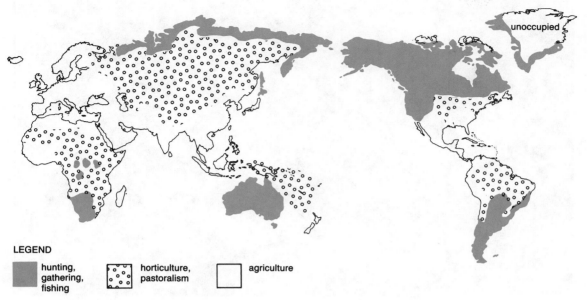

LEGEND

▓ hunting, gathering, fishing

⬚ horticulture, pastoralism

☐ agriculture

FIGURE 3.2 *Subsistence Technologies of* A.D. *1600*

This map shows the worldwide range of subsistence technologies in A.D. *1600.*

SUBSISTENCE ADAPTATIONS AND THE ENVIRONMENT

The study of subsistence is the study of how people obtain the necessities of life, particularly food, from their environment. It is in the study of food getting that we see most clearly how the forces of nature set limits and provide possibilities for human social and cultural life and how human subsistence technologies, the tools and techniques for obtaining food, help people adapt to their environments around the world.

Foraging

The oldest and simplest of human subsistence technologies is foraging, a food collecting system based on fishing, hunting wild animals, and gathering wild plant foods. Human beings have subsisted by foraging for more than 99 percent of their existence. Thus, foraging has been a very successful and adaptable way of surviving. Depending on their environments, foragers place different relative emphasis on the gathering of plants, hunting, and fishing. Those foragers who emphasize plant collecting have the least specialized subsistence technology and the least emphasis on separation of the roles of men and women.

The principal subsistence tools in those few remaining cultures that still live by foraging are digging sticks, clubs, spears, bows and arrows, fishing devices, traps, fire, and containers for storing, cooling, and transporting food. Tools are general purpose and few in number, since they must be made on the spot when needed or transported as the people move from place to place in the quest for food. According to Lomax and Arensberg (1977), who surveyed the subsistence systems of 1,308 societies, "The emphasis is on hand skills rather than tools" (p. 668). Since individual skill is critical to success in the quest for food, foragers generally socialize their children to be independent and assertive and to rely on their own initiative rather than to be compliant to the demands of others.

Since hunting and gathering technologies rely on naturally occurring wild foods, foragers are unable to live year-round in groups as large as those supported by food domestication. Therefore, social mechanisms more complex than the family are not necessary for organizing the political and economic lives of foragers. Foragers lack governments and warfare. They tend to be highly mobile, especially when hunting provides a major portion of their food supply.

Considering the small size of their social

FIGURE 3.3 *Foraging*

Hunter-gatherers, or foragers, rely on the fish, game, or plants readily available in their environment for food. One of the oldest forms of subsistence, foraging is being replaced in many areas of the world by some form of agriculture more suited to feeding large numbers of people. These Kalahari San are digging for bulbs after the rainy season.

groups, it is hardly surprising that foragers generally have been less politically powerful than food domesticators. In competition with food domesticators, foragers have usually been at a disadvantage. As a result, they continue to exist primarily in those areas of the earth of marginal interest to the plant and animal domesticators: the arctic wastes (the Inuit of the Arctic), the tundras (the Chuckchi of Siberia), deserts (the southwest African !Kung San Bushmen and Hottentots and the Shoshoni Indians of the Great Basin in the United States), and tropical environments (the Mbuti pygmies of the African Ituri Forest).

The foraging technology forms the subsistence base of a societal type known as the band. According to Julian Steward (1955) and Elman R. Service (1962), the hunting and gathering technology places certain functional demands on the social organization of the band-level culture. Bands are typically small groups based on kinship, with labor divided only by age and sex, sharing of resources, temporary leadership roles, material possessions limited by nomadism, and ideals reflecting these features. Wild foods are a sparse resource for people with no other means of survival. The poor environments occupied by foragers in recent times are unable to support more than about one person per five square miles and in some places as few as one person per 500 square miles.

Group structure. Permanent social groups cannot be very large. The local group that works and lives together averages about 50 people in contemporary band societies and rarely exceeds 100 people. The local groups of band cultures may have been somewhat larger in earlier times, when bands occupied areas with more abundant resources than are now found in the marginal areas to which they have been restricted by the expansion of more powerful societies. Nevertheless, wild food resources cannot maintain large local groups except in very lush environments, since the larger the group is, the farther individuals must travel from their base of operations in their quest for food.

As a general rule, in the small, local groups of band cultures, all individuals will be related, either by descent or marriage. Kinship is the basic institution in a band society for organizing the education of children, social etiquette, and economic, political, military, and judicial practices. In these largely familial groups, ancestry is most commonly traced through both men and women.

Division of labor. The only specialization of labor in a band culture is that based on differences of sex and age. In a band society supported by the sparse resources of wild foods, the most economical division of subsistence labor usually assigns the work of hunting to the men, while the gathering of wild plants near the camp is done by the women and older children. The sexual aspect of this specialization of labor is an adaptation to pregnancy in the female and the need for prolonged nursing of infants. Although these two biological facts might hinder her as a hunter, the woman still can be an important provider of plant foods gathered locally during periods of pregnancy and lactation. Elman R. Service (1962), R. B. Lee and Ivan DeVore (1968), and J. Tanaka (1977), have estimated that women sometimes provide as much as 80 percent of the calories in the diets of people who survive by hunting and gathering. However, in circumstances where a rigid differentiation is not important for the survival of the group, men, women, and children may be allowed to play overlapping roles. In hunting and gathering societies in areas with plentiful wild foods, men may often gather wild plants as well as hunt; men, women, and children may frequently work together in cooperative hunting activities, even though hunting is thought of as more central to the male status.

Ernestine Friedl (1975) has suggested that the sexual division of labor in foraging societies takes one of four major forms, depending on the subsistence adaptation of the foraging groups to their specific environments. The four basic subsistence adaptations of the foragers are individual foraging, communal foraging, plant-focused foraging, and animal-focused foraging.

Individual foraging. Subsistence based on individual foraging is common in environments in which meat is a relatively unimportant resource. In individual foraging, both men and women are expected to gather their own plant foods but men provide primarily for themselves while women forage for themselves and their children. Only a small amount of time is devoted to hunting in this subsistence pattern. Men and women are typically equal in social power and prestige in these foraging societies.

Communal foraging. In environments where the major meat resource is fish or small game and plant foods are most easily collected by cooperative labor, communal foraging is common. Hunting is usually accomplished by driving animals toward nets where they are killed by the men of the group. In communal foraging, the game is normally divided at the site among all the families who participated, so no particular prestige is gained by men from their role in hunting. The joint participation of women and men in the subsistence activities of communal foraging societies usually results in a relative equality between the sexes.

PYGMY NET AND ARCHERY HUNTING IN THE ITURI FOREST

The Ituri Forest Pygmy of the Congo are a foraging people with an emphasis on hunting. Their adaptation to a tropical forest environment, described by Colin Turnbull (1961), illustrates the interplay of technology and environment by which a society adjusts to its surroundings while meeting its subsistence needs. The Pygmy are divided into two major groups that differ in their primary food-getting technology and that have resulting differences in their social organization. One part of the Pygmy population, the Efe, emphasizes archery, the other, called Mbuti, are net hunters.

For about ten months of each year, the net hunters live deeper in the forest than do the archers, in communities of up to thirty families. Their hunt is a communal affair. According to Turnbull (1961), "The net-hunting technique calls for each family to set up its net and fasten it to the net on each side (every elementary family owns one net, up to three hundred feet in length). As the men and youths are silently forming this semicircle, the women and girls form an opposite one, and at a given signal from the men, close in, beating the undergrowth with branches and making a distinctive whooping cry.

"Any animal falling into the nets is immediately killed with a spear, and the owner of the net into which it fell will give it to his wife to put in her basket. If the animal is too large for this, it is cut up and divided on the spot; otherwise the division takes place back in camp. The ultimate sharing follows no clear-cut kinship lines, though the owner of the net and the owner of the spear that killed the animal have first priority. Momentary individual needs seem to be given much more consideration, and portions will be given to those who were unable to come on the hunt or whose nets trapped no game" (pp. 296–297).

The remaining two months of the year are a time of plenty in the forest. Game is so abundant during this period, called the honey season, that smaller groups of related families can readily provide for their own needs without participating in communal hunts. During this period, the community tends to break up into smaller groups that go their own way until food becomes scarce enough to warrant cooperating in larger groups again.

The bow and arrow hunting Pygmies follow an opposite yearly cycle of dispersal and congregation. They occupy lands near the edges of the forest that are less productive than the interior areas, partly because these areas have been changed by the presence of commercial plantations, mining activities, tourism, missions, and roads. Through most of the year the archery Pygmies wander in groups of three or four brothers and their families. Hunting is done only by men, who climb trees near game trails and wait for the opportunity to shoot animals that pass by or are flushed by the hunters' dogs. The food is carried back to the camp, where it is divided. Women in these groups do not participate in the hunt, but collect vegetable foods near the camp and take care of domestic chores. The archery hunters also supplement their food gathering by engaging in trade with nearby farming villagers outside the forest, a resource that is less used by the net hunters.

Once a year, during the honey season, game becomes abundant enough even in the territories of the archers to make communal hunts more productive than archery. During this short season, the bow and arrow hunters coalesce into a larger community that cooperates in a hunt very like that of the net hunters, although no actual nets are used. According to Turnbull (1961), the communal hunt of the honey season "not only reaffirms the unity of the archery band as a whole, it also provides an opportunity for discussion of matters of general interest, such as betrothals, or the election of a new headman. . . . It is a time for general socializing, for song and dance (much of which is of ritual significance), and ultimately for the realignment of the smaller sections whose composition is never the same year after year. Petty hostilities and jealousies are removed during this festive season, which lasts about two months; old friendships are renewed and new friendships formed" (p. 301).

The contrasting yearly cycle of the two groups of Pygmies is an interesting illustration of how environmental differences can influence the customs of a culture. Cultures are adaptive systems, whereby a people adjust to their circumstances. Although historical documentation does not recount the actual development of these two patterns of Pygmy life, it is conceivable that they arose in response to a decline in game in the forest fringes due to road building and other exploitation of forest resources by the non-Pygmy newcomers. As net hunting became less productive for most of the year, this type of aboriginal subsistence technology might have been abandoned as uneconomical. This reconstructed history is only hypothetical, but it illustrates the concept of interaction between an environment and a society's technology and food-getting customs as an important factor in the adjustment of a way of life to people's subsistence needs.

Plant-focused foraging. Societies in environments where plant resources can readily supply the majority of the food from areas nearby for periods long enough to permit hunting expeditions far from the campsite engage primarily in plant-focused foraging. While men are occupied with hunting larger animals that may have to be pursued for long distances over a period of days, women gather plant foods near the camp, an activity that typically provides between 60 and 70 percent of the group's food. Nevertheless, men's social prestige and power are often high when compared with women, because whenever they bring more meat to camp than their own families can use, they share the surplus with the hunters of other families and as a result are given high status by their neighbors. In contrast, the plant foods that women provide their own families are the basic staple of life. They are readily available to all, so there is no need for women to share the fruits of their labor

FIGURE 3.4   *Inuit Whale Hunt*

Foragers of the far north, Inuits hunt whales, seals, fish, caribou, and bear for food. Here they are cutting up whale meat, but as the whale population dwindles, hunting and fishing societies experience pressure to depend on more industrially processed food.

outside their own families. Thus, women lack access to a means for raising their status in the way men do. In this unbalanced system, when men share food with nonrelatives their status rises in a way that emphasizes the dependence of women on men for the important resource that men provide.

Animal-focused foraging. Environments that offer little in the way of plant foods may be occupied by foragers when fish and animal life are abundant enough. In animal-focused foraging, fish and large game hunted by men are the basic food. In this subsistence system, women do not contribute directly to the food supply, but bear domestic responsibilities including the processing of the meat and skins brought in by the men. Often in those societies, men make the tools that women use. Especially where the meat resources are large game animals, the pursuit of which can encourage high levels of competitiveness and aggression in hunters, the economic dependence of women on men can result in low social status for women.

Optimal Foraging Theory

Nowhere do people use every possible available resource in their environment. Insects, for instance, are a source of protein that is ignored by a great many cultures. Dogs and cats are quite common in North American and European societies, but are culturally defined as pets rather than potential foods. Some species of dogs were raised specifically for their food value by the Aztecs, and both dogs and cats are marketed in various parts of the Orient where milk products traditionally have not been favored as foods. This selectivity in the cultural definition of potential food resources exists even in societies that rely on the simplest of food-getting technologies that permit only foraging for wild foods.

Optimal foraging theory is a way of trying to explain why some foods are emphasized more than others and why some are regularly ignored by collectors of wild foods. Basically, optimal foraging theory asserts that the likelihood of foragers using potential food resource is directly proportional to the calories it offers as food per unit of effort required to obtain and prepare it for eating. The greater the caloric cost of obtaining and preparing a given food, the less likely it will be sought. When all potential foods in a given environment are ranked from the one with the highest rate of return on effort expended to the one with the least payoff, it will be found that those foods at the top of the list will be the ones that are most commonly used in the diet. Items lower on the list will be less and less often used. When the full dietary requirements of a foraging group are considered, there is some point on the entire list below which it is unlikely that foods will ever be sought except under unusual circumstances.

Optimal foraging theory is useful for answering a number of questions about food collecting activities. For instance, it would be ethnocentric to suggest that insects are not used as foods by most societies because insects are unaesthetic as foods. The idea that their nutritional value is lower than that of other animals is simply incorrect. However, the tendency of many societies to ignore the nutritional value of many insects that exist in their environment does make sense on the purely practical level suggested by optimal foraging theory: The high amount of effort that an individual would usually have to expend to gather enough of to them to prepare a meal simply makes most insects too costly to be worth the effort in most environments most of the time. Of course there are exceptions. The aboriginal Shoshoni of the Great Basin desert of the United States were regularly plagued by infestations of grasshoppers in sufficient numbers so that it was quite cost-effective to simply dig a trench, cover its bottom with hot coals, and then just wait until it filled itself with roasted grasshoppers. In such a situation, the usual predictions of optimal foraging theory would not be violated if grasshoppers became a temporary important addition to the normal yearly diet, as it did regularly for the Shoshoni.

Of course, a plant or animal may be collected for reasons other than its value as food. The tribes of the United States Plains hunted the bison as an important food resource, but they also used its hide for leather, its tendons for making bows, and its horns and bones for making various tools. Similarly, an animal or plant low on the list as a food resource might be sought and eaten anyway when its other uses added to its food value make the effort worthwhile. However, the basic principle of optimal foraging theory is not really violated by such considerations. The essential idea that the return on invested effort is the best predictor of the likelihood of a resource being utilized remains constant whether the return is calculated in terms of food calories or in terms of any other valid units of value that contribute toward survival of a social group.

Food Production

Although the shift to food domestication was traditionally viewed as progress, the current anthropological thinking is that foraging had its advantages too. Judging from the few groups that still practice hunting and gathering, ways of life based on foraging are usually quite satisfactory in their ability to meet the needs of people. Population density is generally low, and the communities of cooperating individuals are never very large. Under these circumstances, it is simple for the local group to move quickly from place to place. As a result, food shortages are rare among hunters and gatherers. Nomadic or seminomadic hunters and gatherers do not live amidst their own refuse, one contributor to many of the diseases with which more sedentary peoples must contend. This factor, plus the low population densities that are characteristic of foragers, means that the epidemics that often plague peoples who live under crowded conditions are also rare. Furthermore, Marvin Harris (1977) has pointed out that foragers have a much shorter work week than do food domesticators. For instance, the southern African !Kung foragers need to work only about three hours a day to obtain a nutritious diet, even though their desert environment is not nearly so lush as most of the areas occupied by hunting and gathering peoples before the rise of farming.

The Trend Toward Food Domestication

Despite these advantages of foraging, as early as 20,000 years ago certain changes laid the foundations for the eventual domestication of plants and animals. About this time people practicing generalized hunting and gathering ways of life began to develop more specialized subsistence practices in the Near East: the gathering of different wild foods in different seasons and their preservation in storage pits for off-season use. This planning ahead made a more sedentary life possible even while exploiting wild cereal crops that were native to the area. These wild cereals could be harvested easily by lightly beating the stems so that the seeds would break loose and fall into a basket. After grinding with stone tools, the tough seeds could be prepared for eating in a variety of ways.

This use of the abundant wild grains in zones of sufficient rainfall along the hilly flanks of the mountains of the Near East resulted not only in a more sedentary life but also in population growth. Or population growth itself may have forced people to develop agriculture and animal domestication to better provide for their growing numbers (Boserup, 1965).

The rise of population that may have led to food domestication can be accounted for by the interplay between human fertility and sedentarism (a settled rather than nomadic life style). Rose Frisch and Janet McArthur (1974) and Rose Frisch (1975) have demonstrated that following the birth of a child, a woman will not again begin ovulation so long as less than 20 to 25 percent of her body weight consists of fat. This figure represents the approximate amount of calories that a fetus needs to develop full term to birth. That is, before a fertile woman will be able to conceive, her body must store enough calories of energy to nourish a developing fetus for a nine-month pregnancy. In active nomadic populations this threshold of body fat is more difficult to achieve than in sedentary populations, since the foragers burn more food energy themselves and their diets are likely to be lower in carbohydrates and higher in protein. Since nursing one child takes about 1,000 calories a day, it is unlikely that a woman will become pregnant so long as she is nursing if she lives in a semi-nomadic hunting and gathering society. Since nursing is likely to continue for at least three years in most societies, the level of fertility is, on the average, much lower in hunting and gathering societies than in sedentary societies using domesticated foods. The span of childbearing years is also shorter, for the onset of menstruation occurs later in hunting and gathering societies because a hunting and gathering diet is rich in protein. In demonstration of these theories, Richard B. Lee (1972) and Gina B. Kolata (1974) have reported growth in fertility and population among those !Kung hunter-gatherers who abandoned their native semi-nomadic way of life for a more sedentary food production economy.

Another explanation for the adoption of a comparatively sedentary way of life in the Near East is simply the availability of an abundance of native wild grains. Robert Sussman (1972) argues that such a change in the lifestyle and diet of these early foragers would have resulted in an increase in the people's fertility and rate of population growth. Accelerated population growth, in turn, would have created pressure for even more effective control over the food supply. Specifically, population growth eventually made it necessary for people to move into less productive areas around the margins of the zones where wild grains grew in natural abundance. Lewis Binford (1968) and Kent Flannery (1971) believe that it was in these marginal zones that people found it necessary to seek more direct human control over their food supply. People began to keep near to the home base a few animals such as sheep, goats, dogs, and cattle, which had previously been hunted. This practice ensured a steady supply of meat as well as other useful products such as hides, milk, and milk products. By experimenting in how to plant seeds, people acquired grains as dietary supplements in areas where they had not been common previously.

Whatever the reasons for the growth of food domestication, by about 9000 B.C. goats and sheep had been domesticated in the Near East, and barley and wheat were domesticated by 7000 B.C. in the same area. Cattle and pigs also were under human control by 7000 B.C. The domesticated grains differed from their wild relatives in that the crop domesticators favored larger seeds. As the seeds evolved to a larger size under human influence, the grain came to be more firmly attached to the stems and could no longer be harvested easily by shaking the stems over a basket. Thus, the domestication of grains required the simultaneous evolution of a new technology for use in the harvest, including knife-blades and sickles for cutting bunches of stems. Such tool kits were in use in the ancient Near East by 7000 B.C.

Horticulture. Domestication of plants and animals began about 13,000 years ago. The earliest form of food domestication technology was horticulture, or primitive farming. Horticulture differs from true agriculture in that such factors as the plow, draft animals, soil fertilization, crop rotation, and irrigation are

FIGURE 3.5 *Horticulture*

The subsistence technology of horticulture provides people with food in a simple uncomplicated way. This African woman in a village on the Ivory Coast is pounding grain into flour.

largely absent. The most common hand tools used in primitive labor-intensive horticultural societies are the digging stick and the hoe. Most horticulturalists have some domestic animals with which they supplement their diets, but animals are never the source of the bulk of their diet.

A horticultural technology provides a more reliable subsistence and produces more food per acre than does a hunting and gathering technology, so peoples with horticultural technologies live in larger communities than do foragers. Their denser populations give them correspondingly greater political power than foragers have, so horticultural societies are much more widespread. Four hundred years ago, they were found primarily in the tropical forest areas of South America, in many parts of North America, in most areas of Africa, throughout the islands of the Pacific, and in some of the Asian mainland. Nevertheless, the simple tools of horticulturalists give them relatively little control over the produc-

tivity of the land they cultivate, so there are natural limits on their distribution throughout the world. They were typically found in areas with warm or temperate climates favorable to the domestication of plants.

There are two common forms of horticulture: slash-and-burn and dry land gardening. Slash-and-burn horticulture is also known as swidden horticulture, or shifting cultivation. This form of food cultivation is common in tropical forest environments or in savannas, where clearing the land requires heavy labor. The trees and vegetation that are cut away are left to dry and then burned before a crop can be planted. Garden plots are cultivated for several years during which they may become less and less productive as their nutrients are depleted. Then the fields are allowed to lie fallow for a period of up to nine or ten years before they are cleared and worked again. Typically, gardeners who use the slash-and-burn technique have several gardens, each of which has been cultivated for a different length of time, so that each year the oldest may be abandoned to nature while another, abandoned previously, is again prepared for use. Ultimately, after several cycles of use and abandonment of plots, the soil will have become so depleted that the forest does not grow back, and entirely new gardens must be prepared. Eventually, gardens may be so far from the original village that an entire settlement of several hundred people may be relocated to a more convenient area.

Dry land gardening is carried out in arid environments. The major problem in dry land gardening is getting sufficient water to the crops. Some small canals may be used to channel available water resources such as the seasonal runoff of rainwater from higher land. However, in the absence of major, reliable water sources such as rivers, large irrigation projects that require heavy cooperative labor are not a part of this system. In drier periods water may have to be hand carried to individual plants in gardens.

In nonforested regions where cereal crops predominate, the settlements of horticulturalists may be more permanent than those of tropical forest farmers. Particularly in drier climates, horticulturalists may engage in some hand watering of plants or limited irrigation of fields, but irrigation is not so common or complex as in agriculturally based societies.

FIGURE 3.6   *Slash-and-Burn Horticulture*

Horticulturalists use simple tools such as hoes and digging sticks to plant their crops. In order to clear a plot of land for planting, they cut down or slash the trees and brush and then burn them. The ashes that remain act as fertilizer for the soil. This type of food production is also known as shifting cultivation since a new plot of ground may be started every planting season.

Control over the food supply allows horticulturalists to live in larger local groups than foragers. Villages of several hundred people may live together throughout the year. Housing is more permanent and house construction more elaborate than are the temporary shelters of foragers. Village life necessitates greater accommodation to the presence of others, so childrearing necessarily emphasizes compliance and responsibility over independence and assertiveness in children. Family organization tends to be more elaborate among horticulturalists than among foragers, since a large number of family members may reside in the same location over many generations.

The authority of the family organization in the lives of its individual members is great, since the family is the basic governing institution in horticultural villages. Each family organization may be a politically autonomous component of the village except in matters that affect the common welfare. Such matters tend to be dealt with by a council of family leaders from the entire village who seek to achieve a consensus on how to handle the problem.

The greater numbers and more complex social organization of horticulturalists and the need for control of the land as a source of income makes warfare a common element of life in horticulturally based societies. Nevertheless, just as horticuturalists have tended to be more politically powerful than foragers, horticulturalists have tended to be politically less powerful than agriculturalists. For this reason, they tend now to be restricted to arable areas of the world that are less desirable to the agricultural societies.

THE SHUARA OF BRAZIL

The Shuara are a horticultural people, popularly known as the Jívaro, who have been described by Michael Harner (1973). They live within the higher reaches of the Amazonian tropical forest of eastern Ecuador and Peru. Their basic subsistence food is a starchy root crop called manioc, but they also grow maize, sweet potatoes, squash, beans, peanuts, bananas, plantains, and papayas. These foods are supplemented by fish and game such as monkeys, birds, and peccaries.

Gardens are prepared near the living site by a group of men who belong to the same family. Undergrowth is cleared from a garden area, and the small trees are ringed by removing a strip of bark from the entire circumference of each one to weaken them. When the larger trees are felled, originally with stone axes and in more recent times with steel axes, they take with them the smaller weakened trees in their vicinity, since their canopies are interwoven with vines and other jungle growth. Several months later, after the brush and trees have dried, the garden area is burned. Then the gardens are planted and an elliptical, palm-thatched house is erected. The gardening itself is done by the women of the group.

Men hunt to supplement their families' diets with meat. Small game such as monkeys and birds are shot with blowgun darts that are coated with curare, a poison that suppresses the breathing reflex of the animal. Since a monkey is likely to try to pull out the dart, it is notched so that it will break off easily and leave the poisoned tip inside the animal. Within a few minutes, animals shot with the poisoned darts drop from the trees. Since the blowgun is such a silent weapon, it is often possible for a skilled hunter to pick off several monkeys from a troop before the others become alarmed. Larger game may be killed with spears, or in recent times, with shotguns or rifles. Fish are taken with traps, nets, or spears. The Jívaro (Shuara) have an unusual technique of poisoning the water and the fish in it. They build a dam to contain the fish and, using natural plants such as barbasco shrub and masu, pour the sap into the water. The poison stuns the fish so then they can be speared. Little ecological damage is done by this method.

Pastoralism.   A more specialized form of domestication technology is pastoralism, which focuses on animal husbandry as the major source of food. It tends to be found in areas unsuited to agricultural pursuits and is probably of more recent origin than horticulture. Indeed, it is commonly argued that pastoralism in most parts of the world developed as farming peoples expanded into environmentally less productive zones and adjusted by relying more heavily on domestic animals as their basic source of income. Most pastoralists do supplement their diets with food grown in simple gardens, but plant growing is always subordinated to the demands of their animal husbandry. Thus pastoralism typically requires large areas of land and a somewhat migratory way of life, called transhumance, using, in different seasons at least two primary foraging areas for their animals. Pastoralism is the predominant means of subsistence in environments such as deserts, grasslands, savannas, and mountains that are unable reliably to sustain horticultural or nonindustrialized agricultural production.

There are several types of pastoralism that occupy somewhat different environments depending on the animal that is the primary subsistence resource. Cattle herding was most common throughout sub-Saharan Africa, particularly throughout equatorial and East Africa, southern Africa, and parts of Madagascar. Cattle herding was also found in limited areas in the northern part of South America among the Goajiro, a people of mixed Native American and African origins. Many of the cattle herding peoples combined pastoralism with some plant cultivation. Camels were the basis for pastoralism throughout northern Africa and the Arabian Peninsula. Reindeer herding was particularly important among various peoples of the far north, including the Lapps of the northern Scandinavian subarctic and various peoples in Siberia. Yak herding was limited to the high mountain regions of the Himalayan area. A similar, geographically limited form of pastoralism was found in the Andes of South America, where llama herding in combination with agricultural production was important for societies such as the Inca who dominated the area at the time of European contact. Mixed pastoralism, the predominant type throughout western Asia north of India, combined a variety of animals such as sheep, goats, horses, and cattle.

Since they occupy territory that is often marginal and unproductive, pastoralists are

FIGURE 3.7   *Pastoral and Ranching Societies*
The Masai tribe of Kenya follow their herds in a pastoral tradition. They have great affection for their cattle, calling them each by name, and never slaughtering them.

generally unable to produce everything they need. Therefore, they must obtain some goods from neighboring horticultural or agricultural peoples. This is often accomplished by trade, but sometimes it is more profitable to raid their more sedentary neighbors. Especially when the animals they keep, such as horses or camels, give them great mobility, these peoples can carry out their raids rapidly with little warning and leave quickly afterwards.

According to Lomax and Arensberg (1977), "Pastoralists overproduce as a guarantee against famine and a sign of prosperity and pride, but large herds overgraze, and pastoral overgrazing has created deserts where gardens once were" (p. 676). Since the herds of pastoralists are vulnerable to theft, pastoralists must be constantly with their herds and live in perpetual readiness for conflict. Warfare is a prominent fact of life in pastoral societies. Thus, childrearing emphasizes obedience, deference to authority fig-

ures, and a competitive and socially dominant role for male warriors.

THE NORTHERN TUNGUS REINDEER HERDERS OF SIBERIA

The Northern Tungus occupy much of eastern Siberia. Their environment is in the treeless tundra and forested taiga zones of the northern polar region where plant cultivation is impractical. Their source of livelihood is reindeer herding and hunting.

The Tungus keep a domesticated variety of reindeer that they milk and use for riding and as pack animals, much as horses are used among their southern neighbors. Natural dangers such as wolves make it difficult to increase the herd, and as many as half the herd may be lost each winter. Normally, herd reindeer are only eaten at a few ceremonial events or when a weak animal is

FIGURE 3.8 *Nonindustrialized Agriculture*

Agriculture makes use of more complicated technology than horticulture to produce food. The use of plows pulled by draft animals and simple organic fertilizers characterize the complexity of nonindustrialized agriculture.

culled from the herd to prevent it from breeding; they are not a regular source of meat. The primary sources of meat in the Tungus diet are wild reindeer, deer, elk, bear, wolves, and boars that are obtained by hunting and trapping.

The Tungus must travel with their herds as they migrate between their summer and winter pasturages. The northern tundra is the preferred feeding ground during the short summer because lichens and other foods are more plentiful than in the forest lands to the south. During the four months of summer, the herds are plagued by mosquitoes and gadflies, so the reindeer feed at night and congregate in the daytime around smokey fires built by the Tungus to repel the pests. For the rest of the year, the herds move south and pasture during the day, so that they can be protected at night from wolves.

The summer home of the Tungusic family is a birch bark lodge. In the winter, when the herds must travel constantly to forage for food beneath the snow, the home is a small skin tent occupied by a nuclear family. The husband is responsible for trapping and hunting and heavy labor around the camp, while the wife milks and cares for the herds and takes charge of the routine domestic chores. The husband's hunting and trapping activities are important, since they provide

food, skins for clothing and tents, and furs that are used to trade for useful items such as rifles and metal utensils. This leaves the wife with a great deal of responsibility for the herds in the absence of her husband, including moving it to new grazing areas when this is necessary.

Agriculture (Intensive cultivation).   More intensive than horticulture in the use of land for food production, agriculture or intensive cultivation relies less heavily on human energy than on animal and technological power. The greater productivity of agriculture is made possible by the use of tools and techniques like the plow, irrigation, soil fertilization, and animal traction. Domestic animals such as the horse, cow, and ox are harnessed to pull the plow and to transport produce, and their excrement may be used to increase the fertility of the soil. Agriculture is much more recent than horticulture, being a scant 6,000 years old, but it has proven to be a very successful form of subsistence. An agricultural way of life creates large food surpluses. This surplus permits a much larger population to develop and makes it possible for large numbers of specialists to devote their full-time labor to nonagricultural pursuits. These features, in turn, greatly increase the political power of agricultural societies relative to those with a simpler technological foundation. Therefore, agriculturalists have become the largest, most widespread, most dominant peoples in the world and occupy the most productive parts of the world's surface.

The simplest form of intensive cultivation is nonindustrialized (or traditional) agriculture. In this form, the major tools are hand implements such as the hoe, shovel, and animal-drawn plow. Crops are grown for local consumption, but the use of the plow, animal-derived fertilizers, and irrigation results in greater productivity than is usual in extensive cultivation, so that market crops may also be produced. Use of the plow and animal or human fertilizer to enhance the productivity of the soil makes agriculture more land-intensive than labor-intensive. Horticulturalists can expand their populations only by opening new land to cultivation. However, land-intensive agriculture can allow farmers to support population growth by increasing the output of their fields. The towns occupied by agricultural peoples commonly number in the thousands or tens of thousands. Such large groups require a high degree of specialization and the presence of a system of government that is not based solely on the authority of the family organization. Agricultural societies frequently have class distinctions with inherited differences in political power and wealth within the local communities.

CLASSIC MAYAN RAISED FIELD FARMING

During the golden age of Mayan civilization, the so-called classic period from A.D. 200 to 900, the ancient Mayan occupied the Yucatan Peninsula, including what is now Honduras, Guatemala, Belize, and the Mexican states of Campeche, Chiapas, Tabasco, and Yucatan. Their land was dominated by tropical forests, savannas, and swamps. Their seasonal round consisted of a hot, dry season from February through May and a wet winter season that brought as much as 160 inches of rain.

In this tropical environment, the Maya built a civilization based on slash-and-burn gardening and an innovative system of raised field intensive farming that combined plant cultivation with aquaculture. Raised field agriculture was practiced in swampy areas and along slow moving rivers. These fields were built by digging a series of canals around the growing areas and piling the soil thus obtained on the fields to raise them above the water level. The chest-deep canals between the fields were home to water lilies, on which fish fed that could also be harvested. Periodically the canals were dredged, and the water plants and muck from their bottoms were added to the fields to enrich the soil.

The major crops grown by the Maya were maize, squash, beans, chili peppers, amaranth, manioc, and cacao. These were supplemented by fish from the canals and a variety of forest foods, including avocados, deer, turkeys, peccaries, tapirs, and rabbits. This combination of wild foods and domestic produce supported a population of perhaps two million, divided into a number of petty states, each ruled by its own *mah k'ina* or "Great Sun Lord," who was served by an administrative class of nobles, called *cahals*. These in turn governed in the smaller cities of each state and paid tribute to their lord.

Industrialized agriculture is the form of food production that relies most heavily on technological sources of energy, rather than human or animal labor. Currently, the tool kit of industrialized agriculture includes motorized equipment such as tillers, tractors, and harvesters. Chemical fertilizers are used to enhance the productivity of the soil, herbicides are used to minimize unwanted plants that compete with crops for water and soil nutrients, and pesticides play an important role in minimizing crop destruction by insects. Industrialized agriculturalists not only irrigate their fields, but also may employ various techniques for modifying the effects of adverse weather conditions—for instance, by shading crops or artificially maintaining higher temperatures around their plants during periods of cold weather. Industrialized agricultural techniques create high yields with relatively little investment of human labor. At the same time, food producing becomes increasingly

FIGURE 3.9 *Industrialized Agriculture*

An extremely efficient method of food production is an agriculture that utilizes the mechanization of industry such as this twin rotor combine harvesting soybeans.

expensive in terms of the investment in complex technologies, and the specialists in food production must rely heavily on others to produce and service the equipment that they use.

High-yield production techniques, coupled with an industrialized system of transportation to carry the produce over great distances, have made possible the rise of farms of tremendous acreage. An industrialized agriculture nevertheless operates at great costs, when one measures the amount of energy required to produce its food output. But it is so productive that in the United States, for instance, less than 3 percent of the population is involved in food production.

Societies whose subsistence technology is industrialized agriculture invariably support full-time governments that monopolize political power. The populations united under a single central government commonly number in the millions or hundreds of millions. Indeed, individual cities in industrialized societies may number in the millions.

SUMMARY

The natural environments of the world place limits on the characteristics of the cultures that societies have developed in different parts of the world. For instance, each environment also contains the particular resources that a society may use to meet its people's survival needs. The use of some resources provide opportunities for the development of large social groups and tremendous social complexity, while the use of others may severely restrict the size and complexity of a society. One popular way of categorizing the world's natural environments divides the world into nine basic habitats: mixed forests, scrub forests, tropical forests, mountain lands, grasslands, arid lands, boreal forests, and polar lands. Each of these environments has a unique set of resources that provide opportunities and set limits on cultural development. In adapting to the world's various environments, human societies have developed a variety of subsistence technologies, including foraging, horticulture, pastoralism, traditional agriculture, and industrialized agriculture.

**KEY TERMS
AND
CONCEPTS**

mixed forests 50
scrub forests 50
tropical forests 50
mountain lands 50
grasslands 51
steppes 51
prairies 51
savannas 51
arid lands 51
boreal forests 51
polar lands 51
ice-zone 51
tundra 51
taiga 51
carrying capacity 52
adaptation 52
natural selection 52
subsistence 53
subsistence technologies 53
foraging 53

band 54
individual foraging 55
communal foraging 55
plant-focused foraging 56
animal-focused foraging 57
optimal foraging theory 57
sedentarism 59
horticulture (gardening, extensive
  cultivation) 59
slash-and-burn   60
swidden horticulture 60
shifting cultivation 60
dry land gardening 60
pastoralism 62
transhumance 62
agriculture (intensive cultivation) 64
nonindustrialized (or traditional)
  agriculture 65
industrialized agriculture 65

**ANNOTATED
READINGS**

Cohen, Y. (Ed.). (1974). *Man in adaptation: The cultural present*. Chicago: Aldine. A collection of articles about the environmental adaptations of pastoral and farming societies.

Douglas, M. and Isherwood, B. (1979). *The world of goods: Toward an anthropology of consumption*. New York: W. W. Norton. Discusses economic theories of consumption and how anthropologists might study consumption.

Harris, M. (1986). *Good to eat*. New York: Harper & Row. A collection of essays on the reasons for cultural differences in what is eaten, by the founder of the cultural materialistic approach to studying culture.

James, P. E. (with collaboration by Hibberd V. B. Kline, Jr.). (1959). *A geography of man*. Boston: Ginn. One of the major and influential attempts to classify the world's major natural environments.

Kroeber, A. (1939). *Cultural and natural areas of native North America*. University of California Publications in American Archaeology and Ethnology, vol. 38. The first systematic anthropological demonstration of the relationships between cultural areas and natural environments.

Lustig-Arecco, V. (1975). *Technology: Strategies for survival*. New York: Holt, Rinehart and Winston. An examination of the role of technology in the adaptation of hunters, pastoralists, and farmers.

Rappaport, R. (1967). *Pigs for the ancestors: Ritual in the ecology of a Papua New Guinea people*. New Haven, CT: Yale University Press. A cultural ecological analysis of the Tsembaga Maring that emphasizes the role of pig herding as a regulatory mechanism in Tsembaga warfare.

Vayda, A. (Ed.). (1969). *Environment and cultural behavior: Ecological studies in cultural anthropology*. New York: Natural History Press. A classic collection of writings that illustrates the cultural ecological approach to understanding human customs in the social, demographic, and environmental contexts in which they are found.

In this chapter we will discuss how economic systems work in different societies. We will first examine how cultures differ in their definitions of what is valued as a potential economic commodity. We will consider how the relative values of commodities may vary from culture to culture, how cultural values as well as survival needs may influence the level of demand that may exist for a given commodity, and how cultures differ in the motives that are defined as normal reasons for economic exchanges. Economic systems will then be examined in terms of cultural differences in the control and use of resources, the production of valued goods and services, and in the distribution and consumption of goods and services.

4

Economics

DEFINITION OF ECONOMIC SYSTEMS
The Cultural Definition of Commodity
The Cultural Definition of Value
PRODUCTION: THE CONTROL AND USE OF RESOURCES
Use Rights
Ownership
Division of Labor
DISTRIBUTION
Reciprocity
Redistribution
Markets
CONSUMPTION
Subsistence Economies
Status Income
SOCIAL AGENTS OF ECONOMIC CONTROL
Community Control of Production
Kin Control of Production
Association Control of Production
Social Class

FIGURE 4.1 *Market Exchange*

Market exchange involves the buying and selling of goods. It is a relatively impersonal type of transaction since the exchange depends on supply and demand rather than on kinship status. This Mestizo Indian is selling ponchos and carpets in Central Equador.

Yen. Pieces of eight. Bull market. Penny candy. How long do you think you or your family could survive if you had to grow all the fruit and vegetables you needed? Or how many cows do you think you could raise on a tiny balcony on a high rise apartment on the East Side of New York City? What kind of house do you think you'd live in if you had to build your own from the resources available in your immediate area? If your neighbor had more trees than you did and you had more chickens, what system would you devise to exchange the items you both need?

DEFINITION OF ECONOMIC SYSTEMS

The system by which people obtain or produce, distribute, and consume valued material goods and services is called economics. An economic system includes the subsistence customs that are most especially concerned with the production of needed goods that we discussed in the previous chapter as well as the rules that govern what is done with those goods and how they are used. In this chapter, we will examine in more detail how people organize themselves socially to facilitate the production, exchange, and use of goods and services.

The Cultural Definition of Commodity

Cultures differ in what they define as useful or valuable, that is, as commodities. People work to produce food, provide themselves with shelter, and defend and reproduce themselves in all cultures. However, as was pointed out in the discussion of culture, the specific goods and services that constitute food, shelter, or means of defense differ from society to society. Usually people everywhere must work to obtain food, but what is considered food among one people may be ignored or judged unacceptable by another. For instance, milk and dairy products were unacceptable foods in traditional Oriental cultures, while North Americans reject the use of dog or snake meat, both of which are eaten in various parts of the Orient. These differences may be accounted for in part by an extension of the principle that underlies the concept of optimal foraging theory discussed in the previous chapter. Essentially, this is the idea that people tend to work to obtain the greatest return from their efforts. Although few would argue with such a principle in general, it alone is not sufficient to account for the diversity of things that people endow with economic value throughout the world. For instance, nowhere do people rely on one food alone as an overzealous application of this rule would imply. We humans also seek diversity, resulting in cultural differences in food tastes as well as in how people fill their other survival needs.

Cultural differences are even greater when we consider the range of variation that exists in pleasurable activities that are not mandated by survival needs. Consider, for instance, art, recreation, and religion. Although each category is a cultural universal and even though the psychological principles that guide people's behavior in each category may also be universal, the specific behaviors and objects people find beautiful, sacred, or fun are not readily predictable. Similarly, sex, though valued in all cultures for its role in the survival of the group, is not accepted as a purely pleasurable activity in all societies. Sex may be part of at least general reciprocity in all cultures, but it is not always an item of barter or sale as it has been in some market economies.

Intangible property. Cultural variation in the definition of commodities to be produced, exchanged, and consumed is not limited to tangible things. Intangibles too, may be defined as commodities. Navajos, for example, consider the sacred chants used in their curing ceremonies to be personal property, and an individual must pay an appropriate price to be taught a chant known to another. Northwest Coast Indians of North America considered titles of nobility to be a form of property, the ownership of which had to be validated by gift-giving. North Americans also assert ownership over the expression of ideas and songs in their copyright laws.

The Cultural Definition of Value

Cultures also differ in how much value they place on any commodity. The same things are not everywhere of equal worth. The sacred zebu cow of Hindu India would not command a high price at a North American cattle auction, and the dogs that so many North Americans esteem as household pets are seen as too dirty to be pets by Iranians I have known.

COMPARATIVE WORTH IN THE UNITED STATES

Current discussions of pay equity or comparative worth in the United States is a good illustration of the role of cultural values in people's conceptualization of economic worth. United States employers have, traditionally, placed an emphasis on a supply and demand concept to explain why they pay

FIGURE 4.2 *Chinese Market*

Cultures place different values on the type of goods they use and the food they eat. North Americans enjoy their hamburger and fries whereas Indians protect their cows as sacred and let them roam freely through the streets. Dogs and cats are popular pets in North America yet are hung as food to be sold in this Chinese market.

different salaries for different jobs. The idea has been that when many potential employees apply for a position, that position can be filled at a low salary. On the other hand, when few apply for a specific position, the employer will have to offer a higher rate of pay. This view that the market itself determines the worth of particular jobs has led many employers to argue that the major reason for the lower average income of women employees compared with male employees has been that women simply prefer to apply for kinds of work that command lower levels of pay!

Others, however, have recognized that discrimination may also play a role in what positions employers may be willing to hire women for and what they may be willing to pay a female applicant. For instance, Toth (1986) has shown that as women in the United States have moved into the traditionally high paying field of public relations, salaries have fallen, as has the social rank of this profession. Today, the United States work force is 44 percent female, but nearly 80 percent of public relations positions are filled by women. In spite of this attempt of many women to enter a prestigious and well paid profession, they are typically paid from $6,000 to $30,000 less than their male counterparts who have had a similar education and the same number of years in service. Indeed, the gap between men and women with a 10-year career can be over 1 million dollars.

It has been argued that because of discrimination and other nonmarket factors in creating lower than average salaries for women and other minorities, a simple supply and demand argument is inadequate as the sole basis to determine the salary that a position should command. Adherents of the comparative worth position hold that the dollar value of the pay for a job should be determined only in part by the supply and demand factor, and the characteristics of the job itself should also be considered. For instance, the length of previous experience and the level of education or training required to perform the work; the level of technical or verbal skill it requires; the amount of responsibility it entails for equipment, operations, or the safety of others; the degree of mental or physical effort the job demands; and the nature of the working conditions such as noise or hazards are possible factors to consider when determining the pay scale for a job. A position that is hazardous and requires great skill and previous training might be paid more than a safe job that requires little skill and training. Furthermore—and this is the crucial point of the comparative worth approach—two very different jobs in the same company that are equivalent in these characteristics should receive equivalent pay. Thus, first year clerk-typists and construction workers, entry-level secretaries and mechanics, or nurses who must spend two to four years in college and carpenters who must serve up to a four-year apprenticeship, might represent positions in a three-tiered pay system in the same company.

Such pay schemes have been initiated in a number of larger United States corporations such as AT&T, BankAmerica, Chase Manhattan, IBM, Motorola, and Tektronix already, and they have been considered legislatively in about 30 states. Whether a comparative worth viewpoint will become the predominant United States system for setting pay scales remains to be seen.

Supply and demand as cultural constructs. A good illustration of the cultural element in determining the value of commodities is the law of supply and demand so widely discussed in American marketing as if it were a law of nature that operates uninfluenced by culture. Such a view of supply and demand overlooks the fact that the value of a commodity is culturally defined. Sahlins (1976), for instance, has pointed out concerning food in American culture, that cut for cut, meat is priced higher the less closely the animal from which it comes is symbolically associated with human beings. Thus, dogs are named and live within the house like one of the family, so the eating of their meat, though perfectly nutritious, is tabooed. Horses too are named, but they live outside the house and work for people like servants instead of living with them as kin. Americans are somewhat grudgingly willing to admit that horses are edible, but they are not commonly eaten. Pigs and cattle are clearly defined as foods, but the pig which lives closer to the human domain as a barnyard animal and scavenger of human food scraps usually commands a lower market price than the cow. This system that influences the demand for various animals as food in American culture cannot be applied directly to other cultures.

The profit motive as a cultural construct. In the United States, people often speak of the profit motive as the basic economic incentive. Indeed, one theme of this text has been that material benefits are important predictors of customs. However, the profit motive concept is often used in an overly narrow sense, one that implies that *material* benefit is the sole motivator in economic transaction. This extreme view, common in American society, overlooks the important role of culture in defining value. Since it is a symbolic quality of commodity, anything may be given value. Thus, efforts to obtain valued commodities are not limited to the acquisition of material things. People also work to obtain intangible goods. For instance, people may willingly accept material loss for spiritual merit or for increased social honor. Prestige, respect, admiration, personal honor, mana, luck, or a reward after death may be sought after at the cost of material commodities. Thus, when the profit motive is understood as noth-

ing more than the claim that people will always try to maximize their immediate material gain in any exchange of goods, it is understood much too narrowly.

KWAKIUTL BARTERING: BIDDING UP THE PRICE

A narrow, materialistic view of the profit motive can make customs in which people seek to enhance their social rank and reputation at material cost seem irrational. Consider for example the case of the Kwakiutl, whose potlach giveaway competitions were described in chapter 2. For the Kwakiutl, prestige was a major factor to be considered in important economic transactions. After all, paying too low a price could mark one as poor, and selling high could merit the reputation of stinginess. The hallmark of Kwakiutl bartering was for the buyers to insist on paying a price high enough so that their honor was enhanced. One such transaction was the exchange of blankets for a *copper*, an engraved flat piece of metal which was a major symbol of wealth among the Kwakiutl. Benedict (1934) describes a purchase in which the buyers began with an offer that represented only a fraction of the copper's worth. Then the seller, praising himself, demanded more and more, reminding the would-be buyers that the price must reflect the current owner's greatness. Each demand was accepted by the buyers, until finally the seller was satisfied with a presentation of blankets, beautiful boxes to put them in, and three canoes, the entire offer valued at four thousand blankets:

> The owner answered, "I take the price." But it was not done. The purchaser now addressed the owner of the copper, saying: "Why, have you taken the price, chief? You take the price too soon. You must think poorly of me, chief. I am a Kwakiutl, I am one of those from whom all your tribes all over the world took their names. You must always stand beneath us." He sent his messengers to call his sister, his princess, and gave to his rivals two hundred blankets more, [a final payment known as] "the clothes of his princess." (p. 197)

By paying more than the seller had been willing to accept, the buyer's honor was enhanced by his demonstration of wealth. From examples such as this we can see that the old British advice "Buy cheap, sell dear," would not be a useful guide to the practice of trade in every culture.

PRODUCTION: THE CONTROL AND USE OF RESOURCES

Just because a resource is available to people does not mean that they have the right to use it. In every culture, the right to exploit resources is divided up among the members of a society based on concepts such as use rights and ownership.

Use Rights

The right to use a resource may belong to individuals or groups. For instance, according to Allan Holmberg (1950), among the Sirionó, a nomadic hunting people of eastern Bolivia, when a wild fruit tree was found in the forest it was marked with a notch as a sign that its finder had claimed the right to harvest its fruit for at least the current season. The Waorani, who are horticultural villagers in Ecuador, have more complex customs concerning the ownership of wild trees. They value the fruit of the wild Chonta palm, but the trunk is impossible to climb because it is ringed with spikey thorns. When a wild chonta palm is discovered, its finder claims it by planting a cecropia tree next to it. Years later, when the cecropia is large enough, the owner harvests the chonta fruit by climbing the cecropia. The fruit is shared with other members of the village, but the chonta is considered to be owned by its finder, and is even inherited by the families of its original discoverer.

The right to use a resource may also be based on such social status characteristics as rank, age, or sex. Use right may be allocated by rules such as "first come, first served." This is common, for instance, among seminomadic foragers where it is more efficient for each group to simply begin its foraging in a location that is not already being used than to compete with others who began their work first.

Ownership

The right to use and the right to deny use rights to others temporarily is called <u>ownership</u>, a right that is held even when it is not being exercised. Thus, people are expected to obtain permission to use property owned by others. Ownership itself can be given, bought, or sold.

SHOSHONI vs. PIONEER CONCEPTS OF LAND IN THE GREAT BASIN

The aboriginal Shoshoni of the United States Great Basin were a foraging people who occupied a desert environment. Their territory was a sparse land with food resources that supported only about one person per 50 square miles. So their society was fragmented into small groups. Throughout most of the year, the Shoshoni wandered in search of food in family groups of only four or five people. When families happened upon one another in their nomadic quest for food, they might visit and even cooperate in communal net hunts if one of the families had a net and if they were lucky enough to have come together when large enough numbers of jackrabbits were also in the area. Luck, however, of that kind was the exception rather than the rule. Most of the time it was more economical to remain distant enough from other families so as not to compete for the same limited resources. Naturally, the Shoshoni conception of their relationship to the land was not one of ownership. Instead, they thought of themselves as merely users of the resources within their native lands, and the right to use a resource could not be permanently owned by a migratory people who, throughout most of the year, had to be continually on the move in order to survive. The Shoshoni culture's rule governing the control of natural resources might be translated as "first come, first served."

In the 1840s, Mormon pioneers entered the Great Basin as settlers, bringing with them an agricultural technology. Their way of life was a sedentary one that exploited the ability of the soil to raise planted crops in enough abundance to support large, permanent populations. These farmers have a different relationship to the land than migratory foragers. Farmers who live in permanent houses near the fields they plan to work for years have a special attachment to the land. They expect to own the food they produce and the idea of ownership of land rather than temporary use rights is a likely part of their culture's ideology.

In many parts of frontier America, there was a natural conflict between these two different concepts of the human relationship to nature. In the Great Basin, the conflict took a special twist. Mormon pioneers sought to avoid the direct hostility that had occurred elsewhere when arriving settlers had simply taken possession of land by force. Under a motto of "Better to feed the Indians, than to fight them," many of the immigrants offered to "buy" agricultural land from the Shoshoni. The Shoshoni seemed to take the goods offered them willingly and went on their way. The Mormon farmers were bemused when the Shoshoni returned a year or so later and tried to "sell" them the same land again.

As might be expected, the Shoshoni view of the matter was quite different. To them the land was not something to be owned, bought, or sold. They had merely given up their temporary use rights to the foreigners in return for the goods given to them. Imagine their surprise when they again passed through their traditional hunting lands and found that the foreigners had not merely passed through but had settled down, fencing the land, and even hoarding the food they got from it. The Shoshoni regarded this as a most improper way of acting for they valued the act of sharing and look upon generosity as a defining quality of human beings.

Division of Labor

Production is never accomplished by requiring everyone to perform the same work. In all societies that anthropologists have visited, the labor of production is divided up by age and sex. In horticultural societies, one also finds the beginnings of occupational specialization by age, sex, and groups. Specialization becomes increasingly important, the larger and denser the local groups become; it is particularly important in large industrialized societies throughout the world today.

Age and sex. Where specialization is limited to age and sex differences, the various productive forms of work are thought of as simply roles that males and females of various ages play as members of their families and local groups. Work as an activity is not divorced from one's family or community relationships and is not thought of as a specialized activity to be done for hire. Children are socialized to help the adults in their productive activities and are gradually given greater responsibilities in these tasks until they achieve adult proficiency. In most societies, the contributions of children add to the total productive resources of the family. The most productive years tend to be from puberty until the beginning of old age, when intensive work efforts are often replaced by more organizational and managerial roles.

Sex differences in the division of labor seem everywhere to be based on the expectation that routine and domestic labor will be done by females and the heavier and nondomestic labor will be done by males. For example, men are typically expected to hunt the larger game animals, fish in offshore waters, herd large animals, clear the land in preparation for planting, do the heavier work of house construction, and manufacture stone and metal implements as well as trade-goods. Women may cooperate in communal hunts of smaller game, gather aquatic foods near the shores, herd smaller animals, weed and harvest gardens, take primary charge of domestic chores such as cooking and childrearing, weave textiles, and make pottery. This pattern of dividing up the work of men and women is certainly not the only conceivable one. There are societies that are exceptions in individual activities, such as the Toda of southern India in which men prepare the meals or the Dani of New Guinea where men are the weavers of household textiles. However, the overall division of labor by sex in most societies follows the traditional pattern.

Occupational specialization. In societies without domesticated food resources, work tends to be unspecialized except by age and sex. Though individual skill varies, everyone is expected to develop the basic skills that are shared by everyone of their sex. In horticultural societies, some occupational specializations are normally found within each sex. Individuals may devote time to specialized tasks such as pottery making or weaving that most men or women do not have skill in. The products of their labor are then exchanged for other things that they need.

Specialization by group. In food producing societies, entire groups may also specialize in certain productive activities. Villages in somewhat different habitats may produce different crops which they then exchange. Thus, in the Andean empire of the ancient Inca civilization, villagers who lived between sea level and 11,000 feet grew maize and potatoes. Between 11,000 and 14,000 feet, potatoes were the primary crop. Above 14,000 feet, villagers specialized in raising llamas, alpacas, and quinoa, a grain that was capable of growing at high altitudes. The specialized crops of different altitudes could be easily transported from one part of the empire to another with the aid of llamas as pack animals.

Social groups such as families or age mates may also work together in some specialized productive activity. So for example, among the pig-herding Tsembaga Maring who were discussed in chapter 3, children and young adults specialized in tending the pigs, while adults worked the fields to produce root crops such as sweet potatoes.

DISTRIBUTION

The movement of resources or goods from where they are found or produced to where they will be used is referred to as distribution. There are three major economic systems by which distribution is controlled: reciprocity, redistribution, and market.

Reciprocity

The system of exchange in which goods or services are passed from one individual or group to another as gifts without the need for explicit contracting for specific payment is called reciprocity. Unlike buying and selling, reciprocity does not involve bargaining over what is to be given in return. There is merely the understanding that the sharing is mutual and will be eventually evenhanded.

The enforcement of reciprocity is based primarily on the desire of the participants not to be excluded, rather than on formal sanctions. So long as everyone involved partici-

FIGURE 4.3 *Reciprocity*

Social interdependence in most hunter-gatherer societies is the basis for reciprocity, the giving and taking of goods without the exchange of money. These San hunters are drying strips of meat before distributing them to others.

pates to everyone else's satisfaction, the rules of the exchange do not even need to be discussed. However, if one group or individual fails to engage in its fair share of gift giving, it may be censured or excluded by the others. In economically more complex societies, reciprocity is found within families and between acquaintances, and it typically involves symbolic goods and services such as holiday greeting cards or parties. Whereas in very simple societies, the gifts that are shared may be life-sustaining ones, such as food. In such cases, participation is likely to be self-enforcing even if it is not mandatory, since exclusion from the system may be life-threatening. As noted by Sahlins (1972), reciprocity takes three basic forms: generalized reciprocity, balanced reciprocity, and negative reciprocity.

Generalized reciprocity. Gifts given with no expectation of immediate exchange are part of generalized reciprocity. The persons involved are most likely to be motivated by a sense of obligation toward the welfare of the others. For instance, in families goods and services are provided for children by their parents even though the children may not reciprocate in kind even later in life. Generalized reciprocity may also be exemplified by the care that is given to the elderly or incapacitated who are unable to respond with a return of goods or services of equal value.

The feeling of obligation that minimizes an expectation of an immediate return of favors can be based on a sense of community as well as on the bonds of kinship. In foraging societies, generalized reciprocity is the basic economic mechanism for ensuring that everyone within the local community, nonrelatives included, is provided for. Where generalized reciprocity is practiced, generosity is likely to be an expected characteristic of normal behavior. Thus, for example, in the language of the foraging Shoshoni of the Intermountain region of the United States, the word *dzaandə* meant both *good* and *generous*. The good human was a generous person, and since generosity in sharing was understood to be a natural attribute of the normal person rather than an unexpected or surprising behavior, no word or phrase existed that was equivalent to the English "Thank you!" Similarly, although Apache and Navajo, spoken in the southwestern desert of the United States, did have a word, *eehe'he*, with which to express thanks, it was used only for extremely valuable goods or services such as a gift of a horse or to thank someone for having saved your life. To say thanks in response to other forms of sharing, such as food or the offer of overnight hospitality to strangers caught in a storm, would have implied that the gift was unexpected—a possibly deadly insult among a people who considered generosity to be practiced by any normal human.

Balanced reciprocity. Between persons who lack a sense of kinship or community obligation toward one another, but who each have something that the other would like to have, balanced reciprocity is likely to occur in which a return gift is expected within a relatively short time. It is commonly practiced by members of neighboring communities that each specialize in the production of different goods or that control different resources. Even

FIGURE 4.4   *Generalized Reciprocity*

The family as an entity is sustained by generalized reciprocity, a system of giving in which the welfare of others is of primary importance; there is no immediate expectation of a return. This type of reciprocity is exemplified by the support of children by their parents, the care given to an elderly parent, or the exchange of gifts at holiday time. Most families in the United States and Canada enjoy exchanging gifts at Christmas.

without direct bargaining, balanced reciprocity may be maintained to the benefit of both groups. At appropriate opportunities each group gives that which it has in surplus to recipients known to desire such a commodity. Although no immediate return is demanded, the gratefulness of the recipients and their continued interest in the commodity will ensure that they will reciprocate within a reasonable time with gifts of their own.

One of the most interesting examples of balanced reciprocity that has been noted by ethnographers is a form called *silent trade*. In this kind of exchange, there need to be no direct interaction between the trading partners once the relationship is established. Each simply leaves surplus goods known to be of use to the other at a place where it will be found later by the other. Each occasionally checks the cache site to see if anything has been left and, if so, leaves something in return. The Mbuti

FIGURE 4.5 *Balanced Reciprocity*

A more immediate exchange of goods and services is expected in a system of balanced reciprocity. These Mennonite farmers spend their time and labor helping their neighbor in a traditional barn raising with the expectation that they each will also be helped when the need arises.

Pygmy foragers of the Ituri Forest carried out trade of this kind with horticultural villagers who lived outside the forest. In return for garden produce, iron knives, and pots the Mbuti partner would leave game and other forest foods. Similar silent trade has been noted in a variety of other cultures in different parts of the world, such as the Semang foragers and Malay farmers of the Malaysian Peninsula.

Balanced reciprocity may include the exchange of services as well as goods. For instance, the Quechua-speaking peoples of the South American Andes had a concept of reciprocal work obligations between communities known as the *mink'a* in pre-Spanish times. Members of a *mink'a* group cooperated in helping in difficult work such as harvesting, canal repair, or housebuilding. American *barn raisings* and *harvest bees* of frontier days were a similar form of balanced reciprocity of services.

The economic organization that operated within the caste system in India was probably the most organized example of balanced reciprocity of both goods and services in a complex society. In each local community, individuals were organized into a system of occupations deemed appropriate to members of the various castes. This *jati system* provided for the economic needs of all members of the community because each person was obligated to provide goods or services to everyone else. The miller ground grain for all of the farmers, while the farmers provided some of the food they produced to all members of the community. The barber cut hair, and the weaver gave gifts of fabric to other members of the community. Each occupation benefited others without direct and immediate payment, and so long as everyone received as well as gave, the needs of all could be met.

THE KULA RING

Malinowski (1922) described the classic example of balanced reciprocity in his account of the Kula ring, a ceremonial exchange system between members of a ring of islands in Melanesia. In Kula trade, there were only two kinds of valuables that were exchanged: long, red shell necklaces called *soulava* and white shell bracelets called *mwali*. Both were passed from island to island around the ring as the necklaces were traded for the bracelets. The necklaces moved only clockwise around the islands and the bracelets were traded only counterclockwise.

The necklaces and bracelets exchanged in the Kula ring were objects of prestige that gave evidence of their owners' participation in the Kula system. Each necklace or bracelet carried with it a personal history of its past ownership, so, like an heirloom, its value increased with age. Each owner kept a particular necklace or bracelet only for a year or so and then gave it as a gift to a trade partner. Men who participated in Kula expeditions had specific trade partners on islands in either direction. When they traveled on a Kula expedition, they were received as honored guests by their partners, and bracelets and necklaces were given ceremoniously with appropriate ritual speeches accompanying each bestowal. If, at that time, a partner had no object of equivalent prestige, it was understood that he was expected to work to acquire an appropriate gift to give in return on a later expedition.

Uberoi (1962) has discussed a number of social functions of the Kula ring. For instance, since the exchange of Kula valuables was a form of balanced reciprocity, trade partners should not profit at one another's expense from the exchange. What then motivated the islanders to participate in the long and sometimes dangerous sea voyages that the Kula ring required? Certainly there was an element of socializing and entertainment in the process. However, there were also some practical benefits. Although the exchange of Kula was the pretext for a voyage, utilitarian objects were also exchanged after the ceremonial greetings were completed. Thus, the Kula gift giving helped to maintain an amicable relationship between trade partners from different islands. The partnerships were long-standing ones, since they were inherited by another family member at the death of a partner. So trading partnerships perpetuated friendly relationships over the generations between residents of potentially competing islands. Trading expeditions kept alive the traditions of the islands as the gift-givers recited the histories and legends associated with each Kula item bestowed.

Over time new participants were intro-

duced into the Kula exchange system. Scoditti (1983) noted that younger men took part in Kula expeditions after they had been given necklaces or armbands by relatives or in return for building canoes. Of course, the necklaces and armbands received in this way were likely to be among the less prestigious ones. With frequent and long participation, the reputation of younger traders could rise as they acquired more valued armbands and necklaces. Campbell (1983) suggested that possession of valuable Kula objects also symbolized high social rank, since the most valued items were usually owned by the more experienced participants who were good navigators, respected expedition organizers, and—in earlier times—successful warriors. Finally, Kula expeditions were also occasions for practical as well as ceremonial exchanges. Foodstuffs, tools, and other items of economic importance were bartered by participants in the expedition. Some islands produced foods not grown on other islands, and those people who lived on islands that were not very food productive specialized in manufacturing pieces of technology such as canoes. These items were exchanged during the Kula expeditions to the benefit of all participants. Since the islands in the ring specialized in the production of different commodities, the Kula ring played an important economic role in the lives of its participants, even though it appeared to have only ceremonial significance.

Negative reciprocity. When one group or individual in a reciprocal exchange system attempts to get more than it gives, we speak of negative reciprocity, in which the return has greater value than the gift. Negative reciprocity varies from simple miserliness on the part of one participant, through deceit in bargaining, to outright theft. Here the bonds of obligation are the lowest, and the desire for personal benefit is the greatest. This form of reciprocity is most common among strangers within the same communities or members of different communities, especially communities that differ in cultures. The traditional Apache raiding of their more sedentary neighbors exemplifies a pattern of negative reciprocity in which the neighboring groups were seen not so much as enemies to be exterminated as they were viewed as a kind of resource to be exploited.

Redistribution

Redistribution is the second major economic system for the distribution of goods and services. In redistribution, commodities are contributed by all members of the social group to a common pool from which they are then distributed to where they will be used. While reciprocity is a two-party affair involving givers and receivers, redistribution requires an intermediary, a third party who coordinates the process and exercises control over the flow of goods and services. The mediating individual or group is likely to gain both prestige and power from the position of control over whatever is exchanged in this economic system. Examples of systems of economic redistribution in complex societies include taxation, social security, retirement funds, unemployment compensation, and insurance.

Redistribution, like reciprocity, is an economic practice within families around the world. It occurs when members of a family take part in saving for a common goal. However, as a major societal mechanism within the economic system beyond the family, redistribution is not present in all societies. It is conspicuously absent in foraging societies, and it has been argued that it first arose after

the rise of food domestication. Service (1962) believes that redistribution developed in sedentary agricultural societies that occupied distinctly different ecological zones in which local residents specialized in their economic production activities.

Harris (1974) also ties the rise in importance of redistribution to the presence of agriculture, but he thinks that yearly differences in productivity rather than local specialization is the central cause. He sees redistribution as merely part of a larger set of economic practices that encourages food growers to work hard enough to produce surpluses in most years. The extra produce is normally chanelled to a production manager who has exhorted others to the extra labor, and this person redistributes the goods. The underlying payoff in such a system comes in lean years when climatic conditions or other crises lead to poorer than expected harvests. Furthermore, neighboring communities are not always affected by the same difficulties and may lend a helping hand at such times, if they have been beneficiaries of the suffering community's previous redistributive investments.

Those who manage the redistribution of goods and services are typically rewarded with prestige and sometimes with power and wealth. Anthropologists have been particularly interested in two kinds of redistribution managers found in societies of middle-range complexity: big men and chiefs.

FIGURE 4.6 *Redistribution*

A hierarchical organization is the most efficient means of distributing surplus goods and services in large communities. The items are first brought or sent to a central area from where they are distributed. This system is depicted on a frieze at Persepolis where these Persians are bringing goods and livestock to the king.

FIGURE 4.7   *The Big Man*

The status of big man is one that is earned. The big man is usually wealthy, generous, eloquent, and male. He may be also physically and spiritually superior to others in his tribe. He functions as a headman of a village unit. This Kapauku big man of New Guinea is delivering a political speech.

Big men. The economic entrepreneurs of horticultural societies are <u>big men</u>. They are not true officials who have power to demand the cooperation of others; rather they are prominent individuals within their community, charismatic leaders who encourage relatives and other members of their community to follow their lead in the production of surplus goods. The goal of this production is to host the followers of other big men within a community or members of neighboring communities in a festive gathering of conspicuous generosity and hospitality that promotes the prestige of the host group and its big man.

Chiefs. In somewhat larger horticultural or agricultural societies in which social ranking becomes an important fact of social life, the role of big man merges with that of the local political official, the chief. The <u>chief</u> is a person of authority and prestige who is the major political official and the economic manager of the local community. Unlike the big man, the chief does not generally participate in the productive labor of the redistributive econ-

omy. Instead, the chief is a full-time political official whose duties include coordination of the redistributive practices.

In redistribution involving chiefs, festive occasions may still be celebrated using goods collected in the chief's warehouse. A more important role, however, of redistribution emerges in this system: the use of the centrally controlled goods to finance public works and services. A significant portion of the redistributive economy is chanelled into such activities as building and maintaining irrigation projects, supporting a local police force or militia, and similar undertakings that enhance the general welfare of the community.

A redistributive economy that is controlled by full-time officials clearly lends itself to potential abuse. It is true that the ability of chiefs to siphon off redistributive goods for their own use allows the chiefs and their relatives in many such societies to form a social elite with special prerogatives and a higher standard of living than that of other members of society. But there is a surprisingly large number of cases in which the chiefs and their families are so strongly expected to use the goods they control for the benefit of others that they return more than they take into the system and live in poverty despite the great respect accorded their status.

Markets

The market economy is the third major approach to exchange, one that has become the major economic force in the industrialized societies of the world. The concept of the <u>market</u> is based on the idea of direct exchange, that is, buying and selling as opposed to mutual gift giving of valued items or services.

Marketing may occur spontaneously in any society, but it is most developed in sedentary societies in which the large number of people involved makes it convenient to establish traditional marketplaces to carry out the exchange. Especially in larger societies where marketplaces may bring together strangers and persons who see each other infrequently, market exchange, like negative reciprocity, may place little emphasis on mutual obligation, since each party becomes responsible for his or her own welfare in the transaction. Thus, self-interest rather than generosity often becomes the guiding principle. This, of course,

FIGURE 4.8 *Market Economy*

When communities become so efficient at food producing that a regular surplus is created, they establish a marketplace where the surplus goods and foods are sold for some form of money. This Indian vendor in Equador is selling surplus herbs and spices for medicine.

is moderated, particularly in small-scale societies and even smaller communities within larger societies, by the fact that market exchange may be part of a long-term relationship between the parties.

Barter. In smaller societies that have market systems, exchanges may be primarily the trading of one object or service for another, a form of exchanged called barter. In barter a potter and a farmer might exchange a water vessel for a bag of grain or an itinerant worker might chop firewood in return for a meal and night's lodging.

Money. When the goods that people need are produced close at hand, barter can be the basic form of exchange, but when this is not the case the concept of money may be employed. Money is a standard medium of value that is itself not usually consumed. Its value lies in the fact that even if it is not itself a

usable commodity outside the context of exchange, its users mutually agree that it may be exchanged for other usable commodities. Something of value in its own right may be used as money. For instance, in many parts of the world, salt has been used as money. Money is fundamentally a *symbol* of value, and the only thing necessary to transform anything into money is the mutual agreement that it will be a standard of value. Contrary to popular opinion, there is no inherent need for a government's promise to redeem paper money with any specific commodity such as gold to make that currency useful as a standard device to transfer ownership of commodities. The key ingredient is simply the agreement to accept the paper in lieu of the commodities they wish to exchange.

Money may be either specialized or generalized. Special-purpose money (Bohannan, 1963) is a medium of exchange that is restricted to the buying and selling of a single

FIGURE 4.9 *Barter*

The trading of specific items whose relative value is carefully calculated is often conducted between groups rather than individuals. These New Guinea natives are bartering fish for yams, taro (a starchy rootstock), and other agricultural products.

commodity or at most a restricted number of designated commodities. Coins or tokens that can only be used for gambling, operating video games, or paying for bus rides, and stamps or coupons that are saved to exchange for premiums are examples of specialized money. Bohannan (1955) reports that among the Tiv metal rods were used as a special-purpose money for buying cattle, slaves, or white cloth, all items of prestige within the Tiv economy. Subsistence goods, on the other hand, were exchanged by barter. Among native North Americans of the Northwest Coast culture area, blankets were a special-purpose money for food, but were not a medium of exchange for other items. In various parts of Melanesia, shells are a medium of exchange for stone tools, pottery, and pigs, but not for other everyday commodities.

General-purpose money is a universal medium of exchange, one that is not restricted in its use for only certain commodities but that can be used to buy and sell any item. General-purpose money is particularly useful when local populations are so large that people obtain most of their daily needs by buying and selling. When many different kinds of items are regularly bought and sold, both barter and the need for several special-purpose monies

can be inconvenient ways of doing business. In such situations, a single general-purpose money may replace the other forms of exchange for most transactions.

YAPESE STONE MONEY

The symbolic nature of money is well illustrated by an old anthropological story about the Yapese people of the Caroline Islands in the Pacific. On the island of Yap, large, doughnut-shaped stones were used as special-purpose money for major ritual exchanges between villages. Since the stones were large, they were not easily transported; therefore they were not used in everyday transactions. However, on important occasions that warranted the use of a large number of human laborers, a stone might be moved from one village to another.

On one occasion when one of the stone cartwheels was being rafted across a lagoon between two villages, the vessel sank with its precious cargo. Try as they might, there was just no way to recover the stone from the sea bottom where it still lies. The crisis was overcome when the Yapese recognized some often overlooked facts: The real value of money is not due to its

82

intrinsic worth but is assigned to it for the convenience of its users; and since the value of money is symbolic rather than intrinsic, physical possession of the symbol of value is not necessary to its use. Both villages agreed that although the stone could not be recovered, everyone knew where it was, so its ownership could still be transferred from one group to the other!

CONSUMPTION

In simple, foraging bands there is little difference in the wealth and lifestyle of individuals from one local group to another because individuals in each local group engage in the same basic productive activities. There are few specialized economic activities that supply goods to only some individuals, and reciprocity tends to level out even temporary wealth differences that may arise from time to time due to fluctuations in productivity of a local environment. But, with the development of food domestication and the occupational specializations that generally arise with it, opportunities increase for some individuals, families, and local groups to consistently control more wealth than do others in the same society. It is axiomatic that the more complex and productive a society's economy is, the more opportunities arise for differences to develop in consumption, the final use of goods and services.

Subsistence Economies

People regularly consume most of what they produce in a subsistence economy. This is the usual economic form in foraging societies and in simple food domesticating tribes because not enough surpluses are produced for a permanent exchange of goods to obtain what is needed. Rather, each family produces goods for their own consumption, their own subsistence income. All families produce more-or-less the same goods, and there is little need for trade. Thus, in subsistence economies, permanent differences of wealth are unlikely to arise.

FIGURE 4.10 *Special Purpose Money*

When an item is designated as a specific means of exchange for a particular category of goods it is considered special-purpose money. These may consist of things such as shells, brass rods, pigs, or anything a society designates. The Yapese people of Micronesia use huge stone disks as special-purpose money.

Status Income

When surplus goods are consistently available, the distribution process becomes increasingly important in determining who has the greatest opportunity for control over the final use of the excess. The control of goods by big men and chiefs over and above subsistence needs, called status income, then becomes a symbol of social rank. In the case of big men, most of such wealth is given as gifts to other groups in return for the prestige such gift-giving brings. Both the redistribution of wealth to the needy within a local community and the channelling of some surpluses to host neighboring groups as a source of prestige is also a practice in many chiefdoms. However, the prestige accorded chiefs for their authority to exact tribute from their subordinates sometimes results in the chiefs and their noble relatives enjoying a higher standard of living than their subordinates. In such cases, the actual consumption of surplus goods by the elite becomes a symbol of their high standing. The use of status income as a display of social rank, a practice called conspicuous consumption, is found in many chiefdoms and is a characteristic of the elite in all societies in which market economies predominate. The high standard of living enjoyed by the British monarchy, the European "Upper Ten Thousand" or the American "jet set" typifies the use of income as conspicuous consumption.

SOCIAL AGENTS OF ECONOMIC CONTROL

Economic processes such as decision making about what to produce, what resources to use, and who will do the work is controlled by various people in various ways. In small-scale societies such as bands and tribes, control over productive work may be vested in the community as a whole, in the kin groups of society, or in special associations. In tribes and chiefdoms, the redistributive decision makers include individuals whose influence is based on prestige and power. In complex societies, decision-making power over production and distribution is often in the hands of members of the upper social classes but exercised indirectly through their control of corporations or governmental bureaucracies.

Community Control of Production

In foraging bands in which the local groups are quite small and consist of members of only a few different families, decisions about the production and allocation of needed goods is sometimes a matter of discussion by the entire local group. This is especially true among foragers such as the Arctic Inuit, the Great Basin Shoshoni, and the Yahgan and Ona of Tierra del Fuego, who spend much of the year in very small local groups. It is also common among groups such as the Andamanese Islanders or Mbuti pygmy in which the local community of 20 or 30 persons functions much like an extended family group.

Kin Control of Production

The local kinship group is the most common institution for controlling production and allocation of goods among most foragers, horticulturalists, and pastoralists. Among foragers, this is merely a matter of the members of the nuclear family deciding about their daily needs and how best to fill them. Among pastoralists who typically have larger local populations than do foragers, it is often the extended family that exerts ownership over the basic means of livelihood such as the fields and herds. Thus, for instance, among the horticultural Hopi of the southwestern United States, gardens were owned by kinship groups rather than by the individual woman who managed them day to day. Although she controlled the produce of her alloted plot, she could not dispose of the land without permission of her kinship group.

Association Control of Production

In other tribal societies, associations that cut through family lines and residential areas within a community may control important parts of production. For instance, the Cheyenne bison hunters of the North American Plains relied heavily on sudden kills of large numbers of migrating bisons in cooperative hunts. A single hunter who began to shoot too soon could frighten the herd and spoil the success of the hunt for the rest of the community. So control of the hunt was vested in the Cheyenne military association who could police the responsibility of hunters by punishing

FIGURE 4.11   Board of Directors

In complex societies where groups of producers are organized into corporations, the production and distribution of goods is directed by a group of people who are knowledgeable about its operation.

those who did not abide by the rules that governed the bison hunt. The Tahitian islanders in Polynesia also illustrate the role of associations in tribal production. They used several specialized associations or guilds for the production of expensive commodities such as chiefs' houses and boats. Chiefs' houses were built on a grand scale and could attain a length of nearly 400 feet. While a house was being erected, the carpenters of the guild that were hired to build such a house were fed by the chief who was paying to have the house built. Each guild was governed by its own chief, and the builders who belonged to it were respected specialists who were divided into ranks based on their training and experience. The guilds had special emblems, deities, and ceremonies that set them apart from others, and different guilds competed with one another to achieve prestige and social recognition for the quality of their work.

Social Class

Social class also plays a role in controlling the production, distribution and consumption of goods in complex societies. Commonly, members of the higher social classes have the greatest control over the means of production and receive the greatest share of goods. Members of the social elite may sit on corporate decision-making boards. They also have greater influence than do other persons on government policy-makers to the benefit of their corporations.

Corporation and governmental decision making. Associations of employers and employees that produce goods or provide services and that are legally entitled to act as a single person are corporations. They may exercise the same rights of ownership that persons may hold over the goods members produce or the services they provide. Corporations can outlast the lifetimes of its individual members, so they can produce more than any individual and can develop tremendous economic power as their productive properties increase. Corporations may be privately or governmentally owned, but in either case those who make decisions about what corporations produce and at what prices they sell their goods and services are members of the higher social classes.

The balance of power between governmental officials and private individuals in the control of the means of production varies among complex societies. In some cases, the economic decision-making of private owners of corporations is only loosely regulated. This allows the owners to play a major role in the economic life of such societies. One common outcome of this way of organizing economic decision-making is a competition between corporations for sales. If the basic needs of consumers are met by the system of production, competition for sales may become nonessential. In such a consumer market, the economic focus is on convincing the consumer to purchase nonessential goods and services. Some nonessentials are sought by consumers because they enhance their standard of living rather than simply meet basic needs. They make life easier and more comfortable. Nonessentials, especially those that do not improve consumers' standard of living, may still be marketed successfully because the buyers gain higher status by demonstrating their ability to purchase them. In its extreme, buyers may engage in conspicuous consumption, the use of goods merely as a display of their wealth.

STATE ECONOMIC MANAGEMENT IN THE SOVIET UNION

The Soviet Union's approach to economic planning is one of the world's most centralized. Although some private enterprise does exist in the Soviet Union, control of the economy is vested primarily in the government. Banking and foreign trade institutions are government owned, as are industrial manufacturing plants and state farms. Private enterprise is limited to work done by individuals such as small plot gardening or private taxi operations as sources of supplemental income.

The State Planning Agency is responsible for setting goals for the productive sector of the economy. Theoretically, an advantage of a centrally coordinated system for setting nationwide production goals can be great efficiency in the overall economic system, since central planning can eliminate needless competition and duplication of effort within the nation. And the Soviet economy has achieved some notable successes. For instance, according to Goldman (1986), "Within a little over sixty years, it has achieved a radical redistribution of the wealth and has transformed an agricultural country to a highly industrialized and urbanized one. It has raised the standard of living of the overwhelming majority of Soviet citizens as compared to the lifestyles of their parents in the 1920s and 1930s and their grandparents before the Revolution of 1917."

On the other hand, centralized, government-controlled economic planning can fall prey to the problem of setting economic goals for reasons of political ideology rather than economic need. And this difficulty has also plagued the Soviet economy. For instance, the decisions of the State Planning Agency are heavily influenced by Communist party policy as well as by economic facts such as grass-roots forecasts of the yearly output and resource requirements of the production sector. This political influence on goal setting has inhibited the growth of the Soviet consumer market. Luxury goods are expensive and difficult to obtain. Thus, a prospective purchaser may have to wait as many as seven years for an automobile to become available. Even many basic consumer items can be hard to acquire. Buyers may have to wait in lines for hours to purchase basic commodities such as meat and vegetables. In spite of the fact that housing is a constitutionally guaranteed right of citizens, couples may have to wait several years for their own accommodation.

The poor development of the consumer economy should not be interpreted as an inherent difficulty of central economic planning, but a byproduct of a political policy that might or might not create barriers in any society. In the Soviet case, the failure of the productive sector is largely a result of the unwillingness of the government to invest heavily in the consumer market; instead the Soviet government has felt an urgent need to devote its resources to building up its military and to developing its economic competition with the West.

SUMMARY

Cultures differ in what they define as useful or valuable and in how much worth a given commodity may be thought to have. Commodities may, for instance, include intangible things such as sacred stories or titles of nobility, and a nurse and a carpenter may receive similar or very different incomes in two different societies. Nevertheless, economic systems in all cultures are constructed out of the same building blocks—rules that govern the production, distribution, and consumption of valued goods and services. Production or obtaining commodities involves concepts of use rights, ownership, and a division of labor. Distribution involves some combination of reciprocal exchange, centralized redistribution of goods, and markets. Patterns of consumption depend on how much is produced for use by the producers themselves, how commodities are used in increasing the prestige of some members of society through different levels of status income and conspicuous consumption. All societies have ways of controlling the economic system. Control may be divided between members of the community, the kinship group, associations such as guilds, corporations, or governmental officials.

KEY TERMS
AND
CONCEPTS

economics 70
commodities 70
ownership 73
distribution 75
reciprocity 75
generalized reciprocity 75
balanced reciprocity 76
negative reciprocity 78
redistribution 79
big man 80
chief 80
market 80

barter 81
money 81
special-purpose money 81
general-purpose money 82
consumption 83
subsistence economy 83
subsistence income 83
status income 84
conspicuous consumption 84
corporation 85
consumer market 86

ANNOTATED
READINGS

Harris, M. (1986). *Good to eat*. New York: Harper & Row. An application of the cultural materialist perspective to the problem of cultural differences in the definitions of edible foods.

Herskovits, M. J. (1940). *The economic life of primitive peoples*. New York: Alfred A. Knopf, Inc. The classic statement of the general principles of economic anthropology.

Lee, R. (1984). *The Dobe !Kung*. New York: Holt, Rinehart & Winston. A very readable description of the economic life of a foraging society in southern Africa.

Malinowski, B. (1922). *Argonauts of the western Pacific*. New York: E. P. Dutton.

The first ethnographic account of the role of cultural values in the economic life of the Trobriand Islanders, with special focus on the Kula ring.

Nash, M. (1966). *Primitive and peasant economic systems*. San Francisco: Chandler. An anthropological account of economic systems that focuses on the economics of social change in non-industrialized societies.

Neale, W. C. (1976). *Monies in societies*. San Francisco: Chandler and Sharp. A careful outline of the different kinds and different roles of money in various societies.

*N*owhere is political power, the ability to make and implement decisions about public goals, shared equally by every member of society. Whether people share power broadly throughout the entire community, divide power between their family organization and specialized associations, or place power in the hands of full-time governmental officials depends largely on the size and complexity of their societies. But whatever its form, there is always some system for maintaining social order and reestablishing order when rules have been broken. Some combination of childhood socialization, values, morality, religion, rewards for conformity, and threats of punishment everywhere is used to create an ordered society, but never with perfect success. When conflicts do arise, there are a variety of ways, both peaceful and violent, by which people seek to reestablish an orderly life.

5

Politics

FIGURE 5.1 *Social Power*

The UN Interim Force in Lebanon (UNIFIL), April 1978, was authorized to use its power to confirm the withdrawal of Israeli forces from Lebanon, restore international peace and security, and assist the government in restoring its authority. This Nepalese soldier serving with UNIFIL chats with two Lebanese boys in Naqoura.

According to Swartz, Turner, and Tuden (1966, p. 7) politics is the way in which power is achieved and used to create and implement public goals. As such, politics is involved in organizing and controlling human social behavior. It is through its political system that a society exercises power to maintain order internally and to regulate its relations with other societies. In the study of politics, it is important to consider how power is delegated, since not every use of power in society is legitimate.

89

FIGURE 5.2   U.S. Supreme Court Justices
The legal authority to govern others may be vested in the family organization, the local community, or legitimate elected or appointed officials. In the United States, the ultimate arbitrator in social and legal issues is the U.S. Supreme Court. Here, the Justices sit for their official portrait in 1988.

Those to whom the right to power is delegated are said to have <u>authority</u>, the legitimate right to use force or to threaten the use of force to achieve social goals. In the study of politics, then, we are interested in the authorized use of social power.

TYPES OF POLITICAL ORDERS

Anthropologists have noted a variety of ways in which political power is channeled in different societies. Complex societies have full-time political systems with officials who monopolize the legal authority to govern others. Simpler societies make use of other mechanisms for creating and implementing common goals. For instance, governing authority may be vested in the local community, in the family organization, in voluntary associations, or in officials whose authority is limited to those areas not governed by the family, community, or voluntary associations.

Bands: Government by Community

Societies in which people survive by foraging for wild foods in small local groups are <u>band</u> societies. They consist typically of 50 or 60 people who cooperate in economic activities. Since most political problems affect the entire local group, it is generally the seat of legal authority. When a legal problem arises the entire community will discuss the issue in a kind of town meeting until everyone has had ample opportunity to express an opinion. The consensus that evolves out of the give and take of group discussion is the band equivalent of law.

"HOMICIDE" AND INUIT TRIALS

The native Inuit of the northern coasts of North America occupied a harsh environment that placed heavy demands on people. In a territory that offered few plant foods, hunters were under higher than normal stress to provide for their families. Game included some rather formidable animals such as the polar bear and large sea mammals that were not easily taken. It is little wonder that successful Inuit hunters were strong-willed and aggressive men. In spite of rules of etiquette that demanded humility, politeness, and generosity, tempers sometimes did get out of hand, and violent deaths involving disputes about food and women were not rare.

Homicides were often dealt with by the families of the deceased. Revenge killings were legitimate, but might in turn lead to vengeance by the original killer's kin. So ultimate legal authority was vested in the community as a whole. It dealt with aggressive repeat offenders who were seen as threats to the common welfare. Boas (1888) described the role of community law enforcement among one group of Inuit:

> There was a native of Padli by the name of Padlu. He had induced the wife of a native of Cumberland Sound to desert her husband and follow him. The deserted husband, meditating revenge . . . visited his friends in Padli, but before he could accomplish his intention of killing Padlu, the latter shot him. . . . A brother of the murdered man went to Padli to avenge the death of his brother; but he also was killed by Padlu. A third native of Cumberland Sound, who wished to avenge the death of his relatives was also murdered by him.
> On account of all these outrages the natives wanted to get rid of Padlu, but yet they did not dare to attack him. When the *pimain* (headman) of the Akudmirmiut learned of these events he started southward and asked every man in Padli whether Padlu should be killed. All agreed; so he went with the latter deer hunting . . . and . . . shot Padlu in the back." (p. 582)

Because the entire community had acted as a judicial body and authorized the killing, it was a legal execution, and they had no need to fear any retribution by Padlu's relatives.

Tribes: Government by Family and Associations

Societies with simple food domestication technologies that support local populations and that are small enough to need no full-time governmental authorities are known as tribes. Legal authority is held by the families of the local group and by voluntary associations, or sodalities, whose members are drawn from at least several of the families of the community. Family law typically rules in domestic matters such as the contracting or divorcing of marriage, and the punishment of family members for violation of one another's rights. Voluntary associations often play a role in the military defense of the local community and in policing the community itself, at least in matters that are not traditionally regarded as within the realm of family law.

The political role of voluntary associations is well illustrated by the tribes of the North American plains which typically had a dozen or so military societies in each community. In some tribes, young men graduated from one society into the next as they aged. In others, the associations were equal rivals for members who had to choose which they would join. The military associations of the Plains Indians had many roles. They exercised legal authority as a governing agency by preserving order in the camp, during hunts, and while camp was being moved, and by punishing lawbreakers. But they also performed social, recreational, and economic roles in hosting feasts and dances, holding intersociety competitions, keeping tribal traditions, and providing information about the location of buffalo herds.

Policing authority among Plains Indians was usually held by a single military society for only a year, so that this responsibility was rotated among the associations of a community, and no one monopolized the right to police power. Enforcement of tribal laws by military societies was also limited to crimes that harmed the community welfare. Thus, on communal buffalo hunts, someone who began too soon and frightened the herd away before others were prepared was likely to be punished. The emphasis was on making the culprit an example to discourage similar behavior by others. Punishments that were made public included the destruction of a wrongdoer's property, banishment from the camp, and death.

The Plains Indians relied heavily on the migratory buffalo that passed through their territories each year and competition for this valuable resource brought the highly mobile, horseback hunting tribes into recurrent conflict. The military associations protected their communities against other plundering tribes.

FIGURE 5.3 *Chief of Fijian Village*

The chief's political power is sometimes hereditary and generally permanent. In Fijian chiefdoms he is responsible for redistribution of goods, coordinating labor, supervising religious festivals, and directing military activities. This high chief is presiding at a village meeting.

The greatest defenders of the tribe in each military society were rewarded with honor and the plunder of war. In ceremonial meetings, these warriors recounted their exploits in battle, and it was from these men that the more formal political leaders were selected for the tribe.

Plains military societies also played an important role in public recreation. They performed dances as public exhibitions and generally interacted with the audience in their celebrations. Among themselves members of the military associations provided fraternal camaraderie and a place in which deep friendships could evolve.

Chiefdoms: The Rise of Officialdom

A society that unites a number of villages under the legal control of a government that recognizes the right of families to exercise some autonomous legal authority is a chiefdom. A chiefdom's government lacks the monopoly of legal authority that is characteristic of more complex societies, but it can legitimately use force in matters that concern the common welfare. The authority of the government in a chiefdom is independent of family authority, and its officials may exercise authority over persons to whom they are not kin. Nevertheless, families still exercise a great deal of legal autonomy. For instance, laws that govern marriage and divorce are typically matters of family law. Similarly, the enforcement of laws concerning petty theft is often a responsibility of kinship groups in chiefdoms. Major crimes that concern the entire community, however, crimes such as grand theft, homicide, or insults to the dignity of a chief are typically punishable by the government alone.

In chiefdoms, the everyday functions of government such as the military defense of society, the policing of local communities, the conduct of judicial activities, or the drafting of labor for various public works projects are possible, because governmental authority includes the right of taxation. A major economic function of chiefs is their service as coordinators of a redistributive economy in which all families are required to contribute part of their produce to a common pool which the chief may draw upon to pay for community services.

Chiefdoms lack true social classes, but they are not egalitarian either, since their kinship groups are ranked in a social hierarchy in which some families have greater social power and prestige than others. Political offices are usually inherited so that they remain within certain families, and the highest ranking families normally have control over the most important political offices.

Chiefdoms are typically theocratic societies in which the chiefs are endowed with both religious and secular authority. Indeed, some of the higher ranking political officials may be considered so filled with religious aura that their very persons are sacred.

States: The Official Monopoly of Law

Because chiefdoms vary in their degree of social complexity and the power of their governments, the social differences between a complex chiefdom and a small state society may be slight. They are essentially differences of political ideology: a state is a political unit in which centralized governments monopolize the right to exercise legal force and control the affairs of local communities. It has power to levy taxes, pass laws, and draft people into work or war.

Carniero (1970) has suggested that states arose in circumscribed environmental zones—areas surrounded by mountains, deserts, or other natural barriers to easy emigration—when population growth caused increased social competition for natural resources. This competition led to social stratification and the domination of some groups by others. Political centralization created powerful elites who were able to exact tribute and taxes from the dominated groups. Circumscribed habitats made it difficult for those who were losing in the competition to withdraw to other areas, since emigration to different kinds of environmental zones would have necessitated adopting different ways of making a living. According to Carniero (1979), once states developed they tended to expand at the expense of less powerful neighboring peoples who lacked state organization.

The principle that a state monopolizes the legitimate use of force is well illustrated by Ashanti law. The Ashanti, described by Rattray (1923, 1929), were a west African kingdom in what is now the state of Ghana. The Ashanti kingdom was ruled by a divine king who, like Louis XIV of France, represented the very source of the state's authority. So sacred was the king's personage that cursing the king was punishable by a heavy fine. Indeed, to curse the king was such a terrible thing that it could only be spoken of by the euphemism, "to bless the king."

Only the divine king or his duly authorized representatives had the authority to use any force. Since any crime involves the use of force, crime was, in a sense, theft of the king's authority and an insult to the sacred ancestors he represented. All crimes were punishable by death. The greatest of crimes was murder; only the king had the right to kill an Ashanti.

The explicit view that crimes were punishable primarily because they undermined the authority of the state and only secondarily because they victimized others led to another interesting point of Ashanti law. Suicide, like murder, involved taking the life of an Ashanti. Like murder, it was a contemptible affront to the king and the ancestors. So the body of a suicide was tried and, if found guilty, decapitated. By so doing, Ashanti law symbolically demonstrated the sanctity of the state's authority.

SOCIAL CONTROL: THE IMPOSITION OF ORDER

All societies have a variety of mechanisms by which the social behavior of people is controlled to maintain order or to reestablish order once rules have been broken. Social efforts to create orderly behavior begin at birth and continue through life. Some mechanisms for bringing about and maintaining conformity with acceptable behavior include early teaching of accepted customs and instilling values that motivate people to conform. Other mechanisms are punishments for rule violations and rewards for conformity. Malinowski (1926) pointed out that rules may be obeyed for a number of reasons: They may be self-enforcing due to their practical utility; they may be followed because violating them brings public ridicule, because playing by the rules brings more rewarding interaction with others, because they are sacred and supernatural punishment will result from breaking them, or because they are matters of law that are enforced by the machinery of society.

Socialization

The basic way we learn to fit into a social order is in our childhood socialization or enculturation. We learn about our culture, and we come to see the common expectations that others have about our behavior. Those habits that are learned early in life set the pattern for later relationships outside our home and community. Effective socialization can head off problems by establishing patterns of behavior that others find acceptable.

Values. Part of socialization is learning to feel that some ways of behaving are better than others. Values may be defined as our attitudes or feelings about right and wrong behavior. This broad category may then be divided into various types such as moral, spiritual, or environmental values. Moral values are the rules that govern our relationships with our fellow human beings. Piety or spiritual values define our relationship to the supernatural and may be circumscribed by specific religious rules of behavior such as the Jewish kosher laws, rules against blasphemy, or rules about working on a sacred day. Environmental values deal with our relationship to our physical environment, so that concerns here would include pollution and the protection of endangered species. In many societies, morality and environmental values may receive support from religion. Although morality and environmental values may be understood in purely practical terms such as the need for an orderly social life, or an awareness that needed resources are limited, people may accept the moral and environmental rules of their society simply because they are tradition or because they are supported by religious teaching. Note, for instance, the Judeo-Christian Ten Commandments begin with rules of piety such as "Thou shalt have no other gods before me" but also include moral rules such as "Thou shalt not steal."

Religion and Social Control

Another major force for the maintenance of social order is religion. The rites of passage that symbolize stages in the life of the individual as a member of society are typically religious rituals. Myths and legends also contribute an aura of sanctity to a way of life and increase people's respect for the social order. Taboos and ceremonial obligations further structure life in ways that demand predictable conformity from members of a community. Finally, in some societies, religious ideology directly mandates a moral life with the prom-

FIGURE 5.4 *Witch Burning, Sixteenth Century*

Witchcraft and sorcery, uses of supernatural power to work evil, are thought to have existed in many cultures throughout the world. Witches are thought to cause sickness, death, crop failure and all sorts of other ills. One way of controlling these evils is to destroy the witch. A common European method was to burn a witch at the stake as illustrated in this copper engraving.

ise of supernatural rewards for proper social conduct and punishments for wrong living.

The role of religion in maintaining social order is illustrated by the Hopi Indians of the southwestern United States. As embodiments of evil among the Hopi, witches were called *Two Hearts*. They were the antithesis of normal humans and loved darkness, death, and other things that humans despise. Witches were put to death if they did not confess their evil deeds. So the accusation of witchcraft was a powerful force in bringing people into line with acceptable behavior.

The Hopi were a communally oriented society in which support of community values was prized over individual prowess. The person who excelled too much or too often might be suspected of being a witch. Thus, a child who won more races than others would be advised to run more slowly to allow others a chance to win. In a society in which generosity and sharing were valued, the accumulation of too much personal wealth might also lead to suspicion of witchcraft. In this case, a suspect might sponsor a communal festivity in which goods were distributed to others, an act that eliminated the surplus wealth and curried the favor of others simultaneously. Essentially, any deviance was an invitation for suspicious gossip and this suspicion helped pressure people into conforming behavior, much like the legal system in state societies is intended to do.

Rewards

Societies do not rely on punishments alone to maintain social order. Rewarding acceptable behavior also encourages conformity. The praise and esteem of other members of the community is one such reward. Promotions and salary increases provide incentives to support corporate goals. Similarly, various forms of public recognition reward contributions to the social group that are valued by its members. In addition to money, honor, and respect, people may be rewarded by granting them greater power such as positions of authority within the military, police, or judicial system.

Gossip and Community Pressure

The esteem of others is valued by most people, so gossip and community pressure can be a powerful force in keeping people in line. The key to the effectiveness of gossip is that word eventually gets back to the person being criticized. The nonconformist then has the opportunity to try to regain the respect of others by changing the behavior that others have found unacceptable. Direct confrontation is another form of community pressure that is sometimes resorted to when gossip has failed.

Law

Order is also maintained through law, the cultural rules that regulate behavior through the threat of punishment (Hoebel, 1954). Legal rules may be formally defined and codified into a recognized body of laws, but they may also be said to exist informally, defined by custom rather than code. Pospisil (1972) has demonstrated that law in all societies has four characteristics: legal authority, universal application, legal rights and duties, and sanction. Legal authority is the legitimate right to compel others to obey legal requirements, either by the use of force or by the threat of force, and to punish violators of the law. All societies vest

FIGURE 5.5 *Law Enforcement*

Maintaining order in a society is accomplished by enforcing a set of laws. This village court in Sierra Leone is administered by a tribunal of local leaders headed by the chief. The defendant (with shaved head) is accused of stealing. The chief's policy officer (to the defendant's left) was not able to save his client from a sentence of three months at hard labor and a fine.

legal authority in one or more individuals who are charged with the responsibility to maintain order. They may be political specialists, heads of voluntary associations, designated members of a community, or a family. Universal application is the principle that the legal authority should apply the same laws uniformly in similar situations. It is the expectation of consistency in the application of law that invests legal systems with tradition. Of course, legal authorities may violate this principle, but the inconsistent application of law, or favoritism, is regarded as an abuse of power in all societies. Legal rights and duties are the rules that define relationships between persons by specifying what recompense an injured person is entitled to receive and the obligation of the injuring person to make the recompense. These are the rules that legal authorities are expected to follow in enforcing contracts between persons when one or both believe their rights have been violated. Finally, sanction is the action taken by legal authorities responding to the violation of law or motivating others to follow the law. A sanction may be either a punishment or the loss of a privilege or benefit to which a person was entitled before breaking a law. Sanctions include such things as ridicule, ostracism, corporal punishment, or fines.

THE LAWS OF ESHNUNNA IN ANCIENT MESOPOTAMIA

The most ancient known Semitic law code was written on clay tablets about 1850 B.C. in the kingdom of Eshnunna, now the Diyala region east of Baghdad, Iraq. The city of Eshnunna and the surrounding territory that formed the kingdom was controlled by the Amorites during the three centuries from the end of the Third Dynasty of Sumerian Ur, about 2000 B.C., to the founding of the Empire of Hammurabi in 1728 B.C.

The Eshnunna code contained 62 laws that regulated the lives of the citizens. There was no overall expression of general principles or theory of law in the code, but only individual rulings on particular situations that evidently arose frequently in the society. The laws could be easily subdivided into two parts: The majority were regulatory or definitive, setting forth rates for various transactions and responsibilities in various

situations; the rest were punitive and set forth various fines and punishments.

The first two laws of the code established the fixed rates of exchange to be used in the kingdom. Section one defined the value of various commodities, including barley, in terms of silver. Section two did the same in terms of barley. Although silver was being used as a medium of exchange, the importance of barley in the same role was indicative of the strong agricultural base in this society's economic life.

After the first two laws came a series of laws that gave rates for the rent of property and for the wages of workers. Included here were fines for such things as damage brought about by the negligence of a hired person, wrongful confiscation of another's property, and failure to fulfill a contract.

The penalties for trespassing in the fields of a free citizen or for unauthorized entry into a citizen's house were set forth in the twelfth and thirteenth sections. These penalties depended upon the time of the trespass: If it happened during the day, a fine was to be imposed. At night, the owner had the right to kill the trespasser on the spot.

Next came laws that governed economic rights in civil matters. First, rates of interest were specified (usually about 20 percent) and rules for settling cases were established: Disputes over the ownership of the bride-price under various circumstances, the legalities of betrothal, the ownership of slaves who had been forcibly detained as payment for an outstanding debt, the disposition of fugitive slaves, penalties for assault, the unjust divorce of a woman by a husband who merely wished to take a new wife, and the responsibilities of citizens pertaining to the safe maintenance of their property and the protection of others from damage by their animals.

The single most outstanding characteristic of the Eshnunna law code was that none of the laws were considered public law in the strict sense. Although there were courts, they seemed to function as adjudicators of conflicts between citizens rather than between wrongdoers and the state. It apparently remained the responsibility of persons to enforce their own rights and to seek the judgment of the court if they did not receive satisfaction. The court was available to parties in a dispute as an impartial source of judgment, but the winner of the case was the enforcing agent.

THE RESOLUTION OF EXTERNAL CONFLICT

In all societies conflicts occur and in all societies there are customary ways of trying to resolve conflicts. In some cultures there are accepted ways of acting that tend to head off problems and so avoid conflict. But no society is totally successful in avoiding conflict. Once problems exist, conflict resolution may rely heavily on the good will of those involved or it may be based on the socially accepted use of force by legal authorities.

Peaceful Conflict Resolution

Antagonistic parties may sometimes resolve their conflict if both decide that it is no longer in their best interest to continue or that their losses have been restored. Even when an injury cannot itself be made right, compensation may be accepted because the payment symbolizes an admission of responsibility by the wrongdoer and allows the injured party to withdraw from the conflict honorably. For instance, the concept of compensation has been applied in many societies even for major acts such as murder. The idea of payment to recompense the death of a person was called wer-gild, or "man-payment," in Anglo-Saxon England before the Norman invasion of 1066. According to Evans-Pritchard (1940), the same idea was practiced by the Nuer of the Sudan in recent times, among whom the payment took the form of cattle given by the family of the murderer to the surviving relatives.

Peaceful resolution of conflict requires communication between the parties involved. Negotiation can be carried out by the disputing parties themselves, but it is often accomplished through mediation. Mediation is negotiation carried out by a go-between. It is generally easier than direct negotiation between parties, providing the mediator is neutral. A mediator has no authority to enforce a decision on those involved in a conflict. Instead, as he draws on the desire of the parties involved to avoid a continuation or escalation of their dispute, he also relies on his own prestige and his ability to mobilize community pressure to influence the parties to settle.

Among the Nuer, the person holding the prestigious status known as leopard skin chief

FIGURE 5.6 *Leopard Skin Chief*

The Nuer, tribal cattle herders, turned to a mediator to settle disputes between segments of the tribe in a blood feud. The leopard skin chief used threats of supernatural retribution to persuade both sides to come to a peaceful solution while providing refuge in his village for the accused until the matter was solved.

had no official authority over others but had ritual responsibilities and served as a mediator between families that were in dispute. Because these roles were important ones, the position of leopard skin chief was held only by a much respected individual. The home of a leopard skin chief was a sanctuary to which a murderer might flee for safety while a conflict was being resolved. He performed a ritual purification of the murderer and then approached the family of the murderer to determine the number of cattle they were willing to pay to the family of the deceased. Then he visited the aggrieved family to see if they would accept the offer. If the immediate relatives pressed for retaliation, the leopard skin chief might seek the support of more distant relatives to encourage them to accept a settlement. Distant relatives were likely to press for a settlement, since they were less directly involved in the problem, but would have to side with their kin if the matter escalated to retaliation and feuding between families. Usually a settlement of about 40 cattle was finally accepted. Since an unrecompensed death could lead to a feud between the families, the role of mediator was an important one in maintaining social order.

Community action is another approach to conflict resolution. The entire community would be mobilized to respond to and resolve the conflict in societies that lack complex kinship organizations and that also have small enough communities to create a sense of vested interest in resolving the conflict among all members of the local group.

INUIT SONG DUELS

Native Greenlanders had various ways of resolving personal conflicts, including head-butting, wrestling, and boxing contests. Perhaps the most interesting method was the song-duel described by Rasmussen (1922), quoted in Hoebel, (1954). When an individual lacked the physical strength to challenge an opponent to a test of strength, the song-duel was an alternate way of seeking justice. The song-duel was carried out in front of other members of the community. Following traditional rules for composing the songs, the parties to the conflict would alternately sing insults against their opponent. The songs would outline the grievance or defense and deride the other person. The audience participated by their laughter and applause. As the duel wore on, the audience's laughter sided more and more against one party until the public ridicule was too great for the loser to endure and he would withdraw.

Hoebel recounted a case of a divorced man whose wife married another. The first decided he wanted his wife back and sought to do so by publicly shaming his rival in a song duel that he began with words that accused his rival of wife stealing:

Now shall I split off words—little, sharp words
Like the wooden splinters which I hack off with my ax.
A song from ancient times—a breath of the ancestors
A song of longing—for my wife.
An impudent, black-skinned oaf has stolen her,
Has tried to belittle her.
A miserable wretch who loves human flesh—
A cannibal from famine days.

The rival then responded:

Insolence that takes the breath away
Such laughable arrogance and effrontery.
What a satirical song! Supposed to place blame on me.
You would drive fear into my heart!
I who care not about death.
Hi! You sing about my woman who was your wench.
You weren't so loving then—she was much alone.
You forgot to prize her in song, in stout contest songs.
Now she is mine.
And never shall she visit singing, false lovers.
Betrayer of women in strange households.

Such singing continued back and forth, each contestant hoping to win over the audience and thereby defeat his rival. Songs might be prepared and rehearsed in advance, and in some areas the relatives of each contestant provided a backup chorus in support of their own family member.

A court is a formalized institution that asserts authority over parties in a dispute and over persons accused of violating the law. A court has power to decide cases and impose sanctions. Courts are part of political systems in which governing authorities have the right to exercise control over persons outside their own kinship group, so true courts are found only in chiefdoms and states, societies with centralized political officials.

According to Black (1976), when governmental agencies of law enforcement are weak, then other means of social control are likely to be more important. As he put it, "Law varies inversely with other social control" (p. 6). Religion is one of the more prominent social institutions that play a role in social control. The most well-known examples of religious mechanisms for conflict resolution in a legal setting are oaths and ordeals. Oaths are ritual acts of swearing innocence on pain of punishment by deities. Where religious belief is strongly held by people, oaths can be a powerful force in determining guilt, since the guilty may fear supernatural retaliation too strongly to take a false oath. Ordeals are a test of guilt or innocence in which parties in a conflict are challenged to undertake a dangerous or pain-

FIGURE 5.7   Inuit Band Authority

Inuit bands had no centralized authority figure who made decisions for the group. Instead, the community as a whole, or the best qualified member in a given situation, took the lead in such matters as organizing a whole hunt, distributing the meat, and arranging an equitable solution to a dispute.

ful act with the understanding that supernatural influences will grant them success only if they are innocent. Again, the guilty are likely to refuse such tests or fail them, because their religious convictions undermine their confidence. For instance, the Philippine Ifugao people tested the innocence of persons accused of criminal acts by requiring them to reach quickly into a pot of boiling water and remove pebbles from the bottom. The arm of the person who underwent the ordeal was smeared with grease so that if he acted quickly enough, his arm would not be burned. Those who acted out of a confidence born of innocence probably were more likely to pass this than were those whose guilt made them hesitate. Similar tests have been reported for medieval Europe and for the Tanala of Madagascar where the arms of the accused were unprotected from the boiling water by grease. However, a period of several days was allowed to pass before the arms were examined; this lapse of time presumably favored the innocent who acted with less hesitation than the guilty, since those with less severe scalds were more likely to have healed by then.

Violent Conflict Resolution

Conflicts cannot always be ended peacefully. There are a variety of forceful ways in which people attempt to regulate their relationships with one another, including retribution, feuds, raids, and warfare.

In many simple societies that have no centralized governmental authority for the enforcement of law, the responsibility for the punishment of wrongs is a legitimate authority of the person whose rights have been violated. In such cases, law enforcement is synonymous with <u>retribution</u>, the personal use of force to redress wrongs. Retribution as a legal principle is not the same as anarchy, since it is legitimate in societies that condone it only when other members of the community recognize that the aggrieved party has a valid complaint that deserves redressing. Uses of power that are not condoned by the larger community will be seen as illegitimate and punishable.

<u>Feuds</u> are armed conflicts between two kinship groups that are initiated by one of the groups to avenge a wrong, most often the

murder of one of its members. Feuds may occur between kinship groups that reside in the same community as well as between neighboring groups from different communities. They are most common in societies in which bodies of related males, called fraternal groups, work together and feel obliged to protect one another's common interests.

Raids are organized violence by one group against another to achieve an economic benefit. Raiding is generally a more recurrent and ongoing process than is feuding, since the latter is stimulated by a specific grievance and may eventually be settled. On the other hand, the economic advantages gained are likely to be a continuing motivation for organized violence. In raiding, the goal is not to eliminate or even subjugate the enemy permanently, but rather to accomplish a limited objective such as the acquisition of food, cattle, or other valued goods. Where raiding is common, the enemy is likely to be treated as a resource that must be left available for future exploitation.

The most extensive form of organized violence is war, armed combat between political communities. The nature of war differs according to the complexity of the societies involved. Otterbein (1970) examined cross-cultural data of 50 societies and found that societies with more centrally organized political institutions had more complex military organizations, more effective weapons and tactics, and greater mortality in their engagements than did societies with little or no political centralization. In general, warfare was less complex among bands and tribes than among chiefdoms and states. For instance, professional soldiers were lacking in the former societies, while they were typical in the latter. The tactic of surprise was more characteristic of simpler societies, while warfare was generally more formally arranged and conducted in complex societies.

Otterbein (1970) also found that the purposes of warfare also differed for the two groups. In bands and tribes, wars were fought by groups of individuals who were individually motivated to participate. For instance, opponents might be chosen because of personal grudges, and group strategy was not characteristic. Defense and plunder were the predominant motives in bands and tribal societies. Of course, more complex societies also fought wars for these reasons but were also guided by motives that were less characteristic of warfare in bands and tribes. Prestige was an especially common motivation for participation in war in chiefdoms, societies in which social ranking of individual families was a prominent characteristic. On the other hand, prestige was a less common motive in states where social ranking was secure and part of the structure of broad social classes. Apparently, warfare carried out to achieve economic and political control over other communities was a motive found in some of the more complex chiefdoms but was especially characteristic of states.

Otterbein (1970) also distinguished between internal warfare in which the combat is between neighboring political communities that share the same culture, and external warfare in which the conflict is between political communities with different cultures. Internal warfare is especially common among foraging bands and horticultural tribes, while external warfare is more commonly practiced by more complex chiefdoms and state societies. According to Divale and Harris (1976), internal warfare is particularly associated with the systematic subordination of women. Harris (1974) has summarized the impact of this form of warfare on male and female roles:

> Male supremacy is a case of "positive feedback," or what has been called "deviation amplification"—the kind of process that leads to the head-splitting squeaks of public-address systems that pick up and then reamplify their own signals. The fiercer the males, the greater the amount of warfare, the more such males are needed. Also, the fiercer the males, the more sexually aggressive they become, the more exploited are the females, and the higher the incidence of polygyny— control over several wives by one man. Polygyny in turn intensifies the shortage of women, raises the level of frustration among the junior males, and increases the motivation for going to war. The amplification builds to an excruciating climax; females are held in contempt and killed in infancy, making it necessary for men to go to war to capture wives in order to rear additional numbers of aggressive males. (p. 87)

Since female children are often unwanted in these societies because they lack social power but still need to be fed, female infanticide has been the major means of population control in

FIGURE 5.8   *Warfare*

Organized large-scale warfare is generally the province of complex state societies. The Dugum Dani of central New Guinea, however, are exceptions to this rule. Using simple bows and arrows, spears and sticks, they engage in formal battles with agreed upon sites, times, and battle lines.

most societies throughout human history. Divale (1972) studied foraging and horticultural societies that practiced warfare and found that the ratio of boys to girls aged 14 and under was 128 to 100. Since throughout the world about 105 boys are born for every 100 girls, the extra 23 boys per 100 girls in Divale's sample indicates a higher death rate among girls in these societies.

The female subordination that occurs with internal warfare does not accompany external warfare, in which men are absent from home for prolonged periods while fighting with distant enemies whose languages and customs are different from their own. Under conditions that lead to external warfare or prolonged absence of men for other reasons such as long-distance trade, the rank of women is likely to be much higher. It is women who make the day-to-day economic and internal political decisions of the village while the men are away. In such societies, the gardens and houses are often the property of women, female infan-

ticide and polygyny are likely to be uncommon, and inheritance is usually through the line of female ancestry. In societies of this kind, the power of men over their wives is minimized by their lack of ownership over their wives' home and gardens. Their power is also limited by their lack of authority over their wives' children, who are members of their mothers' families, not their fathers'. The male head of the household will not be a woman's husband but her brother, who belongs to her own family.

There are diverse theories about the cause of warfare. Ember (1982) examined cross-cultural data and found that scarcity of resources such as food and fuel, especially when they were unpredictable, was useful in predicting the frequency of warfare. Vayda (1976) has pointed out that slash-and-burn horticulture is a factor that stimulates internal warfare in many societies, because taking land that has already been worked by neighboring groups may be easier than clearing new land and preparing it for cultivation. Warfare allows horticulturalists to expand geographically when its population growth overtaxes local abilities to produce enough food. Divale and Harris (1976) believe that internal warfare is part of a system that helps to limit population growth because warfare fosters male dominance, subjugation of women, a preference for male offspring, and therefore high rates of female infanticide. Female infanticide has a major impact on population growth, since the number of women in a society is much more important than the number of men in determining how many children will be born.

Naroll (1966) examined possible causes of the frequency of warfare in societies. He determined that a high degree of military sophistication did not act as a deterrent to war. In fact, societies with a sophisticated military were not only more aggressive than were militarily less organized societies, but they were more likely to be attacked as well.

POLITICS IN SUMERIAN CITY-STATES

Sumer was the world's earliest civilization. It arose in southern Mesopotamia about 3500 B.C. and consisted of about a dozen independent city-states, cities that were organized around their own autonomous governments. In the third millennium B.C., Sumerian government seems to have been relatively democratic, with decision-making power divided between a council of elders, the military, and the king, who was both head of state and commander-in-chief. The specific balance of power probably differed from city to city and from time to time depending on the circumstances and personalities involved. Certainly, the debates, politicking, and power plays that occur in contemporary governments were not foreign to ancient Sumer, as attested by some interesting historical documents.

Samuel Noah Kramer (1959) has translated and discussed some of the records of Sumer's political life. One of these records describes a war of nerves between the city of Kish, the traditionally paramount city of early Sumer, and the city of Erech, which came to rival Kish in power. In 2800 B.C., Agga, the ruler of Kish, threatened Erech with war unless its people acknowledged him as overlord. Gilgamesh, the greatest of

Erech's kings who also was called the lord of Kullab, convened an assembly of elders to approve his wish to resist the dominance of Kish. In the words of the Sumerian scribe, as recounted by Kramer (1959, p. 32):

> The envoys of Agga, the son of Enmebaraggesi,
> Proceeded from Kish to Gilgamesh in Erech.
> The lord Gilgamesh before the elders of his city
> Put the matter, seeks out the word:
> "Let us not submit to the house of Kish, let us smite it with weapons."
> The convened assembly of the elders of his city
> Answers Gilgamesh:
> "Let us submit to the house of Kish, let us not smite it with weapons."

However, Gilgamesh was not satisfied with the counsel of the elders. To bolster his position, he convened the young fighting men for support:

> Gilgamesh, the lord of Kullab,
> Who performs heroic deeds for the goddess Inanna,
> Took not the words of the elders of his city to heart.
> A second time Gilgamesh, the lord of Kullab,
> Before the fighting men of his city put the matter, seeks out the word:
> "Do not submit to the house of Kish, let us smite it with weapons."
> The convened assembly of the fighting men of his city
> Answers Gilgamesh:
> "Do not submit to the house of Kish, let us smite it with weapons."
> Then Gilgamesh, the lord of Kullab,
> At the word of the fighting men of his city his heart rejoiced, his spirit brightened.

After pitting the hawks against the doves, Gilgamesh had his way, and the war was begun. The view of the prevailing side might be summed up by the 5,000-year-old Sumerian proverb, "The state weak in armaments—the enemy will not be driven from its gates" (Kramer, 1957, p. 125), an idea still expressed by some contemporary governmental figures. Erech won the war and became the dominant power in the region.

The people of Erech prospered politically under Gilgamesh, but his conquests also had their costs. The Sumerians also had a proverb that expressed the dangers of a ruler who exercised too much power: "You can have a lord, you can have a king, but the man to fear is the 'governor'!" (Kramer,

1959, p. 126). Gilgamesh was a tyrant. He drafted men and set them to work rebuilding the walls of the city, fought wars, caroused so wantonly that he "left no virgin to her lover," and so oppressed his people that they prayed to the gods for help. Perhaps their prayers were answered, for according to legend Gilgamesh finally wearied of conquest and worldly pursuits and departed the city on a quest for the tree of life that would give him immortality.

THE RESOLUTION OF INTERNAL CONFLICT

Mediation, feuds, and warfare are typical means of resolving the conflicts that may occur between groups or societies such as tribes, chiefdoms, or states. Within the boundaries of societies with similar political or cultural views, however, conflicts may arise that necessitate a different pattern or means of resolution. Internal conflicts include crimes such as theft and murder, acts all societies regard as disruptive. Internal conflicts may also overturn a government. Revolution and rebellion are dramatic forms of conflict that seek to redress the wrongs a society perceives are being perpetrated by its government.

Crime

No society is free of crime, the harming of a person or of personal property by another. But societies do differ in the frequency and likelihood of various kinds of crime and in how they deal with it. People who live in small groups have little opportunity to harm another member of the group while remaining anonymous and profiting by the act. In large societies crime is more feasible because of the anonymity permitted by large populations. The motivation, however, to violate other's rights for personal gain is certainly not accepted by everyone in such societies, so population growth alone cannot be thought of as the cause of the greater rates of crime in such societies. It appears that crime in large societies is most likely to be resorted to by those who are unable to fulfill the values that a society's culture encourages. In societies with large populations, two related factors that dif-

ferentiate people in this respect are social class standing and income.

A study carried out by the United States National Commission on the Causes and Prevention of Violence (USNCCPV, 1969) found that violent crimes were 11 times as common in cities of over 50,000 people than in rural areas, and most crimes were committed by young, low-income males who lived in urban slums. Poverty, unemployment, poor education, and inadequate housing seemed to be major factors that created motives for criminal behavior. People in such conditions had standards of success that they were unlikely to achieve by legitimate means, and were therefore more likely than other members of society to undertake illegitimate actions to improve their lot.

Crime varies in frequency from extremely low levels in societies such as the !Kung San foragers of southern Africa (Lee, 1979, 1984) and the Semai horticulturalists of the Malay peninsula (Dentan, 1968) where crime has been described as almost nonexistent to societies such as the Yąnomamö (Chagnon, 1968) in which about 23 percent of the men of each generation die violently. Nevertheless, people in all societies have some concept of crime and consider some harmful acts to be legitimately punishable. Theft, assault against members of one's own community, and murder are probably regarded as crimes everywhere.

CRIME AND VIOLENCE AMONG THE SEMAI OF MALAYSIA

The Semai of the Malay peninsula have been described by Dentan (1968) as a nonviolent people. Their culture included the concept that anger made people prone to accidents, so victimized persons were highly motivated to seek redress for their grievances, but in ways that did not accentuate their anger. A person who felt wronged by another approached the offender and requested compensation. The other person was under some pressure to acknowledge his fault and make amends to avoid further responsibility for accidents that might befall the already injured person if compensation was not forthcoming. Even when social problems were not adequately resolved, violence did not result. The injured party might spread gossip and otherwise insult the wrongdoer. These acts were enough pressure for some to resolve the problem finally, but even if they failed, escalation of the hostility did not occur among the Semai. Dentan supported his description of a society without violence with the fact that the Semai could not remember an instance of homicide.

That it was situational forces and not just personality that molds people to crime or conformity was illustrated by a further fact about Semai behavior. During the 1950s, the Malayan government was involved in military conflict with Communist guerrilla forces. When Semai men joined the military and participated in combat, they became noted for the extremes of their fervor in battle. Although in their native society, even killing an animal for food was done with reluctance, they seemed not only able to kill their enemies in battle, but actually to enjoy it. The extreme contrast between Semai nonviolence and violence-proneness in these two situations has led to an interesting debate about Semai personality, culture, and the causes of violence in recent anthropological publications (e.g., Nanda, 1988; Robarchek, 1979; Robarchek and Dentan, 1987; Dentan, 1988).

Although theft is probably regarded as wrong in every society, the definition of theft differs from culture to culture. Outsiders may be considered fair game, and in many societies personal property may be freely borrowed without asking unless the owner expressly indicates that an item is not to be taken. This is particularly likely in societies in which generous sharing of resources within the group is common. For instance, Goldman (1972) described property rights among the Cubeo, a horticultural tribe of the Colombian Amazon Basin: "The attitude of the Cubeo toward personal possessions is best described as casual. They are not indifferent to objects but they regard strong proprietary feelings as improper. Their attitude toward ownership is governed by the important status principle that giving is honorific. Among kin [persons who share common ancestors] objects circulate freely; the closer the tie between people the more active the exchanges. Sisters exchange ornaments and trinkets and men borrow freely from one another with or without

permission. They seem to be most free with objects of economic utility, such as a canoe, weapons, implements, and somewhat more possessive with objects of personal adornment" (pp. 75–76). In this context of rather nonchalant attitudes about property rights and borrowing, Goldman recounted an interesting story about borrowing among the Cubeo: "On one occasion a visitor from an upriver sib [kinship group] rose to leave, after having spent most of the day in amiable talk, and in a most casual voice said, 'I will take my spear with me.' A young man then went to his quarters and fetched the spear, which the visitor took as he departed. The young man explained that he had been at this man's house during a drinking party. He saw the spear and admired it and took it home without saying anything about it. Theft to the Cubeo is not a matter of purloining an object. It is entirely a matter of attitude. They ask, in a manner of speaking: Is the taking of an object an act of friendship or of hostility?" (p. 76).

Societies also differ in the likelihood of theft. For instance, in foraging bands of 50 or 60 people, it would be difficult if not impossible to steal the personal property of another and remain undetected. Furthermore, it is generally advantageous to let others borrow one's tools rather freely, since the fruits of everyone's labor will benefit the entire group. Thus, the very motive for theft can be undermined by cultural practices such as the implied permission common in many hunting and gathering societies for others to use any implement that is left outside the hut.

Homicide is universally regarded as a criminal act, but cultures vary in what they define as homicide. There is probably no society in which the taking of some human life by someone is considered under all circumstances to be murder. Killing is an accepted part of warfare wherever war is found. Avenging a murder by killing the murderer is typically accepted in most societies. Accidental killing is probably not thought of as murder in any society. Nevertheless, the intentional taking of another life without justification, however justification happens to be defined, is considered murder practically everywhere. An interesting exception to this general rule was reported by Jenness (1922), who asserted that among Copper Eskimo men, the likelihood of their killing at least one person was so high that only repeated offenses were considered to be murder. This was an important distinction, since murder was a capital offense and taking the life of everyone who had killed just once would have been impossible.

Legal response to crime. In less complex societies, the enforcement of legal rights is largely left in the hands of individuals and their families. When crimes are committed, restitution or retribution are common motives that guide the action taken by victims and their supporters. Bands and tribes are likely to act in legal matters in ways that are designed to return the group to the balance it had before a law was broken. Where the magnitude of the crime threatens to disrupt the community permanently, corporal punishment, confiscation of property, ostracism, or even death are possible sanctions.

The exacting of legal punishment has followed the principle of retribution in many societies. For instance, Beattie (1964) reported

that the Berbers of North Africa expected exact equivalence in revenge for a death: "So if a man in one group kills a woman in another, the object of the injured group will be not to kill the murderer, but to kill a woman on their opponent's side" (p. 175). This is the same principle of an eye for an eye that was set forth in Hammurabi's famous code: "When a patrician has destroyed the eye of a member of the aristocracy, they shall destroy his eye. If he has broken another patrician's bone, they shall break his bone. . . .If a patrician has knocked out a tooth of a seignior of his own rank, they shall knock out his tooth. . . . If a patrician struck another patrician's daughter and has caused her to have a miscarriage, he shall pay ten shekels of silver for her fetus. If that woman has died, they shall put his daughter to death."

Law enforcement in complex societies tends toward an emphasis on punishment of the criminal. This is probably because crime in societies with full-time law enforcement offi-

FIGURE 5.9   *Rebellion*

In many countries around the world those groups who become disenfranchised or who live in occupied territories may express their frustrations in the form of peaceful protest or violent opposition. In the Gaza Strip, this Palestinian youth was beaten unconscious by Israeli soldiers following a violent demonstration.

cials tends to be viewed as a threat to the legitimacy of the government's authority. The reaction of the enforcement system in such societies is to eliminate, imprison, or otherwise punish the wrongdoer; punishment typically becomes more important than seeing that restitution is made to the victim. In recent times in the United States and other industrialized countries, efforts have been made to pass various victim compensation laws, but the predominant emphasis in industrialized societies remains punishment; it is still usually regarded as the victim's obligation to seek recompense through civil suits.

Rebellion and Revolution

The most dramatic forms of internal conflict are rebellion and revolution. Rebellion is an organized and violent opposition to the legitimacy of a society's current governing authority. It is most likely to occur when a significant number of those who are subject to the government's authority feel themselves to be disenfranchised or inadequately represented by their leaders. In other words, a sense of powerlessness to influence official policies where the members of society feel a right to such influence is a major stimulus for rebellion. Rebellion seeks to influence the policies of government and how they are carried out, but is does not attempt to change the nature of the governmental system itself. Revolution is the organized use of force to alter the very form of government. It is fostered by the same conditions that lead to rebellion, but is likely to occur when those involved view the very system of government as the source of its illegitimate policy and practices. Both rebellion and revolution have much in common with warfare, since all three represent conflicts, often violent ones, between at least two groups, each of which asserts the legitimacy of its own right to use force for its own political ends.

SUMMARY

Politics, the use of social power to implement public goals, takes different forms in human societies. Governing authority may reside in the local community, a typical trait of band societies. It may be vested in the kinship group and in specialized associations that draw their members from the entire community, as in the world's tribal societies. Or it may be the special domain of full-time officials who make up a specialized government, which shares legal authority with its society's kinship groups, as in chiefdoms, or which claims a monopoly over all legitimate uses of political power, as in the states.

However they are organized, political systems have a variety of mechanisms for maintaining social order and for reestablishing order when rules are broken. These mechanisms include socialization, values and morality, religion, rewards and punishments, informal community pressure, and law. Law, the most formal means for enforcing obedience to the rules of social life includes both peaceful and potentially violent means for resolving conflict. Extreme levels of violence such as warfare and rebellion occur when conflicts exist either between governments or within a single society. Such conflicts occur when different groups regard their opponent's use of political power as illegitimate.

KEY TERMS
AND
CONCEPTS

ANNOTATED
READINGS

Fried, M. (1967). *The evolution of political society: An essay in political anthropology.* New York: Random House, Inc. A theoretical examination of societal differences in terms of their political structures.

Hoebel, E. A. (1954). *The law of primitive man: A study in comparative legal dynamics.* Cambridge, MA: Harvard University Press. The first major attempt to carefully formalize the anthropological analysis of legal ideologies and practices.

Maine, H.S. (1879). *Ancient law: Its connection with the early history of ideas, and its relation to modern ideas.* The classic Victorian text on the anthropological study of law from a cultural evolutionary perspective.

Malinowski, B. (1926). *Crime and custom in savage society.* London: Routledge & Kegan Paul, Ltd. A short examinaiton of law by the founder of the American functionalist approach to anthropological analysis.

Nader, L. (Ed.) (1965). The ethnography of law. *American Anthropologist,* special supplement to Vol. 67, pp. 3–32. An important synthesis of anthropological viewpoints on the study of law.

Nader, L., and Todd, H. F., Jr. (1978). *The disputing process: Law in ten societies.* New York: Columbia University Press. An important collection of ethnographic descriptions of how disputes are settled in a cross-section of the world's societies.

Pospisil, L. (1971). *Anthropology of law: A comparative theory.* New York: Harper and Row. A systematic theory of law based on cross-cultural research by an anthropologist who was also trained in the classical study of Roman law.

Roberts, S. (1979). *Order and dispute: An introduction to legal anthropology.* New York: St. Martin's Press. A short book devoted to the understanding of how order is maintained within societies traditionally studied by anthropologists.

PART III

Society and

Humans are not isolated creatures but social ones. It is in our nature to interact with others of our species for reasons of companionship and survival. Chapter 6 details how groups are organized by status, rank, and role behavior in society and describes the rituals within the life cycle that mark the passage of individuals through stages in their life. Chapter 7 describes the systems used to identify our relationships to other members of our family. Chapter 8 illustrates the many forms that marriage takes in societies around the world. An intimate social relationship, it is the basis for the creation of the family, the primary group to which we belong and the basic institution of social life throughout human existence.

Social Life

*N*owhere are all people treated equally. In every society, people are organized into groups and levels of honor and social power. Categorizing people on the basis of distinctions such as the kind of work they do or their relationships to each other has the benefit of making social life efficient, orderly, and predictable. But some ways of categorizing people lead to inequalities that are unrelated to people's innate abilities. Such discriminations are made on arbitrary bases such as race and sex. After examining patterns of social organization and the complexities of racial and sexual statuses, we consider how some of the social statuses we acquire follow one another in a definite sequence from birth to death known as the life cycle.

6

Social Organization and Life Cycle

ORGANIZATIONAL PATTERNS
Groups
Statuses and Roles
Division of Labor
Rank
Contextual Cues
Master Statuses

BIOLOGICAL TRAITS AND SOCIAL STATUSES
Statuses Based on Biological Distinctions
Innate Differences vs. Socially Learned Roles

THE LIFE CYCLE
Rites of Passage

Pregnancy, Childbirth, and Naming
Enculturation, Childhood, and Adolescence
Courtship and Marriage
Parenthood
Divorce
Old Age
Death

FIGURE 6.1 *Status*

By his position in his society, this Ghanian chief is accorded a high ranked status. At his installation ceremony in Accra, he is surrounded by his family.

Tinker. Tailor. Soldier. Sailor. Rich man. Poor man. Beggar man. Thief. Imagine yourself digging through old greasy tinfoil and moldy orange peels for your daily dinner. Or imagine yourself in a London Fog trenchcoat on a foggy London morning cautiously peering around a corner to catch a glimpse of the spy carrying an alligator briefcase. Imagine yourself growing up black in the hills of South Africa or white in the Australian outback. Wherever you find yourself in society is determined both by biology and by culture. Throughout human history, cultural continuity has been maintained by symbolic communication among members of a particular society.

111

ORGANIZATIONAL PATTERNS

The pattern of that communication is determined by how society is organized. The social organization of a society consists of (1) the various groups from which the society is built, (2) the statuses that individuals may hold, (3) the division of labor, the way in which the tasks of society are distributed among individuals and groups, and (4) the rank accorded to each group and status.

Groups

Every human society is itself a group. Its members perceive their common identity because of the culture that binds them together. All human societies that have ever been studied have been subdivided into smaller groups that coalesce from time to time for specialized activities. When a group gets together, it has geographical boundaries, specifiable members, a common activity engaged in by its members, and a division of labor. Football fans scattered across the country are not a group, but football spectators at a specific game are. When a group is formally organized, it may have an explicitly formulated ideology, a goal-oriented "game plan" or set of procedures for carrying out the activity that brings its members together.

The members of social groups generally identify themselves symbolically with a name or some other emblem of their group identity. Commonly, the identifying emblem indicates the activity that draws the members together or represents some other important aspect of the group's characteristics. Thus, the group identity of the United States of America is symbolized by a flag that portrays the political unity of that society's 50 states by a group of 50 stars. The Great Seal of the United States of America contains the image of an eagle clutching an olive branch and arrows, symbols of peace and war, which suggest that the major purpose of the nation as a political entity is to maintain internal order and to defend the group. A smaller, more face-to-face group, such as a religious congregation, may identify itself as a unified body by naming the congregation and by symbolizing its religious purpose with some symbol of its religious ideology, such as the Star of David, a church spire, a cross, or a denominational flag.

There will also be structured relationships between groups in every society. Interactions by groups are culturally patterned, and there may be a hierarchical ranking giving them different degrees of honor and social power. Group relationships are sometimes called the social structure of a society, to distinguish this aspect of social organization from other aspects such as individual statuses and roles (Service, 1962).

Statuses and Roles

Besides groups, each pattern of social organization also includes several kinds of relationships. Each relationship that a person may have with another is called a status. Statuses are the kinds of things we can be for one another: government official, doctor, lawyer, teacher, taxicab driver, husband, lover, mother, child. Since each status is actually part of a relationship, the statuses of any society exist in pairs, such as doctor and patient, husband and wife, parent and child, or friend and friend. The status pairs of a society are of two types: those in which the holders of the statuses are expected to behave in different but mutually compatible ways and those in which the holders of the statuses are expected to behave in a similar way towards one another.

Status pairs in which both parties are expected to behave in different but compatible ways are called complementary statuses. Neither status in such a pair can function without the other, and the complementarity of their relationship is symbolized by referring to each status in such a pair by a different word. The status of doctor requires the existence of the complementary status of patient, that of parent implies that of offspring, and without the status of student there could be no teacher. In each of these cases, the holder of one status of the pair is expected to behave differently from the holder of the second status.

Statuses such as friend, neighbor, enemy, colleague, or ally, on the other hand, imply the existence of two or more holders of the same status who are expected to act toward one another in similar ways. Statuses paired in this way are called symmetrical statuses. One cannot be an enemy unless there is someone who will respond in kind as an enemy, too (Watzlawick, Beavin, & Jackson, 1967).

In every society, each person may be involved in many different kinds of relationships. Each person therefore has many different statuses. The same person may be a wife, a mother, a student, an employee, a friend, and a political activist. The statuses that we are allowed to have are often based on our age or sex and, in some societies, on the family or racial groups into which we were born. Such statuses, known as ascribed statuses, are assigned to us at birth. Other statuses must be acquired during our lifetimes. These statuses, such as team captain, college student, or club member, are known as achieved statuses.

The ways in which the holder of a status is expected to behave are called the roles of that status. Every status has several different roles, each of which is considered appropriate for certain times and places. In a culture in which emotional reserve and independence are valued, a parent may be expected to play the role of comforter to a distressed 10-year-old in private, but to maintain a more detached supportive role toward the child in public, particularly when the child's friends are around.

By conforming their behavior to the role expectations of others, holders of a particular status symbolically communicate that they hold that specific status and that they wish to be responded to in a manner appropriate to it rather than to some other status that they might also hold. The team captain is expected to direct action without discussion on the field; off the field, the same person may be expected to listen to and respect the opinion of another with whom he or she shares the status of friend.

Because each status has its own role expectations, the various status pairs of a society form a pattern of predictable relationship expectations that guide the interactions of society's members with one another. Due to this pairing, the process of communicating to others that one possesses a particular status simplifies the establishing of a social relationship since it also communicates the nature of the role that one wishes them to play in return. When team members accept another's status as team captain, they know that during a game their appropriate relationship to the leader is that of followers. Without such role agreements, ball games—and social life—would be somewhat chaotic.

Division of Labor

The day-to-day work that must be done in any society is allocated to people through their statuses. By playing their various roles, people accomplish that work. This makes it possible for the members of society to be organized efficiently into a clear-cut, well-known, and effective division of labor by which all the tasks of life are accomplished.

Even in the simplest of human social systems, where few specialists exist, there is some division of labor. In those societies that have the simplest social organizations—those in which people survive by foraging for wild foods—age and sex are the primary bases for assigning the work of life. Even though tasks may overlap and distinctions may not be strictly enforced, males and females in all societies are generally expected to specialize in somewhat different economic activities, as are the members of different age groups. Typically in the foraging societies, men are assigned the status of hunters, while women specialize as gatherers of wild plants. Children may provide some help around the campsite, fetching water or gathering branches for the fire. Older members of the group may be relied on for their experience in interpersonal and intergroup relations to mediate disputes, negotiate with strangers, or arrange marriages. In more complex social systems other forms of specialization develop, and the division of labor may become much more intricate. For instance, in societies in which people grow their own food, individuals or entire villages may specialize in the growing of a particular crop or the manufacture of woven goods or pottery. These are traded to other people or villages in return for their specialties. In industrialized societies, there are so many specialized occupations that a monetary system is needed to organize the exchange of labor. In these divisions of the work of life, some kinds of work are valued more highly than others, introducing the social effects of rank.

Rank

Rank is a measure of the relative importance accorded to groups and statuses. Holders of highly ranked statuses and members of highly ranked groups generally have more ready access to whatever is valued in

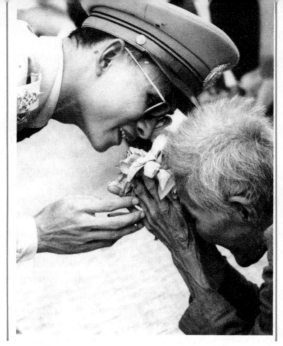

FIGURE 6.2 *Rank*
A status pair consists of two individuals who relate to each other in a way that depends on their rank in society. King Bhumibol of Thailand commands the respect and honor of one of his subjects.

their culture than do other members of their society. That is, depending on whether the rank is high or low compared to other groups, the rank of a group aids or hinders its members' quests for attaining the most valued goals of their culture.

Power and honor. Rank has more than one component. According to Kemper (1978), the two characteristics of a status that determine its social rank are the amount of social power and honor[1] associated with it. Power and honor are measures of one's ability to influence others successfully. Power is the ability to exercise coercion in obtaining what is sought and to punish the failure of others to comply. Someone is honored if others freely choose to give benefits to that person.

Groups, too, may be ranked in the degree of power and honor that they command. For instance, secret societies and vigilante groups are often characterized by high access to power, but their level of honor may be judged low by others. Service associations may have

1. Kemper uses the word "status" to refer to what is here called "honor." This reflects the lack of standardization in the terminology of the social sciences. Kemper (1978, p. 378) defines status as ". . . relationship in which there is *voluntary compliance* with the wishes, desires, wants and needs of the other" [italics in original]. To avoid confusion I will continue to use the word "honor" in this discussion wherever Kemper uses "status."

little power to obtain social benefits for their members coercively, but they may be high in the honor accorded their members.

Like groups, individual statuses may be ranked. Within a status pair, one status may be thought of as the superior of the two and may have access to a greater amount of honor, social power, and/or wealth. Thus, parents are expected to train and control their children rather than the other way around, and it is the teacher who tests and assigns grades to the student. Statuses that are not part of the same status pair may also be ranked with respect to one another. In the United States, the occupational statuses of doctor or senator are generally considered more desirable and their holders given more social power and greater incomes than are the holders of the less valued occupations of sales clerk, mail carrier, or carpenter.

Societies differ in which statuses are most highly ranked. For instance, in industrialized nations where many of the important relationships in life are based on jobs, occupational status is a major determinant of the rank most people hold. In these societies, the loss of income that comes with retirement is often accompanied by a loss of rank. In socially simpler societies in which kinship relationships determine the most important roles, it is common for rank to increase with age and experience.

Class. Ranking of diverse statuses is more common in those societies that have large populations and many differentiated, highly specialized statuses. These societies are organized into a hierarchical structure that sometimes is subdivided formally into ranked classes of statuses. A class is a broad stratum that cuts across society and is made up of unrelated families that have more or less equal access to income and prestige. The larger and more complex a society is, the more likely it is to distinguish between the holders of various statuses on the basis of a system of ranked classes. Sometimes class membership is determined by birth and the statuses that individuals may hold during their lifetimes are limited to those of the class into which they are born. In such a case, when people are not permitted to move from one formally demarcated class to another by acquiring a new status, the classes are called castes.

CASTE IN INDIA

Caste in India has been described by many anthropologists, including Beals (1974, 1980), Dumont (1970), Kolanda (1978), and Mandelbaum (1972). The system of organizing people socially by grouping them into castes is an ancient practice that is couched in religious concepts. The system of castes is complex and differs somewhat in various parts of India. In simplified terms there are four major kinds of castes. The first of these, the Brahmin caste, is ranked highest in ritual purity and closeness to God. Members of this caste are priests in theory, although in fact most practice other occupations. Socially, members of the Brahmin caste are accorded greater honor than are those of the lower castes even though they have less power and wealth than many members of other castes. The Kshatriya—warrior-rulers, nobles, and landowners—are next in honor. They are thought to be less ritually pure than the Brahmins and are subject to fewer dietary and ritual restrictions than the priestly class. Next come the Vaisya, the commoners, and, finally, the Sudra, who are the farm artisans, servants, farmers, and laborers. Below all these are the people of no caste, the so-called Untouchables who perform the polluted tasks of life such as removing dead cattle from the village, tanning hides, working leather, and removing human waste.

Although Indian society accords greater honor to the higher castes, it does not link freedom with this honor. Members of the higher castes are hedged about by various restrictions, most notably dietary restrictions. The Brahmins and Vaisya are expected to be strict vegetarians, although the Kshatriya may eat goat, considered a relatively clean animal, and may drink liquor. The Sudra may eat chicken (a less pure animal) as well as goat, and the Untouchables may eat any meat, including beef and pork. The members of higher castes also are expected to avoid physical contact with the members of lower castes in varying degrees.

Within each caste there are many occupational subcastes or jatis that are also ranked by ritual purity. Members of each jati have rights over and responsibilities to the members of other jatis. For instance, potters of the artisan class are expected to make pottery for the farmers, while the farmer is expected to present the potter with a traditional portion of his harvest. The relations between the jatis are most noticeable when a ritual is performed. For instance, Brahmins must officiate, using bowls made by the Potter jati and wearing clothes provided by the Weaver jati and washed by the Washer jati. Such rituals portray the interdependence of the various jatis and reassert the rights of each to belong to the community, since all public rituals require the cooperation of all jatis. In everyday economic life, few people in modern India actually make their living on the basis of their jati occupation. Washers often do so, and a local artisan may provide services in return for a portion of the harvest. However, many people may provide services for a fee or follow an occupation different from their traditional jati occupation, since most jatis have more members than are necessary for performing the service. Thus, jati occupations represent a system of ritual rather than economic ranking.

Hostilities sometimes arise within the system because the different castes have access to different amounts of honor, power, and wealth. The Hindu religious ideology helps to minimize these conflicts by asserting that individuals who conform well to the rules that govern their position in life will be rewarded by future rebirth into a higher caste. By accepting the caste system and following its rules, one may eventually attain a sufficient spiritual development to avoid being reborn into the world and its misery. Those who rebel against the rules of caste purity will be reborn at a lower position, thereby prolonging the cycles of reincarnation and human suffering.

In socially less complex societies, statuses are not ranked into complex hierarchies, but a given status may outrank others. For instance, a person may be the best basketmaker or the chief hunter, the firstborn child, the head of the largest family, or the spokesperson for the group. However, widely differing statuses are not ranked with respect to one another as they are in all industrialized societies.

Contextual Cues

No matter how simple or complex a society, each of its members will hold more than one status. Each role of each status has a

FIGURE 6.3 *Caste*

The caste system in India is a complex social and religious system of ordering the members of its society. The highest rank is the Brahmin caste and the lowest, the Sudra. Beneath these are the Untouchables, not considered a part of the caste system.

particular situation in which its manifestation is considered appropriate. In other words, people learn to play each of their numerous roles as they are directed by culturally defined contextual cues which might be the location in which the actors find themselves, the date and time of day, or the statuses of other persons who are present. Thus, in the United States and Canada, holders of the status of student who find themselves in the context of a classroom during a scheduled class meeting time are expected to play one of their student roles that is appropriate to that set of cues. Elsewhere, students may continue to relate to a teacher through another of their student-appropriate roles, but one that is more appropriate to the nonclassroom setting. When the teacher leaves, the student's behavior may shift radically as they begin to play the roles of entirely different statuses.

Sometimes conflicting contextual cues occur in the same situation, calling for behaviors appropriate to different statuses. In such circumstances, depending on how different those statuses are from one another, the individual may experience an extreme degree of psychological disorientation and confusion technically called role conflict. For instance, the first time a newly married couple is visited by their parents in the couple's home, a degree of awkwardness may arise when the young couple attempt to play the role of heads of household in the presence of their parents, who have previously had a monopoly over that superior status.

Master Statuses

The usual pattern in which the setting determines which of a person's statuses may be manifested is violated by a few unusual statuses, called master statuses. Master statuses are those that are so strongly imbued with importance in the minds of people that it is difficult to forget or ignore them, even in situations where they are not the most appropriate. Either the status in question is so highly valued by others that it outshines its holder's other statuses or it elicits such a negative reaction that it overshadows its possessor's other more positively valued statuses. Thus, a master status may be said to carry its own context. If the Chief Justice of the United States Supreme Court or a well-known actor were to appear in a college classroom on a parents' visiting day, this visitor would not be treated as just another parent in the audience. More likely, instead of the situation's defining the status of the visitor, the situation itself would be redefined to fit the visitor's master status, and the classroom hour would be radically altered.

When people's statuses have significantly different degrees of rank, they will tend to adopt the highest status that is appropriate to

116

the situation. The greater the importance that ranking has in a society, the more its members will attempt, wherever possible, to avoid appearing in roles of subordinate statuses. The exception to this rule is that a person who is very clearly of a high master status, such as a senator or a Nobel Prize winner, may play the role of a much lower status as a way of showing respect for his or her subordinates. United States presidents have been photographed in their shirt sleeves on tractors, and Diana, Princess of Wales, has driven a tank while visiting a British military base as ways of "humanizing" themselves in the public eye.

Another category of people who may not follow the usual pattern of adopting the highest status appropriate to the situation is those with low-ranked master statuses. They may have formally acquired other more highly ranked statuses, but their master statuses bar them from access to a higher degree of social rank. Because of their lack of social honor and power, the master statuses of low social rank are sometimes given the special designation of minority statuses. Minority statuses in United States society include ascribed statuses such as female, black, Chicano, or Native American, and achieved statuses such as drug addict, prostitute, ex-convict, physically handicapped, or mentally ill.

Even though these statuses are commonly called *minority groups*, the minority status is not a matter of numbers. In the United States, for instance, females make up slightly more than 50 percent of the population, and blacks constitute large numerical majorities in many cities and counties. Yet, irrespective of numbers, birth into either of these statuses may bar acquisition and successful use of highly ranked social statuses. Thus, U.S. women currently hold only about 8 percent of elective offices in a society in which they compose over half of the total population, and adult black males in the United States suffer from an unemployment rate that is twice that of the adult male work force as a whole.

THE EDUCATION OF DR. POUSSAINT: A STUDY IN MASTER STATUS[1]

Alvin Poussaint, a black psychiatrist, has given a powerful account of the black experience in a white-dominated society. The

FIGURE 6.4   *Master Status*

In most situations, people will adopt a role appropriate to their highest status. The one exception might be the person of obvious high master status who elects to play a role associated with a lower status in order to show respect or concern for his or her subordinates. Pope John Paul II holds this small Mexican child in the village of Cuilapan. He visited this region to reassure the peasants that he understood their problems and pledged to work on their behalf.

following passage illustrates that despite his professional status, in the 1960s his master status as a black in the United States sometimes called forth strong expectations that he should adopt a subordinate role in interacting with whites.

Once last year as I was leaving my office in Jackson, Miss., with my Negro secretary, a white policeman yelled, "Hey, boy! Come here!" Somewhat bothered, I retorted: "I'm no boy!" He then rushed at me, inflamed, and stood towering over me, snorting, "What d'ja say, boy?" Quickly he frisked me and demanded, "What's your name, boy?" Frightened, I replied, "Dr. Poussaint; I'm a physician." He angrily chuckled and hissed, "What's your first name, boy?" When I hesitated he assumed a threatening stance and clenched his fists. As my heart palpitated, I muttered in profound humiliation, "Alvin."
He continued his psychological brutality, bellowing, "Alvin, the next time I call you, you

come right away, you hear? You hear?" I hesitated. "You hear me, boy?" My voice trembling with helplessness, but following my instincts of self-preservation, I murmured, "Yes, sir." Now fully satisfied that I had performed and acquiesced to my "boy" status, he dismissed me with, "Now boy, go on and get out of here or next time we'll take you for a little ride down to the station house!" (p. 53)

1. From "A Negro Psychiatrist Explains the Negro Psyche" by Alvin F. Poussaint, August 20, 1967, *The New York Times*, pp. 52–53, 80.

BIOLOGICAL TRAITS AND SOCIAL STATUSES

In every human society, some of the statuses that people hold are assigned on the basis of biological facts. Factors such as sex, degree of biological maturation, physiological handicap, or skin color have been commonly used as the grounds for assigning statuses and role expectations.

Statuses Based on Biological Distinctions

In all human societies that have been studied by anthropologists, the physiological differences between males and females have been the basis for expecting individuals to adopt life-work and ways of acting thought to be appropriate to their gender. For instance, in the simplest and oldest form of human society, survival is based on the search for non-domesticated foods. In such societies, the status of hunter is commonly assigned to the males of the group, while the gatherers of wild vegetable foods are usually females.

Similarly, all human societies have used differences in the biological aging process to place individuals into different statuses. Everywhere, social distinctions involving different behavioral expectations, rights, and responsibilities have been made between infants, children, adults, and the aged.

The blind, deaf, mentally retarded, and other individuals considered to have unusual physiological characteristics are also often set apart in status. They may be expected to behave differently from other people because of these characteristics, even if their biological characteristics might not force them to do so.

FIGURE 6.5   *Racial Discrimination*

In the Republic of South Africa, Apartheid became official State policy when the National Party took power in 1948. A ruling coalition of Dutch-speaking Afrikaaners and English-speaking Europeans allowed the meetings of whites for political purposes, but denied those of nonwhites.

In many societies today, racial differences are also used as an important fact of social life, and persons may be categorized and given different statuses on the basis of race. Holders of these different racial statuses may then be expected to play vastly different roles. The behavioral expectations that are placed on them may be highly arbitrary, with no basis in the actual physiological characteristics that differentiate the status holders.

Innate Differences vs. Socially Learned Roles

We humans may differ from one another in behavioral capacities or generalized tendencies, such as activity level, aggressiveness, or responsiveness to stimuli. Such differences are present when we are born and may result from biologically inherited hormonal and neurological factors. However, social roles are not inherited biologically. As cultural phenomena, social roles are learned. Our inborn predispositions may influence the style with which we play a role, but they do not determine the content of our roles.

Although biology does not control the content of social roles, beliefs about biology may. People who share some biological characteristic may be socialized into playing roles that their culture claims are a natural result of those biological traits. The result is a self-fulfilling prophecy in which playing the learned role seems to prove the culture's association of the behaviors with biology. For instance, an active female child may be subject to intensive social training that leads her to conform to a more passive and nonaggressive role because her society considers these traits attributes of the female status. Similarly, Scott (1969) has described an interesting process by which persons with poor vision may acquire the status of blind persons. Having been labeled blind by legal criteria, such persons may begin to interact with various care-giving agencies. In the process of providing their services, these agencies may unwittingly encourage their poorly sighted clients to learn to perceive themselves as helpless. Learning to play the blind role inhibits the use of what vision the clients actually possess.

When statuses are assigned to people because of biological characteristics, the roles that they are expected to play are commonly thought of as a natural and inherent result of those biological conditions. In societies where men hold the powerful statuses, the culture is apt to contain beliefs that men are somehow naturally more dominant than women. Where one racial group dominates another in the same society, the race whose members tend to hold the more highly ranked statuses will generally be described as inherent leaders, while the subordinate race will be commonly portrayed as naturally lazy, less intelligent, and in need of guidance. This practice of attributing differences in role expectations to the supposed biologically inherited qualities is especially widespread in views commonly held in many parts of the world about racial and sexual differences. The belief that role expectations of members of different racial groups are actually hereditary characteristics

is known as racism. The belief that role differences between women and men are biologically caused has a parallel name, sexism.

Racism. Though inaccurate and demeaning, racism has evolved because it serves a variety of societal needs such as supporting the political and economic goals of various segments of society. Racism goes a step beyond the mere belief that different races exist. It states that people of different "races" differ in behavioral abilities and that they therefore should play different social roles which, of course, generally reflect the ethnocentric prejudices of the racist, the superior roles being reserved for those who belong to the racist's group.

The racist approach to describing society is predicated on confusing biological heredity with learning culturally assigned roles. In the United States, nearly everyone has heard such racist stereotypes as "White people are natural leaders," "Blacks are natural athletes and have rhythm in their blood," and "Jews are born businessmen." The continued existence of such stereotypes that contend that certain ways of acting are inherited through one's biological race readily supports a society's ongoing practice of treating the holders of different racial statuses in different ways.

Such publicly held racist ideas tend to inhibit social change by supporting current discriminatory policies. Even the so-called minority groups may use racist stereotypes— "Whites are naturally racist"—to gain more power by uniting members of their group in opposition to the status quo. Racism of this type also serves as political leverage when applied against the guilt that many people of the dominant status groups feel about the inequitable past treatment of minority groups.

Whether serving the values of the dominant or subordinate members of a society, racist stereotypes are frequently based on the prejudices of the group that is doing the labeling and may be highly inaccurate. For instance, when Jackie Robinson was attempting to become the first black to enter major league baseball in the United States, newspaper editorials throughout the country contended that to allow blacks to play on major league teams would lower the quality of the game. In that day, blacks were regarded as naturally inferior athletes. Now that it has become commonplace for blacks to be recruited to professional sports, one is more likely to hear the equally racist idea that blacks are inherently superior athletes.

Sexism.   Like racism, sexism treats individuals as if they are by nature constrained by whatever traits are socially imputed to their group, often even after they have demonstrated that the stereotype does not fit them personally. People forget that the role expectations that society may place on a group may be arbitrary and socially learned rather than innate.

Sexist concepts include the ideas that men are instinctively aggressive and females innately passive or nurturing. A father who chooses to remain home to care for his children or a mother who seeks employment outside the home may be thought of as "going against nature" and as somehow abnormal. The fact that individuals are capable of violating the traditional role expectations of their group is evidence that there is, in fact, no instinctive impulse for them to follow that role.

THE LIFE CYCLE

Rites of Passage

Arnold van Gennep (1960) has pointed out that as we move from one status to another within the life cycle, our changes in status and role expectations are commonly proclaimed to other members of society by formal rituals known as life crisis rites or rites of passage. Rites of passage symbolically dramatize how important status changes are in the eyes of society. Four public symbolic rituals are commonly celebrated throughout the world: naming ceremonies, which confer human status on the new member of society and proclaim the parenthood of its caretakers; puberty celebrations, which confer adult status; marriages, which legitimize new sexual, economic, and childrearing obligations; and funerals, which proclaim the loss of human status by the deceased and restructure the ongoing social order.

There are many other status changes that are less widespread or peculiar to specific societies. The Navajo celebrate the first smile

of a baby with ceremonial gift-giving (Kluckhohn & Leighton, 1946). In the United States, high school graduation is an important life change as is one's first full-time job. Divorce is found in every society, although in most, the majority of marriages do not end in divorce. Where the family organization is an important economic and political force, parents undergo a status change when their first child is born.

Rites of passage help to maintain stability and order in society while the social order adjusts to culturally significant changes in people's lives. The acquisition of a new status calls for the successful adoption of a new set of roles by the person who is moving into the new phase of life. The formal dramatization of these changes in a ritual of status change may be psychologically beneficial to those who are beginning roles that they have not practiced before and to other members of society who must also adopt new ways of relating to them.

Our concept of who we are is intimately related to our ability to be comfortable in the roles we play. A rite of passage gives us dramatic encouragement to adopt a new set of roles and admonishes others to respect the change. Thus, a rite of passage may provide us with a greater sense of confidence in our new social identities. But in the dominant North American culture, some of the traditional rites of passage are relatively weak or sometimes lacking. For instance, few people in the United States experience any form of puberty ritual as they near adulthood. This lack often creates confusion about the roles we are expected to play and leaves individuals alone to wrestle with what in the United States culture are commonly called "identity crises." The existence of this expression in the everyday language is evidence of how extensive role confusion is in this society. It suggests the benefits that rites of passage may provide to a society's members by helping them maintain a greater sense of self-confidence as they undergo the normal changes experienced by members of their group.

Pregnancy, Childbirth, and Naming

The first life-cycle change is associated with birth. Yet even before that obviously major event, our parents are experiencing the status changes of pregnancy. The biological facts of conception, pregnancy, and the birth process are interpreted differently among cultures. After birth, each society also has specific ways of raising us.

Pregnancy. In all cultures, people are awed by the mystery of a child's growth within its mother's body. Most peoples believe that pregnancy is a result of sexual intercourse, but conception is explained in a variety of ways. Often the child is thought of as developing from semen, menstrual blood, or both. In many societies, both the mother and the father are believed to contribute to the conception and sometimes the growth of the child during intercourse. Sometimes, however, the role of one parent is given more weight in explaining the origin of the child. For instance, in ancient Greece, the father was thought to plant the child in the mother as one might plant a seed in the field. The mother merely carried the father's child as it grew. Such a metaphor was not uncommon in horticultural societies in which men were dominant. In other societies, where men and women had equal status, the symbols of procreation might emphasize the role of both father and mother in conception. In a few cases, women were thought to become pregnant without the aid of a husband.

CONCEPTION WITHOUT SEX IN THE TROBRIAND ISLANDERS' IDEOLOGY

Very few societies view conception as being caused spiritually rather than sexually. Most notable, though, for such beliefs are the native peoples of Australia and the native inhabitants of the Trobriand Islands. Bronislaw Malinowski (1929), who contributed to the development of anthropological research and analytic methods, lived for years among the Trobriand Islanders during World War I. He reported their beliefs about conception in a book ethnocentrically entitled *The Sexual Life of Savages*, from which the following account is derived.

The Trobrianders' ideas about conception were related to their beliefs in reincarnation. The Trobrianders believe that after death the spirit (*baloma*) of a person goes to Tuma, the Island of the Dead, where it enjoys a happier life than that of mortals.

Periodically it rejuvenates itself until it decides to return to the world of mortals. Then it transforms itself into a small spirit-infant. The spirit-infant is brought to a human mother-to-be by an older controlling spirit, who usually appears to the woman in a dream to inform her that she is about to become pregnant. This controlling spirit is most often a maternal relative of the woman, or her father.

After revealing its intentions, the controlling spirit lays the child in the woman's head, causing blood from her body to rush there before descending to the womb with the spirit-child. Actual entry may be by way of the vagina, since the Trobrianders insist that a virgin is unable to conceive because of her "tightness." Although intercourse may open the way for the child, it is not thought to cause conception, which may occur thereafter without sexual relations. After conception the woman's menstrual flow is said to cease because the mother's blood nourishes the body of the infant and helps to build it.

According to Malinowski, the combination of mystical and physiological features of these pregnancy beliefs provided a complete theory of how human life originates. In addition, Malinowski notes that Trobriand social, economic, and political life was carried out within a matrilineal society in which the members of social groups shared maternal ancestors. Thus, in day-to-day social life maternity was a much more influential fact than paternity. Malinowski concluded that the Trobriand ideology of reproduction " . . . also gives a good theoretical foundation for matriliny; for the whole process of introducing new life into a community lies between the spirit world and the female organism. There is no room for any sort of physical paternity" (1929, p. 179).

Malinowski contrasted the Trobrianders' mother-oriented system of thought with the more male-oriented ideology of the missionaries who sought to convert them to a Christian belief system:

We must realize that the cardinal dogma of God the Father and God the Son, the sacrifice of the only Son and the filial love of man to his Maker would completely misfire in a matrilineal society, where the relation between a father and son is decreed by tribal laws to be that of two strangers, where all personal unity between them is denied, and where all family obligations are associated with mother-line.

We cannot, then, wonder that paternity must be among the principle truths to be inculcated by proselytizing Christians. Otherwise the dogma of the Trinity would have to be translated into matrilineal terms, and we should have to speak of a *God-kadala* (mother's brother), a God-sister's-son, and a divine *baloma* spirit. But apart from any doctrinal difficulty, the missionaries are earnestly engaged in propagating sexual morality as we conceive it, in which endeavor the idea of the sexual act as having serious consequences to family life is indispensable. (pp. 186–187)

The Trobrianders vehemently opposed the idea of physiological paternity, a belief that is well suited to a society with a strong patriarchal ideology but not to their own. They characterized the missionaries' belief that sex is the cause of conception as an absurdity and the missionaries, therefore, as liars. For example, Malinowski quotes one of his informants as saying, "Not at all, the missionaries are mistaken, unmarried girls continually have intercourse, in fact they overflow with seminal fluid, and yet have no children" (p. 188). By native logic, if sex were the cause of pregnancy, the unmarried girls would become pregnant more often than older married women, since they engage in sexual intercourse much more often. Yet it is the older married women who have the most children. Another informant argued, "Copulation alone cannot produce a child. Night after night, for years, girls copulate. No child comes" (p. 189), contending thereby that the empirical evidence did not support the view of a relationship between sex and pregnancy. Malinowski also tells us that, "one of my informants told me that after over a year's absence he returned to find a newly born child at home. He volunteered this statement as an illustration and final proof of the truth that sexual intercourse had nothing to do with conception. And it must be remembered that no native would ever discuss any subject in which the slightest suspicion of his wife's fidelity would be involved" (p. 193).

According to Weiner (1976), the contemporary Trobrianders, who no longer disagree with Western ideas about procreation, continue to use the concept of "virgin birth" as a way of avoiding public shame over infidelity. Weiner, relying on myths and old people's beliefs, argues that the Trobriand ideas about spirits causing pregnancy may have served this purpose even in Malinowski's day. She believes that the implicit understanding that both sexes are part of the process of reproduction existed in ideas that, although spirits cause the pregnancy, sexual intercourse is necessary for the development of the fetus *after* conception: "A man develops and maintains the growth of the fetus through repeated sexual intercourse with his wife" (p. 123).[1]

The Trobriand Islanders' denial that sex causes conception symbolically supported their emphasis on inheritance of both property and familial authority through the mother's line. The concept of a paternal role in the creation of a child would challenge the kinship system around which their political and economic life was built. The emotional intensity of the Trobriand rejection of the idea of paternity makes more sense as evidence of their reaction to its ideological significance than as evidence of lack of knowledge.

1. From *The Sexual Life of Savages: An Ethnographic Account of Courtship, Marriage and Family Life Among the Natives of the Trobriand Islands, British New Guinea* (pp. 170–193), by Bronislaw Malinowski, 1929, New York: Harcourt, Brace and World, Inc. Copyright 1929 by Bronislaw Malinowski.

On the surface, some societies appear to be unaware of the link between intercourse and conception. Walter E. Roth claimed that the indigenous people of the Tully River of North Queensland, Australia, were ignorant of the role of sex in pregnancy:

A woman begets children because (a) she has been sitting over the fire on which she has roasted a particular species of black bream, which must have been given to her by the prospective father, (b) she has purposely gone a-hunting and caught a certain kind of bullfrog, (c) some men may have told her to be in an interesting condition, or (d) she may dream of having the child put inside her. (quoted in Leach, 1969, p. 87)

On the other hand, Tully River people were aware that copulation causes pregnancy in animals. It is unlikely, therefore, that they were unaware that sex caused pregnancy in humans in a purely physiological sense. However, in any culture, people's ideas about humans are never straightforward descriptions of observed fact, uninfluenced by their values. Their denial of the role of sex in human pregnancy was not simple ignorance; it was a symbolic affirmation of their ideologically important values. According to Leach (1969), the pregnancy beliefs of the people of Tully River are ways of affirming that "The relationship between the woman's child and the clansmen of the woman's husband stems from public recognition of the bonds of marriage, rather than from the facts of cohabitation" (p. 87). The people of Tully River believe that pregnancy is "caused" by a woman's catching the right kind of bullfrog in the same sense that Christians believe that a wife's fertility is "caused" by the rice thrown at her at the end of her wedding ceremony.

Pregnancy rituals. Pregnancy is a time of potential anxiety, since it's fraught with possible negative outcomes such as miscarriage, physical defects in the baby, or death in childbirth for either the infant or the mother. Such anxieties cause people to turn to symbolic pregnancy rituals to protect the child and pregnant woman and to aid in a successful birth. These rituals are frequently expected to apply to the husband as well as the pregnant woman. They generally take the form of taboos against doing things that have some similarity to the feared outcomes. For instance, the Great Basin Shoshoni forbid a pregnant woman or her husband to eat either the mud hen, which they called the "fool's hen," or the trout, which flops about when one catches it, since the former might result in the child's being stupid and the latter in its becoming entangled in the umbilical cord during labor.

Among the Aztecs of Mexico, pregnant women were forbidden to look at an eclipse of the sun, which they called *Tonaltiu qualo*, meaning "The sun is being eaten," since to see this phenomenon might result in a lip defect, such as harelip, in the unborn child. As a prophylactic against the effects of accidentally seeing an eclipse, the Aztec mother-to-be might wear an obsidian blade over her breast to protect the child. Formerly, in many parts of the United States one heard advice against eating strawberries or raspberries during pregnancy, because they might result in birthmarks.

On the other hand, some pregnancy rules require behaviors that are similar to the characteristics of a good birth. The Shoshoni father was encouraged to hunt the otter, since this animal is known for its enjoyment of sliding down slippery riverbanks, much as the child was hoped to pass easily through the birth canal. In some groups in the United States, women are encouraged to involve themselves in artistic pursuits such as listening to classical music to increase the chances of the child's becoming artistically inclined.

Birth. In most societies, when the woman enters labor she is attended by one or more women who have already experienced childbirth themselves and who help her through the process. Most commonly, birth occurs with the woman assuming a kneeling or squatting position, a posture that facilitates the birth process more than the reclining position traditionally used in many Western hospitals. These upright birthing positions have a beneficial effect on the angle of the birth canal and take advantage of gravity in aiding the passage of the infant.

It is only in recent years that Western medicine has begun to abandon its customary treatment of women in labor as if they were ill patients undergoing a surgical procedure. With pressure from women's groups, the role of the woman in her labor has been redefined as an active partner with others involved in the birthing process, and changes have begun to be made in the woman's posture during childbirth that facilitate her role and not simply that of the medical personnel.

NISA'S FIRST LABOR

Marjorie Shostak (1983) has written a fascinating biography of a !Kung San woman, Nisa. The !Kung San are foragers who occupy lands in Botswana, Namibia, Angola, and South Africa. !Kung San women face childbirth without medical facilities or the help of traditional midwives, although they may be helped to give birth by their own or their husband's female relatives. About one woman dies for every five hundred births, and infant and child death is common. Nisa's account of her first birth is dramatic:

I lay there and felt the pains as they came, over and over again. Then I felt something wet, the beginning of the childbirth. I thought, "Eh hey, maybe it is the child." I got up, took a

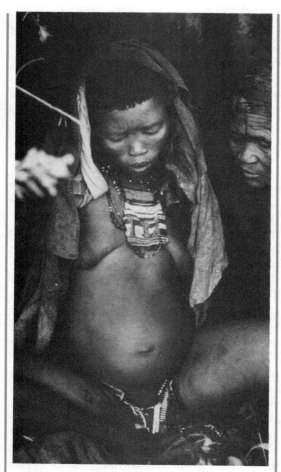

FIGURE 6.6 *Birth*

The most common method of giving birth in non-Western societies is for the woman to assume a natural squatting position. This !Kung San woman is preparing to give birth.

blanket and covered Tashay with it; he was still sleeping. Then I took another blanket and my smaller duiker skin covering and I left. Was I not the only one? The only other woman was Tashay's grandmother, and she was asleep in her hut. So, just as I was, I left.

I walked a short distance from the village and sat down beside a tree. I sat there and waited; she wasn't ready to be born. I lay down, but she still didn't come out. I sat up again. I leaned against the tree and began to feel the labor. The pains came over and over, again and again. It felt as though the baby was trying to jump right out! Then the pains stopped. I said, "Why doesn't it hurry up and come out? Why doesn't it come out so I can rest? What does it want inside me that it just stays in there? Won't God help me to have it come out quickly?"

As I said that, the baby started to be born. I thought, "I won't cry out. I'll just sit here. Look, it's already being born and I'll be fine." But it really hurt! I cried out, but only to myself. I thought, "Oh, I almost cried out in my in-laws' village." Then I thought, "Has my child already been born?" Because I wasn't really sure; I thought I might only have been sick. That's why I hadn't told anyone when I left the village.

After she was born, I sat there; I didn't know what to do. I had no sense. She lay there moving her arms about, trying to suck on her fingers. She started to cry. I just sat there, looking at her. I thought, "Is this my child? Who gave birth to this child?" Then I thought, "A big thing like that? How could it possibly have come out from my genitals?" I sat there and looked at her, looked and looked and looked.

The cold started to grab me. I covered her with my duiker skin that had been covering my stomach and pulled the larger kaross over myself. Soon, the afterbirth came down and I buried it. I started to shiver. I just sat there, trembling with the cold. I still hadn't tied the umbilical cord. I looked at her and thought, "She's no longer crying. I'll leave her here and go to the village to bring back some coals for a fire." (1984, pp. 193–194)[1]

1. From *Nisa: The Story of a !Kung Woman* (pp. 193–194) by Marjorie Shoshtak, 1983, New York: Random House. Copyright 1981 by Marjorie Shostak.

The couvade. A few societies, most commonly gardening societies that occupy tropical forest environments, have a custom known as the couvade in which the husband acts as if he is going through labor while his wife is giving birth to their child. This ritual is often performed with the intent of providing religious protection for the newborn child by misdirecting any potentially harmful supernatural powers away from the actual birth that is in process elsewhere.

Why would such a practice be more likely in tropical forests? The groundwork for answering this question was laid by John Whiting (1964) who showed that in societies with protein scarcity—e.g., many tropical forest crops do not have all the amino acids necessary for protein building—children tend to be nursed for long periods. This protects the child from suffering from protein deficiency in its early developmental period. Prolonged nursing is facilitated by rules against the nursing mother's having sex for several years after the birth of a child, since another pregnancy would require weaning the first child. The sex taboo, however, does not prevent the husband from having other wives and continuing his sex life during this period in their households. One result of this arrangement is that a male child spends his early years with no male role model in residence in his mother's household.

If male solidarity is extremely important—for instance, where warfare is common—painful male puberty rites may be one way of helping the boy finally break his sexual identification with his mother and prove clearly that he has entered the masculine domain. Munroe, Munroe, and Whiting (1973) have argued that the *couvade* was a possible alternative to severe male puberty rites in protein-deficient environments. Painful puberty rituals force the boy to prove his manhood by enduring pain. Where this is not done, the psychological identification with the female role is never fully lost, and the *couvade* occurs as a symbolic acting out of the female role at the time of childhood. Be this as it may, the link between the *couvade* and protein-deficient environments is clear. For instance, the *couvade* is not found in certain tropical forests such as those of Southeast Asia where pigs and chickens have been domesticated or where vegetable foods are grown that provide all the amino acids necessary for protein synthesis by the human body.

Although many do not accept Munroe, Munroe, and Whiting's rather Freudian interpretation of the significance of the *couvade* as a completely satisfactory explanation of its presence in protein-deficient environments in the absence of severe male initiation ceremonies, the custom does make sense in a rather pragmatic way: Since the father will be absent from the home in which his child will be raised, it becomes even more important than usual that his paternity be proclaimed publicly. This is symbolically accomplished through the *couvade* ritual. In this ritual the husband of a woman who enters labor affirms his new status as father of the child by acting as if he himself were experiencing the pains of labor and giving birth to his own new infant. Thereafter, there is no public doubt about who the legal father of a child is, even though the parents may have minimal contact during a period of many years.

Naming.   The next important symbolic act in the life of a newborn baby is its naming ceremony. In this ritual the baby is officially received into the community of human beings and symbolically given human status by giving it a human name. In the birth or naming ritual, the infant is commonly brought into contact with those aspects of life that are of central concern to the members of the society into which it is being received. Thus, among the Samoans of Polynesia and the Yahgan of southernmost Argentina (Cooper, 1946; Murdock, 1934; Service, 1978), both of whom relied heavily on sea products as their main source of food, the newborn child was bathed in the sea shortly after birth. The Mbuti Pygmy of the Ituri Forest of Africa (Gibbs, 1965) grow no food but obtain all their basic needs from the uncultivated resources of the forest; they therefore speak of the forest as their parent and their provider. They initiate their children into the human group in a ritual in which vines from the forest are tied around the children's ankles, wrists, and waists, thereby bringing them into contact with their future livelihood.

In the industrialized societies of Europe and North America where millions live together under single governments, many of life's problems relate less to uncertainties about control over the food supply and more to the difficulties of interacting daily with strangers with whom one has no close ties of kinship or residential unity. Strangers are more likely than family or co-residents to act against one another's interests and to violate each other's rights for their personal gain. So, in societies in which people must interact frequently with strangers to accomplish major goals, concern over issues of social morality are mirrored in the common practice of baptism, a ritual washing away of the effects of human sinfulness.

Enculturation, Childhood and Adolescence

From birth through adolescence, we humans are raised in some kind of family setting according to the dictates of our culture. Our upbringing usually includes some restrictions on free expression of our sexuality, including taboos against intercourse with certain family members. In many societies, our attainment of

FIGURE 6.7 *Christening*
In this Greek Orthodox ceremony a newborn is named and initiated into the community with the ritual use of water as a symbolic cleansing. The baby will typically be sponsored by two people who then become its godparents or coparents and aid in its spiritual and sometimes financial upbringing.

sexual maturity is marked by special puberty rites honoring our passage into adulthood.

The enculturation process. The process by which children learn the culture that guides the life of members of their society is known as enculturation or socialization. Even before they begin to communicate in the language of their society, those around them have begun to mold their behavior so that it will conform to the rules for living that make up their culture.

Anthropologists have long asserted that enculturation occurs partly by imitation and partly by direct teaching through language. According to Hall (1959) the psychological effect of enculturation on individuals depends on whether the learning of a custom is based mostly on imitation or direct teaching by language. In the latter case, the effect will depend on whether language is used primarily for admonition or for explanation when a custom is taught. Imitative learning, which Hall calls informal learning, results in a greater tolerance for individual stylistic variation and gradual adaptations of older ways of doing things to new situations. Much of what we have learned informally is done automatically, without awareness or concentration and with little or no feeling. When the informally-learned rules for doing things are broken, however, anxiety mounts rapidly in all present until someone acts to deal with the rule violation.

Learning that occurs when language is used to admonish us for violating a custom is called formal learning. In formal learning, customs are taught when we break a rule and are corrected by someone else. The teacher expresses disapproval of our behavior and suggests an alternative way as the proper, moral, or good way to act. We are conscious of the rules we are following if we learned them formally, since talking about them was part of the learning. Formal ways of doing things are endowed with deep feelings by the participants, and their violation leads to tremendous insecurity in those who rely on them to order and structure their lives. Since strong emotions are associated with practices learned through the formal method, adherence to the custom as taught is an important affair. Therefore, formally learned customs are slow to change.

It is also possible to teach a custom by talking about it but without expressing disapproval or disappointment of the learner's rule-breaking behavior. Instead, the new way of acting is explained by giving the logical reason that lies behind it. This form of learning has been called technical learning by Hall. People are most highly conscious of technically learned behaviors since they include explanations of the reasons and benefits of the behaviors. Due to the emphasis on explaining the rationale, little emotion is associated with material learned in this way and it may be replaced readily by new technical ways of dealing with the same situation.

Childhood sexual socialization. Before we are able to play the role of adults with complete success, we must acquire knowledge of the sexual customs of our society. Most societies deal with this necessity in a fairly matter-of-fact way. According to Ford and Beach (1951), 34 percent of the 95 societies whose sexual customs they surveyed had little or no restriction on sexual experimentation in childhood. Examples of peoples whose attitudes toward childhood sexuality were permissive are the Lepcha, an agricultural society in the Himalayas, and the Trobrianders, who lived on one of the Melanesian islands. According to Ford and Beach (1951), the Lepcha believed that sexual activity is necessary in order for girls to grow up. Therefore, most girls were regularly engaging in full sexual intercourse by the age of 11 or 12. Among the Trobrianders, boys of 10 to 12 years of age and girls of 6 to 8 years are given explicit sexual training by older companions.

Fifty-one percent of the societies Ford and Beach studied were semirestrictive: Young people were expected to follow certain rules of etiquette in their exploration of their sexuality, although no severe punishments were imposed for violations. Only 15 percent of these societies were truly restrictive of childhood sexuality. Restrictions were most common where male solidarity was economically or politically important and where class distinctions or differences in wealth or the control of property were important matters. This is certainly understandable, since adults in such societies are likely to have a greater vested interest in the future marriage plans of their children. The more carefully the sexuality of unmarried persons is controlled, the greater are their parents' options in selecting the marriage partners of their children.

Puberty rituals. Near the time individuals reach biological maturity it is common for an adulthood ritual, commonly called a puberty ritual, or adulthood ritual to be held. This ritual signals the transition from childhood to adulthood and impresses on both the child and his or her community that the old roles of childhood are to be set aside and that others should treat him or her as an adult thereafter.

Not all societies practice puberty rituals, but they are quite common. In Cohen's examination (1964) of 65 societies, 46 had puberty rituals, while 19 did not. He divided these societies into two groups: those with nuclear families only (minimal families that consist only of parents and their children) and those with complex family organizations such as lineages and clans in which many related individuals participate in family affairs (see Chapter 7). He found that in societies based on the nuclear family—a situation in which children would be trained from an early age to be socially independent—the probability of puberty rituals was smaller. On the other hand, of those societies with more complex families—and in which children would have to be trained to play an interdependent, cooperative role with many other family members to become adults—almost all had puberty rituals.

Social circumstances that foster interdependent role playing can lock people into their current roles and make change difficult without the aid of a mechanism for transformation from one status to another. The puberty ceremony symbolically redefines the child as an adult in a dramatic, public fashion that is difficult for those involved to ignore. The ritual proclaims the changes in rights and responsibilities that everyone in the group must recognize for the change to occur. By symbolically transforming the child to an adult, the puberty ritual creates barriers against everyone's falling back into their previous habits of interaction.

Puberty rites for males. For boys, puberty rituals seem to be most dramatic when the transition from boyhood to manhood is potentially difficult. Under such circumstances, male puberty rituals are often severe and painful ordeals, involving ceremonies such as circumcision, scarification of the body (decorating the body with a pattern made of scars), tattooing, and the filing or knocking out of front teeth as indicators of adult status.

Whiting, Kluckhohn, and Anthony (1958) found that circumcision as a part of initiation rituals is especially associated with three social customs: a taboo on sex between husband and wife for a year or more after the birth of a child, the sharing of sleeping quarters by mother and child with the father's quarters elsewhere, and the establishment of residence by a married couple near the husband's relatives. The first two of these customs make it

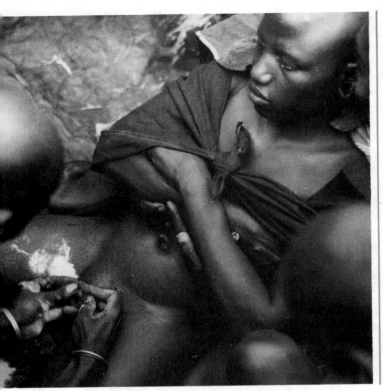

FIGURE 6.8 *Puberty Ceremony*

Circumcision is a ritual initiating the young male into adulthood. This Maasai shows no emotion throughout the ceremony. Afterward he will have a three month healing period during which he will wear black and the "Olemasari" headdress, will not wash, be seen eating, or have his food touched by a woman.

more difficult for a male child to identify with the male role, since the most available adult role model is the mother. The third, residence of couples near the husband's relatives, is common where male solidarity is important among adults. The conflict between the need to identify with the male group as an adult and the relatively weak childhood tie between father and son make the transition from childhood to adulthood a stressful one. Hence the dramatic ritualizing of the status change by painful rites through which a boy proves to the adult male community that he is capable of adopting the adult male role.

Puberty rites for females. Brown (1963) found that about half of a sample of 60 societies practiced puberty rituals for girls. Girls' puberty rituals are most likely to occur in societies in which the residences of newly married couples are established near the wife's relatives. The more important a woman's labor is to the family food supply, the more likely it is that female puberty rituals will be practiced. According to Brown, female puberty rituals are painful in only 30 percent of the societies that practice such rituals. As with male initiation rituals, painful ceremonies are most likely in societies where mothers and daughters share sleeping quarters while the father sleeps elsewhere.

FEMALE CIRCUMCISION AND THE SUBORDINATION OF WOMEN

Many cultural practices serve to keep women in subordinate roles, restricting their freedom. Some societies keep women in restrictive clothing, for instance, or under veils. Certain others in which male dominance over women is an important fact of life mutilate the genitals of female children, a practice called female circumcision. Hosken (1980) describes the most common forms of female circumcision, their effects, and the cultural settings in which they occur.

Infibulation—an operation by which the sides of the vulva are closed over the vagina—is particularly common where the virginity of wives is especially important, since this childhood operation ensures virginity. Following infibulation, sexual intercourse is not possible until the barrier created by the operation is cut by the husband. Excision—removal of the pleasure-sensitive clitoris—is performed to reduce a woman's sexual sensations and, thereby, her interest in sex. This is thought to increase her fidelity in marriage, especially in societies where polygyny (where men are permitted to have more than one wife) is practiced and legitimate opportunities for heterosexual intercourse are less common for wives than for husbands. Excision is sometimes thought to increase female fertility, so it is also practiced to ensure that a woman will have many children.

Female genital mutilation is most common today in the most populous areas of East, Central, and West Africa, in some Middle Eastern countries including Egypt and the southern Arabian Peninsula, and in some parts of Indonesia and Malaysia. Though these mutilations are particularly common today in Moslem areas of these parts of the world, they should not be thought of as Moslem practices. Excision, for instance, is practiced by Christian Copts in Egypt as well as by Egyptian Moslems and by non-Moslem groups in the 26 African countries where it has been documented. Furthermore, although infibulation was not a traditional Western practice, excision was practiced by European and American surgeons into the twentieth century (Barker-Banfield, 1983) as a supposed cure for masturbation and nymphomania, a negative label for sexual desire in females.

Courtship and Marriage

Following the puberty or adulthood ritual, the next common rite of passage is marriage. Cultures handle courtship and mate selection in many different ways. In many societies, marital partners are selected by parents. In others, especially in those in which children will establish their own households that are economically independent of their parents, courtship and choice of spouse is a responsibility of the young adults themselves.

Sex without marriage. Following puberty, the majority of societies are quite tolerant of sexual experimentation before marriage. Ford and Beach (1951) found that of 95 societies surveyed, 81 had little or no restriction on premarital sexual relations. The least permissive societies are, as might be expected, those in which parents have the greatest interest in controlling the marital choices of their children, societies in which people are ranked by differences in wealth or class membership, and societies in which male solidarity is economically and politically important.

COURTSHIP IN SAMOA

In traditional Samoa before contact with Europeans, children were unshielded from the facts of sex, birth, and death. Growing up sharing a house with no walls with 50 or 60 relatives, they did not develop the kind of shame that is connected with sex in societies where privacy is more common. Chas-

tity in daughters was a mark of prestige for families, but as in all societies sexual experimentation occurred discreetly. Mead (1928) believed that both men and women were equally free to choose their partners, and her informants claimed that the European concepts of fidelity and jealousy were unheard of.

Etiquette required that a rendezvous be arranged through a go-between, called a *soa*. An unmarried woman might invite a suitor to spend the night with her in her family's home if she did not wish to meet him elsewhere. In such a case, the young man might remove his girdle and grease his body to make it slippery before entering the house after dark when other family members were already asleep. It was expected that he would be discreetly gone before others arose.

This form of courtship gave rise to a custom known as sleep crawling, in which an unpopular youth or jilted lover might sneak into the house of a young woman without invitation, in the hope that she might be expecting another lover and allow him to stay once she had discovered the deception. Freeman (1983) regards this as a form of rape and believes that a great deal of competition occurred among young men in this practice, due to the great emphasis that Samoan families placed on competition for status and on the chastity of their daughters as a symbol of their family honor. If the woman was not favorably disposed to the sleep crawler, she had the option of rousing her household to chase, ridicule, and beat the intruder for adopting such tactics. If he were publicly identified, a sleep crawler was disgraced and would not be entertained or considered for marriage by other women.

Informal clandestine love affairs in Samoa would eventually lead to the development of more or less permanent primary sexual liaisons between couples that were, in effect, a form of trial marriage. If the couple desired to formalize their relationship by marriage, a courtship process was required in which a go-between would accompany the lover to the woman's family and plead his case for him. After repeated visits, the actual proposal of marriage would be made by the go-between. If the marriage was acceptable to the family, a ceremony would be arranged in which elaborate gift giving took place between the two families.

FIGURE 6.9   *Marriage Ritual*

The marriage ritual differs greatly from culture to culture. This bride and bridegroom sit next to Brahmin priests in a typical high caste wedding in South India.

The marriage ritual. Once an agreement for marriage partners has been achieved between the families, the actual ritual of marriage may occur. Marriage rituals vary tremendously from society to society, but they generally involve symbolism dramatizing the union being created between the two families. They may also portray the relations, especially those of a stressful nature, that are expected to exist between the couple and their respective in-laws. For instance, among the Aztec of Mexico the bride was carried, like a burden, on the back of the old woman who had acted as her matchmaker to the place of the marriage. After lectures by the elders of both families about their new responsibilities as married persons, the capes of the couple were tied together into a knot by which they were joined in marriage.

An occasional form for marriage rituals involves a mock battle in which the bride is captured by the bridegroom and his family or friends from her defending relatives. G. W. Stow (1905) described a South African !Kung San marriage by mock capture. During the wedding feast the groom was expected to seize hold of the bride. Then the two families began to fight while the bride's family focused their attention on beating the groom with their digging sticks. The groom had to succeed in holding on to his bride during this beating for the marriage ritual to be complete. Had he failed, he would have lost his bride.

Parenthood

With marriage may come children, turning the social unit into a family. The relationship between spouses generally changes at the birth of the first child. It creates new obligations for the husband and wife and new demands on their time and energy. Their domestic roles must be adjusted to accommodate their new status as parents. No longer will they have as much exclusive time for each other.

In societies in which the family organization is important economically and politically, entry into parenthood may be formally indicated by a change in the parents' names. By this custom, called <u>teknonymy</u>, a parent might be called Father of Lynn or Mother of Kay. Teknonymy is most often practiced by men in societies in which the couple takes up residence with or near the wife's family. It occurs for women as well, but in fewer societies. In either case, it reflects an elevation in the social rank of the individual, since because of the birth of the child he or she is no longer such an outsider to the family with which the couple resides. The name change calls attention to the greater bond that now exists between the new parent and the in-laws.

Divorce

Not all marriages last until the death of a spouse. In the United States, for instance, between 30 percent and 40 percent of marriages begun in 1989 are likely to end in divorce. Around the world, there are societies with higher and lower rates of divorce. Reasons for divorce vary, but impotence, infertility, infidelity, laziness, and simple incompatibility are common justifications. In probably three quarters of the nonindustrialized societies that have been studied by anthropologists, women and men have been more or less equal in their right to divorce (Murdock, 1957).

Cross-cultural variations in divorce rates make it possible to discover some of the factors that make divorce less likely. The payment of a marriage gift to the bride's family gives her family a vested interest in the stability of the marriage, since the groom's family is likely to demand return of the payment if the marriage is dissolved. The dowry, a transfer of wealth in the opposite direction, has a similar effect of stabilizing marriage ties. When the couple lives in an extended family, relatives are also likely to have a stabilizing effect on their marriage. Matrilocality, discussed in chapter 8, Marriage and Family, also is associated with a low divorce rate. Perhaps this is because the control over property this form of residence gives to women is associated with greater than usual social power and honor for women and little familial authority for the husband, who resides with his in-laws. Under these conditions, the frequency of abusive behavior by the husband is also likely to be relatively low.

FIXED-TERM MARRIAGES IN IRAN

Although it is possible to conceive of the marriage bond as continuing after the death of a spouse, as for instance the Nuer do, it is more common for marriage to be automatically terminated with the death of a partner. Where divorce is available as a voluntary means for terminating a marriage during the lifetimes of the partners, it is still commonly associated with a marital crisis such as incompatibility, infertility, or infidelity. The Shi'ah Moslems of Iran have developed another, creative use for the concept of divorce that is not associated with difficulties within the marriage itself—two persons may contract a marriage for a specific period of time after which the divorce is automatic.

Temporary marriages *mut'ah,* (lit. 'plea-sure') originally grew out of situations in which men were away from home and separated from their permanent wives for prolonged periods, as for instance during a war or pilgrimage. The men might establish fixed-term marriages that would last only until their return home. In permanent marriages, a payment to the bride, called indirect dowry, similar to a dowry is required but neither the amount nor its time of payment need be fixed in the marriage contract. If both parties agree, it may be paid following the actual wedding ceremony, although the wife does not become bound by the usual obligation to have sexual intercourse with her husband until the indirect dowry is paid. Fixed-term marriages also require an indirect dowry, but given the temporary nature of the unions, Shi'ah custom requires that it be a fixed and definite amount, and paid at the outset of the marriage. Children of a temporary marriage have the same rights of support and inheritance as those of a permanent marriage, but either the husband or wife in a fixed-term marriage are free to prevent the conception of a child without the other's permission. In permanent marriages, on the other hand, contraception requires the agreement of both spouses.

Islam, as understood by Shi'ah Moslems forbids sex outside marriage and prostitution. Nevertheless, sexual abstinence, going counter to the God-given sex drive, is not a desireable state. In the Shi'ah Moslem view of human nature, temporary marriage makes it possible for human beings to fulfill their sexual drive without sin in situations that make permanent marriage impractical.

Old Age

We all want to grow older, but we do not want to grow old. The negative feelings we have about aging are partly related to the loss of health and strength that accompany the biological process. Socially, aging may also bring a loss of our accustomed rank. What are the factors that contribute to the loss of social power and honor that old age brings in societies such as our own? Cross-cultural research sheds some light on this question.

When postmarital residence rules require a couple to live near one spouse's parents, it is easier for the parents to continue their roles as family heads into their old age. In societies in which the family is a cooperating economic or political group, the status of family head can be a major determinant of an older person's rank in life. According to a study of nonindustrialized societies by Lee and Kezis (1979), nuclear families lack a structure in which parents can maintain into their old age their role of family heads. Older people are more likely to have high ranked statuses in societies in which they live with related married couples and in societies in which descent is traced through only one of the parents (patrilineal or matrilineal societies) rather than through both. However, if an extended family is too large to be easily led by a single family head or couple, the family heads may govern in name only, while family decisions are actually made by smaller groups within the extended family. When the political power or wealth of a family is not consistently related to a particular family line, parents' rank is not so likely to rise with age as in a system in which rank is intimately connected to a particular inheritance line.

In all societies, the elderly are accorded more respect if they are economically productive. Thus, in industrialized societies where rank is associated closely with wealth and income, the social rank of the elderly tends to decline markedly at retirement.

Death

Death is more than a simple biological process. It involves distinctive psychological and social changes as well.

Simple and obvious criteria such as the absence of breathing, heartbeat, or reaction to pain have been used in societies throughout the world to determine when biological death has occurred. With the development of a technology to measure brain functioning directly, in the United States and other industrialized societies, more emphasis seems to be directed toward defining death as the cessation of activity in the cerebral cortex of the brain, the center of intellectual and conscious processes. However, these criteria may not always agree with one another. For instance, the cerebral cortex may no longer be active while the heart and lungs continue to operate, or a person may be comatose and unresponsive to pain, yet later report having been fully aware of the surroundings. Life-support systems used to maintain the vital functions of comatose patients whose heart and lungs have stopped functioning further complicate the process of determining biological death.

Psychological death refers to the process by which people prepare themselves subjectively for their impending biological death. According to Elisabeth Kübler-Ross (1969), who studied dying patients' responses to their circumstances in United States hospitals, the initial reaction of most patients to learning that their illness is terminal is *denial*. Patients refuse to accept the correctness of the diagnosis, insisting that some error has been made or that their records have been confused with those of someone else. Their basic attitude might be summed up as "There must be some mistake; this cannot be happening to me!" When they finally accept that they are in fact dying, denial is replaced by a period of *anger*, which is characterized by rage, envy, and resentment. In this period, the dominant question is "Why me, why not someone else?" The anger may be directed at anyone at hand—other patients, doctors, nurses, even family members who come to visit and comfort the person. The third stage is one of *bargaining* for more time. In this stage, patients seek a slight extension of their deadline—to allow doing something "for one last time" or some similar request, in return for which they vow to live a better life. In the fourth stage, *depression* predominates, while the dying person mourns because of the approaching loss of people and things that have been meaningful in his or her life. Finally, a stage of *acceptance* may be reached, a stage of quiet expectation. This is not a stage of happiness, but one of rest in which there are almost no strong feelings and in which the patient's interests narrow as he or she gradually withdraws from everyday life in preparation for what is about to happen. This may be a time of great distress for the patient's family, since they may feel rejected by his or her withdrawal and lack of interest in their visits.

Socially, death brings about the final change of status in the human life cycle—the change from a human status to a nonhuman one. Social death is the point at which other people begin to relate to a dying person with behaviors and actions that are appropriate toward someone already dead. Like psychological death, social death may occur before biological death. W. H. Rivers (1926) reported that among the Melanesians, the word *mate*, which means "dead person," was applied not only to the biologically dead but also to individuals who were gravely ill, close to death, and to the very old who were likely to die soon. The Melanesians, of course, distinguished between biological *mate* and social *mate*. The purpose of referring to those who were close to death as *mate* was that they were treated socially as if they were dead. Such persons might be buried alive so that they could proceed to a more pleasant afterlife rather than linger among the living under the unpleasant circumstances of extreme age or terminal illness. Among the Inuit of the Arctic, the survival of hunting families would be endangered if they slowed their wanderings through arctic wastes in search of food to allow the aged or infirm to keep up. Eventually, at the urging of the afflicted party, the Inuit might hold a funeral ceremony and say goodbye to the one who had to be left behind to die so that others might live.

Since all societies must restructure their social relations so that the work of the world may be continued after the death of a member, social death is found in each society. The most dramatic aspect of this social custom is manifest in funeral rituals. Funeral rituals provide a mechanism for dealing with and disposing of the body of the deceased and, at the same time, provide a setting in which the survivors can be encouraged to adjust themselves to the person's now permanent absence. As a part of this second role of funeral rituals, issues of inheritance of property rights and of passing on the statuses of the deceased to new persons are dealt with in many societies during or immediately following the funeral.

THE MAPUCHE DEATH AND BURIAL RITUAL

The Mapuche, a native people of southern Chile, believed, according to Louis Faron (1961, 1968), that death is caused by spiritual powers. The forces of evil known as *wekufe* were usually brought into play by a sorcerer-witch called *akalku*. When a person died, the corpse became dangerous to those who

FIGURE 6.10 *Burial Ceremony*

A major change in a family or society is the death of one of its members. Many societies have elaborate rituals to help the spirit of the deceased in its journey in the afterlife as well as to help those left behind adjust to the loss. This Lama, a Tibetan monk, presides at a cremation ceremony in Nepal.

had to deal with it. One or two members of the household washed the corpse, clothed it in its finest garments, and laid it out for display on an altar in the house. After four days, the body was transferred to a canoe-shaped coffin that had been carved from a split tree trunk.

The relatives, especially the women of the family, mourned and lamented the loss, tore their garments, and promised revenge for the death which they believed to have been caused by sorcery. Then came the wake or "Black Gathering." First, the house was purified of evil spirits to prevent them from capturing the soul of the deceased. This was done by horsemen who surrounded the house and shouted at the evil spirits who invariably came in search of the souls of the dead. A four-day-and-night vigil by the relatives followed. This was important, since how the deceased spent eternity—either among the ancestors or in the underworld of witches—depended not on how he or she had lived but on how the mourners conducted themselves during the death ritual. It was their behavior that prevented the witches from stealing parts of the corpse for use in creating a new evil spirit.

After the four days of vigil, the corpse was taken to a bier in a field. There the deceased was praised in several speeches. The coffin was then painted black and decorated with cinnamon, apple, and the shrub

133

maqui. A large wooden cross, a symbol borrowed from Catholicism, was placed at the head of the coffin, which faced toward the east.

When the chance that the spirit of the deceased would be captured by evil forces had been dealt with, the guests, who might number over 1,000, assembled in the mourning houses and were fed a ceremonial meal provided by the family of the deceased. The men were greeted by the host and the female guests by a female relative of the deceased, in separate groups.

Although many feared to do so, it was customary for the guests to look on the face of the corpse. Small gifts, belongings, and a packet of food were dropped into the coffin to accompany the deceased on the journey to the afterworld of the ancestors.

Only the closest relatives finally accompanied the coffin to the graveyard. As they returned from the cemetery, ashes were scattered along the way to prevent the spirit from returning to bother the living.

SUMMARY

None of us operates totally independently as isolated, self-sufficient individuals. Each of us lives within a society, and all societies organize their members into groups of various sorts and divide labor among their members. Our social life is also characterized by relationships with many people, each of which involves a status. Furthermore, each status carries various role expectations defined by our society. Statuses are ranked in power and honor by our society, with some—master statuses—considered so significant that their high or low rank outweighs that of all our other statuses. Low ranked master statuses are the defining feature of minority groups.

Statuses are sometimes assigned on the basis of observable biological facts, such as age, sex, and skin color. Sometimes people are socially grouped into minorities because they share some biological characteristics. Those who believe that the social roles played by minority groups reflect biological realities are called racists or sexists. Racist and sexist thinking typically bars minority group members from access to economic and political power with the rationalization that they cannot handle it. But the role expectations that accompany minority group status have little or no relationship to our innate characteristics; they are cultural phenomena, socially learned and enforced.

We change in many ways through life, but some of our changes are not unique to us. Rather, they are signs that we are passing through predictable stages in the life cycle. The major stages discussed here are birth, socialization during childhood, marriage, family formation, old age, and death. Societies shape these changes in culture-specific ways, with only a few universals or near-universals such as the incest taboo. Along the way, life cycle changes may be marked by customs such as pregnancy taboos, *couvade*, naming ceremonies, puberty rituals, marriage negotiations, marriage rituals, establishment of residence, divorce, and funeral rites, each of which has specific cultural meanings and purposes. Many cultures also have specific expectations about whom one can marry and with whose family the new couple should live.

KEY TERMS AND CONCEPTS

social organization 112
group 112
social structure 112
status 112
status pair 112
complementary status 112
symmetrical status 112

ascribed status 113
achieved status 113
role 113
division of labor 113
rank 113
power 114
honor 114

ANNOTATED READINGS

Dahlberg, F. (Ed.). (1981). *Woman the gatherer*. New Haven, CT: Yale University Press. Six articles on women's roles from cross-cultural and evolutionary perspectives.

Dalby, L. (1985). *Geisha*. New York: Vintage Books, Random House. A beautifully written and copiously illustrated description of geisha life.

Friedl, E. (1975). *Women and men*. New York: Holt, Rinehart and Winston. A brief but information-packed overview of sex roles and their relationships to variations in culture. Must reading for the major in anthropology.

Kenyatta, J. (1968). *Facing Mount Kenya: The tribal life of the Gikuyu*. New York: Random House. An excellent description of Kikuyu life by a Kikuyu anthropologist. Especially good chapters on life cycle rituals.

Martin, M. K., & Voorhies, B. (1975). *Female of the species*. New York: Columbia University Press. An examination of the status of women in societies of varying social complexity.

Montagu, A. (Ed.). (1980). *Sociobiology examined*. New York: Oxford University Press. Biological determinism critiqued by 16 anthropologists.

Rosaldo, M. Z., & Lamphere, L. (Eds.). (1974). *Woman, culture, and society*. Stanford, CA: Stanford University Press. Discussions by female anthropologists of their observations of the status of women in a variety of societies.

Sanday, P. R. (1981). *Female power and male dominance: On the origins of sexual inequality*. New York: Cambridge University Press. A cross-cultural examination of sex role inequality and the ways in which sex role differences are symbolized.

Service, E. R. (1975). *Primitive social organization: An evolutionary perspective*. New York: Random House. An excellent and insightful interpretation of primitive social organization.

Shostak, M. (1982). *Nisa: The story of a !Kung woman*. New York: Random House. A fascinating account of the life history of a woman in a foraging society.

Simmons, L. W. (Ed.). (1942). *Sun Chief: The autobiography of a Hopi Indian*. New Haven, CT: Yale University Press. A fascinating autobiographical account of the life of a Hopi chief, Don Talayesva.

Stephens, W. N. (1963). *The family in cross-cultural perspective*. New York: Holt, Rinehart and Winston. A good discussion of family, sexual restrictions, mate choice, marriage, and related topics.

Van Gennep, A. (1960, originally published 1908). *The rites of passage* (S. T. Kimball, trans.). Chicago: University of Chicago Press. The classic discussion of the major changes in status that are celebrated in ritual.

Wilson, E. O. (1978). *Human Nature* Cambridge MA: Harvard University Press. The Pultizer Prize winning exposition of sociobiology applied to the human species.

*H*uman beings in all the world distinguish their kin from other people. In this chapter, we will see how the concept of kinship is based on various ways of thinking about how children are descended from one or both of their parents and how these parent-child descent ties are used to build up a network that defines those people that are related to one another by kinship. You will learn to recognize different descent systems, some based on the concept of descent from only one parent in each generation and others based on the concept of descent from both parents. We will then consider how different kinds of kinship groups can grow out of these different ways of viewing kinship. Finally, you will be introduced to the most common kinship terminologies, the systems for naming relatives that are related to the ways in which people think about descent and, therefore, their kinship relationships.

7

Kinship and Descent

DESCENT
Descent Rules

Descent Groups
KINSHIP TERMINOLOGY

FICTIVE KINSHIP

FIGURE 7.1 *Totem*

A totem is an object, plant, or animal that is a symbolic representation of a kinship group or of an individual. It derives from the term ototeman of the Algonquin tribe of the Ojibwa of eastern North America and originally meant "his brother-sister kin." In different societies a particular totem may be viewed as a companion, ancestor, or protector.

Kinship is a very human concept. It is the way we keep track of our relationships with others who are connected to us by ties we trace through parents and their offspring. You are my kin if we can find a chain of connected parent-child ties that stretch from you to me. My children are linked to me, their common parent, by a chain one link long. Kin are connected to each other by chains of two similar links. My only niece is my mother's eldest daughter's daughter: she is three parent-child links away from me among my kin. And so it goes, as far as we are taught to keep track of such things.

DESCENT

In a purely biological sense, all members of the human race are relatives, but kinship does not attempt to keep track of all possible biological relatives. Kinship is a much narrower concept than that. In any human community, some people are thought of as "kin" and others as "not kin," and a particular society's way of defining who are kin may not give equal weight to all connections between biological parents and their offspring. As we shall see, for instance, in many societies, children may be thought of as kin to only one of their parents. Thus, more formally, kinship is a system for classifying people who are socially related through accepted parent-child ties.

Descent Rules

The cultural recognition of children as kin of one or both of their parents is called descent. If parents came in only one sex, it would be a lot simpler to define our kin. Since they

FIGURE 7.2   *Interpreting Kinship Diagrams*

Kinship diagrams are drawn using a variety of standard symbols. Those shown here are among the most common, and will be used later in this text. The simple family diagram at the bottom could be easily expanded using the same symbols to show ego's uncles, aunts, and cousins. Can you figure out how to do it?

SYMBOL	MEANING
ego	The person whose genealogy is being traced
	RELATIVES
Mo	Mother
Fa	Father
Br	Brother
Z	Sister
So	Son
Da	Daughter
IICu	Parallel cousin, a cousin linked to ego through parents of the same sex (i.e., ego's mother's sister's child or ego's father's brother's child)
XCu	Cross cousin, a cousin linked to ego through parents of the opposite sex (i.e., ego's mother's brother's child or ego's father's sister's child)

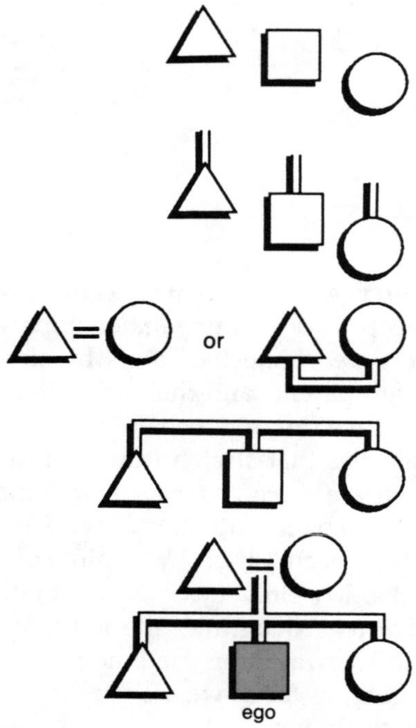

SEX:
Male
Person
Female

DESCENT:
Son of
Child of
Daughter of

MARRIAGE:
A husband and wife

SIBLINGS:
Brother of
Sibling of
Sister of

FAMILY:
Ego, ego's brother and sister, and their father and mother

ego

come in two varieties that play different roles in the production of children, the story becomes more complex. For instance, a brother and sister relationship can be traced by the links to a common mother or by links to the same father. Either way works, and my own culture, like that of the Siberian Chukchee or the American Great Basin Ute, considers either chain to be equally valid. So it lets me simply say that my sister and I share the same parents and lets it go at that. This system is based on the principle of <u>bilateral descent</u>, a rule that asserts that we are equally descended from both parents and lets us count relatives on both our mother's and father's side of the family. The bilateral system is a common approach. In about 36 percent of societies, people consider links through either parent to be equally valid ways of reckoning their kin.

A variation on the bilateral theme is the idea that we may consider ourselves descended through parents of either sex, but we must choose only one parent for each link that connects a group of relatives. This system, followed in less than 1 percent of societies, is <u>ambilineal descent</u>. Using the concept of ambilineal descent, a child might be designated as a relative of either the mother's kin or the father's kin, but not both. A decision had to be made in each generation which parent's group the children would be part of, but the connection might be established through the father in one generation and through the mother in another. The ancient Scottish clans were built up in such a way, so that the relatives who made up a particular clan all could trace themselves back to the founding ancestor of the clan, but not consistently through parents of the same sex.

When grouped by bilateral descent, relatives spread out on both sides of a person's family, creating two groups of equally related kin for each person. In the ambilineal approach, a less predictable group of relatives is created, a group made up of individual families who belong to the entire group in some cases because the father is a member and in other cases because the mother is a member. These two descent systems are sometimes referred to by the general terms <u>cognatic</u> or <u>nonunilineal descent</u> systems. Most societies have a narrower way of building up a group of kin that follows a principle called <u>unilineal descent</u>, descent through a single sex line rather than through both parents equally. The ancient Greeks, the Lau of Fiji, the Mission Indians of southern California, or the Mossí of the Sudan and about 44 percent of all societies that anthropologists have studied follow the system of reckoning kin by insisting that kin are only those who are joined by *father*-child ties; that is one of the reasons why a good definition of kinship has to contain a phrase such as "believed to be related" or "socially

FIGURE 7.3 *Bilateral Descent*

In bilateral descent, ego is considered to be descended equally from both parents and, therefore, from an increasing number of ancestors on both sides of his family—that is, to all of ego's relatives between the dotted lines.

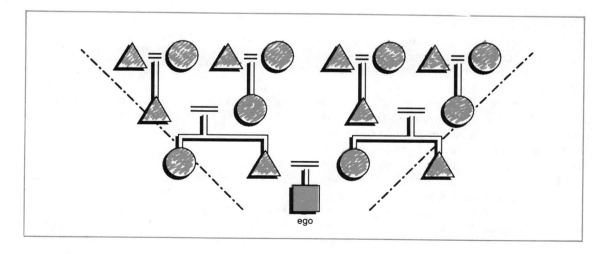

ego

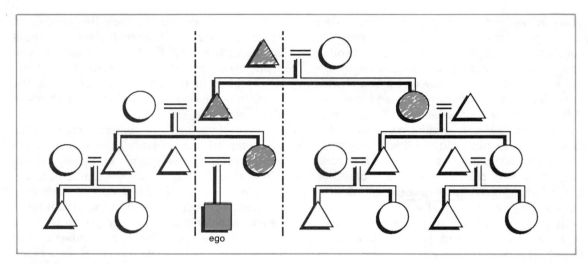

FIGURE 7.4   Ambilineal Descent

Ego's relatives are shown in red. In ambilineal descent, ego's ancestors—those relatives between the dotted lines— can be traced through either the father or mother, but not both. Membership in the traditional Scottish clans was based on genealogies that were traced in this way.

accepted parent-child ties." This rule for grouping relatives is called <u>patrilineal descent</u>, since it defines children as offspring of their fathers only.

On the other hand, the Navajo of Arizona, the Taureg of the Sahara Desert, and the Caribbean Goajiro are equally convinced that mother-child links alone should be used. Their approach to counting kin is based upon the principle of <u>matrilineal descent</u>. It is shared by about 15 percent of the world's societies. In about 5 percent of societies, a person may have two separate sets of kin, one designated only through mothers and the other only through fathers. Such a kinship determining rule, called <u>double descent</u> or <u>double unilineal descent</u>, would be a useful way of keeping track of relatives if, for instance, some property— say, houses and gardens—were inherited from the parent of one sex and other property—say, religious rituals and gardening tools—were passed down through the opposite line.

Considering all these diverse ways of counting kin, it is clear that even though the concept of descent is understood in most cultures as a biological relationship between children and parents, it is not identical to the biological concept of a genetic relationship. Rather, descent is reckoned through one or both parents in ways that are socially relevant to the lives of each people. The descent system followed by a particular people depends on

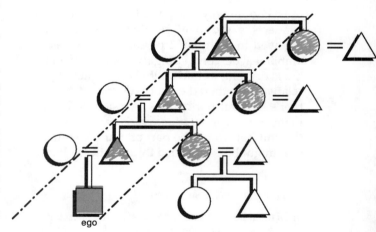

FIGURE 7.5   Patrilineal Descent

In patrilineal descent, a chain of father-child ties links ego to his or her ancestors, the males between the dotted lines. Each generation within the descent line consists of siblings who belong to the line of their father and his siblings. Only children of males will continue the line. The children of female members of a patrilineal descent line will belong to their husband's descent line. Ego's patrilineal relatives are shaded red.

the kinds of role played by a person's relatives in day-to-day life. It was noted already, for instance, that double descent might play a role in channeling different kinds of inheritance down through the generations. Patrilineality is

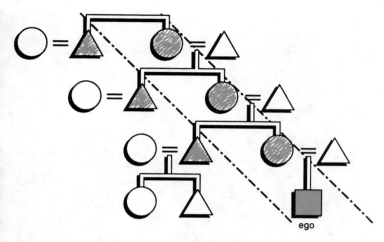

FIGURE 7.6 *Matrilineal Descent*

In matrilineal descent, a chain of mother-child ties links ego to his or her ancestors, the females between the dotted lines. Each generation within the descent line consists of siblings who belong to the line of their mother and her siblings. Only children of females will continue the line. The children of male members of a matrilineal descent line will belong to their wife's descent line. Ego's matrilineal relatives are shaded red.

commonly followed in situations that require male solidarity, for instance, in work requiring heavy cooperative labor or in feuding between neighboring groups. Matrilineality is an effective means of unifying groups of women as decision-making bodies. It is commonly followed as a principle of kinship in societies

where men are often absent from the local community. Just as patrilineal and matrilineal descent may coexist, ambilineal or bilateral descent may co-occur with matrilineal or patrilineal descent so long as there is some socially useful reason for keeping track of each group.

Descent Groups

In all societies, there are social groups whose membership is based on descent. Membership in descent groups may be defined either by the sharing of a common ancestor or by the sharing of a common living relative. The first approach may be based on patrilineal, matrilineal, or ambilineal descent reckoning; the second is associated with bilateral descent.

Lineal (corporate) descent groups. Social groups that are based on a matrilineal or patrilineal descent system are called unilineal descent groups. Those that are based on ambilineal descent reckoning are ambilineal descent groups. Both of these share one important characteristic: they are corporate groups, or organizations that continue to exist even though their individual members change over the generations and they can legally perform social functions such as owning property, conducting ceremonies, regulating marriages, disciplining their own members, or engaging

FIGURE 7.7 *Double Unilineal Descent*

In double unilineal descent, ego is considered to be a member of his patrilineal descent line for some purposes and his matrilineal descent line for others. For instance, among the Yako of Nigeria, a man's house and land are passed down his patrilineal descent line to his sons when he dies, but his livestock and other moveable property are passed to the males of the next generation in the matrilineal descent line to which he belongs, i.e., to his sister's sons.

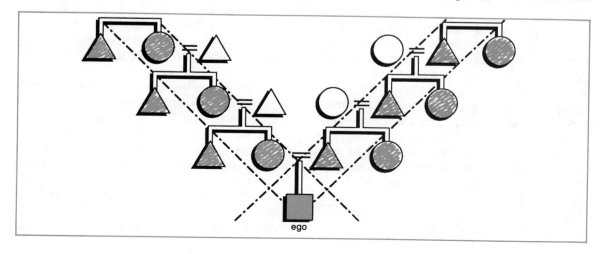

in legal processes or warfare with other groups. Corporate groups are typically named to symbolize their existence as a social entity.

A lineage is a group of kin who trace their descent from a known common ancestor. When members trace their genealogical ties to the common ancestor through matrilineal descent, the lineage is known as a matrilineage; a lineage based on ties of patrilineal descent is a patrilineage. Lineages that are formed using an ambilineal descent principle are called cognatic lineages or sometimes ramages or septs. In all three cases, the body of kin who consider themselves relatives based on their descent from the common ancestor has the special quality of continuing to exist as generations pass. Older members may die, and new members may be born, but so long as the common ancestry is remembered the surviving members can view themselves as part of a common body of relatives that can carry out common goals. A lineage is, in other words, a corporate group. Lineages are typically named for the common ancestor from which its members are descended.

Since each succeeding generation may produce more offspring than made up the previous generation, a lineage may gradually increase in the size of its membership. Thus, lineages may be as small as 30 or 40 people, but may grow to encompass thousands of members. Since growing populations tend to spread out from the location of their ancestral homelands, local segments of a lineage may become involved in activities in which it would be unwieldy and unnecessary to call together all members. So, growing lineages often fission into smaller sublineages over the generations.

As generations pass, lineage membership may reach such numbers and such distance from the common ancestry that their exact genealogical ties are no longer remembered even though surviving members of the total group still regard themselves as relatives based on their descent from the common ancestor. A corporate kinship group of this type is called a clan or sometimes a sib. Clans may also be differentiated by the rule of descent through which membership is defined. Thus, anthropologists speak of either matriclans, patriclans, or cognatic (or ambilineal) clans, depending on the descent rule.

FIGURE 7.8 *Scottish Clan*

The tartan, a cross-checkered repeating pattern of stripes or lines woven into a woolen cloth, has come to have great significance in tracing the ancestry of a Scottish clan. The earliest tartan was designed for the Highland 42nd Regiment of Foot, or Black Watch.

The common ancestor of a clan may be so far removed in time that his or her identity may no longer be remembered accurately. As the ancestor's life story is passed down the generations, it may become altered and embroidered with tales that represent the values of clan members more than historical fact. The ancestor may take on heroic proportions and as portrayed by succeeding generations may become more mythological than real. The process by which the folk memories of an important person may become increasingly filled with symbolism that can elevate him or her to a superhuman level is one that operates even in literate societies. In the United States, for instance, children hear mythologized stories of George Washington's inability to tell a lie, and the setting of stories about his having thrown a silver dollar across a river has been moved in some versions from Virginia's smaller Rappahannock to Washington, D.C.'s nearly mile-wide

Potomac River. Abraham Lincoln, the Great Emancipator, is remembered as having freed all the slaves in the United States, rather than as just having promised freedom to Southern slaves who joined the Union in fighting the Confederates. When such stories continue to be embellished over many generations, a time may come when it becomes difficult to identify the historically real from the mythological, and the stories about clan ancestors in traditionally nonliterate societies are frequently so filled with superhuman elements that it is impossible to demonstrate that the founder of the clan really existed except in folklore. Indeed, a symbolic ancestor of an existing clan may not even be a human at all. For instance, symbolic clan ancestors are often important animals, plants, or—less often—geographical features in the environment such as the Bitter-Water or Salt clans of the Navajo.

Clans may have tens or even hundreds of thousands of members. By virtue of their large membership, clans can be very powerful organizations. Like lineages, they are corporate groups that perform a variety of social functions, such as carrying out major ceremonies, owning land or other property, maintaining peaceful relationships between their individual members and the lineages that make them up, handling the legal matters, and regulating the marriage options of their members.

NAVAJO CLANS

The Navajo who reside in Arizona are a pastoral people who herd sheep and grow corn and other crops in a dry, desert region. They number today over 180,000 people who occupy a reservation territory of more than 25,000 square miles. Though individual families may live miles apart, their unity is aided by a continued reliance on matrilineal clan membership as a source of economic and social cohesion. In the 1940s Kluckhohn and Leighton (1962) found that the Navajo had approximately 60 clans, each bearing the name of a locality. Each clan is likely to have members who live in different communities, and a given local group may be composed of families who belong to 15 or 20 different clans.

A Navajo is born a primary member of the mother's clan, but members of the fa-

ther's clan are also considered to be relatives, so a Navajo might describe him or herself as "born to Bitter-Water [the mother's clan] for Salt [the father's clan]." Clans play an important role in regulating marriage, and Navajos are traditionally forbidden to marry either members of their own matriclan or of their father's matriclan. This rule of exogamy forces marriages to link members of different clans in each generation and is one of the means for maintaining ties of allegiance between members of the various clans in a community.

Considering that there are a large number of Navajos and the clans are spread over a large territory, each Navajo is likely to have many relatives whom he or she has never met. Nevertheless, a clan member is a relative, and the obligations of kin are strong. Two Navajo strangers who discover their common clan membership have the same familial obligations of hospitality and mutual help as they do to their previously known relatives.

Traditionally, the clan was collectively responsible for the crimes and debts of its members. This fact, of course, meant that the clan also had authority to control irresponsible behavior in its members. Grazing land, for instance, could not be freely bought or sold by individual persons without permission of other clan members. Clans also originally controlled inheritance. Goods passed to children from the members of their mother's clan.

Family loyalty still receives support from the traditional clan system of shared economic responsibilities in spite of the fragmenting effects of employment of many Navajos in the industrialized economy of the non-Navajo society that surrounds them. For instance, a Navajo religious ceremony—which might be necessary for the curing of an illness, the reunion of a family member after a period of residence at a nonreservation university, or the celebration of a girl's passage into adulthood—may cost a thousand or more dollars to carry out, an expense that can be too costly for a single household to bear. Such expenses may be supported mutually by nearby members of the person's clan for whom the ritual must be held, a practice that reinforces a tremendous sense of family loyalty, reciprocal responsibilities, and gives great cohesion to contemporary Navajo family life.

In addition to lineages and clans, there can also be larger unilineal descent groups within a society. A group of clans that are thought to be related by kinship at a level higher than the clan ancestors is called a phratry. It does not necessarily grow from a common ancestral clan. The kinship connection between the clans of a phratry may be merely a social fiction that allows its members to interact as a larger corporate group. That is, a phratry is a group of two or more clans whose members believe and act as if they are somehow related, whether they are really related or not.

Sometimes the kinship groups of a society are organized into two major categories or groups, called moieties from a French word meaning "half." Each moiety in this kind of organization is a unilineal kinship group that may consist of a clan or phratry. Moieties usually play a role in the regulation of marriage, by the requirement that the members of each moiety take their spouses from the opposite group. According to Lévi-Strauss (1967), the relationships between moieties may "range from the most intimate cooperation to latent hostility" (p. 10), and in addition to providing spouses for one another's members, "[s]ometimes their role is confined to activities of a religious, political, economic, ceremonial, or merely recreational character" (p. 10). Thus, the two moieties of a society may play other socially reciprocal roles such as providing funerals or hosting feasts for each other. Moieties may also facilitate social specialization by playing complementary roles. For instance, among the Toda of southern India, the clans of one moiety owned all of the sacred herds of dairy cattle and the dairies in which they were kept, but the dairymen of the sacred herds, who were the priests of Toda society, could be chosen only from the other moiety.

Combinations of lineal descent groups. More than one kind of lineal descent group may operate simultaneously within the same society. For instance, lineages may be the only descent group present in a society; a clan may exist without lineages being differentiated within it; or a clan may be subdivided into identified lineages, each of which carries out activities within the entire clan. Lineages, clans, and phratries may be organized into moieties. As a matter of fact, with one excep-tion, any combination of lineages, clans, phratries, and moieties may occur in a particular society. That exception is merely that when phratries are present, there must also be clans, since phratries are defined as groups of two or more clans.

Bilateral (noncorporate) descent groups. Descent groups that are not based on descent from a single common ancestor may also exist. Such a group, called a kindred, is defined by the kinship relationship all its members have to a living person. A kindred consists of all relatives on both the paternal and maternal sides of the family who are known to a single individual. Bothers and sisters will have the same kindred, but other relatives will have kindreds with somewhat different members. For instance, if kindreds included only first and second cousins then my own second cousin's kindred would include *their* second cousins who would be too distantly related to me as fourth cousins to be part of *my* kindred.

A person may call upon her or his kindred for aid and support, and kindred can act together as a group on behalf of the individual or siblings to whom they are all related. Unlike unilineal descent groups, kindreds exist only in respect to the particular living group of siblings that they share at a given time in history. When those brothers and sisters die, their kindred no longer has a uniting focus, so it ceases to exist. Thus, kindreds do not have the quality of being corporate groups that exist beyond the lifespans of the individuals that are born into and die out of them. Kindreds, therefore, are not normally responsible for such corporate responsibilities as owning property or conducting religious ceremonies. Rather, their existence is usually ephemeral. They may be called together for a particular purpose by the individual or sibling group that seeks the support of a body of relatives, but they cease to work together as a group when the purpose is accomplished.

Such kindreds include relatives on both sides of their families, they are the typical descent group of societies that race ancestry bilaterally. They are most common in circumstances in which small family groups are more adaptive than are larger ones and in which individual mobility is high. Thus, they are typical of industrialized societies such as those of North America where children do not typ-

FIGURE 7.9   *La Grande Famille*
A kindred consists of all relatives on both the paternal and maternal sides of the family who are known to a single individual. This family gathers for a photo at the wedding of their son in Charente Maritime, France.

ically inherit their homes and occupations from their parents and may even have to leave their home towns to obtain employment. Kindreds are also typical of foraging societies since small family groups that pursue a migratory life can more readily obtain the wild foods they need to survive in most environments than can larger, permanent family organizations such as lineages or clans.

The evolution of descent groups.   The oldest and simplest of human social systems, those founded on foraging economies, do not usually have descent groups. Economic cooperation between intermarried families may create a local extended family of bilaterally related kin in the next generation, but when growth in the local kindred group makes food getting difficult, a break-up is likely to occur. Since the life-style is based on a wandering quest for food, conditions do not foster the easy perpetuation of ongoing kinship ties between neighboring groups over many generations. Nor is there any specific need to do so. Within a generation or two, bilateral kindreds may still be called together for common economic or political action, but conditions that call for the development of permanent unilineal descent groups do not seem to be present in most such societies.

On the other hand, unilineal descent groups are common in horticultural, pastoral, and agricultural societies. In such societies,

when an extended family divides, each smaller group of relatives is likely to establish its new residence within easy access of the other. This pattern of geographical and social dispersal can easily support the formation of lineages or other corporate descent groups as generations pass, if it is economically or politically advantageous to do so. For instance, lineages, clans, and phratries lend themselves readily to the maintenance of cooperating family-based military groups when warfare is an important feature of social life.

Interestingly, larger, socially more complex and specialized societies sometimes shift again toward a bilateral descent system. Where lineages and clans are the basic social building block, these kinship groups typically perform many of the governmental functions that are carried out by specialized non-kinship groups in some of the more complex societies. Thus, for instance, if a society develops a political system that takes over the military role previously played by unilineal descent groups, then bilateral descent reckoning is likely to replace the lineal system that existed before. Similarly, increasing social complexity can fragment the extended family. This can happen because geographical and occupational mobility increases the viability of smaller, economically independent nuclear family groups whose children are best off if they are considered kin to both of their parents' relatives. Both of these conditions are

145

common in the most industrialized societies of the world today where bilateral descent is the rule.

KINSHIP TERMINOLOGY

Kinship terminology is the way in which people communicate about the familial relationships. It symbolically portrays the distinctions between relatives that are important in their lives. Kin terms may be based on many different distinctions. For instance, kinship terminologies of different societies commonly either use or ignore the potential contrasts between: (1) paternal versus maternal side of the family; (2) generation; (3) relative age; (4) sex; (5) descent ties versus marriage ties; (6) own versus linked descent line; and (7) when descent lines are noted, sex of the linking relative. Thus, actual kinship terminologies are highly varied. Nevertheless, individual systems can be grouped into six common types, called *Hawaiian, Eskimo, Omaha, Crow, Iroquois* and *Sudanese.* The first two of these are types found in societies with bilateral descent systems in which relatives on the maternal and paternal sides of the family are equally important in a person's life. The others tend to be associated with societies that use unilineal descent reckoning.

Hawaiian. This is the simplest kinship terminology in the sense that it is the system with the fewest terms. In the Hawaiian kinship terminology system, the key distinction is one of generation. Relatives are not distinguished by side of the family (e.g., "aunt" may be either a mother's sister or father's sister). One's affinal descent line is not distinguished from linked or collateral descent lines, those that parallel one's own line back to a common ancestor. Thus, in Hawaiian kinship terminology, cousins and their parents are called by the same kin terms as are one's siblings and one's own parents. Thus, siblings and both paternal and maternal cousins are called by the same terms, commonly translated as "brother" and sister"; and one's father, father's brother, and mother's brother are all referred to as "father"; and mother, mother's sister and father's sister are likewise designated by a single term. In its simplest form, Hawaiian kinship terminology may not make any distinction by sex, reducing the system to three basic kin terms: parents, siblings, and children.

The Hawaiian kinship system is especially common where extended families or some other form of corporate descent group, within which the nuclear family does not function autonomously, live and work together. It is more common in societies that make use of bilateral or ambilineal rather than unilineal descent systems (Textor, 1967). In other words, Hawaiian terminology emphasizes the cohesion of the extended family or corporate groups, distinguishing only between the generational differences which are important in the etiquette of family interaction in all societies. It should be noticed that the Hawaiian

FIGURE 7.10 *Hawaiian Kinship Terminology*

Hawaiian kinship terminology is most common in societies in which an extended group of relatives joined by bilateral descent live together and share work and child-rearing obligations. Its main emphasis is on distinguishing the members of the family's two adjacent generations—the generation of the parents and the generation of the children. Ego calls his or her parents and their siblings by the same two terms, translatable as "mother" and "father" and calls his or her cousins by terms that can be translated as "brother" and "sister."

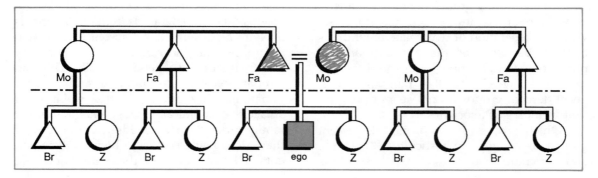

system automatically extends the field of persons who have the same kinds of rights and obligations as members of one's own nuclear family. Thus, on the death of a child's biological father, there are likely to be several other men who will be expected to take responsibility for the childrearing activities that the child's "real" father would have performed. Similarly, the incest taboo is extended to cover a much broader range of relatives, such as cross cousins, than is typical in other systems.

Eskimo. This kinship terminology is the second general type of bilateral kinship system. It is the type with which most North Americans are familiar. In Eskimo kinship terminology, the terms for mother, father, brother, and sister are not used for any relatives outside the nuclear family, and the terms for other relatives such as aunt, uncle, or cousin are the same for the maternal and paternal sides of the family. Cross cousins and parallel cousins are not distinguished by different terms and cousin terms may not even differ by sex.

The simplicity of Eskimo terminology is related to the fact that this system is typically found in societies such as foraging or industrialized societies or in other circumstances in which ego's most important relatives are ego's closest relatives. Thus, Eskimo terminology is commonly associated with economically independent nuclear families, bilateral descent and kindreds rather than unilineal or ambilineal descent and lineages, clans, or other corporate

descent groups. Data compiled by Murdock (1967) for 71 societies in which Eskimo terminology was used indicated that only 4 had large extended families, and only 13 had unilineal descent groups. Fifty-four, in fact, had no corporate descent groups.

The remaining major kinship systems are those associated with unilineal descent systems. They distinguish between maternal and paternal kin, but differ in other ways.

Omaha. This kinship terminology is an example of a bifurcate merging system, one that derives its kin terms from two major characteristics: the contrast between paternal and maternal relatives (hence, "bifurcate") and the use of a small number of kin terms to refer to many different kin within each of these two groups (hence, "merging"). The Omaha system is found in societies that have patrilineal descent systems. In the Omaha kinship terminology system, members of one's mother's patrilineage are distinguished only by sex regardless of generation. Thus, one term is used for all males of that group (e.g., for mother's brother and mother's brother's son) and another for all females including ego's mother, her sister, and her brother's daughter. In ego's own patrilineage, father is merged with father's brother. Parallel cousins in both lineages are merged with ego's brother and sister, and their children are called by the same term as ego's own children. The bifurcation is a useful way of contrasting the lineage of ego's mother from that of ego's father, while

FIGURE 7.11 *Eskimo Kinship Terminology*

Eskimo kinship terminology is most common in societies that trace relationships bilaterally and in which the isolated nuclear family—a husband and wife and their own offspring—is the economically independent work-group of society. This kinship system emphasizes the separateness of ego's nuclear family (ego's parents and siblings) from other relatives by contrasting mother and father with aunts and uncles and by contrasting brother and sister with cousins.

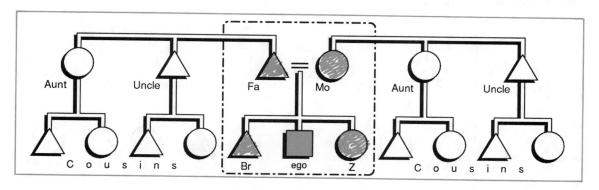

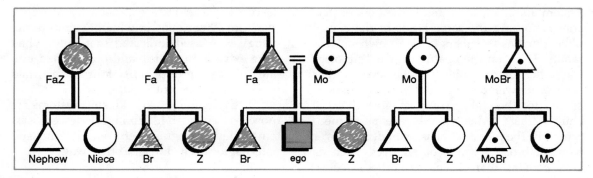

FIGURE 7.12   *Omaha Kinship Terminology*

Omaha kinship terminology is most often associated with patrilineal descent reckoning. Its terms for relatives contrast those related to ego through patrilineal descent ties (noted in red) to the equivalent relatives of his or her mother's patrilineal group (indicated with a dot). The terminology is more elaborate for ego's own patrilineal relatives than for ego's mother's patrilineal relatives for whom the same terms (Mo and MoBr) are used in both generations. Can you figure out which of ego's cousins are potential spouses and which are not?

the merging of terms for parents and their same sex sibling has the effect of emphasizing lineage cohesiveness. Since the mother's lineage is relatively unimportant in ego's daily life, generational differences in status can be ignored, but in ego's own patrilineage—which is the important corporate group in life—different terms for men of the father's generation and men of ego's own generation are distinguished in recognition of the differences in power and honor that they are likely to have.

Crow.   The Crow system is also a bifurcate merging system, but it is the mirror image of the Omaha pattern. Named for a Native North American society, Crow kinship termi-

nology is found in many matrilineal societies throughout the world. In it the relatives of ego's father's matrilineage are distinguished only by sex, regardless of age or generation, while generational differences are noted within ego's own matrilineage. As with the Omaha system, Crow kinship is highly compatible with a powerful unilineal descent system, in this case emphasizing the importance of the matrilineal kin organization.

Iroquois.   Like the Omaha and Crow systems, Iroquois kinship terminology is a bifurcate merging system. It, too, assigns different terms for maternal and paternal relatives, while merging father with father's

FIGURE 7.13   *Crow Kinship Terminology*

Crow kinship terminology is most often associated with matrilineal descent reckoning. Its terms for relatives contrast those related to ego through matrilineal descent ties (noted in red) to the equivalent relatives of ego's father's matrilineal group (noted with a dot). The terminology is more elaborate for ego's own matrilineal relatives than for his or her father's matrilineal relatives for whom the same terms (Fa and FaZ) are used in both generations. Can you figure out which of ego's cousins are potential spouses and which are not?

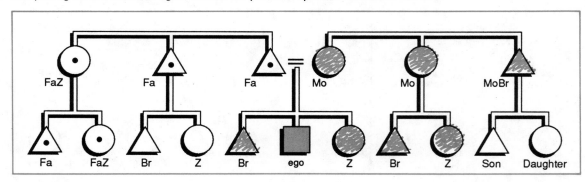

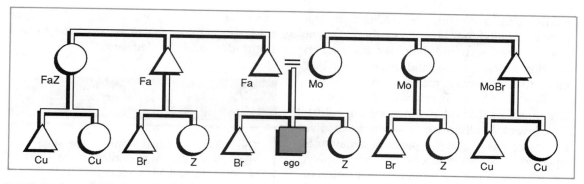

FIGURE 7.14 *Iroquois Kinship Terminology*

Iroquois kinship terminology tends to be found in societies that use unilineal descent reckoning, especially among those that trace ancestry through matrilineal descent. Societies that follow the Iroquois system instead of the Crow or Omaha systems are believed to place less importance on the solidarity of their unilineal kinship groups and are more willing to permit marriage with cousins on either side of the family. For this reason, paternal and maternal cross cousins are not distinguished from one another, and in some variants of the Iroquois system, parallel cousins are not called "brother" and "sister" as shown in this figure but by another term—thereby indicating their acceptability as potential spouses for ego.

brother and mother with mother's sister. The terms for parallel cousins are similarly merged with the terms for brothers or sisters. The important distinction that separates Iroquois from the Omaha and Crow systems is that in the Iroquois system there is no merging of generations in the lineage that marries into ego's lineage. Rather, ego's cross cousins in both lineages are merged, minimizing the lineage contrast for members of this one group of kin.

Like Omaha and Crow, Iroquois kinship is most often found in societies with unilineal descent, and it is particularly common in matrilineal societies. Crow, too, is associated with matrilineal social organizations, and Leslie White (1939) suggested that the reason for the

presence of one rather than the other may be that the Crow and Omaha patterns are most likely to develop in a society that is firmly unilineal, while the Iroquois system is most likely in either an incipient or weakening unilineal descent system. Goody (1970) has added the idea that the Iroquois pattern is likely to develop when circumstances favor marriage with either maternal or paternal cross cousins rather than with just the cross cousin of one side of the family.

Sudanese. This kinship system has the largest number of kin terms, so it is sometimes also called <u>descriptive kinship terminology</u>. As do many kinship systems, <u>Sudanese kinship terminology</u> distinguishes parallel cous-

FIGURE 7.15 *Sudanese Kinship Terminology*

Sudanese, or descriptive, kinship terminology is common in societies that trace descent patrilineally when status distinctions between individual members of both ego's patrilineage and ego's mother's patrilineage are important. Accordingly, the Sudanese system uses a different term for each relative in each patrilineage.

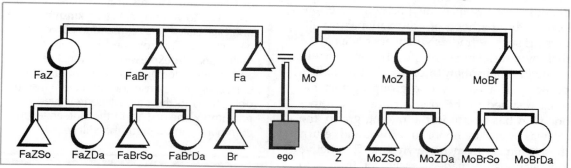

ins from cross cousins. In addition to the nuclear family terms for mother, father, brother, sister, son, and daughter, this system includes cousin, uncle, and aunt terms that distinguish maternal from paternal relatives.

Referring to each relative by a separate term suggests that the distinctions are culturally relevant. In other words, when descriptive terminology is present, a person's behavior is expected to be different toward each relative. For instance, a person would have a different relationship with a maternal cross cousin than with a paternal cross cousin. Relatively few societies have circumstances in which such diversity of kin relations would be necessary, so the descriptive kinship system is a rare one. When it does occur, it is in association with patrilineal descent. Sudanese terminology occurs most often in North Africa.

FICTIVE KINSHIP

Sometimes societies create relationships that are thought of as more or less equivalent to kinship relationships between persons who would otherwise not be considered relatives by either descent or marriage. These so-called fictive kinship relationships include adopted relatives who become legal equivalents of relatives by birth. They also include persons thought of as ceremonial or quasi-relatives, whose relationships are secondary to those based on descent or marriage. Such ceremonial kinship relationships are established to fulfill special purposes such as establishing a stable economic bond between two persons or providing foster parents upon the death of the biological parents. Thus, in addition to fully adopted relatives, fictive kin include various kinds of "blood brotherhood" and co-parenthood or "godparenthood." Among the Rwala Bedouin, for instance, men sometimes established a brotherhood of *akh* relationship with persons such as traders who were not a part of their own residential groups. This relationship created an obligation to protect the outsider's property. If a raid by one group against the other resulted in the loss of camels by someone who has an *akh* in the raiding group, the *akh* was bound by honor to recover and return those animals from his own kin. This fictive kin relationship made it easier for traders to

travel safely from group to group to conduct trade, an activity that was beneficial to both the traders and the Bedouin.

GODPARENTHOOD AMONG THE CHAN KOM MAYA

The village of Chan Kom in the state of Yucatán, Mexico, was studied in the 1930s by Redfield and Villa Rojas (1934). Its 250 people were Maya Indians whose customs had been influenced by 300 years of Spanish colonial domination. One European custom adopted by the people of Chan Kom was the *padrinazgo*, choosing of godparents for their children at important ceremonial transitions during the life cycle.

The most important godparents were selected at the time of a child's baptism. The godfather, or *padrino*, and godmother, or *madrina*, took on the obligation to act as parents to the child and to aid it in growing up. In return they were treated with particular respect by the child's parents.

Godparents who had less responsibility were chosen for later changes in the life cycle of the child. The second such event was at the time of the *hetzmek*, the native Maya celebration of the change from infancy to childhood which occurred when the child was old enough to be carried on its mother's hip instead of in her arms. Godparents were also chosen in preparation for marriage. The same-sex godparent instructed the bride or bridegroom in the marriage ritual and gave advice about the responsibilities that came with marriage. Marriage godparents might also admonish their godchildren at later times for not living up to their marriage responsibilities.

Godparents provided support for community values throughout the life of their godchildren and so helped to maintain their sense of responsibility to follow the customs of Chan Kom. Parents and godparents also entered into a kind of fictive kinship relationship called the *compadrazgo*, or co-parenthood. This relationship involved formality and the expression of mutual respect and concern for one another's welfare. By extending the sense of intimate kinship obligations to the field of nonrelatives, co-parenthood helped to further integrate the community throughout the village.

SUMMARY

The ways in which people think about kinship depend upon how they conceive of descent. Children may be thought of as offspring of their mother, their father, or both. Thus, throughout the world, we find systems of kinship based on matrilineal, patrilineal, ambilineal, or bilateral descent. The groups of people thought of as relatives may be organized into corporate groups such as lineages, clans, phratries, or moieties, or into noncorporate kindreds. The various kinds of kinship groups are related to the economic and social conditions in which they are found. Similarly, kinship terminology, of which there are six common types, tend to reflect the kinds of conditions with which people must cope as they work together as relatives. Therefore, the six patterns of kinship terminology are also related, though not perfectly, to the kinds of descent systems that are found in each society.

KEY TERMS AND CONCEPTS

kinship 138
descent 138
bilateral descent 139
ambilineal descent 139
cognatic (nonunilineal) descent 139
nonunilineal descent 139
unilineal descent 139
patrilineal descent 140
matrilineal descent 140
double descent (double unilineal descent) 140
double unilineal descent 140
unilineal descent group 141
ambilineal descent group 141
corporate group 141
lineage 142
matrilineage 142
patrilineage 142
cognatic lineage (ramage, sept) 142
ramage 142

sept 142
clan (sib) 142
sib 142
matriclan 142
patriclan 142
cognatic clan (ambilineal clan) 142
phratry 144
moiety 144
kindred 144
Hawaiian kinship terminology 146
Eskimo kinship terminology 147
bifurcate merging 147
Omaha kinship terminology 147
Crow kinship terminology 148
Iroquois kinship terminology 148
Sudanese kinship (descriptive kinship) terminology 149
descriptive kinship terminology 149
fictive kinship 150

ANNOTATED READINGS

Fox, R. (1967). *Kinship and marriage: An anthropological perspective*. Baltimore: Penguin. One of the most easily understandable analyses of kinship and descent available. This book is a good start for the middle range student who wants to understand the workings of kinship as well as the basics.

Keesing, R. M. (1975). *Kin groups and social structure*. New York: Holt, Rinehart and Winston. A study of kinship theory for advanced students.

Graburn, N. (1971). *Readings in kinship and social structure*. New York: Harper & Row. Articles on a wide range of topics and perspectives concerning kinship and society.

Pasternak, B. (1976). *Introduction to kinship and social organization*. New York: Macmillan. Includes an evaluation of theories of kinship and residence.

Schneider, D. M. (1980). *American kinship: A cultural account*. (2nd Ed.). Chicago: University of Chicago Press. A symbolic interpretation of U.S. kinship.

Schneider, D. M., and Gough, K. (Eds.). (1961). *Matrilineal kinship*. Berkeley: University of California Press. Discussions of kinship in a number of matrilineal societies.

Schusky, E. L. (1971). *Manual for kinship analysis*. (2nd Ed.). New York: Holt, Rinehart & Winston. A short course on the basic tools of the trade for recording and analyzing kinship systems. A good starting point for the student who wants an overview of the basics.

Schusky, E. L. (1975). *Variation in kinship*. New York: Holt, Rinehart and Winston. Another good introduction to kinship, descent, and residence.

In this chapter, marriage will be defined as a social, economic, and sexual union that takes many forms. You will be introduced to the most common marriage forms such as monogamy, polygyny, polyandry, and group marriage, as well as to less common forms such as symbolic, nonsexual, fictive, and homosexual marriage. You will learn about the common rules that govern and restrict the choices of potential marriage partners, and the ways in which marriages are negotiated in traditional societies. Finally, the contrast between nuclear and extended families will be introduced, and you will learn how three or more generations of kin can be united into a single family by different patterns of postmarital residence customs in the world's societies.

8

Marriage and the Family

MARRIAGE
Definition of Marriage
Functions of Marriage

Types of Marriage
Atypical Marriages
Marriage Choice

Negotiating Marriage
FAMILY
Postmarital Residence

FIGURE 8.1 *Moscow Wedding*

Marriage as a social, economic, and sexual union between two or more people is common in most cultures of the world. However, the rules and customs that govern marriage differ from culture to culture. This wedding party is leaving the Tomb of the Unknown Soldier in Moscow which they visited following their wedding ceremony.

Sex and reproduction are cultural as well as biological phenomena. In all societies, there are customs governing how and under what circumstances they should occur. Marriage plays a central role in these customs. Typically, people marry to legitimize sexual unions and to facilitate child rearing. Nevertheless, the reasons for marrying are diverse, and the families created by marriage differ in many ways from society to society.

MARRIAGE

Ethnographers have reported marriages that are contracted by parents before the birth of a child, marriages that are highly ceremonialized, marriages that simply establish a common residence, and marriages between more than two persons, to name but four examples. What then are the minimum defining characteristics of marriage?

Definition of Marriage

Marriage is a socially accepted sexual and economic union involving a lasting commitment between two or more people who have parental rights and obligations to any children within the union. Legitimate sexual relationships are recognized in many societies outside the bonds of marriage. For instance, data from the Cultural Diversity Data Base (White, 1987, p. 30) indicate that only 27 percent of 186 societies surveyed have customs that imply the importance of female virginity at the time of marriage. Societies also may approve of sexual relationships outside of marriage between persons who are already married to others. The same Cultural Diversity Data Base (p. 31) indicates that only 44 percent of a sample of 109 societies forbid extramarital sex to both husbands and wives. Another 44 percent accept such behavior by husbands, and 12 percent permit extramarital sex by wives.

The Toda of southern India recognized the legitimacy of formalized sexual liaisons between a married woman and certain other men, such as priests, to whom she was not married, so long as the woman's husband was consulted for his approval. For the husband to refuse such requests was considered bad form. The Kalinga of the Philippines institutionalized the taking of mistresses by married men. Children born to the mistresses normally inherited smaller portions of the family property than did the children of the wife. This practice was not followed by all families, but if a wife were barren, taking a mistress was the only legitimate means of perpetuating the man's family without divorce and remarriage—so the wife would often help her husband in the selection of a partner. Gregerson (1966, pp. 163–4) reminds us that sacred prostitution—often performed as part of the rites

of a god in a sacred setting such as a temple—was accepted in much of the ancient Near East, India, and Greece and that, according to Herodotus, "every Babylonian woman must have sexual intercourse with a stranger in the temple of Mylitta [a variant of Ishtar or Astarte, a goddess Herodotus equates with Aphrodite] once in her life." Though sexual unions such as these may be socially approved, they are not examples of marriages.

Marriage is thus defined as an economic partnership as well as a sexual one. It includes the concept of economic interdependence between partners who are bonded in a relationship that is expected to be a long-lasting one. Those economic rights created by marriage generally include (1) a division of labor in the production and consumption of the family's income; (2) defined property rights with respect to other goods brought into or created during the marriage; and (3) specified inheritance rights for the survivor or the children upon the death of a marriage partner.

Marriage is also typically a union between the families of the marriage partners. It creates two sets of in-laws who have obligations to those in the marriage and also to one another as relatives of the partners. The children produced will be the next generation of one or both of the parents' families. A marriage may lack one or both of these characteristics, but it will not be a typical marriage in its society, and its members may be considered unfortunate by others. In most societies, for instance, the presence of in-law ties provides a measure of economic security to the family created by a marriage. The birth of children ensures the continuity of one or both family lines, so in many societies, the failure of children to be born to a union is valid grounds for divorce.

To say that marriages are normally expected to be long-lasting—even life-long—unions is to recognize that marriage involves a commitment of the partners to one another and to their socially acknowledged partnership. For this reason, marriage usually includes an expectation of fidelity. Cross-cultural data reported by Ford and Beach (1951, pp. 115–116), indicates that in a sample of 139 societies, 61 percent required women to be sexually faithful in marriage, and 53 percent had the same requirement for husbands. Reiss (1987) argues that even in cultures that may

FIGURE 8.2 *Families of Marriage Partners*

Marriage generally creates two sets of in-laws, the families of the partners who assume obligations to the couple as well as to each other. They may provide an economic and emotional support for the couple. In this receiving line at a Christian wedding in Tokyo, Japan, the married couple and their families greet the guests.

have lenient rules regarding marital fidelity, jealousy is still associated with infidelity.

To strengthen the commitment of marriage partners, the establishment of their married state always includes some kind of public proclamation of their new status. Similarly, the dissolution of a marriage also includes some way of letting others know that the commitment is ended. Marrying and divorcing may be as simple as announcing the change to one's peers, or they may require complex secular or religious rituals, but all societies distinguish between more committed marital relationships and more casual nonmarried involvements. Data from the Cultural Diversity Data Base (p. 21), a recent cross-cultural sample that is a refinement of an earlier collection of data begun by Murdock (1967), indicates that a common residence for husbands and wives is characteristic of 90 percent of the sample's 186 societies.

Functions of Marriage

The apparent universality of marriage as an institution suggests that it plays an important role within society. It fulfills a variety of functions in the maintenance and perpetuation of human social life.

Perpetuating the kinship group as a corporate entity. It is through the marriage ties established with other families that kinship groups perpetuate themselves as children are born to the marriage. In many of the world's societies throughout most of human history, the kinship group has been the basic institution that guides and directs people's daily lives. Where family is the basic work group and kinship groups such as lineages or clans play the roles that are fulfilled by governments in socially more complex societies, the perpetuation of the kinship group to which one belongs will naturally be a very important process. This is why marriages are typically expected to fulfill a child-bearing and child-rearing role which results in heterosexual marriages being accepted as the basic marriage form, even in societies that recognize other forms of marriage as well.

Division of labor by sex. Societies may place greater or lesser emphasis on the idea of segregating roles and the division of labor by sex, but these practices seem to exist in all the world's societies up to this point in history. Heterosexual marriages in particular function to maintain these sex-role distinctions since they bring together partners who have typically received somewhat different gender so-

155

cialization and who, in turn, are likely to serve as role models for different sex-roles as they rear their own children. Even in societies such as the United States where women have made increasing inroads toward economic and political equality with men since the 1950s, most heterosexual families still maintain a gender-based division of labor that continues to influence children's perception of sex differences.

Socialization of children. The presence of both male and female adults in the family created by heterosexual marriage facilitates the process of child rearing in societies that distinguish between male and female roles and that divide up the work of life between the sexes. Since children of both sexes will be born into most families, heterosexual marriages ensure the presence of adult role models of both sexes who pass their skills to their same sex children through socialization.

Regulating inheritance rights. In addition to providing for the socialization of children, marriage is commonly the means of ensuring the inheritance rights of the offspring by establishing their legitimacy as members of the family.

Minimizing sexual competition. It is generally held that another function of marriage is to minimize the potentially disruptive effects of sexual competition. When people marry, the role change typically defines them as no longer being appropriate sexual partners for members of the unmarried group within which courtship is a common pursuit. Thus, the move from the more tumultuous period of unmarried courtship to a more stable period of married life helps to minimize the social effects of competition for sexual partners. Being part of a stable relationship thereby permits each partner to devote time previously taken up by the courtship process to other socially desirable pursuits.

SEX AND REPRODUCTION AMONG THE NAYAR OF INDIA

In societies throughout the world, the maintenance of a stable sexual relationship, reproduction of the family, child rearing, and the economic division of labor that includes the work of both males and females, are normally carried out within the single institution of marriage. However, all societies recognize that a given marriage may lack one or more of these features, and individual societies sometimes provide nonmarital ways of fulfilling one or more of these functions. Although marriage is commonly said to be a cultural universal, there is at least one major group within a larger society, the 30–40,000 Nayar of Kerala State in southern India, that has no marriages as they have been defined in this chapter.

According to Gough (1959, 1961), the nineteenth-century Nayar were a landowning caste whose men by tradition pursued the occupation of soldiers who hired themselves to the rulers of several neighboring kingdoms. This meant that men were often away from home for extended periods of time. Among the Nayar, children were members of their mother's family and household. Land was owned by a group of relatives who were related through the female line and who lived together as a household. This group, called the *taravad*, was headed by the eldest male of the household.

Each Nayar *taravad* had a special partnership with several others in the community. At intervals of every ten or twelve years, the girls of each *taravad* would go through what was called the *tali*-tying ceremony with a man selected from the linked *taravads* who tied a *tali*, a gold ornament, around the neck of the girl. Although this ceremony is considered a marriage ceremony, it also marked the transition of the girl into adulthood. The couple spent three days and nights together in a room in her household, and sexual relations were permitted if the girl was old enough. However, the "husband" had no further obligations to his "bride," and her only responsibility to him thereafter was to perform a certain ceremony upon the occasion of his funeral. Thus, this marriage was essentially a symbolic one.

Having gone through the *tali*-tying ceremony, the woman was now entitled to enter into *sambandham* relationships with other men of the same or of a higher caste than her own. These, too, might be called "marriages," but they also lacked most of the defining features of marriages elsewhere. Preferred partners were men of the higher-ranking Namboodri Brahmin caste who could not, by rules of their own caste, accept the children of the Nayar "wives" as their own heirs.

The first of these *sambandham* relationships began with a simple ceremony, as did any others that were intended to involve a lasting sexual relationship. Temporary relationships with other *sambandham* partners involved no ceremony. *Sambandham* "husbands" were allowed to spend the evening with their "wives" and were expected to bring small gifts with them at each visit, but a common residence was not established. The Nayar woman continued to live with her own *taravad*, where her brothers took responsibility for the costs of rearing her children. The woman's *taravad* benefited from her *sambandham* relationships in several ways: The woman's children became members of her own *taravad* and constituted the next generation of her family, and she might receive various services from each of her husbands who were likely to have a variety of occupations.

Children born to a Nayar woman were legitimate only if paternity was acknowledged by one or more of her *sambandham* husbands. The designated father was usually one of the men who had been sexually involved with her during the appropriate time for the child's conception, but might also be the man who was currently in the role of a "visiting husband." The fatherhood ceremony consisted of the payment of the midwife's fee, but the "father" had no further economic or social responsibilities for rearing the child. The failure of any of the husbands to acknowledge paternity was considered evidence that the woman had fathered the child with a man of a lower caste or a Muslim or Christian, an offense that was punishable by death or banishment of both the mother and child.

Types of Marriage

Marriages take several forms. Four basic types seem to exist: monogamous, polygynous, polyandrous, or group marriages. These four types differ in the number of persons of one or both sexes who form the marriage relationship and in the circumstances under which each tends to be the idealized form of marriage.

Monogamy. In monogamous marriages one man and one woman are joined as husband and wife. Monogamous marriages are the most common form of marital unit in all societies, even where other forms may be idealized as more desirable. Yet Ford and Beach (1951) found that less than 16 percent of their sample of 185 societies formally *restricted* marriage to the monogamous form. The recently developed Cultural Diversity Data Base (p. 22) supports the Ford and Beach finding with a similarly low figure of 14 percent of a sample of 180 societies and indicates that another 19 percent prefer monogamy without forbidding other marriage forms.

Serial monogamy. In societies such as the United States in which monogamy is the accepted form of marriage, a high rate of divorce and remarriage creates a particular pattern sometimes called serial monogamy. Serial monogamy has some characteristics of polygamy, the form of marriage in which a person is permitted to have more than one spouse at the same time. In serial monogamy, persons are permitted to have more than one spouse during their lifetimes, but only one at a time.

Polygyny. The form of polygamy in which one man is married to more than one woman is described as polygynous marriage. This was actually the *preferred* form of marriage in 83.6 percent of 185 societies surveyed by Ford and Beach (1951). The highest frequency of polygynous families is found in societies in frontier areas; in societies where warfare is common; in societies in which the ratio of adult women to men is high (a condition that is common in either of the two preceding circumstances); and in groups where rapid growth of families is beneficial to family survival. Since the ratio of male and female children is about equal in all societies, relatively few men actually are able to practice polygyny even in societies where it is the preferred marital form. Typically, it is practiced most commonly by individuals of high social standing while most men of lower social standing remain monogamous. Since it generally takes some time and effort to achieve the social standing that makes it possible for a man to have more than one wife, polygyny often involves an age difference between spouses, with older men taking much younger

FIGURE 8.3 *Wedding Ceremony*

While marriage takes many forms, it is a universal phenomenon. This Togolese chief, here posing with a number of his wives, practices polygyny.

wives. White (1988) has demonstrated that polygyny is organized into two basic patterns: sororal polygyny and male-stratified polygyny. In sororal polygyny a man marries two or more closely related women, often sisters. White has suggested that the traditional term, *sororal polygyny*, be referred to as male-ranked polygyny with related co-wives, since this is a more descriptively accurate label for this marriage form. In societies that practice this form of polygyny, social ranking is primarily a matter of individual achievement. A small number of men, such as outstanding hunters, warriors, or shamans, demonstrate their success by marrying a second or third wife. In these societies, male labor is the major contribution to the subsistence income of the family and extra wives are a drain on the man's wealth. In effect, the man exchanges his individually achieved wealth for wives, and his ability to support them demonstrates his success at achieving high social rank.

Male-stratified or wealth-increasing polygyny is more common in societies in which there are hereditary classes. In this form of polygamy, a small number of men who hold positions of rank and authority, often older men of wealthy families, marry a larger number of wives, perhaps 20 or 30. In these societies, the labor of women is often economically valuable, and each new wife increases the wealth of the family and its social prominence. It also becomes easier for the husband to acquire yet another wife. In contrast to sororal polygyny, where the wives and their husbands often reside together, these wives often have their own residence so that their economic activities can be carried out with a minimum of direct competition between co-wives.

Polyandry. It is rare for a single woman to have several husbands, as in a polyandrous marriage. It is the idealized family type in probably less than 0.5 percent of the world's societies. The most common form of polyandrous union is one in which a woman is simultaneously married to several brothers, a form of polyandry known as fraternal polyandry. Polyandry is advantageous where resources are extremely limited and it is beneficial to keep the growth of the family at a minimum. Regardless of the number of her husbands, a woman is not likely to become pregnant any more often than she would in any other type of marriage. Polyandrous unions have been reported among Southern Indian and Tibetan peoples where land is at a premium and cannot easily be further subdivided from one generation to the next. It was practiced by the Shoshoni of the Great Basin— a man might temporarily share his wife with a younger brother until he was old enough to

FIGURE 8.4 *A Polyandrous Wedding Ceremony*

One variation in the structure of marriage is the polyandrous type in which one woman marries two men. This Nepalese woman, in the veil, is marrying the two brothers on the left.

make his own way as an independent hunter with his own family. Like polygyny, polyandry is actually practiced by a minority of women in societies where it is the preferred marital form and gives evidence of a woman's high status.

The Toda of Southern India, described in detail by Rivers (1906), are one of the few peoples of the world where polyandry and group marriages were the rule. Marriages were arranged by parents when children were as young as two or three years of age. A marriage united the girl not only to the boy for whom she was originally selected but also to any brothers he might have, including those born after the ceremony. Thus, a Toda wife typically had several husbands who were usually brothers, although she might also enter marriage with other men. Since a woman was considered to be the wife of any of the brothers of a man she married, if brothers entered into marriage with more than one woman, the result was a group marriage in which several women might be wives simultaneously to several men.

Both polyandry and group marriage made it infeasible to keep track of biological paternity, so this concept was unimportant to the Toda. However, since Toda families were patrilineal, fatherhood in its social sense was important. Therefore, the Todas employed a ritual of fatherhood, a ritual that designated a particular man to be the social father of any children a woman bore for a period of years thereafter, whether or not he was their natural father.

Since fatherhood was established by a ritual act, the concept of adultery was irrelevant to the Toda view of family relations. Not only was sexual infidelity by a wife not grounds for divorce—since it would not have affected the legitimacy of a child's rights to inherit from the socially defined father—but it was also so unimportant a concept that there was not even a word for adultery in the Toda language.

Group marriage. When several males are simultaneously married to several females, they are called group marriages. Group marriage and polyandry typically occur together, but group marriage and polygyny do not. This is because polyandry and polygyny are not simple mirror images of one another. Women in polyandrous families are likely to have higher status than those in polygynous families. For instance, the sexuality of plural wives

159

in polygynous families is often jealously guarded by their husbands, but this is unlikely in a polyandrous society in which married women will have plural mates as a matter of course. On the other hand, no such contrast exists for husbands in these two family types. The sexuality of husbands in polyandrous societies is no more likely to be abridged than it is in polygynous ones. So polyandrous societies typically have no rules against husbands sometimes also marrying plural wives, something that wives in polygynous societies are not likely to be permitted to do. When one of a woman's husbands in a polyandrous society marries another woman—often a sister of the original wife—the new bride also becomes the wife of co-husbands in the original marriage as well. Such simultaneously polyandrous and polygynous families are also group marriages.

CO-MARRIAGE AMONG THE INUIT OF NORTH ALASKA

According to Burch (1970, 1975), the Inuit of North Alaska engaged in monogamy, polygyny, polyandry, and a nonresidential form of group marriage that he calls co-marriage. Co-marriages were typically contracted to create a kind of fictive sibling relationship between the same-sex partners. This quasi-siblinghood continued into succeeding generations, since the children of both couples in a co-marriage were considered siblings, and their children in turn were accepted as cousins. Thus, co-marriages established long-lasting cooperative bonds between people and their descendants who resided in different locations, a very useful practice in a highly mobile society in which autonomous nuclear families might lack a network of relatives to call upon for help wherever they traveled.

A co-marriage was established when, by mutual agreement, the husbands and wives had sexual intercourse with each other's residential spouse. This formality established a co-husband relationship between the men and a co-wife relationship between the women, relationships that included a continuing obligation of mutual aid similar to that of siblings. Such relationships were both emotionally and practically important among the Inuit, since siblings had strong moral responsibilities toward one another, and life in the cold, arctic environ-

ment they occupied could be a difficult one for small foraging families when other relatives were not available in the same location for cooperative activities.

Atypical Marriages

In addition to the most commonly idealized forms of marriage, monogamy, polygyny, and polyandry, there are a variety of other types of marriage that may also occur. These atypical marriage forms may be rare or quite common, depending on the society in question, but are rarely the preferred type in any society. Atypical marriages include symbolic marriages, nonsexual marriages, fictive marriages, and several forms of homosexual marriage.

Symbolic marriages. As we have seen, marriage is normally created in all societies as a vehicle for establishing economic and social ties between kinship groups and for providing a means of perpetuating the group. However, under some circumstances societies may sanction the establishment of marriages in which these functions do not apply. Such symbolic marriages may serve other purposes, as when religious specialists consider themselves married to a deity. The Roman Catholic nun who wears a ring symbolic of her status as a bride of Christ, and who is therefore taboo to others as an object of romantic love, is a Western example of a participant in a symbolic sacred marriage. Mormon religious practice provides another striking example of symbolic marriage: It includes a contrast between a "marriage for time" and a "marriage for eternity." A temporal marriage is one performed by a judge or minister, including a Mormon minister. Such marriages end at the death of one partner, lasting only "till death do us part." Eternal marriages, on the other hand, are performed only in a Mormon Temple and are believed to be valid "for time and all eternity" in the eyes of God. An outgrowth of this belief is the practice of performing vicarious marriages between deceased persons and their surviving spouses or even between two deceased persons who were married only temporally while alive. This system of symbolic marriage has a polygynous bias in the Mormon subculture, since a woman whose "eternal husband" has predeceased her may remarry "for time" only, while a man may enter into several "eternal marriages" serially, if one or more of his wives dies before him. When a man who has entered several "eternal marriages" dies, Mormons believe that he will be reunited with all his wives after death.

Nonsexual marriages. Marriages sometimes fulfill their usual economic, kinship, and even child-rearing functions in the absence of a sexual union between the partners. Such nonsexual marriages can occur for a variety of reasons. For instance, they may occur in societies that have class differences, for the political or economic benefits to the marriage partners or their relatives, as when a royal marriage is negotiated to stabilize a political alliance between two societies. Among Mormon pioneers in the United States, an elderly woman sometimes entered into a nonsexual marriage as a plural wife for companionship or economic security in a precarious environment. In such a role, she might participate in the domestic life of the family in providing companionship, helping with housework, and sharing childrearing responsibilities with her co-wives.

Fictive marriages. A marriage can exist legally without a family being established in order to allow one or both partners to obtain social benefits that would be unavailable otherwise. Such a marriage is called a fictive marriage. For instance, immigration and naturalization quotas in the United States have resulted in the practice of marriages between U.S. citizens and potential immigrants or resident aliens for no purpose other than to facilitate the immigration or acquisition of citizenship by the noncitizen partner. In such a case, the parties to the marriage may not establish a common domicile or sexual relationship; indeed, they need not be acquainted before the marriage nor see each other again afterwards. This particular example of fictive marriage is one that is legally rejected by U.S. immigration authorities, and those who are involved may be punished by law, but analogous fictive marriages do exist in societies where they are openly accepted as valid means to an end. For instance, among the

Kwakiutl it is possible for a man to marry the male heir of a chief as a means of inheriting certain privileges from the father-in-law. When there is no heir to marry, a man may marry the chief's arm or leg as a legally valid way of becoming an inheritor.

Probably the most widespread forms of fictive marriage are the levirate and the sororate. The levirate, a custom mentioned in Deuteronomy 25, is the obligation of a dead man's next of kin, usually one of his brothers, to marry the widow. Commonly, at least the first child of this union is considered to be the offspring of the first husband. This custom is especially important in societies that stress the importance of the line of descent through males, since it provides a way for men who die without heirs to have descendants. It also cements anew the marriage alliance between the two families whose children were originally united in marriage. At the same time, it provides the widow with someone who will continue to perform the duties of a husband. The sororate is a similar custom in which a widower, or sometimes the husband of a barren woman, marries his first wife's sister. Again, at least some of the children born to this second marriage are considered children of the first wife, a particular benefit in societies where ancestry is traced primarily through women. Like the levirate, the sororate ensures that the marriage tie between the two in-law families is not dissolved by the death of one partner and that the survivor will continue to have a mate.

GHOST MARRIAGE AMONG THE NUER OF THE SUDAN

Evans-Pritchard (1951) described an interesting form of fictive marriage practiced by the Nuer, a cattle-herding people who live in the savannah region of the Upper Nile in the Sudan. Ghost marriages occur when the close male kinsman of a man or boy—married or unmarried—who died before he had any legal heirs, marries a woman in the name of the deceased relative. The living vicarious husband gives the family of the bride a number of cattle, as the deceased man would have done, had he married the woman while he was still alive. Legally, the woman will be the ghost's bride, and all of the children she bears will be his. However, the vicarious husband will be treated in all other respects as if he were the woman's real husband, something that is not true in the case of the levirate. As with the levirate, the purpose of a ghost marriage is to bear children who will be heirs to the deceased husband. However, ghost marriage differs from the levirate in several important ways. In a leviratic marriage, the marriage ritual, including any economic requirements, was performed by the original husband. The wife in a ghost marriage is not the widow of the deceased, so the marriage arrangements and ritual are carried out after the death of the ghost husband, who may have been a boy who never married while alive.

Ghost marriages among the Nuer are almost as common as simple marriages between a man and woman. This commonness is partly because each ghost marriage tends to create anew the circumstance which requires ghost marriages in the minds of the Nuer: a man who enters a ghost marriage as the vicarious husband obtains no descendants through that marriage; but his own brothers are likely to assert their right to marry wives of their own before he is permitted to marry a wife in his own name. Such a vicarious husband may well die before he is able to found a lineage of his own, and it will be up to one of his brothers or nephews to enter a ghost marriage in his behalf. Thus the Nuer "solution" to the "problem" of men who die without children perpetuates the very situation it is intended to eliminate. Such a situation suggests that there is more to the story than meets the eye, that some pragmatic benefits may accrue to Nuer families who practice ghost marriage.

How might Nuer ghost marriage benefit the living? An answer to this question is suggested by other customs related to ghost marriage. The Nuer not only assert that a dead man may be the legal father of children born long after his death, but also that a ghost may continue to own property. When a man dies without heirs, any cattle he may have owned do not revert to the larger family herd, but remain *ghok jookni* "cattle of the ghost." Such cattle are sacred and may not properly be used for any purpose other than as payment to a bride's family for her bearing of children in the name of the ghost. This restriction has further implications: According to Evans-Pritchard (1966:111), "When Nuer raid a herd to seize cattle in compensation for some injury they will not take cattle reserved for the marriage of a ghost." So the idea that uninherited cattle remain the property of the dead benefits the survivors. Such property is still under their control. They may milk the cows while they hold them in trust for the deceased owner, and they may be used for obtaining a wife for one of their living sons so long as he enters a fictive marriage in behalf of the dead owner of the cattle that pays for the marriage, but they cannot be taken from the family in payment of debts as their other cattle can. Thus ghost marriage is part of a larger web of cultural concepts that includes economic benefits similar to those of family trusts in the United States.

Just as legitimate marriages may exist without a sexual component, nonreproductive marriages may still fulfill the other functions of marriage and be socially accepted. Marriages of this type include those by persons past their reproductive years and homosexual marriages, both of which are legitimate in a large number of human societies.

Homosexual marriage.   Various forms of homosexual marriage, both male-male and female-female marriages, have been legitimate in a number of human societies. Like nonreproductive heterosexual marriages, they can fulfill other functions of marriage besides procreation. Indeed, as we shall see, homosexual marriage does not preclude the birth of children or child rearing.

A number of native North American societies had a social status that has come to be known as the *berdache*, a female or male—who had adopted a sex role that mixed the gender characteristics of both sexes. The *berdache* was particularly common among men of Plains Indians tribes where warfare was an almost sacred preoccupation and where the male role placed strong emphasis on demonstrations of pride, bravery, and daring. So the presence of the berdache has long been thought of as a cultural alternative for men who lacked the skill or interest in the aggressive pursuits of the traditional male role (Hoebel, 1949, p. 459). Such a man might instead opt for the life of a berdache by adopting the dress, work, and mannerisms of a woman.

The *berdache* was a sacred status in many Native American societies. Often these people played important ceremonial roles in society, and in some cases all shamans were required to be *berdaches*. A female who became a *berdache* actually moved up the status hierarchy and might achieve wealth and social prominence, since the change allowed her to participate in advantageous male pursuits such as trade. A *berdache* "man" might marry and even raise children by having another man impregnate his wife or a *berdache* "woman" might hire another woman as a surrogate mother.

Similar same-sex marriages are accepted in many cultures throughout the world. Such relationships have been called pathic (Gregerson, 1983) or intragenerational marriages (Adam, 1986), since the term *berdache* has so often been used for the North American examples in particular. Intragenerational marriages involve two partners of the same sex who belong to the same generation. Often, but not always, one of the partners adopts the opposite sex role of his or her own biological sex, including the practice of transvestism, cross-sex or gender-mixed dressing. This association of transvestism with same-sex marriage in societies in which pathicism is socially accepted contrasts with the pattern found in the United States and probably in other industrialized societies in which same-sex relationships have been stigmatized historically. In such societies, transvestism seem to be most common among heterosexually married males. Same-sex marriages between partners of more or less equal age also may be culturally approved without transvestism or a change in the sex role behavior of either partner. This form, sometimes called homophilic marriage to distinguish it from pathicism which usually includes gender-mixing or transvestism, is the form most commonly found in industrialized nations.

Little information exists on the prevalence of institutionalized female transvestism, but in cross-cultural studies of male transvestism, Downie and Hally (1961) and Munroe, Whiting, and Hally (1969, pp. 87–91) found that, "Societies that tolerate the sharing of roles by the two sexes will also tolerate a role that enables a man to take over the functions of the female sex" (Downie & Hally, 1961, p. 8). This seems to go counter to the traditional view that transvestite role change is a cultural escape from the demands of the male sex role in societies that strongly differentiate between the roles of men and women. However, the traditional view does seem to hold up in one respect. Munroe and Munroe (1977, pp. 307–308) determined that male transvestism is more likely to be found as a culturally valid option in societies in which men play the predominant role in the subsistence economy.

In a recent study, I compared societies that accepted pathic marriages with those that did not and found that the former were more likely to have a variety of other social traits that also are associated with a need for flexibility and adaptation to changing economic circumstances (Crapo, 1987). These social traits include bilateral descent, ambilocal residence or the absence of patrilineal kin groups when patrilocal residence is followed, and social rank based on individual achievement rather than birth into a high status descent group. Male labor is particularly important in the food-getting activities of these societies, but women have relatively high status both politically and domestically. Polygyny is one indicator that a male is particularly successful as a provider, since the major source of income is male labor. So polygyny is practiced only by a few outstanding individuals who are able to support a small number of wives, usually sisters, the form of polygyny that White (1988) has termed male-ranked polygyny with co-wives or sororal polygyny. By taking a pathic wife, a man may actually increase the income of his family and improve his chances of being able to afford a third wife even sooner. So in these societies, pathic marriage is respected and is even a means for the nonpathic husband to achieve wealth, respect, and a polygynous family sooner than would otherwise be possible.

NUER WOMAN MARRIAGE

Evans-Pritchard's (1951) study of the Nuer of the Sudan reported a form of marriage that he called "woman marriage," in which one woman marries another. She does so exactly as a man does, paying a bride price of cattle to her bride's family. The female husband in such a family acquires cattle when her own kinswomen marry just as her brothers do and may inherit cattle from her father as if she were a son. Children born to her own wife through the services of a man she chooses for that purpose "are called after her, as though she were a man" (p. 109). Her children address her as "father," and she is "treated by her wives and children with the same deference they would show to a male husband and father" (p. 109). When her daughters marry, she receives the cattle that are normally given a father in payment of the bride price.

Woman marriages may also occur when a female relative of a deceased man marries a wife in the name of the dead kinsman. According to Evans-Pritchard (1951, p. 111), "The persons involved in a marriage of this kind are the dead man, his kinswoman who marries a wife in his name, the wife, and the man who is brought in to cohabit with the wife." The children of this union are legally those of the dead man and will inherit from him.

One other form of homosexual marriage is found in a variety of the world's cultures, a form that has been variously labelled male mentorships (Herdt, 1981), intergenerational marriage (Adam, 1986), or pederasty (Greg-erson, 1983). Male mentorships are ways of initiating younger, unmarried men into the culture of a society in which men play a socially dominant role, and exercise sexual rights over persons of lower rank, such as women, youths, and slaves (Adams, 1981, 1986). It is commonly associated with the marriage of the highest ranked men to several wives as a way of symbolizing their high social standing and of perpetuating their power by ensuring that they will have large families. Among other things, male mentorship relationships help to prevent younger males from competing with their social superiors for wives, since one or both of the partners in a male mentorship will be denied the right to marry until he is older. The mentorship relationship makes this temporary taboo on heterosexuality easy to follow by providing an alternative sexual outlet in a context that emphasizes male solidarity and superiority over females.

The older male in a mentorship relationship socializes the younger apprentice, who in return may aid his mentor in his pursuit of higher status within the male community. These marriages are not exclusively homosexual. If the older male is not currently also the husband in a heterosexual marriage, he will be expected to enter one at some point in his career, and the apprentice will, himself, eventually graduate into the rank of mentor, and, either then or later, into that of a heterosexually married man. Male mentorships are often a part of the military training system in male-dominant, warlike societies. In such societies they may also be associated with training in specialized religious settings, where younger males are secluded from contact with females during their training.

My own (1987) examination of societies that have institutionalized male mentorships indicates that they are typically patrilineal and patrilocal societies that are characterized by male dominance over women. Successful competition in the male prestige system is rewarded by polygyny of a kind that White (1988) has termed male-stratified or wealth-increasing polygyny, in which the most prominent social leaders are a small number of older males who have a large number of wives, and whose labor is an economic asset. Each wife in this system increases the wealth of the family and adds to the likelihood that other wives will be married.

GREEK AND AZANDE WARRIOR MARRIAGES

According to Dover (1978) and Boswell (1980), the Greeks of classic times made no distinction between homosexuals and heterosexuals as is commonly done in contemporary Euro-American cultures. Rather, homosexual and heterosexual relationships complemented each other, and both were entered into by the same men. The basic form of Greek homosexual marriage occurred in a military context. Greek warriors often fought in pairs, bound by an oath of sacred loyalty. The loyalty between the warrior apprentice and his senior mentor was the highest of Greek loyalties, and the bond that unified them as a fighting pair was rooted in their sexual affection. No fighting man not so bonded could ever be trusted to fight as dearly for a fellow warrior as a lover would by virtue of his emotional bond with his partner. It was to their homosexual military partnerships that the ancient Greeks attributed their success in war, and this was the reason for their having regarded homosexual love both as a spiritual union and as the epitome of masculinity.

Sexual mentorships were also found in other settings in ancient Greek society. Respected teachers, including men such as Socrates and Aristotle, were expected to have male lovers among their students. The sexual and emotional bond was believed to foster the teaching relationship in which the mentor played the role of nurturer and teacher, while the student was inspired to learn by his love for his teacher.

The ancient Greeks regarded homosexual marriages as both more masculine and spiritually superior to male-female marriages, but the senior partners in homosexual unions were not exclusively homosexual. They also entered into heterosexual marriages, unions through which they could engender children who would continue their family lines into the future.

Male mentorships similar to those of the ancient Greeks have been noted by anthropologists in a variety of societies in more recent times. For instance, they appear to be particularly common in Melanesia, where they have been reported among the Big Namba of Malekula (Deacon, 1934), the Marind Anim (Baal, 1966), the Etoro (Kelly, 1976) and the Keraki (Williams, 1936) of New Guinea. Here they tend to be associated with warfare and a strong ideological emphasis on the importance of male ritual homosexuality as part of a system of symbolic protection from what they considered the spiritually polluting effects that females have on men. Other examples of male mentorships have been reported in societies as geographically widespread as Java (Weis, 1974), Bali (Duff-Cooper, 1985), Libya (Abd Allah, 1917, Cline, 1936), native Australia (Strehlow, 1913; Mathews, 1900), Amazonia (Hugh-Jones, 1979), and Japan (Ihara, 1972).

Evans-Pritchard (1937, 1970, 1971) has described a mentorship system among the Azande of the Southern Sudan that illustrates the similarities of male mentorships in the cultures in which they are found. As did the ancient Greeks, the Azande expected homosexual marriages to supplement the practice of heterosexual marriage. Homosexual marriage was integrated into a form of universal military conscription based on age. During their period of military service, young warriors married boys who played the same roles as female wives played for older men. The husband in such a marriage addressed the parents of his boy-wife as "father-in-law" and "mother-in-law," and the boy provided routine domestic services for the husband as a female wife might also do. When the husband grew older, he gave up his boy-wife and entered the heterosexual phase of his life. In turn, his wife-apprentice graduated into warriorhood and took his own boy-bride.

Male members of the Azande aristocracy, those with the largest and wealthiest households, entered heterosexual marriages with multiple wives and simultaneously maintained within their households pageboys who were also lovers. The pageboys originally entered the households as a form of tribute exacted from lower status households within the Azande empire. They increased the wealth of the households for which they worked, and when they were old enough, they married heterosexually. Their marriages were possible because they were given the bride wealth necessary by the head of their household just as were the sons of the household.

Azande women had lower social rank than men, and their social status derived from the men in their lives, their fathers, brothers, and husbands. Female homosexuality, therefore, could not play the same role as male homosexuality of validating aristocratic power. Lesbian relationships did exist among co-wives in a household, but they were not idealized. Rather, they were seen as potentially in conflict with male societal dominance. They were regarded as supernaturally dangerous to men, and the Azande believed such a relationship would cause a man to die if he witnessed it.

Marriage Choice

Each culture includes various rules that influence the choice of marriage partners. Some of these rules restrict the choices that may be made by proscribing certain persons as possible partners. Other rules require marriage within defined social categories. Some

FIGURE 8.5 *Berber Marriage Festival*

The Berbers of Morocco conduct a mass marriage ceremony annually in September. Eligible men and women gather at Marabout, the grave of their holy man, to find a mate. Women are divided into two groups identified by their headdresses. Widows and divorcees wear a peaked hood as seen here, where a couple agrees to marry. She must be guaranteed a marriage gift of new shoes, a head scarf, and a small amount of money.

define particular kinds of persons as preferred partners. All three kinds of rules help to narrow the range of appropriate mates from which the selection is made.

Social restrictions on partner choice. When marriages are of practical significance to a family, the culture often has formal guidelines about whom a person ought to marry. Such rules increase the likelihood that the practical well-being of the kin group will be fostered.

The most common example of such marriage guidelines is the exogamy rule, a rule that requires marriage outside a designated group. Since marriage always involves legitimation of a sexual relationship, the existence of an incest taboo requires marriage outside the group of kin with whom sex would be incestuous.

One rule regarding sexual behavior seems to be found in almost all cultures. This is the incest taboo, which forbids sexual intercourse between parents and their children, between brothers and sisters, and frequently between other kin as well. There are a few cultures in which exceptions to this rule exist. For instance, the Hawaiian royalty, the kings and queens of ancient Egypt, and the Inca em-

perors were expected to perpetuate their lineages by brother-sister marriages. They were regarded as sacred and were expected to violate the incest taboo that applied to all others.

Except for the few societies or special social groups in which the usual incest taboo is not applied, the rule of exogamy always requires marriage outside the nuclear family, and usually it also prevents marriage with first cousins. However, rules of exogamy are more than mere extensions of the incest taboo. Incest taboos specifically govern sexual behavior. Rules of exogamy do more than this: They govern marriage rights. Therefore they may exclude from consideration for marriage a broad circle of persons with whom sex is not necessarily forbidden. Thus, rules of exogamy may require marriage outside one's own residential unit as well as outside one's own family. In some societies the local group is divided into two groups, or moieties, which are each exogamous—so that members of one moiety always marry persons from the opposite moiety of their society. This arrangement divides each local group into two units that have reciprocal rights and obligations to one another. For instance, members of one moiety may host funerals when a member of the opposite moiety dies.

Endogamy rules, on the other hand, require that both marriage partners be members of a certain kinship, social, or local group. For instance, a rule of endogamy may require marriage into one's own village, church, or social class. In the traditional castes of India, marriage partners were strictly limited to members of one's own caste.

Marriage preference rules single out certain kin as ideal marriage partners. Although the exogamy rules of most societies promote marriage beyond the circle of one's cousins, there are many that in fact prefer marriage between cousins. Most of these cultures have a rule of preferential marriage between cross cousins—cousins who are linked by parents of opposite sex, as children of a brother and sister. In both patrilineal and matrilineal systems of reckoning kinship, cross cousins belong to different lineages. With such marriages, members of each family gain in-laws outside their own lineage to whom they can turn for aid in times of need. A common form of cross-cousin marriage is one in which a brother and a sister marry cross cousins who are also sister and brother to each other. In societies where the inequality of the sexes is marked, this is often described as two men exchanging sisters. In such cases, marrying one's brother-in-law's sister does create an added social bond between two men, a bond that may benefit them both politically and

economically. Sister exchange or, more accurately, bilateral cross-cousin marriage, repeatedly links two lineages over many generations (see Fig. 8.6) This system is called "bilateral" because a man's wife is both his mother's brother's daughter and his father's sister's daughter.

A less intense pattern of intermarriage between two lineages is one in which a male of one lineage marries a woman from another lineage in one generation, and his daughter marries into that lineage a generation later. This permits his sister to marry into a third lineage, thereby extending the marriage alliances into an even greater circle of people. This system has been called patrilateral cross-cousin marriage because, from the male's point of view, the preferred marriage is with one's father's sister's daughter. Patrilateral cross-cousin marriage permits many lineages to be linked into a circle in which marriage partners flow in one direction in one generation and in the other direction in the next generation (see Fig. 8.7).

An even more common pattern is one in which several lineages are linked into a circle in which the women of each lineage always marry in one direction around the circle, while their brothers marry into the lineage next to theirs in the opposite direction (see Fig. 8.8). This marriage system is like the patrilateral marriage system, but the direction of mar-

FIGURE 8.6   *Bilateral Cross-cousin Marriage*

Various clans or groups of people define their kinship by an elaborate system of descent. This diagram shows marriage occurring between cousins who are linked by parents of the opposite sex.

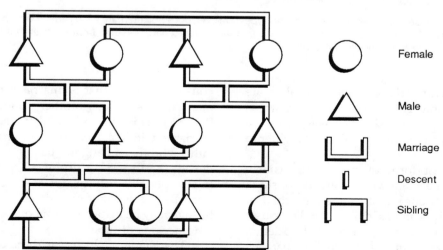

Female

Male

Marriage

Descent

Sibling

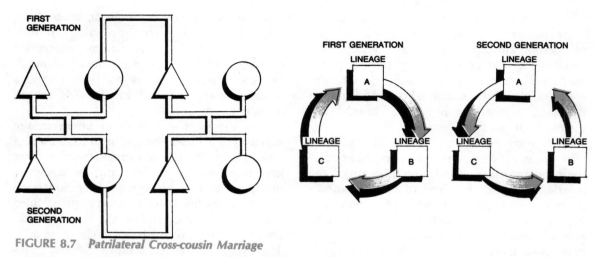

FIGURE 8.7 *Patrilateral Cross-cousin Marriage*

A circular type of lineage occurs in this form of marriage. In one generation the marriage partners are chosen in one direction on the diagram, and in the next generation they are chosen in the opposite direction.

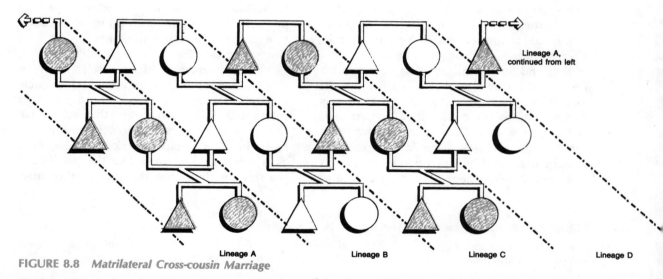

FIGURE 8.8 *Matrilateral Cross-cousin Marriage*

Similar to the patrilateral cross-cousin system, this type, however, does not alternate each generation. The women of each lineage marry someone in one direction as diagrammed on the chart, and their brothers marry into the lineage next to theirs but in the opposite direction.

riages is asymmetric and does not alternate each generation. This system also is known as matrilateral cross-cousin marriage, since a wife is always a mother's brother's daughter to her husband.

The rarest form of preferential cousin marriage is marriage with a parallel cousin (a cousin who is one's mother's sister's child or one's father's brother's child). Parallel-cousin marriage is found among many Arab societies. It is called *bint'amm* or patrilateral parallel-cousin marriage, that is, marriage between a man and his father's brother's daughter (see Fig. 8.9). This rule is useful in maintaining solidarity within a lineage, since a man and his father's brother's daughter belong to the same lineage (Barth, 1954, Murphy & Kasdan, 1959). It is especially helpful, for instance, among Arab Bedouins where members of the same lineage may be dispersed from one another for long periods of time.

The levirate, which was discussed earlier

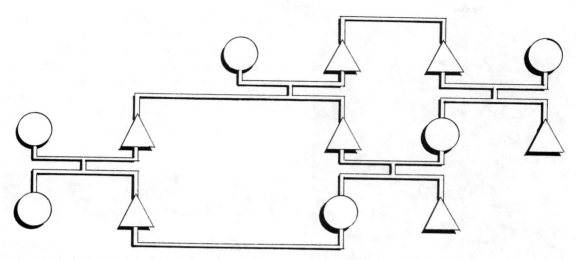

FIGURE 8.9 *Patrilateral Parallel Cousin Marriage*

This system of kinship maintains unity in a lineage because a man always marries his father's brother's daughter.

in this chapter, is a more specialized marriage rule that requires the kin of a deceased man to provide his widow with a new husband, often a brother of the dead husband. A more or less opposite practice, the sororate, requires that the family of a deceased wife provide the surviving widower with another wife from among the women of their own family. Both of these rules illustrate that in kinship-based societies, a marriage is actually a contract between two families who have continuing obligations to each other even after the death of a spouse. In matrilineal societies, a surviving wife may be expected to marry the heir of her deceased husband, generally the dead man's sister's son. This fulfills the same basic function addressed by the levirate and, at the same time, symbolizes that the dead man's heir has assumed not only his property but also his rights and obligations, including the obligation to care for the surviving wife.

Negotiating Marriage

Negotiations before marriage between the two families will emphasize pragmatic issues, such as the size of the payment one family may make to the other, the work and domestic skills of the future spouses, and the like. Less rational matters such as the feelings of the prospective bride and groom for one another are not given as much weight as they carry in societies in which large kinship groups are not

the major economic and political units of society. The feelings of the couple for each other need not be neglected, but they may play little role in such negotiations, for neither their sexual gratification nor their emotional compatibility is of greatest interest to their respective families. Rather, the couple to be married form a link by which those families are joined in their society's larger arena of politics and economics.

Bride wealth.   In perhaps three quarters of the world's societies, marriage negotiations involve the determination of how the prospective groom's family shall recompense the family of the bride-to-be for the loss of her productive and reproductive services (Coult & Haberstein, 1965; Murdock, 1957). This compensation may consist of gifts, known alternatively as the bride price, bride wealth, or progeny price. The amount of the bride wealth compensation will reflect the importance of the bride's family compared with that of the groom's since the bride's status as a married woman and the status of her children will be greater if the compensation is a high one. Bride wealth is found in 60 percent of those societies that anthropologists have investigated. It is particularly common among simpler food-producing societies, such as tribal horticulturalists and noncommercial pastoralists, those that raise animals only for their own use.

FIGURE 8.10   *Bride Price*

In some societies, marriage negotiations involve paying the family of the bride for their loss of her services. In this New Guinea village, a man is counting out cowrie shells in payment for his prospective bride.

Bride service.   Alternatively, compensation to the bride's family may take the form of a period of work to be performed by the groom for his wife's family, in which case it is known as the bride service. The bride service has been reported in about 24 percent of societies that anthropologists have studied. It is particularly common among foragers who lack the accumulation of wealth necessary for paying bride wealth.

Bride service also typically differs from bride wealth in that bride wealth is paid at one time, or over a short period, at the beginning of the marriage and permanently validates the marriage, while bride service continually recompenses the bride's family for a prolonged period that may last the life of the marriage. In the words of Schlegal and Eloul (1988, p. 294), in bride service, "marriage is in a constant state of economic negotiation." Nevertheless, even when the bride service is performed for a fixed period of time, the spouses usually have

sexual access to one another from the beginning of the period of service, and the legitimacy of children is not affected by being born before the end of the service. Under the custom of bride wealth, however, children may not be considered fully legitimate, particularly in respect to inheritance rights, until the entire progeny price has been paid.

JACOB'S SERVICE FOR RACHEL AND LEAH

Then Jacob went on his journey, and came to the land of the people of the east. As he looked, he saw a well in the field, and lo, three flocks of sheep lying beside it; for out of that well the flocks were watered. The stone on the well's mouth was large, and when all the flocks were gathered there, the shepherds would roll the stone from the mouth of the well, and water the sheep, and put the stone back in its place upon the mouth of the well.

And Jacob said to them, "My brothers, where do you come from?" They said, "We are from Haran." He said to them, "Do you know Laban the son of Nahor?" They said, "We know him." He said to them, "Is it well with him?" They said, "It is well; and see, Rachel his daughter is coming with the sheep." He said, "Behold, it is still high day, it is not time for the animals to be gathered together; water the sheep, and go, pasture them." But they said, "We cannot until all the flocks are gathered together, and the stone is rolled from the mouth of the well; then we water the sheep."

While he was still speaking with them, Rachel came with her father's sheep; for she kept them. Now when Jacob saw Rachel the daughter of Laban his mother's brother, and the sheep of Laban his mother's brother, Jacob went up and rolled the stone from the well's mouth, and watered the flock of Laban his mother's brother. Then Jacob kissed Rachel, and wept aloud. And Jacob told Rachel that he was her father's kinsman, and that he was Rebekah's son; and she ran and told her father.

When Laban heard the tidings of Jacob his sister's son, he ran to meet him, and embraced him and kissed him, and brought him to his house. Jacob told Laban all these things, and Laban said to him, "Surely you are my bone and my flesh!" And he stayed with him a month.

Then Laban said to Jacob, "Because you are my kinsman, should you therefore serve me for nothing? Tell me, what shall your wages be?" Now Laban had two daughters; the name of the older was Leah, and the name of the younger was Rachel. Leah's eyes were weak, but Rachel was beautiful and lovely. Jacob loved Rachel; and said, "I will serve you seven years for your younger daughter Rachel." Laban said, "It is better that I give her to you than that I should give her to any other man; stay with me." So Jacob served seven years for Rachel, and they seemed to him but a few days because of the love he had for her.

Then Jacob said to Laban, "Give me my wife that I may go in to her, for my time is completed." So Laban gathered together all the men of the place, and made a feast. But in the evening he took his daughter Leah and brought her to Jacob; and he went in to her. (Laban gave his maid Zilpah to his daughter Leah to be her maid.) And in the morning, behold, it was Leah; and Jacob said to Laban, "What is this you have done to me? Did I not serve with you for Rachel? Why then have you deceived me?" Laban said, "It is not so done in our country, to give the younger before the first-born. Complete the week of this one, and we will give you the other also in return for serving me another seven years." Jacob did so, and completed her week; then Laban gave him his daughter Rachel to wife. (Laban gave his maid Bilhah to his daughter Rachel to be her maid.) So Jacob went in to Rachel also, and he loved Rachel more than Leah, and served Laban for another seven years (Genesis 29, *The Oxford Annotated Bible*, Revised Standard Version).

Dowry.   In the dowry, the benefits flow in the opposite direction from those of the bride wealth or bride service. Here, goods belonging to the bride's family accompany her into the marriage. The wealth is most often controlled by the bride within her new family, but it sometimes is held in trust for her by her husband or his relatives, or it may simply become the property of the husband's family (Goody & Tambiah, 1973, p. 2). The dowry is likely when a woman's economic contributions

to, and therefore her potential status within, the family are low. When the dowry is controlled by her husband or his family, it is apt to be perceived as a compensation for the economic burden of supporting the woman. Thus, the dowry is not a mirror-image of the bride wealth or bride service, even though it flows in the opposite direction. Like bride wealth and bride service, dowry reflects the status of the woman in a marriage. The first two forms are more likely when a woman's economic contribution is important to a family; the dowry, on the other hand, is more likely when women are considered an economic burden (Schlegel & Barry, 1986).

The dowry is most common in more complex societies, especially those whose economy is based on complex agriculture or commercial pastoralism, that is in societies in which commodities are produced for market exchange and in which there are wealth differences between families. The dowry may be viewed as a kind of advance on a woman's inheritance from her own family. It keeps wealth within the family by ultimately benefiting the grandchildren of the donors.

Indirect dowry.   Goody (1973) has noted a variant of the dowry that he has called the indirect dowry, a payment of goods made by the groom or his family to the bride, either directly to her or to her father who then passes it to her. Sometimes the father may keep some of this payment before passing the rest on to his daughter to cover the costs of the marriage preparations or to recompense him for having raised the girl. As with the dowry, the goods that go to the bride in the indirect dowry are intended to provide security for the bride and her children, especially if she becomes widowed. Coming from her husband's family, the payment may symbolize their commitment to the well-being of the daughter-in-law in her new setting away from her paternal home.

Gift exchange.   Sometimes the flow of goods between the families who are party to a marriage goes in both directions. Called gift exchange, this reciprocal sharing of objects of more or less equal value between the two families emphasizes the ties of future interaction and mutual aid that will characterize the relationship between the families.

Women exchange. Schlegel and Eloul (1988, p. 292) have pointed out that gift exchange is not perfectly balanced, since one family loses a child, while the other gains a relative by marriage. However, there is one system that overcomes this imbalance. Women exchange is a system in which no gifts are passed between the families. Instead, each family gives a female, usually a daughter, as a bride to the other family. Since each family loses a daughter but gains a daughter-in-law the exchange between the two families is completely balanced.

FAMILY

Marriage legitimizes a sexual union and provides an institutionalized means for producing the next generation. Some group must be charged with the responsibility for rearing the children born from the marriage union. The group in which children are raised is known as the family. This group need not be structured solely around the individuals who are united to one another in marriage. When the family does consist of parents and their children, it is called a nuclear family. This is the family type that is most familiar to peoples of Western societies in recent times, and it is also typical of foraging societies. However, as the sole basis for households it is a rare family form.

Almost all societies throughout most of human history have had more complex family forms than the nuclear family. These more complex family forms, known collectively as extended families, include more individuals than a husband and wife and their children. They are formed when the married couple sets up their residence with one of their families. Extended families usually include three generations: either a pair of grandparents, their sons, the wives of their sons, and all the children of their sons, or a pair of grandparents, all their sons and daughters, and all the children of their daughters. These two basic types of extended family may be further elaborated, depending on the marriage forms involved, since the extended family may include plural spouses in the parental and grandparental generations.

Extended families may live under a common roof or in several closely assembled dwellings. Thus, they may make up a single household (residential unit) or several households. In any case, the number of individuals involved in childrearing responsibilities will be much larger in extended families than in nuclear families. Therefore, extended families are likely to have more formally established rules regarding the rights and obligations of various family members to one another than do societies in which nuclear families are the norm.

THE SAMOAN EXTENDED FAMILY AND HOUSEHOLD

Ella (1895) and Mead (1928) described the traditional Samoan family system, which provides a marked contrast to North American families and households. Among the Samoans, a single household was led by a *matai* or headman, a titled member of the family selected to act as their patriarchal head. The *matai* had life-and-death authority over members of the household and was responsible for carrying out religious rituals for the family. As family head, he also owned the land that was worked by the family members and assigned them their share to work.

Within the extended family group, children were tended by their older siblings. The mothers were thus freed for other activities and all adult relatives were viewed as having rights over the children of the group. Besides baby-tending, boys under eight or nine years of age and girls who had not yet attained puberty were expected to help adults in many other ways contributing to the work and welfare of the household. On the other hand, if the demands of the family became too great, children were free to leave home and take up residence with other relatives in another household that they found more congenial.

Postmarital Residence

Although marriage joins two kinship groups as allies, the couple joined by the ritual of marriage may be more involved in the daily life of one of their parental kinship groups than the other, depending on where they are most likely to set up their new residence.

FIGURE 8.11 *Gift Exchange*

In this Fiji village, the two families who will be involved in a marriage exchange gifts of food. It is a reciprocal sharing of goods of equal value intended to emphasize the mutual respect of both families.

According to research by Murdock (1957), in about two thirds of the world's societies newly married couples are expected to set up residence in or near the residence of the husband's family. This form of residence, called virilocality or patrilocality, is most often found where the solidarity of the male group is very important. Naroll (1973) found that the best single predictor of virilocality was the man's predominance in food production. Its likelihood is increased by other factors that strengthen males' solidarity: e.g., where hunting is a primarily male activity; where food production requires heavy labor; where warfare involves fighting between neighboring groups that share a common culture and language; where men have more than one wife; where men wield authority in a political organization that is a source of prestige; or where male accumulation of property is a sign of rank.

The second most common residence pattern is uxorilocality, formerly known as matrilocality. Uxorilocality is found in about 15 percent of societies and involves the setting up of a residence in or near the residence of the bride's family (Coult & Haberstein, 1965; Murdock, 1934). This is most likely to be practiced where food is provided by simple gardening in environments that do not require heavy labor and in warlike societies where belligerence is most common between distant groups.

A third residential pattern is bilocality or ambilocality: Residence may be in the home area of either the bride or the groom. This form of residence is practiced in 5 to 10 percent of societies. It permits flexibility of choice in societies in which cooperation within large kinship groups is important but in which it is useful to be flexible about which group a new couple joins, as in agricultural groups where land is limited.

In neolocality the couple sets up a residence in some new place apart from either family. This residence pattern provides maximum flexibility in electing a place to live and is most common when the nuclear family of two parents and their children is economically independent and responsible for its own survival. Only about 1 in 20 societies emphasizes neolocal residence. It is most common in industrialized societies.

Finally, in avunculocality residence the couple takes up residence in or near the house of the groom's mother's brother. This rare form of residence is common in less than 5 percent of societies and occurs only in matrilineal societies where the men of the matrilineage must stay together, as when warfare is common.

SUMMARY

Marriage is a socially accepted sexual and economic union that unites members of previously separate families in a committed relationship that typically involves childrearing expectations. The most commonly recognized marital types are monogamous, polygynous, polyandrous, and group marriages. However, in many societies there are also symbolic, nonsexual, fictive, and homosexual marriages. Since marriages unite separate families into an in-law relationship with each other, their creation has practical implications for more persons than just the spouses. So the choice of marriage partner is restricted in all societies by a variety of rules, such as rules of endogamy and exogamy, and marriage preference rules. In most societies, the creation of a new marriage traditionally has also involved various practical considerations, such as the payment of goods or service to the family of the bride and the dowry. The family established by marriage may vary in size from the nuclear family that is common in Western societies today to the more traditional extended family that has been common in most of the world since the rise of food domestication. The size of the family is directly related to customs that govern where a newly married couple is expected to set up their residence.

KEY TERMS AND CONCEPTS

marriage 154
monogamous marriages 157
serial monogamy 157
polygamy 157
polygynous marriage 157
sororal polygyny 158
male-ranked polygyny with related co-wives 158
male-stratified 158
wealth-increasing polygyny 158
polyandrous marriage 158
fraternal polyandry 158
group marriages 159
symbolic marriages 160
nonsexual marriages 161
fictive marriage 161
levirate 161
sororate 161
ghost marriages 161
homosexual marriage 162
berdache 162
pathic 163
intragenerational marriages 163
transvestism 163
homophilic marriage 163
male mentorships 164
intergenerational marriage 164
pederasty 164
exogamy rule 166
incest taboo 166

endogamy rules 167
marriage preference rules 167
cross cousins 167
sister exchange 167
bilateral cross-cousin marriage 167
patrilateral cross-cousin marriage 167
matrilateral cross-cousin marriage 168
parallel cousin 168
bint'amm 168
patrilateral parallel-cousin marriage 168
bride price 169
bride wealth 169
progeny price 169
bride service 170
dowry 171
indirect dowry 171
gift exchange 171
women exchange 172
family 172
nuclear family 172
extended family 172
household 172
virilocality 173
patrilocality 173
uxorilocality 173
matrilocality 173
bilocality 173
ambilocality 173
neolocality 173
avunculocality 173

ANNOTATED READINGS

Bohannan, P., and Middleton, J. (Eds.). (1968). *Marriage, family, and residence.* New York: Natural History Press. A still widely read collection of articles about marriage, family and residence patterns in various societies.

Ember, M., and Ember, C. R. (1983). *Marriage, family, and kinship: Comparative studies of social organization.* A collection of cross-cultural studies that test various explanations of human social organization.

Fox, R. (1968). *Kinship and marriage.* One of the easiest to follow texts that has been produced on kinship and marriage.

Frayser, S. G. (1985). *Varieties of sexual experience: An anthropological perspective on human sexuality.* New Haven, CT: HRAF Press. One of the most recent attempts to use cross-cultural data to examine the diversity of human sexual customs through time and across cultural boundaries using data from Murdock and White's Standard Cross-Cultural Sample. This book includes important discussions of marriage, family, child rearing, and divorce.

Gregerson. E. (1983). *Sexual practices.* New York: Watts. A well-illustrated and informed discussion of the major topics of the cross-cultural study of human sexuality.

Needham, R. (Ed.). (1972). *Rethinking kinship and marriage.* London: Tavistock. A collection of essays that focus on the cross-cultural study of kinship and marriage customs.

Pasternak, B. (1976). *Introduction to kinship and social organization.* Englewood Cliffs, NJ: Prentice Hall. One of the standard sources on kinship, this book contains information about theories of marriage and the family.

PART IV

Ideology and

Humans have built a superstructure of culture using their ability to symbolize, to explain their place in the universe, and to understand the concept of their own mind and its relationship to others in a society. Chapter 9 looks at patterns of language and learning, the system of symbolizing and communicating meaningful ideas to others. Chapter 10 discusses the most abstract of symbolic systems, the varieties of religious ideologies and rituals that societies develop to give meaning to their place in the universe. Chapter 11 focuses on the individual's relationship to culture, illustrating how it shapes personality, influences states of consciousness, and identifies psychological disorders.

Symbolism

*H*uman ways of life are far more varied and complex than those of other animals. Both the diversity and the complexity are possible, in part, because the human animal's ways of adjusting to its environment are readily modified by learning. We human beings are born with a tremendous capacity for learning any way of life to which we are exposed. The development of ways of life that are much more complex than those of other animals is facilitated not only by our remarkable capacity to learn but also by our distinctive ability to communicate the intricacies of these lifeways to other members of our group. Unlike other animals, we tend to portray our concepts by highly arbitrary but mutually accepted symbols, including languages. In this chapter, we will examine these two capacities, learning and symbolizing, which are so fundamental to the origin and perpetuation of the human pattern of life.

9

Learning and Symbolizing in Human Behavior

FIGURE 9.1 *Karachi Classroom*

Human cultures and traditions are learned either at home or in the more structured environment of the classroom. These girls are sharing books in a classroom in Karachi, Pakistan.

Dude. Boombox. Beetlejuice. Jive. Lift. Bonnet. All words of the English language. Would you understand what they meant if you were 18 years old? or 80? Lived in California? London? In all parts of the world, and at all ages, humans learn to communicate with each other using a complicated system of vocal sounds that symbolize complex concepts. It is the primary ability that distinguishes us from other primates.

179

LEARNING AND CONCEPTUALIZING

Like all organisms, we human beings interact with our environment. In the process, we gain experience and change our behavior to interact more effectively with our environment. Such changes in behavior are commonly called learning. In mammals, the process of learning is controlled by the neocortex, the newly evolved surface area of the brain. The neocortex gains information about the environment through the animal's senses. The senses enable animals to see, hear, smell, taste, feel pain, moisture, temperature and texture, judge whether they are lying or standing, and monitor several processes occurring within their bodies.

Building Concepts

In humans, and possibly in other mammals as well, information gained through the senses is gradually organized into mental models of things that are perceived. These models are called concepts. As mental models, concepts are the basis for memory. They also provide the organism with a knowledge of some part of its environment and help it to interact more effectively with its surroundings. We humans can manipulate concepts mentally to arrive at expectations about the behavior of things in our environment. This ability increases our effectiveness in dealing with those things and therefore our ability to survive.

Each concept is built from many smaller bits of information called percepts. A percept is a perceived quality or attribute of the object or event. The more ways in which any object or event is perceived (e.g., from different angles, at different points in time, or with different senses) the more complete and useful the concept becomes. Consider the concept "chair," for instance. When a child first sees a chair, the image cast on the retina of the eye is different at each angle from which the child might view the chair. In these original perceptions of the chair, if the child glimpses it at separate times from two different perspectives, this inexperienced being might not even recognize that what it has seen is a single object. Gradually, the learning child integrates the percepts into the concept "chair," thereafter recognizing it to be the same object no matter from which side it is seen.

Correcting Incomplete Perceptual Data

Our conceptual models of the world can never be perfect or complete reflections of reality, for two reasons. First, the number of different perspectives from which perceptual data concerning any object or event may be obtained is infinite. Second, our senses are limited in their perceptual abilities. Thus our concepts are always to some degree incomplete or distorted, and no concept may be said to be correct in any absolute sense. The real test of a concept is not its truth but its utility; some conceptualizations are simply more useful than others in helping it cope with its environment.

Inasmuch as our experiences always suffer from some degree of incompleteness, we often fill in missing parts of the conceptual model, making it seem complete. This is necessary so that the model may be used to provide needed information about aspects of the thing with which we must deal even though we have not experienced them directly. Distortion occurs when some percepts are not integrated into a conceptual model because they do not dovetail neatly into the pattern formed by the other percepts.

The tendency to treat conceptual systems as if they were more complete, perfect, and correct than the incoming perceptual data is called closure (Wertheimer, 1938). Closure implies that a conceptual system has more parts and relationships than are actually perceived. Closure occurs when we build concepts based on assumptions such as the following: (1) when things occur together they belong together; (2) when things are similar they belong together; (3) when percepts can be combined into a single concept by the addition of a small amount of missing information, this is superior to an alternate combination that requires the brain to supply missing information; or (4) when we can group percepts so they match concepts that we already have, it is acceptable to do so.

Closure involves going beyond the available perceptual facts of experience and can, therefore, lead to errors and incorrect anticipations. Nevertheless, it does often offer some

FIGURE 9.2   The Concept of Closure - Mbuti Pygmy Hunters

The density of the forest environment for these Mbuti pygmy hunters necessitates their use of closure to accurately shoot their prey without seeing it entirely. Closure is successful because with the concept of the animal in the hunter's mind, he is able to imagine the whole thing even if he sees only part of it.

advantages by making it possible to make a necessary judgment before all the perceptual data are in. For instance, in the mid-1960s the Mbuti archers of the Ituri Forest of Zaire lived in a dense forest environment. It was often necessary for a hunter to fire an arrow quickly on hearing the sound of his prey before he was able to see clearly its outline in the foliage (Turnbull, 1965). To wait for a complete experience of the animal before acting would have made hunting an unprofitable business. In this case, the ability to make closure allowed the hunter to recognize the presence and approximate location of a game animal based on limited information. The hunter was then able to react quickly enough to obtain an adequate food supply.

CULTURAL AND ENVIRONMENTAL INFLUENCES ON PERCEPTION

Since closure is often based on congruity with previous experiences, our cultural background and environmental setting have a great impact on how we interpret our experiences. An example of the impact of cultural differences on how people interpret

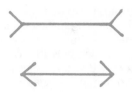

FIGURE 9.3   Müller-Lyer Illusion

The perception of visual illusions appears to be culturally and/or environmentally determined. In the figure above, most Europeans, for example, would judge the top line to be longer than the bottom one, whereas the natives of Murray Island and South India would interpret the line lengths as nearly equal.

experience has been reported by W. H. R. Rivers (1901, 1914), who showed the Müller-Lyer diagram to Papuan natives of Murray Island and to the Toda of South India. Both groups interpreted this figure more accurately than did English people. The Müller-Lyer figure consists of two horizontal lines of equal length, one of which terminates with diagonal lines pointing away from the center, while the other terminates in diagonals angled back towards its center. English subjects tend to report that the first horizontal line looks longer than the second.

The causes of this illusion have been investigated by many later researchers. In one interesting study by Segall, Campbell, and Herskovits (1966), 1,878 people from 14 non-European societies were shown this illusion. The researchers found that the lengths of the lines in this figure were most deceptive to people who lived in a "carpentered world" and whose way of life gives them experience with two-dimensional portrayals of things. In effect, the people who were fooled by the illusion lived where houses had flat walls that met at right angles, forming a straight line along their intersection, and especially where people were accustomed to judging flat pictures and diagrams as representations of three-dimensional forms. The perceptual habits developed in those societies led people to see the first line as if it were farther and the second as if it were nearer to the observer. Since the lines are of equal length, the one judged to be farther away will seem to be longer, as it would have to be for it to have the same apparent length on paper.

Another famous illusion is the full moon illusion. When seen near the horizon—even in pictures—the full moon seems much larger than when it is seen high overhead. Again, cross-cultural research has shown this illusion to be culturally and environmentally patterned. Segall et al. (1966) showed that this illusion was especially effective in environments that offer an open view of extended vistas. It fails to work with people who live in restricted environments, such as dense forests. The interpretation of this difference is similar to that of the Müller-Lyer illusion. People who have unrestricted views of the horizon become habituated to unconsciously judging the distance of things by how close to the horizon they are; they learn that a distant object will appear to be the same size as a nearby one only if the distant object is larger. When they see a picture of an object such as the moon near a horizon and compare it with a picture of the same object with no horizon shown, the first is likely to seem larger, since it will unconsciously be thought of as a distant object.

Turnbull (1961) reports the interesting case of a Mbuti archer named Kenge who had grown up in a densely forested environment, where he had never had the opportunity to see objects at any appreciable distance. Turnbull took this individual on a drive out of the forest into the open savannah. When a herd of about 150 buffalo came into view in the distance, the Mbuti man asked what kind of insects they were. Turnbull unsuccessfully tried to explain that they were not insects: "When I told Kenge that the insects were buffalo, he roared with laughter and told me not to tell such stupid lies" (p. 253). After another passenger also claimed that the "insects" were indeed buffalo, Kenge "strained his eyes to see more clearly and asked what kind of buffalo were so small. I told him they were sometimes nearly twice the size of a forest buffalo, and he shrugged his shoulders and said we would not be standing out there in the open if they were" (p. 253). In an effort to convince his companion, Turnbull drove the jeep toward the herd. According to Turnbull:

> . . . as we got closer, the "insects" must have seemed to get bigger and bigger. Kenge, who was now sitting on the outside, kept his face glued to the window, which nothing would make him lower. I even had to raise mine to keep him happy. I was never able to discover just what he thought was happening . . . that the insects were changing into buffalo, or that they were miniature buffalo growing rapidly as we approached. His only comment was that they were not real buffalo, and he was not going to get out of the car again until we left the park. (p. 253)

Generalizing Concepts

The ability to make closure—that is, to use incomplete data to build seemingly complete concepts—is possible only because concepts are by nature idealizations. If concepts were accurate models of real things, it would be necessary to have a different concept for each different thing, no matter how similar they were to one another. But concepts are idealizations of things, not one-to-one replicas of them. So two similar things also may be treated conceptually as if they were the same.

Since concepts are idealizations, a single concept may be created that refers to no one real or existing thing but to a class or category of nonidentical but similar things. Children need not see every existing cat before developing a generalized concept of cats; the concept is constructed out of those characteristics that they have perceived in most of the cats they have observed so far. Insofar as these perceived similarities are, indeed, traits shared by all cats, the abstract generalized conception will enable a person to recognize and appropriately respond to a new such animal on meeting it for the first time. This is so even though each cat is individually different in many respects from any other. Thus, the ability to develop a generalized concept from a limited amount of information increases the ability of the human being to function in spite of limited experience.

Perceiving Contrasts

Unfortunately, since we create concepts using limited information, we sometimes make erroneous judgments based on our concepts. Witness the classic anecdote of the child who, on seeing a skunk for the first time, tries to pet the "pretty kitty." To be really useful, concepts must be formulated by noting relevant differences as well as similarities.

The kaleidoscope of patterns and colors perceived visually can be discriminated as "objects" and "background" because of visual contrasts that isolate the form of the object from the whole visual field. For instance, an object may be noticed when it moves: Some of the patterns and colors are seen to move as a group in contrast to the stable background. The necessity of contrasts in perception is illustrated dramatically by a process known as the ganzfeld phenomenon, the inability to perceive when contrast is not maintained (Cohen, 1957). For instance, when experimental subjects stare at a large, plain white wall or have two halves of a cut ping-pong ball taped over their eyes so that only a diffused white light can be seen, the visual centers of the brain have no contrasts to analyze. After about 20 minutes, persons who are experiencing no visual contrasts lose the awareness of vision itself. In such a state, subjects wearing ping-pong balls are no longer aware of the diffused white light and often even are unable to determine whether their eyes are open or closed. Control over eye movements is also lost, and the subjects cannot determine in which direction their eyes are looking.

Experiential contrasts are the building blocks of concepts. So the percepts out of which a concept is built can be described formally with a set of statements about the presence or absence of perceivable differences between objects. For example, according to Katz's analysis (1972) of the percepts that define the significance of the concept "chair," the recognition that an object is a chair requires that an observer be able to notice, among other things, that the object under observation is physical (rather than mental), nonliving (versus living), manufactured (versus natural), and that it has a backrest and a seating capacity of one. Such an object is conceptually contrasted by English speakers with a "stool," which is perceptually the same as a chair in all the above characteristics except one—the absence of a backrest.

The number of percepts required to define the boundaries of a concept is not fixed. Generally, the more in common that two things have, the smaller is the number of percepts necessary to distinguish them conceptually. For instance, an awareness of the absence of a backrest is relevant to distinguishing the class of stools from those conceptually categorized as chairs, but no such perceptual fact is needed to distinguish between stools and tables. Similarly, the presence or absence of horns might be relevant in conceptually distinguishing between horses and cows, while distinguishing cows from chickens would require a consideration of the presence or absence of such attributes as wings.

The conceptualizing process is different from the process of visualizing or mental imaging. Mental imaging involves remembering a total experience. Concepts, on the other hand, are abstractions from experience and are composed of a limited number of percepts that are relevant to some particular problem-solving situation, such as thinking, analyzing, or communicating.

SYMBOLS AND SIGNS

Analyzing one's experiences, whether internally in thought or externally in communication, involves the manipulation of concepts. In communicating, another capacity is also called into play. To transfer the information embodied in a concept from one person to another requires the use of an observable object or event to represent that concept, since one person's concept is not directly observable by another person. It is this ability to represent ideas in an external form that makes possible the communication of ideas from one person to another. Communication is the most distinctive of all human behavioral attributes, and serves as the foundation for the extremely complex ways of life found in all human groups.

Most aspects of human cultures are transferred from one person to the next, through the generations, by intentional acts of communication. The process of communication is the use of objects and events to represent other objects and events. There are two different classes of communicative acts: those that use signs to transfer information and those that use symbols. Both humans and other animals communicate by means of signs, but humans are the only animals known to communicate naturally with symbols.

Distinguishing Between Signs and Symbols

A sign is an object or event used to represent some other object or event in a nonarbitrary manner. The meaningfulness of a sign is determined by factors of the communicator's biology or by the inherent physical properties of the sign itself (Cassierer, 1944). Thus, reflex acts and biologically inherited instinctive acts that convey meaning may be called signs. When a snarling dog bares its teeth, the act is highly expressive as a warning sign, and, in the context of muscles tensed and ready for sudden action, the meaning of the act is clear. Even when a sign is learned, the meaning is based on its intrinsic qualities, such as the sharpness of the dog's teeth. Sometimes an animal may have a biologically based predisposition to recognize the meaning of a sign, while in other cases it may have to learn the meaning of the sign by being repeatedly exposed to the sign and its referent.

The meanings of symbols, on the other hand, must be learned. A symbol is also an object or event that is used to represent another object or event, but the meaning of a symbol is arbitrarily created by its users (White, 1971). The relationship between a symbol and what it represents is not determined by the inherited biological tendencies of the communicator to relate the two to one another. Furthermore, a symbol need not share any physical similarities or physical proximity with its referent. There is, for instance, no reason dictated by human biology or the physical properties of the wavelengths of light that red had to be used to mean "stop" or green to mean "go" in traffic signals, nor is there any compelling reason in human biology or in geometric properties for a stop sign to be octagonal rather than triangular in shape. There may be causal factors in one's history or environment that influence the form of a symbol, but its meaning is arbitrary in the sense that it is not based on the intrinsic qualities of the symbol itself but exists solely because the users of the symbol agree to use it. Any symbol may be used to designate any referent.

Once the meanings of a symbol come into general acceptance, they may seem as natural to its users as do the meanings of a sign. But, since the meanings of symbols are a matter of social convention or consensus rather than nature, they can change quite readily even within the lifetimes of their users. It is the fact that humans can freely assign new meanings to objects or actions that allows people to communicate extremely complex and subtle messages to one another.

Human vs. Nonhuman Communication

Homo sapiens is not the only species of animal that communicates. Many nonhuman animals make use of both biologically innate and learned signs in communicative acts. However, the creation and use of symbols is characteristic of humans alone. Furthermore, we human beings are prolific in our constant use of symbols. When consciously attempting to communicate, human beings use symbols more frequently than signs. Even when acts do have rather natural meanings as signs, we often alter the meanings or the forms of these acts symbolically. In other words, we tend to transform almost anything into symbols for other things.

In human beings, only the simplest of meaningful signs—those that communicate simple feelings in nonconscious or nonintentional ways—are biologically preprogrammed. For instance, we express heightened interest in whatever we are observing by an increase in the dilation of the pupil of the eye, a change controlled on an unconscious level by the autonomic nervous system (the part of the nervous system that controls the functioning of nonvoluntary actions such as the beating of the heart). This sign, though unintentional, is communicative, and other persons perceive the change and respond appropriately to it as evidence of personal interest. Similarly, the increased muscle tension that signals rising anger is often communicative enough to cause an observer to begin acting more carefully.

In some other animals, even complex communications may be governed by biologically controlled behavioral tendencies. For instance, a fighting timber wolf may indicate its submission by freezing its stance and exposing the vulnerable area of its throat to the attacking fangs of its opponent. This act might seem highly inappropriate and dangerous in the heat of battle, yet the timber wolf has a biological predisposition to signify its acceptance of defeat in this way. And the sign is responded to appropriately: Although the victor grasps the throat of its victim with its mouth as if to bite, its muscles tremble as if strained by the effort to control its enraged attack, and it does not bite to kill. If the submitting wolf remains rigid and unmoving, it will not be bitten, and the victor will continue to strain as if it desires but is unable to bite until, finally exhausted, it releases its hold and begins to walk away. Even now, if the submitting wolf starts to move, a renewed attack will begin until the sign of submission is given again. The process may be repeated several times until the loser manages to escape from the repeated attacks of the gradually tiring dominant animal.

In humans, on the other hand, all complex messages are transmitted by symbols. This tendency to create symbols—to continually use one thing to represent something else and to alter the meanings again and again after they have once been created—distinguishes humans from all other animals. Other animals, to be sure, are capable of learning to react to one item as if it were another, but only if these separate items are in some way similar to one another or are always experienced together at the same time or in the same spatial location. Humans alone seem to have a tendency to create meaningful relationships between things that neither share great physical similarities nor occur together in nature.

HUMAN COMMUNICATION WITH AND WITHOUT SYMBOLS: HELEN KELLER

The dramatic impact that symbols have on human behavior is well illustrated by the case of Helen Keller, a person in whom the acquisition of symbols and, hence, the ability to communicate symbolically was delayed until she was almost seven years old. Stricken by illness at the age of 19 months, Helen was left both blind and deaf. Helen lacked the senses through which we normally learn the arbitrarily agreed-on meanings of our communicative acts and through which we usually perceive those symbolic acts themselves. Nevertheless, she needed to communicate and did so by her own signs, acts whose meanings were implicit in the quality of the acts themselves. In her own words:[1]

My hands felt every object and observed every motion, and in this way I learned to know many things. Soon I felt the need of some communication with others and began to make crude signs. A shake of the head meant "No" and a nod, "Yes," a pull meant "Come" and a push, "Go." Was it bread that I wanted? Then I would imitate the acts of cutting the slices and buttering them. If I wanted my mother to make ice cream for dinner, I made the sign for working the freezer and shivered, indicating cold. . . .

About three months before Helen's seventh birthday a teacher, Miss Anne Sullivan,

arrived to attempt to train her to communicate by finger spelling. Gradually, Helen learned to spell several words, but she simply used these as she had previously used her own self-invented signs. That is, she had not yet recognized the essence of symbols: Since their meaning is arbitrarily assigned by their users, a symbol may be created to refer to anything. In the words of Anne Sullivan:

Helen has learned several nouns this week. "M-u-g" and "m-i-l-k," have given her more trouble than other words. When she spells "m-i-l-k" she points to the mug, and when she spells "m-u-g," she makes the sign for pouring or drinking, which shows that she has confused the words. She has no idea yet that everything has a name. (p. 253)

In a month of intense teaching, Helen learned only 25 nouns and 4 verbs. Here is her own description of this period of her slow learning of the fingerspelling signs:

The morning after my teacher came she led me into her room and gave me a doll. The little blind children at the Perkins Institution had sent it and Laura Bridgman had dressed it; but I did not know this until afterward. When I had played with it a little while, Miss Sullivan slowly spelled into my hand the word "d-o-l-l." I was at once interested in this finger play and tried to imitate it. When I finally succeeded in making letters correctly I was flushed with childish pleasure and pride. Running downstairs to my mother I held up my hand and made the letters for doll. I did not know that I was spelling a word or even that words existed; I was simply making my fingers go in monkey-like imitation. In the days that followed I learned to spell in this uncomprehending way a great many words, among them *pin, hat, cup* and a few verbs like *sit, stand,* and *walk*. But my teacher had been with me several weeks before I understood that everything has a name. (p. 35)

Helen's slow rate of sign learning was superseded by a remarkably accelerated rate of learning that began when her inborn symbolic abilities became activated in a single dramatic incident. This change was recorded by her teacher in a letter:

April 5, 1887.
I must write you a line this morning because something very important has happened. Helen has taken the second great step in her education. She has learned that everything has a name, and that the manual alphabet is the key to everything she wants to know.

In a previous letter I think I wrote you that "mug" and "milk" had given Helen more trouble than all the rest. She confused the nouns with the verb "drink." She didn't know the word for "drink," but went through the pantomime of drinking whenever she spelled "mug" or "milk." This morning, while she was washing, she wanted to know the name for "water." When she wants to know the name of anything, she points to it and pats my hand. I spelled "w-a-t-e-r" and thought no more about it until after breakfast. Then it occurred to me that with the help of this new word I might succeed in straightening out the "mug-milk" difficulty. We went out to the pump-house, and I made Helen hold her mug under the spout while I pumped. As the cold water gushed forth, filling the mug, I spelled "w-a-t-e-r" in Helen's free hand. The word coming so close on the sensation of cold water rushing over her hand seemed to startle her. She dropped the mug and stood as one transfixed. A new light came into her face. She spelled "water" several times. Then she dropped on the ground and asked for its name and pointed to the pump and the trellis, and suddenly turning around she asked for my name. I spelled "Teacher." Just then the nurse brought Helen's little sister into the pump-house, and Helen spelled "baby" and pointed to the nurse. All the way back to the house she was highly excited, and learned the name of every object she touched, so that in a few hours she had added thirty new words to her vocabulary. Here are some of them: *Door, open, shut, give, go, come,* and a great many more.

P.S.—I didn't finish my letter in time to get it posted last night; so I shall add a line. Helen got up this morning like a radiant fairy. She has flitted from object to object, asking the name of everything and kissing me for very gladness. Last night when I got in bed, she stole into my arms of her own accord and kissed me for the first time, and I thought my heart would burst, so full was it of joy.

1. From *The Story of My Life* by Helen Keller, 1954, Garden City, NY: Doubleday & Company, Inc. Reprinted by permission.

Cultural Complexity and Symbolic Communication

Since the meanings of symbols are arbitrarily assigned, they may be changed whenever doing so can aid the communication process. For example, a teacher might explain, "In this discussion, when I say *money*, I mean anything used by people as a medium of exchange, not just officially issued currency."

Similarly, new symbols can be created readily whenever they are needed to express new ideas. Fifty years ago, English lacked the words *quark, smog,* and *ethnocide.* Because of this ability to change the meanings of symbols and to create new ones at will, human symbolic communication can transfer information about complex and subtle details of experience, including new insights concerning the external world and inner experience that have never before been expressed. Such uses of symbols make human communication far richer and more complex than the sign communication of any other animal.

Since symbols may be physical objects that are arbitrarily endowed with meaning, a people's socially shared beliefs and values can be portrayed in long-lasting form, such as monuments, works of art, flags, and written documents. Such symbols can help to preserve information and public tradition over long periods of time. This makes possible the gradual accumulation and reevaluation of information over many generations. The total body of shared human knowledge may gradually become larger and more sophisticated than any one individual or group of cooperating individuals could hope to create. Thus, the human symbolic ability makes possible a growing degree of complexity that is not possible in any other social animal.

NONVERBAL COMMUNICATION

The two most active forms of interpersonal communication are nonverbal communication and language. Nonverbal communications, the subject of this section, are messages we convey to each other without words. Often these messages are unconscious expressions of our emotions and may not even be intended as communications. They range from grins and hugs to the spaces we place between ourselves in conversation and our handling of time (as in arriving early or late for an appointment).

Nonverbal Signs

The simplest forms of nonverbal communication are physiological signs, not symbols. For instance, blushing, which communicates embarrassment, is a direct reflection of one's emotional state and is controlled by the autonomic nervous system. Smiling, although it can be consciously controlled and assigned other symbolic meanings in special contexts, is also more generally a direct reflection of happy feelings. As such, it can be observed in deaf-blind individuals as well as in others. Slumping posture will signal submission or defeat without conscious effort; prolonged eye contact can indicate aggression or interest in maintaining contact; staring blankly while avoiding eye contact may signal fear or a desire not to interact.

Culturally Patterned Nonverbal Symbols

Nonverbal signs communicate the same meanings in every culture. Samoan, Navajo, or Chinese, we all express happiness with the same spontaneous smile, confusion with a distinctively human knit brow, and boredom with a yawn. Nevertheless, we humans have the distinctive tendency to play with meanings, and we sometimes take natural signs and give them an arbitrary cultural form or meaning. We make symbols even of signs. Our nonverbal symbols, such as parting gestures, flirtatious uses of the eyes, and hand gestures of contempt, vary from culture to culture. For instance, throughout Europe when people want to point out the location of something they gesture in the appropriate direction with their hand. The finger closest to the thumb, appropriately called the "pointing finger" in colloquial English, may also be extended. Shoshoni Indians of the North American Great Basin use no such gesture unless they have changed their habits to accommodate imported European nonverbal symbols. Their traditional gesture, still used today, is with their lips. Many North Americans use a "thumbs up" gesture to express their feeling that things are going well. In Japan this gesture would likely be interpreted to mean "boss" or "father." The German who points to the side of his forehead communicates the same idea—"crazy!"—that the North American may convey by tracing a circle next to the head with the index finger. North Americans point at their chests to indicate "self"; Japanese point to their noses with the same significance. Since such symbolic gestures have meanings that

FIGURE 9.4 *Andamanese Greeting and Parting Customs*

Andaman Islanders of either sex greet each other after absences of a few weeks by one sitting in the lap of the other and weeping. Since their etiquette demands crying as a means of expressing sentiment, the Andamanese learn to shed tears on demand.

must be learned, we tend to be much more conscious of how we are using them and what we wish to communicate when we use them than we are of the multitude of meaningful nonverbal signs that we use spontaneously.

Our most common nonverbal symbolic communications tend to be performed with the highly visible upper extremities of the body—the hands, arms, shoulders, head, and parts of the face. They are often used in situations of purposeful communication: (1) where verbal communication is impossible, as when persons are too distant from one another to hear one another well; (2) where verbal communication is inappropriate, as when the actor wishes to send the message to only one member of a group (but knows others would overhear a verbal message), or when the sender feels that a verbal communication would be too direct or strong in impact; and (3) where their use will provide added emphasis while speaking verbal symbols.

Cultural variations in such symbols may inhibit full communication between people of different cultures, even on a nonverbal level. Greeting is not signified everywhere by a handshake: A kiss, an embrace, or a nose rub will do as well. Among the Toda of India, a woman indicates respect in greeting an elder kinsman by kneeling and lifting his foot to her forehead (Murdock, 1969). A wave of the hand that the European would interpret as a farewell might elsewhere be used as a request to approach. Such differences can lead to misunderstandings between well-intentioned persons from different societies who do not realize that their behaviors are only arbitrarily endowed with meaning and that the same behaviors might denote something different to people from another society.

Proxemics

Even the distance we place between ourselves and others conveys subtle nonverbal meanings. Edward Hall (1969) has studied the ways in which people symbolically structure their nonverbal manipulation of spatial relationships between themselves and others. He refers to the study of people's use of the space around them as proxemics. One finding of proxemic research is that the distances that people choose to place themselves from others communicates how they feel about the interaction. According to Hall, there are four main distances to which North Americans adjust themselves in their business and social relations: intimate, personal, social, and public distances.

Intimate distance, which is reserved for occasions when caressing and touch are appropriate, varies in the United States from direct contact to one and one-half feet, where persons are still close enough to touch one another easily. We experience others in this zone intensely by many of our senses. They fill our field of vision, their breathing is audible, and we are aware of their presence by the senses of touch and smell as well. This intensified experience of the presence of another person in our lifespace brings a heightened awareness of how changes in ourselves result in changes in the other and vice versa. This intimate awareness often leads us to experience the other as an extension of our own self rather than as a separate entity. Intimate distance is normally regarded as too close to be used by adults in public. In crowded situations such as elevators or subways, when one is forced to remain within the intimate distance of strangers, individuals communicate that they are not intentionally intruding on the intimate zone of others by staring impersonally at a distant spot.

The second meaningful zone to which North Americans adjust themselves, called personal distance, indicates a close friendship relationship. It is the zone from one and one-half feet to four feet. A husband and wife generally place themselves within the first half of each other's personal zone in public or conversational situations, while other friends will normally occupy the farther half of this zone. In many other cultures, the distances for this personal zone are somewhat closer than they are in the United States or northern Europe. This can make it difficult for persons of differing cultural backgrounds to communicate their interest in one another. An Anglo-American may feel ill at ease if a stranger from another society adopts a distance that in the stranger's homeland indicates friendship but which to the Anglo-American seems overly intimate or pushy. When the Anglo-American backs away to a distance at which he or she feels comfortable among friends, the other may mistakenly interpret the nonverbal com-

FIGURE 9.5 *Proxemics - Social Use of Space*

Specific social and cultural rituals determine how people use their individual space. The Taiwanese monks greeting each other (A) are careful to observe a formal social distance. In other cultures (B) the greeting may include close physical contact such as a handshake or a hug.

munication as disinterest. Such misunderstandings can be avoided only if one becomes aware that even the most habitual of human behaviors, being very specific and symbolic, have no universal meanings but vary from society to society.

Beyond personal distance is social distance of 4 to 12 feet, which is used in more impersonal interactions of a cordial type such as in business transactions. Public distance, which is greater than 12 feet, is the final zone. The usual distance placed between a teacher or public speaker and most audiences is 12 to about 25 feet. Distances greater than this are used to distinguish important public figures.

Hall (1969) has studied several societies and has found that the distances to which people adjust themselves for intimate, personal, social, or public activities are not the same in every society. For instance, among Germans personal space is expanded to include visible areas far beyond the North American's four-foot space. People are expected to greet formally anyone of their acquaintance who comes into sight and is within hailing distance. This difference shows up in the German preference for solid doors that clearly separate each room in homes and work places, a preference that contrasts with the common North American rooms connected by doorways that have no closeable doors. The closeable door allows the German to indicate more clearly his or her personal space with a definite boundary. Typically, the traditional German home or apartment has a lockable door on every room, including the kitchen. The North American walk-through floor plan with kitchen and dining areas open to and clearly visible from the living room would strike the traditional German family as strange, indeed. Arab homes, on the other hand, are much more open than those in North America. Privacy is obtained not by physical boundaries but by withdrawal from communication, which may simply mean moving outside personal distance. To North Americans who identify their "selves" with their bodies, this intimacy might seem an invasion of their persons. Yet for Arabs, who have had to adjust to higher population densities in which contact with strangers is difficult to avoid, it is adaptive to learn to isolate their sense of personal identity deeper within their bodies than North Americans do.

Kinesics

Nonverbal communication often accompanies speech, providing the context within which speech is interpreted. Signs such as posturing of the body, gestures, and the use of the eyes communicate variations either in a person's interest and involvement in the others present or in the subject being discussed. Nonverbal communication is able to transfer information about emotions such as love, hate, fear, dependency, submission, dominance, interest, disinterest, or boredom. It therefore defines and expresses the nature of the relationships of which the actor is a part. Without the maintenance of a successful nonverbal relationship between people, verbal communication may become impossible. For instance, if their body movements are too unsynchronized with each other or if they indicate hostility, successful verbal communication may be impossible.

The study of the body movements that complement speech as a means of communication is called kinesics. Ray Birdwhistell (1970) has developed a system for recording those movements with precise detail. He has discovered, for instance, that the human face can make a quarter of a million different expressions. For study purposes, 26 symbols are enough to record the basic facial positions. Birdwhistell's system for recording the movements of the entire body uses less than 100 symbols.

Birdwhistell has demonstrated that the ability of the human brain to process visual data about other people's body movements is astounding. He estimates that people are capable of processing as many as 10,000 bits of information or percepts per second. People's nonverbal interaction is subtle and complexly patterned. Birdwhistell's coding of the communicative body movements that people use and respond to involves a recording sheet of at least 100 separate lines for each participant. Each of these 100 recorded items is relevant in the normal communication process, and it requires about an hour's time to record all the information about body movement represented by one second of film. Children obviously have a great deal to learn in order to acquire the complex patterns of nonverbal behavior that are characteristic of their own society.

Some nonverbal signs can be brought under more or less conscious control and become overlaid with symbolic significance that will alter their basic significance as signs. Yet such nonverbal signs are not sufficiently free of their basic tendencies to reflect the emotional state of the actor for them to be used as a productive communication system. A true language is a system of verbal symbols that makes possible the easy translation of concepts into grammatical sequences that represent the relationship between those concepts. This facilitates the transmission of complex messages. By contrast, nonverbal communication tends to be used for the sending of simple, often unconscious messages about one's feelings and about the ideas being expressed in language, if any (Watzlawick, Beavin, & Jackson, 1967).

LANGUAGE

Language is a symbolizing system that does not rely on the expression or acting out of the meanings it represents. Language is therefore said to be an "open" system of communication because its subject matter is unlimited. New messages can be invented to express anything that can be thought. Language can be used not only to communicate emotional responses concerning things or persons being perceived at the moment of communication, but also to talk about nonexisting things and things that are not visible because they are displaced in space or time. Language is a meta communication system—one that can be used to communicate about the process of communication itself. In the following sections, we will examine the distinction between speech and language, the biological basis of humans' capacity for language, the structure of language, the interactions between language and culture, and the processes by which languages change and diverge from each other.

Language vs. Speech

Within the human supply of symbolic skills, language is the most singularly outstanding and systematically organized component. It is formally defined as a verbal system of symbolic communication. It should be noted that by this definition language is not the speech sounds uttered by speakers of a language (Chomsky, 1965). Speech consists of sounds used by communicators as symbols of their conceptual models of reality. Language, on the other hand, is the shared *system* that underlies the act of creating speech sounds in a patterned way. This system is made up of three sets of shared rules: (1) rules for forming the particular speech sounds used in the language, (2) rules for putting the sounds of speech together into words that symbolize concepts, and (3) rules for putting the words together into sentences that portray the relationships between concepts. The existence of a shared system for organizing speech symbols increases the amount of information that can be communicated with those symbols. If speakers could do no more than simply produce an unstructured list of vocal symbols, then a hearer could associate these utterances with a series of mental concepts. Yet the hearer would have no way of deciding which relationship between the communicated ideas the speaker had in mind. Language enables the hearer to accomplish this—to share complex ideas.

When children begin learning language, they not only learn the vocal symbols of the speech which they hear uttered by others around them, but they also discover the meaningful pattern to the arrangement of these speech sounds. The number of sentences that can be spoken in any language is effectively unlimited. But the existence of a system that governs the organization of words into sentences makes it unnecessary for children to actually hear and memorize each separate sentence before they can communicate any idea they wish to express to someone else (Chomsky, 1971). They need only learn a finite number of words and a finite set of grammatical rules for arranging those verbal symbols into patterns that express relationships between the concepts for which they stand. They are then able to arrange and rearrange their words in ways that can communicate ideas and relationships which they had never heard expressed before. In summary, having a socially shared pattern for representing concepts by strings of vocal symbols makes it possible (1) to produce new sentences one has never heard before, (2) to communicate about new concepts, and (3) to interpret correctly new utterances that one hears for the first time.

This is in direct contrast to the sign communication techniques of other animals, which set major limits on their communicative abilities.

Is language unique to the human species? We are now attempting to understand the communication patterns and language potential of other animals including our own closest relatives. Biologically speaking, human beings are members of a group of animals known as *primates*. The other primates are the apes, the monkeys, and the small tree-dwelling prosimians. Biologically, these other primates are more like the human species than are any other animals. As a group, the primates also tend to be social and communicative animals. Nevertheless,

the uniqueness of the human language capacity is apparent when one compares it with the communication systems of the other primates.

According to Altmann (1973), "For the most part . . . the social signals of monkeys and apes are not semantic: the messages do not stand for something else. They are simply social signals to which a response is given. In this they are much more like the cry of a newborn infant than they are like the speech of human adults." Similarly, Marler (1965) observes, "It begins to appear that a repertoire of from about 10 to about 15 basic sound-signals is characteristic of nonhuman primates as a whole. In some it may prove to be smaller or larger, but it is doubtful if the limits will be exceeded by very much. . . . Comparison with other highly vocal groups of vertebrates that have been closely examined reveals an approximately similar repertoire size." Thus, the nonhuman primates do not seem much different

FIGURE 9.6 *Chimpanzee Signing*

In several different experiments chimpanzees have been taught to converse with their trainers using American Sign Language. Here this chimpanzee asks to hug the cat and gets his wish.

from other comparable animals in their vocal communicative abilities. Symbolic language seems to be a distinctively human trait.

In recent years, the limits of nonhuman primate communicative abilities have begun to be explored through attempts to teach various forms of language to chimpanzees (Mounin, 1976), possibly the most similar to human beings in their biological characteristics. These efforts have revealed a striking capacity in chimpanzees to expand their communication skills. One such study was started in 1966 by Allen and Beatrix Gardner (1969, 1985). A major problem in earlier attempts to teach a human language to chimpanzees (Kellog, 1968, Hayes & Nissen, 1971) had been the chimpanzee's difficulty in forming the sounds used in human speech. The Gardners overcame this problem by teaching a modified version of *American Sign Language (ASL)*, the gestural language of the deaf in North America. Chimpanzees naturally make use of a variety of gestures when communicating in the wild, and the Gardner's use of ASL proved to be a breakthrough. Within four years, Washoe had mastered more than 130 signs of ASL. In addition to using signs appropriately to name objects (e.g., dog, flower, or shoe), attributes (e.g., red, dirty, or funny), and actions (e.g., give, want, or drink), Washoe learned to combine signs into sequences such as "give" + "tickle." The Gardners and Washoe's later trainer, Roger Fouts, claim that Washoe has mastered something equivalent to grammar in human language. In six successful studies they believe they have proven that chimpanzees have at least a basic ability to use language in the human sense. Others disagree. Terrace (1979) has worked with chimpanzees and has also analyzed videotapes of human/chimpanzee sign language interaction. He and several colleagues, Terrace, Pettito, Sanders, and Bever, (1979) claim that many of the apparent examples of chimpanzees' combining signs into grammatical sequences are not spontaneous but have resulted from the chimpanzees' responding to subtle cues that the trainers gave. Rumbaugh, Warner, and Von Glasersfeld (1977) began training chimpanzees to communicate by pressing keys embossed with geometric signs. They agree (Savage-Rumbaugh, Rumbaugh, & Boysen, 1980; Savage-Rumbaugh, Pate, Lawson, Smith, & Rosenbaum, 1983) with Terrace that chimpanzees can learn to associate signs with objects and actions and to use signs to make simple requests, but that the chimpanzees that have been taught ASL do not demonstrate a grasp of grammar. Rather, they merely string together any signs they know that are relevant to the situation in which they are making a request. Savage-Rumbaugh and her colleagues (1980:60) assert that the most important difference between chimpanzee communication and that of human children is that chimpanzees make requests but do not spontaneously begin to describe their environment. They make sequences like "give orange me give eat orange me eat orange give me eat orange give me you," but they do not make comments such as "The orange is cold" or "The orange juice is sticky" while they are eating the orange.

On the other hand, in more controlled settings, it has been possible to train chimpanzees to demonstrate some of the skills used in spoken language. Ann and David Premack (1972) have trained a chimpanzee, Sarah, to use colored geometric shapes to express herself. The shapes and colors were unrelated to the objects and processes they represented, and Sarah was able to master abstract concepts such as "same" and "different." She learned the meanings of about 130 geometric shapes and was able to arrange them into the order that words occur in English sentences. Rumbaugh (1977) and Savage-Rumbaugh, Pate, Lawson, Smith, and Rosenbaum (1983) have reported that other chimpanzees, taught to communicate with their trainers using computer-linked keyboards, were able to learn to press the keys in correct sequences, and could recombine the keys into different sequences to express different ideas, both characteristics of human language. They were also able to communicate about things they were not directly observing. These studies suggest that chimpanzees do have many of the capacities that are important in human languages.

Another primate language training study has been carried out by Francine Patterson (1978; see also Hill, 1978) with a gorilla named Koko. Like Washoe, Koko has been taught American Sign Language. Her vocabulary is over 400 words. It includes words for emotions, such as sadness and shame, and Koko can communicate about her own feelings. She has spontaneously used descriptive phrases, such as "finger bracelet" for ring, to refer to things for which she had learned no word from her trainer, an

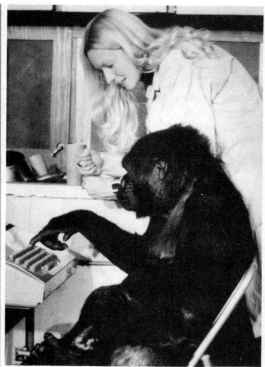

FIGURE 9.7 *Koko Communicating*

Koko, the gorilla made famous by her affection for kittens, has also been taught American Sign Language. Here she is using a computer which synthesizes human speech from symbols.

ability that also had been demonstrated by the chimpanzee Washoe. Koko has been caught lying, when she tried to blame a human for something she had broken. Koko has mastered sign language well enough to take an intelligence test designed for human beings and to score in the low-average range!

We have much to learn about nonhuman primate communication skills—what they have in common with and how they differ from human language. Considering the abilities that nonhuman primates have demonstrated, an intriguing question that remains to be answered is why they have not put these skills to use in the wild, where their communication with one another seems limited to a small number of signs that have very natural expressive meanings. One project now underway that may eventually help us answer questions like this one began at the Institute for Primate Studies in Oklahoma. There, a group of chimpanzees—including Washoe—who have learned American Sign Language were placed together on an island to see how they would use ASL with each other, whether they

would learn signs from each other, and whether their skills would be passed on to the next generation (Linden, 1974). In 1980 the project was moved to Central Washington University where the study of communication between chimpanzees has been continued. Roger Fouts and his colleagues (R. Fouts, D. Fouts, & D. Schoenfeld, 1984) have reported that by 1984 Washoe's adopted offspring, Loulis, had learned 28 signs from her mother. By mid-1986 the number had reached 65 (D. Fouts, personal communication, July 15, 1986).

In evolutionary terms, chimpanzees and gorillas are our closest living relatives. Perhaps they do have the same basic symbolic capacities as human beings, but the controversy about how closely their communication skills parallel our own continues. The communication skills of these nonhuman primates are tremendously impressive, but whether they can use the "languages" they have been taught as symbols and not just as systems of meaningful signs remains to be seen. So far none of the primates in these studies have demonstrated that they have Helen Keller's distinctively human insight that *everything* can be given a name.

The Biological Basis of Language

The exceptional human linguistic ability—an ability that has allowed the creation and perpetuation of complex cultures—is made possible by a biologically inherited, specialized set of structures in the brain. The human brain is a complex affair, as yet imperfectly understood. It consists of three major subdivisions: (1) the brain stem, which regulates involuntary processes such as breathing and heartbeat and controls basic drives such as hunger; (2) the cerebellum, which coordinates muscular activity; and (3) the cerebral cortex, the largest and most recently evolved part of the brain, which monitors the senses, controls mental activities, and initiates voluntary activities (see Fig. 9.8).

The cerebral cortex is the area of the brain that analyzes sensory experiences and initiates conscious action. Seen from above, it is divided in half into two major components or hemispheres. Each hemisphere is creased by numerous folds. The specialized language mechanisms of the cerebral cortex are located

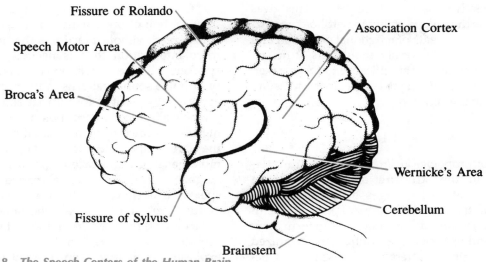

Fissure of Rolando

Speech Motor Area

Broca's Area

Association Cortex

Wernicke's Area

Cerebellum

Fissure of Sylvus

Brainstem

FIGURE 9.8 *The Speech Centers of the Human Brain*

Without the complex structures in the brain, humans wouldn't have the ability to transform sensory experiences into speech. The speech center is located in the left hemisphere of the cerebral cortex. Wernicke's area receives speech sounds and interprets them as meaningful. The association cortex coordinates information from other sensory stimuli to allow the brain to select a proper verbal response. Broca's area, including the Fissure of Rolando, controls the grammatical sequence of words and the physical movements necessary to produce speech.

on only one side of the cerebral cortex—on the left hemisphere for almost all individuals.

Below one of the major creases is Wernicke's area, an area of the cortex that receives incoming information about speech sounds. Wernicke's area seems to be the seat of comprehension of the meaning of speech, for it seems to perform the function of interpreting the meanings of words. This area also is involved in the formulation of verbal messages. Here concepts are apparently translated into their corresponding word representations.

From Wernicke's area, the word information is passed on to a larger region of the cerebral cortex called the association cortex. The association cortex coordinates information from various other parts of the cerebral cortex—such as the hearing centers, the visual centers, and the centers of physical sensation—with the vocal message by providing Wernicke's area with the conceptual information that guides its selection of the appropriate word symbols.

From the association cortex, the linguistic message is sent forward to an area in the front half of the cerebral cortex known as Broca's area. There, it organizes the message grammatically and controls information about the sequences of movements necessary for the production of speech. Broca's area is directly in front of an important fold in the cerebral

cortex known as the Fissure of Rolando, which controls the voluntary movements of various parts of the body. The part of the Fissure of Rolando directly next to Broca's area is the speech motor area. This area controls the movement of the vocal cords, tongue, jaws, and lips. Thus, Broca's area seems to be directly in charge of causing this area of the brain to move the vocal apparatus in the proper sequences to produce the speech sounds of the message.

There are no *direct* connections between the parts of the association areas that deal with vision, those that pertain to hearing, and those that are related to the motor activities of speech. Lancaster (1968) has pointed out that in monkeys and apes the only way of making these connections involves another region of the brain known as the limbic system. The limbic system consists of some of the deeper and evolutionarily older areas of the cortex that deal with emotional experience. This may be why vocal communication in the nonhuman primates such as the apes and monkeys is limited to the expression of internal motivational states. In human beings, on the other hand, indirect connections that do not involve the limbic system (and emotion) can be made between the areas of the association cortex, which are connected with the other sensory centers, and the association areas connected to the speech centers (DeVore, 1965). This gives humans the unique ability to withhold vocalizations in moments of emotional excitement and to communicate vocally about facts of no immediate emotional significance to the speaker, abilities of fundamental importance for symbolic communication.

The Structure of Language

Anthropological linguists who are interested in the structure of languages have shown that all languages have definite patterns in the sounds that their speakers use, in how those sounds are combined to form symbols, and in how those symbols are organized into meaningful utterances. These three structured parts of language are called phonology, morphology, and syntax.

Phonology. Phonology is concerned with the basic building blocks of a language. It is the study of the sounds that are used in speech and the rules for producing the various sequences of sounds that occur in a particular language. The human vocal apparatus is capable of forming a very large number of different sounds. However, the range of sounds actually produced in human languages is relatively small. Although there are at least 3,000 languages in the world, it is possible to record any human language using the International Phonetic Alphabet, a special alphabet that consists of fewer than 100 sound symbols.

The description of a specific language begins by using some of the symbols of this alphabet to record the phones, sounds made by speakers of the language. This record is called a phonetic description of the language. A phonetic transcription of a language records more sound detail than would seem necessary to native speakers. A simple phonetic transcription of verse from the well-known English poem, "The Walrus and the Carpenter" by Lewis Carroll looks like this:

ðə tʰãym hæz kʰãm
ðə wɔlrʌs sɛd
tʰu tʰɔk əv mẽni θĩŋz
əv šuz ænd šɪps
ænd silĩŋ wæks
əv kʰæbəjəz ænd kʰĩŋz
ænd way ðə si ɪz bɔylĩŋ hat
ænd wɛðər pʰɪgz hæv wĩŋz.

One important reason that a phonetic transcription of one's native language is difficult to read without practice is that it records more information than is needed by fluent speakers who are unconscious of many of the predictable sound patterns in their speech. In every language, it is found that some of the phonetically recorded sounds are not meaningfully distinct from one another. Instead, they are simply variants, or allophones of a more general sound called a phoneme of that language. For instance, a native English speaker is likely to say that the letter *t* in the words "top" and "stop" are the same sound. In fact, this is not the case. In the first word the pronunciation of the *t* ends with a definite explosion of air that is not present following the *t* in the second word. This difference can be demonstrated by pronouncing each word while holding the end of a strip of paper against the upper lip. The paper will flutter only when the word "top" is pronounced.

Once it is determined how the phones of a language are grouped into phonemes, it is possible to record the language phonemically using a smaller alphabet designed especially for that language. A phonemic alphabet is made using only one symbol for each phoneme of the language. The phonemes of such alphabets are the units of sound that native speakers of a language think of as different sounds. A phoneme is a psychologically distinct sound of a language in the sense that the meaning of a word will not be changed, in the opinion of native speakers, if one allophone is substituted for another, while substituting one phoneme for another can create a new word. The phoneme is the smallest meaningful unit of sound in a language, in the sense that substituting one phoneme for another can change the meaning of a word. Thus, if the word *stop* is pronounced so that the *t* is followed by the explosion of air found in its allophone in the word *top*, the word will still be heard by listeners as *stop*. However, substituting the phoneme *l* for *t* will create a different word, "slop."

A phonemic alphabet records the distinctions in sounds that are psychologically relevant to the native speakers of a language. It records their language in a way that native speakers are likely to describe as "spelling words the way they sound." In a phonemic transcription of spoken English the word *hiss* would be written as *his*, and the word *his* would be written as *hiz*. Typically, only between 20 to 45 phonemes are necessary for writing a language. English, for instance, has 45 phonemically distinct sounds. Since the 26-letter alphabet used by English speakers for writing their language is not phonemically accurate, English speakers must learn a complex system of spelling to decipher the conventions they use in writing their language.

Grammar. Grammar is the analysis of the regular and predictable ways that the sounds of a language are combined to form meaningful utterances. Grammar has two subdivisions. The first of these is morphology, the study of how phonemes are combined into the smallest meaningful units, called morphemes. *Alligator, love,* and *Arkansas* are morphemes of English. These morphemes are called free morphemes because they can stand alone as words in sentences. English morphemes such as *-s*, meaning "plural," and *pre-,* meaning "before," are called bound morphemes because they cannot serve as words in sentences. Bound morphemes only occur as suffixes or prefixes of other morphemes. Sometimes several morphemes carry the same meaning, for instance *-s*, *-z* (written as an *s* in English), *-en*, and *-ren*—all of which mean "plural." Such morphemes are considered variants of one another, since it is predictable which will be chosen by English speakers to pluralize another morpheme. Thus, *child* combines acceptably only with the plural morpheme *-ren*. Morphemes that carry the same meaning in this way are called allomorphs of one another.

Syntax is the second subdivision of grammar. It is the study of the rules for combining morphemes into complete and meaningful sentences. All languages do an adequate job of expressing meanings, but each language has its own distinctive rules that control how one goes about expressing those meanings. Although we each find the conventions of our own language quite natural, seeing how differently other languages operate can give us some idea of the fact that what seems natural to us as native speakers is merely one of many possible conventions.

Languages such as English use word order to indicate differences between the actor and the acted-upon. For instance, there is an important difference of meaning between the two English sentences, *The dog bit the child,* and *The child bit the dog.* In many languages, the distinction between subject and object is instead indicated by subject and/or object suffixes. For instance, in the Latin sentence *Canis infant-em momordit* (literally, "Dog child-object bit"), the suffix *-em* indicates the object. Languages that distinguish subjects and objects in this way can become quite free in their word order. Thus, in Latin *Infant-em momordit canis* also would be used to mean "The dog bit the child." Often, in languages that do not rely on order to indicate subject-object relations, differences in order may convey differences in emphasis. In the two Latin sentences just used, the first might be translated as "The *dog* bit the child," while the second would be "The dog bit the *child.*" Some languages have special ways of marking an emphasized word. For instance, in the Andean language Quechua the bound morpheme *-qa* indicates the emphasized topic of a sentence: *Alqu wawa-ta-a kʷan-irqa* (literally, "dog child-object-topic bites"), which might be translated as "The dog bites *the child,*" but *Alqu-qa wawa-ta-qa kʷani-n* would be "*The dog* bites the child."

Quechua greatly elaborates the process of modifying single words with suffixes to express complex meanings. Thus, the two-word Quechua sentence *Mana kasu-wa-na-yki-chiq-ri-chu* (literally, "Not obey-me-for-you-plural-nicely-question") means "Is it not for you to obey me nicely?" Other languages such as Chinese use but one morpheme per word, so that the Chinese equivalent of "The dog bit the boy" would be "*Gǒ yǎo le shǎohái*" (literally, "Dog child bite completed"), the time of the action being specified by a particular word *le* that indicates that the action of the verb *yǎo* is completed.

The many languages of the world differ tremendously in their phonologies and grammars. Despite the great diversity in how languages organize a small number of sounds into meaningful sentences, all languages seem equally able to express ideas. As natural as your own language may seem to you after years of use, it is no more fundamentally human in its workings than others. Like all symbolic systems, languages convey meanings effectively simply because their users have learned the same conventions for interpreting those meanings.

Linguistic Relativity

In their study of languages spoken in both simple and complex societies, anthropologists have not found a language that might be described as "primitive." All languages are equally able to be used as vehicles for the expression of complex and intricate ideas. Languages differ from one another simply in the superficial ways of organizing the verbal elements used to express concepts. Individual languages differ in the sounds they use for forming words, but in all languages it is possible to form a new verbal symbol whenever speakers wish to express a new concept. They differ in the order in which they arrange the subjects, verbs, and objects with which they express relationships between the things and processes that all human beings are capable of thinking about. They differ in that some use prefixes where others use suffixes and where still others use separate words instead of either prefixes or suffixes, but one of these methods is as effective as the others in getting the hearer to become aware of some finer aspect of form, quality, or process than the original word symbolizes.

The vocabularies of different languages also differ from one another, but this reflects no difference in the ability of speakers of one language to create, whenever the necessity arises, a new word for a concept already symbolized in the vocabulary of another language (Boas, 1966). Vocabulary differences are simply a reflection of current differences in what needs to be talked about in different social groups. Thus, the vocabulary of English includes terms for electron microscope, short-stop, and hero sandwich, while Navajo has a term *shosh* that means "to place slender stiff objects (like sticks or pencils) side by side (in a parallel position)" and a word, *hózhó*, for "the beauty, harmony, good, happiness, and everything positive or ideal as embodied in the environment as a whole." As circumstances change and a social group acquires new things to talk about, the vocabulary of the language used by that group also changes.

Basic conceptual processes are universal in the human species, and the specific products of these processes, which differ from group to group, can be symbolically expressed in any language. Nevertheless, the vocabulary and grammatical differences of different lan-guages do have an impact on (1) which things will be habitually noticed, labelled, and thought about in a highly conscious way and (2) how speakers will habitually organize their conscious expression of the relationships between these things (Sapir, 1949). The idea that language influences thought processes is expressed in the theory of linguistic relativity, sometimes called the "Sapir-Whorf hypothesis" after two of its originators. According to linguistic relativity, what a people habitually think about is a reflection of what the current vocabulary of their language impels them to notice, and at least some aspects of how people think will be affected by the grammatical relationships demanded by their language. Human thinking, in other words, is not simply a matter of universal biological cognitive processes. Human beings also habitually organize their thoughts in patterns guided by the grammatical structure of their own language. Although language structure does not *determine* how its speakers think, most anthropological linguists recognize that language does have some effects on what we think about most readily and on how we think much of the time.

Effects of morphology. Benjamin Lee Whorf was an originator of the idea that the superficial and arbitrary grammatical patterns that distinguish one language from another influence the ways in which its speakers habitually think about the world. His strongest case is for the effect that the morphology of a language can have on its speakers' tendency to notice some things readily while failing to pay attention to others. For example, Whorf (1971) pointed out that one place in which industrial fires frequently begin is the room in which so-called "empty" containers are stored. The word *empty* is a symbol that refers to two somewhat different concepts: It is used to mean (1) "containing only residues, gases, vapor, or stray rubbish," and also, in a more basic sense, to mean (2) "vacuous, inert, or containing nothing." Those who label the room as a storage area for "empty containers" are using the word in its more specialized association with the first concept, but other persons are likely to behave around these containers of sometimes volatile residues and gases as if they were inert and vacuous. A worker who would never consider lighting a cigarette near a "full" gasoline drum might casually do so near an "empty" one, never stopping to think that the volatile gasoline fumes that remain in the empty containers are much more likely to ignite explosively than is the liquid gasoline of the full containers. According to Whorf, the use of a single symbol that represents two different concepts is not uncommon in hazardous situations.

Whorf (1971) argued that people's names for things often influence how they behave around those things even more than the physical traits of the things themselves. He cited the blower as an example. Physically, a blower is a machine that simply causes air to move. Yet when it is used to make air pass through a room—such as a room for drying materials—because it is called a *blower*, workers are likely to install it so that it *blows* air into the room instead of *pulling* air out of the room. The former method of installation is no more efficient and is much more hazardous, since an electrical fire in the machine itself will be blown into the room where the contents may also ignite. Once begun, the fire will be fanned by a blower installed in this way as long as it continues to function.

Sometimes labels are changed in the hope of avoiding undesirable conditioned responses or of calling forth some hoped-for result. Thus, unpopular wars are called "pacification programs" and the American War Department was renamed the "Defense Department." Similarly, tuna did not become a popular food in the United States until one company began to label it "Chicken of the Sea." And those who wished to support what they called more workable "legal controls" over drug use or prostitution soon recognized that it was better to use such labels for their legislative proposals than to refer to them as attempts to "legalize" these activities. Western science provides a further example of conditioning effects of verbal symbolic labels: European scientists noted that when they "added heat" to an object, its weight did not change. So for years they searched for evidence of other "weightless substances" before they realized that heat, even though it is labeled by a noun, is actually a process rather than a substance.

Effects of syntax. Syntactical processes may also affect how speakers of a language think about the world and how they behave,

although the influence of syntax is probably not so great as the effects of morphology. One finds numerous examples of correlations between a society's customs and values and the grammatical characteristics of its language. For instance, the Navajo language is highly verb-oriented; even inactive verbs have a structure that implies a state achieved by motion. The language describes the universe as kinds of motion to which subjects may attach themselves but for which they are not causally responsible. This feature parallels perfectly the Navajo world view, in which the universe is seen as being in a state of dynamic flux and humankind is seen as subordinate to a more powerful nature, with which humans may interact and to which they may adapt but never master. Similarly, in the Navajo language, it is ungrammatical to use a verb meaning "to cause to do" with a human object. The closest Navajo translation of "I made him go home" would run something like "Even though he did not want to go home, when I asked him to, he did." This is in perfect parallel to Navajo social values, in which coercion is strongly rejected.

Harré (1984) cites examples of Inuit grammar that parallel Inuit ideology. If the Inuit respond to the question "Who is preparing dinner?" their answer, *uva-nga*, does not translate as "I am" but as "The being here-mine." The English "I hear him" becomes in Inuit *tusarp-a-ra*, literally, "his making of a sound with reference to me." In general, where English grammar portrays a person as an "entity" who has attributes and intentions and who intiates actions, Inuit designates a person as the "location" at which qualities and relations occur. This characteristic of Inuit grammar mirrors and supports Inuit social life, in which one's position within the group is much more important than one's characteristics as an individual. Responsiveness to others is the hallmark of Inuit social interaction: When one laughs, all laugh; when one cries, everyone cries. According to Harré, "At least with respect to a large and varied catalogue of public performances, individual feelings, intentions, and reasonings play a very minor role" (p. 88).

Such parallels between syntax and culture are best viewed as systems like that of the chicken and its egg: It is not clear which came first. Syntax may change to reflect the culture in which the language is spoken, but the habits of thought embodied in that syntax may help to maintain conformity to the rules of the culture by making those rules feel very natural to those who speak the language.

An interesting parallel between grammar and ideas is found in English religious literature concerning the existence of God. According to the believer, "Creation itself demands a creator." If one examines this argument in terms of English grammar, it takes on a different significance than is intended when it is used as an argument for the existence of God. *Creation* is formed of two meaningful elements, the root *create* and the suffix *-tion*, which was borrowed from Old French into English. This suffix means "that which has been _____ed." Indeed, many dictionaries define *creation* as "that which has been created," forcing the reader to consult another entry for a complete definition. In English, a noun-focused language, no declarative sentence (one that makes a contention about the nature of some part of reality) may occur without a subject that can carry out the action of the verb used. Therefore, the existence of the verb *create* (which is "demanded" by the existence of the noun *creation*) requires the existence of a noun that can serve as its subject in a declarative sentence. Many nouns can serve as the subject of the verb *create*. However, the noun that corresponds most closely to the verb *create* in the role of subject is the noun *creator*, which is formed of the same root and the Old French suffix *-tor*, which means "one who _____s." Thus, what the argument "Creation itself demands a creator" really indicates is that the existence in English of a noun of the form *crea-tion* implies the existence of a verb *create* which, in turn, requires the existence of a subject noun of the form *crea-tor*. Whether the existence of the universe, which may arbitrarily be labeled with the symbol *creation*, "demands" the existence of a preexisting deity who brought it into existence is another matter entirely. Although English speakers may be swayed by the "logic" of the sentence, this argument for the existence of God loses its impact when it is translated into many other languages.

Language, then, seems to have an effect on the way people relate to the world. It is a conscious vehicle of habitual thought. The vocabulary of any language selects out segments

of reality of which its speakers must become aware when they learn to use their language. And the grammar is a built-in logic system that leads its users to relate the parts of the world to one another in the same way that the grammar organizes the relationships between the words that stand for those parts of the world.

Changes in Language

Since languages are symbol systems and much of the pattern of grammatical organization of a language's verbal symbols is itself generally arbitrary, languages are highly susceptible to change. Language change may occur as the language is passed, by learning, from one generation to the next. A language may also change as its speakers are influenced by their interaction with speakers of other languages. In the following sections, these processes of linguistic change will be described in detail.

Changes over time. Since the sounds used to form the verbal symbols of a language have no necessary connection with the meanings of those symbols, it is possible for both the sounds and the meanings attached to them to change as time passes. Likewise, the customary ways of organizing the verbal symbols into meaningful word order to communicate relationships between the concepts may also change as time passes. Thus, with the passage of time, languages may change in their sound system, their semantic or meaning system, and in their grammatical system. Consider for instance, the differences between contemporary versions of the Lord's Prayer and this Old English version written before the year 1066:

> Faeder ure, thu beube eart on heofonum, si thin nama gehalgod. Tobecum thin rice, Gewurthe thin willa on eordhan swa swa on heofonum. Urne gedaeghwamlican hlaf syle us to daeg. And forgyf us ure gyltas, swa swa we forgyfadh urum gyltendum. And ne gelaed thu us on costnunge, ac alys us of yfele. Sothlice.[2]

2. From *Old English: An Introduction* (p. 19) by Robert J. Kispert, 1971, New York: Holt, Rinehart and Winston. Copyright 1971.

Since language change involves change in the systems that comprise it, the changes show up in systematic or patterned ways. For instance, the change of one sound to a new one expresses itself in every word of the language in which that sound occurs. Compare a list of Old English words of about 1,000 years ago with their modern English equivalents:

Old English	Modern English
hus	house
mus	mouse
ut	out
hu	how

In this list, the Old English *u* represents a sound that would be pronounced approximately as *uw*. Consistently, these same words are pronounced today by English speakers as the vowel sequence *ao*, variously written as *ou* or *ow* in contemporary spelling. That is, the Old English sound *uw* became *ao* in Modern English, consistently changing the pronunciation of all English words in which it occurs.

Subdivisions within a language. Such changes in language occur gradually with the passage of time. Yet, at any given time, the need to communicate effectively within a social group necessitates a certain degree of mutual sharing in the sounds used to form words, in the meanings of words, and in the grammatical patterns for combining them. So, as a language changes, it changes in the same way for all members of the group. However, when a group is subdivided, either geographically or socially, a characteristic of those divisions is the tendency for members of each group to communicate more frequently with members of their own group than with others. One result of such isolation is that new ways of speaking that arise in one of the groups may not pass over into the others. Thus, the language originally spoken in all these groups can gradually change until it is made up of separate dialects (Bloomfield, 1933). For instance, the English now spoken in England differs from the varieties of English spoken in the United States and Australia, although all three varieties developed from the same English that was spoken but a few hundred years ago by emigrants from Great Britain.

Dialects of the same original language can gradually become so different that their speakers are no longer able to understand one another. English and German are examples of two languages that were at one time in history a single language. This language, called Proto-Germanic by modern students of language, was spoken on the mainland of Europe in what is now northern Germany. The people who spoke this language were known as the Angles and Saxons. They left the mainland about 1,500 to 2,000 years ago to become a separate social group in the British Isles where their isolation allowed the language to change in different ways than it did on the mainland. Since the process of change was systematic in both groups, one finds a system of consistent parallels between the two "daughter" languages, German and English. Compare, for instance, the initial sound of the following word lists from German and English, and notice that the German *z* (written as upper case Z in the case of nouns), which is pronounced *ts*, is consistently a *t* sound in English:

German	English
zu	to
zwanzig	twenty
zwölf	twelve
zwitschern	twitter
Zinn	tin

Word-borrowing. Change in language also occurs when words are borrowed by the speakers of one language from other languages with which they come in contact, especially those spoken by their politically and economically more powerful neighbors. Such changes generally involve the borrowing of foreign words for items and activities that are introduced into society by speakers of another language or by interaction with more prestigious speakers of a foreign language. For instance, following the Norman invasion of England in 1066, English speakers began to be influenced by the Old French language of the more powerful Normans. Today, about half of the vocabulary of the English language traces its origins to borrowed Old French words. Approximately two and one half centuries after the invasion, an early historian, Robert of Gloucester (1300) described in his *Chronicle* the effects of the language of the Norman rulers on English:

Thus cōm, lọ, Engelọnd intō Normandïes họnd; And thē Normans ne cōuthe spẹ̈ke thọ bote hor owe spẹ̈che, And spẹ̈ke French as hii düde at họm, and hor children düde alsọ tẹ̈che,

Sọ that heie men of this lọnd that of hor blōd cōme Họldeth alle thülke spẹ̈che that hii of hom nọme; Vor bote a man conne Frenss me to teleth of him lüte. Ac lowe men họldeth tō Engliss, and tō hor owe spẹ̈che zhüte.[3]

(Lo, thus England came into Normandy's hand; and the Normans speak nothing but their own speech, and spoke French as they did at home, and did so teach their children, So that high men of this land that came of their blood Hold the same speech that they received of them; For except a man knows French men speak little of him. But low men hold to English, and to their own speech yet.)

Those English speakers who had the most contact with the Norman rulers began to adopt Old French terms for elements of Norman life, although the speech of the English commoners was less influenced. For instance, contemporary English has inherited a distinction between the cooked and live forms of several meat animals. *Mutton*, *pork*, and *beef* were adopted into English from Old French (*moton*, *porc*, and *boef*) for use when serving foods to the Norman rulers. When the animals were still alive and in the keeping of the English peasants they were called by their original English names, *sheep*, *swine*, and *cow*. These latter three terms have their counterparts, not in French, but in the German words *Schaf*, *Swein*, and *Kuh*, a derivation that reflects the recent separation of English and German from a common ancestral language. Similarly, the word *roast* represents a borrowing from Old French—*rostir*, a verb used by cooks when speaking about preparing meat for their Norman rulers. This aristocratic term did not, however, replace the original English word *bake*, which continued to be used in the peasant households for the same method of preparing meat. *Bake* itself stems from the same original word as the German word *backen*, which means "to bake or roast." Notice that in modern English, one still "roasts pork" (both words being of Old French origin) or "bakes ham" (both Germanic words). Although the

foods themselves and the cooking procedures may be identical, the two idioms reflect two socially different speech contexts (Leaf, 1971).

Basic Vocabulary

The tenacity of these Germanic words for things that were important in households suggests that domestic terminology may be somewhat more stable and resistant to externally induced language change than are other parts of a vocabulary. The part of a language that best reflects its internal history consists of those words that are learned by individuals early in their lives in their home setting. Such words are used frequently in normal speech situations. The habit of their use is not easily overcome, and foreign terms are not likely to supplant them (Gudschinsky, 1964). The part of a vocabulary that has these qualities is known as the basic vocabulary of a language. It includes such words as *father*, *mother*, *brother*, *sister*, *head*, *hand*, *foot*, *eat*, *water*, *drink*, *fire*, *house*, *earth*, *sky*, *sun*, *moon*, *star*, and others that designate basic elements of people's social, biological, and physical environments.

By comparing the basic vocabularies of two languages, it is possible to determine whether they developed from the same common ancestral language, proof that may not be evident in comparing the entire contemporary vocabularies of the languages. For instance, although over 50 percent of the entire English vocabulary is derived from French, the frequency of French words in English does not indicate that both languages arose recently from a common ancestral language. This distinction becomes clear when one examines the English basic vocabulary. In this more stable part of the vocabulary, English words generally have their closest counterparts not in French but in the Germanic languages spoken in the region from which the Anglo-Saxon immigrants to England originally came. The recent common origin of English and German is illustrated by the following basic vocabulary lists:

English	German
father	vater
mother	mutter
brother	bruder
sister	schwester

3. From *A Middle English Reader* (p. 210) by Oliver Farrar Emerson, 1923. New York: Macmillan. Copyright 1923.

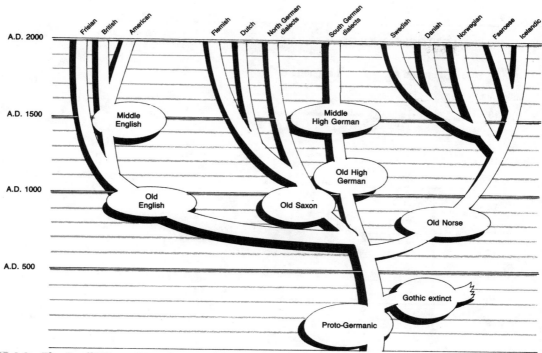

FIGURE 9.9   *The Family Tree of Northern European Languages*

The root or parent language of Northern European languages is called Proto-Germanic. It in turn is derived from an earlier Proto-Indo-European base, the ancestor of many languages in India as well as Europe.

hand	hand
house	haus
mouse	maus
water	wasser
sun	sonne
moon	mond
fire	feuer

Language Families

Such lists of basic vocabulary terms make it possible to compare languages to find how many of these items they share. It is assumed that the more of these stable items two languages share in common, the more recently they began diverging from a single parent language to become separate languages in their own right. Using this assumption, it is possible to reconstruct a family tree of related languages. When one compares the languages of northern Europe by this method, a family tree results that looks like the one in Figure 9.9. The points of branching on this language family tree correspond to major occurrences in the histories of the societies that led to the separation of the speakers of the original language into socially separate subdivisions.

Thus, the point of separation of Old English from the other branches that arose from Proto-Germanic reflects the migration of the Anglo-Saxons from the northern German coast to the British Isles about A.D. 500. After this time the islanders were no longer in intense enough communication with their mainland counterparts to maintain a language unity.

This process of language family tree construction has been used to demonstrate the common ancestry of most European languages and also to show that they are but one part of a family of languages stretching from Europe through India. This family of languages diverged from a single common ancestral language, called Proto-Indo-European by linguists today. It was spoken almost 5,000 years ago. The languages of other parts of the world also have been grouped into similar language families.

A method also has been developed to estimate the minimum number of years since the divergence of any two related languages. The method, called glottochronology, makes it possible to assign dates to the various branches in a language family tree. By comparing the basic vocabularies of languages that

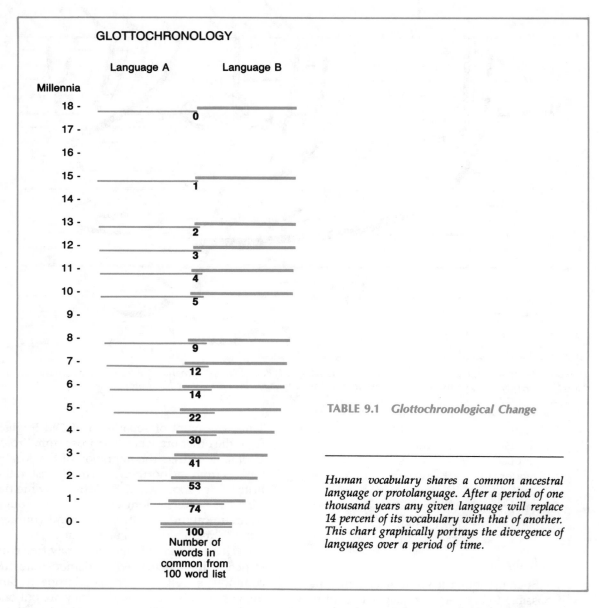

TABLE 9.1 *Glottochronological Change*

Human vocabulary shares a common ancestral language or protolanguage. After a period of one thousand years any given language will replace 14 percent of its vocabulary with that of another. This chart graphically portrays the divergence of languages over a period of time.

belong to different language families and have had long written histories, researchers discovered that about 14 percent of a 100-word basic vocabulary was replaced by new words every 1,000 years in all the languages that have been examined in nonisolated societies (Gudschinsky, 1956). Thus, the rate of change in the basic vocabulary, being a constant, can be used to compute the length of time that two languages have been diverging from one another. Since about 14 percent of the basic vocabulary of a parent language will be lost in any daughter language after a 1,000 years of change from that original state, each daughter language will maintain 86 percent of the original vocab-

ulary. Therefore, 86 percent of whatever items any other daughter language has maintained from that original vocabulary will be found in the base vocabulary of any other daughter language. Consequently, if one compares lists of 100 basic vocabulary items for two contemporary languages and discovers that they share about 74 basic vocabulary items (86 percent of 86 items), then one may calculate that they were in fact a single language 1,000 years ago. Two languages will share about 55 (74 percent of 74) of the original 100 basic vocabulary items after 2,000 years of separation and about 41 items (74 percent of 55) after 3,000 years of separation (see Table 9.1).

Contemporary World Languages

It is estimated that there are at least 3,000 languages spoken in the world today. Some estimates are nearer 5,000. The exact number is difficult to determine because of dialects—geographical or social variants of the same language. The dialects that make up a language can be very similar to one another or so distinct that two linguists might not agree on whether they should be called dialects or separate languages. Consider German and Dutch. Although speakers of Bavarian German dialects would be unable to comprehend the dialect spoken in a German village in Schleswig-Holstein near the border of Denmark, the change from one local dialect to the next is too gradual to claim that there is more than one German language in the country. Similarly, the dialects spoken in small towns on either side of the German and Dutch borders may be so similar that the inhabitants of both towns can understand one another. Yet people speak of German and Dutch as if they were separate languages. In fact, some southern German dialects differ more from the nationally preferred way of speaking the modern standard German "language" (which is mostly based on northern German dialects) than some northern dialects in Germany differ from Dutch.

Some languages are spoken by relatively few native speakers. For instance, only a few thousand people speak Shoshoni today. On the other hand, some languages are spoken by many societies with very different cultures. Such languages may cross the borders of modern nation-states and be spoken by millions of people. For instance, English is one of the official languages of India as well as the native tongue of peoples as geographically distant from one another as England, Canada, South Africa, the Falkland Islands, and Jamaica.

The languages spoken by the largest numbers of people today are those that have become the national languages of major nations. The Beijing dialect (formerly called Mandarin) of China is spoken by about 713 million people. English is the next most commonly spoken language of the world, with about 391 million speakers. Table 9.2 shows the 20 most widely spoken languages of the world as of 1981.

In some parts of the world, many different languages are spoken by people who differ relatively little in their culture. Canada maintains two nationally recognized languages, French and English; political speeches and advertising must be carried out in both. In Nigeria about 400 languages are spoken, of which only 3 have been designated as official languages. Such a diversity of spoken languages can create enormous political problems in administering governmental affairs throughout the country. The elevation of one or more languages to official status is intended to alle-

TABLE 9.2 *The World's Twenty Most Commonly Spoken Languages*

Language	Speakers (in millions)	Language	Speakers (in millions)
1. Mandarin (China)	713	11. Malay or Indonesian	112
2. English	391	12. French	105
3. Russian	270	13. Urdu (Pakistan and India)	70
4. Spanish	251	14. Punjabi (India and Pakistan)	64
5. Hindi (India	245	15. Italian	61
6. Arabic	151	16. Korean	59
7. Bengali (Bangladesh and India)	148	17. Telugu (India)	59
8. Portuguese	148	18. Tamil (India and Sri Lanka)	58
9. German	119	19. Marathi (India)	56
10. Japanese	118	20. Cantonese (China)	54

Note. From *The World Almanac and Book of Facts* (p. 164) by S. S. Culbert, 1982, New York: Newspaper Enterprise Association.

The use of one language by a great many people depends as much on population in a given area as it does on political and national status of the language.

viate some of these problems. Since government business is largely conducted in an official language, speakers of other languages are expected to learn one of the official languages or find an interpreter when they wish to deal with government administrators. Where national languages exist, they are likely to be the ones used in the school system, with the idea of teaching all citizens to use the national language. Although the selection of one of a society's languages as an official one may simplify some of the problems of governing a linguistically diverse country, the designation of an official language is not without its problems. For instance, speakers of a nonofficial language may find themselves at a political or economic disadvantage compared with others who speak the national language. Such circumstances can lead to political rivalries and conflicts that are difficult to resolve.

SUMMARY

The basis for the complexity of human cultures is our ability to form and communicate concepts. Whereas signs are communications that express our feelings directly, symbols are forms of communication in which one thing is arbitrarily used to represent another, according to socially agreed-on and learned conventions. Human communication is highly symbolic and therefore extremely flexible. While some nonverbal messages such as our gestures, facial expressions, body language, and distances from each other are spontaneous signs of our emotions, even nonverbal communications may be symbolic. Verbal communication—language—is totally symbolic, for speech sounds, written words, and ways of arranging them are uniquely and arbitrarily assigned symbolic meanings within each culture.

The capacity for creating and using complex language systems seems to reside within certain areas of the human cerebral cortex. Research suggests that some nonhuman primates may have similar, though more limited, capacities but do not use them unless they are carefully taught to do so. Languages and cultures are so closely linked that the forms and patterns of our speech both affect and reflect how we perceive the world. Languages, like their cultures, change over time and with influences from other cultures and their languages. The part of a language that is most resistant to change is its basic vocabulary, which consists of household words taught and used from childhood. Differences and similarities in basic vocabularies allow linguists to trace the historical growth of language families into the many languages and dialects spoken in the world today.

KEY TERMS AND CONCEPTS

learning 180
neocortex 180
concepts 180
percepts 180
closure 180
ganzfeld phenomenon 183
communication 183
sign 183
symbol 184
nonverbal communication 186
proxemics 188
intimate distance 188
personal distance 188
social distance 190

public distance 190
kinesics 190
metacommunication system 191
speech 191
language 191
American Sign Language (ASL) 193
brain stem 194
cerebellum 194
cerebral cortex 194
Wernicke's area 195
association cortex 195
Broca's area 195
Fissure of Rolando 195
speech motor area 195

limbic system   195
phonology   196
International Phonetic Alphabet
  (IPA)   196
phone   196
phonetic   196
allophones   196
phonemic   196
phoneme   196
grammar   197
morphology   197
morpheme   197

free morpheme   197
bound morpheme   197
allomorph   197
syntax   197
linguistic relativity   198
Proto-Germanic   201
basic vocabulary   202
Proto-Indo-European   203
glottochronology   203
dialect   205

ANNOTATED READINGS

Birdwhistell, R. L. (1970). *Kinesics and context: Essays on body motion communication.* Philadelphia, PA: University of Pennsylvania Press. An exposition of the techniques used for analyzing body movement in nonverbal communication.

Blount, B. G. (1974). *Language, culture and society: A book of readings.* Cambridge, MA: Winthrop. A basic collection of articles on anthropological linguistics in the 1970s.

Burling, R. (1970). *Man's many voices: Language in the cultural context.* New York: Holt, Rinehart and Winston. A basic introductory text about anthropological linguistics.

Carroll, J. B. (1956). *Language, thought and reality: Selected writings of Benjamin Lee Whorf.* Cambridge, MA: M.I.T. Press. The primary writings of Whorf on the effects of language on thought and action.

Greenberg, J. H. (1968). *Anthropological linguistics: An introduction.* New York: Random House. A good nontechnical introduction to anthropological linguistics.

Hall, E. T. (1959). *The silent language.* Greenwich, CT: Fawcett Publications. An interesting look at the rules for nonverbal communications in a variety of cultures.

Hymes, D. (1964). *Language in culture and society: A reader in linguistics and anthropology.* New York: Harper & Row. A collection of seminal writings in the various subfields within anthropological linguistics. Somewhat dated, but still the most comprehensive collection of its kind.

Lenneberg, E. H. (1967). *The biological foundations of language.* New York: Wiley. The basic text on the biological basis of speech.

Linden, E. (1974). *Apes, men, and language.* New York: Penguin. A popular account of the history of work with chimpanzees and American sign language.

Mandelbaum, D. G. (1968). *Selected writings of Edward Sapir in language, culture and personality.* Berkeley, CA: University of California Press. A well-chosen collection of the classic writings of the father of American anthropological linguistics.

R *eligion is an organized system of shared supernatural beliefs, which gives meaning to perplexing parts of human society and its environment, and a system of rituals by which human beings strive for greater control over themselves and their social and natural environments. Psychologically, the beliefs and rituals of a particular religion symbolically express the kinds of stresses and anxieties that are common among the members of that society. In this chapter we will examine both the psychological and the social aspects of religion.*

10

Religion

FIGURE 10.1 *Avalokitśvara, Sovereign Lord of the Universe*

This image of Avalokitśvara is at the Buddhist Tikse Monastery in Ladakh, India. He represents compassion, one of the major aspects of the Buddha's nature. His current incarnation is the Dalai Lama.

Ghosts. Demons. Angels. Witches. Buddha. Shaman. Christ. Do you whistle in the dark as one way of dealing with the unknown silence? Do you sleep with a nightlight? Do you avoid stepping on cracks in the sidewalk or walking under ladders? Do you light candles to ward off the demons of darkness in your soul or your world? Every culture has evolved a system of symbolic beliefs and rituals which it uses to define its place in the universe.

209

THE DEFINITION OF RELIGION

Religious beliefs and rituals take so many forms across the world that anthropologists have found it difficult to define religion in a way that encompasses them all. Aspects of a global definition of religion include belief in supernatural beings and power, symbolic expression of feelings, and ritualized behaviors.

Belief in Supernatural Beings

Over a century ago, Sir Edward Burnett Tylor (1871) attempted one of the first anthropological definitions of religion as the belief in supernatural beings, such as the soul, ghosts, spirits, and gods. It was Tylor's belief that religion served an important role in providing human beings answers to perplexing questions, such as the cause of unconsciousness, sleep, dreams, and hallucinations. Early humans, he contended, created the idea of the soul to account for such phenomena. Unconsciousness, fainting, sleep, and even death could be explained as the soul's departure from the body; dreams are memories of the soul's experiences as it travels outside the body during sleep; and visions or hallucinations are simply apparitions of souls and other spirit beings, for the idea of the soul implied the possibility of other spiritual entities, such as ghosts, genies, angels, and gods.

Although Tylor's views were useful in pointing out the role that religion plays in providing people with ways of understanding parts of their experiences for which they have no pragmatic explanations, his perspective was narrow in its concern for the intellectual aspect of human functioning. For Tylor, a nineteenth-century Victorian scholar, religion was a product of the human intellect. Its relationship to human emotional life was of less interest to him.

Belief in Supernatural Power

An even greater limitation of Tylor's definition was its ethnocentric narrowness in excluding from the realm of religion the belief in formless supernatural powers. Robert Marett (1909) raised this criticism of Tylor and introduced the Melanesian word _mana_ to refer to the concept of spiritual power. _Mana_, which

FIGURE 10.2   *Serpent-Handlers*

In trying to control the forces of evil in their lives some sects actually learn to handle venomous snakes. This serpent-handler in Appalachia, West Virginia, takes her power from New Testament Scripture which says the followers of Jesus will not be harmed.

might be thought of as a kind of supernatural electricity, may reside in objects such as a rabbit's foot, a four-leaf clover, in powerful natural phenomena such as thunderstorms, or in anything strange, rare, or dangerous. In doses too large, it can cause harm, illness, or even death, but properly channeled it can be used by human beings to accomplish ends that are unattainable by other means. _Mana_ can increase one's luck, skill, and ability to gain knowledge of hidden things. _Mana_ is the force behind magic; it is the holiness in the ground around the burning bush; it is the sacredness of the Host in the Eucharist; it is Luke Skywalker's Force. As the embodiment of spiritual power in its rawest form, _mana_ inspires the sense of awe and reverence that people of every religion experience when they perceive themselves to be in the presence of the Holy. Though _mana_ makes things more powerful than they normally would be, it does not come and go of its own accord. Like its secular equivalent, electricity, it must be manipulated by human beings to benefit from its power. However, unlike electricity, the manipulation of _mana_ is accomplished through rituals.

Mana is one of the simplest and most widespread of religious ideas. Marett believed that the concept of *mana* was a more primitive religious idea than that of spirits. He asserted that it was therefore a more ancient religious idea, one that arose not from intellect but from the sense of awe and fear that is inspired by the unusual or the strange.

Where *mana* plays a prominent role in religion, the concept of taboo is also likely to be important. A taboo is a rule that forbids contact with sacred or dangerous things, those filled with so much *mana* that careless contact with them may harm the unwary. The term was derived from a Polynesian word, *tapu* or *tabu*, which means both forbidden and sacred. Polynesian chiefs were sacred, and their bodies contained so much *mana* that it was taboo for commoners to touch them, since to do so might kill an ordinary person. *Mana* and taboo need not be immediately involved with beliefs about spirits or gods, so Tylor's definition failed to encompass an important aspect of religious practice and ideology. Marett broadened Tylor's definition to include *mana* by defining religion as the belief in supernatural things in general.

THE ARK OF THE COVENANT

The protection afforded by taboos is well illustrated by a story in Exodus about the Ark of the Covenant. The ark was a sacred box of acacia wood overlaid with gold. Its top was crowned with a throne for God. In the ark were kept the most sacred things of the Israelites: the Tables of the Law, a pot of manna (food miraculously provided to the Israelites in the wilderness), and Aaron's staff. So sacred was the ark, so full of spiritual power, that it was not to be touched by human hands. The ark was transported by authorized priests who carried it with poles that were passed through rings mounted on the sides of the ark. On one occasion when the ark was being transported on a cart, the oxen stumbled and the ark began to fall. Uzzah, a soldier, tried to prevent the ark from falling, but when his hand touched the box he died. His good intentions offered no protection from the terrible sacredness of the ark which was taboo for good reason.

His death followed his act, not as punishment for a sinful act in any moral sense but as effect follows cause in the world of *mana*.

Recently, a number of anthropologists have addressed the problem of clarifying some ambiguities of the word supernatural, which has almost always been a central element in Western anthropologists' definitions of religion. Traditionally, the supernatural has been understood to be a realm which transcends that of the natural senses. It consists of things that are believed to be very powerful but that do not seem to conform to the normal laws that govern the behavior of things in the world of everyday experience. Since the dichotomy between a natural and a supernatural realm has long played a central role in the distinction between science and religion in Western culture, few have felt that the term "supernatural" needed further clarification. However, Cohn (1967) has pointed out that the distinction between a natural and a supernatural realm is not made in most of the world's religions. Neither is there a word in most of the world's languages that translates as "religion." How, then, have anthropologists decided to call behavior religious when they were studying cultures in which there is no word for religion and no explicit concept of a supernatural realm?

Anthropologists have adopted several different ways of coping with the difficulties that a concept of the supernatural creates when it is used as the central feature in a definition of religion. One approach has been to find an alternative concept to use as the hallmark of religion. Another has been to broaden the idea of religion by dropping the concept of the supernatural from its definition. An example of the former approach is found in the work of Stewart Guthrie (1980), who undertook a major survey of the studies of religion and showed that the common denominator in religious thinking is anthropomorphism—assigning human qualities to that which is not human. It is, according to Guthrie, the systematic use of anthropomorphism to create beliefs in those beings and powers that traditionally have been called supernatural that is the essence of religious thinking. Thus the word *anthropomorphism* can take the place of *supernatural* in a definition of religion: a system of (1) beliefs in which the nonhuman realm is portrayed as having humanlike qualities including the ability to respond to symbolic communication, (2) feelings related to those beliefs, and (3) ritual practices that elicit and control those feelings and are carried out either to portray the beliefs or to influence the universe by symbolic communication.

Symbolic Expression of Feelings

The second approach to bypassing the problem of the supernatural, that of dropping the concept altogether, usually involved emphasizing the emotional side of religion over its cognitive aspect. This view of religion saw it as an expression of feelings, not beliefs. An early example of such an approach to religion is embodied in the work of the French anthropologist Emile Durkheim (1915) who focused on the sacred feelings that religion creates in a community of people. By sacred, Durkheim meant the feelings of awe, respect, or reverence that were inspired by things that were set apart and forbidden. Durkheim was concerned with the question of what lies at the roots of religious ideas and what maintains them through the generations. He suggested that religious ideas are symbolic representations, metaphors of those aspects of society and culture that inspire feelings of respect, fear, and awe. Durkheim believed that by maintaining and manipulating these feelings in symbolic form, religion perpetuated the sentiments that people must have toward their society if it is to survive. Thus, for Durkheim, religion was society's symbolic worship of itself.

A more recent definition of religion that emphasizes its role in expressing feelings to lend stability to society is one still used by many anthropologists that was formulated by Geertz (1966): "A religion is (1) a system of symbols which acts to (2) establish powerful, pervasive, and long-lasting moods and motivations in [people] by (3) formulating conceptions of a general order of existence and (4) clothing these conceptions with such an aura of factuality that (5) the moods and motivations seem uniquely realistic" (p. 4). By elim-

inating the concept of the supernatural from his definition, Geertz has broadened the traditional concept of religion to include any ideological system that people turn to as the ultimate source of their most deeply held feelings. Geertz's definition emphasizes important similarities in the deep commitment and behavior of followers of theologies such as Islam or Christianity and of adherents of political ideologies such as Marxism.

Geertz's approach, like that of Durkheim, focuses on the role of religion in validating people's allegiance to their society and culture. With this definition, Geertz reminds us that the purpose of these ideologies is to help people perceive the world as their value system teaches them it ought to be. Religion, in this view, consists of important symbols that affirm culturally valued beliefs by providing people with ritual settings in which those valued beliefs seem to be true. According to Geertz, it is by participating in religious rituals that people repress any contradictions between the world as it ought to be and the world as it is, since the symbolism of the rituals they perform make sense only if their beliefs are true. This is why political and religious ideologies that offer people a way of understanding themselves and the world around them represent ultimate truths by those who espouse them.

Ritual Behaviors

Other anthropologists have shifted their interest away from both beliefs and feelings toward the ritual behaviors that are always a part of the practice of religion. Ritual differs from other sorts of behavior in three important ways: it is symbolically meaningful and is often performed in a repetitive, stereotyped, and predictable way, with the intent of manipulating nature through the power of symbols rather than by mechanical means. Typical of those who view ritual as the central element of religion is Anthony F. C. Wallace (1966), who contends that ritual is the central element of religion performed to bring about or to prevent changes in human beings or in nature. Religious beliefs give meaning to the rituals by explaining and interpreting them and by directing the energy of the ritual performance.

Religion: A Summary Statement

In spite of the various emphases that different anthropologists have had in their approaches to religion, the various definitions which they have proposed agree that a full description must include consideration of at least four major factors: Religion is a social phenomenon; it includes an ideological component of beliefs; it inspires special feelings; and it manifests itself in rituals. When a social group shares a religion, it shares beliefs that differ from the ordinary day-to-day beliefs that grow out of a mechanistic view of things. Religious beliefs portray the world anthropomorphically rather than scientifically. They postulate a world of human-like beings and powers: Gods, angels, demons, ghosts, or forces that respond to symbols. Religion always inspires special feelings, usually of awe and dread that are associated with unusual things regarded as sacred or holy. Finally, people manifest their religious beliefs and feelings in rituals, those ceremoniously performed behaviors that express ideas and feelings about sacred things. The rest of the chapter will examine each of these different elements of religion. Religious ideology, the realm of beliefs and feelings, will be examined first. Religious ritual will be discussed next. This will be followed by an overview of the social organization of religion. Finally, the question of why religions seem to be found in all of the cultures of the world will be addressed.

IDEOLOGY IN RELIGION

Religious ideology, the realm of religious beliefs and sentiments, has fascinated writers for centuries. The religious beliefs of different societies are extremely diverse, more so than any other aspects of cultural ideologies. Variability in nonreligious beliefs is directly constrained by their immediate practical results. An oar must be an effective tool for moving a small boat through the water, so ideas about how to build and use an oar do not differ greatly from one society to another. Feminine and masculine roles may vary across cultures and time, but all cultures must call attention to at least the biological distinction between male and female or become extinct. Cultures with

automobiles may direct their drivers to drive on the left or the right sides of streets; simply allowing drivers to decide spontaneously how best to pass oncomers would probably be too costly to any society. Religious belief is more insulated from such practical considerations, but variations between religions do seem to have some relationship to the people's varying social, technological, and environmental circumstances.

Diversity of Beliefs

Consider first some examples of religious diversity. Chastity, sexual fidelity, and even celibacy are venerated in some religious traditions. But if you were to visit a certain part of India, you would find people for whom sexual intercourse is a means of attaining the highest state of spiritual ecstasy and among whom temple dancers share themselves sexually with the devotees as a sacred act. Not all witches fly on broomsticks. The Nyakyusa, a farming and herding people of Tanganyika, believe that there are witches living as pythons in the bellies of their human victims, whose insides they gnaw away to satisfy their cravings for flesh (Wilson, 1951). Cannibalism was a sacred act among several peoples in the not too distant past, notably among the Kwakiutl of the British Columbia coast where the Cannibal Society was the highest ranked religious association. Among the Aztec of Middle America, cannibalism may have played a role in the system of human sacrifice by which the Aztec gods were placated. Estimates of how many people—mostly enemy soldiers—the Aztec sacrificed to the gods and then devoured every year, range from about 15,000 to 250,000 people.

Souls? They come in many sizes and shapes. Among the Shoshoni of the American Great Basin, the soul was thought to be shaped like a small ball of feathers that resided in the forehead. The Jívaro, who were native to the forests of Ecuador, believed that a person might have three kinds of souls: the *nëkás*, the *arutam*, and the *muisak*. The *nëkás* was an ordinary soul that resided in the bloodstream and perpetuated the individual's personality after death. The *arutam* was a power-conveying soul that had to be acquired by prayer and fasting. It protected the possessor from death

FIGURE 10.3 *Aztec Human Sacrifice*

Cannibalism may be one way for a society to impose order on chaos, to regenerate itself or to communicate with the supernatural. Recent evidence indicates that Aztecs sacrificed humans to placate their gods and engaged in ritual cannibalism. This drawing from the Codex Florentino (ca. 1577) shows the sacrifice of a captive warrior impersonating Tezcatliopoca.

FIGURE 10.4 *Thaipusam Ceremony*

One manner of honoring the gods in certain societies is by self-sacrifice. This man, with a skewer through his cheeks, is participating in the Thaipusam festival at Kuala Lumpur, Malaysia, honoring the Hindu war god Subrahmanya.

unless it was first lured away by magic. The *muisak* was an avenging soul that came into being only at the death of a powerful warrior who had a special kind of power-conveying soul. Once it was formed, it sought to kill the murderer.

Many people have worshipped both female and male deities. Others have venerated various types of animals or worshipped deformed children or other humans as deities. The adherents of some North American religions believe themselves immune to poisons, the bites of venomous snakes, or the weapons of enemies as long as they exercise sufficient faith, practice the rituals of their religion assiduously, or wear the proper charms. The possibilities of religious belief and obligation have been limited only by the bounds of human imagination. From the unicorns of medieval European folklore to the cannibalistic stone giants of contemporary Shoshoni stories, if it can be imagined, it has probably been a part of the religious ideology of some people somewhere.

The Adaptive Basis of Religious Beliefs

The view espoused in this text is that differences in religious ideologies must be accounted for as adaptations of culture to differing social, technological, and environmental circumstances. Religious ideology that conflicts too greatly with the nonreligious beliefs and values of a culture, including its survival strategies, will not be readily adopted by the people. For this reason there is a predictable degree of harmony between a people's religion and the rest of their culture.

One famous proponent of this view, Leslie White (1971), contended that the degree to which people view the world around them in religious terms is inversely related to the complexity of their technology. The more complex the technology, the more they relate to the world in mechanistic rather than spiritual ways. In other words, as people develop direct, pragmatic control over their environment, they may become less likely to seek help from supernatural powers. Growth in technological complexity also tends to accompany growth in population and increasing social complexity and specialization. These factors make it increasingly likely that people will feel lost in a sea of strangers, lacking the power they would like to have in day-to-day social life. When such people are alienated from society, they are less likely to believe in the supernatural. Since religion is a system of rituals wherein people reaffirm their commitment to the fundamental goals and values of their society, stresses experienced by the socially alienated tend to be channeled into coping mechanisms other than the society's traditional religion.

Social structure also may affect religious ideology. Guy Swanson (1960) has tested the notion that religious beliefs are symbolic representations of what he calls the "sovereign groups" of society, the groups that have "original and independent jurisdiction over some sphere of life" (p. 20) and, thereby, the power to inspire respect and compliance in their members. Using a sample of 50 societies from around the world, he found that strong statistical relationships existed between several common religious doctrines and social traits that could logically be expected to be symbolized by those doctrines.

Swanson found that monotheism, the belief in a high god, a supreme being who either created and ordered the universe or at least maintains order within it now, is most likely to be found in societies in which the sovereign, decision-making groups are organized hierarchically so that one of them is superior in rank to at least two levels of groups below it. In such societies, one sovereign group, like a supreme god, can create and maintain order among subordinates.

Polytheism is the belief in superior (but not supreme) gods who control major parts of the universe, such as the weather, the oceans, or agriculture. According to Swanson, polytheism reflects specialized purposes in human affairs. A society with many unranked occupational specialties is more likely to have a polytheistic religion than is a society with few such specialties. Similarly, societies with social classes are more likely to have polytheistic religions than are egalitarian societies, since the purposes of different social classes differ one from another. For instance, traditional Indian society with its hereditary social castes

and numerous jati occupations had equally diverse specialized polytheistic deities.

According to Swanson's research, ancestral spirits remain active in human affairs when the kinship organizations that perpetuate the purposes and goals of their deceased members are more complex than the transitory nuclear family. Belief in reincarnation is most common in societies in which continuity from one generation to the next is maintained by small, isolated groups whose members are economically interdependent and occupy a common settlement smaller than a village. Belief in some form of human soul, the embodiment of an individual's personality and personal memories, is almost universal. But Swanson distinguishes between societies in which the soul is believed to be lodged in the individual's body and those in which the soul transcends the body. People are more likely to believe in souls that are intimately tied to the individual's body if they live in societies that have: (1) many different sovereign groups to which everyone must belong, (2) situations in which individuals with conflicting objectives that cannot be reconciled by such means as courts must work together as a group, (3) situations in which groups of individuals whose relationship is not based on their common consent must function as a group to achieve the members' common goals, (4) large-sized settlements, (5) debts, or (6) no sovereign kinship group. All these social traits increase the degree to which individuals are set apart from each other.

Although all societies have moral and ethical rules that govern the conduct of individuals toward each other, not all societies use the threat of supernatural punishments for the violation of their moral rules. Supernatural sanctions for violations of moral rules are most common where interpersonal differences in wealth are prominent, that is, where different groups within society benefit unequally from those rules.

According to Swanson, sorcery—the use of rituals to harm another person supernaturally—is most common in societies in which individuals must interact with each other but in which socially approved means for one individual to control another do not exist. In an earlier study of sorcery, Beatrice Whiting (1950) showed that sorcery was most likely to be practiced in societies that lack "individuals or groups of individuals with delegated authority to settle disputes" (p. 90) and in which retaliation by peers is the main tool of social control. In addition, beliefs in sorcery and witchcraft—a related phenomenon in which the evildoer has an innate ability to harm others without using rituals—are most common in societies that engender severe anxiety about the expression of aggression or sexuality in children during their socialization (Whiting and Child, 1953).

INDIA'S SACRED COW

Religious beliefs often serve practical purposes, though these purposes may not be obvious. Such is the case with the sacred cows of India.

Since the British colonial occupation of India, the English phrase "sacred cow" has stood for any custom that is maintained in spite of all rational reasons for its change. The zebu cow, held sacred by Hindus of India, symbolizes gentleness, life, and India itself. The cow is so greatly revered that its protection was written into the constitution. The cow may be neither killed nor molested as it wanders the streets. To the British, for whom cattle were an important food resource, it seemed the height of folly for a society in which hunger and even starvation were significant social problems to support cow reverence instead of cow eating. In spite of the thinly veiled ethnocentrism in this opinion, there is some intuitive merit to the idea that protection of the cow is irrational when its use as food might alleviate a major social problem.

Marvin Harris (1974), who believes that the material conditions of life have a greater impact on an ideology than an ideology

FIGURE 10.5 *Sacred Cow of India*

The cow is sacred to Indians because it is economically and ecologically more sound to preserve it than to slaughter it. A curious sight to Westerners is the cow sharing the road with automobiles and the sidewalk with people.

does on those conditions, has argued that the custom of cow reverence is integrated with other facts of Indian life in such a way that using cows for food would create more problems than it would solve. Those whose only contact with cattle is the meat section of their local supermarket may be unaware of the great expenditure of resources that goes into the raising of cattle as food. In the United States, for instance, beef cattle are fed from farm-grown foods. Three fourths of the agricultural land in the United States is devoted to growing food for cattle. Since American farmers still are able to produce sufficient food for domestic consumption and export, this cost is well within their means. In India, though, the establishing of this kind of beef industry would remove acreage from the production of food for human beings. The result would be the displacing of millions of farmers and an increase in food costs and hunger.

Indian farmers pen their cows at night but allow them to wander the streets during the day, scavenging their own food. Eating the weeds and plants they find along the way, the cows consume things that are not edible to humans for about four-fifths of their diet. The custom of permitting cows to range freely greatly reduces the amount of labor and feed that farmers must devote to the upkeep of their animals. Allowing cows to wander the streets and fostering cow love benefits the poorest farmers who otherwise could not afford to own a cow or keep it during times of hardship.

Although the cow is not food for its owner, it is an important part of that farmer's means of food production. Teams of oxen are harnessed to pull plows. Cows are milked to provide a small amount of milk for their owners and a few milk peddlers. Cattle also produce dung, which is valuable as fertilizer and fuel in India, a country with little oil, coal, or wood. Cattle dung takes the place of expensive petrochemical fertilizers. It also is burned within the home. Finally, when cattle die from natural causes, the meat is not wasted, for most of it is eaten by members of the lowest castes. The custom of cow worship ensures that the meat reaches the tables of those who could least afford to buy it if it were a market item sought by all.

Perhaps someday beef will be routinely eaten in India, but under current circumstances beef-eating would not be cost-effective, whereas cow reverence is. Far from being a case of the irrationality of religious symbols, the sacredness of the zebu cow in India reflects the real importance of the cow as a resource and means of livelihood in India under the current economic conditions.

Mythology and Legends

Myths are religious stories that recount the origins of things. They explain such things as the history of the gods, how the universe came to be, how human beings, animals, and plants were created, how human ways of life began, the origin of death, and the nature of the afterlife. Usually myths are placed in the distant past and involve supernatural beings. For example, the Shoshoni of the Great Basin desert tell a myth of a time when the sun was so close to the earth that people were dying and the plants of the earth were burned up so there was no food to be found. Cottontail, one of the creatures of the earth, determined to kill the sun and set things right. He took some rocks as weapons and traveled toward where the sun rises until it got too hot for him. Then he began to burrow until he got to his destination. He made a hunting blind and waited until the sun came up. When the sun arose, Cottontail threw a rock at the sun and killed him. It was so hot that Cottontail was scorched, which left him brown, as he is to this day. After a while, the sun revived, but Cottontail removed the sun's gallbladder and told the sun that he must go up higher in the sky so that all people might have light to gather food, but not be burned. Out of the sun's gallbladder, Cottontail fashioned the moon, which also went up to the sky. Since the moon turned out basket-shaped, it is not always round in the sky, but shows phases, depending on which side is facing the earth.

Legends are much like myths, and it is not always easy to decide whether a particular story is best classified as a myth or as a legend. In general, the distinction between myths and legends is that legends usually deal with a more recent period of time than myths, and the central characters of legends are heroes and heroines of great stature who are responsible for the beginnings of a particular society. Although they are usually regarded as real persons, these heroines and heroes are often thought to possess superhuman qualities and to embody the central values of their society. The legendary figures of American culture are noted for their individualism, self-reliance, strength, and cleverness. They stand up for their ideals against great odds, triumphing over adversity. George Washington is one American legendary figure who actually existed. Yet time has endowed him with stature somewhat above that of a real person. He is remembered in American folklore as being unable to lie even as a child. At one time, it was said that he was strong enough to have thrown a silver dollar across the Rappahannock. In many parts of the country, the river in this story has become the much wider Potomac. Other American legends are based on purely fictional characters, like Paul Bunyan, whose exploits included the creation of Puget Sound.

Religious Feelings

Supernatural things are believed to be a source of great power that can be influenced for human ends. Whether perceived as gods, spirits, or mana, they have the quality of being both nonhuman yet human-like in their response to symbols. Because they are both powerful and mysterious, they are capable of inspiring strong feelings in humans who approach them. Rudolf Otto (1923) described these intense feelings as the uncanny or eerie sense of awe and dread that people sometimes experience when they are confronted by mysterious things. Such feelings are easily interpreted as a perception of a transcendent, supernatural presence that often inspires ambivalent feelings. They can fascinate even while they are feared since they are a source of great power that can both benefit and destroy those who approach.

Religion can be an ecstatic experience as well as a dreaded one. The "religious thrill" of the ecstatic experience is often associated with trance and is typically thought of as being caused by the overpowering presence of supernatural beings or power. Religious ecstasy is accompanied by unusual behaviors such as convulsions and glossolalia, a behavior that can vary from groaning to uttering unintelligible sequences of sounds that are commonly called "speaking in tongues" by followers of

FIGURE 10.6   *Ghost Dance Shirt*

The Ghost Dance ritual originated among the Plains Indians in the 19th century as a response to the encroachment of the white man on Indian lands. In each version of the dance the idea was to destroy the white man and bring back to life the spirit of the dead Indians. The Sioux warriors wore Ghost Dance shirts in the belief they would be protection against bullets.

some North American religions, such as the Holiness churches. Similar ecstatic states have been described in non-Western cultures. For instance, Benedict (1934) described the dance of an initiate into the Cannibal Society, the most sacred society of the Kwakiutl Indians of British Columbia: "He danced wildly, not able to control himself, but quivering in all his muscles in the peculiar tremor which the Kwakiutl associate with frenzy" (p. 180). Similar behavior is found in the spirit possession trances of many cultures around the world, such as the Shoshoni and Koreans whose possession trances are exemplified later in this chapter.

RITUAL IN RELIGION

Of the many cultural arenas in which ritual behavior is common, such as play and art, religion is the most publicly encouraged system for the ritual expression of people's concerns and anxieties.

This section will examine the three main roles of ritual in religion: (1) to unite a community emotionally, (2) to portray or act out important aspects of a religion's myths and cosmology, and (3) to influence the spiritual world and thereby the natural world for human beings or, conversely, to help human beings adjust to the conditions of the natural and spiritual realms. These roles of ritual as symbolic communication may be present simultaneously in a single ritual and are not always clearly distinguished in the minds of the participants themselves.

Ritual as Communitas

Victor Turner (1969) has emphasized the role of ritual in helping people achieve a sense of unity with each other, a kind of social relationship that he calls communitas. During the state of communitas, the normal structure and hierarchy of society is forgotten and members of the group experience themselves as a community of equals whose individuality may even be submerged into a general sense of fellowship. According to Turner, every society needs the experience of communitas as a source of deeply felt bonding and allegiance—a kind of "mystery of intimacy" (p. 139)—between the members of the group. However, communitas is also potentially dangerous and disruptive to society, since it challenges the basic structure of social hierarchy, rank, and power differences as they are usually experienced in day-to-day interaction. The dangers that communitas might otherwise pose to society's power structure are restrained by the fact that this state is typically achieved only during the ritual process.

Rituals, Turner noted, are often described as having three phases. In the first phase, sometimes described as a period of "separation," the participants in the ritual literally may be removed from their normal place of work to a place set apart for the purpose of disentangling themselves from the web of symbols that define the ordinary reality of their culture. The second phase of a ritual is often described as a period of pilgrimage within a spiritual landscape. Turner calls the transition stage between the beginning and end of a ritual the liminal period. It is during the liminal phase of a ritual that communitas is characteristic of the participants' feelings toward each other. Finally, participants in rituals are returned to an awareness of the mundane world of normal social life during the phase of reintegration. This tripartite pattern of ritual is particularly common in the rites of transition which societies commonly use to mark the status changes that occur during the life cycle. However, liminality, the state of being "betwixt and between," is also found in social settings where people experience themselves as marginal or inferior in the eyes of others. Thus, people with low ranked or marginal social statuses—such as slaves, prostitutes, or street people—may experience a strong sense of camaraderie such as is experienced by mainstream members of society only during the ritual process.

Ritual as Portrayal

Religious ideologies always include myths, beliefs about the activities of spiritual beings and powers, especially at the beginnings of things. The symbolism of rituals often portrays several such stories simultaneously. For instance, the Christian ritual that is sometimes called the Sacrament of the Lord's Supper, in which wine and broken bread are shared by members of a congregation, may remind them of the final meal that Jesus and the disciples had together before Jesus' arrest and crucifixion. At the same time, the broken bread and the wine may symbolize or become the body and the blood of Jesus, who Christians believe died as a vicarious sacrifice on behalf of humankind. In addition, the ritual may represent purification and renewal of the spiritual bonds that unite members of the congregation with their religion as they receive and eat the sacramental meal. Similarly, the baptism by immersion that is practiced in some Christian churches may represent simultaneously: a washing away of sin; a portrayal of the death, burial, and resurrection from the dead that most Christians believe Jesus experienced; the spiritual death and renewal by which the individual enters the Christian religion; or the individual's own future death, burial, and hoped-for reawakening to a life beyond the grave. Part of the beauty of a ritual for its participants lies in the multiplicity of meanings it may have for them, a characteristic that may give them the feeling that the ritual embodies meanings transcending those of ordinary symbols.

Ritual as Influence

In their attempt to influence the spiritual or natural worlds for the sake of human beings, some rituals are believed to be coercive in their effect. Others are thought to be more like requests for aid. Usually, rituals are more coercive in nature when people feel an urgent need for more control over events than they have by nonreligious means. The most coercive rituals are known as magic. Magical rituals are often performed with mechanical precision and careful attention to details, especially when the successful outcome of the magical act is crucial to the performers.

Sir James Frazer (1922) noted long ago that magic the world over seems invariably to make use of the same two principles: imitation and contagion. Imitative magic uses a principle called the Law of Similarity by anthropologists. This principle seems to be based on the idea that acts that are similar to the desired outcome increase the probability of its occurrence. Magical rituals that follow this principle imitate the thing that they are designed to bring about. Christians who immerse a convert in water to "wash away sin" and Pueblo who whip yucca juice into frothy suds to "bring rain" are both making use of the Law of Similarity. So is the American child who takes care to step over the cracks in the sidewalk, following the admonition in the childhood rhyme, "Step on a crack, and you break your mother's back"—in which there is a similarity in the sound of the words "back" and "crack" and in the appearance of the line of sidewalk blocks and the line of vertebrae in the spinal column.

SHOSHONI LOVE MAGIC AND THE LAW OF SIMILARITY

During my fieldwork on an eastern Nevada reservation, one 65-year-old Shoshoni informant described Shoshoni love magic or, as he called it, "girl medicine." His description made it clear that the concept of similarity was a rationale for the ritual actions involved:

Weasel is used for girl medicine. It is good. You take the heart out before it is dead and talk to it. You take it off someplace by yourself and talk to it. . . . You put it under your pillow for five nights, to dream about girls. The heart is mixed with *pisappih* [red face paint clay] all ground up. If you don't dream something about girls, it won't work, so you throw it away. If you do, it will work.

If you see a girl you like, but she won't pay attention to you, get a little piece of rock about half the size of your fingernail and put the medicine on the rock. Then go by her and hit her with it. When she feels it, that's a ghost. For half an hour or so, you walk around where she can see you. Then after a while she's getting worse and worse. After a while she follows you and talks to you. That's how you catch a girl, the oldtimers say.

Weasels are pretty little things, especially in the winter. That's why they chose it to catch a girl.

The Law of Contagion involves the idea that once two things have been in contact with each other they remain in contact on a spiritual level, so that the magical manipulation of one will also affect the other. Contagious magic may be performed on anything that has had contact with the person to be influenced: A lock of the person's hair or a piece of his or her clothing are ideal; fingernail or toenail clippings, dirt from under the nails, or excrement will do just fine; even dirt from the bottom of a footprint will help. In magic designed to harm, the magical poison can simply be poured into the victim's footprint itself. The Law of Contagion is one reason why many people all over the world have two names, one for public use by others and a true, private name known only to themselves and perhaps a few close relatives. Since the name is an extension of the self, so the logic goes, to know someone's true name is to be able to use it as a form of contact in speaking a magical spell. This is why in some parts of the world people customarily change their names as a part of the cure of an illness that is thought to have been magically induced, thus denying the sorcerer a chance for continued mischief by magical contact through the victim's name.

Often, magic employs elements of both the Law of Similarity and the Law of Contagion at the same time. My grandmother in Arkansas practiced the custom of protecting her children from tetanus by carefully washing

FIGURE 10.7 *Divination*

By ritually manipulating a system of signs and symbols such as tea leaves or playing cards people hope to obtain information about the future as well as determine what might have occurred in the past. This Indian at Batu Caves, Malaysia, is reading a palm, a common method of determining a future course of action.

the farmyard nail that had been stepped on, covering it with lard, and placing it on the kitchen windowsill. This magical ritual made use of the object that had inflicted the wound—the Law of Contagion—and treated it in a way that would prevent germs from reaching it—the Law of Similarity.

Obtaining hidden knowledge. An important use of rituals to obtain supernatural aid is <u>divination</u>, obtaining knowledge by supernatural means. People have been quite creative in developing methods of divination. Examining the entrails of animals for unusual signs, considering the flight direction of birds or the shapes formed by molten lead poured into water, or checking the lines on people's hands or the date of their birth have all been used as means to answer questions. Casting of the *I Ching*, spreading of *tarot* cards, and random selecting of Bible verses have served the same purpose. Methods of divination fall into two main categories: those in which the results can be easily influenced by the diviner

and those in which the results cannot be readily influenced. The former include practices such as reading tea leaves or interpreting an astrological sign, since there is much latitude for subjective interpretation by the diviner. This category also includes methods such as trance-speaking and "water witching," in which the movement of a willow branch held by the diviner is interpreted as evidence of water, since the diviner can influence the movement or speech, consciously or unconsciously. These methods permit the diviner's knowledge of the client's circumstances to play a role in providing answers that are psychologically satisfying to the customers.

Methods that give responses that the diviner is unable to control include techniques such as casting lots or checking whether an object floats on water to answer a question. Like flipping a coin, these tend to randomize the answers. This approach to divination is especially useful when conflicting secular information or divergent opinions must be dealt with.

THE AZANDE POISON ORACLE

Evans-Pritchard (1937) described an interesting system of divination that uses poison. The Azande, who live in the Republic of the Sudan, Zaire, and the Central African Republic, consult the poison oracle on all important matters. They may use it to diagnose the cause of an illness, to decide how to most safely conduct vengeance by magic, or to determine who has used magic against them. The poison oracle also is consulted to find out if a journey may be undertaken safely or to prepare for any dangerous or socially important activity.

Consulting the poison oracle usually occurs in the bush far from the homestead to maintain secrecy and to avoid people who have not observed the taboos necessary for the oracle to work. Participants must not have sexual intercourse or eat elephant's flesh and a number of other foods for several days before consulting the oracle. Smoking hemp will pollute the oracle as well.

The diviner, who with only rare exceptions is a male, scrapes a hole in the ground and places into it a large leaf to hold the *benge*, or oracle poison. He fashions a brush of grass to administer the poison to chickens, several of which are brought by each questioner. When everyone is seated, it is decided how each question will be framed to provide the most information. The diviner then pours water into the leaf bowl and adds the powdered poison. After mixing the paste with his brush, the diviner squeezes the liquid from the brush into the beak of one of the chickens. While several doses are given, the questioner asks the first question repeatedly, ending each time with a request for the poison to kill or to spare the fowl if the answer is affirmative. For instance, a question about whether adultery has occurred might be ended by the questioner's saying:

Poison oracle, poison oracle, you are in the throat of the fowl. That man his navel joined her navel; they pressed together; he knew her as woman and she knew him as man. She has drawn *badiabe* [a leaf used as a towel] and water to his side [for ablutions after intercourse]; poison oracle hear it, kill the fowl. (Evans-Pritchard, 1957, p. 138)

The poison used is a red powder prepared from a jungle creeper. The alkaloid that it contains has effects similar to strychnine. Some chickens seem unaffected by it. Others die immediately or soon after it is administered.

In poison oracle divination, there are always two tests of each question, one framed positively and the other negatively. One chicken must die and another must survive to confirm an answer to a question. If both live or if both die, the oracle must be consulted at another time to obtain an answer to the question.

Affecting health. Influential magic also may be used to cause ill health. Illness is a problem with which people must cope in all parts of the world. Although health-related magic is most common in societies that lack complex secular medical technologies, one finds religious rituals for the curing and causing of illness in all the world's many societies.

According to Forest Clements (1932) there are six major theories of disease in the world's societies: natural causes, magic, the intrusion of disease objects into the victim's body, soul loss, spirit possession, and taboo violations. Each of these is associated with an appropriate approach to curing the illness.

Those diseases or infirmities that are thought to be the result of natural causes are treated by pragmatic techniques such as setting broken bones and the use of herbs. When magic is used to bring about illness or death in a victim, favored materials include things that have been in intimate contact with the victim such as hair clippings, nail parings, excreta, or pieces of the victim's clothing. Magic-caused illnesses must be cured by countermagic.

Sending a foreign object, called a disease object, into the body of a victim by magic is another favored technique of sorcerers and witches for bringing about illness or death. When a foreign object such as a barbed stick or a stone is believed to have been supernaturally projected into the victim's body, thereby causing pain and illness, the object is removed by massage and sucking.

The third spiritual cause of illness is soul loss. When a soul has left a person's body—whether dislodged from the body by a sudden fright, simply lost during its nightly wanderings, or stolen by another's magic—the body is left without the vitality it needs to survive. If this is believed to be the cause of the victim's ill health, a healer must coax the wayward soul back into the patient's body or recapture it and bring it back.

Spirit possession, the control of a person's behavior by a spirit that has entered his or her body, requires a ritual of exorcism to remove the offending spirit. Taboo violation is the only one of the six causes of illness in which magic may not play a role. In many cultures, it is believed that illness may come not as punishment but simply as a natural consequence of breaking a supernatural rule. Thus taboo violation includes willful breaking of the taboos but may also include rule breaking that was accidental or even done without the actor's awareness. So the rule breaker is not necessarily held morally responsible for the act, as in the Western concept of sin. For instance, Apache Indians of the southwestern United States believe that illness may result from using as firewood, wood that has been urinated on by a deer, even though one is unlikely to know that this is the case. Furthermore, in some societies the illness that follows a taboo violation may strike someone other than the rule breaker. When taboo violation is thought to be the cause of illness, confession will play a role in the cure.

What determines whether people will believe that the malicious acts of others, such as sorcerers or witches, are the cause of illness or will attribute illnesses to other causes? As has been noted above, Beatrice Whiting (1950) and Guy Swanson (1960) cited the presence of societal conflicts in the absence of effective social means of resolving conflicts as a major cause of the belief in sorcery to work harm. The specific social conflicts surrounding sexual jealousy also have been suggested as a basis for witchcraft and sorcery. On the other hand, the two forms of belief that illness may be caused by nonhuman spiritual beings—that is, spirit possession or punishment for the violation of a taboo—are not related to the development of secular authority or to the severity of socialization anxiety. These beliefs may be found with the other four theories of disease, but they also are found in societies where the others do not occur. Bourguignon and Greenberg (1973) found that spirit possession is most common in societies in which people are expected to be submissive and compliant and that spirit loss is most common in societies in which people are socialized to be independent and self-assertive. In both cases, the supernatural concept of illness seems to symbolize anxiety about the kind of social role one is expected to play. Illness as a result of taboo violation is found in societies in which conformity to rules is important. For instance, taboo violation is an important cause of illness among the arctic Inuit, whose environment can be quite deadly if one is lax or careless in following the established rules of life.

Death by magic. In some cases, victims of sorcery actually die. Anthropologists have tried for decades to understand the phenomenon of death by magic.

Cannon (1942) analyzed cases of so-called "voodoo death" and suggested that the actual cause of death in such cases may be prolonged shock induced by extreme fear. Cannon quotes Herbert Basedow (1907), who graphically described the terrifying effect of sorcery by bone-pointing (see Fig. 10.8) in native Australia:

> A man who discovers that he is being boned by an enemy is, indeed, a pitiable sight. He stands aghast, with his eyes staring at the treacherous pointer, and with his hands lifted as though to ward off the lethal medium, which he imagines is pouring into his body. . . . His cheeks blanch and his eyes become glossy, and the expression of his face becomes horribly distorted, like that of one stricken with palsy. He attempts to shriek but usually the sound chokes in his throat, and all that one might see is froth at his mouth. His body begins to tremble and the muscles twist involuntarily. He sways backwards and falls to the ground, and after a short time appears to be in a swoon but soon after he begins to writhe as if in mortal agony, and, covering his face with his hands, begins to moan. After a while he becomes more composed and crawls to his wurley [hut]. From this time onwards he sickens and frets, refusing to eat, and keeping aloof from the daily affairs of the tribe. Unless help is forthcoming in the shape of a counter charm administered by the hands of the "*Nangarri*" or medicine-man, his death is only a matter of a comparatively short time. If the coming of the medicine-man is opportune, he might be saved. (Cannon, 1942, p. 181)

FIGURE 10.8   *Bone Pointing*

A man in the Northern Territory, Australia, shows how the magic bone is pointed at a victim while he is being "sung." It is said that when a victim learns of the ritual even though it is done in secret, he or she may actually die.

Normally, both fear and anger stimulate the sympathetic nervous system, which regulates the inner organs and the circulatory system. This stimulation prepares the body for prolonged muscular exertion by discharging adrenalin and accelerating the heart rate, by constricting blood vessels during the exertion, and by dilating the bronchioles within the lungs so that more oxygen may be available to the muscles and more carbon dioxide may be expelled. All of these changes prepare the body for the muscular action that may be necessary for the escape from danger. However, when the energy thus made available cannot be used for a prolonged period, the physiological stress of remaining in this state of preparedness for intense action will eventually result in exhaustion and damage to the bodily organs, which may result in death. As Hans Selye (1976) pointed out in his description of the stress response, which he termed the General Adaptation Syndrome: These are nonspecific changes that occur in the body as a result of any stress, and even adaptation to a stress-producing event eventually ends in a state of exhaustion. Adaptation to unusual levels of stress cannot go on indefinitely.

In fear-induced shock, the prolonged con-

striction of the small blood vessels occurs especially in the extremities and the abdominal viscera. The lack of an adequate supply of oxygen in the visceral capillaries causes their thin walls to become more permeable, and blood plasma escapes into the spaces surrounding these small blood vessels in the abdomen. This reduces the volume of blood available in the circulatory system until adequate circulation is no longer possible. The result is a lowering of the blood pressure, which in turn leads to a deterioration of the heart and other organs that normally ensure an adequate circulation of blood to the body. If the cycle is not broken, death is inevitable. The process by which it happens is often speeded by the fact that the victim may cease to eat and drink, thereby adding even greater stresses to the body. Recently Eastwell (1982) has argued that dehydration may be the actual cause of death. Since stress that is brought on by fear of sorcery cannot be eliminated by any practical action, death may indeed result unless the fear can be eliminated by a ritual cure.

DEATH BY SORCERY IN DOBU

R. Fortune (1932) gave a graphic account of the use of sorcery to kill among the Dobuans, inhabitants of the Melanesian Islands near New Guinea. The sorcerer and one or more assistants approached the area of the victim's garden in the forest. They rubbed their bodies with magically powerful herbs to make themselves invisible and then crept to the edge of the clearing where the victim was working in the garden. Suddenly, with a characteristic scream, the sorcerer jumped into the clearing. The victim, taken by surprise, would recognize what was happening from the cry and actions of the sorcerer. He or she would be overcome by fear and fall immediately into a faint. The sorcerer was then free to prance about and dramatically act out, in symbolic form, the surgical opening of the victim's abdomen and the magical removal of the entrails and vital organs. After closing the magical wound, the sorcerer would ask the victim, "What is my name?" The victim could not respond, ensuring that the sorcerer would not be identified.

After the sorcerer departed, the victim gradually recovered enough to stagger home and crawl up the ladder to his or her house. Relatives, recognizing the expression of shock and fear on the victim's face, knew what had transpired and began to make arrangements for the funeral. The victim lost all appetite and could die from shock within the next few days.

Spiritual healing. Just as ritual is believed to play a prominent role in the causing of illness or even death, religious power is called on in many societies to cure illness. Curing illness is the primary concern of <u>shamans</u>, or inspired religious healers. In societies in which shamans are able to congregate in sufficient numbers, they may form organizations in which they discuss their practices, cooperate with one another in curing patients, and initiate apprentices into the shared secrets of the trade. For instance, among the Iroquois, a native American people who lived in northern New York and were described extensively by Morgan (1851), various illnesses were treated by the members of specialized medicine societies. Among these were the False Face Society, the Bear Society, the Pygmy Society, the Otter Society, the Chanters for the Dead, and the Eagle Society. Each specialized in the treatment or prevention of particular ills and had its own songs and rituals. Those who asked a particular society for a cure became members of that society if the cure was successful, as did persons who dreamed that they must join a society. Thus, following a cure, individuals acquired a new social status and were expected to play a role in the curing of others who became afflicted by the same disease.

The False Face Society was a powerful religious curing society among the Iroquois of the northeastern United States. These cures were accomplished with the use of wooden masks representing various spirits that were worn by the members of the society during its ceremonies. The masks characteristically had distorted features and were created by carving the face into the trunk of a live tree (see Fig. 10.9). During the carving, prayers

FIGURE 10.9 *Iroquois False-Face Society*

These are samples of the kind of face masks worn by an Iroquois curing group known as the False-Face Society. Carved into the trunk of a tree and representing spirit forces, they were later worn by shamans who visited the victim's house to drive out the evil spirits causing illness.

were made to the spirit force that it represented. After tobacco had been burned before the mask, it was cut free, painted, and decorated with hair made from cornsilk or horsehair.

Curing ceremonies took place at the request of the patient's family in the longhouse where they lived. The members of the False Face Society would don their masks and travel in a group to the patient's house. As they came, they mimicked the spirits represented by the masks. Upon entering the patient's house, they sprinkled the afflicted person with ashes and shook their turtle carapace rattles over him or her to drive away the illness. In return for their work, members of the False Face Society were paid with gifts and food.

THE SOCIAL ORGANIZATION OF RELIGION

A hallmark of religion is ritual involvement with others. By participating in the religious rituals of their society, people express a sense of togetherness, unity, and belonging.

225

This group aspect of religious practice fosters deeper loyalty to one's society. To be sure, all religions include rituals that individuals may perform for their own benefit: private prayer to petition the spirits and gods for aid, magic to achieve the same ends more coercively, taboos that are followed to avoid misfortune, and positive acts that foster luck, skill, and safety. However, no religious system is built solely from these individualistic ritual activities. All religions have at least part-time religious specialists who perform rituals for others, and some are organized into more complex communal or ecclesiastical religious groups (Wallace, 1966).

Ritual Specialists

Ritual may be performed by any adherent of a religion, but all religions also have some individuals who specialize in the use of spiritual power to influence others. These include shamans, sorcerers, and witches.

Shamans. The most common kind of ritual specialist in human societies is the medical-religious curer that anthropologists refer to as the shaman. The term "shaman" was originally borrowed from a seminomadic Siberian people called the Chuckchee, among whom shamanism was a male occupation. According to Waldemar Borgoras (1907) the Chuckchee shaman was a man who was socially withdrawn, listless, and prone to falling into trances before entering the shamanic career. Like healers in other societies, in other words, Chuckchee shamans tended to be social deviants. This fact was institutionally recognized: Shamans were expected to adopt the dress of women as a symbol of their unusual status. Having been chosen by another world, shamans were set apart socially by the transvestite role. In fact, those shamans who, besides adopting the clothing of women, took on the behavior of a woman and entered into sexual relationships or marriages with men, were thought to be the most powerful among the shamans.

Eliade (1964) has shown that the central feature of shamanistic practice is the ecstatic experience achieved in trance. In the trance state, shamans may send their spirits on errands in service to their clients, or they may invite powerful spirits to enter their bodies and give them power. In spirit travel and possession trances, shamans experience the ecstasy of visions of a world not seen by ordinary eyes. Noll (1985) has argued that the training that sets the shaman apart from other people in the skill of entering trances and experiencing visions is facilitated by practicing visual imaging. With practice the shaman's visions become more vivid and lively, and the shaman learns to control when the visions begin and end and what their content will be. Peters and Price-Williams (1980) describe the vivid shamanic trance as similar to waking dreams and guided imagery. Further, Price-Williams (1985) believes that the true shamanistic trance involves passing over from simple visual imaging into an altered state of consciousness in which the shaman experiences personal "participation and immersion in the imagery content" (p. 656).

BECOMING A SHAMAN AMONG THE AVAM SAMOYED

Where shamans are formally initiated by others of their kind, the initiation ceremony often enacts a kind of symbolic death, journey through the spirit world where the novice is trained and given the powers of a shaman, and rebirth into the human world. This formula is well illustrated in a story told by Popov (1936) about the vision of a Siberian Avam Samoyed man who received the power to cure. While lying near death from smallpox, his Sickness spoke to him on behalf of the Lords of Water and gave him the new name, Diver. After climbing a mountain, Diver met a naked woman, the Lady of Water, who took him as her child and suckled him at her breast. Her husband, Lord of the Underworld, gave him two guides who led him to the Underworld. There he learned of the diseases, both physical and mental, from which people suffer. Then he visited the Land of Shamanesses where voice is strengthened, since song is used in cures. On an island in one of the Nine Seas, he found the Tree of the Lord of the Earth. There he was given the wood for making three of the drums that shamans use in their ceremonies. After he received instruction in the medicinal use of seven herbs and in other techniques for curing, he was told that he must marry three women.

Then the initiate was led to another high mountain where he met two women clothed in the hair of reindeer. Each gave him a hair to be used when he used his power to influence reindeer. He crossed a great desert to another mountain. There he was dismembered, and his body parts were boiled in a great cauldron by a naked man who forged his head on an anvil that was used to forge the heads of great shamans. This man taught him to divine whether a cure would be successful, reassembled his body, gave him new eyes capable of seeing into the spirit world, and pierced his ears so they could hear the speech of plants. After all these things, he awoke and found that during the three days of his coma, he had been so close to death that he had almost been buried.

Sorcerers.   The antisocial equivalent of a shaman is the sorcerer, a person who uses supernatural power to harm human beings. Sorcery may be used to cause misfortune, illness, and death. As dangerous as a sorcerer may be, acknowledged practitioners of the art may be tolerated by their neighbors, since their noxious powers may occasionally be sought by others. A sorcerer might, for instance, be hired by persons who believe themselves to have been wronged by others and who seek vengeance by sorcery. Since persons who discover that they have been cursed by a sorcerer may seek the removal of that curse by making amends for the wrong of which they have been accused, the sorcerer's role in society is sometimes similar to that of the law enforcers in complex societies.

NAVAJO SKINWALKERS

Among the Navajo of the southwestern United States, it is said that a curer may be seduced by the dark side of power. No human being is all good or all evil. In the Navajo view, we each have both qualities or, more accurately, the capacity to do both good and evil. According to Witherspoon (1977), the goal of Navajo life is to bring

FIGURE 10.10   *Navajo "Sing"*
One way the Navajo counter the forces of evil in the universe or in man is to perform a ritual chant or "sing." This Navajo mother is holding her sick child while sitting on a sand painting and chanting rituals intended to restore the child to health or a state of hózhó.

one's impulses under control so that one grows and develops through a complete life in a condition of *hózhó*—the state of beauty, harmony, good, and happiness—and then dies naturally of old age and becomes one with the universal beauty, harmony, and happiness that make up the ideal positive environment.

A person's *ch'indi*, or potential for evil, can be controlled by rituals that restore one to a state of *hózhó*. Although the state of inward beauty achieved through living in outward harmony with the ideal environment can be disrupted by contact with dangerous (*báhádzid*) things or by the sorcery of others, perhaps leading to illness or to death, such states can be countered by a traditional ritual chant, or "Sing," of which there are over 60. Rituals channel supernatural power by reenacting the Navajo creation myths, which relate the deeds of the gods, both good and evil.

Navajo singers, the curing shamans of the Navajo, also can learn to use the power of ritual to harm other people. Initiation into the world of sorcery carries a high price: The initiate must consent to the death of a close relative. In using rituals to upset the ideal balance of life in others, the sorcerer's *ch'indi* grows stronger and may overwhelm him. Sorcerers live a life that inverts the ideals of the Navajo: They gather at night in places avoided by others to do their rituals; they dig up corpses to grind their bones into poisons; they don the skins of wolves and transform themselves into animals. Skinwalkers, as they are called, can travel great distances faster than ordinary humans can imagine. They cast their poisons into the smoke holes of their victims' hogans or magically shoot harmful substances into their bodies.

Witches. Witches share the world of supernatural power with sorcerers and shamans. Like sorcerers, they are believed to do evil to human beings. Unlike sorcerers, who must learn the rituals with which they work their harm, witches are thought to be born with the power to harm. The evil of a witch works so spontaneously that it may do its damage to others even without the witch's conscious intent. Witches are often viewed as the epitome of evil, and they may be described in terms that invert the normal qualities of human beings: Witches love the night; they commit incest and kill their own relatives; they may travel on their heads instead of their feet, and may fly as fireballs through the sky. Since witches are so different from ordinary humans, the very presence of persons who are believed to be witches may not be tolerated, and convicted witches are likely to be killed.

Shamanic Religions

Of all forms of religious organization, shamanic religions are the socially simplest and perhaps the oldest. Shamanic religions are based on rituals performed by nonspecialists for their own benefit and by the shaman for the benefit of nonspecialists. Shamans may perform rituals to divine the future or to gain answers to their clients' questions. As spirit mediums, they may be called on to increase the success of a hunt, the fertility of the game, or the growth of crops. The charms they make protect their clients from harm or increase their luck and skill. However, shamans are best known for their skill at manipulating the supernatural to cure illness. Their spiritual powers do not differ in nature from those that

nonspecialists may use in their own behalf, but their special status grows out of their reputation for greater skill at manipulating these powers. In addition to their spiritual powers, shamans often possess an impressive body of knowledge about the natural medical effects of a broad range of native plants and other curative materials and techniques. Shamans also draw upon the awe and reverence of their patients for religious power, thereby increasing the patients' confidence in the likelihood of recovery.

On the reservation in Nevada where I did my fieldwork, a Shoshoni *puhakanten*, literally a "possessor of power," still cured the sick. The shaman's power to cure was not a human power but a spiritual power brought to him by a spirit partner, a *newe puha-pea*, the Eagle, who first appeared to him in a vision and gave him the power to cure.

When a prospective patient approaches this shaman, the first task is to determine whether he will be able to perform the cure. At the direction of his spirit partner, certain cases—such as those he diagnoses as cancer—must be referred to a medical doctor. To facilitate the diagnosis, the individual who has consulted him may be given an "eagle wing," a fan made of eagle feathers to place above his or her bed that night. That evening, the shaman consults his spirit partner for a diagnosis. On the next day, he will either accept or reject the petitioner as a patient, depending on the diagnosis.

A cure usually begins at sunset in the shaman's home. It is sometimes attended by other interested members of the community. Attendance at a curing ceremony is believed to foster good health in general among those who participate. The patient, who has bathed that morning at sunrise in a local hot spring, provides tobacco that is smoked by the shaman as part of the ceremony. After smoking, the shaman begins a chant that he was taught by his spirit partner in his virst vision. This chant is a call to the Eagle to come down from his mountain abode and enter the shaman to give him power to cure his patient's illness. He alternately smokes, chants, and massages the patient's body to remove the illness. Following the ceremony, the patient may be given some tasks to perform to complete the cure. For instance, a patient who is suffering from nosebleeds may be required to collect the blood and dispose of it on a red anthill. Patients are required to abstain from alcohol to ensure the efficacy of the cure.

Korean religious tradition also includes an important role for shamanic rituals that are performed by a class of female shamans called *mansin*. They obtain their power by becoming possessed by powerful spirits and deities. While possessed they carry out rituals that benefit both individuals and groups. They divine the causes of both psychological and physical illnesses, undertake the cures, communicate with the spirits of the dead, placate angry gods, and purify villages that are plagued by evil spirits.

Brian Wilson (1980) has described a *kut*, or spirit possession ritual, conducted by a *mansin* to cleanse a village of angry spirits that had caused a series of tragic deaths, a murder and several suicides. The shaman, whom Wilson calls Mansinim, had diagnosed the cause of the problems to be the village's tutelary spirit, who was angry because some members of the community had cut down some trees.

> According to Wilson, "Mansinim began the *kut* with the *pujong*, or ritual cleansing of the [village] shrine and surrounding area of all polluting elements. While the *paksu* (male shaman) who was working with her this day beat a rapid beat on the drum and gong and chanted the invocational *tokkyung*, Mansinim walked around the concrete *sŏnang* shrine with salt water and ashes and sprinkled the surrounding area using her *Changgun* sword to sprinkle the water. Then she took a bowl of salt and walked around the shrine and sprinkled the salt to drive away any harmful spirits that might have been lurking about. She took two cymbals (*para*) attached to each other by a strip of white cloth and began beating them in a slow, almost funereal rhythm. She walked out in the field, clanging the cymbals, and when I later asked why she said it was to notify the gods and spirits that she was here and that the *kut* was about the begin. The field was marked off with straw rope from which were fluttering red, blue, and green bits of cloth. She marched toward an old tree beside which were the two guardian posts inscribed with the customary *ch'onha tae changgun* [male general of heaven] and *chisang yo changgun* [female general of earth]. She circled the tree three times and bowed, then walked to the base of the mountain overlooking the village and bowed to *San Sin*

> [the Mountain God]. Walking back to the *sŏnang*, still clanging the cymbals, she bowed before every tree along the side of the path.

> She entered the *sŏnang* shrine and bowed. Then she put on the red vest and blue sash of [the god] Sinjang, the Arrester, and her hands, pressed together in a prayer-like position, began shaking. This is the outward sign that the god has possessed her. She took the sword and trident and began jumping in front of the *sŏnang* shrine. Inside the little house-like shrine was the offering of a pig tied to an upright stone. The stone is the *sŏnang* spirit which guards the village. The villagers say it was miraculously washed up during a flood and deposited in the village.

> The *paksu* changed the beat to a dance rhythm and Mansinim took the divinatory flags and danced with them, circling the shrine. Then she danced with a fan and bells. She danced over to the chairman of the Elders' Association and pulled him into the shrine, where he bowed and placed a money offering at the foot of the stone. Mansinim fanned him with both fans. The gods were pleased.

> She took the *sin tae* (spirit stick used in divination) and danced with it. A bow signaled the end of that *kori* [one segment of the ceremony].

> After lunch the *kut* resumed. Mansinim put on the blue vest and black hat and the *Taegam* [Greedy Provincial Official] danced. Then she put on the *Changgun* ["General's"] costume, took two swords and danced with them inside the shrine compound. Her motions became very mannish and brusque. She stopped dancing and her body shook. *Changgun* had descended. She took her sword and tried to balance it on the flat end of the handle but the wind kept blowing it over. She went out and got the trident while the *paksu* picked up the beat with drum and gong. This time the trident stood, a sign of the favorable presence of *Changgun*. Her body shook again and she began dancing, becoming more animated as she danced and then she began jumping. Finally she faced the assembled villagers and the General spoke to them through her:

> > You are ungrateful! (*kwaessim hada*)
> > Do you know which General has come down?
> > *Tosol Changgun* ["Heavenly General"] has come down in order to help the people who live in this mountain valley. I come to this village letting three *mansins* go ahead,

In order to make a success of human
wishes.
Because three mansins fervently pray,
Because all the spirits cooperate to make
a success of human wishes,
Because villagers ask the *Son Hwang* [the
tutelary spirit of the *sŏnang* shrine] spirit
for their wishes,
Because villagers offer a whole *ssiru*
[steamed rice],
Because villagers offer a whole pig and
pray fervently,
Don't worry, I will solve your problem,
I will also open the door to a bright
future.

Later in the afternoon, at the end of the *kut*,
Mansinim drove the offending *subi* [goblins],
magwi [demons], *kwisin* [ghosts] and other
evil spirits into a dead branch to which had
been tied pieces of red and green cloth. With
the chairman of the Elders' Association trail-
ing behind she ran across the field and then
across another field to the foot of a hill where
she untied and burned the colored cloth and
'planted' the tree in the hillside." (pp. 8–10)

Lewis (1971) pointed out that spirit possession is a religious practice in which socially
powerless members of society are able to assert themselves in ways that society ordinarily
forbids and "press their claim for attention
and respect" (p. 32). This view of the psychological role of spirit possession seems valid
when applied to the *kut*, a spirit possession
trace that is practiced by women in Korea, a
society in which the social roles of women
provide few opportunities for achieving high
public status. In a discussion of the role of the
spirit possession trance of the usually female
shamans known as *mansin* in Korea, Wilson
(1980) has painted a poignant portrait of how
Mansinim sought the fulfillment that was denied by other means to her because of her
gender.

Mansinim had had a difficult life: Her
father had died when she was three years old,
and she worked as a housemaid as a teenager.
She entered into an arranged marriage with a
man she had never met, and had to live alone
in a bomb shelter when her husband went into
the army during the Korean war. After the
death of two of her children, she suffered from
dizzy spells and fits of crying, and was frequently ill. After a violent quarrel with her
husband about an affair he had been having,
she found her calling as a shaman when she

became possessed by the spirit of her mother-
in-law during a *kut* ceremony. Wilson has
noted that similar hardships seem characteristic of many of the female shamans whose lives
he studied.

Yet according to Wilson, Mansinim's role as
a shaman was not simply the manifestation of
psychological stresses. As a shaman, Mansinim
came to be possessed by a variety of powerful
spirits and deities such as Tosol Changgun,
whose name means "Heavenly General." During her states of possession on ceremonial
occasions, Mansinim was able to abandon her
prescribed role as a submissive woman, and
speak with a religiously legitimated power and
authority usually reserved for men in Korean
society. In Wilson's opinion, her dominant behavior when possessed fit her natural predispositions in a healthier way than did any other
role available to her:

Earlier Mansinim had told me that as a child
she had been a tomboy, a troublemaker, beating up boys in the village. Her mother called
her *son mosum* ('tomboy'). She said that she
had 'always wanted to be a man,' and that
when she dies she hopes to be 'a great general' in the spirit world. She complained that
her husband is 'quiet and mild and never
behaves like a man.' Since Mansinim cannot
become a general in real life she becomes a
general in *kut*. And since she rejects the
subordinate role that a wife is expected to
play to a husband, she reverses that role by
being ritually transformed into the husband's
mother who, as parent and departed ancestor, commands the husband's respect. What
is interesting about this situation is that it is
not just a bit of craziness—this 'acting out' of
spiritual roles expresses a keen insight into
the reality that is presented by the dynamics
of interaction in this family. For in fact Mansinim *is* the dominant member of the family
by virtue of a personality and character that
are much more aggressive, assertive, forceful,
'masculine' (by Korean standards) than her
husband. Therefore the ritual role reversal is
simply a symbolic way of recognizing and
even utilizing what is already a fact in the
power structure of this family. Once Mansinim is released from the necessity of playing
the subordinate role of submissive wife she
can, in *kut*, unfurl her 'real self' . . . and play
this 'self' with gusto. Which she does. When
she dons the red robe of the *Changgun* with
the gold breastplate and metal helmet you'd
better *believe* that she is a general! Her entire

manner and bearing changes from her normal circumspect mode of behavior, and she stomps heavily around with her sword almost daring anyone to challenge her.

Possessed of a god, Mansinim was able to express a part of her personality that was otherwise forbidden by her culture. Thus, Mansinim's shamanistic religion offered her a healthy outlet for parts of herself that, otherwise being denied, might have been a source of psychic distress.

Wilson described a dramatic recollection of Mansinim that encapsulates his view of how the shamanistic role provided an alternative outlet for ambitions that were denied her within Korean secular life:

> I vividly recall . . . Mansinim, standing on a mountainside dressed in the red and green costume of *San Sin*, the Mountain God, weeping and crying out as her husband knelt at her feet, 'If I had been born a man, I would have been a great general.' In many subsequent consversations Mansinim expressed her dissatisfaction over the limitations and restrictions placed upon her simply because she was a woman. And yet in her life she had resolved contradictions that appear to baffle behavioral scientists: While passionately resenting her circumscribed lot as a woman she nevertheless had learned to cope successfully with the demanding and sometimes conflicting role of wife, mother, and ritual specialist. I measure 'success' domestically in terms of the obvious affection and respect that passed between Mansinim and her husband, children and grandchildren, and professionally by the heavy demand for her services. (p. 3)

Communal Religions

A slightly more complex form of religious organization adds the practice of rituals by groups of nonspecialists to those found in the shamanic religions. These communal religions are found in more societies than are the shamanic ones. They tend to be found in societies that have slightly larger local groups than those in which shamanic religions predominate. In societies with larger social groups, communal rituals serve to celebrate the cohesiveness of the group or ease the transition of individuals from one status to another by publicly proclaiming that change in a rite of passage. Like shamanic religions, they are found in many societies where people survive by foraging wild foods. Communal religions also are found in societies where horticulture and pastoralism are practiced.

The group rituals permit broader social participation in the shared concerns of the community or of groups of specialists than do individual or shamanic rituals. They focus on matters that concern groups rather than individuals and increase the sense of social solidarity among those who participate. The group rituals that are most often celebrated in communal religions are: rituals to increase the fertility of game or ensure success in hunting; annual rituals to influence the weather, the fertility of crops, and the harvest; social rituals to celebrate changes in status or reinforce the importance of social divisions by sex or age; and ceremonies to reenact the mythology of the group or commemorate the memory of culture heroes, ancestral spirits, or particular deities.

THE RAINBRINGING RITUAL OF THE JIGALONG PEOPLE

According to Tonkinson (1974) the most important yearly ritual of the Jigalong people of the western Australian desert is the rainbringing ritual, called *Ngaawajil*. This ritual reenacts the story of Winba, an old snake-man ancestral being and other rainmaking beings, controllers of rain, clouds, thunder, lighting, hail, and other elements of the weather. If the people perform, the annual return of the rains is ensured, as is the increase in the kangaroo and other game animals that depend on the rains for water in the desert environment where the Jigalong people live and hunt.

Since the ritual lasts for many days and consists of a number of ceremonies performed simultaneously in different locations, it requires the cooperation of five male and four female groups, each with its own name, insignia, and ritual responsibilities. Throughout the ritual there is a division of the participants into the two-generation-level moieties of Jigalong life, groupings that unite members of alternate generations (grandparents and grandchildren) and separate members of contiguous generations (parents and children). Thus, the ritual reinforces a major aspect of Jigalong social life by incorporating the moiety division into the structure of the ritual.

The ritual activities occur at two locations, the Camp—where men, women, and children participate together in the ritual—and the "men's country" away from the camp—where only initiated males are involved in the ceremonies. At the Camp, men and women of appropriate status prepare food for the participants, and members of each moiety engage in chanting and throwing water at members of the other moiety. Away from the Camp, the ritual requires two piles of sacred objects used to encourage the rainmaking ancestors to bring the rains: lightning, thunder, hail, and rainbow stones and other objects. These objects are sprinkled with blood symbolic of rain, covered with down feathers symbolic of clouds, and "fed" with ceremonial food and water. The desire for rain is communicated to the rainmaking ancestors by rainmaking snakes believed to live in the piles of sacred objects.

Ecclesiastical Religions

The ecclesiastical religions make use of all the previous ways of organizing some of their rituals, but they add to them a series of rituals performed by members of a professional clergy or priesthood. These religious practitioners are called priests to distinguish them from their more charismatic counterparts, the shamans. Whereas shamans serve individual clients when called upon to do so, priests perform rituals for a congregation on a full-time or at least regular basis. Priests may be organized into a bureaucracy which both organizes the activities of its members and regulates the ritual calendar of the congregations. Unlike shamans, who often are highly charismatic individuals who creatively follow the inspiration of the moment in modifying their ritual performance to fit the needs of their clients, priests tend to be much more concerned with the maintenance of the traditional forms of the rituals they have learned. Ecclesiastical religions tend to be found in agriculturally based societies, particularly in those with large enough populations to support a variety of full-time specialists. They are characteristic of the world's most complex societies.

Ideologically, the earliest recorded ecclesiastical religions had polytheistic beliefs in which a variety of high gods each required the service of special religious practitioners. Wallace (1966) has called these early ecclesiastical religions the Olympian religions to distinguish them from the later monotheistic religions in which the supernatural pantheon of ranked gods is superseded by one in which the highest deity is regarded as a truly Supreme Being, if not the only god in the pantheon. The ancient Greeks, Egyptians, Babylonians, and Romans followed the Olympian pattern, while monotheistic religions are represented today in Judaism, Christianity, Islam, and in modern philosophical Hinduism, in which all of the gods of earlier Hindu tradition are said to be merely various manifestations of a single, all-encompassing deity.

MORMON PRIESTHOOD AND PANTHEON

Mormonism was founded in 1824 in the eastern United States by a charismatic leader, Joseph Smith, following a series of visionary experiences, including a visitation by God the Father and Jesus. Today, this religion claims over five million members worldwide.

Mormonism is an ecclesiastical religion. Its priesthood, which is held only by male members of the church, is organized into a complex hierarchy, presided over by a president. The president of the church is also referred to as the *Prophet, Seer, and Revelator* of the church. As the presiding official of the church, the Prophet is believed to receive direct guidance from God whenever this is necessary for the work of directing the church. Below the Prophet is the Quorum of Twelve Apostles, which is presided over by its own president and two counselors. Below this level are intermediary officers down to the local congregations, called *wards*. The presiding official of the ward is the *bishop*. The bishop is a nonpaid minister, as are all local members of the priesthood. His responsibilities are not to deliver weekly sermons but to organize and preside over each Sunday's worship services and all other business of the ward. In this work he is aided by his own counselors and a series of priesthood quorums within the ward.

The local priesthood quorums are themselves organized into an age-graded system which is divided into two major components, the lower, or Aaronic Priesthood and the higher, or Melchizedek Priesthood. Boys are typically inducted into the Aaronic Priesthood at the age of 12 as Deacons. Their assignments include passing the Sacrament to members of the ward during the Sacrament meeting each Sunday. At 14 boys are ordained Teachers and are permitted to prepare the sacramental bread and water used in the service. Sixteen-year-olds become Priests, at which time they receive the authority to bless the Sacrament and to baptize. Eighteen-year-olds receive the full authority of the Melchizedek Priesthood as Elders, including the authority to confirm a baptized person as a member of the church and, by the laying on of hands, to give that person the right to receive direct and personal guidance through the Holy Ghost. At this time, it is expected that worthy males will spend a two-year period as unpaid, full-time missionaries for the church. For most, the next major change occurs at age 45 when men are inducted into a High Priest's quorum.

The women's organization is an auxiliary program, since all policy-making and governing authority is vested in the priesthood. The men's and women's organizations are structurally equivalent, but they differ in authority and responsibility, with the women specializing in supportive service roles. Mormon ecclesiastical values reflect the secular differentiation of male and female roles. According to Shepherd and Shepherd (1984), Mormons are taught to idealize a family pattern in which the husband, as the family's sole source of income, plays a presiding role and in which the wife, as counselor to her husband, specializes in domestic responsibilities. In addition to a Father in Heaven, Mormon theology includes a divine Mother in Heaven (Heeren, Lindsey, & Mason, 1985). However, Her role in Mormon theology is an auxiliary one, like that of the women's organization within the church or of the wife within the idealized Mormon family. She is never explicitly mentioned in Mormon scriptures, She has no governing authority within the Godhead, and She is not approached in worship in any rituals of the church.

The recurring pattern of presidents and

two counselors within the church structure mirrors Mormon theology, which includes a divine pantheon of many gods presided over by God the Father, Jesus Christ, and the Holy Ghost. Jesus, the firstborn spirit child of God, and the Holy Ghost, another spirit son of God, are believed to be fully separate individuals from the Father. Their role in the Godhead is much like that of the counselors to the earthly Prophet of the church. Thus, church organizational structure reproduces forms that Mormons think of as divine in origin and that reinforce the value of a presiding role for males.

WHY ARE PEOPLE RELIGIOUS?

Although cultures differ considerably in their religious beliefs, practices, and organizations, there is no known human culture in which religion is absent. There is archaeological evidence that religion has been practiced by our ancestors since at least the time of the Neanderthal, 125,000 years ago. In trying to explain the universal existence of religion in our species, anthropologists usually have considered the role that religion plays in making our social life more successful and the psychological benefits that religion gives us as individuals. The question of whether people also are responding to a true supernatural realm is, itself, not accessible to anthropological study.

The Maintenance of Social Order

Religion teaches people that they have a place in the universe and a relationship to it. Through the ideology of a religion and through its rituals, people gain a sense of identity and a feeling that life is meaningful. The practice of a religion creates greater solidarity among its participants, enabling them to work more effectively together and accomplish more.

Religion provides guidelines and values about how human life is properly conducted. In so doing, it motivates people to follow the customs of their society even in the absence of practical insights about how their actions may benefit their society. For instance, farmers suffering the effects of a prolonged drought may be too discouraged to dig yet another well after several failures until a "water witch" assures them of the presence of water at some location. Without such religious sources of motivation, the short-term costs of trying one more time in the face of the previous failures might seem to outweigh the potential long-term benefits.

Social rules that are necessary to the maintenance of order may be supported by the threat of supernatural punishments for their violation or supernatural rewards for their acceptance. This can be especially beneficial to a society that lacks secular means of ensuring obedience to the rules. Viking men were promised the reward of Valhalla for valor in warfare, and Aztec warriors were assured that death in battle led to an eternity in the most glorious of the Aztec heavens, that of their war god, Huitzilopochtli. Among the Rwala Bedouin of northern Saudi Arabia, the pains of Hell awaited those who lied, and for the ancient Egyptians a similar fate was reserved for the stingy.

In situations in which disagreement might be divisive, religion may provide the means to achieve consensus without hard feelings. For instance, divination can be used to find the answer to a question about which the group is hopelessly divided. That solution then can be accepted by all without loss of face.

Finally, the rituals of religion provide emotional release from stresses that might otherwise lead to socially disruptive behavior. When Zuñi farmers blame their crop failures or illness on the malevolent activities of sorcerers in another town and take action to protect themselves through rituals, they may be sparing themselves the strife that might otherwise disrupt their own village if they took out their frustrations on neighbors or relatives.

The Reduction of Anxiety

In addition to benefits to society at large, there are psychological benefits for the individual in the practice of religion. People do not always have as much control over their lives or circumstances as they need to feel secure. When this is the case, the performance of rituals for control through supernatural means can alleviate debilitating anxiety. This is especially true when the anxiety stems from prob-

lems for which no secular remedies are known. More than one anthropologist has noted parallels between shamanistic curing rituals and Western psychotherapeutic practices.

In frightening situations, religion can be a source of strength to stand up to one's fears and overcome them. The prayer uttered privately or the blessing given by another before a dangerous act is undertaken may provide just enough confidence to ensure success. Guilt can be overcome by acts of penance and sacrifice, and shame may be counteracted by demonstrations of piety that restore one's reputation. People who are unable to remove unjust obstacles in their lives can release their anger by acting it out with rituals that direct the power of magic against the source of their frustrations. At times of loss, religion may console the grieving. In these and other ways, religion helps people cope with troubling emotions.

The Cognitive Role of Religion

Religion's role in shaping beliefs also may be helpful to people. One important function of religious belief is to give people answers to important questions for which they have no scientific or definitive answers: Why do I exist? What will become of me after I die? What are the sun, moon, and stars, and how did the earth itself come into existence? Who were the first humans, and how did they originate? To such questions, religious ideology usually provides satisfying answers based on supernatural authority.

Some questions that religion answers, existential questions that deal with meaning and purpose, are questions with which science is not equipped to deal. However, others are questions that had no scientific answers at one time but which had come to be answered at a later time. The rise of scientific specialists in Western societies led to new answers to many questions that had been handled previously by religious leaders. This change resulted in social conflict between advocates of science and religious leaders, which, as society became more secular and dependant on rational explanations for natural phenomena, gradually resulted in a major loss of social and political influence by religious professionals. Education, for instance, increasingly came under the control of secular educators. A natural byproduct of the conflict between science and religion was the evolution in Western culture of the idea that scientific and religious ideologies are fundamentally different, perhaps even irreconcilable. This idea is dramatically illustrated in the ongoing attacks on scientific knowledge about the age of the earth or about human evolution by Christian fundamentalist religious leaders in the United States who reject the notion that scientific insights should be allowed to influence their interpretation of Scripture.

It is true that science and religion differ in the methods and assumptions that they employ to create new ideas. However, it is an error to assume that the cognitive processes involved in religious thinking differ radically from those applied in science. Guthrie (1980, p. 181) has shown that "people hold religious beliefs because they are *plausible* models of the world, apparently grounded in daily experience" (emphasis added). Guthrie believes that anthropomorphism (using human qualities to explain the nonhuman realm) is fundamental to religion and that it is anthropomorphism that all religions have in common. He observes that our experiences are initially ambiguous, and we reduce this ambiguity by interpreting them in human terms. Whether we do so religiously or scientifically, we interpret our experiences by creating models for them, based on phenomena that seem to us to be analogous to the experiences we wish to explain. Humans make very plausible models for many of the things we experience for three reasons: (1) Humans are complex and multifaceted, so they have similarities to many phenomena; (2) human beings are likely to be found wherever the human observer may be; (3) humans are the most important factor in the human environment. Therefore, anthropomorphic models are readily used by human beings to interpret their experiences, and it is these models and interpretations of the universe as created and governed by unseen humanlike beings that we call religion. Guthrie's view that there is nothing psychologically implausible about religious ways of interpreting experiences implies that when we ask why people are religious, we may be asking the wrong question. Perhaps we should be asking why people sometimes think in nonreligious ways.

CREATIONISM: A CONTEMPORARY AMERICAN RELIGION

Fundamentalist religious leaders in the United States have opposed scientific views about human evolution since Darwin first proposed them. In the nineteenth century, Darwin outlined the natural mechanisms that could guide evolutionary change in living things. Such mechanisms were a potential threat to religious ideas, since they did not require a role for God in the process, and incorporating them into a religious model would have required a major change in the fundamentalists' literal approach to interpreting Scripture. Instead, they chose to oppose the introduction of evolutionary ideas into the United States school system. They successfully supported efforts to pass laws that forbade the teaching of evolution in states where their followers had sufficient numbers to command the respect of legislators. In 1925, John Scopes, an Arkansas high school teacher, was convicted and fined $100 for teaching his biology students that humans had evolved from simpler animals.

In the past decades, a new form of religious fundamentalism has developed in the United States, taking for itself the name *Creation Science*. The major creationist organizations are The Institute for Creation Research, which makes its home at Christian Heritage College, and the Creation Science Research Center. Creationist organizations do not carry out original scientific research in the traditional sense. Instead, they gather material published by scientists in any field that they judge relevant to their interests in creationism and use these within their argument for a creationist view of the universe. They also participate actively in lobbying to bring about legislation that forbids the teaching of evolution within the public schools without giving equal time to creationist ideas.

What do creation "scientists" believe? This is not an easy question to answer, since their views are not built up systematically as is usually the case within the sciences. Individual creationists differ in their opinions on specific issues, but some broad boundaries can be drawn that would probably surround them all. Generally, creationists are outspoken anti-evolutionists, refusing to believe that either life or the universe itself has evolved through time, even under Divine direction. They believe that the universe came into existence suddenly by the act of a Creator. Contrary to the dominant opinions of astronomers, physicists, geologists, biologists, and anthropologists, they believe that the universe, the earth, and all living things came into existence at about the same time, probably between 6,000 and 13,000 years ago. Individual creationists are divided on whether the process took six days or 6,000 years. They agree that the basic "kinds" of living things were created with essentially the same traits that they have today. There seems to be no accepted definition of what constitutes a "kind," but creationists are in agreement that whatever it is, the only change that can occur in living things is within a "kind" and that one "kind" cannot evolve into another. Fossils of extinct living forms, creationists believe, were creatures that died suddenly as a result of a major, catastrophic, world-wide flood.

If creationist beliefs sound as if they were based on a fundamentalist religious interpretation of Genesis, it is probably no coincidence. To join the Creation Research Society, one must sign a statement that reads in part, "The Bible is the written Word of God, and because we believe it to be inspired throughout, all its assertions are historically and scientifically true."[1] The logo of the Creation Science Research Center surrounds the phrase, "In the beginning God. . . ." The religious basis for their beliefs seems clear, but their work of lobbying for the teaching of creationism within the public schools requires that they portray their views as "scientific" to sidestep the Constitutional prohibitions that prevent state supported schools from teaching or promoting sectarian religious doctrines.

1. From *Conference on Evolution and Public Education: Resources and References* (p. 80) edited by P. Zetterberg, 1981, St. Paul, MN: University of Minnesota Center for Educational Development.

SUMMARY

Religion is found in all cultures but is subject to greater diversity than any other aspect of culture. Universal aspects that define religion in all societies are the belief in supernatural beings, the belief in supernatural power, the symbolic expression of feelings, and ritual behavior. The great diversity in belief systems may be related to variation in people's social, environmental, and technological contexts and may be seen as helping them adapt to those particular circumstances. Ritual religious behaviors may serve any of three general functions: uniting a community emotionally, portraying human needs or sacred beliefs, or influencing the supernatural. Rituals may be the province of solo practitioners—shamans, sorcerers, or witches—in small-scale societies. In somewhat larger societies, religion is often a communal matter, with group ceremonies. In large, socially stratified societies, religious specialists are commonly full-time practitioners, organized into hierarchical systems known as ecclesiastical religions. However organized, religion seems to help maintain social order, reduce individual anxiety, and help people make sense of the often puzzling world around them.

KEY TERMS AND CONCEPTS

religion 210
mana 210
taboo 211
supernatural 211
anthropomorphism 211
sacred 212
ritual 212
monotheism 215
polytheism 215
ancestral spirits 215
reincarnation 215
human soul 215
supernatural sanctions for violations of moral rules 215
sorcery 215
witchcraft 216
myths 217
legends 217
glossolalia 218
communitas 219
liminal period 219
magic 220
imitative magic 220

Law of Similarity 220
Law of Contagion 220
contagious magic 220
divination 221
disease object 222
soul loss 222
spirit possession 223
taboo violation 223
sin 223
voodoo death 223
bone-pointing 223
General Adaptation Syndrome 224
shamans 225
sorcerers 227
witches 228
shamanic religions 228
communal religions 231
ecclesiastical religions 232
priests 232
Olympian religions 232
monotheistic religions 232
creationism 235

ANNOTATED READINGS

Evans-Pritchard, E. E. (1956). *Nuer religion*. Oxford: Clarendon Press. Based on years of intensive study by one of the greats in British anthropology, this is a classic study of religion in an African society.

Furst, P. T. (Ed.). (1972). *Flesh of the gods: The ritual use of hallucinations*. New York: Praeger. A collection of articles on the use of hallucinogens to achieve altered states of consciousness in religious settings.

Kluckhohn, C. (1944). *Navaho witchcraft. (Papers of the Peabody Museum of American Archeology and Ethnology, Harvard University, 22(2))*. Cambridge, MA: Harvard University Press. An interesting look at a fascinating part of Navajo religious beliefs.

Lehmann, A. C., & Myers, J. E. (1985). *Magic, witchcraft, and religion: An anthropological study of the supernatural*. Palo Alto, CA: Mayfield. A thorough and up-to-date collection of articles on religion.

Lessa, W. A., & Vogt, E. Z. (Eds.). (1979). *Reader in comparative religion* (4th ed.). New York: Harper & Row. The classic comprehensive reader for the anthropology of religion. Must reading for the anthropology major.

Radin, P. (1937). *Primitive religion*. New York: Dover. A classic and insightful view of religion by an excellent writer.

Sharon, D. (1978). *Wizard of the four winds: A shaman's story*. New York: Macmillan. An insightful biography of a Peruvian shaman.

Swanson, G. E. (1960). *The birth of the gods: The origin of primitive beliefs*. Ann Arbor, MI: University of Michigan Press. An often overlooked, but important exploration of the Durkhdeim view of religious belief as a reflection of the organization of society. An important reference book for the anthropology major.

Wallace, A. F. C. (1966). *Religion: An anthropological view*. New York: Random House. Probably the most thorough and influential interpretation of religion as a psychological and cultural phenomenon to have been written by an anthropologist. Must reading for the anthropology major, but worthwhile for any thoughtful student of religion.

Worsley, P. (1957). *The trumpet shall sound: A study of "cargo" cults in Melanesia*. London: MacGibbon and Kee. The classic comparative study of religious revitalization movements in Melanesia.

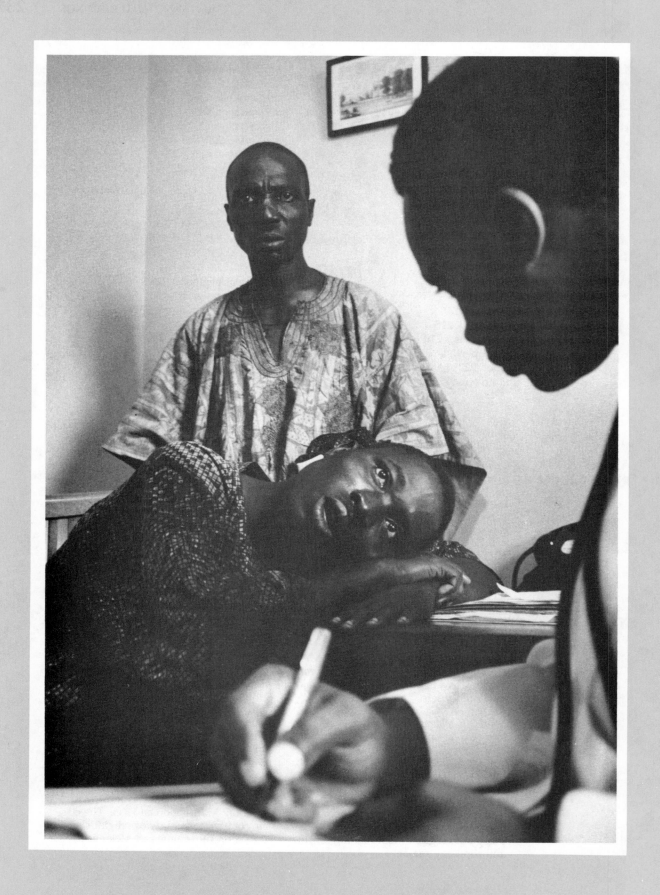

W e like to think of ourselves as unique individuals, yet we tend to be somewhat similar to other people in our society. Our personalities are not merely our own. They are shaped to a great extent by our culture. In this chapter, we will look at how culture provides the limits within which we can express our unique qualities. Culture also provides various ways for interpreting deviant behavior. Such behavior may be valued as creative or it may be stigmatized. Deviant behavior grows out of attempts to relieve the stresses peculiar to life in our own society. If these attempts do not fit within the bounds of what others consider normal behavior appropriate for our roles, we may be labeled mentally ill.

11

Culture, Personality and Psychological Process

FIGURE 11.1 *Caring for the Mentally Ill*

First psychiatrist of Nigeria, tribal chief's son, Dr. T. Adeoye Lambo, runs a clinic in Abeokuta, Nigeria.

Stressed out. Cool. Yuppie. Druggie. All-American. Are you self-confident? shy? bright? frightened? Do you listen to AC/DC? or Mozart? Do you play the violin? or basketball? Do you drink Coke? or Pepsi? Who we are and who we become depend on numerous influences both in our family and our culture.

PERSONALITY AND SOCIAL ORGANIZATION

In psychological terms, our personality may be defined as our consistent pattern of behaviors, resulting from a more or less enduring set of inner forces. Although we generally think of our personality as something located within ourselves, anthropologists are more interested in examining personality in relation to external cultural and social pressures. An anthropological view of personality portrays it as one part of a complex cultural system, most of which lies outside the individual. The governing mechanism of this system is culture, a network of assumptions, ideas, and feelings that guides the social life of a people who share them, much as the rules of a game guide its playing. Personality from this perspective is seen as an individual's pattern of behavior that results from the various social roles that he or she has learned to play. Whereas psychologists tend to be interested in the consistent ways of behaving regardless of the role being played, anthropologists are more likely to be interested in how differences in the individual's style of behaving vary from role to role, depending on the time, place, or social context of the role playing.

Socialization and Modal Personality Types

Our culture is incorporated into our personality through socialization, the process by which a culture is passed from one generation to the next. Much of this socialization occurs during our childhood. Every society has its own customs by which children are raised toward adulthood. For instance, Margaret Mead (1950) pointed out that the warlike, aggressive Iatmul of New Guinea encouraged aggression in their children by allowing them to cry for long periods before feeding them and then frustrating their attempts to take food. The nearby Arapesh, on the other hand, having a peaceful way of life, indulged their children.

It is to be expected that the adults of each society, having personalities influenced by their culture's childrearing customs, will share many common personality traits. This fact is expressed in the concept of modal personality type—the idea that beyond individual differ-

ences a typical pattern of personality traits can be found in each society.

Childhood socialization practices. During childhood, our personality is shaped by factors such as how we are fed and cared for, the degree to which we are touched and comforted, how long we are nursed, how we are weaned and toilet trained, and how and what we are taught about human sexuality. For instance, Cora DuBois (1944) reported that Alorese children in Indonesia received very inconsistent care from infancy. Mothers had to return to work in the fields within two weeks after the birth of a child, and infants received little attention until they were nursed when their mothers returned late in the afternoon. Once an Alorese child learned to walk, it received even less attention during the day. Weaning occurred before the birth of another child and was promoted by teasing, punishment, or even by sending the child to stay with relatives. As one might expect, Alorese children grew up to be suspicious and pessimistic, with shallow friendships. Alorese religion and art reflected their upbringing. Like parents, Alorese gods were not to be relied on. They had to be placated to avoid their anger. But this was done grudgingly, and

FIGURE 11.2 *Socialization*

Children in many parts of the world are nursed for three or four years, as is this !Kung San child from the Kalahari Desert of South Africa.

religious art was only carelessly crafted, without devotion. Frustration and resentment were central themes of folk tales and stories.

The family setting also is influential in childhood socialization. Whiting (1959) has shown that societies composed of extended family households are more likely to punish aggression than are societies in which households are made up of nuclear families. When extended family members live under the same roof, aggression among children is more likely to constitute a problem that will be punished by adults. Similarly, Minturn and Lambert (1964) found that it was particularly those families who live in cramped quarters that are the ones most likely to punish aggression. In such societies it is to be expected that children will experience greater anxiety about the control of aggression and that folk tales will reveal a preoccupation with aggression.

Subsistence patterns also seem to have a significant impact on personality development. Barry, Child, and Bacon (1959) compared agricultural societies with societies in which people survive by hunting and gathering wild foods. They found that the cultures of agricultural societies are more likely to stress compliance in children, while hunting and gathering people are more likely to teach their children to assert themselves as individuals. Whereas self-reliance is an important survival trait among hunters, following an established routine seems more important in the daily lives of agriculturalists. Children who play with and scatter the stored food reserves of agricultural peoples or who get underfoot in their more crowded settlements are not likely to be well tolerated.

Institutions that affect personality. Kardiner (1946) held that children's personalities are most directly influenced by a society's primary institutions, those involved in childrearing, and that out of people's personalities arise the secondary institutions of society, those most central to the ideology of a culture, such as religion, folk tales, and art. Just what are the primary institutions? According to Whiting and Child (1953, p. 310), "The economic, political and social organs of a society—the basic customs surrounding the nourishment, sheltering and protection of its members—seem a likely source of influence on child training practices."

LeVine (1973) has elaborated these relationships. He contends that a society's adaptation to its specific environment determines its economic and social structure, what he calls the society's maintenance system. This system, in turn, determines the society's childrearing practices, which—mediated by the biological needs, drives, and capacities of these children—result in the development of children's personalities. As children grow into adulthood, the basic patterns of their personalities influence how they work and play and are the source of cultural products such as fantasy, forms of recreation, and basic ways in which the world is understood—e.g., whether the environment is viewed as benevolent or dangerous. Finally, the modal personality of adults is also reflected in crime rates, suicide rates, and leisure activities and is the basis of cultural traits such as religious beliefs, art styles, and theories of disease.

Socialization, personality, and culture. Cross-cultural research has resulted in various findings that do lend support to the idea that there are connections between socialization practices, personality traits, and other parts of culture. For instance, George Wright (1954) has examined the theme of aggression and has found that it is most common in the folk tales of societies where children are severely punished for aggression. In a similar way, proverbs, riddles, and jokes seem to reflect the psychological preoccupations of people in each society.

Proverbs, like myths and legends, embody the basic values of a culture, but in a much shorter form that can readily express issues that concern people in a particular society. Their brevity makes it possible for proverbs to be inserted into conversations, where they can be used to cast light on the topics being discussed, comment on the propriety of a state of affairs, call others to take action, or even mildly rebuke another person without direct confrontation. In accordance with the work ethic, Americans remind each other that "the early bird gets the worm." The Aztec leader who was informed about disputes among the commoners might have responded, "My task is to guard turkeys. Shall I peck at those who peck at one another?" He meant that it was no more his fault that the commoners contended among themselves than it was the fault of the turkey guardian that turkeys pecked one another. Those who leave their own culture may remember proverbs that they learned years before but be unable to recall the meanings of those proverbs, since they embody symbolism relevant to specific cultural contexts that are no longer present.

Riddles are mental puzzles told for entertainment. By describing common things in novel ways, they challenge hearers to exercise their ability to see similarities between common things that are not usually associated with one another. They are a source of information about the things that a people consider noteworthy in their environment, how they classify things, and what aspects of things they judge to be relevant. For instance, Aztec riddles about spindles often relate them to pregnancy. Perhaps the most obvious analogy in these riddles is that the spindle grows in size as it is filled, just as one does in pregnancy. However, a more subtle message carried by these Aztec riddles is one of classification: They reiterate the idea that the spindle is symbolically associated with the woman's role.

Jokes and other forms of humor have long been recognized for their role in helping people relieve the tensions to which their way of life exposes them. Since the major anxieties differ from society to society, so does the type of humor. Consider the Inuit of northern Alaska and Canada. They live in a harsh environment that challenges the limits of their skill. The ability to endure pain and to cope skillfully with potentially disastrous situations is necessary for survival in the far north. The people's reaction to many near-disasters is one of mirth. For instance, they might laugh uproariously at the tale of a party of travelers who are spilled into the wet snow and lose their dogs when their sled tips over, slides from the trail onto rotten sea ice, and breaks through the ice, immersing its contents in freezing water. In spite of the inconveniences involved, the disastrous possibility of the party's being thrown into the freezing seawater has been escaped. Even the party that was involved in the situation might react with immediate laughter at their relief, before settling down to the unpleasant task of retrieving their dogs and damaged goods.

Play that is formally structured into

TABLE 11.1 *Games of Strategy and Social Complexity*

Games are metaphors for social situations people are likely to encounter. Researchers have found that the more complicated a society is, the more likely it will be to engage in complex games of strategy.

	Games of Strategy Present	Games of Strategy Absent
Societies with Low Social Complexity	5	18
Societies with High Social Complexity	14	6

Note. From "Games in Culture," by J. Roberts, M. J. Arth, and R. R. Bush, 1959, *American Anthropologist, 61*, p. 600. Copyright 1959. Adapted by permission.

games has been examined by Roberts, Arth, and Bush (1959). They view games as models of the conflict-producing situations in society that create anxiety during childhood. Games provide both adults and children an outlet for the expression of these anxieties by permitting reenactment of these conflicts in a nonthreatening setting, as well as a safe chance to practice the skills needed in conflict situations. Societies with a simple social organization are unlikely to use games of strategy; they are usually present in societies with a complex social organization (see Table 11.1).

Roberts and Sutton-Smith (1962) found that games of strategy are most popular where obedience is stressed in childrearing. Such games may well reflect anxiety about powerlessness among children who lack the determination to achieve many of their goals directly. Games of chance, on the other hand, are more popular in societies in which duty and responsibility are stressed during socialization. Such games may represent a form of defiance, a psychological release from anxiety about having to be responsible. These researchers also found that games of physical skill tend to be preferred when independence is emphasized during childhood socialization.

Fischer (1961) compared the pictorial art of complex, socially stratified societies with the art of egalitarian societies (those that are usually organized into small, self-sufficient communities, with little differentiation of activities, statuses, or rank). He found that, regardless of the specific symbols used, art in egalitarian societies tends to use symmetrical designs and repetition of simple features. Much of the available space is left empty, and figures are not enclosed by a formal boundary. In stratified societies, by contrast, pictures tend to be asymmetrical and composed of dissimilar elements that are integrated into the full design. The tendency is for little empty space to be left within the field of works of pictorial art, and figures are often enclosed by well-defined boundaries.

Fischer speculated that symmetry may reflect the basic similarity of the generalized statuses within the egalitarian communities; repetition of simple elements may reflect the similarity of individuals. He suggested that the asymmetrical design of the art of stratified societies may reflect the specialized differences and ranking of statuses; the integration of diverse elements into the design may mirror the high degree of specialization and integration of diverse statuses in complex societies. Fischer also suggested that the greater use of empty space in the art of simple egalitarian societies may represent their relative isolation and self-sufficiency. By contrast, the filling of empty space in the art of complex societies may stem from the lack of isolation of individuals, who learn to find security through establishing a place for themselves in the network of statuses that makes up the community. Similarly, the enclosing boundaries may represent the imposition of controls on the behavior of individuals—since many rules imposed from above is a social trait most characteristic of the socially stratified societies.

Music and dance. Music was studied in great detail by Alan Lomax (1968), who found the songs of complex societies to be wordier than those of simple societies. He pointed out that precision in enunciation also tends to increase with social complexity. Lomax noted that choral singing is most common where cooperative labor is the hallmark of work. Polyphony, the singing of two or more melodies simultaneously, is most common in societies where women contribute at least half of the food. Counterpoint also is most common where women contribute the bulk of the food, especially among societies of food gatherers.

Lomax looked at dance as an art form that is culturally patterned. He found that "movement style in dance is a crystallization of the

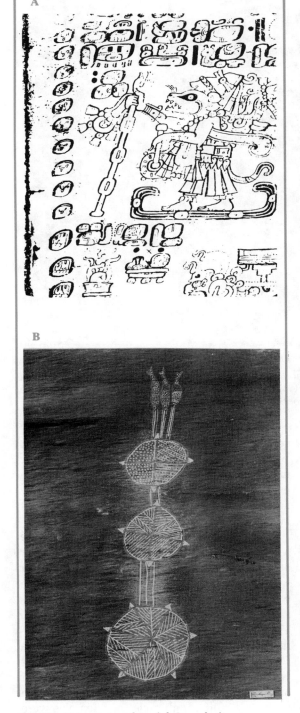

FIGURE 11.3 *Art and Social Complexity*

In this segment (A) of the Dresden Codex, the Opossum God carries the image of the Maize God to a shrine at the entrance of the town. This is an example of art produced in a stratified society. The bottom illustration (B), by contrast, is produced in an egalitarian society. Its design is simple, repetitive, and surrounded by space.

FIGURE 11.4 *Javanese Dancers*

The dances of Java are divided into two categories, Putri and Wajang Wong, depending on the social status of the performers and the audience permitted to see them. These Wajang Wong dancers use precise disciplined motions of the body and head to depict set story motifs which symbolize social and environmental concerns.

most frequent and crucial patterns of everyday activity" (1968, p. 237). For instance, the postures adopted in work frequently are found in the dance style of a society.

Socialization of gender differences. Anthropologists have noted that in every society there are socialization practices that result in differences in the typical patterns of male and female personalities. Cultures vary greatly in the particular ways in which gender differences are organized.

The well-known anthropologist Margaret Mead did fieldwork (1950) among three New Guinea societies in which the ideologies about sex roles were quite different. Her description of these societies makes it clear that concepts of what it means to be masculine or feminine are highly variable and determined by culture rather than by any absolute dictates of biology. Although there were gender role differences among the Arapesh, no basic temperamental differences were thought to exist between males and females. Neither men nor women were believed to be driven by spontaneous

sexuality, and violence, although tolerated, was not linked with either sex. Men were expected to be gentle, unacquisitive, and cooperative, and women were taught to passively accept anything out of the ordinary without curiosity.

The people of a not-too-distant tribe, the Mundugumor, were quite different in their attitudes about the sexes. The Mundugumor were headhunters and cannibals, and their life was characterized by fighting and the competitive acquisition of women from their enemies. They assumed that there was a natural hostility between members of the same sex. As a result, inheritance crossed sex boundaries with each generation from father to daughter and from mother to son. Compatible with their way of life, both males and females were raised to have violent social personalities and to place no value on sensuality. For instance, breastfeeding of infants was done in a utilitarian way, with no hint of pleasure; nursing was carried out only to give food and never for comfort from fright or pain.

Finally, the Tschambuli, a third nearby

group, did distinguish presumed personality differences between men and women, although these expectations differed radically from role expectations of men and women in North America. The Tschambuli preferred marriages in which a man had many wives and traced their ancestry through the men of the family, who owned the houses and the land and officially "owned" their wives. But in practice women held the main power in society, both in control of the economic system and in social initiative. Tschambuli women were socialized to be sexually aggressive, while the men, who were shy in adolescence, were thought to be not so urgently sexed.

Mead (1950) summarized her findings in these words:

> Here, admittedly looking for light on the subject of sex differences, I found three tribes all conveniently within a hundred mile area. In one, both men and women act as we expect women to act—in a mild parental responsive way; in the second, both act as we expect men to act—in a fierce initiating fashion; and in the third, the men act according to our stereotype for women—are catty, wear curls and go shopping, while the women are energetic, managerial, unadorned partners. (p. vi)

These extremely contrasting examples demonstrate that the personalities of men and women in any one society are not unambiguous manifestations of inherent characteristics that are fixed by nature. Rather, they are manifestations of each society's culturally patterned role expectations.

MALE AND FEMALE ROLES IN IRAN

For an in-depth example of socially patterned status differences between males and females, we can look at Iranian men and women. According to Behnam (1985), the traditional Muslim family traced its ancestry through the father, tended toward marriage between cousins, favored polygyny, and was male dominated. The Iranian family was an autonomous economic unit in production as well as consumption. This lent it great cohesiveness, and the decision making for the domestic group lay in the hands of the male hierarchy within the family. According to

Nessehi-Behnam (1985), the economic role of the family made marriage an important union between two family lines, so marital choices were a matter of great importance, with preparations sometimes beginning at birth.

In wealthy Iranian families, the symbolic distinction between the private intimacy of the household and the profane external world of strangers was portrayed by dividing the house into two areas, the private (*andaruni*) interior of the home, the area of the wife, and the public (*biruni*) area of the man, the threshold between the home and the outside world. Although the men of the family could enter the private areas of the home, the women were excluded from the public areas.

The responsibility of the woman for domestic work was emphasized by the Islamic religious traditions. The exemplary models of the division of labor within a marriage were Ali, the brother of Muhammad, and Ali's wife, Fatimah. In Islamic *hadith* or sacred tradition, Fatimah took responsibility for the domestic affairs, such as grinding the flour, baking the bread, and sweeping the house, while Ali took responsibility for all works outside the door of the house, such as bringing the firewood and obtaining food for the family. In the words of Allah as recorded in the *Qur'an* (4:34), "Men are the protectors and maintainers of women because God has given the one more (strength) than the other, because they support them from their means." Men, in other words, are thought to excel women in natural strength, so it is their responsibility to support their wives. Since a son will bear the economic responsibility of supporting a wife, a daughter need not inherit as much as a son. The *Qur'an* (4:11) specifies that, "God (thus) directs you as regards your children's (inheritance): to the male, a portion equal to that of two females."

In the Islamic view, men and women differ not only in strength but also in temperament. The woman is thought blessed by God with a tender spirit and greater emotional sensitivity. This temperament is in harmony with her role as a nurturer of children and as the conscience of her husband, but in legal matters the objectivity of her judgment may be tainted by emotion. The *Qur'an* (2:282) therefore treats the testimony of two women as equal in weight to that of one man: " . . . and get two witnesses out of your own men, and if there are not two men, then a man and two women such as ye choose for witnesses, so that if one of them errs, the other can remind her."

The man is thought to be endowed by God with greater rationality and the natural ability to become a leader. In the words of the poet Iqbal, "The virtue of man shines without any outside help; but the virtue of woman depends on another (i.e., man) to bring it out" (as quoted in *Mahjubah*, November 1984, p. 19). Thus, the Prophet has said: "The most honoured women before Allah are those who are obedient to their husbands and remain within the boundaries of their homes" (as quoted in *Mahjubah*, November 1984, p. 18).

Industrialization has created many strains on the traditional Iranian family structure. Urbanization has drawn many people away from rural areas. This shift has created higher divorce rates, especially as men have left their families in search of work in the cities. The older extended family networks that controlled the economic life of families have been undermined by the movement of couples away from their parents into the cities. Housing problems in the cities make it difficult for extended families to maintain a common residence, further fragmenting the earlier family hierarchies. Industrialization also created increasing opportunities for women to be employed. This opportunity has made divorce easier, since employment permits women to support themselves following divorce. Thus, the divorce rate is three times as high in urban areas as in rural areas (Nassehi-Behnam, 1985).

The revolution of 1979 brought attempts to reestablish the old male/female distinctions, with an increased application of Islamic religious principles in family law and values and repeal of the Family Protection Laws passed in 1972 that granted women the right to divorce, the right to an education and to work without their husbands' consent, and the right to custody of the children, as well as restrictions on polygyny. The wearing of the veil by women in public has become mandatory, women's employment has been restricted, and coeducational schooling has been terminated as contrary to Islam.

The war between Iran and Iraq has increased the death rate among men, so polygyny has been officially encouraged to provide for the widows. Islam permits a man to have as many as four wives. This makes it unnecessary for women to remain without the support of a man and decreases the need for women's employment. Once again only the man has the legal right to divorce. Under Islamic law, a man may declare himself divorced from his wife. A wife, on the other hand, cannot divorce herself from her husband without the decree of a judge, but even in civil law a divorce is more readily granted a man than a woman.

It is to be expected that Iranians who share the contemporary official Iranian view of men's and women's divinely instituted roles would have very different ideas about legal equality than are common in the West. For instance, the high percentage of employed women in Western countries is sometimes described by Iranians as a form of exploitation of women, in which women are expected to continue their "natural" responsibilities of childbearing and childrearing while taking on the duties of men as well. Thus, Western "emancipation" of women is seen as a clever device of men to overload women with work that the men should be doing themselves. According to the editors of *Mahjubah* (November 1984), an Iranian magazine for Muslim women, "Islam has liberated woman from the turmoils and troubles of the outside world; so that she may concentrate on the duties of domestic affairs" (p. 18).

Personality and Social Roles

In guiding behavior, culture defines the nature of a society, the kinds of roles the participants may adopt, and, hence, the ways that people can interact. For instance, among the Cheyenne of the North American plains, the Contrary Warrior was expected to interact with others in a different way from other Cheyenne (Grinnell, 1961; Llewellyn & Hoebel, 1941). When Contraries wished to affirm something, they were required to say "No"; to deny they said "Yes"; when they were asked to go away, it was anticipated that they would approach. Contraries were expected to be the bravest of warriors and possessed of visionary power, inspiring other warriors to fight their hardest. To set the status of Contrary apart from others, Contraries were expected to do all things backwards, displaying buffoonery even during otherwise solemn occasions.

Status-appropriate roles. Patterns for behavior are laid down in the culture's ideology as rules outlining the status-appropriate roles that people may play when interacting with one another and how those roles should be played. Personality therefore can be seen as a cultural phenomenon as well as an internal, psychological one—that is, as a culturally controlled pattern in an individual's role playing. Whenever people interact in settings where one of their statuses is appropriate, they normally manifest those parts of their personality that embody the roles of that status.

Each human group is made up of several statuses that the group defines as mutually compatible. When a person attempts to enter a new group, members interact with the newcomer to determine her or his potential to hold an available status that the group recognizes as appropriate for its members. This process determines which roles of the group's various statuses the newcomer is capable of playing. In initiating the process, newcomers "present face," that is, communicate to the others the possible social value they claim for themselves. Once admitted to the group, individuals are expected to play a role that supports that face, or social standing. They will be evaluated by the others based on how well they continue to live up to that initial self-portrayal.

SORORITY RUSH: AN EXAMPLE OF ESTABLISHING FACE

Whether we are being interviewed for a job, discussing the news of the day with a group of potential new friends, or joining a sorority, our first interactions with others are an attempt to demonstrate that we can be of value to them. If we convince the group that we can fill a role that would benefit it and if the group convinces us that we have something to gain from playing that role, then we will be taken into the group. Depending on how formally the group is organized, the process may be more or less highly structured, but it is essentially the same in content wherever it occurs.

Consider the case of sorority rush, a more formal example of face-work. On the Utah State University campus, Greek Rush Week begins on Monday when the three sororities set up a registration table in the Student Center. Young women who wish to join a sorority pay a $5 registration fee to demonstrate the seriousness of their intent. They fill out an application giving their names, hometowns, grade-point averages, and interests, as well as identifying immediate relatives who have been sorority sisters. On Tuesday, applicants attend a movie that explains the Greek system: the "philanthropies" engaged in by each House, the intramural sports between the Houses, the parties and social events that each hosts, and the activities of Greek Rush Week that they are participating in as applicants. The applicants are then divided into groups of 30 or 40 for House Tours. Each group is guided through the three sorority Houses near the campus.

During the next three days of Greek Rush Week, the applicants and sorority sisters become more familiar with each other. The sisters must study all applicants' information, learning their names and as much as possible about them. On Wednesday they host half-hour "Halloween Parties" for each group of applicants. The activities include singing and dancing. The applicants and House sisters meet personally at this time. On the next day each House invites a smaller group to return to a "Beach Party." This group includes only those applicants in which each House is most interested. At this party, the sorority sisters talk with the applicants, trying to become better acquainted personally. After the party, the sisters meet to hold an open discussion and vote on each applicant.

On Friday an even smaller group of the most preferred applicants are invited to return to the "Preference Party." The selectiveness of the process works both ways, for even if the applicants are invited by all three Houses, they may attend only two events. Preference Day is the most intimate and emotional of the three days. The goal of the House at this party is to show the value of the sorority to its members, to communicate the closeness of the sisters and how they feel about each other. There is singing, and the senior sisters give talks about what the sorority means to them.

After the Preference Parties, the applicants must indicate their first and second choices of a House on a signed document. Once it is signed, their choices cannot be changed. The sisters of each house write the names of their top choices, and all applicants are ranked based on the total votes

FIGURE 11.5 *Sorority Rush*

One example of a mutually compatible group is a college fraternity or sorority. Various houses on campus represent a particular attitude or ideal and every year new students seek to be admitted through a series of activities and interviews.

they receive. The Greek Council meets and compares the lists from each House with the preferences of the applicants, and each applicant is assigned a House.

On Saturday the applicants pick up the "bids" which inform them which house they have been assigned. They go immediately to the sorority House, where the sisters are waiting outside for them. They are greeted with song and a welcoming party. At a formal ceremony, applicants now become Pledges, a status they will hold for about eight weeks. At the end of that period, if the Pledge wishes to finalize her entry into the House, she will be initiated into the status of a full member.

Face-work. Much of our day-to-day social interaction is aimed at promoting and protecting our own face and the face of other members of our group. In general, the more highly ranked our social status, the more effort others will expend to protect our face. Erving

Goffman (1955) has described as face-work the process by which we are maintained in the roles we have been assigned to play. Often, when one first behaves in a way that contradicts the face one has initially espoused, such violations are ignored, and no damage to face occurs. It is then possible for a person to return to the usual role, and social interaction continues according to the normal game plan. If, however, a violation of the norms is brought to public attention—that is, if it becomes publicly labeled as a violation of one's expected "normal behavior"—some work must be done to repair one's damaged face. This face-work is necessary if one is to be accepted again as a fully participating member of the group.

This repair process generally follows a definite sequence, which Goffman has characterized as (1) the challenge, (2) the offering, (3) the acceptance, and (4) the thanks. In the challenge, the person who has injured or threatened another's face is confronted with the warning that the threatened face will be defended. In the offering, the offender (or, occasionally, another person) is permitted to make amends, perhaps by indicating that the apparent threat was meaningless or unintentional, that it was only a joke, or that it had been unavoidable. The offering may also take the form of excusing the actor from responsibility, as when one attributes an otherwise serious violation of rules to intoxication, fatigue, or illness. At the same time, compensation may be offered to the offended party, and the offender may take on a self-imposed punishment. The recipient of the offering may now indicate acceptance of its sufficiency for reestablishing the original symbolic balance of the group. If this is done, the offender expresses thanks for the forgiveness.

As individuals manifest their personal qualities in social interaction, their behavior is thus constrained by culturally defined rules for maintaining social order. The personality traits that are considered normal are those that can be integrated successfully into the interactions. Roles that consistently disrupt the recurring exchanges are likely to be seen as abnormal or deviant. Each society exists in a unique environment and has particular techniques for obtaining what its people need to survive there. Each society therefore has its own unique structure, with interactions among individuals guided by cultural rules that express that society's needs and values. Thus, the cultural ideals of "normal" interaction will be defined differently from society to society.

Individuality and Deviance

Although a culture's ideals and rules for behavior work to create conformity, none of us are identical to anyone else, and each of us brings with us our own unique predispositions including how we each respond to our socialization. Thus, the actual behavior of individuals varies from the expectations embodied in their culture about how people will act in various situations. The ways in which individuals may successfully deviate from their culture's rules about behavior and the degree of individual deviation that is tolerated by others is also different from culture to culture.

Deviance. To the average speaker of English, the word *deviance* has a rather negative connotation. In a more technical context, however, deviance is not limited to behavior that others consider bad. Deviance is merely behavior that differs enough from what other members of society expect, that they notice and react to it (Becker, 1963, pp. 8–9; Erikson, 1962, p. 308; Scheff, 1966). The reaction may be positive as well as negative. Deviance may be welcomed and praised or rejected and punished. Thus, creativity may be considered a kind of deviance from cultural expectations but it generally results in a valuable new contribution to society and may be rewarded. It is also true that deviation from cultural norms may bring public censure and stigma, the loss of rank that accompanies the social rejection of persons who have violated accepted role behavior. For instance, poets or actors sometimes have been imprisoned or confined in mental hospitals by governments who perceived their political commentaries as "bad," "pornographic," or "insane."

Inadequate Role Playing and Emotional Distress

Failure to play our roles as we are expected to may bring us personal distress as well as stigma. Every status has a culturally

FIGURE 11.6 *Cultural Deviance*

Ezra Pound (1885–1972) was an American poet most known for his extensive collection of Cantos. In his concern about the causes of World War II, he condemned American participation in broadcasts from Italy. Returning to the United States he was arrested, tried for treason, and finally found insane and mentally unfit for trial. He spent 12 years in St. Elizabeth's Hospital for the criminally insane in Washington, D.C., where he continued to write.

defined rank. To maintain face, the holder of each status is expected to use a particular amount of power and to receive a certain amount of honor. Failure to play one's roles in a way that uses the appropriate level of power or demands the appropriate amount of honor results in emotional distress for the role player.

The most basic form of this subjective distress is anxiety, a general sense of powerlessness and foreboding. Depending on the context in which the stress occurs and on how the individual interprets the situation, anxiety may alternate with more focused distressful feelings (see Table 11.2). Anxiety will take the form of the more concrete emotion fear if the sufferer feels that he or she is playing a role with insufficient power to remain safe from the noxious effects of some specific problem. Anxiety alternates with guilt when stress arises from an awareness that one is exercising

TABLE 11.2   *Emotional Responses to Inadequate Role Playing*

In a given situation, when we fail to respond in a manner appropriate to our status or role, we experience emotional distress.

Problem (Context of Stress)	Individual's Interpretation of the Role Playing Difficulty	Individual's Physiological and Behavioral Responses to Tension State**	Individual's Subjective Feeling
UNKNOWN DANGER, NON-SPECIFIC AROUSAL	"I need to act but I don't know what to do. I cannot cope with this."	generalized visceral tension, hyperventilation, breathlessness, tightness of chest, stomach spasms, diarrhea or constipation, rapid heartbeat, respiratory distress, fainting, nausea, sweating, tremor and agitation	ANXIETY (includes frenzy, helplessness, inner conflict, worrying, feelings of loss of self-control)
KNOWN DANGER	"I have too little power."	*facial pallor, coldness of hands and feet, rapid and shallow breathing, rapid heartbeat, immobilization or retreat	FEAR (includes terror, apprehension)
HARM TO ANOTHER	"I have used too much power."	head lowered (lower than in shame), gaze averted with only quick glances at other people, avoidance of eye contact, wringing of hands, face takes on "heavy" look with tightness around eyes, dryness of mouth, tightness of sphincter muscles, preoccupation with concepts of fault and wrongdoing	GUILT (includes self-reproach, remorse)
REJECTION, LOSS, ISOLATION	"I have too little esteem; I am worthless."	*sadness with or without tears, headaches, nasal congestion, swelling of eyes, feelings of hopelessness	GRIEF (includes loneliness, sadness, sorrow, pensiveness)
LOSS OF FACE	"I have claimed too much esteem, and others know of it."	*blushing, lowering or covering of face, gaze averted down and to one side, confusion, body curved inward on itself, curled up, makes self look smaller, eyes closed	SHAME (includes embarrassment, shyness, contriteness, sheepishness, mortification)
FRUSTRATION	"Someone/something stands in my way."	*violence of movement or speech, repetitiveness	ANGER (includes hate, rage, annoyance)

*From "The Distancing of Emotion in Ritual," by T. J. Scheff, 1977, *Current Anthropology, 18* (3), 483–506.
**Alternatively, any of these may be realized as emotionless and/or distraction.

Note. Ideas of power and esteem adapted from *A Social Interactional Theory of Emotions* by T. D. Kemper, 1978, NY: John Wiley and Sons.

more power than is personally acceptable. Grief or sadness may be present when the stress-causing situation is understood by the sufferer as the inability to obtain voluntary esteem from others. Alternatively, anxiety may take the form of shame or embarrassment when there is a possibility that the present esteem of others may be withdrawn, that is, when the stress stems from discovering that one is receiving more honor than one's skills deserve. Any of these four negative concrete emotions—fear, guilt, grief, and shame—may be avoided if the sufferer has learned to respond to others with anger instead. We feel anger when we hold another person responsible for causing our own distress.

Stress and Anxiety

Stress is the body's attempt to prepare itself to take action against any problem, whether organic (e.g., a drug-induced change in brain chemistry), psychological (e.g., learned habits that make it difficult to interact successfully with others), or external (e.g., a major life crisis, such as a divorce). Normally, we prefer to channel the energy mobilized by stress into direct attempts to eliminate the problem. When such pragmatic action is not possible, either because (1) we have not correctly identified the problem, (2) we have not learned a means of dealing with it adequately, (3) we lack the skill to take action successfully, or (4) we have no opportunity to take action, we begin to experience anxiety, conscious awareness and preoccupation with the stress we feel. Depending on how we interpret the situation, anxiety may be a general, nagging sense of foreboding, or it may take on the more concrete form of one of the distressful emotions: fear, guilt, grief, shame, or anger. Some persons so control the expression of anxiety that they experience affectlessness, a kind of emotional lethargy.

Emotional Distress and Trance

One common result of intense or prolonged anxiety is the experience of trances. Trances, which are sometimes also called altered states of consciousness, are subjective states of mind in which experiences are temporarily not interpreted in terms of the normal symbolic categories of one's culture. They are experienced regularly in various ways by all human beings as a normal response to the stresses of daily life that we all experience. Trances may be rather mild and undramatic experiences, such as the state of daydreaming or fantasy that we all engage in occasionally when we are tired or bored with our current environment. They also may be rather vivid and dramatic occurrences, such as the hypnotic trance you may have seen in a stage performance. They also occur during sleep as dreams.

Psychologist Arnold Ludwig (1972) reports that the major characteristics of altered states of consciousness are: (1) alterations in thinking, (2) disturbance of the sense of time, (3) change in emotional expression, (4) change in body image, (5) distortions in perception, (6) change in the perceived meaning or significance of things, (7) a sense that the experiences cannot be described, (8) hypersuggestibility, and sometimes (9) a sense of loss of control, and/or (10) feelings of rejuvenation. Most of these changes may be results of stress, which may inhibit the usual role of the left hemisphere of the cerebral cortex in initiating action and controlling a person's behavior during symbolic interaction with others.

Biological explanations of trances. To understand altered states of consciousness, we must first look at the effects of stress on the brain. In the discussion of a biological basis of language (see Chapter 9), we noted that the human cerebral cortex is divided into two major halves or hemispheres, and that the left hemisphere is more specialized than the right. The left hemisphere has specialized centers that make possible the symbolic skills embodied in language. Since normal human interaction is predominantly a series of symbolic interchanges, the left cerebral hemisphere tends to be dominant in initiating and controlling most human activities. Stress, however, interferes with the symbolic capacity of the human organism. This leaves the right hemisphere, the side of the cerebral cortex that takes the lead in nonsymbolic behavior, to play the dominant role during the expressive acts that are common in rituals. This is a role to which it is well suited, since the right hemisphere's predominant way of operating involves communication by direct representation, that is, by signs.

The alterations in thinking that are common in altered mental states include increased difficulties in concentration, attention, and memory, all of which are understandable results of stress. There is also a shift away from thinking in terms of cause and effect—a left hemispheric way of organizing thought—toward a mode of thought in which opposites may coexist. The coexistence of opposite meanings is a hallmark of communication by signs: A smile may indicate friendship or sarcasm, tears may signal sorrow or joy, and laughter may express either relief from stress or mounting embarrassment.

It has been noted repeatedly in studies of differences between the left and right hemispheres that the ordering of information in a sequence, such as a chronological listing of events, is a left hemispheric trait. However, the experience of time as a passage of events one after another at a constant, measurable pace is alien to the way in which the right hemisphere orders its memory of events. Therefore, the disturbed time sense common in altered mental states may be a result of a shift away from the predominant influence of the left hemisphere's symbolic conceptualization of time.

The change in emotional expression in altered states may involve an increase or decrease in emotional reaction to events. This change may happen because the right hemisphere is more closely tied to the limbic system (which influences degrees of emotional reaction) than is the left hemisphere.

Body image change may occur because the left hemisphere's body image concepts are abstract symbolic representations of its body image ideals while the right hemisphere's body image information is stored in direct representations. Any clash between the two systems of body imaging is likely to be highlighted during periods of right hemispheric dominance, as during an altered state of consciousness.

Perceptual distortions take their most dramatic form as hallucinations, which are like vivid dreams in a waking state. According to Buchsbaum (1979), studies of how the left and right hemispheres communicate suggest that hallucinations may result from the failure of the left hemisphere to suppress incoming information about the fears of the right hemisphere. Normally, this may involve an inhibitory chemical, serotonin, produced in the brain during waking hours (Goleman, 1978; Jacobs, 1978). Both dreams and daydreams are normally produced by brain stem stimulation of various brain centers on a 90-minute cycle (Krupke & Lavie, 1975; McCarley, 1978), and daydreams may be the waking state manifestation of dreams in a washed-out form. Under stressful circumstances, the levels of serotonin in the brain may decline, allowing daydreams to be experienced in the vivid form of hallucinations.

The change in the perceived meaning or significance of things often experienced during altered states is sometimes called the eureka experience. It is a sudden sense of deep insight into things "as they really are." This experience may occur because the right hemisphere analyzes experiences not by breaking them up conceptually into parts that are then related to one another by abstract logic, but by weighing the experience in its totality. The left hemisphere solves problems and discovers meaning by the symbolic process of analysis, while the right operates in a more holistic way that finds answers in sudden flashes of insight. Therefore altered state experiences may be described later as ineffable, that is, as not expressible in words, language being a left hemispheric means of communicating.

The hypersuggestibility of people in altered mental states may be because the right hemisphere is capable of understanding language and responding to simple commands or suggestions given to it in language. The experience of loss of control—which is not always present in altered states—may be nothing more than awareness that the logic-oriented, left hemispheric centers of decision making are temporarily subordinated to the more spontaneous and intuitive right hemisphere. This experience may or may not be distressful to individuals, depending on how important it is to them to keep their overt behavior in harmony with a preexisting, well-ordered set of conscious symbolic norms. Finally, the rejuvenation sometimes felt after altered states may simply be the cathartic sense of release from stress that is afforded by the sudden shift from an anxiety-laden state into an altered state of consciousness.

Causes of trance states. Ludwig (1972) reports five main ways of producing altered states of consciousness: (1) a prolonged reduction of sensory input and/or motor activity; or (2) the opposite conditions, namely, sensory and/or motor overload; (3) prolonged increased alertness or mental involvement; or (4) the opposite condition, a prolonged decrease in mental alertness or involvement; and (5) changes in body chemistry. The first of these may be exemplified by trances induced by solitary confinement, so-called "highway hypnosis," or the sensory deprivation associated with *kayak angst*. Examples of the second process are brainwashing, the trances of whirling dervishes, and the frightening encounter or tickling that leads to *latah*. Increased alertness as a path to altered mental states may be seen in the effects of fervent prayer or sentry duty. Decreased alertness is used in some forms of meditation to achieve a mystical mental state. Changes in body chemistry include all the drug-induced altered states of consciousness. All these methods for bringing about altered states interfere with the normal functioning of the central nervous system and produce stress, the source of signalized ritual behavior.

Trance and ideology. Interestingly, altered states of consciousness may play a part in the development of the ideology of a culture. Whenever people attempt to describe or account for the experiences they have had during an altered mental state, they must use the medium of language, a left hemispheric system of communication. Whatever the particular beliefs by which people make sense of altered state experiences, these beliefs share one thing in common: They invariably involve some degree of what Leslie White (1971) has called a confusion between self and not-self. This altered perception may take one of two forms: either (1) that which lies outside the individual is considered an extension of the individual, as when lightning is thought to be nature's response to a sinful thought; or (2) that which actually occurs within an individual, such as a dream or an hallucination, is spoken of as a truly external event. Ideas developed in this way are not pragmatic responses to the practical problems of day-to-day life. The function they perform is to relieve the personal effect of stresses. They do so not

FIGURE 11.7 *Drug-induced Altered States of Consciousness*

One means of inducing an altered state of consciousness is to ingest a drug. Here, anthropologist Napoleon Chagnon participates in a Ya̧nomamö ritual of sniffing a hallucinogenic through a long tube.

by eliminating the objective cause of the stress but by relieving the resulting inner feeling of distress.

Cultural Shaping of Altered States of Consciousness

To the extent that altered states of consciousness are responses to stress, they may be culturally shaped, in two dimensions. One dimension is the cultural nature of the stress itself; the other is the way in which altered states of consciousness are culturally molded as responses to stress. Areas in which the relationships between altered states and cultural patterns have been demonstrated are the use of dreams to control the supernatural, trance states, play, and art.

Dream-control of the supernatural. D'Andrade (1961) compared societies in which people attempt to contact and control the supernatural with dreams with those societies in which dreams play no such role. He found that societies in which young men move far

FIGURE 11.8   *Altered States of Consciousness in Shamanism*

A Tapirapé shaman (A) in a tobacco-induced spirit trance is helped to walk by two companions. A Cayuga man (B) is dressed as a shaman who performs rituals while under the influence of the spirit whose mask he wears.

from their parents when they marry are more likely to make such use of dreams. And societies that have the capacity to store food are less likely to use dreams for supernatural purposes than are societies that are less able to preserve quantities of food. Since the latter type of society is also likely to emphasize independence and self-reliance as a natural consequence of its low accumulation of foodstuffs, Bourguignon (1974) regards the use of dreams to control supernatural power as a response to stresses generated by the lack of human support.

Socialization and trance states. A relationship between socialization for independence and the nature of trance states also has been noted in cross-cultural research. Bourguignon and Greenbaum (1973) have noted that different cultural patterns lie behind two different forms of trance, which may be called spirit travel trance and spirit possession trance. The first is characterized by passivity or even unconsciousness during the altered mental state, which is interpreted as a "trip"

in which the spirit leaves the body and communes with supernatural entities. Possession trances, on the other hand, involve a great deal of bodily activity thought to be under the control of a spirit visitor. These trances are often entered with the aid of repetitive chants and dancing. Unlike participants in spirit travel trances, people who engage in possession trances often experience amnesia about what they said and did while possessed. In spirit travel trances, hallucinations may be vividly recalled and drugs are more likely to be used as an aid to entering the trance.

The spirit travel trances are most likely to be found in societies that place the heaviest stress on independence and assertion. Spirit possession trances, on the other hand, are most common where compliance is expected. Thus, Bourguignon and Greenbaum believe that the variety of trance that is more common in a culture is a kind of emotional safety valve for relief from the most common kind of stress in that culture. In cultures in which people normally are expected to behave in an independent way, spirit travel trances permit persons to be taken care of physically by others while they are on a spiritual trip. The spirits they visit offer help and assistance in a way that is not generally available in normal social settings, thereby fulfilling dependency needs that go unsatisfied in the participants' day-to-day social life. In contrast, in cultures where people usually play a more compliant and dependent role, some may satisfy their normally unfulfilled desires for power and autonomy during a spirit possession trance in which they take on the personalities of the powerful, dominant spirits that animate their bodies. During these possession states they can behave in ways their normal roles do not permit, speaking boldly and acting powerfully. Later, they are not held responsible for behaving aggressively, since they did so in the role of a passive vehicle for the spirit that controlled them and may even claim no recollection of their own trance behavior.

According to Whiting and Child (1953), spirit travel trances were especially common in Native North America where they were found in 94 percent of the societies examined. In contrast, only 25 percent had spirit possession trances. In Sub-Saharan Africa, on the other hand, spirit travel trances were much less common: Only 36 percent had spirit travel trances. Spirit possession trances were about as common in Sub-Saharan Africa as in North America: 26 percent of the Sub-Saharan societies had this form of trance.

Emotional Distress and Ritual

Prolonged or intense anxiety may also result in changes in behavior. The behavioral changes that often accompany spontaneous trances begin with a breakdown of old patterns leading to residual rule breaking, behavior that violates the unspoken, taken-for-granted rules of our culture. Sometimes this less typical behavior may result in a creative new solution to the original problem. More often it does not. In such cases, our residual rule breaking settles down into highly expressive ("signalized") actions that portray how we feel about the unresolved problem. Whenever it recurs, we are likely to respond with the same expressive acts. Thus, stress-induced residual rule breaking coalesces into <u>ritual</u>, stereotyped repetitive behavior that expresses problems by acting them out. Although ritual acts have no pragmatic effect on the original problem, they do have the psychological effect of reducing our anxiety.

Ritual and the control of anxiety.   We all spontaneously use rituals when we experience stress that we have not learned to handle in any practical way. Many of our rituals are organized into culturally established patterns that are shared by many people and thought of as *religious* acts. In times of crisis, these religious rituals are available as a source of comfort. Rituals give us something to do when we feel that we must act but do not know what to do. They permit us to channel some of the excess energy of stress into physical action and thereby relieve some of the physiological problem of stress. An even more important role of rituals is to distract us from the stress sensation by focusing our attention elsewhere.

Religious rituals are especially effective in this, since they are supported by an ideology that asserts that they are a source of supernatural power that can help in the problems we face.

Following major disasters, such as the 1985 earthquake in Mexico, individuals often seek comfort from grief and fear through prayer, both privately and in groups. More idiosyncratic rituals also appear, spontaneously created and carried out with the same emotional benefit of relief from anxiety. For example, people sweeping the steps of a now-demolished house reassure themselves that order can be maintained in the midst of chaos. Others gain solace after the death of loved ones by temporarily denying the loss in word and deed—by preparing food for them as usual at mealtime or even by talking to them as if they were still there. We reassure ourselves in much the same way when we bring flowers or gifts to the bed of someone in a coma, keeping alive the hope of recovery by ritual communication. When we understand the real benefits that rituals give us in emotionally trying situations, we can see that a phrase such as "empty ritual" overlooks the importance of rituals to our emotional well-being. Rituals may not solve the problems that cause us stress, but they help us continue to function in spite of that stress.

Sometimes, however, our rituals fail to sufficiently allay our worries. When this hap-

FIGURE 11.9 *Ritual Prayer*

In this village in the populous highlands of Guatemala in 1976, the residents gather for mass after an earthquake that left one million people homeless.

pens, we may elaborate the rituals in a vain attempt to gain control over the anxieties they have not succeeded in eliminating. Then our rituals can interfere with other parts of our lives and become part of a vicious cycle in which we function less and less effectively. It is these rituals that others are most likely to see as evidence for insanity. Nemiah (1975) has reported the case of a young man whose rituals began over his anxiety about not performing well but eventually interfered with his performance:

> A man of 32 who worked on the assembly line of an electronic concern developed the following compelling ritual: before he could solder one piece to another, he had to tap on the workbench 3 times with his left hand and 3 times with his right, followed by stamping 3 times on the floor first with his left foot, then with his right. For a time this merely slowed down his work performance, and he was able to continue his job.
>
> Gradually, however, an element of doubt crept into his mind. After completing a sequence of tapping and stamping, doubting thoughts would flash into his consciousness: "Did I really do it right? Am I sure I tapped 3 times? Did I stamp with my left foot first?" In response to these questions, he had to repeat the ritual to make sure it was perfectly done; but, the more he performed it, the greater his doubt. Before long, almost his entire working day was taken up by his rituals, and he was forced to leave his job. (p. 1246)

Signalized behavior has lost many of the communicative characteristics that are necessary for the exchange of symbolic information. Such communication remains highly expressive of feelings and intentions, but it is not very useful as a vehicle of abstract fact. Human communication generally consists of the use of symbols such as words and sentences and the simultaneous use of expressive signals such as the tone and volume of the speaker's voice, posture, muscle tension, and unconscious gestures. Normally, such signs provide a powerful context that helps us recognize which of the possible meanings of another person's symbolic behaviors are the intended ones. For instance, although the words are identical, the two sentences "That *dress* looks good on you" and "*That* dress looks good on you" will be interpreted in very different ways simply because of the sign difference in specifically which word is emphasized by greater volume and voice tenseness. When we are under stress, the usual contrast between symbols and signs breaks down and the significance of our words and other normally symbolic actions is less easily interpreted. At these times, our behavior, including our speech, becomes less clearly symbolic and portrays our feelings very expressively. Such behavior is best interpreted on the level of signs. Thus, as behavior is transformed into ritual, its significance as communication tends to take on meanings with more universal significance than the

256

TABLE 11.3   *The Stress Process*

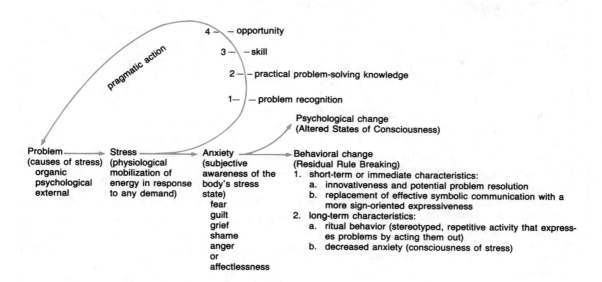

We tend to want to directly solve problems that cause stress. This may not be possible if 1) we fail to recognize the problem; 2) we haven't learned how to solve the problem; 3) we haven't the skill or 4) the opportunity for dealing with it. When we cannot solve problems directly, anxiety results, which leads to psychological and behavioral changes that are common in deviant behavior.

same behavior might otherwise have in its culturally defined symbolic role (see Table 11.3).

SIGNALIZED SPEECH

Since we normally pay attention to the symbolic aspects of speech, it is instructive to notice that when people are under stress the expressive element of their speech becomes more prominent. At such times, speech may fail to convey facts very effectively. Its meaningfulness will be best understood on the level of sign communication—as communication that expresses the speaker's feelings and needs through the connotation of words and the style of their delivery more than through the denotation of the words and the context the other words provide. Since context does not limit the conscious meaning of an individual word, the words of signalized speech appropriately may be interpreted as representing all its possible meanings at the same time. The meaningfulness of signalized speech, like that of ritual behavior, may thus transcend its performance. The expressive nature of signalized speech also gives it a similarity to poetry. Both are often

best understood by considering the allusions of the words, the recurring themes, and the multiple meanings hidden in them, rather than by merely looking for the concrete story line.

Lehmann (1975) has reported the case of a schizophrenic secretary who wrote the following memo:

> Mental health is the Blessed Trinity, and as man cannot be without God, it is futile to deny His Son. For the Creation understands germany in Voice New Order, not lie of chained reaction, spawning mark in temple Cain with Babel grave'n image to wanton V day "Israel." Lucifer fell Jew prostitute and Lambeth walks by roam to sex ritual, in Bible six million of the Babylonian woman, infer-no Salvation. (p. 896)

We search in vain for a coherent message, but the expressive concerns leap out in repeated themes: health, religion, warfare, sex, sin, and punishment. Notice the plays on words that unite several themes: *Germany* represents concern about the nation involved in World War II and about germs, a cause of illness. *New Order* reminds us of the politics of Germany under Nazi rule but also can represent the mental patient's struggle for internal order. To *lie* is to deceive, but the word also has a sexual connotation. A *chained reaction* calls to mind the atomic weapons born in World War II, but it is also true that the patient is "chained" as a reaction to her guilt. Like the Jewish prisoners of German concentration camps, the patient is confined—in a mental hospital. Is *mark* both the stigma of mental illness that she bears as a sign of her sin and the name of the illegitimate son she "spawned" and futilely tries to deny? In this signalized communication, it is possible with effort to find the remnants of a story line, but the information is so hidden by the expressive aspects of the message that any interpretation is at best a guess: After the patient "roamed" and became pregnant, she felt like a prostitute because of her wantonness. For her sin, she has been punished with a loss of mental health. She finds no solace in religion, for she is doomed to suffer pains of the *inferno*, and from her circumstances she can *infer no salvation*.

Social Stress and Deviant Personality

People who suffer the stigma and emotional distress that can accompany inadequate role playing may occasionally experience spontaneous altered states of consciousness and find themselves engaging in ritual behavior that expresses their distressful feelings. Sometimes, however, individuals become habituated to ritualized behavior and trance states, and this interferes even more with their ability to play acceptable social roles. Such individuals may find themselves reassigned to deviant master statuses, such as "immoral," "possessed," or "insane" persons.

Deviant statuses. A deviant is a person who has been labeled by others for his or her role-playing errors. The specific deviant status assigned will depend on the way in which a person misuses socially assigned power and prestige. The user of an excess of power will be seen as *hostile* and will be described as being prone to anger. The person who consistently uses less power than expected will be seen as *timid* or *fearful*. One who claims the right to an unrealistically high level of esteem will be viewed as *conceited* or *megalomaniacal*.

The overly self-denigrating individual will be labeled as *depressive* or *insecure*. Each culture elaborates these four basic categories with labels for subtypes that occur with high frequency. For instance, in American culture there is a special term for the person who manifests the hostile use of power by insulting the rank of another person: Such a person is said to be *catty*. One who uses an excess of power to prevent another from terminating a conversation, while remaining overtly oblivious to his or her own violation, will be called a *bore*.

Categories of cultural rules. Rule violations in the use of culturally appropriate levels of power and prestige are common enough in all societies so that every culture is likely to specifically label and define realms within which violations of rules can be grouped. For instance, in the United States, rule violations will be seen as violations of *law* if they result in harm to persons or property. Violations of rules of prestige, which differentiate members of one class from another, are violations of *etiquette*. *Aesthetic* standards are those current values about beauty. They include judgments about what things may be compatibly organized together. For instance, North American aesthetic standards preclude the use of Greek columns on a ranch style house, although I suspect that if one grew up with such a style it would not seem strange. As do all symbolic categories, aesthetic standards change. For instance, before the film *Flashdance*, wearing a torn sweat shirt in public was considered unaesthetic in most of America. Law, etiquette, and aesthetics are but three of a much longer list of formally labeled American rule categories.

The precise list of rule categories varies, of course, from culture to culture, and categories that are important in one society may be absent in another. In most societies, for instance, there is no formal category of rules labeled *religious* rules, since the concept of religion as a separate aspect of human life is rare (Cohn, 1967). The one universal fact in categories of rules is that, regardless of how long the list may be, there will always be rules left over that belong to none of the categories. These may be said to make up the *miscellaneous* or residual rules of that culture.

Violations of residual rules. Even if a residual category is not formally named, the violation of any of these rules elicits a similar reaction from members of society. Scheff (1966) has pointed out that it is the violation of residual norms that results in the labeling of a person as *insane* by other members of society. The violation of legal rules may be abhorred. But it is precisely because most members of society can conceive of situations in which they themselves might be tempted to violate the rights of others that such violations are deemed punishable. Likewise, violation of etiquette is undesirable, but this "poor taste" is understood as evidence of a failure to have achieved a desirable level of social ranking, something that not everyone is expected to be able to accomplish. The residual rules, on the other hand, are the rules that are taken for granted, conformity to which is assumed to come naturally to all normal individuals.

Residual rules are the prohibitions that need not be taught; it literally "goes without saying" that they are not to be done. Indeed, the prohibitions embodied in these miscellaneous rules could never be fully codified and formally taught since the list is, for any culture, an open-ended one that could be added to *ad infinitum*. It is doubtful that any Americans have ever been taught not to remove their shoes and juggle them while carrying on a conversation with a minister. Yet most if not all Americans would immediately recognize such behavior as a rule violation were they to witness it. If the actor, on being queried, failed to provide an acceptable rationale to American observers by the standards of their common ideology, the observers would be likely to judge the act and perhaps the actor as insane.

The concept of insanity is found in cultures throughout the world. According to Miller (1974) and Murphy (1976), people are judged to be insane when they seem to lack control over their deviant behavior. Typically, the insane status that such people acquire is one of the most highly stigmatized in all societies. People who hold this status are thought of as embodying the antithesis of whatever their societies regard as normal. Thus, for instance, languages as diverse as Shoshoni and English express the idea of insanity with a word that means "not sane."

Those who consistently violate the residual rules of their own culture need not be thought insane. For instance, they may be thought of as "rebellious" or "bad" if they are believed to be breaking rules intentionally. But if the residual rule breaking is extreme, others may decide that the rule breakers lack the basic ability to control the unacceptable behavior, an ability that others—including "bad" as well as "normal" persons—are assumed to have. It is then that the insane label is likely to be used. Thus, insanity typically is a more stigmatizing label than are labels such as "bad" or "immoral." And since insane behavior is believed to be "out of control," its very unpredictability may be frightening as well as unacceptable to others. This, too, adds to the stigma of insanity. From this perspective, it can be seen that insanity, the process of acquiring the master status of *insane person* or *residual rule breaker* may be viewed as a cultural process as well as a psychological one.

Stress and residual rule breaking. In the opinion of Scheff (1966), the causes of residual rule breaking are diverse. They include: (1) organic sources such as genetic, biochemical, and physiological problems; (2) psychological sources, such as problems in upbringing and training or maladaptive habit patterns that interfere with one's own success; (3) external stress such as drug ingestion, danger, lack of food and sleep, or sensory overload; and (4) volitional acts of innovation or defiance. The common denominator of all these causes is that residual rule breaking is likely to occur when the individual is experiencing stress, regardless of its sources. Stress is a physiological state that has been studied for years by Selye (1976), who defines it as the nonspecific response of the body to any demand. In the beginning stages of the stress state the human body is mobilizing itself for action. This state of readiness involves such general bodily changes as increased movement, heightened blood pressure, excess perspiration, and accelerated heartbeat.

In some situations leading to stress, the culture offers no practical avenues of acceptable action that will eliminate the cause of one's stress. In such a situation the energy inherent in the stress state may be channeled into ritualized behavior that expresses the stress feelings. Such behavior is repetitive since the stress that motivates it is not eliminated by the behavior. Yet it is associated with temporary emotional relief as the excess energy of the stress state is drained off.

When one's culture has provided no normal response to a stressful situation, residual rule breaking does have the potential of being adaptive. By doing things that are not in the normal behavioral repertoire of the culture, the stressed person may discover a creative practical solution to the original stress-inducing problem. In such cases, residual rule breaking may be a source of cultural innovation and change when problems arise in a society. However, such innovations will be adopted by society at large only if enough other members of society are trying to cope with the same kind of problem and therefore recognize the benefit of the innovation (Wallace, 1961). When this is not the case, other members of society are likely to regard the residual rule breaking as a startling and undesirable form of deviance from the usual behaviors that they expect from one another. This is one reason why people labeled insane for their strange-seeming behavior are sometimes feared as potentially dangerous. When few others are experiencing the same stresses in life and society fails to recognize the adaptive benefit that residual rule breaking may have for the rule violator, the person runs the risk of being redefined by others as insane.

From childhood through adulthood, our personality is thus shaped by our society. The ways we behave when we are with others are guided by the roles considered appropriate for our status. We may feel considerable distress if we do not live up to our role expectations, sometimes leading to ritualized expressions of the feeling of stress. Each society has its own rituals for dealing with deviance, from facework processes for restoring status to deviant labels for those who persistently err in the use of power and prestige. Behaviors that fall totally outside social expectations are categorized as insanity.

MENTAL DISORDERS AND CULTURE

Insanity is recognized in all cultures by its social inappropriateness. Edgerton (1976, p. 63) has defined insanity as a situation in which

" . . . a person's thought, emotions, or behavior appear to others in his society to be unreasonable or irrational, or when his ability to cope with the ordinary demands of life are impaired." As a case in point, Edgerton (1976, p. 64) reports the example of " . . . an elder Sebei man of Uganda who for some years spent most of his waking hours hanging upside down from the limb of a tree or a rafter in his house. His only comments were: 'I have a chicken in my head' or 'I have countless wives.' Most Sebei easily agreed on labeling him psychotic."

Some concept of insanity exists in every culture, but its causes are understood in many different ways. A widespread way of thinking about insanity is the belief that it is related to the supernatural: The insane may be possessed or controlled by malevolent spirits; they may be suffering the effects of sorcery; or they may be witches or sorcerers themselves. Harris (1974, pp. 207–24) pointed out that such views were common in Europe during the fifteenth through seventeenth centuries, a time when the political influence of the clergy was being challenged by a series of grass-roots religious revitalization movements that prophesied the end of the traditional Church-State connection. During this period when religious revivalism threatened the established coalition of clergy and the political elite, social deviants, including the insane, were often stigmatized as possessed or in league with the Devil. Treatment for their condition included the execution of witches and painful exorcism rituals that were designed to make the bodies of possessed persons too uncomfortable for evil spirits to remain.

According to Scull (1979, pp. 13–49), as the power of the European monarchs grew and that of the clergy waned, the religious model for deviance declined and socially troublesome deviants, including vagrants, minor criminals, the physically handicapped, and the insane, were increasingly confined at the expense of the state. Then, during the century between the mid-eighteenth and the mid-nineteenth centuries, a major change occurred in which the insane came to be distinguished from other deviants and viewed as mentally ill. This was a period of population growth, commercialization of agriculture, and the proliferation of workhouses and other similar institutions for housing the growing number of unemployed who had been dispossessed from the rural areas by the economic changes wrought by industrialization.

In the growing urban centers of Europe, the numbers of unemployed persons were a significant and disruptive social problem. The solution was sought in various forms of confinement: prisons for incarcerating and punishing the criminal poor and vagrants who "refused to work," almshouses and workhouses for helping and training the indigent who were willing but unable to work, and madhouses for the troublesome insane whose bizarre behavior marked them as "incapable" of surviving in the new wage-based economy or abiding by the rules of the almshouses and workhouses. The madhouses were run by medical practitioners whose background and training in the handling of the medically incapacitated was thought to be appropriate for handling the new class of incapacitated mentally ill.

The illness model of insanity was born under economic circumstances that fostered a more secular view of the world than had predominated in previous centuries. It grew up in times during which a distinction between those who were labelled "bad" because they were able but unwilling to work and those who were labelled "ill" because they were incapable of working was economically useful in the eyes of the social elite, the leaders of government and of business.

Implicit in the view of the insane as incapacitated was the idea that those who suffer from mental diseases should not be stigmatized, since they are no more responsible for their strange behavior than are other ill persons for the symptoms of their diseases. Even though the medical approach to insanity has been increasingly accepted by the public as the basis for the *treatment* of what are now called mental disorders, the public has been much slower in accepting the idea that those who suffer from mental disorders should not be stigmatized for what those in the mainstream of society see as bizarre behavior. Although the stigmatization of mental illness is certainly less widespread today than in the past, its decline seems primarily to be a result of the fact that as the mental health professions have increased in numbers, so have the

FIGURE 11.10 *Catatonic Schizophrenia*
An individual with catatonic schizophrenia sometimes maintains the same uncomfortable position for extended periods of time. This may be one way to avoid the anxiety of interacting with other people.

number of persons who are acquainted with someone who has been treated for some form of mental disorder. As was pointed out by Phillips (1963) almost three decades ago, the rejection of the mentally ill for being different was significantly less common among those who had a friend or relative who had sought help for their problems, than among other persons.

Psychiatric Categories

Contemporary psychiatric classification includes three categories of mental disorders that are held to be of psychological origin: schizophrenia, mood disorders, and neuroses. The various problems called schizophrenia are generally seen as disorders of thinking that result in bizarre forms of self-expression, often accompanied by hallucinations. In the terminology of this text, schizophrenic disorders may be defined as problems in the process of communication, especially in role acquisition and the presentation of face.

The mood disorders are defined as problems of feeling. Sufferers of the depressive variety of affective disorders characteristically experience deep emotional lows, attended by subjective judgments of personal inadequacy, loneliness, and worthlessness as well as by slowness of thought and movement. Depression refers, in other words, to problems related to the actor's sense of inadequate social value or esteem. Sometimes mood disorders begin with a brief period of mild depression that is replaced by a period of exhilaration and high activity known as a manic episode. It is believed that the manic episode helps the sufferer avoid experiencing the distress associated with depression.

The neuroses include a variety of problems in handling anxiety. From a cultural perspective, they may be seen as problems related to a sense of inadequate social power. The most commonly reported forms of neuroses are hysteria, phobias, anxiety states, hypochondriasis, and obsessive compulsive disorders.

In hysteria, an overwhelming anxiety, fear, or sense of powerlessness may be avoided by disassociating oneself from awareness of some aspects of the personality. For instance, in amnesia distressful memories are blocked out of conscious memory. This process occurs without the direct awareness of the afflicted individual. Hysteria may also take the form of conversion of anxiety into what appears to be an organic problem. Some part of the body ceases to function normally, even though there is no medical evidence of real organic impairment. For instance, in hysterical paralysis certain muscles can be used for some activities but not for others that are associated with emotionally stressful aspects of the individual's life. Tics, tremors, or an inability to speak are other examples of hysterical conversion reactions. As in amnesia, the failure of an organic function seems to occur without the person's conscious recognition or intent.

In phobias, conscious awareness of the true source of anxiety is avoided by displacing fear onto some object that is symbolic of whatever produces the anxiety. The overtly feared object is often something regarded as completely harmless by nonphobic individuals. Phobics may fear kittens, dirt, open fields, closed-in spaces—almost anything.

An anxiety disorder may involve a chronic state of tension and mild apprehension, or temporary but acute and terrifying panic-like reactions that are not associated with any real danger.

In hypochondriasis, there is an intense preoccupation with physical health and the body, a magnifying of sensations of normal bodily fatigue, aches, pains, and a recurring but unfounded fear that the sufferer's complaints are evidence of some dire disease.

In obsessive compulsive disorder, consciousness of anxieties is avoided by engaging in repetitive thoughts and acts that distract the individual from the anxiety. However, the repetitive acts or thoughts generally have characteristics that are symbolically indicative of the underlying anxiety. Usually the person suffering from these obsessive compulsive reactions considers them undesirable but feels they cannot be controlled without the experience of great emotional stress.

Culture-Specific Forms of Hysteria

Although the basic psychological mechanisms by which schizophrenia, mood disorders, and the neuroses are produced may be common to all peoples throughout the world, the symbolic forms taken by the problems are molded by the shared meanings that behaviors have in particular cultures. Anthropological fieldworkers have reported a variety of culturally specific forms of mental disorders in traditional non-Westernized societies. The most commonly described examples have been hysterical disorders.

The hysterias. *Amok* is a disorder found in New Guinea (Langness, 1965; Newman, 1964). Only young men ages 25 through 35 seem to be afflicted by the disorder, which is a hysterical reaction of the dissociation type. After an initial depression, the victim enters a phase of anxiety and depression in which experiences take on an unreal quality, and the victim broods over offenses by others. Finally, in a burst of energy, the victim "runs amok," screaming and attacking people and their property. During this stage, the sufferer seems delirious and sometimes unable to hear what others shout at him. After exhausting himself, the victim returns to consciousness but has no memories of what he has done. Among the Gururumba of New Guinea, the individual who was affected by *amok* was not expected to recompense the losses he inflicted, for his behavior was believed to have been beyond his control, caused by the bite of an aggressive ghost or some similar factor that made him not responsible during the attack. Additionally, his susceptibility to the attack was seen as evidence of a weakness in his resistance to the normal stresses of Gururumba social and economic life. Therefore, payment of his previous economic debts was no longer vigorously sought by others. Disorders similar to *amok* were also reported in Malaya, Indonesia, Polynesia, and the Sahara.

Latah was found in Southeast Asia and Mongolia (Aberle, 1961; Van Loon, 1926). It is a hysterical dissociation brought on by a sudden startling encounter with things such as dangerous objects or even by tickling. After an initial fright reaction, such as tremor and collapse, the victim engages in compulsive imitation of the actions and speech of others. In Southeast Asia and Indonesia, *latah* was most common among women, but in Mongolia it was said to be more likely to afflict men.

Imu, which is perhaps simply a variety of *latah*, was found among the aboriginal inhabitants of northern Japan, the Ainu (Winiarz & Wielawski, 1936). Like *latah* in Southeast Asia, *imu* mainly afflicted women. Brought on by a sudden frightening experience, such as hearing a loud sound or being bitten by a snake, it begins with an aggressive or fearful startle reaction. This reaction is followed by automatic obedience or its opposite, negativism, and the compulsive imitation of sounds and gestures until the victim is exhausted.

A similar disorder, arctic hysteria or *amurakh*, was found among the Yakut and Tungus of northeastern Siberia, where it also was most common among women (Czaplicka, 1914). Like its counterparts elsewhere, it involves compulsive imitation of sounds and gestures. At least in the form experienced by spiritual healers, or shamans, the original attack is brought on by a sudden fright.

Another hysterical disorder with dissociation characteristics was found among the native Greenlanders of northern Greenland (Foulks, 1972; Gussow, 1960; Wallace, 1972). This affliction is known as *pibloktoq*. It was found somewhat more commonly in women than in men. After a period of irritability and withdrawal, the victim becomes highly agitated, violent, and talkative. Some victims may tear off their clothing and run naked into the snowfields. Finally, after collapsing from exhaustion and falling into unconsciousness, the victim may recover from the attack with no memory of it.

Since *pibloktoq* was most common in the winter, increased life stresses caused by the work of coping with the rigorous arctic winter in small communities might be a triggering factor in this disorder. However, Wallace (1972) has argued that the basic cause of *pibloktoq* was the Greenlanders' calcium-deficient diet. Since vitamin D—produced by the body when it is exposed to sunlight—is necessary for the body to absorb calcium from food, the seasonal increase in *pibloktoq* could be explained by the decreased sunlight in winter. Calcium deficiency would impair the functioning of the central nervous system, producing the *pibloktoq* symptoms of nervous excitability and distortions in thought processes. Other researchers (Foulks, 1972) failed to find significant differences in the serum calcium levels of *pibloktoq*-prone and normal Greenlanders, so Wallace's calcium deficiency hypothesis remains controversial.

Hsieh-ping is a hysteria found in traditional Chinese societies (Wittkower & Fried, 1957). Sufferers, most commonly women, are believed to be possessed by spirits of dead relatives or friends to whom they have failed to offer the proper respect. It includes symptoms of tremor and disorientation, with clouding of consciousness, delirium, speaking in tongues, and hallucinations.

Saka is an hysterical disorder found among the Wataita in Kenya (Harris, 1957). Sometimes preceded by restlessness and anxiety, an attack begins with convulsive movements in which the upper body trembles and the head shakes from side to side. Occasionally, the victim may repeat actions or sounds thought to be in a foreign tongue. A trance or loss of consciousness and rigidity of the body may follow. Attacks may be precipitated by the sight, sounds, and smells of men or foreigners or even by things associated with them, such as the train whistle or the smell of a cigarette.

Social roots of hysterias.   Each of these hysterical disorders is ideologically patterned in such a way that the people among whom it is found understand the symptoms according to their culture's unique system of meanings. Yet, all these disorders share several important characteristics with each other and with the varieties of hysteria described in the Western psychiatric tradition. For instance, in most of these cases, the affliction is more likely to strike women than men, a finding that may reflect women's traditional lack of socially granted power. In those cases where men are prominent victims, they are often failing in the goal-oriented masculine roles of their culture, where power is expected to be exercised successfully. Attacks are often set off by a sudden frightening shock or by other stimuli that may call the victims' attention to how little power they have compared with others. Attacks are followed by great agitation and even violent behavior that is powerful in form, if not in fact. Alternatively, instead of violent agitation, one may find its opposite: behavior that dramatizes the powerlessness of the victim, such as automatic obedience or robot-like imitation of others' sounds and gestures. In either case, the hysterical behavior is generally performed in a mentally clouded, disoriented state of mind. Finally, after termination of this intense and ritualized drama of powerlessness, the victim, who may fall exhausted into a state of unconsciousness or sleep, is likely to experience amnesia concerning the attack itself.

Hysteria and culture.   Hysterical disorders are most common in certain kinds of societies. Seymour Parker (1962) has summarized the traits common to societies in which hysteria is prevalent: (1) early socialization is not severe and there is a high level of gratification of dependency needs; (2) there is a corresponding emphasis on communalistic values and expectations of mutual aid; (3) the female role is ranked markedly below that of the male; and (4) the religious system often provides models of hysteria-like behavior in spirit-possession rituals. In other words, child-drearing practices foster high expectations that others may be relied on to fulfill one's dependency needs; therefore, self-reliance does not reach a high level. Community values support these traits by providing a substantial level of support from others. At the same time, this communal orientation creates a strong emphasis on conformity to community values.

In certain areas of life, these expectations that one's needs may be met by others breaks down. The dependence on others rather than on oneself for fulfillment of one's needs implies that a person's self-esteem is contingent on the interpretation of his or her value in the eyes of others. Many times, this support for self-esteem is consistently available: children are not dealt with harshly, their wants are quickly fulfilled, and mutual aid among adults communicates their value. But in several areas of life, this system for gratifying the need for a sense of well-being breaks down. Women, for instance, are repeatedly reminded that their status is inferior to that of men in both esteem and power. By and large, women in these societies therefore carry a heavier burden of their day-to-day stress as private concern about their self-worth. They also are more likely than men to react to sudden dangers by fright reactions that lead to hysterical breaks with reality and that manifest their anxiety about having too little power to take care of themselves. Similarly, symbolic reminders of their inferior status may lead stressed women to fall into hysterical trances that manifest the same anxiety.

Social outcasts of either sex are not supported in their self-esteem by these societies. Rather, the communities use subtle and not-so-subtle sanctions to withdraw their support from deviant individuals. For the individual whose self-esteem is dependent on the support of others, this can be disastrous. For example, in traditional Chinese societies, the woman who failed, either out of laxity or poverty, to make the expected offerings to the dead could find herself losing the needed support of her community. This might lead quickly to great anxiety in a person not socialized to self-reliance. Since a married woman left her own family to reside with her husband and his kin, she lacked support from her own kin at times of emotional stress. The hysterical reaction that resulted was believed by those around her to be a manifestation of spirit possession. In performing a cure, the community would reintroduce her into its good graces and the hysteria would subside.

Men who are less active or who fail in the pursuit of the male goals in these societies also may develop anxiety about their inadequate personal power. This is likely in situations where they do not have others to whom they may turn for aid without denying the masculinity that they are expected to demonstrate by their independence. When arctic hysteria struck men, it usually struck those whom Edward Foulks (1972, p. 11) described as " 'nervous' young men aspiring to become shamans," that is, young men who were somewhat marginal in secular male pursuits and wished therefore to become spiritual healers.

Other Culture-Specific Disorders

Besides the hysterias, other disorders uniquely shaped by specific cultures have similar underlying patterns.

Kayak angst has been found among the native people of Greenland, especially those of western Greenland (Freuchen, 1935; Honigmann & Honigmann, 1965). It strikes males while they are alone and the sea is calm. The stress is that of physical immobility and environmental monotony in a potentially dangerous situation. The reaction begins with confusion, dizziness, and blurring of vision and depth perception. The victim becomes immobilized by fear of capsizing the kayak, a fear that is increased by a sudden chilling of his lower body, which he believes to be caused by water entering the kayak. These attacks may recur and be so incapacitating that the man may refuse to leave shore again, in spite of the economic importance of doing so. *Kayak angst* may be classified as a phobic disorder.

Susto, sometimes called *espanto* or *pasmo*, is most common in Latin America (Rubel, 1960). Following an experience of shame from failure to meet an important social obligation, the victim, whose soul is believed to have been lost because of a sudden fright or some other spiritual cause, becomes withdrawn, listless, and irritable. In addition, the victim loses appetite and experiences rapid heartbeat, nausea and vomiting, diarrhea, and restless sleep troubled by nightmares. *Susto* seems to combine some elements of depression with its primary symptoms as an anxiety reaction.

Koro has been associated most commonly with China and other parts of east and southeast Asia (Hsien, 1963, 1965; Yap, 1963, 1965). Like many other neurotic disorders, *koro* attacks often follow a sudden fright. Male victims report that their penis feels cold, numb, and no longer a part of themselves. They fear that it is shrinking and being absorbed into their abdomen, leading to death. Among women, the fears center on the belief that their breasts are being similarly absorbed and that they will die. The cultural parallel of this anxiety about masculinity or femininity is clear: The traditional ideology of Chinese culture classified all things as masculine and feminine on the basis of the *yin* and *yang* or "female" and "male" essences they contain. In China, *koro* is believed to be caused by an imbalance of *yin* and *yang* in the victim. For instance, it is believed that *koro* can be brought on in men by the loss of semen through masturbation or frequent sexual intercourse, since semen is held to be a source of *yang*, which represents masculine vitality and strength. Like *susto*, *koro* is an anxiety reaction.

Frigophobia or *pa-ling* is a Chinese disorder that involves the obsessive-compulsive need to change clothing repeatedly and to wear it in several layers to avoid heat loss from the cold and from winds (Kiev, 1972; Yap, 1951). The attendant fear of the cold and wind is rationalized by the victim of *pa-ling* by the belief that either of these may upset the balance of *yin* and *yang* necessary to health. It is believed that the resulting loss of vital essence may lead to death. In contrast to the normal use of layered clothing in China, sufferers of *frigophobia* may spend so much time changing clothes that they are unable to function in their normal responsibilities.

ANOREXIA NERVOSA: A CULTURE-SPECIFIC DISORDER IN THE U.S.

The unique social stresses of the modern United States also lead to culture-specific disorders, including one syndrome in which some young women literally starve themselves to death. Contemporary American culture emphasizes slenderness as a mark of beauty in women. Fashion models are much more slender than the average American woman. Advertisements and movies reinforce our image of a desirable figure. The stars of our motion pictures are rarely of average build, and the overweight actress is most often found in a comic role. Diet foods fill an entire section of our supermarkets.

United States culture also stresses the desirability of youth, another element in our concepts of beauty and attractiveness. In spite of an increasing awareness that sexism harms us, practically and emotionally, the word "girl" traditionally has been used as if it were a synonym for "youthful woman."

In a society in which youth and slenderness are highly valued, anxiety about weight gain and growing older is also common. As many as 1 in 250 American females between the ages of 12 and 18 years may suffer from a disorder called anorexia nervosa. The central characteristics of this disorder are an intense fear of becoming obese, an inaccurate body image, a significant loss of weight, and a refusal to maintain even a minimal normal body weight. Victims of anorexia nervosa are almost always female. They are frequently described as perfectionistic "model children." The disorder usually starts in late adolescence. The patient refuses to eat and may lose 25 to 30 percent of her body weight. Although the most common pattern is a single episode followed by full recovery, some 15 to 21 percent of cases end in death by starvation.

Anorexia nervosa has been described as an obsessive compulsive attempt to maintain a slender body build and an expression of fear of the transition from childhood to womanhood. Anorexics commonly feel inadequate in their social roles and incompetent in their work or school performance.

It is clear from these examples that the culture-specific disorders have much in common with one another. Indeed, the underlying psychological process seems to be the same. Individuals who are faced with stresses that they are unable to relieve by pragmatic action experience emotional distress about their inability to deal with their problems successfully and begin to show that stress by breaking the residual rules of their cultures. These various culture-specific disorders differ from one another mainly in their overt manifestations: The responses to stress are symbolic behaviors that are appropriate to the particular culture.

Causes of Mental Disorders

Some people use altered states of consciousness as coping mechanisms for dealing with stress and then return to their normal behaviors; others get lost in altered states. What prevents some individuals from maintaining an acceptable social role while suffering from stress? The failure may be due in part to individual characteristics that make some people unusually susceptible to the effects of stress. It may be due in part to the nature and level of the stresses involved. Finally, it also may be partly because the social reactions of others do not give each individual the same opportunity to escape from the anxieties that stress creates.

Individual susceptibility. Those who prefer to examine insanity from a psychological or biological perspective argue that insanity is at least partially a result of objective abnormalities within the sufferer rendering him or her incapable of dealing with stresses that most people can handle. This viewpoint is not strictly a Western one. Jane Murphy (1976) points out that one element of insanity in cultures around the world is the belief that those who are truly mentally ill are *unable* to control the spontaneous rituals and the onset of their altered states of consciousness. This approach often portrays individual genetically inherited differences as being predisposing factors that are insufficient by themselves to cause insanity. That is to say, genetic inheritance may play a role in setting an individual's level of tolerance for stress, but social stresses—which differ in form from culture to culture—are believed to be the critical triggering forces that precipitate episodes of insanity.

The social context. Those who prefer to apply a cultural perspective to the analysis of insanity reject the notion that it is an illness (Szasz, 1970). They assert, in other words, that it is not a problem that arises primarily due to some inherited inadequacy of the individual. The proponents of this approach believe that it is more enlightening to see insanity as a social process in which problematic situations force some members of society to play the role of sick or inadequate individuals. Those who maintain this position argue that the inability to control ritualized behavior and altered

TABLE 11.4 *Social Class and Schizophrenia*

The higher a person's rank in a complex society, the more he or she is allowed unusual behavior without being labeled as insane.

Social Class	Number of Persons in Each Social Class	Number of Schizo-phrenics in Each Social Class	Percentage of Social Class Under Treatment for Schizophrenia
I	358	6	1.67598%
II	926	23	2.48380%
III	2,500	83	3.32000%
IV	5,256	352	6.69711%
V	2,032	383	18.80216%
Total	11,077	847	7.64647%

*Adapted from August B. Hollingshead and Frederick C. Redlich, "Social Stratification and Psychiatric Disorders," *American Sociological Review* 18:163–169, 1953.

states of consciousness—used in many cultures as a criterion for judging a person to be insane—need not always be the result of a real biological incapacity of the individual who plays the sick role.

Another social aspect of insanity is that the same rule violation may be ignored when engaged in by one person, excused when done by another, and seen as evidence of "mental illness" in a third. What accounts for such differences in people's reactions to norm violations?

Research in complex societies has made it clear that the higher one's rank, the easier it is to behave in unusual ways without being labeled as insane. For instance, Hollingshead and Redlich (1953) examined data from New Haven and surrounding Connecticut towns. They found that there was an inverse relationship between social class and schizophrenia. The higher the class, the lower was the percentage of people being treated for schizophrenia (see Table 11.4). The lowest of five classes made up 17.8 percent of the community's total population but 36.8 percent of the psychiatric population. It appears, then, that one's social rank may be a factor in determining whether one enters into the role of a schizophrenic.

The situation in which a person deviates from the norms of the group may also influence whether or not the behavior is judged insane. For instance, the individual who engages in acts of autistic reverie will not be thought insane if this silent musing is confined to times when he or she listens to music. The person who carries on half of a dialogue with what seems to be an unseen partner will not

be thought to be mentally ill if there are cues such as age or setting that suggest an alternative explanation—for instance, a child may talk to an "invisible playmate," and an actor or university professor may rehearse lines for a play or public address. Even the person who claims to hear voices that others do not hear or who "speaks in tongues" and makes unintelligible sounds need not be thought of as strange, if he or she does so only during the services of an appropriate religious organization. On the other hand, these same activities performed in other contexts may lead to the practitioner's being labeled insane.

Since the status of the insane is a master status with low access to both power and prestige, once people have been labeled insane they are likely to continue to be thought of as insane, irrespective of their future behavior. One American researcher, David Rosenhahn (1973), had himself and several other researchers admitted to a number of American mental hospitals as patients. He and his co-researchers discovered that once they had been admitted, even though they behaved normally, the hospital staff, including psychiatrists, psychologists, and psychiatric nurses, failed to recognize that they were actually sane.

The implication is that the researchers' predicament mirrored what happens in social life outside institutions. Once we are branded with a deviant status associated with an altered state of consciousness, others will assume that all our actions spring from an altered state of consciousness and therefore withhold power and prestige from us, severely restricting the roles we are allowed to play.

SUMMARY

From an anthropological perspective, personality is an individual's patterns of behavior that express the various social roles he or she has learned to play. As children, we are socialized to fit into the patterns of our society. As we take on roles, we learn the behaviors that are considered appropriate for them. These behaviors are what others perceive as our personalities. The socialization customs of each society engender different anxieties in children, and these are expressed in various ways, including the themes of folk tales, the kinds of games children like to play, the art, music, and dance of a society.

The socialization that is the source of our personality differences results in the typical male and female personality characteristics that are found in societies throughout the world. The social roles which define our personalities are also not the same in every culture. Each society includes different statuses, each with its own culturally defined role. Normal day-to-day behavior in any society is a matter of trying to play those roles appropriately. However, not everyone plays the roles assigned to him or her in a uniform way. In every society, people deviate from their expected roles in ways that may be approved as creative or stigmatized as unacceptably deviant.

The stigma of inadequate role playing is often accompanied by emotional distress and sometimes by trances, altered states of consciousness that are interpreted in most societies as evidence of the influence of supernatural forces. Ritual behavior is another common result of anxiety. Those who have such experiences too frequently may be reassigned to a master status such as that of insane person, a status that implies an inability to control one's own behavior. The insane status is found in every culture, but cultures differ in how it is understood.

ANNOTATED READINGS

Barnouw, V. (1985). *Culture and personality.* (4th ed.). Homewood, IL: Dorsey. An introductory-level text on psychological anthropology.

Bateson, G. (1936). *Naven: A survey of the problems suggested by a composite picture of the culture of a New Guinea tribe drawn from three points of view.* Cambridge, MA: Cambridge University Press. The analysis of a Iatmul ritual that led to Bateson's revolutionary theory of schizophrenia.

Hsu, F. L. K. (Ed.). (1972). *Psychological anthropology: Approaches to culture and personality.* Morriston, NJ: Schenkman Press. A basic survey of the field of psychological anthropology for the advanced student.

LeVine, R. A. (Ed.). (1974). *Culture and personality: Contemporary readings.* Chicago: Aldine. A useful collection of papers on cultural and psychological aspects of the human condition, including cultural interpretations of the abnormal personality.

Marsella, A. J., DeVos, G., & Hsu, F. L. K. (Eds.). (1985). *Culture and self: Asian and Western perspectives.* (New York: Tavistock Publications. A current examination of the experience of self from a cross-cultural perspective.

Price-Williams, D. R. (1975). *Explorations in cross-cultural psychology.* San Francisco, CA: Chandler and Sharp. A short but somewhat technical examination of cross-cultural psychology with emphasis on cultural relativism in the interpretation of human psychology.

Simons, R. C., & Hughes, C. C. (1985). *The culture-bound syndromes: Folk illnesses of psychiatric and anthropological interest.* Boston: D. Reidel Pub. Co. The most comprehensive survey of the culture-specific mental disorders available. Each disorder is described and then analyzed in terms of contemporary Western psychiatric classification.

Wallace, A. F. C. (1961). *Culture and personality.* New York: Random House. A short and insightful examination of culture and personality.

PART V

Cultural Change

Human cultural systems are dynamic. The pace of change is rapidly accelerating today as societies communicate more easily with one another and learn to adapt more readily to a complex, technological way of life. Chapter 12 details this process of cultural evolution, focusing on the interrelationships among technology, social organization, and ideology. Chapter 13 illustrates how this process affects contemporary world societies. Chapter 14 takes a unique anthropological view of contemporary American culture.

and Diversity

271

*H*uman cultural systems do not remain forever stable. In adjusting to the world around them, to the effects of population growth, and to the influence of other groups, human beings adopt new and different ways of manipulating their environment, of organizing themselves, and of thinking and communicating. Over the millennia, societies have evolved from simple hunting and gathering ways of life to extremely complex ones based upon industrialized technologies. We can reconstruct the process of cultural evolution on the basis of evidence provided us by the contemporary diversity of human cultural systems. In this chapter we will explore the process of cultural change, the levels of cultural complexity, and the rules that govern movement toward greater complexity. The chapter ends with the discussion of whether technological progress is simultaneous with progress in quality of life.

12

Process of Cultural Evolution

THE PROCESS OF CHANGE
Cultural Dynamics
Interrelationships Among Technology, Social Organization, and Ideology

LEVELS OF CULTURAL COMPLEXITY
Bands

Tribes
Chiefdoms
States
CULTURAL EVOLUTIONARY THEORY
Archaeological Evidence of Cultural Evolution

Specific and General Evolution
Stabilization vs. Evolutionary Potential
Leapfrogging
Progress?

FIGURE 12.1 *Yąnomamö Archer*

The Yąnomamö, a contemporary tribe in the jungles of Brazil, have until recently resisted the effects of industrialized culture.

Tai Chi. Cannes. Beta Max. Chernobyl. Challenger. Are we becoming a global culture? Is there any area of the world that has not seen the golden arches? Or not felt the influence of a microchip? How do we maintain individual and cultural autonomy in a world that is becoming culturally unified?

THE PROCESS OF CHANGE

Cultural traits are subject to many change-promoting influences, both internal and external. As one trait changes, others also shift, ultimately altering the nature of the entire cultural system.

Cultural Dynamics

No culture is completely static. Cultural changes may arise within a society, or they may result from the cultural influence of one society on another.

Innovations that arise within a society are of two types: discoveries and inventions. A discovery involves noticing something that has not been noticed before. Discoveries are made, of course, on the basis of what the current cultural pattern of thinking prepares people in the society to notice in their environment. Although they must be new and different from previous ideas, they must not depart too radically from the current way of thinking or they will seem bizarre. In such a case they will not be accepted. In a culture with a high degree of role specialization, it is possible for some members of society to have experiences that are so uncommon in society at large that the insights they produce will be regarded as insignificant, foolish, or of no practical use. Gregor Mendel, a nineteenth-century Austrian monk, spent years cultivating plants and in the process developed revolutionary new ideas about genetics that were shelved for years. It was only much later that growing interest in evolutionary theory among biologists provided a place where Mendel's discoveries proved to be very useful and enlightening to the scientific community. Similarly, inventions, which might most simply be defined as putting previous cultural elements together in some new way, must be seen as valuable in terms of the prior values of a way of life or they will not be adopted by a people.

Cultural changes that occur as a result of the influence of one society on another are referred to as diffusion, the passage of a cultural trait from one society to another. Anthropologists generally distinguish between two forms of diffusion: direct borrowing of traits and stimulus diffusion, in which the idea of the trait rather than the trait itself passes from

FIGURE 12.2 *Diffusion*

One way a society's culture is influenced by another is through diffusion. Here, a young Yugoslavian woman's manner of dressing contrasts sharply with the traditional style worn by the women behind her.

one people to another. In both cases, the trait is likely to be modified in form, use, and meaning as it diffuses from one culture to another. Such adjustments allow it to fit into the ongoing way of life of the recipient society. But the greatest changes in a trait are likely to occur when the idea is borrowed and then the trait is created anew on the basis of the idea in the borrowing society.

Tobacco provides an example of changes in a directly borrowed trait. It was originally commonly used as an important religious ritual item in the Native American cultures. It was borrowed from one society to another until it is now found in all parts of the world. In the process, both the crop and methods of its preparation have been greatly modified. It is now used in many parts of the world as what might be called a recreational substance, smoked for enjoyment rather than for religious reasons (Linton, 1936). The development of writing in Egypt also illustrates how the form of a trait may be changed when it is borrowed.

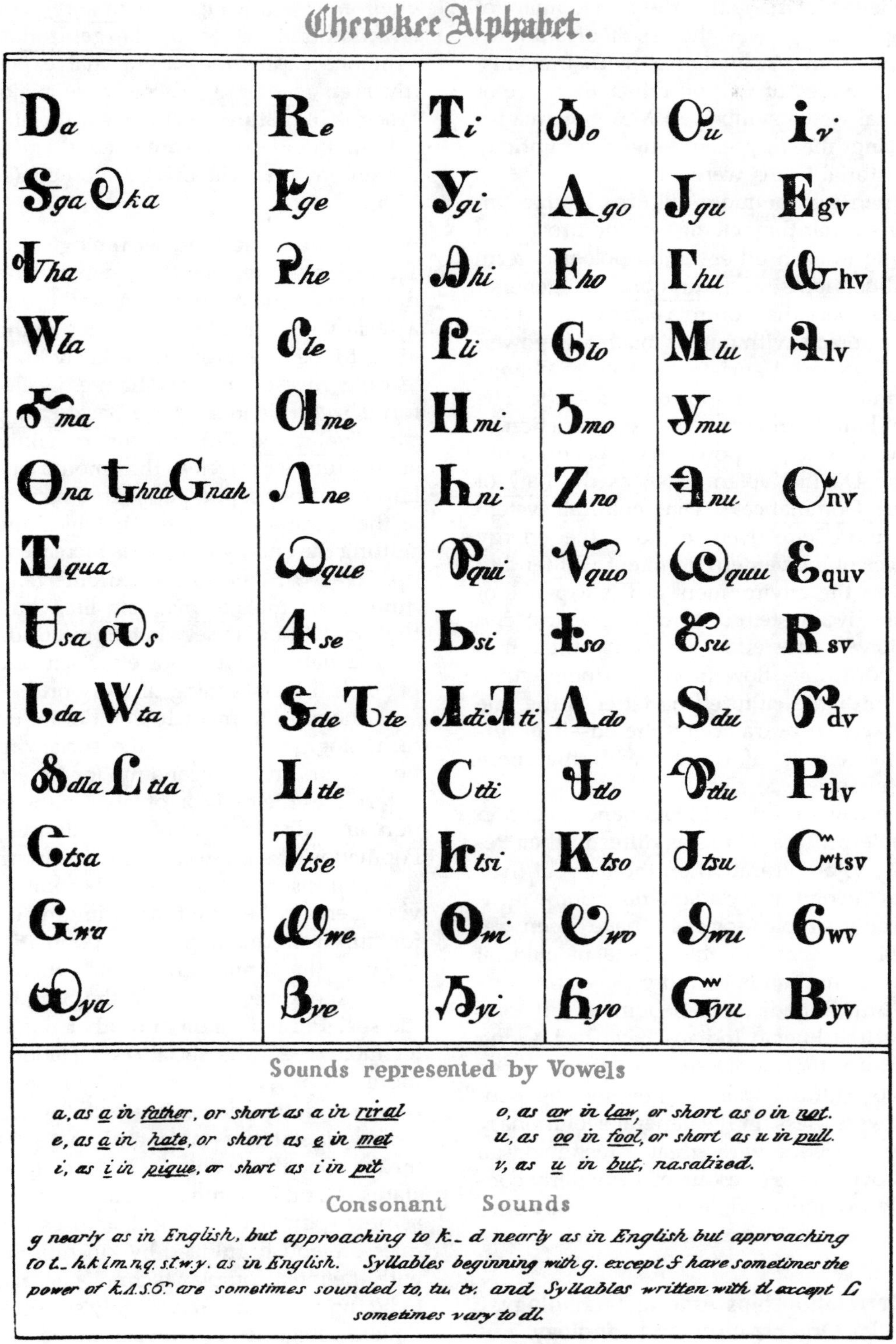

Cherokee Alphabet.

Sequoyah's alphabet, or syllabary, for writing Cherokee.
Smithsonian Institution.

FIGURE 12.3 *Cherokee Alphabet*

Language is fundamental to acquiring, storing and communicating knowledge and thus is crucial to the development of culture. Sequoyah, the Cherokee Indian, developed this alphabet for his tribe.

It is believed by many that the development of writing in Egypt was the result of stimulus diffusion from Mesopotamia, with transmission of the idea of writing rather than use of the actual visual symbols of Mesopotamia for portraying the Egyptian language. Entirely new pictorial forms were chosen.

When two or more cultures interact intensely so that they change in the process of adjusting to each other, anthropologists term the adjustments acculturation. In general, when a society that controls a great amount of power interacts with one of much less power, the less powerful society is likely to change more than the more powerful society. The general long-term effects of the interaction of societies of unequal power have been formulated by David Kaplan (1960) as the Law of Cultural Dominance: "That cultural system which more effectively exploits the energy resources of a given environment will tend to spread in the environment at the expense of less effective systems." Any interacting cultures have some effect on each other. But, since more traits flow from the dominant to the subordinate culture, the latter is the one more likely to be radically altered—if it survives the effects of contact with the more powerful society at all.

The Law of Cultural Dominance is not an invariable process. Cultures differ in their receptivity to acculturation on the basis of their degree of evolutionary adaptation. Some technologically simple societies have been remarkably resistant to the effects of cultural change at the hands of more powerful societies. Ruth Benedict (1934) pointed out long ago that the Pueblo Indians have had a long history of rather successful resistance to the effects of cultural traits of neighboring peoples. Nevertheless, in the general evolutionary scheme, societies with greater technological control over energy resources have fairly consistently expanded while technologically simple societies are becoming fewer each year.

Interrelationships Among Technology, Social Organization, and Ideology

Change may begin within any aspect of culture but is likely to then affect other aspects as well. The major goals of culture-guided behaviors are manipulation of the external environment (through technology), social interaction (the role of social organization), and symbolic expression of internal experiences (through ideology). These three major subsystems of culture—technology, social organization, and ideology—are related, and change within any one will affect the others (see Fig. 12.5).

Evolution through technological change. Technology—the means by which energy is drawn from the environment and used within a society—is considered by some anthropologists to be the area most likely to be the leading edge of cultural change. Leslie White formalized this idea as the Basic Law of Cultural Evolution: "Other factors remaining constant, culture evolves as the amount of energy harnessed per capita per year is increased, or as the efficiency of the technological means of putting the energy to work is increased" (1971, pp. 368–369). Due to the extreme reliance of humans on tools to maintain life, changes in the tool kit of a society have profound effects on the nature of the society itself and on a people's understanding of the world.

The most immediate point of influence of technological change on the social organization occurs in the economy, for its structure determines the division of labor in the production and distribution of subsistence goods. Population size is affected too: The more effective a subsistence technology becomes at providing energy beyond the minimum necessary for survival, the larger the population will grow. As the population expands, there will be a corresponding increase in the complexity of the social organization and other parts of the technology. As the social organization grows more complex with increasing numbers of statuses and specialization—and interdependence of statuses—new and more complex means of political control will develop. Kinship statuses tend to become socially less important as new specialized political statuses take over roles previously fulfilled by kinship. Societies with the most complex technologies also tend to be those that are most highly stratified with ranked categories of statuses, some of which have access to greater amounts of power, prestige, and control over the material wealth of the society.

These technological changes will be reflected in ideological adjustments, first as new

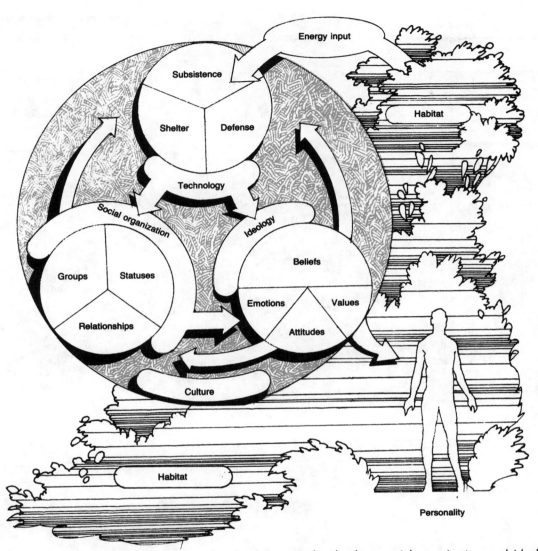

The chart shows the relationship of the cultural subsystems of technology, social organization, and ideology. Change in any one will affect the others.

informal patterns of ideas and feelings arise and later as the formal, conscious ideology finally accommodates to the new circumstances. The ideology may reflect technological or social innovation by actually adding new beliefs. For instance, changes in a society's tool kit may provide people with added insight into the nature and functioning of the world around them. However, it is probably more often the case that ideological change involves the modification and replacement of earlier beliefs and feelings with newer ones, rather than the simple addition of new elements.

A classic example of the effects of technological change on social organization and ide-

ology is the case described by Sharp (1952) of the effects of the introduction of steel hatchets to the Yir Yiront, an Australian hunting and gathering society that previously had known only the stone axe. Among the Yir Yiront, stone axes were manufactured only by adult men and were the property of adult males only. They were, however, commonly used by women, by men who owned no axe of their own, and by children. Whenever these persons performed a task requiring an axe, they had to borrow one from an adult male kinsman. The process reinforced the authority of the kinship system that structured the society, and the axes served as symbols of masculinity

FIGURE 12.5   *Acculturation*

The process of two cultures interacting so they become more like each other is called acculturation. Here we see in A, a family of Tierra del Fuego Indians in primitive dress standing in front of their modern style house; in B, a Kikuyu tribal dancer on a Nairobi municipal bus; and in C, Arabs carry home their supply of Pampers.

FIGURE 12.6 *Technological Evolution of Culture*

Technology is the leading edge of cultural change in a society. These donkeys and cars share a street in Addis Ababa, Ethiopia.

and male dominance in the social and economic system. Enter the European missionaries, who attempted to help the Yir Yiront "improve their conditions of life" by distributing or trading steel axes which, being technologically more efficient tools, were to help the natives "progress." Through the missions, it became possible for women, young men, and even children to possess their own axes. This change undermined the authority of the adult males of the society and eventually had a disruptive effect on the economic system of the Yir Yiront as well, since their trade with neighboring peoples was motivated by the need to acquire stone to manufacture stone axes. The festive annual gatherings at which trade previously had occurred began to lose their social importance and excitement as trading partnerships weakened. A man might find it easier to obtain a steel axe from white men by selling his wife's favors than by traditional means, an outcome hardly foreseen by the European missionaries!

Evolution through social change. Cultural change may begin not only within the technological subsystem but also within the social organization. As a population grows, the number of social relationships increases, and new ways of coordinating society are needed. New statuses and institutions arise in response to these pressures. In very simple societies, the family is the fundamental institution of social control. It educates the young, produces food and other economic goods, carries out judicial activities when members violate important rules, and performs other "governmental" functions. As societies increase in population and density, new institutions arise to help coordinate human interaction. One important new institution is the special-interest nonkinship association—groups such as the local militia composed of all young men of the group, the voluntary fire brigade, or the harvest cooperative group. Larger-scale societies begin to develop full-time specialists and other new statuses and groups such as full-time governmental specialists, draft laborers, religious leaders, and standing armies.

As the social organization becomes more complex, these changes are reflected in the society's technology and ideology. For instance, when producers begin to specialize in the manufacture of the same item, wares tend to become more standardized in form. Ideologically, as governmental specialization develops, members of the society increasingly value order and stability, even at the expense of individual autonomy.

Evolution based on ideological change. Adjustments in the cultural subsystems that are initiated in the ideological realm may be exemplified by processes such as the birth of a new religious or political philosophy. When successful, the new doctrine is proclaimed by a social body organized by the author of the new teachings. New ideologies thus give rise to new social structures, which influence the functioning of the culture's technology.

An ideology may, on the other hand, slow the process of change. The Old Order Amish of Pennsylvania are a well-known example of a social body that for ideological reasons has remained highly resistant to the complex technological changes that have occurred among their neighboring Americans. The Amish have maintained a horse-and-buggy transportation system, a horse-drawn plow subsistence technology, and a home life unaffected by the presence of radios, televisions, and other common North American household appliances.

LEVELS OF CULTURAL COMPLEXITY

As human technologies evolved historically from hunting and gathering through horticulture to agriculture, corresponding changes occurred in the social organization and ideology of human cultural systems. These changes will now be outlined using five societal types—bands, tribes, chiefdoms, agrarian states, and industrialized states—in order of increasing cultural complexity. All types still are present in the contemporary world, but the trend is toward industrialized states, with band and tribe forms becoming increasingly rare.

Bands

The foraging technology forms the subsistence base of a societal type known as the band. According to Julian Steward (1955) and Elman R. Service (1962), the hunting and gathering technology places certain functional demands on the social organization of the band-level culture. Bands are typically small groups based on kinship, with labor divided only by age and sex, sharing of resources, temporary leadership roles, material possessions limited by nomadism, and ideals reflecting these features. Wild foods are a sparse resource for people with no other means of survival. The poor environments occupied by foragers in recent times are unable to support more than about one person per five square miles and in some places as few as one person per 500 square miles.

Group structure. Permanent social groups cannot be very large. The local group that works and lives together averages about 50 people in contemporary band societies and rarely exceeds 100 people. The local groups of band cultures may have been somewhat larger in earlier times, when bands occupied areas with more abundant resources than are now found in the marginal areas to which they have been restricted by the expansion of more powerful societies. Nevertheless, wild food resources cannot maintain large local groups except in very lush environments, since the larger the group is, the farther individuals must travel from their base of operations in their quest for food.

As a general rule, in the small, local groups of band cultures, all individuals will be related, either by descent or marriage. Kinship is the basic institution in a band society for organizing the education of children, social etiquette, and economic, political, military, and judicial practices. In these largely familial groups, family ties and ancestry are most commonly kept track of through the men.

Division of labor. The only specialization of labor in a band culture is that based on differences of sex and age. In a band society supported by the sparse resources of wild foods, the most economical division of subsistence labor usually assigns the work of hunting to the men, while the gathering of wild plants near the camp is done by the women and older children. The sexual aspect of this specialization of labor is an adaptation to pregnancy in the female and the need for prolonged nursing of infants. Although these two biological facts might hinder her as a hunter, the woman still can be an important provider of plant foods gathered locally during periods of pregnancy and lactation. Elman R. Service (1962), R. B. Lee and Irven DeVore (1968), and J. Tanaka (1977), have estimated that women sometimes provide as much as 80 percent of the calories in the diets of people who survive by hunting and gathering. However, in circumstances where a rigid differentiation is not important for the survival of the group, men, women, and children may be allowed to play overlapping roles. In hunting and gathering societies in areas with plentiful wild foods, men may often gather wild plants as well as hunt; men, women, and children may frequently work together in cooperative hunting activities, even though hunting is thought of as more central to the male status.

Ernestine Friedl (1975) has suggested that the sexual division of labor in foraging societies takes one of four major forms: individual foraging, communal foraging, plant-focused foraging, and animal-focused foraging, discussed in more detail in Chapter 3, Environment, Adaptation, and Subsistence.

Economy. Beyond age and sex specialization, all persons are economic generalists. Without economic specialists, the band economy functions by a simple mechanism known as reciprocity, the mutual sharing of surpluses in the form of reciprocal gift-giving. The trait of generosity, so characteristic of band peoples, is actually a very effective economic device for insuring the survival of the entire group. For a hunter, the sharing of one's excess during times of successful hunts serves as a kind of insurance against his own future times of need. Every hunter is bound to experience some periods of poor luck in the chase. Generosity to others in one's own times of plenty is more than a mere act of good will; it is an investment. Those with whom a hunter has shared food or other useful goods in the past will make return gifts of their own later surpluses to insure the continuation of his good will in the future when they again are the ones

in need. In the long run, the economic system of reciprocity maintains a balance in the distribution of goods. No one prospers at the expense of others, but neither does anyone need fear the specter of starving alone during the inevitable periods of personal failure or illness when one cannot hunt.

Leadership. As might be expected, band societies lack sufficient resources to support any full-time educational, economic, religious, military, judicial, legislative, or executive specialists. All leadership is charismatic. That is, a man or woman becomes a leader in some activity because of a personal talent in that area. Leadership also is unofficial; it is maintained only so long as a person demonstrates the qualities of excellence that draw a following. Charismatic leadership confers no authority, no power to coerce. A leader can only lend advice or take the initiative. Coming from a man or woman of respected abilities or wisdom, the advice or action is apt to be followed by others. The leader in the hunt is likely to be a man of proven ability in locating, tracking, and capturing game. A less effective hunter does not assert himself in matters of the chase but may nevertheless be a respected leader in political matters where his broad experience and proven wisdom bring greater attention to his judgments than to those of other members of the group. However, as abilities decline, so does the leader's following.

Nomadism and material culture. Since the wild food resources near enough to be conveniently obtained from any given home base soon will be depleted or scattered too far to make their search and retrieval worthwhile, camp must be moved frequently. Without a domestication technology, people must follow their food supply. This seminomadic pattern has a feedback influence on the nature of a band society's material technology. The band society's tool kit is influenced by the number of things the group can carry when it moves on to a new hunting ground. Band-level peoples cannot afford to have as many different kinds of specialized tools as are commonly found among more sedentary peoples. Each tool must be able to serve many different functions. For instance, the Australian boomerang served not only as a throwing weapon used in the hunt but also as a flat working surface when making other tools, a digging tool, a club, a scraping tool, and a percussion musical instrument.

Ideology.   Since a hunting and gathering technology has an impact on a band society's ideology, it is possible to outline ideological characteristics that are common to band cultures. Like members of all human societies, band-level people learn to gain pleasure from their way of life; their likes and dislikes grow out of the experiences available in their own culture, as do their values. Perhaps the primary characteristic value of band cultures is that of generosity, for members of the group must adhere to the economic principle of reciprocity if all are to survive. Unlike the ideologies of settled horticultural and agriculture peoples, band ideology includes no concept of private ownership of land. Such an idea would be maladaptive to a society that must follow the game to survive. Of course, the belief system also must include accurate factual knowledge of subsistence and shelter techniques needed for survival by those who hunt and gather the wild products of nature.

The social organization of band societies also has an effect on their ideology. Some of these may be illustrated in terms of religious ideology. In an egalitarian society there is no hierarchical arrangement of the groups that initiate and control aspects of social life. In such societies, the supernatural realm will be equally unranked in its membership: There is no concept of a high god who rules over other lesser gods and spiritual entities. Hunters are more likely to be concerned with their personal spiritual relationship with animals and with spiritual entities and powers that may improve their hunting effectiveness.

In a society where a person's survival depends to a great extent upon her or his own talents and prowess, this autonomy of the individual is reflected in a belief in personal souls that reside in and animate the bodies of individuals. The ideologies of band societies also commonly include a belief in the reincarnation of the spirits of individuals. Reincarnation embodies the idea that the spirits of one's ancestors continue to be interested enough in the goals and purposes of the group that they return to it, thus symbolically expressing the

FIGURE 12.7   *Shoshoni Winnowing*

The Shosoni wandered in search of their food supply from season to season. This woman on the Lemhi Reservation, Idaho, in 1904, is winnowing wheat using the traditional Shoshoni method.

continuity across generations of the personal interests and goals that are central to the life of the small local band.

Human health is another major concern of the religious ideology of the band. Since many illnesses lie beyond the control of the band-level medical technology, human anxiety concerning health is alleviated by the belief that such illnesses are caused by (and can be cured by) spiritual forces. The forces commonly believed to cause illness are witchcraft, spirit possession, the intrusion of a foreign spiritual substance into the body, or spiritual contamination due to the violation of some ritual rule.

THE GREAT BASIN SHOSHONI: A BAND SOCIETY

Steward (1938) described the native culture of the Great Basin Shoshoni. The Shoshoni occupied a territory that stretched all the way from near Death Valley, California, through central

Nevada, northern Utah, and southern Idaho to central Wyoming. It generally is believed that the Shoshoni moved into the Great Basin from somewhere near the Death Valley area some 1,000 years ago. Throughout their territory, the Shoshoni spoke dialects of the same language, closely related to those of their Great Basin neighbors, the Northern and Southern Paiute and the Ute, who practiced a similar way of life.

The Shoshoni were a highly mobile people who hunted game and gathered wild plant foods in a sparse desert environment. Variations in rainfall made the location and amount of plant and animal foods highly variable from year to year. The Shoshoni spent much of the year in search of food, wandering in small groups of one to three nuclear families. During the spring and summer months, their food consisted of foraged seeds, berries, roots, and small game such as insects, larvae, rodents, and other small mammals.

Occasionally, several families who usually hunted separately would happen upon a large congregation of rabbits. If one of the families owned a rabbit net, a collective hunt would be held. The rabbit net was about eight feet high and several hundred feet long. It was laid out in a great semicircle, and everyone would fan out to drive the rabbits toward the net. When the rabbits became entangled in the net, they would be clubbed or shot. These hunts provided both meat and furs which, cut into strips and woven into capes, provided warmth in the cold winter season. Similar communal hunts were held when antelope were available. After the hunt was completed and the meat eaten, families would again go their own ways in the search for food.

In the late summer, Shoshoni families would move toward the mountain ranges where pine nuts would soon ripen. The best locations at which to gather pine nuts varied, so families would congregate at different locations each year as fall approached. They gathered pine nuts in the fall and stockpiled enough to feed themselves during the cold winter months.

During the winter months, 20 to 30 families would camp in the same vicinity. Winter was a time for socializing. Dances and gambling were popular recreations. The most common dance was a communal one in which men and women arranged themselves in a great circle and sidestepped in one direction. This dance was believed to

have some general health benefits for those who participated. Gambling took many forms. Especially popular was the hand-game, played with two short sticks, one banded and the other plain. One member of each of two teams would alternately conceal these sticks, one in each hand, while a member of the opposing team would attempt to guess which hand concealed the banded token. Rapid singing was used to confuse the person who was guessing.

At the end of the winter, families began to disperse once again, some having added a new member or two by marriage. New wives left their families of birth and traveled with the families of their husbands, for marriage among the Shoshoni was patrilocal. The Shoshoni were flexible about their marriage forms, which included polygyny, some polyandry, and group marriage as well as monogamous marriage. When a man married several women, it was preferred that they be sisters. Young men frequently would marry each other's sisters, thereby cementing their two families more firmly together. Since winter encampments brought different groups together at different locations each year, marriages created kinship ties between families that were widely dispersed. This gave the nuclear family relatives in many different locations with whom they could cooperate whenever they met in their wandering quest for food.

Cooperation within and between families was the basis of Shoshoni economic and political life. There was no governing authority among the Shoshoni outside the family even during the winter encampments. Prior to European contact, there was no warfare among the Shoshoni. Property was limited to what people carried with them as they traveled, so there was little conflict over property rights. What few conflicts arose could usually be settled within the group on the basis of familial authority. Conflicts between different families were most often concerned with witchcraft accusations or wife-stealing. These might be settled by a feud, but the wandering way of life lent itself to conflict avoidance or even to settling of conflicts by each family's simply going its own way rather than pursuing the matter.

Shoshoni religion focused on the acquisition of spiritual power, called *puha*, which increased its possessor's skill, luck, and strength. *Puha* could be used to make love or gambling magic, to ensure the success of a hunt, and to cure or to kill. Religious specialists, who devoted more time than others to the acquisition and use of *puha*, were known as *puhakanten*, "power possessors." Some *puhakanten* had the particular ability to attract antelope. Their skill was especially useful during communal antelope drives, since they could help draw the antelope into the corral. Other *puhakanten* devoted themselves to the curing of illnesses when called upon to do so. These spiritual healers were likely to have had a visionary experience in which they acquired a spirit ally known as a *puha newepea* or "power partner." During curing ceremonies, the healer would alternately chant and smoke tobacco until his spiritual ally would come and endow him with the power to cure.

Shoshoni religious beliefs included creation stories, known as Coyote Stories, in which anthropomorphic animals were the central characters. Coyote, the creator of human beings, was a Trickster, a deity who enjoyed playing practical jokes and whose own curiosity and lack of self-control often got the best of him. Coyote invariably refused to take good advice, almost always to his own detriment. Human beings entered the world by escaping from a bundle he had opened in spite of having been told to leave it closed. He later obtained pine nuts for the hungry Shoshoni by stealing this food from wealthier tribes to the north. He and his elder brother, Wolf, were instrumental in removing the teeth from women's vaginas, a problem that plagued people in mythological times. In addition to many tales of animals who, like Coyote, spoke and acted like human beings, there were stories of other creatures who bothered human beings. One popular story was that of the giant Rock Ghost who frequently would come down from her mountain cave home in search of Shoshoni children to eat. Coyote stories were enjoyed during the winter encampments but were generally not told at other times, since the telling of a Coyote Story could bring on a storm.

Tribes

When the hunting and gathering subsistence technology gave way to the domestication of plants and animals, functionally related changes came about in the social organization, in the ideology, and in other aspects of the technology, giving rise to a new societal type called the tribe.

In most tribal cultures, the subsistence technology emphasizes horticulture as the basic means for acquiring food, the planting, weeding, harvesting, and storage of foodstuffs. Techniques for irrigating the gardens may or may not be present, but there is no use of the plow, fertilization of the soil, or crop rotation, all of which are characteristic of more complex agricultural technologies.

Group structure.   Increased control over the food supply leads to understandable changes in the organization of society into a horticultural tribe. Population may grow to approach 10 people per square mile. Local groups must maintain more or less permanent residence near the planted gardens from which they draw their food. These groups can grow to be quite large in comparison with the local groups of hunting and gathering peoples. According to Marshall D. Sahlins (1960) the communities of contemporary horticultural societies have up to 200 to 250 residents. While the local groups in bands may be composed of anywhere from one to a dozen families that are loosely interrelated by ties of marriage, a tribal community may consist of as many as 20 residential families. Often, these families may be grouped into a number of lineages and clans, groups that are united to one another by ties of common ancestry.

Another common practice for helping to organize the activities of people is to divide all the families, lineages, or clans into two major groups, the moieties discussed in Chapter 7, Kinship and Descent. Each moiety of such a society has reciprocal rights and responsibilities toward the other. For instance, members of one moiety may be expected to find their mates from the other moiety; one moiety may perform rituals such as funerals for members of the other moiety; or each moiety may specialize in performing the rituals of a particular season.

The increased specialization provided by the creation of lineages, clans, and moieties allows the institution of kinship to accomplish more as a means of organizing day-to-day human affairs than if it were limited to a mere extended family group. According to Robin Fox (1967), in societies where people are independent but sometimes need help, they are likely to create groups in which membership and obligations to help are based on having a kinship relationship. Such a group, which consists of all persons related in some way to a particular living individual who is not their common ancestor, is called a kindred, discussed in more detail in Chapter 7. It is a personal group and cannot function as a corporate entity like a clan, which may own land. It may, however, provide useful benefits to the individual around whom it is focused, such as helping him or her in work activities when called upon to do so.

Although family organization is still the basic institution around which most of daily tribal life revolves, even complex systems of kinship relationship such as the clan, the moiety, and the kindred are not adequate for dealing with the great variety of social problems that may arise in communities of several hundred members. In tribes, problems that concern more than one family may be dealt with by a number of nonkinship associations. These include associations based on one's age, military and religious associations, secret societies, and other groups that draw their membership from all parts of a community. Such associations that have neither a kinship nor a residential basis are organized to carry out some basic activity that cannot be performed as effectively by the kinship organization of the tribes. These activities may be political, economic, or religious in nature, such as defense of the community, control of community members during group activities, conduct of trade, or the performance of curing ceremonies or other religious rites. In all cases, their uniting of members in a common cause forms the roots of an incipient system—though it may be generalized and diffuse—of secular government within the tribe. Most issues of law and polity, however, remain matters of legitimate familial concern at the tribal level of social organization, and tribes have no true centralized government.

As in bands, tribal leadership is charismatic. It is achieved by an individual's personal ability to convince others that it is in their own self-interest to follow his or her lead. Thus, leadership is a matter of skill rather than the power of an inherited status. By and large, tribal society is egalitarian like the band soci-

ety in that every individual has more or less equal opportunity to obtain the necessities of life and the esteem of others in leadership activities.

Economy. Tribal society continues to make use of reciprocal sharing, both along kinship lines and between kin groups. But the division of labor in the realm of production is more highly specialized than in bands. Tribal societies often have economic entrepreneurs who encourage higher levels of productivity among their coresidents. These are the so-called big men whose activities were outlined in Chapter 4. Also, in addition to having a division of labor along age and sex lines, tribal communities include among their residents individuals and groups who specialize in economic activities other than food production. These specialists can be freed from subsistence activities to engage in other occupations, since tribal communities have a more secure control over their yearly food supply than do band peoples.

Religion. Tribal religion involves a practice that is uncharacteristic of foragers: the ceremonial worship of gods—great spiritual beings who personify the major forces of nature that are of concern to food producers who must control the land from which they obtain their livelihood. These include gods of the wind, rain, plant and animal fertility, land, and war. The gods are not arranged in hierarchies. On different occasions, individual deities may rise in prominence and importance. Gods of war may be extremely important at times of war, and agricultural deities may be most important in times of drought. But the overall importance of the various deities balances out in the long run.

Pastoral tribes. Those tribes found in environments where gardening is too unproductive to support a sedentary tribal population make their living by pastoralism, the herding of animals such as reindeer, horses, sheep, goats, camels, and cattle. The pastoral forms of tribal society are found mostly in arctic and subarctic areas, deserts, mountains, and grasslands. Because of the marginality of their environments and the resulting specialized emphasis on animals as their basic food resource, pastoralists must often interact with neighboring agricultural peoples to secure materials that they cannot produce themselves, including foodstuffs. This may be accomplished by peaceful trade or, in some cases, by raiding the more sedentary agricultural peoples.

THE TODA: A TRIBAL SOCIETY

Rivers (1906) described the Toda, a pastoral tribe of India. The Toda lived on a high plateau in southern India. They made their living by herding buffalo. Since they practiced no agriculture, the Toda supplied neighboring tribes with dairy products from their herds in return for farm products, pottery, ironware, and other goods and services. As might be expected, buffalo were extremely important to the Toda. Cows were individually named, and their pedigrees were carefully remembered. Some herds even were regarded as sacred. These herds were tended by special dairymen at sacred dairy temples. Their care involved elaborate rituals, and the dairymen who tended them lived the lives of priests, lives filled with rituals and special taboos. The ancestors of these sacred herds played an important role in the creation myths of the Toda, who believed that when the first 1,600 sacred buffalo were created by one of the gods, the first human appeared holding onto the tail of the last buffalo—an apt symbol of the Toda's economic dependence on their herds.

Socially, the Toda were divided into two endogamous moieties. The more highly ranked of these, the Tarthar, owned all of the sacred herds of buffalo and their dairies. The sacred dairymen who tended the herds all belonged to the second moiety, the Teivali. Both of these groups were further divided into exogamous patrilineal clans, each with its own territory. Clans served as land and herd-owning groups. The major villages and most sacred herds of buffalo were the property of entire clans rather than of the individual families that made up the clans.

Although families and clans were the main decision-making bodies among the Toda, the pastoral life of the Toda had created a population density that was too great for all problems to be settled without some mechanism that stood above clan membership. This mechanism was an incipient government organization, a tribal council known as the *naim*. Its five members always came from certain families of specific clans. Lacking the authority of the true governments of more complex societies, the *naim* had no voice in criminal matters. Its primary functions were to regulate ceremonies and to settle disputes between individuals, families, and clans when called upon to do so.

Population growth was limited by the Toda's location. Their land was bounded on all sides. In the southern directions, cliffs dropped from 3,000 to 5,000 feet. To the north were agriculturalists. With no room for expansion, the Toda had sought to solve the problem of population growth by limiting the number of women and therefore the number of children born in each generation. This was accomplished by the practice of infanticide in which unwanted infants, especially girls, were suffocated shortly after birth. This led to a surplus of men in each generation. To rectify this imbalance the Toda practiced polyandry.

Marriages were arranged, and they occurred between children as young as two or three years of age. The girl was considered to be the wife of the boy with whom the marriage ceremony was performed and of all his brothers, including those born thereafter. Until she was 15 or 16, the bride lived with her own parents. Shortly before puberty, she had to be initiated into sex by a man selected from the moiety to which her family did not belong, that is, to a man whom she would not be permitted to marry. If this ceremonial loss of virginity did not occur before puberty, the bride was stigmatized for life, and her marriage would be cancelled.

Since the Toda based their clan membership and inheritance on the principle of patrilineal descent, fatherhood was an important matter. But, since a woman had many husbands, fatherhood had to be designated on some basis other than the idea of biological paternity. Among the Toda, a man became a father by performing a fatherhood ritual. This was one of the most important rituals of the Toda. For a child to be born without its having been performed was a great scandal. In this ritual, a man and a pregnant woman went into the forest where the man carved a niche in a tree, placed an oil lamp into it, promised the woman a calf, and ceremonially presented her with an imitation bow and arrow. She held the bow and arrow to her forehead and watched the lamp until it burned out. Afterwards, he prepared a meal, and the two spent the night together. From this time forward, he would be the father of all children to whom she would give birth, until some other man performed the same ceremony with her to supersede him as father of her children. Although it was usual for one of a woman's husbands to hold the status of father of her children, it was possible for a man who was not one of her husbands to perform the bow-giving ceremony with her.

Chiefdoms

Another level of cultural complexity—the chiefdom—is typically found in the simplest agricultural societies. Chiefdoms are sometimes known as rank societies because their social systems are not egalitarian like those of the bands and tribes (Fried, 1967; Service, 1963, 1978).

Social, political, and economic structure. As in the bands and tribes, most day-to-day social life in chiefdoms revolves around the family, but the families in each local community are organized into broad social groupings that are ranked with respect to one another. Some families are more wealthy, prestigious, and politically powerful than others. Birth into these families conveys advantages not available to members of other families.

In addition to the family-based mechanisms of government that are found in bands and tribes, chiefdoms possess political specialists who have the right in at least some matters to exercise authority over persons who are not members of their own families. These specialists, the chiefs whose economic role was described in Chapter 4, generally derive much of their authority from religion. The power of the chief or governing council of the chiefdom is more limited than that of the governments of more complex societies, and families may legitimately exercise legal power in many areas of life, such as the contracting and dissolution of marriages or the punishment of individuals for minor thefts. However, the chief is normally called on for the adjudication of more serious infractions of law, such as major thefts or homicide. In some of these matters, he may be expected to play the role of mediator be-

tween the conflicting parties, with the goal of reestablishing peaceful relations between the members of the community. In other cases, the chief may have the authority to determine guilt or innocence and exact punishment for an offense without consulting the members of the offender's family. The position of chief is therefore a true office, and its holder has authority to legitimately wield power over others with whom the chief has no known kinship ties.

The office of chief is most often hereditary, although which relative of a deceased chief will inherit the office may be decided by the surviving family members. In some cases, the community as a whole may have some say in the selection of the new chief from the group of possible heirs.

Each community in a chiefdom is likely to have a chief who acts as its political head, and groups of villages within a chiefdom usually will be unified under a district chief of higher rank than the local village ones. The entire chiefdom, which may consist of several hundred thousand people in various districts, may or may not be unified under a central paramount chief, but the residents of the various districts will think of themselves as a single people in that they share a common language and culture.

Although the office of chief has definite political power, probably his most important function is the economic one of serving as a redistributor of goods and a provider of services. In a chiefdom, all families in a community are expected to contribute a portion of their annual produce to the warehouse. The chief then sees to it that these goods are redistributed, generally at community feasts or festivals, to those most in need. It is often the case that a chief's power and prestige is maintained in direct proportion to his generosity. Indeed, the level of gift-giving expected of a chief may exceed that which comes in from other families, so that the wealth of the chief's family is gradually drained, to the benefit of other less prestigious families.

Specialists. In chiefdoms a high level of specialization of labor is common. Individuals and sometimes entire communities may specialize in the production of goods desired or needed by others. These goods are then ex-

FIGURE 12.8 *Bedouin Tent Dwelling*
Tribal Bedouins make their living herding camels. This 18-year-old boy lives on the men's side of the family tent in the Negev desert.

changed for materials that the specialists do not produce or for labor that the specialists require but do not perform for themselves. Specializations may include crafts, such as pottery making or house building, and services, such as religious or military occupations.

Chiefdoms also generally have a system of drafted military personnel, partly as a result of two factors: (1) chiefdoms, compared to horticultural societies, have larger and more dense populations because agriculture is generally more productive than is horticulture, yet (2) agricultural societies are more likely to experience food shortages due to droughts than are horticultural societies (most of which are in areas of more reliable rainfall). Food shortages among people with dense populations are likely to result in intense military competition for control over land. The presence of a draft army reinforces the police power of the government and lends authority to the chief's office. The trait of official authority is absent in the leadership positions of bands and tribes, where leaders must inspire their following but cannot compel obedience.

Chiefdoms generally have religious specialists who serve the entire community. Indeed, the chief may be the primary religious functionary. The religious ideology in chiefdoms reflects their social complexity. The gods are many and specialized in function, as are the social occupations of the human members of the chiefdom. Guy Swanson (1960) has demonstrated that in those societies in which decision-making power is organized hierarchically into at least three levels, the gods are also ranked in a hierarchy headed by a supreme deity. This level of social complexity is found in many chiefdoms throughout the world, as is the concept of a supreme god—a religious idea that is almost absent among tribal and band peoples.

THE RWALA BEDOUINS: A PASTORAL CHIEFDOM

According to Musil (1928), the Rwala had the largest and most powerful tent-dwelling Bedouin chiefdom of the northern Arabian peninsula. Although much of their life was organized around the concept of kinship, the Rwala also had officials whose authority was felt beyond the boundaries of their own kin. These chiefs or *sheikhs* were officers whose positions were inherited within particular patrilineal lineages. In addition to local *sheikhs* whose authority was felt throughout an entire camp, there also were regional chiefs whose authority derived from a lineage of greater prominence than those of the local chiefs. There also was a paramount chief or *sheikh*, often called a "prince," over all the Rwala. His main duties

288

were to conduct relations with the national government and with chiefs of other Bedouin peoples, but he had little power over the internal politics of the Rwala themselves.

Life in the camps was largely governed by kinship. Each man saw himself as the center of a group of relatives, or kindred, known as the *ahl*. A man's *ahl* consisted of all his patrilineal descendants and ancestors to the third generation. This group of relatives had strong obligations to him and could bear the guilt for his misdeeds. People also were organized into patrilineal clans, called *feriz*. Marriages were preferably within one's own lineage of the clan. In particular, a man was encouraged to marry his father's brother's daughter or his father's father's brother's son's daughter—his patrilineal first- or second-parallel cousin. This woman could marry no other without his waiving his prior claim. Since parallel cousin marriage was forbidden in many societies, anthropologists have debated the reason for this unusual preference. It has been argued that by marrying into their own patrilineage, the Bedouin kept inheritable property from being dispersed and increased the solidarity of the lineage which was divided most of the year into small wandering groups. The marriage preference system counteracted the fragmenting effects of the Bedouin pastoral adaptation to a desert environment (Barth, 1954; Murphy & Kasdan, 1959).

Although polygyny was permitted, few men had more than one wife. Divorce was quite common, and although it was the prerogative of the husband to divorce his wife or grant a divorce, he was expected to divorce his wife if she expressed love for another. Both spouses were free to remarry.

Rwala, like other Bedouins, had black servants who often have been referred to as "slaves." These persons formed a kind of separate caste within Rwala society, since they did not intermarry with the Rwala. They were expected to do much of the drudge work around the camp. These servants could not be bought, sold, or killed and could choose another master if they became disaffected with their previous one. They chose their own spouses, owned property of their own, and were entitled to take food from their master's larder.

The Rwala made their living by herding camels which could be ridden and also provided milk for food and hides and hair for manufacturing items. Camels were traded to merchants in return for cash, weapons, clothing, and other necessities. Trade was important, for the desert environment did not permit the Bedouins to be completely self-sufficient.

Warfare was a central fact of Rwala life, and it tinged many other aspects of their culture. Stolen animals were the main reason for warfare, which consisted most often of surprise night raids on the enemy camp. Weaker groups of Bedouins and villagers paid protection tribute (*khuwa*) to more powerful ones such as the Rwala. The receiver of this protection "tax" was bound to protect those who paid it and to restore any property that was stolen from them by raiders. War was enjoyed because it was an opportunity not only for booty but also for displaying one's skill and courage. Old age was rare for males, since over 80 percent of Rwala men died as a result of warfare.

Blood feuds also were common among the Rwala. Kin were obligated to avenge the murder of a relative, and the murderer's kin shared the guilt to the third generation. The avengers therefore could take the life of a relative of the actual culprit should they happen on one before finding the murderer. Vengeance of this kind was legitimate, a matter of family law. Guilty parties were not permitted to defend themselves against avengers, but instead had to seek the protection of a powerful *sheikh* who aided them in reaching a traditional place of refuge, where they stayed until the avengers agreed to accept a blood price of horses, camels, and weapons to compensate them for the death.

As might be expected, the custom of hospitality was very strong. The power of a chief to protect those under his care was a matter of grave honor. Travelers who entered a Bedouin camp greeted the *sheikh* and were assured of his protection by his salutation of peace, which was binding on the entire camp. This custom helped to alleviate the negative effects of war, as did the custom of tribute "taxes" which obligated the receiver to protect those who paid them. Traders who traveled from group to group insured themselves and their own goods by having an acquaintance or "brother" (*akh*) in each group to whom they paid a fee in return for protection. Should the trader's property be stolen in a raid, it was the obligation of his *akh* in the raiding group to see to it that they were returned when claimed.

States

The most complex society is known as the state. This is an independent political unit in which a central government integrates and has considerable control over the many communities in its territory, theoretically monopolizing the right to use legal force within its boundaries.

Technology. The major technological difference between the chiefdom and the state is that the agriculture of the state society is more intensive than that of the chiefdom. The plow and draft animals are almost always present, and agricultural technology is generally much more complex than in chiefdoms. Irrigation systems play a major role in the agriculture of most states, so much so that one scholar, Karl Wittfogel (1957), has suggested that it was the necessity of controlling and regulating water resources that led to the rise of the world's first states. This view has not been accepted widely because it places too much emphasis on the single factor of irrigation at the expense of others, such as population growth, trade, diplomacy, and warfare. But it reminds us that irrigation was an important technological development that played a role in the increasing productivity of the state's subsistence activities.

Due to the effects of truly intensive agriculture, members of a state society may number in the millions. They occupy densely packed towns and cities in which little or no agriculture may be practiced. They also occupy more rural communities of smaller size that specialize particularly in the production of particular kinds of food in return for the specialized nonagricultural products of the larger communities.

Market economy. The flow of goods over great distances between communities is facilitated by the rise in prominence of the market system. In a market economy, goods and services are made available to people at a common location where they are exchanged. In such a specialized economic system, the role of kinship in the production and distribution of goods is likely to become attenuated. By and large, productive work ceases to be a family activity, since production becomes more a matter of cooperation between groups of specialists. Similarly, the distribution of goods from where they are produced to where they are consumed easily becomes the work of specialists.

Centralized power. States differ from chiefdoms primarily in one important way: Whereas in chiefdoms the right to use force in matters of law is divided between the kinship systems and the political apparatus, in the state, the government monopolizes the right to use force. This difference is at least partly attributable to the growing need for a centralized coordination of society, especially in areas of potential conflict between individuals and groups. The need for centralized control of society is likely to grow as the number and density of people unrelated by kinship increases.

Social ranking. In the state society, statuses are ranked into broad social strata or classes that have differential access to prestige and power. These social classes may be recognized formally in the society's ideology or they may be present informally while the ideology may not recognize their existence. For instance, historically both American and Soviet ideologies have denied the existence of classes within their societies, although in both cases they are a definite part of the social system. In the Soviet Union, attempts have been made to eliminate class distinctions by legislation that forbids the children of individuals who hold political or other prestigious positions to hold the same status in the next generation. The effect, however, has not been to eliminate differences in power and prestige between families but simply to ensure a change in occupations between generations within the same class. Children of a bureaucrat may become scientists or members of a university faculty, thereby maintaining the high rank of their parents.

The rigidity of classes differs even in those societies that recognize them. In some, the movement of individuals from one class to another may be possible, although not common. When changing one's class is not permitted, social scientists refer to the system as a caste system.

FIGURE 12.9   *Tenochtitlan*

This Aztec capital was on an island in a lake in the valley of Mexico, now the site of Mexico City. It was connected to the mainland by a series of causeways. The four quadrants of the city each had its own group of markets, schools and officials.

THE AZTECS: A NONINDUSTRIALIZED STATE SOCIETY

The Aztec capital Tenochtitlan, which was situated on an island in a lake in the Valley of Mexico, had a population of about 250,000 people when the Spanish arrived in 1519 (see Fig. 12.9). Aztec society was supported by agriculture that used corn (maize), beans, and squash as staple crops. Although the Aztecs lacked the plow, the farmers of Tenochtitlan were able to extend their fields into the lake surrounding their city first by driving piles into the shallow lake bottom to form a retaining wall around the new plot and then by filling in this piece of lake with dirt and refuse that formed new, rich soil to farm as it decayed. This innovative technique, called *chinampa* agriculture, was productive enough to support large populations and nonagricultural specialists who lived in the cities.

Tenochtitlan was connected to the mainland by a series of causeways, one of which contained an aqueduct that brought fresh water to the city. The city itself was divided into four great quarters, each with its own market, temple, schools, and local officials. Each quarter was occupied by a number of patrilineal clans (*calpulli*) that owned the lands of the district (Soustelle, 1961). Local affairs were controlled by a council composed of the heads of all families that belonged to the patrilineal *calpulli* district. The head of this council was the *calpullec*. He distributed the lands of the clans to various families according to need. These were to be worked by the families but remained clan property. Those who were lax in the use of the land allocated them would lose their right to work it.

Aztecs were strict in the upbringing of their children. They were lectured frequently on the values of hard work and obedience. Laziness was considered to be among the greatest sins. Disobedient children were beaten, pricked with thorns, or held in the smoke of a fire containing chili pepper. At the age of 15, boys entered the clan boarding school (*telpochcalli*) where they learned the arts of war and government. The sons of nobles received their training in a priestly school (*calmecac*) where they learned writing, astronomy, and religion. Since the Aztec had a written tradition before the arrival of

Europeans, they recorded their own histories and continued to write about themselves after the Conquest (see Dibble & Anderson, 1950 to 1969).

Upon completion of their studies, sons of nobles chose entering the priesthood or the government. In Aztec society, a society of classes, the highest class was composed of military officials and priests. The military governed society, and the priesthood mediated between the people and the gods to ensure the growth of crops and success in war. The highest military leader was the king, or *tlacatecutli*. He presided over a council of 20 speakers or *tlatoani* who represented the 20 Aztec clans. It was they, along with other clan leaders, military officers, and high priests, who declared wars, mediated disputes between clans, and created new laws. The second most prominent official, next to the king, was the Snake Woman (*çiuacoatl*), the man who actually presided over the council of speakers and who was responsible for the administration of housing, tribute, and the judicial system. Aztec priests dressed in black and lived a rigorous life of ritual and self-sacrifice, with self-torture and fasting. Seven times a day, they offered sacrifices of their own blood. It was the priests who educated the children of the nobility.

Although they were not part of the nobility, the traders (*pochteca*) were often among the wealthiest of the Aztecs. These traveling merchants carried on trade far beyond the borders of the Aztec empire and often acted as spies for the military. Any attacks on trading expeditions brought immediate retaliation by the military. At home, the *pochteca* had special privileges because of their particular value to society, forming almost a separate group within Aztec society. Their occupation was hereditary, and the *pochteca* had their own gods and rituals as well as the right to their own court system. Yet, in spite of their wealth, traders often lived lives of outward poverty so as not to incite the anger of the king who might confiscate their property on some pretext if he thought they were becoming too powerful. A multitude of other occupational specialists existed, including metalworkers, jade carvers, feather workers, carpenters, stonemasons, weavers, potters, and farmers.

Below the class of commoners were propertyless laborers (*macehualtin*), who were mostly foreigners with no claim to land, and some Aztecs who had lost their clan rights. These laborers, whose position was much like that of the serfs of medieval Europe, did work such as carrying burdens or working a noble's land. At the very bottom of the social classes were slaves. Slaves were mostly debtors or the children of debtors but also included some younger people delivered to the Aztecs as part of the tribute paid by conquered people. Slavery involved rights over the work of the slave but did not include ownership of his or her person. A slave might own property, marry and raise children, or buy himself or herself out of slavery. For this reason, slaves included people who sold themselves into slavery to pay their previous debts.

War was a central preoccupation of the Aztecs. The chief god of the Aztecs, Huitzilopochtli, was the god of war and the traditional Aztec tribal god from the Aztecs' precivilized days. Valor in war was rewarded by knighthood in one of the two great military orders, the Eagles and the Ocelots. Persons so knighted held the privileges of nobility, although the status was not passed on to their descendants. Dying in battle ensured a man a glorious afterlife in the heaven of the sun god. This fate was shared by women who died in childbirth, since every new child strengthened the Aztec nation. For the same reason, abortion was a capital crime. Marriage also was a legal obligation; refusal to marry was punishable by loss of clan membership, which placed one in the class of unpropertied workers.

The religion of the Aztecs was polytheistic. Atop the great pyramid at the center of Tenochtitlan was a temple dedicated both to Huitzilopochtli, the Aztec war god and the god of the nobility, and to Tlaloc, the god of rain and agriculture, a god of special import to the commoners. A third major god was Quetzalcoatl, the Plumed Serpent, god of wind and air and the patron deity of the priesthood. The great god Tezcatlipoca, or Smoking Mirror, chief god of the Mexicans prior to the Aztecs, also was revered as of great importance. Many lesser deities existed, each with specialized powers. The great gods of the Aztecs were honored in state ceremonies and were nourished with the blood of sacrificial victims who had been captured in war. Thus, warfare was to the Aztecs a sacred obligation and not just a means of expanding the empire.

Industrialized states. The most complex of the state societies are those with an industrialized technology, which harnesses the power of fossil fuels, hydroelectric dams, or more recently tapped energy sources such as atomic energy, solar power, or geothermal power. Compared with nonindustrialized states, the industrialized are even more complex. The percentage of persons engaged in food-providing activities declines radically as new, highly specialized occupations come into existence.

Specialization of labor is the order of the day in state societies. For instance, in the United States—one of the technologically more complex of the contemporary state societies—there are specialists who make their living in these ways: driving trucks in which trash is collected from the individual households of a community, moving the trash from the households to the trucks, operating the machinery for burying the waste products so collected, and supervising the work of the trash collectors and disposers. The building of a simple house to be occupied by a single family may require the work of specialists who dig basements, specialists who lay concrete foundations, carpenters, dry-wall specialists, roofers, electricians, heating specialists, painters, glaziers, and a host of supervisory specialists. When it comes to health care, one must decide whether to visit a general practitioner, a specialist in internal medicine, a heart specialist, a specialist in problems of the digestive tract, a specialist in bone disorders, a skin specialist, or a surgeon, to cite but a few of the vast number of medical specializations. Even then, much of the actual work done when one visits a doctor will be executed by a variety of technical specialists who work for or with that doctor, such as X-ray technicians, laboratory technicians, and nurses. A government publication lists over 20,000 different occupations found in the United States (U.S. Dept. of Labor, Employment and Training Administration, 1977).

Secularism. Perhaps the most outstanding aspect of the ideologies of state societies is that relative to the socially simpler societies, state-level peoples see a much greater part of the world about them in nonreligious terms. The more complex technologies of state soci-

eties require—if they are to be used effectively—that their users think of the parts of the world that they are manipulating with tools in a more pragmatic and matter-of-fact way than do peoples who control less of their environment technologically. Crop rotation, the plow, fertilization of the soil, and efficient irrigation systems make it much less likely that their users will think of the growth of crops as being dependent upon mysterious spiritual forces than do peoples who rely on rainfall gardening for their food supply. Similarly, with an increasing degree of social specialization in state societies, religious ideology is likely to decline in importance, since specialists are likely to see their day-to-day activities in a matter-of-fact, blasé way due to their routine nature. State societies also foster a secular, pragmatic view of life because the interdependent contributions of humans—in contrast with the influence of deity—are quite apparent. The survival of each member of a state society is obviously dependent upon the services performed by an immense number of other specialists.

To take an extreme example, even the work of full-time religious specialists tends to become a matter of routine in state-level societies. Where there are full-time religious thinkers, religious belief tends to place more stress on organized rational theological doctrine, while characteristics such as religious ecstasy and altered states of consciousness which are often found in simpler societies, are likely to be less common. The priests of ecclesiastical religions frequently forbid the performance of shamanistic activities, such as seances, faith healing, prophecy, and psychic readings by separate specialists. They also often frown on similar behavior in the lay congregation and may taboo such practices as spirit possession trances and the ecstatic speaking in tongues by members of the congregation. Thus, when there are full-time religious practitioners who specialize in the routine performance of rituals for the congregation, the role of the congregation moves toward less active participation. Their only active part may be to fit themselves into the ritual pattern, not spontaneously but in a highly predictable way on cue. For the most part, they may be but a passive audience to a ritual that is performed almost in its entirety by the religious specialist. For such a specialist the ritual behavior may become a matter of almost pure routine. Participation in these rituals may be largely motivated by a more or less secular desire to be accepted as a conforming member of society—that is, because people experience what Radcliffe-Brown (1958) has called "secondary anxiety"— rather than because they feel an immediate personal need for the rituals for spiritual reasons. In state societies, even religion has a tendency to become somewhat secularized, in contrast to the religious behavior of people in simpler social systems where labor is less specialized.

CULTURAL EVOLUTIONARY THEORY

The observable differences among tribes, bands, chiefdoms, and states have led a number of anthropologists to speculate about whether these levels constitute developmental stages in the advance toward civilization, the progress of societies from one stage to another, or improvements in the quality of life. In asking such questions, they have tried to formulate general laws that can be applied to the process of cultural evolution in all societies.

Archaeological Evidence of Cultural Evolution

Those societies that became the earliest civilizations developed historically from less complex social forms based on simpler technologies. In 1949 Julian Steward examined the developmental sequences of the early civilizations in Peru, Middle America (Mexico and the Mayan area), Mesopotamia, Egypt, and China. He found that there were important parallels in how complex societies evolved in each of these arid or semiarid regions. On the basis of these parallels, he developed a typology of five successive stages through which these societies tended to pass during the rise of civilization.

According to Steward (1949), the Pre-Agricultural Era was the period in which societies were organized into bands of food collectors. The Era of Incipient Agriculture was one in which increasingly sedentary bands supplemented their diets of wild foods with some farming. The world's first tribal societies devel-

oped during this era. During the Formative Era, chiefdoms arose. Irrigation was practiced on a small and local scale. The emergence of a system of social rank was reflected in a division of the technologies of this period into production of two kinds of goods: objects designed to meet the basic domestic and biological needs of people, and very elaborate and stylized objects symbolic of the higher status of their users. Ceramics, loom weaving, basketry, house building, and the erection of religious edifices were universal, and metalworking was developed everywhere except in Middle America during this period.

In the Era of Regional Florescence, local state governments arose under the control of theocratic leaders. Society came to be organized on the basis of class distinction rather than kinship. Warfare was generally less important than in later times. During this period, the priesthood developed a variety of full-time, nonproductive religious specialists who laid the foundations for the abstract sciences: writing, astronomy, the calendar, and mathematics. The development of the wheel was another hallmark of this era. It was in this period of early civilization that societies had the means to erect their biggest and most impressive monumental architecture. Finally, as population pressures reached, and in some cases perhaps overshot, the carrying capacity of irrigation-based agriculture, competition for arable lands increased, and large-scale militarism became increasingly prominent.

Thus began the Imperial Era of Cyclical Conquests. Theocratic governments gave way to secular, military-based authority, and empires were built as some regions expanded their political and economic domination over neighboring areas. Urbanization increased and walled fortifications became common. Several classes became rigid hereditary divisions in which upward mobility by means of achievement disappeared. These changes were reflected in the religions of the early empires, in that gods of war became the most prominent deities of the pantheons. In some cases this period began with the rise of a central and dominant empire, which then ended in collapse and a decline in population below the levels of the previous era as the agricultural base became overtaxed. This collapse was followed by a period of "Dark

Ages" and then by a period of cyclical conquests between competing city-states during which first one and then another local region would rise to prominence, only to be supplanted by another. Elsewhere, the period of cyclical conquests followed the Florescent Era immediately with no unifying imperial military state initially dominating the rest.

Specific and General Evolution

The existence of extensive parallels in the development of early civilizations suggests that the evolution of ways of life is as lawful as biological evolution. Marshall Sahlins and Elman R. Service (1949) and Service (1971) have clarified the lawful regularity of cultural evolution by pointing out that cultures change in two fundamentally different ways: (1) through a process of specific evolution, or change in the direction of increasing adaptive specialization; and (2) through a process of general evolution, or change in the direction of increasing complexity. In the first form of change, a way of life becomes more adjusted to its specific environmental circumstances—in a word, more specialized. In the second, new parts of a total environment are drawn upon by the cultural system. As a culture becomes more complex, it relates to its environment in radically new ways, harnessing greater amounts of energy for new uses. Qualitative change is the hallmark of general evolution.

While biological changes cannot be passed from one species to another, the traits that arise in one culture may pass over into another. Thus, the evolutionary development of cultures must be seen in terms of the interplay of the specific and general evolutionary changes that occur within cultures and the interactions between cultures.

Stabilization vs. Evolutionary Potential

It is the interaction between cultures that makes possible an interplay between the forces of specific and general evolution. Acting alone, specific evolution leads ultimately to stability. If a culture were ever to achieve a perfect adaptation to its environment, any further change would be maladaptive. If a way of life is relatively inefficient in helping a society to deal with its environment, it is a simple matter for a people to improve their adjustment to the circumstances. However, the more efficient a way of life becomes in making use of the resources available to a people, the more expensive and difficult it becomes to implement each new increase in efficiency, so that change in the direction of greater adaptation gradually slows and a way of life becomes more stable. This fact has been referred to by Thomas Harding (1960) as the Principle of Stabilization. On the basis of this principle, Sahlins and Service (1960) have formulated what they call the Law of Evolutionary Potential, which states that a culture's capacity to move from one general evolutionary stage to another varies inversely with its degree of specific evolutionary adaptation.

If it were not for general evolution, interacting cultures would continue increasing their adaptations to their environments and to each other until a final stability would be achieved among them. But, as we have seen, under certain circumstances cultures may adopt radically new modes of adaptation and undergo a qualitative change in social complexity and power. General evolutionary change inevitably disrupts the previous balance of power between neighboring societies. As each new general evolutionary stage is achieved, societies at the new level expand at the expense of simpler, less powerful cultures. Some of these simpler societies may be absorbed. Others are driven out of their territory or annihilated as the more complex society expands in population and acquires new territory. Still others may adopt the new technology in order to defend themselves by entering the new level of general evolution. The latter will eventually need to improve the efficiency of their use of the technology that made the transition to the new stage possible. That is, they begin to improve their specific evolutionary adaptation to the new technology. As this process occurs, the earlier dominant societies of this stage are likely to achieve a high degree of social stability sooner than latecomers do.

Leapfrogging

When considered in light of the Law of Evolutionary Potential, the earlier stabilization of the first culture to make the transition from one general evolutionary level to the next makes it likely that this culture will be the first to move to an even more complex stage. Rather, it is the backwater cultures, those which are less specifically adapted to their current situation, that have the greatest chance to leap ahead in power and complexity by adopting and implementing radically new technologies. This fact has been formulated into another general law of cultural evolution, called the Law of Local Discontinuity of Progress. This law states that successive stages of general evolutionary change are not likely to be achieved in the same locality. General evolutionary change tends to occur in a kind of leapfrogging way with the dominant centers of world power shifting from one area to another over the centuries.

Elman R. Service (1971) believes that this leapfrogging process is likely to continue into the future. It is his contention that, should no unpredictable factor such as an accidental war intervene, the most likely course of future events is one in which Western civilization will be eclipsed by some of the currently underdeveloped nations. Service writes, "Those nations that are now the most advanced in the present coal and oil complex have less potential for the full and efficient use of the industry of the future than certain hitherto 'underdeveloped' regions which could build a new civilization well-adapted to such a base" (p. 42).

The forces of industrialization, of course, still are spreading gradually throughout the world. In Western Europe and North America, the process of industrialization was a gradual process that grew from quite small-scale industries to the large and complex international industrial corporations of today over a period of centuries. The social, political, and ideological life of these regions was gradually transformed to fit the needs of the developing industrial complex. Those areas of the world that are just now beginning the process of industrialization are naturally seeking to do so quickly. In Service's words (1971, pp. 44–45), "They will begin with the latest and most advanced of the known technologies and attempt to create the complete industrial complex at once, skipping whole epochs of our development. This requires a high capital investment. The economy, therefore, must be socialistic; the government rather than private

persons provides most of the capital by necessity." In the process of worldwide industrialization, Service expects that at least some of the developing nations will surpass the present status of the United States and Russia as the world's dominant powers, both politically and economically.

However, other factors besides a culture's ability to change readily must be considered in assessing current trends in cultural development. Part of the adjustment of a culture to its specific environment is its adjustment to other cultures with which it must interact. In the contemporary world, adjustment to the political and economic influences of the world's superpowers is a major factor in how the rest of the world's cultures are changing today. It is quite possible that the worldwide economic and political power of the superpowers is great enough to inhibit the traditional leapfrogging pattern of cultural change.

Progress?

Does technological progress also produce progress in quality of life? The major changes that occur in societies when technologies harness more energy are an increase in population, increases in the number of different statuses and groups, and an increase in the specialization of roles. Inherent in these changes is an increased dependence of everyone in society on each other. Individuals come to have less autonomy and less ability to fulfill their own needs by means of their own actions, since they must rely upon others to perform necessary tasks for which they themselves lack the skills. In general, the economic role of kinship declines. Family continues to play a role as an economic group in consumption but tends to lose its role as a production and distribution group. The role of kinship as a legitimate political force also declines. In the realm of ideology, more and more facets of life need to be understood in mechanistic rather than spiritual terms, for the role of religion as a source of explanations declines as a culture becomes more generally evolved. All of these trends tend to make the life of individuals less and less secure and stable, factors that have important psychological impact on the modal personality types at different stages of general cultural evolution.

FIGURE 12.10 *Technological Progress*

As a culture develops the technological means to increase production, it also produces psychological alienation in its population. People have little autonomy and control over their lives and little satisfaction in their jobs when they are involved in a form of mass production as in this pineapple cannery in the city of Taitung, Taiwan.

The psychological effects of individuals' decreasing autonomy and control over their own lives is referred to as alienation. The concept of alienation is most strongly associated with Karl Marx (1961), who argued in 1844 that alienation develops when the work of individuals ceases to be carried out as a way of directly satisfying human needs and becomes instead merely a means of satisfying those needs indirectly. In the simplest societies, individual roles are highly generalized and each individual possesses most of the skills necessary for survival. For instance, if a woman is hungry, she takes up a basket and a digging stick (often of her own making) and goes in search of food. This direct relationship between work and personal needs leads to a sense of fulfillment in work. As societies become more complex, however, persons work not to satisfy their immediate physical needs but merely to obtain some object such as money that can later be used to satisfy those needs. The labor is a step removed from the purpose for which it is ultimately performed. A telephone operator may spend the day pushing buttons in service of others, an activity that has no obvious connection with obtaining food or shelter or any other personal need. He or she may receive payment for this work only once a month and is not likely to feel the same personal satisfaction in that daily work as does the hunter in manufacturing the salmon spear or rabbit snare that will be used to obtain the day's meal.

As societies grow more complex and the work of individuals becomes more and more removed from the direct fulfillment of needs, alienation increases. The effects of alienation are multiplied when individuals must work for others in order to survive. Under such conditions, even the direct products of a worker's labor do not belong to him or her. This lack of control over the products of one's labor reduces the sense of satisfaction for having created some useful or aesthetic object.

High specialization of labor in which no

individual has the skills to do everything necessary for personal survival also leads to competition between interdependent specialists. Each attempts to obtain the most possible from his or her goods or services at the expense of others. Such competition also increases the sense of alienation from society as a source of human security and meaningfulness.

The first anthropologist to emphasize the concept of alienation in the study of human cultures was Edward Sapir. He went so far as to suggest that cultures could be rated in terms of how "inherently harmonious, balanced, self-satisfactory" (1924, p. 410) they are, a view that has received little attention from other anthropologists. Although he did not suggest that there is a direct relationship between the complexity of a society and the degree to which its culture is "a spiritual hybrid of contradictory patches, of water-tight compartments of consciousness that avoid participation in a harmonious synthesis" (1924, p. 410), the parallel between his views and Marx's concept of alienation is obvious.

SUMMARY   Cultures change—often in the direction of increasing complexity—through local discoveries and inventions, plus things borrowed from other cultures, including those to which are politically subordinate. As changes occur within the realms of technology, social organization, or ideology, they affect the other realms so that the culture adjusts as a whole. The interrelated signs of increasing complexity are: harnessing of more energy per capita, increased specialization of labor, greater population density, greater status-ranking, decreasing emphasis on kinship, decreasing individual independence, more centralized political control, and more secular ideology. Four general levels of cultural complexity exist today—bands, tribes, chiefdoms, and states.

Historically, the great civilizations of the past are thought to have evolved according to a general pattern, categorized as the Pre-Agricultural Era, the Era of Incipient Agriculture, the Formative Era, the Era of Regional Florescence, and the Imperial Era of Cyclical Conquests. Another way of looking at the changes through which societies pass is to categorize them as specific evolution (adaptation and specialization) or general evolution (qualitative change toward greater complexity). The first tends to stabilize a society (the Principle of Stabilization), while the second moves a society toward increasing complexity, unless such change is inhibited by the effects of the society's previous adaptation (the Law of Evolutionary Potential). Because those cultures that are already well adapted are less likely to change, new leaders in the movement toward complexity may emerge from the previously underdeveloped societies (the Law of Local Discontinuity of Progress). The features of increasing complexity may not be entirely desirable, for in the psychological realm they tend to cause a sense of alienation.

**KEY TERMS
AND
CONCEPTS**

discovery 274
invention 274
diffusion 274
direct borrowing 274
stimulus diffusion 274
acculturation 276
Law of Cultural Dominance 276
technology 276
social organization 276
ideology 276
Basic Law of Cultural Evolution 276
band 280
tribe 284
nonkinship associations 285
chiefdom (rank society) 287
state 290

market economy 290
nonindustrialized state 293
industrialized state 293
Pre-Agricultural Era 294
Era of Incipient Agriculture 294
Formative Era 294
Era of Regional Florescence 294
Imperial Era of Cyclical Conquests 294
specific evolution 295
general evolution 295
Principle of Stabilization 295
Law of Evolutionary Potential 295
Law of Local Discontinuity of
   Progress 296
alienation 297

**ANNOTATED
READINGS**

Chagnon, N.A. (1977). *Yąnomamö: The fierce people* (2nd ed.). New York: Holt, Rinehart and Winston. An Exceptionally well-written ethnographic account of a tribal society. Includes fascinating insights into the ethnographer's personal experience while doing fieldwork.

Sahlins, M. D. (1968). *Tribesmen*. Englewood Cliffs, NJ: Prentice Hall. A short overview of tribal societies.

Sahlins, M., & Service, E. R. (Eds.). (1960). *Evolution and culture*. Ann Arbor, MI: University of Michigan Press. A thoughtful examination of various views on cultural evolution.

Service, E. R. (1979). *The hunters* (2nd ed.). Englewood Cliffs, NJ: Prentice Hall. An excellent brief introduction to the basic characteristics of foraging societies.

Service, E. R. (1978). *Profiles in ethnology*. New York: Harper & Row. A well-written series of ethnographic descriptions of a variety of the world's traditional cultures. Must reading for the anthropology major.

Service, E. R. (1962). *Primitive social organization*. New York: Random House. A very useful reference work on the social organization of traditional societies written from an evolutionary perspective.

Steward, J. H. (1955). *Theory of culture change*. Urbana, IL: University of Illinois Press. A collection of the basic papers on cultural evolution by one of the most influential twentieth-century cultural evolutionists.

Thomas, E. M. (1959). *The harmless people*. New York: Knopf. A beautifully written account of life among the !Kung foragers of the Kalahari Desert of South Africa.

Turnbull, C. M. (1962). *The forest people*. Garden City, NY: Doubleday. A well-written, empathetic, and easy-to-read account of the Mbuti pygmies of central Africa.

White, L. A. (1959). *The evolution of culture*. New York: McGraw-Hill. A review of cultural evolution as seen by the anthropologist who reawakened an interest in the subject in the twentieth century.

*I*n the contemporary world, hunting and gathering cultures that have changed little over thousands of years coexist with rapidly modernizing industrial cultures whose trappings range from superhighways, heart transplants, and cable television to polluted air and water. Between these two extremes, the mass of humanity lives as peasants growing their own foods, with little income for other goods. Anthropologists are concerned about the fates of all three groups: the vanishing primitive peoples, the peasant cultures that cannot quite meet their own needs, and the industrial peoples threatened by problems such as overpopulation, strained resources, and disparities of wealth.

Contemporary World Societies

13

FIGURE 13.1 *Indigenous People*

Many societies native to an area are becoming controlled by expanding state societies. In addition, they are losing their unique cultural characteristics. This baby wears her native Guatemalan bonnet.

As the cultures of the world evolved, societies at each new general evolutionary level were technologically and socially more powerful than those of the preceding levels. Throughout the history of cultural evolution, societies with less dense populations have been displaced by those with technologies that have allowed their populations to grow increasingly powerful. Tribes have displaced bands, and chiefdoms have expanded at the expense of both band and tribal peoples. The process continues today as the state-level societies take control of territories that once belonged to nonstate peoples. As this happens, more and more of the nonstate societies of the world are becoming extinct.

THE VANISHING
OF NONSTATE SOCIETIES

Today, relatively few bands, tribes, and chiefdoms still exist, and the number is declining each year. The expansion of state societies into territories once occupied by nonstate societies has given rise to a new class of people, called indigenous people, who are the native people of an area now controlled by a state political system within which they have little or no influence. Today, about 200 million people—4 percent of the world's population—have this status. As we shall see, however, not all indigenous people continue to live their ancestral way of life. Those who do are an even smaller minority.

There are three general ways in which indigenous cultures disappear: acculturation, ethnocide, and genocide.

Acculturation

When two previously distinct cultures come in contact, they both change. In this process, called acculturation, each of the interacting cultures borrows traits from the other and makes adjustments. Acculturation can change a culture so much that it soon has little in common with its own traditional characteristics.

The process of cultural change may begin before members of the two societies actually meet, as technological traits from one society are passed and traded through intermediary societies until they reach far distant groups. But acculturation occurs most dramatically when two societies are interacting directly. As each adopts the other's technological, social, and ideological traits, they become more like one another. When one of the societies is politically, economically, and technologically less powerful than the other, it will change the most. When this process is carried to an extreme, the subordinate culture can change so much that it is hardly distinguishable from the dominant one. As a more powerful society extends its boundaries and politically subordinates a less powerful people within its own native territory, the indigenous people generally come to have very little influence on the political decision making of the society that governs them.

The process of acculturation can take place forcibly, for instance, through military domination. It also can occur more peaceably through mechanisms such as trade. As members of the less powerful society seek to acquire materials they find useful from their more powerful trade partners, their own way of life changes in the process. Acculturation eventually can lead to the extinction of an entire culture even though its people survive.

Ethnocide

Sometimes the destruction of a traditional way of life is carried out by deliberate, systematic policies of the dominant culture. Such a process is called ethnocide. An example of the systematic attempt to extinguish the traditional cultures of indigenous peoples has been the treatment of Native Americans in the United States. The political subordination of Native American peoples involved prolonged military campaigns as well as economic processes. Following military conquest, the native people often were forced to cede much of their original lands to the United States government. Initially, Native Americans lived as independent societies with whom treaties were signed that recognized their own rights to self-government on their own lands. Later, Native Americans were redefined by their conquerors as "dependent peoples" of the United States government, whose access to political power within the society that claimed to govern them was almost nonexistent. As more and more of their lands were taken for use by other nondependent citizens, Native Americans found themselves forced onto the least desirable lands, called reservations, and in some cases dispossessed of land altogether.

THE CHEROKEE TRAIL OF TEARS

In the 1830s, the Cherokee, or *Tsalagi* as they called themselves, were a farming people who lived in what is now northern Georgia, western Tennessee, eastern North Carolina, and eastern Virginia, where they had lived since at least 1540. They had been greatly influenced by the customs of European immigrants and had adopted many of their ways. Many had attended college.

FIGURE 13.2 *Sequoyah*

The Cherokee Sequoyah created an alphabet unique to his nation. Utilizing only the idea of writing from the Europeans, Sequoyah's symbols represented specific Cherokee syllables. (see Chapter 12)

Most had adopted Christianity. Their homes were generally built in the same manner as those in neighboring white communities. Their clothing was of woven cotton or wool. An 1825 census of the Cherokee Nation authorized by the Council of the Cherokee listed 10 sawmills, 61 blacksmith shops, 18 ferry boats, 31 gristmills, 2,493 plows, 8 cotton machines, 2,488 spinning wheels, and 762 looms. The United States government had signed a treaty in 1785 recognizing the Cherokee's right to perpetual occupancy of their lands. During the War of 1812, Chief Junaluska volunteered over 600 Cherokee scouts to aid the United States army in fighting the Creek Indians at the Battle of Horseshoe Bend. During this battle Chief Junaluska personally saved the life of Andrew Jackson. By 1821 the Cherokee Sequoia had developed a system for writing the language of his people, and within 10 years the literacy rate was greater among Cherokees than among U.S. citizens. In 1832 the Cherokee began printing their own newspaper in both Cherokee and English.

In 1828 a Cherokee boy at Ward Creek, Georgia, sold a gold nugget to a white trader, an act that one observer of its results said sealed the doom of the Cherokees. Cherokees began to be driven off their land by gold seekers. In 1830 the state of Georgia passed a law annexing a large portion of the Cherokee lands and declaring Cherokee laws and government null and void within Georgia. Cherokees were forbidden to mine gold within this area, a law enforced by the Georgia Guard. The Cherokees sought redress through the federal courts and sued the state to keep their lands. The case reached the United States Supreme Court, which was presided over by Chief Justice John Marshall. In 1832 the court ruled in favor of the Cherokees. However, President Andrew Jackson would not honor the Supreme Court's decision; he remarked that "John Marshall has made his decision; now let him enforce it." Jackson became involved in the removal of the Cherokees from their lands. Chief John Ross sent Chief Junaluska as an envoy to plead with President Jackson for protection for his people, but Jackson rejected the pleas of the man who had saved his life. In 1835 the Treaty of New Echota, Georgia, made the evacuation of the Cherokees from all of their lands mandatory. Chief John Ross requested a two-year period for his people to prepare to leave for land in what is now Oklahoma and Kansas.

The Cherokees continued to negotiate their right to remain. But, in 1838 while Chief John Ross was in Washington, D.C., attempting to work out an alternative to the removal of his people, 7,000 soldiers under the command of General Winfield Scott began immediate arrests of Cherokees wherever they were found. Men working in their fields were beaten and driven at gunpoint into stockades. Women were driven from their homes, and children were separated from their families. No time was allowed to take clothing, blankets, or food. Eighteen thousand Cherokees were housed in rat-infested stockades without sanitary facilities. From May until November of 1838, people with as much as one thirty-second Cherokee ancestry were arrested.

One of those evicted was John Ross, nephew of Chief John Ross, who was preparing to leave for Princeton. He was taken from his Georgia home, a two-story brick mansion, with his mother, a full-blooded Scottish woman, after his father was shot in an upstairs room. The mansion was burned as they left. During the fall and winter of 1838, the Cherokees were loaded into 645 wagons, and the 900-mile trek began. Four thousand died in the stockades or on the journey to Oklahoma Indian Territory.

Politically dominant societies may legally require that indigenous peoples send their children to schools that train them in the dominant culture and language of the nation. In some cases these are boarding schools where the children must live for long periods of time, far from their own families. Often the use of their native language is not only discouraged but also forbidden and punished. Removed from the normal process of socialization in their own native culture, they return home ill-equipped to carry on their parents' way of life. Missionary efforts also have contributed to the destruction of native ways of life. This has not been limited to attacks on traditional religious beliefs, for the missionaries often have sought to condemn as immoral other parts of native culture that differed from current customs in their own societies. For instance, Western religious leaders generally have worked for the abolishing of forms of marriage other than monogamy, even though their own religious heritage includes scriptural precedent for polygyny as a once-accepted form (Ribiero, 1971; Walker, 1972).

Genocide

Related to ethnocide, the destruction of a culture, is the practice of genocide, the systematic destruction of a people. Many of the indigenous people of the world have been and are being systematically exterminated. Military campaigns against native peoples have been only one way in which the extinction of whole societies has occurred. Biological warfare also has been used. In the earlier days of United States history, clothing and blankets infected with smallpox and other diseases were distributed to some Native Americans, ostensibly as gifts. Colonial people also have given gifts of poisoned foods to indigenous people and have sometimes hunted them for sport (Bonwick, 1870; Calder, 1874; Horwood, 1969). In the past decade in many parts of Latin America, Indians have been killed by settlers moving onto their traditional lands. This private warfare is carried out with guns, bombs, dynamite, and even rapid-fire weapons from helicopters by private individuals while the national governments have turned a blind eye to the killing. In some cases, government

agencies have declared traditional native lands to be "empty" in spite of the presence of indigenous people and therefore legitimately available for settling by nonindigenous farmers, miners, and land speculators.

Gregor (1983) has reported the historical impact of the immigration of nonindigenous people into one Latin American country:

> In 1500 explorer Pedro Cabral landed on the coast of Brazil and claimed its lands and native peoples for the Portuguese empire. Since that time Brazilian Indians have been killed by European diseases and bounty hunters, forced off their land by squatters and speculators, and enslaved by ranchers and mine owners. Today the Indians, numbering less than one-tenth of the precontact population, inhabit the most remote regions of the country. (p. 1)

The effects of such violence have penetrated even into indigenous groups that have had little direct contact with outsiders. Gregor has described the Mehinaku, a single village tribe that lives in a vast protected reservation in the Mato Grosso of Brazil. Despite their official protection and relative isolation, contact with Brazilians has been sufficient to undermine the security of their lives. Gregor quotes one Mehinaku villager: "Last night my dream was very bad. I dreamed of a white man" (p. 1). According to the Mehinaku, such dreams portend illness. The symbolism is apt since, in the words of Gregor, "In the early 1960s, almost 20 percent of the tribe died in a measles epidemic, and the villagers continue to suffer from imported diseases for which they have neither natural nor acquired immunity" (p. 2).

THE EFFECTS OF INDUSTRIALIZATION

One fundamental factor sealing the doom of many nonstate societies and altering the nature of all the world's cultures has been industrialization. Beginning with the Industrial Revolution in Great Britain in the latter half of the eighteenth century, many cultures have joined the movement away from home production of goods to large-scale, mechanized factory production requiring great inputs of capital. This shift has brought profound alterations in all aspects of life, including changes in economic systems, growth of populations, and concentration of people around cities. Even those societies that have not industrialized are now defined and affected by their lack of industry.

Developed and Underdeveloped Societies

Societies may be categorized in a number of ways. One simple distinction commonly is made on the basis of industrialization. Developed countries are the industrialized nations of the world: the countries of North America, Europe, Japan, Taiwan, and the Soviet Union. Underdeveloped countries are the remaining largely nonindustrialized world societies, including all of Africa, Asia (excluding Japan, Taiwan, and the Soviet Union), and Latin America. The distinction between developed and underdeveloped countries is widely used, but the dichotomy is simpler than the reality it represents. For instance, the world's underdeveloped countries vary from extremely poverty-stricken societies in which hunger and starvation are daily problems to others that have incorporated a great deal of industrialized technology into their economy and will soon be viewed as having become developed countries. Those underdeveloped countries that are making major gains in industrialization are sometimes referred to as developing countries in recognition of the changes they are undergoing. As developing countries are drawn into the worldwide network of industrialized economies, they change in a variety of ways that are discussed in the following sections of this chapter.

As of mid-1985, three fourths of the human population lived in underdeveloped nations (Kent & Haub, 1985). Living standards are very low in these areas, and their current economies often will not support industrial development. Most underdeveloped countries suffer from severe shortages of land, capital, or labor. Land is often largely owned by a small, elite minority, with the remainder severely fragmented into plots too small to do more than meet the minimal needs of the families who farm them. The results of the absence of capital include roads that are impassable when it rains, schools that lack enough books, and per capita incomes that are extremely low. The average per capita gross national product of the underdeveloped nations is 640 U.S. dollars, compared with 10,700 U.S. dollars for the developed world (Haub & Kent, 1988). The population of the underdeveloped world is a more rural one than that of developed countries: While 73 percent of the people in developed societies live in urban areas, only 37 percent of the people in underdeveloped countries do so. These contrasts between the developed and underdeveloped parts of the world are results of the process of industrialization that began two centuries ago.

Economic Change

Industrialization has greatly influenced the economic and social life of societies in which it has occurred. Preindustrial economies are fundamentally matters of family-based production, and the food and other goods produced are used primarily by the producers themselves. Trade exists mostly to distribute the surpluses from the family and community stock rather than to specialize in the production of food or other goods for the purpose of trade. With industrialization comes a major increase in the number of specialized occupations. Industrialization has created a great demand for wage laborers at centralized locations who do not produce their own food. So industrialization is only possible if farming moves from being a family-oriented subsistence activity to a market-oriented enterprise.

Farming to raise cash crops is vastly different from farming to feed oneself. Farming peoples who produce for their own consumption are more likely to diversify their production into as many as 20 to 30 different kinds of crops and animals. This diversity minimizes their risks and maximizes their autonomy. Market-oriented farmers tend to invest in a smaller number of more specialized crops. Industry also fosters the production of nonessential food crops, such as cocoa and coffee, and nonfood products, such as wool for textiles or sisal for twine and cordage manufacture. So industrialization fosters a move of a large percentage of farmers away from staple food production. In an industrialized economy, the food-producing sector of farming becomes increasingly competitive, mechanized, expen-

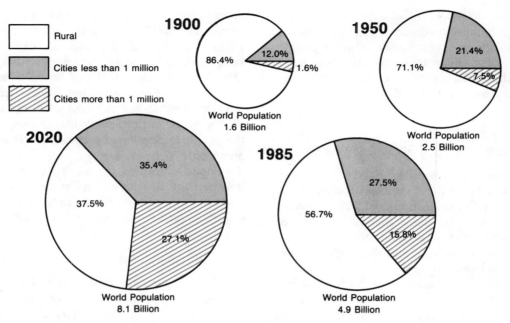

Sources: Kingsley Davis International Technical Cooperation Centre Review, July 1972; World Facts and Figures, 1979; UN Population Division; and Population Reference Bureau.

FIGURE 13.3   *Patterns of World Urbanization*

Industrialization has created the move to cities, increasing their size so that in 1985, eleven cities had more than 10 million people.

sive, and competitive, so that small-scale farms become less and less viable.

Urbanization

Agriculture created towns and cities long before industrialization began, but industrialization greatly fostered the growth of cities. Since the large-scale manufacture of marketable goods and trade go hand in hand as industrialization proceeds, industrialized centers of manufacture tend to be located in urban centers along the routes of trade. As industry produces a growing demand for labor, workers are drawn out of rural areas into the cities to find employment, and urban areas grow in population.

In 1900 only 13.6 percent of the world's population lived in cities. By 1988 the portion of the world's population living in urban areas had risen to 45 percent (Haub & Kent, 1988) and it is expected to climb to 60 percent by the year 2020 (Murphy, 1985; see Fig. 13.3). Part of the process of urbanization has been an increase in the size of cities. In 1950 there were only 2 cities with more than 10 million inhabitants: the New York/New Jersey urban com-

plex and London. In 1985 there were 11 such cities, the largest of which was Tokyo/Yokohama with 19.0 million people (Murphy, 1985; *Statistical Abstract of the United States,* 1989, p. 18, Table 1406; see Table 13.1).

World Population Growth

In addition to becoming more concentrated in cities, the world's population has grown in general as industrialization has increased our life expectancy, through factors described in the next section. The history of human population can be described as a long period of slow growth followed by a relatively recent explosion that reached its fastest rate of expansion in 1965, when world population was increasing at about 2 percent per year. The period of slow growth ended with the development of agriculture about 10,000 years ago, but the truly rapid explosion that we are still experiencing started with the Industrial Revolution.

A third of a million years ago, in the time of *Homo erectus,* the human population of the entire world was less than 1 million people. When food domestication began, about 10,000

TABLE 13.1 *World's Ten Largest Cities*

1950	Population (in millions)	1985	Population (in millions)	2000	Population (in millions)
1. New York-N.E. New Jersey	12.3	1. Tokyo-Yokohama	19.0	1. Mexico City	24.4
2. London	10.4	2. Mexico City	16.7	2. Sao Paulo	23.6
3. Rhine-Ruhr	6.9	3. New York-N.E. New Jersey	15.6	3. Tokyo-Yokohama	21.3
4. Tokyo-Yokohama	6.7	4. Sao Paulo	15.5	4. New York-N.E. New Jersey	16.1
5. Shanghai, Mainland	5.8	5. Shanghai, Mainland	12.1	5. Calcutta	15.9
6. Paris	5.5	6. Greater Buenos Aires	10.8	6. Greater Bombay	15.6
7. Greater Buenos Aires	5.3	7. London	10.5	7. Shanghai, Mainland	14.7
8. Chicago-N.W. Indiana	4.9	8. Calcutta	10.3	8. Teheran	13.7
9. Moscow	4.8	9. Rio de Janeiro	10.1	9. Jakarta	13.2
10. Calcutta	4.6	10. Seoul	10.1	10. Greater Buenos Aires	13.1

Note. United Nations, Department of International Economic and Social Affairs, 1985.

years ago, there were still fewer than 10 million people in the world. By A.D. 1 the figure was about 300 million. It reached half a billion in A.D. 1650, and the first billion was achieved about A.D. 1800. By July of 1986 the figure had reached 5 billion. Using the same beginning point, a population of one billion required a third of a million years to reach. The second billion took only about 130 years, the third just 30 years, the fourth only 15 years, and the fifth a mere 11 years!

Industrialization and the Quality of Life

Industrialization does provide benefits. Its productivity is much greater than that of hand labor. This high productivity frees many members of society to pursue the specialized occupations that do not exist in preindustrial societies. Thus, industrialization brings to society new goods and new services. Overall, the standard of living in industrialized societies is higher and the life expectancy longer than in traditional ways of life. The growth in life expectancy is influenced by many factors. The industrialization of food production can provide better nutrition and security from famine. Improved housing and sanitation also can be created through industrialization. The increased number of specialized statuses in industrialized societies represent new services that also can increase life expectancy. For instance, medical specialists—including doctors and other health care providers—can contribute directly to a declining rate of disease and to lower mortality rates in all age categories.

Industrialization also has its costs.

Growth in industry is paralleled by growth in air and water pollution. As population grows, increased demand for goods can lead to the depletion of nonrenewable resources such as minerals and fossil fuels and to the overuse of potentially renewable ones. The urban growth that an expanding population fosters brings crowding and its attendant problems of unemployment, poverty, poor health and nutrition, and crime. It is an irony that industrialization can create both many new jobs and high unemployment, wealth and poverty, abundant foods and poor nutrition. Many of these problems grow out of the fact that although industrialization creates wealth, that wealth is not necessarily equitably distributed. Without exception, the process of industrialization has been accompanied by increasing disparities in the wealth, power, and honor of the social classes that are part of all state-level societies. At times, these inequities can be the source of major social problems.

PEASANT CULTURES

Since the beginning of urbanization, the contrast between urban centers of power and wealth and less influential rural food-producing areas has been a fact of human life. As societies have grown in social complexity, the discrepancy between the political power and prestige of the urban elite and other members of society changed from a strictly urban-rural distinction to one of social elites versus peasants. Peasants are food producers whose economic life centers on using family-based labor

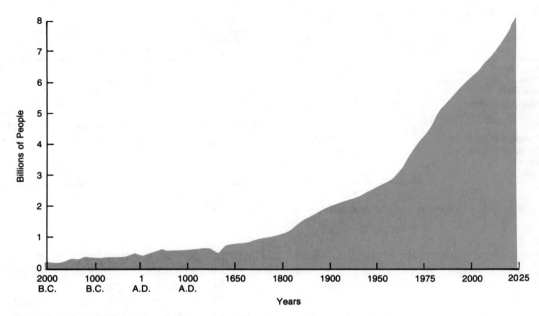

FIGURE 13.4 *World Population Growth Through History*

The growth of the population of the world has historically been a long, slow process until the Industrial Revolution, which initiated a rapid growth period.

and who consume most of what they grow. Since peasants must produce their own food, they do not specialize in cash crops or crops that cannot be eaten. Peasants may produce some crops for sale or hire out their own labor to supplement their incomes, but their cash incomes are too low to change their material conditions or socially subordinate status. They may produce some cash crops for sale in markets, but the income from their sales is used to supplement their diets rather than to increase their food-producing efficiency. Typically, peasants use nonindustrialized, hand-labor techniques that yield only a minimal subsistence for their own families, yet need large families to ensure that they have enough labor to produce the food they need. They are largely rural peoples, but today some peasants do live in urban areas where they can supplement their incomes from small-scale gardening with income from paid labor. Peasants are a subordinate part of a larger society in which they are economically and politically dominated by a governing class of which they are not a part. They rarely control their own political destinies. Their food production is part of the larger society's economy, but they have little influence on its operation. Often, peasants do not own the land that they work.

Feudal Peasantries

In preindustrial times, peasants were part of political systems in which local aristocratic leaders who claimed ownership of the land granted the <u>feudal peasants</u> the privilege to use the land to grow their own food in return for rent or service. According to Dalton (1969), the relationship between peasant and lord in feudal times involved responsibilities and obligations on the part of the land owner as well as the peasant. For instance, the feudal lord provided military and police protection for the peasants, settled disputes, and fed them in times of hardship. Feudal social forms are less common today but can, for instance, still be found in parts of India, El Salvador, and Guatamela. Peasants' lack of land ownership probably always has been a source of dissatisfaction in most feudal societies (Wolf, 1969), but the exploitation of peasants by feudal aristocracies was not as one-sided as one might believe. In the period which followed industrialization, when contracted wage labor replaced the earlier paternalistic feudal system, the peasant was forced to provide for all his needs. In the industrialized economic system, the obligations of the propertied classes ended with the payment of the wage.

Colonial Peasantries

Following the development of industrialized food production and transportation technologies, the subordination of peasantries intensified. Industrialization opened the door for colonial empires to spread into distant parts of the world, where inexpensive peasant labor made possible the cheap extraction of natural resources for the benefit of the colonial administrations and their homelands. Colonial peasants were encouraged, sometimes economically and sometimes by the pressure of military might, to move from the production of food to the production of nonfood export crops and paid labor. As Lappé and Collins (1977) have pointed out:

> Colonialism destroyed the cultural patterns of production and exchange by which traditional societies in "underdeveloped" countries previously had met the needs of the people. Many precolonial social structures, while dominated by exploitative elites, had evolved a system of mutual obligations among the classes that helped to ensure at least a minimal diet for all. A friend of mine once said: "Precolonial village existence in subsistence agriculture was a limited life indeed, but it's certainly not Calcutta." The misery of starvation in the streets of Calcutta can only be understood as the end-point of a long historical process—one that has destroyed a traditional social system. (p. 76)

The colonial subordination of peasantries can be seen as a process in which some societies have been underdeveloped to the benefit of others (Rodney, 1972). Colonial administrations encouraged the production of cash crops such as cotton, cocoa, coffee, sugar, and tobacco for export at the expense of the staple foods that had been produced previously. These export crops were selected for their high price value in the home market relative to their shipping costs and not for their value as foods. The methods used to bring about this shift to cash crop production included physical force and taxation. Since the taxes levied by colonial administrations had to be paid in cash, peasants were forced to grow cash crops. In some cases, foreign governments or private individuals claimed ownership of native lands and forced the native people to work the fields as slaves, wage laborers, or dispossessed tenant

FIGURE 13.5 *Peasant Market*

Most peasants produce food for their own consumption and sell some of their crops at market to supplement their incomes as do these women in the delta region of Senegal.

farmers. The profits of the export products grown remained in the hands of the foreign interests. Thus, through various means, previously self-sufficient farmers could no longer grow enough food to meet their own needs. Ironically, even though peasant peoples throughout the world are basically farmers, the peasant societies have had to become major food importers to feed themselves. This has locked them firmly into the world economy which today is dominated by the industrialized nations.

Contemporary Peasantries

Today, most of the people in the world can be classified as peasants, members of a social class of traditional, family-based food producers who are subordinate to an urban-based administrative class in each of their societies. The economies of these societies are, them-

FIGURE 13.6 *Irrigated Farmlands*

One type of peasant typically works for an absentee landlord. This child works on an irrigated farm near Djenné on the southern edge of the Sahara.

selves, highly influenced by worldwide economic forces that are beyond their control. Because of the small volume of their specialized cash crops, the peasants lack the cash flow to pay for the equipment and services that would be necessary to industrialize their farming techniques. Neither is their economic base sufficient for state taxation to sustain the bureaucratic social benefits available in urban centers. Traditional credit and rental arrangements in peasant communities often are based on commodities rather than money, and exchange is centered on small marketplaces in which individual peasants act as "penny capitalists," selling their few surplus products or selling their labor on a piecemeal basis. Since in many peasant societies much of the most productive land is owned by a wealthy elite—who long ago converted it to the production of cash crops—peasants find it difficult to produce sufficient foods on their "postage stamp" farms to meet their own nutritional needs. Much of their cash income is devoted to the purchase of food, and typically the cash in-

comes that they obtain prove insufficient to meet the expenses of life in an industrializing society.

The varieties of peasant societies. Peasant societies are not all identical. They are found in various environments and use different subsistence technologies. Moris (1981) has outlined the basic contexts in which one finds peasant societies: pastoral and ranching areas, irrigation farmland, large-farm or estate areas, marginal lands and hill farming, intensive peasant smallholdings, organized settlement and frontier areas, labor reserve areas (remittance economy areas), tenancy and refugee farming, and peri-urban squatter settlements.

Pastoral and ranching areas have low-density populations that are spread over large territories. Sometimes the resources they use must be owned communally rather than individually to be effectively utilized. Their need to migrate seasonally with their herds and the low population density make it difficult for them to form a power base to which the centralized government administrators will respond. This lack of political power is especially problematic since these people's needs differ from those of the more sedentary parts of a society with which administrators are likely to be familiar. Their special problems include stock theft and difficulties in establishing effective educational programs.

Irrigated farmlands often are worked by tenant farmers. There is heavy reliance on one or two major crops, such as coffee or hemp, grown for their market value. Tenant farmers may live in large villages near the land they work on behalf of absentee landlords. Peasant-landlord relations have many characteristics of the historically earlier forms of peasantry, since the land worked by the peasant is owned by an elite whose good will the peasant must keep to maintain access to the land. Adequate medical facilities and other social resources are likely to be minimal in the peasant villages.

Large-farm or estate areas are common in the tropics. They are supported by foreign investment and typically grow export crops such as rubber or tea. Here the peasant is simply a laborer and lives in quarters provided by the management. In some cases, these estates may be owned by the local government rather than by members of the private sector.

FIGURE 13.7   *Pastoral and Ranching Societies*

Tribes that follow the pastoral or ranching tradition find it difficult to develop a political power base. They also face problems educating their young and dealing with theft of their stock.

Estate settlements often have very differing social needs from those of neighboring towns, since the entire population of the estate settlement is made up of working-class persons.

Marginal and hill farming is found in isolated pockets of semiarid land and hill country where only hand techniques are usable in farming because of the steep slopes. Crops are limited to those relying solely on the yearly rainfall. Only the surpluses above the peasants' own needs can be marketed. Small stock supplement the subsistence needs of these peasants, but the animals often cause a gradual deterioration of communal lands where they are pastured.

Intensive peasant smallholdings are found where better soil and rainfall allow dairy farming or growing of perennial crops such as tea, coffee, bananas, and cassava. Farming in these areas is basically hoe farming done by hand. Since these areas are sometimes quite productive, hoe farming can yield enough to support population growth. This increase often is followed by a shift toward labor-intensive high-yield crops, such as irrigated rice, and smaller and smaller plots, until the equivalent of urban population densities are achieved in the rural peasant settlements. The people in these areas can become locked into increasingly impoverished conditions by division of land into intensively cultivated smallholdings.

Frontier areas develop when new lands are opened up to settlement by national governments that do not recognize the land claims of the indigenous populations there. The attraction of these areas is often the natural resources they contain, such as timber, gold, and other minerals useful to the industries of the nation. Land speculation is common in these areas, and what seems like a booming economy can lure farmers who are not aware of the riskiness of farming in these areas. Bank loans are made on the basis of the speculative value of the land, not its farm income value. Foreclosures gradually dispossess the farming populations, who become landless peasant workers or tenant farmers.

What Moris (1981) calls labor reserve areas should probably be called remittance economy areas, since they are "rural communities that depend on remitted earnings for cash income" (1981, p. 29). These are communities that experience high levels of out-migration, as workers are forced to leave the communities to meet their economic needs. The local communities are thereby drained of younger working-age men. This lowers the productivity of community labor, and what little income finally reaches the community from absent workers

311

may accomplish little in improving conditions in the home community. Welfare costs of supporting the less productive members of the community who are left behind—the aged, the sick, and persons too uneducated to find employment elsewhere—further undermine the standard of living in the community. Absentee ownership of land may complicate matters in these areas, since those who reside in the communities often are unwilling to pay for improvements to land they do not own. Because of their stagnant economy and lack of services, these communities gradually gain a reputation as "backwards districts," to which young people are not likely to want to return.

MIGRANT LABOR AND WOMEN'S STATUS IN LESOTHO

The case of Lesotho is a particularly interesting example of the domination of peasant economic and social life by forces that lie beyond the control of the people involved. Lesotho is a small, mountainous kingdom that is entirely surrounded by the Republic of South Africa. Its major internal subsistence resources are agriculture and cattle herding, but most of its best agricultural lands were lost to South Africa in a series of wars that ended in 1868.

Since the loss of Lesotho's best agricultural lands, tremendous population growth forced the expansion of cultivation into many areas that had previously been used for cattle grazing. As seasonal pasturage in the highlands came to be used throughout the year, their productivity was undermined by overgrazing and erosion. Lesotho agriculturalists in this century found it became unprofitable to export grain because of import tariffs imposed by neighboring governments; grain must now be imported from South Africa to feed Lesotho's growing population. Indeed, about 40 percent of food consumed in Lesotho is imported. Cash income is also important to Lesotho men, because the traditional bride price required for marriage is now usually made in cash payments. Today, the majority of cash income for the people of Lesotho comes from wages earned by migrant laborers who work primarily in the mines of the Republic of South Africa.

According to Safilios-Rothschild (1985), nearly half (47.7 percent) of Lesotho men are absent from home, working as migrant laborers starting at about the age of twenty years. Males who take employment in South Africa may stay away from one to two years at a time, after which South African law requires that they return home for several months before resuming work. Typically, migrants are away from home for total a period of fifteen to twenty years, between the ages of about twenty and fifty years.

Lesotho women have been forbidden since 1963 by South African law to enter South Africa as migrant laborers, and women are not permitted to reside with their husbands at the mines. Thus, between 40 and 60 percent of Lesotho's married women are left behind to manage on their own (Gordon, 1981, p. 59; Palmer, 1985, p. 18), and between 60 and 70 percent of rural households are headed by women. They can rely on little male help, even from their own kin, in their agricultural work, since the half of the male population who are engaged as migrant laborers are those in their most productive working years. Working husbands may have a portion of their wages remitted to their families in Lesotho, although Mueller (1977) indicates that most migrants prefer to send only small amounts and bring most of their savings home when they return during their leaves. Safilios-Rochschild (1985, p. 304) indicates that 90 percent of migrant miners do not send regular remittances, and only 30 to 35 percent of rural female-headed households receive any at all.

The absence of migrant husbands takes a high toll in the lives of Lesotho women. Gordon (1981) found that the longer migrant husbands had been absent from home, the greater were the levels of stress reported by their wives. This was partly because husbands' commitment to their wives declined the longer they were away from home, resulting in decreases in remittances and increases in divorces or separations. Widowhood is also common among wives of migrant laborers, due in part to the much greater age of husbands in Lesotho marriages and in part to the high death rate in mining.

The economic consequences of separation and divorce are not limited to the loss of a woman's remittance income. Since land is owned only by men, legal divorce results in the loss of access to the former husband's lands. Furthermore, divorced women are not viewed as acceptable spouses by other men if their ex-husband had not paid a full bride price before the divorce.

Widowhood also brings economic hardships. Traditionally, a third of a widow's lands were repossessed by her husband's family, and although this custom is no longer legal, it is still followed by many instances in the more rural areas. Widows also face the prospect of lifelong responsibility for agricultural work that would otherwise be taken over by their husbands at the end of their work in the mines. Nevertheless, few widows remarry, because doing so would require them to give up all rights to their deceased husbands' fields, house, property, and children—all of which would revert to his relatives (Bardill & Cobbe, 1985).

One response to the poverty related to traditional hand-labor-based agricultural production has been the formation of cooperative agricultural associations in which members can pool their resources for their mutual benefit. The government has encouraged such efforts by offering agricultural credit to cooperatives that become legally registered.

Ironically, the poorer, female-headed households in rural areas have difficulty meeting the requirements for registration, since it requires that they have formal training in managerial, cooperative, bookkeeping, and marketing skills. Such training is offered by the government where they find it most convenient and economical to do so—in town centers rather than in rural areas, where the poorest households are found. Thus, less-needy households in and near the towns are closer to the training centers than are rural households in general. Female heads of households in the rural areas also find it more difficult to arrange to do their agricultural work and tend their children while attending such training than do male heads of households. These barriers to women's ability to obtain agricultural assistance are difficult to challenge, since there is a widespread assumption that female-headed households have access to migrant husbands' remittances and are, therefore, less in need of financial assistance than are male-headed households.

A second important response to the economic difficulties of life in Lesotho has been the government's attempt to increase agricultural production through the introduction of industrialized tools and techniques. According to Riley (1989), these efforts have focused on making loans available to farmers for the purchase of irrigation equipment, such as pumps, pipe, and sprinklers, and cultivation equipment such as rototillers, push cultivators, and—in very few cases—tractors. This has increased productivity, but it has also increased labor and expenses among women heads of household. For instance, irrigation has increased the necessity of weeding and transplanting, and harvesting, all of which are traditionally women's work in Lesotho.

Irrigating, on the other hand, is viewed in Lesotho as men's work, so women heads of household are faced with the additional expense of hiring men to do such work as moving irrigation pipe and spinklers.

Thus, along with the increased productivity that industrialized technology is bringing to Lesotho has come a dramatic increase in costs to women. They continue to be responsible for almost all domestic tasks and have larger expenses, more agricultural work, and devote more time to money-producing activities than before development projects started. In spite of these changes, few agriculturists have achieved self-sufficiency in food production, so foreign employment continues to keep a majority of men away from home and unable to break the cycle of increasing work for women as agricultural development proceeds.

Tenant or refugee farms worked by landless and dispossessed tenant populations may develop, according to Moris (1981), when the production system of a traditional society gives way to paid employment of tenant farmers. This change disrupts the traditional system of mutual obligations that gave peasant farmers the right to work land they did not own. After generations in which these rights have been recognized, the peasant farmers suddenly find themselves dispossessed and without any source of income. Modernization in these areas is difficult, since the lands that are worked are not owned by the peasant farmers. The officially recognized landowners are unlikely to be willing to bear the costs of such things as fencing or improved housing or farm structures, since these benefit the tenant farmers, not the owners. Similarly, the farmers are not motivated to make improvements on lands that belong to someone else.

FIGURE 13.8 *Peri-urban Squatter Communities*

Squatter settlements are economically poor and politically without power. They exist near rapidly growing cities. Residents support themselves by growing their own food and working at odd jobs.

Peri-urban squatter settlements are the final category of contemporary peasant-land relationships based on Moris's analysis. These are formed of people "who live in densely settled communities near rapidly growing cities" (1981, p. 30). Peri-urban squatters are especially common in tropical areas, where perennial crops can be grown and multiple cropping makes it possible to grow enough to support families on extremely small "postage stamp" farms. The unofficial settlements created by these peasants outside major cities may lack the recognition that would entitle them to public services or legal title to the land they occupy and work. Sanitary conditions are often extremely poor in these settlements, as are nutrition and health. Incomes are supplemented by petty trading, casual work, gardening, and other services performed for citizens of the nearby cities.

The difficulties of change in peasant societies. The economic limitations of peasant life are not easily overcome. Some observers feel that a major obstacle to change lies in the peasants' own attitudes. According to Foster (1967), life in peasant societies often leads to a rather fatalistic, dreary outlook in which the drudgery of life is not believed to bring much reward, since the achievement of one person can only be accomplished at the expense of another. Foster has called this outlook the image of limited good. Because of this view of life, peasants are commonly jealous of success, and peasant life contains many social pressures not to excel over one's peers. Lewis (1966) saw this life-style as fostering attitudes that cause peasants and other poverty-stricken people to think only of today, to spend and consume what they have right now since saving for tomorrow seems futile. Lewis called this approach to life the culture of poverty. Although this outlook certainly is not the underlying cause of the impoverished conditions of peasants in most parts of the world, it can make it difficult for peasants to take part effectively in opportunities for social change.

Wolf (1966) believes there are more substantial reasons why change is difficult in peasant circumstances. Peasants are slow to combine forces to overcome exploitation because they are individually bound into vertical political ties or "patron-client" relationships with more wealthy and powerful individuals on whose aid they depend in times of need. To work with other peasants for the common good is to sever these personally advantageous ties, so peasant communities are caught in a cycle of competition between individuals and factions.

Scott (1976) points out that the status quo does provide the peasant with a buffer from adversity. Peasant community expectations have a leveling effect that limits the poverty into which any one member of the society can sink. The maintenance of "commons"—lands available to all, for instance as pasturage—is an example of the buffers against adversity that are built into the peasant community. Commercialization, according to Scott, is actually a threat to peasant security, since it undermines the mechanisms that provide that security in impoverished circumstances.

Nelson and Water (1984) argue that prices in peasant markets are quite unstable and seasonally variable, since peasants market only the surplus that their families do not need for food. Peasants tend to rely on relatives for credit and assistance. They lack sufficient cash incomes to support markets that sell factory-produced goods. Nelson and Water believe this situation is self-perpetuating because reliance on family for labor and economic support leads to large family size and increased population growth leads to reduced savings and investment. This, in turn, necessitates greater reliance on family labor and traditional means of production.

Although there are many features of life in peasant societies that make change difficult, it would be a mistake to assume that peasant societies cannot change. Peasants have been ready to revolt against the system that maintains their landlessness and poverty when opportunities for successful uprisings have presented themselves. Many social scientists believe that peaceful improvement of peasant conditions is also possible. Popkin (1979) portrays the peasant life style as a rational response to the tight constraints that limit their production and to the high degree of risk they face in making a living. He contends that when markets and opportunities exist, peasants respond by increasing output.

Applied Anthropology and Cultural Change

As anthropologists have studied the problems of nonindustrial populations, many have felt a growing obligation to apply their insights to achieve constructive change in areas such as overcoming the cycle of poverty in peasant societies. This new subfield of anthropology is called applied anthropology. Applied anthropologists working in developing countries have pointed out that the problems of the developing world are not merely technological in nature. Technological change is intimately connected to social and ideological facts of life, and technological change can sometimes create unforeseen problems in these areas. Yet the social and ideological aspects of development often have been overlooked by the governmental administrators and technicians who have been given responsibility for improving conditions among peasant populations.

Fisher (1972) describes a number of reasons why government-sponsored development projects often fail. The list demonstrates that project failures are more typically social and ideological than technological in nature. Projects intended to improve the lot of the peasant poor often are designed by persons who are unfamiliar with life in the peasant community, and these projects are imposed from the outside. The governments involved sometimes fail to commit resources that are necessary for the projects to succeed. Goals and resource allocations may be revised in the middle of a project without regard to the effects on work in the community setting. Project planning sometimes is not economically sound, and the projects may not incorporate the incentives to which peasants respond. Erroneous assumptions are commonly made about the effectiveness or capabilities of the institutions involved in the project. Projects that look good on paper may not be targeted toward specific clienteles. Often, projects spread their resources too thinly to be effective in any one area. The human element in the real work of project implementation may not be fully taken into account. The various governmental ministries involved in the work may not coordinate their efforts. Finally, demand for the new product created by the peasants is often insufficient for the work to become self-sustaining, and the yield or output projections may be inconsistent with the level of management available.

THE MASAI PROJECT: AN ATTEMPT AT PLANNED CULTURAL CHANGE

Moris (1981) has described the social and political problems that plagued a development project among the Maasai,[1] a Tanzanian seminomadic cattle-herding people. The 45,000 Maasai occupied a 14-million acre territory in northern Tanzania where they herded 1 million head of cattle and about 1.25 million sheep and goats.

Attempts at range management, planning for most effective use of land for raising livestock without depleting the environment, began about the time of Tanzanian independence in 1961. Following recommendations of an American range specialist, the Tanzanian government attempted to form a pilot project Ranching Association near the town of Arusha. Unfortunately, the choice of location for this pilot project was made without considering the social organization of the people who would form the Ranching Association. It necessitated cooperation between Maasai cattle herders and their rival neighbors, the Wa-Arusha, who herded goats and farmed small plots. The program therefore was plagued by political frictions and made little progress for its first three years.

In 1970 the Masai Project was begun with support from USAID (United States Agency for International Development). Five technical experts were hired for work on the project: an animal production specialist, a range ecologist, a livestock marketing specialist, a water development engineer, and an anthropologist. The project took responsibility for range development in Masailand, an area of 24,000 square miles.

Within the first year and a half, four ranching associations had been formed. Cattle dips and range offices were being built, and technical data were being gathered on stocking rates. A vegetation survey was underway, and groundwork was being laid for the formation of a jointly owned breeding herd. Legal action was being considered to stop the spread of bean cultivation into grazing lands. But, at the same time, the Tanzanian government was sponsoring the formation of village-based farming—in what are called "Ujamaa villages"—throughout the country, as part of its political policy of trying to create a socialist system of production. The regional government leaders began to see the Masai Project as interfering with their goal of teaching pastoralists to adopt farming in sedentary, government-sponsored villages.

As the Tanzanian government reorganized its system for administering local areas, Masai Project members were required to report daily to the local government office. Continual reporting of day-to-day matters through the hierarchy of district officials

cut into the work time of project members and slowed routine decision making. According to Moris (1981), plans and personnel were continually in flux:

> The frequent changes and reassessments in the project took their toll upon staff and morale alike. As fast as Tanzanian staff were recruited as range officers, they were called up to do their national service or assigned to counterpart training. Of the initial five foreign experts, three finished their tours or otherwise left. In its first four years the team had had three leaders, reported to four successive regional heads, and worked under three District Livestock Development Officers in Monduli. By the end of 1972 half the project vehicles were not running because of a lack of American spare parts.
>
> The project was continuously under reconsideration, either by Tanzanian leaders or US-AID. Among Tanzanians there were fears that the US experts might oppose the Ujamaa settlement program. When equipment was late in arriving, this was interpreted as a deliberate US action to impede Tanzanian development. Some USAID officials in Washington opposed the project's investment in a socialist country where land was not privately owned. (pp. 105–106)

By 1973 the ranching associations were becoming popular among the Maasai, partly because the Maasai could see that registered ranching associations received more government assistance than did other stock owners. However, instead of forming new ranching associations, neighboring Maasai moved into lands of the existing associations in order to obtain special livestock services. In cooperation with the Tanzanian government, the project then was reorganized and strengthened. Plans were laid to increase to 21 the number of ranching associations and to include a program for settlement of the Maasai into ranches equivalent to the government-sponsored villages.

By 1977 only one of the major issues of the Masai Project had not been solved. The remaining problem was how to integrate the government concept of socialist village settlements into the association structure. And team work time was being diverted into growing areas of responsibility, such as a land capability survey using remote sensing imagery, a U.S.-backed roadbuilding program, and a livestock training center. The growing size of the project team, which had reached 10 technicians and 20 Tanzanian counterparts, and its expanded responsibilities led to internal stresses and disagreements over project priorities. By the middle of 1977, most of the more experienced team members had left the project. Most of the replacements did not speak Kiswahili, the language used in almost all Tanzanian government meetings.

The Tanzanian government received assistance to establish a livestock marketing company. However, this commercial organization was unable to recover its operating costs in remote areas. All but a few dams in the water development aspect of the project washed out, roads deteriorated without maintenance, and the professional staff and equipment were gradually dispersed.

1. After the Masai Project began, Maasai became the preferred spelling for the people of Masailand because it better reflects their native language. The name of their territory maintains its historical spelling.

The Future of the Peasant World

In spite of the difficulties in planned cultural change, the life of peasant villagers, who make up the majority of the world's inhabitants, is changing. For village life in Asia, Hayami and Kikuchi (1981) report that the previous decreasing economic benefit to peasant farming, which resulted when population growth outstripped the ability of peasants to produce, is being counteracted by the introduction of irrigation systems, modern varieties of increased-yield food plants, and fertilizer technology. Where the application of new farming technologies is successful, the income differentials in rural populations are being reversed. In the view of Hayami and Kikuchi, the critical problem in peasant village development is achieving peasant labor productivity sufficient to counteract the strong population pressure on limited land resources. They believe this can be achieved by efforts to control growth, cultivate new land, and develop nonfarm jobs.

Critchfield (1981) has found that several important changes are occurring in peasant villages throughout the world. He believes that "contraception and scientific farming are producing, at last, a change in the general human condition" (p. 320), and sees four changes in all the villages he has studied. First, contraception is now a fact of life in village culture, and "in places as scattered as China, India's Kerala and Karnataka states, Sri Lanka, and Java and Bali in Indonesia, annual population growth rates have plummeted from 2½—3 percent in the early Sixties to 1—1½ percent now—mostly in the five years 1975 to 1980. Elsewhere, though less spectacularly, fertility [the number of children born per woman] has been declining for the first time in the modern era" (p. 322). Second, high-yield, fertilizer-intensive, fast-maturing crops are spreading quickly into the world's villages along with year-round irrigation and multiple cropping. Third, the rural exodus to the cities is being replaced by a return of peasant workers to villages as they become able to feed them. Finally, the underdeveloped countries are becoming increasingly competitive in the world marketplace. Critchfield reports:

During the 1970s more than one hundred and thirty developing countries joined in a new international network linking thirteen agricultural research centers, eight of them set up since 1971. They now pool knowledge and genetic material on all kinds of crops—wheat, maize, rice, sorghum, millet, cassava, potatoes, groundnuts, vegetables, legumes, tubers, and others. New findings are exchanged on livestock breeding, plant and animal diseases and farming systems. This new global scientific network cuts across all political boundaries and ideologies; scientists and trainees come from China, Russia, the United States, India, Pakistan, Cuba, Vietnam, Turkey, African and European countries, every nationality you can name. China's increasingly active role since the late 1970's, and its contributions of samples of basic genetic diversity developed only in China, now allows completion at last of the world's major plant germ-plasm collections. (p. 325)

From changes of these kinds, we may well expect major adjustments in the political and economic role of the currently underdeveloped countries in the next two decades as they move into the status of developed nations.

Population Control in Developing Nations

Since hunger in underdeveloped countries is basically a matter of too little growth in productivity compared with rates of population growth, control of the population growth rate has been one of the major concerns of many of these countries. Government-funded family planning clinics, legalized abortion, and public education programs about birth control are common means of fostering smaller family size. In some developing countries such as the People's Republic of China and Singapore, even stronger measures have been adopted.

Nearly one fourth of the human population, over one billion people, live in the People's Republic of China, and over half of those people are under 33 years of age (Tien, 1983). Both the absolute size of the Chinese population and the large percentage of the population that represents people of reproductive age make population control a major concern in China. A high fertility rate might well overcome China's ability to feed its population in the future, much less achieve the status of a developed nation. For these reasons, the Chinese government has taken more extreme measures than have many developing countries, and these measures appear to have been quite successful at reducing the fertility rate. One means of lowering the fertility rate is to delay the average age of marriage. The current legal age for marriage is 20 for women and 22 for men. However, the main efforts to reduce fertility involve direct intervention in family planning. As Article 53 of the revised 1978 constitution of China states, "The state advocates and encourages birth planning." Using newspapers, radio, and television, the government actively publicizes and encourages the goal of limiting births to one child per family. Bonuses, larger pensions, free health care for the child, priority in housing, and the promise of education and employment priorities for the child are all used as inducements for voluntary commitment to having only one child. County birth planning offices supply contraceptives and subsidize local health centers for IUD insertions, sterilizations, and abortions.

Peer pressure also is used to achieve the goal of one child per family in China. At the local level, the government has organized a system of fertility committees throughout the country. These committees meet with individuals and create social pressure for conformity to government goals in family planning. Families are encouraged in community meetings to publicly commit themselves to having only one child, although—in deference to the strong value that Chinese peasants still place on sons—a second child is considered acceptable if the first is a daughter. The weight of public opinion is brought to bear on individuals who refuse to support the national goal of reduced population growth. A liberal policy on abortion and social pressure to terminate pregnancies after the second birth have reduced China's total fertility rate to only 2.1 children per family, a rate about half of what it was in 1970 and equivalent to that of developed countries.

Singapore, where 2.6 million people occupy a mere 200 square miles, is one of the three most densely populated countries of the world. The government provides free family planning services, including abortion and sterilization. Government policy is to encourage small families. Women receive maternity leave only for their first two children. The medical fees for the delivery of babies are greater for each successive child. Income tax exemptions apply only to the first two children. Subsidized housing is denied to large families. In 1983 the government began offering a cash payment equal to the average yearly income of a family in Singapore to any woman who was sterilized after her second child.

In developed countries where the costs of population growth have not been felt so strongly, it is difficult for many people to accept the degree to which the governments of China and Singapore are intervening in the reproductive lives of their citizens. These measures are more readily comprehended in light of the terrible costs that high fertility rates have had in slowing the process of economic development in much of the world. Remaining underdeveloped takes its toll, not only as an absence of the material luxuries associated with industrialization, but also as hunger and high mortality rates. Life expectancy at birth in the undeveloped countries is now 58 years, compared with 72 years in developed nations. In light of the advantages of successful development, similar governmental measures to control fertility rates may become common in other parts of the developing world.

SUMMARY

Industrialization has dramatically altered life in many nations, though some peoples continue to subsist by ancient foraging methods or simple hand cultivation. The indigenous cultures are becoming more and more scarce, either through adaptations to the dominant cultures that surround them or through forced takeovers of their ancestral lands and outright murder of the people. In more powerful cultures, industrialization has brought profound economic changes, population growth, concentration of population around cities, and both positive and negative effects on the quality of life. The majority of the world's people are affected by these trends but still live as peasants practicing small-scale food production for their own needs. Change in these peasant cultures comes slowly, but some are now cooperating to enhance their position in the world economy.

KEY TERMS AND CONCEPTS

indigenous people 302
acculturation 302
ethnocide 302
reservations 302
genocide 304
industrialization 304
developed country 305
underdeveloped country 305
developing country 305
peasants 307
feudal peasants 308
colonial peasants 309
pastoral and ranching areas 310

irrigated farmlands 310
large-farm (estate) areas 310
marginal and hill farming lands 311
intensive peasant smallholdings 311
frontier areas 311
labor reserve (remittance economy) areas 311
tenant or refugee farms 313
peri-urban squatter settlements 314
image of limited good 314
culture of poverty 314
applied anthropology 315
range management 316

ANNOTATED READINGS

Bernard, H. R., & Pelto, P. J. (Eds.). (1972). *Technology and social change.* New York: Macmillan. An important collection of case studies of the effects of the introduction of Western technology on a variety of cultures.

Bodley, J. H. (1975). *Victims of progress.* Menlo Park, CA: Cummings. A discussion of the destructive effects of contact with industrialized societies on traditional societies.

Geertz, C. (1963). *Agricultural involution: The processes of ecological change in Indo-nesia.* Berkeley, CA: University of California Press. An already classic study of cultural change and the interactions of technology and the agricultural habitat.

Goode, W. J. (1963). *World revolution and family patterns.* New York: Free Press. An examination of the influence of industrialization on the family.

Wolf, E. R. (1966). *Peasants.* Englewood Cliffs, NJ: Prentice Hall. A short but important introduction to the nature of peasant society.

*T*raditionally, anthropologists have taken as their objects of study the cultures of the world's small-scale, technologically simple societies. Few have attempted to analyze the cultures of large-scale societies such as America.[1] By and large, anthropologists have tended to give priority to the study of simple societies because they represented a rapidly disappearing source of information about the human condition. Sociologists have studied social patterns in industrialized societies, but their interests generally have not centered on cultural questions, and far too little empirical fieldwork exists on American lifeways to develop an adequate model of American culture as a whole. Yet, if anthropology has any relevance to students for whom the introductory-level course will be their main exposure to the field, it lies in making their own cultural environment more meaningful. This chapter focuses on those aspects of American culture that seem most appropriate to the theme of this text and to the interests of university students, anthropology majors and nonmajors alike.

14

Contemporary American Culture

AMERICAN SOCIAL ORGANIZATION
The Economic Base
Social Class
Women's Status in the United States
American Politics
Power Relations

Family

THE LIFE CYCLE IN AMERICA
Pregnancy and Childbirth
Infancy and Childhood
Adolescence and Courtship
Marriage

Illness
Old Age and Death

AMERICAN IDEOLOGY
Religion in America
American Drives and Values
The Changing Context of American Values and Drives

The Mets. The Jets. Pizza. Pepsi. Tacos. Sushi. Chop Suey. LaToya. Pavarotti. Springsteen. How would you identify a typical North American culture if you were an anthropologist studying it? Or would it depend on where you first set your sights? Los Angeles. New Orleans. Baltimore. Minneapolis. Has the great melting pot of American society grown too complicated to be defined? Or is that diversity still its strength and its hope?

FIGURE 14.1 *American Culture*

Because of its diversity, a truly American culture is difficult to define. Apple pie and ice cream. Hot dogs and ball games. For every stereotype, one can think of aspects of American culture that defy it.

1. For convenience, *America* will be used in this chapter to refer to the United States only, rather than to all the countries of North, Central, and South America.

321

AMERICAN SOCIAL ORGANIZATION

American society is composed of over 246 million people who live in cities of up to several million. Such a large population can only be sustained with a rather complex social organization that has many highly specialized statuses, social classes, and a hierarchy of political and economic power. We will examine the social organization of American society by considering the basic economic differences in U.S. statuses, the role of race and gender in the United States, and the American political organization and family structure.

The Economic Base

The American people are supported by an industrialized technology based primarily on fossil fuel burning and water-powered generators. About 46 percent of the population make up the employed civilian labor force of over 120 million. Another 19 million are government workers. The American economy is productive enough that only about 30 percent of the labor force is involved in the production of goods, while the rest are service providers. Food is produced for the entire society by less than 3 percent of the labor force, a decline from 38 percent in 1900. America's high productivity has led to a relatively low demand for labor throughout most of its history. As a result of high productivity, the United States rarely has had an unemployment rate less than about 6 percent of the labor force except in time of war, and the unemployment rate often has risen well above 10 percent.

Social Class

Ideologically, Americans have not traditionally viewed their society as one made up of separate classes. Yet, as in other industrialized societies, the people of America do not all have equal access to the goods or services produced by its labor force. For instance in 1983, 5 percent of the United States population received 15.8 percent of the total income before taxes. American society, in other words, is socially stratified into classes (see Table 14.1). The American class system is somewhat ill-defined, in that the American ideology itself has traditionally denied its very existence as a formal structure. Polls have

TABLE 14.1 *Distribution of Wealth in the United States*

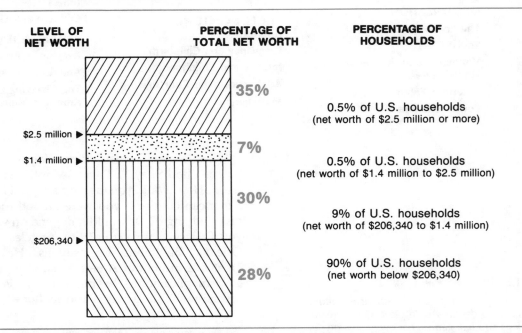

Note. From *Concentration of Wealth in the U.S.: Trends in the Distribution of Wealth Among American Families*, July, 1986, Washington, D.C.: Joint Economic Committee, Congress of the United States.

FIGURE 14.2   *American Class System*

Americans are quick to deny that their democracy supports a class system, but ethnographic studies indicate that economically and socially such a system does exist.

indicated that some 80 percent of Americans claim membership in the middle class. Interestingly, this figure includes both some persons who by technical standards would be considered members of the lower class and others who are technically of upper-class background. The failure of Americans to formally recognize that there are classes within their social system has been made easier by a traditionally high level of mobility within the American class system.

An important measure of one's position within the American class system is one's occupation. The American economy is based primarily on market exchange. Rather than producing goods for direct exchange, most Americans are employed by someone else. In return, they are compensated with an income that they then exchange for the services and goods that they require. The size of their personal income depends largely, though not entirely, on the prestige ranking of their income-producing status (see Table 14.2).

The least prestigious and least well paid of the economic statuses are unskilled laborers. They usually are paid by the hour or by the quantity of goods that their work produces. Unskilled laborers often are hired for part-time or seasonal work such as food baggers at supermarkets, bus persons at restaurants, and farm laborers. Many of these jobs are held by young people who are not yet economically self-sufficient, by a disproportionate percentage of ethnic minorities, and by migrant workers who travel from state to state for seasonal farm work.

Pink collar jobs are occupations traditionally held by women: waitress, sales clerk, secretary, telephone operator, and public school teacher (see Table 14.3). There is some variation in the prestige and incomes associated with these jobs, but in the main they fall

TABLE 14.2   *Occupations Ranked by Prestige in the United States*

Occupation	Score	Occupation	Score
Dentist	88.5	Stenographer	46.4
Mayor	84.2	Building superintendent	43.6
Electrical engineer	83.1	Automobile mechanic	41.2
Chemist	82.8	Dressmaker	39.6
Registered nurse	79.0	Librarian	39.5
Banker	77.1	Baker	39.1
Psychologist	73.7	Sales clerk	36.8
Army captain	60.6	Hairdresser	35.1
Insurance agent	58.1	Telephone operator	32.7
Child-care worker	56.0	Waiter/Waitress	31.8
High school teacher	55.1	Bus driver	28.8
Social worker	54.9	Miner	28.1
Plumber	54.6	Cashier	27.8
Secretary	53.0	Farm laborer	27.4
Firefighter	50.3		

Note. From "Sex and Consensus in Occupational Prestige Ratings" by B. Powell and J. A. Jacobs, 1983, *Sociology and Social Research, 67*(4), p. 400. Copyright 1983. Adapted by permission.

below average in both measures. This category of low-level human service and information processing jobs has been the fastest growing of the occupational categories since about 1950. Since World War II, tens of millions of jobs were opened up in this category. Since they were low-paid new jobs, rather than ones previously held by men, they were readily obtained by women without their being seen as competing with men for jobs (Harris, 1981).

Blue collar workers are manual laborers other than farm workers. Although they command little prestige, some of these statuses have access to above-average incomes due to the economic importance of the commodities and services that they control. Examples of

TABLE 14.3   *Representation of Women in Occupations, 1985*

All occupations	44.1%[a]
Managerial/professional	42.7%
Executive, administrative, managerial	35.6%
Teachers, college and university	35.2%
Teachers, except college and university	73.0%
Professional workers	49.1%
Technical/Sales/Administrative support	64.7%
Sales workers, retail and personal service	68.5%
Administrative support, including clerical	80.2%
Information clerks	90.1%
Service workers	60.6%
Personal service	80.9%
Protective service	13.2%
Crossing guards	73.3%
Precision production, craft, repair	8.4%
Operators, fabricators, laborers	25.4%
Farming, forestry, fishing	15.9

Note. From *Professional Women and Minorities: A Manpower Data Resource Service* (Table 4-7, pp. 75–80) by B. M. Vetter and E. L. Babco, 1986, Washington, DC: Commission on Professionals in Science and Technology. Copyright 1986. Adapted by permission.

Note. [a]Figures show the percentage of female workers in these occupations.

TABLE 14.4   *U.S. Occupations Held Predominantly by One Sex, 1985*

Occupation	Number	Percent Held by Men
Nine Jobs Where Men Are Scarce:		
Prekindergarten and kindergarten teacher	329,000	1.2
Dental hygienist	56,000	1.5
Secretary	4,059,000	1.6
Receptionist	679,000	2.4
Licensed practical nurse	402,000	3.1
Child-care worker	738,000	3.9
Welfare service aides	82,000	7.4
Textile sewing machine operators	760,000	9.8
Librarian	201,000	13.0
Six Jobs Where Women Are Scarce:		
Automobile mechanic	906,000	99.3
Surveyor and mapping scientist	22,000	98.7
Truck driver, heavy	1,838,000	97.9
Aerospace engineer	95,000	95.3
Police and detective	652,000	89.9
College and university teacher	643,000	64.8

Note. From *Professional Women and Minorities: A Manpower Data Resource Service*, by B. M. Vetter and E. L. Babco, 1986, Washington, DC: Commission on Professionals in Science and Technology.

blue collar workers are garbage collectors, dockhands, factory workers, taxicab and bus drivers, janitors, and supervisors of manual laborers.

White collar occupations are clerical workers, sales workers, technical workers, managers, and administrators. Their work is primarily the providing of services. Although many of these occupations are fairly prestigious and relatively well paid, over the years many white collar offices have become more and more like factories in the repetitive nature of the routine work.

Professionals are typically self-employed providers of services whose work generally requires a graduate-level university degree. Included in this category are the most prestigious nongovernmental occupations such as medical doctors, lawyers, scientists, and university faculty. These highly ranked positions, as well as highly ranked governmental positions, generally have been dominated by men (see Table 14.4).

Historically, the simplest means to climb to a higher position within the class system than one's parents had occupied was through the educational system, since higher-ranked occupations generally have required a higher level of education than have lower-ranked ones. Indeed, it is common for many employers in the United States to require an educational background in prospective employees that goes far beyond what is actually needed for the work itself. This system, in which education is strongly rewarded as a means to raising one's rank within the class system, keeps potential workers in school for a longer period of time before they begin full-time work than might otherwise be the case. This has been one means by which the number of people in the labor pool, and therefore the unemployment rate, has been kept lower in the United States than it otherwise would have been.

Although opportunities for upward social mobility have been high in America, so have the chances of moving down in the occupational ranks. For instance, a decline in the demand for a product or service can make it impossible for a person who is qualified for a high-ranked occupation to obtain employment, and persons already employed may lose their positions. Thus, engineers who are educationally too specialized in their skills to move readily from one high-ranked position to another may find themselves bagging groceries, and recent university graduates may be forced to accept employment driving cabs. A great deal of personal anguish may accompany such downward shifts in social rank.

AMERICAN FACTORIES IN MEXICO

Today the international economy of all nations is affected by the economic life of all others. This interdependence of national economies is well illustrated by the role of U.S. corporations in Mexico.

In 1964 the U.S. Congress drastically curtailed the movement of migrant labor from Mexico into the United States. This resulted in an unemployment crisis in Mexico. In response to this problem, the Mexican Border Industrialization Program was established a year later. It encouraged foreign corporations to open assembly plants in Mexico to help alleviate the unemployment crisis. Today in Mexico there are over 1,600 U.S. and Canadian companies, including American Hospital Supply, Chrysler, Coleman Products, Fischer-Price, Foster Grant Corp., General Electric, ITT, Levi-Strauss, Mattel, National Semiconductor, Samsonite Corporation, Sears, Union Carbide, Velcro USA Inc., and Xerox, in a 1,950-mile-long (3,218 kilometers) free trade zone along the Mexican-U.S. border.

Multinational companies now employ over 426,000 Mexican workers in assembly plants called *maquiladoras*. Unassembled parts are stored by American companies in warehouses on the U.S. side of the border and shipped daily into nearby Mexican towns for assembly. For instance, in El Paso, Texas, over 700 trucks ferry parts across the border each day to *maquiladoras* where they are processed by Mexican *maquiladora* workers, who are paid wages that typically range from $3.85 to $5.00 per day.

U.S. multinational companies save thousands of salary dollars for each worker they employ in a foreign assembly plant, but the savings do not end there. The Mexican Free Trade Zone was established with the understanding that corporations that moved there would not be taxed by the Mexican government, and when the assembled goods are returned to the U.S., the value-added tax that is paid to the U.S. government is based only on the low cost of the Mexican labor that went into their manufacture. Since the goods are then sold at U.S. retail market prices, determined as if they had been manufactured in the United States, the *maquiladora* system results in tremendous profits for corporations that participate.

In addition to tax benefits, corporations also save in health and safety expenses. Mexican workers can be employed in conditions that would violate U.S. health and safety regulations. For instance, *maquiladora* electronics employees work with toluene, PCBs, and solvents that can cause chloracne, skin cancer, and leukemia. Company doctors routinely dismiss such problems as unrelated to working conditions. Although Mexican law requires companies to grant female employees liberal childbirth leave benefits, companies routinely require women job applicants to submit to pregnancy tests before they are hired. There is a very high turnover rate among employees—women typically work only about seven months for a given company. Thus in practice, companies rarely have to grant the maternity leave that is guaranteed by law.

Nogales, Mexico, is an interesting example of a border town that has been greatly influenced by the *maquiladora* system. In 1975 there were 50,000 inhabitants there. In 1989 the population had swelled to 150,000 by jobless people who had migrated from other parts of Mexico to find work either in *maquiladoras* or as day-laborers in American Nogales, just across the border. Many of the immigrants live in squatter settlements in crude, self-built shacks. Technically illegal, these settlements have no electricity, sewage facilities, or permanent water supplies. The 65 *maquiladoras* employ 20,000 of Nogales' new residents for about $3.74 a day. Although this might be a good wage in much of Mexico, prices in border towns such as Nogales approximate those of neighboring U.S. towns. Thus, *maquiladora* workers must pay $2.61 for a gallon of milk. Ground beef costs $1.42 a pound, and cheese costs $2.47 a pound.

Many of the *maquiladora* workers in Nogales are single parents, but there are only two day-care centers, each with a capacity of about 45 children, for factory workers' children. So tremendous problems exist related to the large number of "latch-key" children, many of whom have no alternative but to remain at home in the squatter settlements during the day. Since wages are so low in the assembly plants, and since a woman may have to spend more than half her income to pay someone to watch her children, many children 14 years of age and older go to work in the plants.

Hours in the plants are long. Employees work eight-hour shifts broken by two fifteen-minute breaks and a half-hour lunch period. Since the work-week is six days long, many employees work nearly ten hours each day to have Saturday off. Sexual harassment is said to be rampant in *maquiladoras*, and job insecurity creates tremendous pressure for women employees to simply accept it.

The Mexican government has had little effect in trying to improve working conditions in the *maquiladoras*. Typically the assembly plants are nothing more than cinder block buildings that can literally be vacated by the company overnight. Companies have little invested in the properties themselves and can easily move their operations to other Third World countries if the profitability of their Mexican plants declines. Thus the Mexican government hesitates to press too strongly for higher salaries or for better health and safety.

In addition, the U.S. dollars that enter the Mexican economy have become increasingly important to Mexico, especially since the devaluation of the peso in 1976 cut workers' real wages by 50 percent. So the government has had to make some concessions to keep foreign industries that threatened to leave. *Maquiladoras* were exempted from various worker-protection requirements, given the right to dismiss workers without severance pay, and allowed to keep workers on "temporary" status for as much as three months. In the attempt to further attract American companies, Mexican Nogales passed local laws that forbade the formation of unions and made it illegal for foreign companies to pay their workers more than the legal minimum wage. The North American Congress on Latin America (1979) estimated that Motorola was able to save four million dollars a year by moving from Phoenix to Nogales and that General Electric saved between $10,000 and $12,000 per worker by operating its assembly plant in Juarez instead of in the United States. Under these circumstances, it seems unlikely that the lot of *maquiladora* workers is likely to change in the near future.

The day when "Made in America"

meant that a product was manufactured in the United States is gone. Few Americans probably realize that the elevators they ride when going to work, the luggage they carry on trips, or the sterile medical packs that are used in their hospital emergency rooms may have been assembled in plants in Mexico or in similar facilities in other Third World countries.

Economic differences by race. Historically, racial statuses have had an important influence on social relations in the United States. For instance, at one time over three quarters of the states in the United States eventually passed laws prohibiting interracial marriages. That is, those of nonwhite racial statuses were forbidden to marry whites, although nonwhite races were not consistently forbidden to intermarry with one another. Nineteen states still had such laws in 1968, when they were struck down by the Supreme Court of the United States as unconstitutional. Despite legislation that has attempted to eliminate racial discrimination, the class system in the United States continues to reflect the historical discrimination against members of minorities. Holders of minority racial and ethnic statuses in the United States have had unequal opportunities to achieve highly valued social positions and high-income occupations. As a result, races and ethnic groups are socially and economically stratified in the United States. According to the United States Bureau of the Census, whites possess a disproportionate share of the higher socioeconomic statuses and nonwhites are disproportionately relegated to low socioeconomic positions (see Fig. 14.3).

Economic and health costs of racism. Maintenance of different ways of treating socially designated races is not without its cost. Consider this example based on information from the *Statistical Abstract of the United States 1969* and on the *Statistical Abstract of the United States 1989* (U.S. Department of Commerce, 1969 and 1989): In 1900 the life expectancy of males classified as white in the United States was 150 percent that of males classified as black! The difference can be attributed to a

FIGURE 14.3 *U.S. Median Family Income by Race in Constant (1987) Dollars*

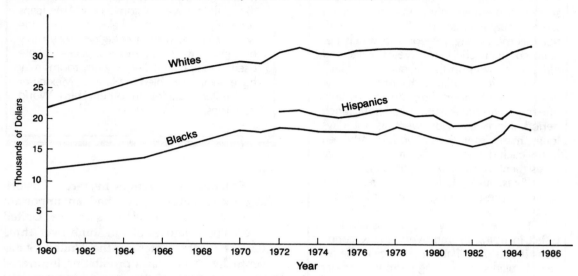

Note. From *Statistical Abstract of the United States: 1989* (109th ed.), p. 495, by U.S. Bureau of the Census.

higher infant mortality rate among blacks, a differential access to adequate medical treatment and hospital facilities, and the debilitating effects of the lower-class jobs available to black men. By 1940, the gap had closed somewhat with a general rise in the standard of living, but the white male population could still look forward to an average of 10 more years of life than was available to the black male population. By 1987, the white male life expectancy reached 72.1 years, 6.7 years more than that of black males. Thus, in effect, in every generation of 72.1 years, 6.7 years of life were denied to the 26.8 million United States males classified as black, an equivalent of 179,761,000 years of human life wasted needlessly. If the method of racial discrimination were death by execution rather than barriers to health and wealth, approximately 46,088 18-year-old black men would have to be executed each year to depress the overall life expectancy of the black male population of the United States as much as actual discriminatory conditions of life seem to have been doing as of 1987.

Effects such as these take their toll on other groups as well. For instance, Native Americans today are so culturally disenfranchised in the United States that three quarters of this group have incomes below the officially designated poverty level. The Native American unemployment rate is about 50 per-

cent on the average. Native American life expectancy is only about 63 years.

It is in effects such as the lowered life expectancies and living standards among those who hold minority racial statuses that racism makes itself felt in its most harmful way. To those who feel its effects, even more abhorrent than ethnocentrism or racial prejudice is the fact that these attitudes may become the basis of social policies, supported by the weight of law or custom, that perpetuate arbitrary and harmful inequalities between peoples. Great harm may be done even without any outward show of prejudice or violence.

Minority statuses in the United States. Minority statuses in the United States include many groups besides those defined by race. Ethnic group identity is based on shared customs, such as those of immigrants from various European countries, especially of southern and eastern Europe. Religious minorities as well, such as Moslems, Buddhists, Rajneesh, Amish, Hutterites, and Mormons exemplify groups that have not received total acceptance as members of the American mainstream. Sexuality and gender are also important in American culture as determinants of minority status. Thus, nonheterosexual Americans continue to experience social, economic, and even legal discrimination as minorities, and many aspects of women's roles in America are most fruitfully understood in the context of women's minority status—an issue that will be addressed in more detail in the following section of this chapter.

One of the most distinctive illustrations of the minority status in American society is the example of Native Americans. According to the 1980 census, there are about one and a half million persons in the United States legally defined as Native Americans. Today, the figure probably exceeds two million. The impact of minority status on the indigenous Americans is clear: Indians have the lowest life expectancy and the highest unemployment rates of any group in the United States. They also fall below the nation as a whole in average income, housing, and education.

Originally, Native Americans were the only inhabitants of the lands now under control of the United States government. Now, they find themselves in the unusual position of being both citizens of the United States and of tribal groups that the Supreme Court has called "domestic dependent nations" of the United States (Cherokee Nation v. Georgia 5 Pet. 10 [1831]). This ambiguous legal state of affairs stems from the political history of relations between the U.S. government and the original Native American societies that it conquered as it expanded its borders.

From the viewpoint of Native Americans, the founders of what was to become the United States entered North America as immigrants. Although the incoming population was originally small, its numbers grew rapidly from continued immigration, and its economic and political power was great due to the industrializing technological base from which it grew. Initially, the U.S. government formally recognized the sovereignty of Indian tribes. The northwest Ordinance of 1787, ratified by the First Congress in 1789, declared "The utmost good faith shall always be observed towards Indians; their lands and property shall never be taken from them without their consent."

Nevertheless, as the immigrant population expanded across much of the North American continent, its citizens entered lands occupied by Native Americans, who found themselves overwhelmed by U.S. military power. When Native American societies did attempt to regulate their relations with the U.S. government and minimize the loss of their own lands and cultural identities by the negotiation of treaties, they were at first treated as foreign nations. Thus, in these treaties, Indian tribes typically ceded some of their lands to the United States while reserving other lands to themselves, and the United States, as a party to these treaties, acknowledged Indian sovereignty over their own lands while sometimes promising economic aid and educational rights to the tribal groups in return for the ceded lands.

Indian-U.S. relations never remained as clear-cut as the contents of these treaties suggest. The expansion of the U.S. domain eventually engulfed the various Indian territories, and left Native American societies in a more powerless position than that of other peoples who had entered treaties with the United States. In 1823, the Supreme Court declared that the U.S. government had the right to govern Indians saying that "The discovery and conquest gives the conquerors sovereignty over and ownership of the lands obtained" (Johnson v. McIntosh, 21 U.S. 542). Thus, lands Indian peoples thought they had reserved to themselves through treaties became officially administered as parts of the United States itself. Indian tribes were no longer to be treated as sovereign nations within their own territories, but as dependent peoples within the United States. This process of reducing the status of Native American peoples from that of independent and equal signatories of treaties with the U.S. government to "wards" of the government was formalized when the U.S. Congress unilaterally passed legislation that declared all Indians born within the territorial limits of the United States to be U.S. citizens.

Following the extension of U.S. citizenship to Native Americans, it was easy to forget that "reservations" were U.S. lands that had been held in trust for Indians who had not yet adjusted to mainstream American life. U.S. treaty obligations to residents of Indian lands came to be seen by many non-Indians as "special treatment" by the federal government. There followed a period during which tribes were encouraged to disencorporate as tribal entities in return for settlement of claims which they had unsuccessfully pursued for lands they had lost to states and to the federal government. Some tribes ceased to exist under this policy. Others remained. Today, there are still 287 Indian reservations in the United States, governed in part by the tribes, in part by federal bureaus, and in part by the states in or next to which they are located.

The uneasy mix of governing powers that control the destinies of reservation residents is a continuing source of conflict both among Native Americans and between reservation governments and non-Indian political bodies. For instance, Cree Indians and other tribes whose traditional lands straddled the U.S.-Canadian border were guaranteed the right to pass unimpeded from one country to the other by an early treaty between the U.S. and Canada. This right is still in force, although U.S. border officials occasionally express annoyance at its use by Indians whose vehicles are immune to the searches they may legally make of other vehicles that cross the border.

Many times the legal conflicts over Indian rights become major court cases because of the economic interests that are at stake. For instance, treaties with Lumhi Indians and several other tribes in the state of Washington have guaranteed them free and unregulated fishing rights. These rights have been challenged by representatives of the commercial fishing industry and by government agencies concerned with recreational fishing, both of which have economic interests in the maintenance of fishing quotas that those treaties prevent them from imposing on members of the tribes. In Utah, important legal cases have been fought in the 1980s over whether the state government has the right to tax oil companies for oil produced by wells on the Ute Indian reservation and over the right of the tribe to exercise police authority over predominantly non-Indian towns that exist within the Ute reservation. In 1989, the Ute government declared that the federal government and the state of Utah had abrogated their contractual obligation to build irrigation projects on the reservation in return for rights to irrigated water that flows from the reservation—opening the way for the tribe to withhold that water in the future. In Idaho, a conflict continues that threatens a major source of revenue for the Shoshoni and Bannocks Indians of the Fort Hall Reservation. For years, sales of goods such as cigarettes at untaxed prices have been

an important attraction for tourist dollars on the reservation. The Idaho state government is now asserting that this practice is illegal, and that the tribe must collect state taxes on all such sales. The tribal government, on the other hand, asserts that the state of Idaho has no authority over tribal business practices, since reservation lands are not legally part of the state.

Sometimes the conflicting views of Indian authority to govern their own lands have reached the point of forceful and even violent confrontations. For instance, in 1986 when the city of Scottsdale, Arizona, refused to renegotiate the rights for non-Indian use of Pima highway, an important commuter road on reservation land, the tribe finally closed the highway to further use by non-Indians. Bonfires and barricades stopped the flow of traffic until the city government capitulated. Most recently, in July of 1989, the New York state police sealed off the St. Regis Indian Reservation because Mohawk Indians had continued to open gambling casinos to tourists from New York, a state that does not allow gambling. After several raids of the reservation casinos by state police, a Mohawk group called the Sovereignty Security Force, blocked the main highway in protest against state and federal agencies that they believed were intervening illegitimately in the internal affairs of the tribe by attempting to prohibit gambling, a source of millions of dollars of revenue that the tribal government had authorized. New York state troopers responded with checkpoints of their own on roads into the reservation, as of September 1989, that conflict was still continuing.

The unusual legal situation of America's indigenous peoples is a complicated tangle of conflicting views about who has sovereignty over reservation lands. Tribal, state, city, and federal governments are all involved. Sometimes the tribes themselves are factionalized over who best represents their interests, and within the federal government conflicts sometimes arise about which government body is responsible for determining policy towards reservations. For instance, usually the Bureau of Indian Affairs is the dominant federal party, but in some cases, policies that influence Indian lands adjacent to national forests or parks are set by the National Forest Service or National Park Service. Since vast sums of money are often at stake in these conflicts, they are likely to continue well into the next century.

Women's Status in the United States

With industrialization, the means of subsistence have shifted for most families increasingly toward sources of income other than food production. In many societies, including European countries during the rise of industrialization and, more recently, in other parts of the developing world, men were drawn more quickly into the industrialized sector of the economy than were women. This process increased the economic dependence of women on men in history, as witnessed in the industrialization in Europe, the Soviet Union, and the United States and is having a similar effect in many other industrializing nations today.

In the United States, women are holders of minority status, a low-ranked master status that tends to overshadow the other statuses they may hold. Like racism, this sexism creates inequalities of opportunity. Thus, women in the United States today make up three quarters of the poor.

Similarities between sexism and racism. Striking parallels may be found in the history of the treatment of women and blacks in the United States. Caroline Bird (1973), a contemporary feminist author, lists some of these parallels.

> To begin with, neither women nor blacks could hide the respective facts of sex or race. Generalizations about blacks and women as workers relegated both groups to inferior status on the job. Both groups were regarded as a labor reserve, denied equal hiring, training, pay, promotion, responsibility, and seniority at work. Neither group was supposed to boss white men, and both were limited to jobs white men didn't want to do.
>
> Blacks were supposed to be better able to stand uncomfortable physical labor; women, boring details. Both had emerged from a "previous condition of servitude" that had denied them the vote, schooling, jobs, apprenticeships, and equal access to unions, clubs, professional associations, professional schools, restaurants, and public places. Strikingly similar rationalizations and defense mechanisms accommodated both denials of

FIGURE 14.4   Women's Status

Since laws against discrimination have gone into effect, occupations formerly closed to women have become more and more available. Diane Sawyer, seen here with Charles Kuralt on a segment of the Sunday Morning television program, has assumed a prominent position in broadcast journalism.

> the central American ideal of equal opportunity. (p. 130)

Ashley Montagu (1974), one of anthropology's most outspoken critics of racism, has noted that:

> In connection with the modern form of race prejudice it is of interest to recall that almost every one of the arguments used by the racists to "prove" the inferiority of one or another so-called "race" was not so long ago used by the anti-feminists to "prove" the inferiority of the female as compared with the male. . . .
>
> In the nineteenth century it was fairly generally believed that women were inferior creatures. Was it not a fact that women had smaller brains than men? Was it not apparent to everyone that their intelligence was lower, that they were essentially creatures of emotion rather than of reason—volatile swooning

FIGURE 14.5   *Employment Rates of Women in the United States*

With the increase in contraception and the necessity to contribute economically to the family unit, over fifty percent of American women are employed outside the home.

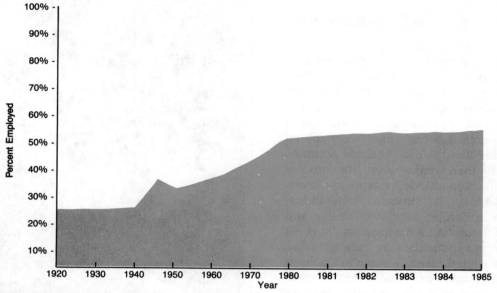

Note. From *Statistical Abstract of the United States: 1986* (106th ed.) [Table No. 674, p. 398] by U.S. Bureau of the Census, 1985, Washington, DC: U.S. Government Printing Office. Copyright 1985 by U.S. Bureau of the Census.

natures whose powers of concentration were severely limited and whose creative abilities were restricted almost entirely to knitting and childbirth? For hundreds of years women had played musical instruments and painted, but to how many great female musicians and painters could one point? Where were the great women poets and novelists? Women had practically no executive ability, were quite unable to manage the domestic finances, and, as for competing with men in the business or professional world, such an idea was utterly preposterous, for women were held to possess neither the necessary intelligence nor the equally unattainable stamina. Man's place was out in the world earning a living; woman's place was definitely in the home. (pp. 186–187)

That the roots of the women's movement for freedom from such sexist stereotyping and for abolition of slavery are intertwined is not surprising. A good example of the interrelatedness of the problems surrounding the unequal treatment of blacks and women is found in the history of Sara and Angelina Grimké, two early nineteenth-century militant American feminists and abolitionists. Because they spoke out strongly for women's rights

and for the rights of blacks to freedom from slavery, no less a figure than John Greenleaf Whittier urged them to stop their work for women's rights because it was undermining the antislavery campaign: "Why then, let me ask, is it for you to enter the lists as controversial writers in this question [of women's rights]? . . . Is it not forgetting the great and dreadful wrongs of the slave in a selfish crusade against some paltry grievances of your own?" (Barnes, 1934, pp. 223–224). To which Angelina, writing for herself and her sister, replied, "What then can woman do for the slave, when she herself is under the feet of man and shamed into silence?" (Barnes, 1984, p. 429).

Occupational discrimination. Several limitations have been formally placed on women in the United States on the basis of the idea that societal norms should reflect the biological differences of the two sexes. Among the strongest of these limitations has been the so-called "protective" legislation that was overtly designed to protect the female, thought of as the "weaker sex," from exploitation in the labor market. In many states, for instance, laws have forbidden employment of women in

TABLE 14.5   *Percentage of Men and Women Holding Political Positions in the United States, 1987*

	Men%	Women%
U.S. Population[a]	48.8	51.2
Office		
U.S. Senate[a]	98.0	2.0
U.S. House of Representatives[a]	94.6	5.4
U.S. Supreme Court	88.9	11.1
Governors[b]	92.0	8.0
State Legislators[a]	84.2	15.8
Statewide Elective Officers	84.2	15.8

Note. [a]From *Statistical Abstract of the United States: 1989* (109th ed.) [Table No. 423, p. 253; Table No. 431, p. 256] by U.S. Bureau of the Census, 1989, Washington, DC: U.S. Government Printing Office. Copyright 1989 by U.S. Bureau of the Census.

Note. [b]From *State Elective Officials & the Legislature: 1987–1988* (p. 1–153) by D. Gona (Ed.), Lexington, KY: The Council of State Governments. Copyright 1987 by The Council of State Governments.

positions that require them to lift more than a nominal amount of weight. On the basis of such laws, many individual women who were perfectly capable of meeting the demands of a particular job have been denied employment "for their own protection," not because of evidence that they lacked the necessary skills, but because they were female.

In the decades beginning with the 1960s, the status of women in the United States has improved as their percentage in the labor force has increased. Nevertheless, although traditionally male occupations are becoming increasingly available to women, the roles of women are still particularly limited in areas of social life such as politics in which social power is wielded (see Table 14.5).

American Politics

The American political system has been dominated historically by two major political parties, and one commonly hears political issues discussed as if Americans fall simply into one of two fundamentally contrasting camps, liberals and conservatives. However, the actual political makeup of Americans is more complex than this suggests. A *Times Mirror* (1987) survey of American political attitudes found that there were three important personal orientations and six values from which the major American voting blocks were really formed. The personal orientations included differences in (1) religious faith, (2) alienation, a sense of powerlessness and distrust of government, and (3) financial pressure. For instance, politically active Americans tended to be more religious than average, and both Democrats and

Republicans had important religious constituencies among their party members. The political value differences that divided groups of American voters were (1) the degree of their tolerance for people with different lifestyles and the expression of nonmainstream ideas, (2) the importance they placed on social justice for minorities and the needy, (3) the level of their anticommunism, (4) the stress they placed on faith in their country's ability to solve its problems, (5) their attitudes about the size and effectiveness of government, and (6) their feelings about the power and influence of business corporations.

The *Times Mirror* survey found that a full 11 percent of Americans were totally uninvolved in public affairs and politics. These people never voted. They tended to be young and poorly educated. Their greatest concerns were unemployment, poverty, and the threat of nuclear war.

The Republican party is most staunchly supported by two main groups: *enterprise Republicans*, and *moral Republicans*. Enterprise Republicans are affluent, educated, almost exclusively white Americans who are particularly probusiness and antigovernment in their values. Moral Republicans as a group are middle-aged Americans with middle incomes who hold strong and very conservative political views. They favor the death penalty and are strongly anticommunist, antiabortion and pro-school prayer. They favor social spending by government except when it is specifically targeted for minorities. Moral Republicans are regular churchgoers, and many are born-again Christians. Like enterprise Republicans, they are largely white.

The backbone of the Democratic party is a coalition of five different groups: *New Deal Democrats, Sixties Democrats,* the *partisan poor,* the *passive poor,* and *seculars.* New Deal Democrats are older Americans who have moderate incomes and little financial stress. Many are of blue-collar and union background. Almost a third of this group are Catholic. They favor restrictions on abortion and support school prayer and social spending except for minorities. The Sixties Democrats are a well-educated group that includes a large number of females and blacks. They favor government spending on social programs, including programs specifically for minorities, and they tend to be somewhat less anticommunist than other groups. The partisan poor is a very low income group that is strongly concerned with social justice issues. They favor social spending but oppose tax increases. They also favor the death penalty and school prayer, but are divided on the abortion issue. The passive poor feel less economic pressure than the partisan poor and are less critical of their society. They favor social spending, oppose cuts in defense spending, and are moderately antiabortion. The seculars are well-educated, mostly white, and generally middle-aged. They are the only nonreligious group in the political spectrum. They strongly support personal freedom, favor cuts in military spending, and oppose school prayer, antiabortion legislation, and increased aid to minorities.

There are three remaining voting groups. These are the *upbeats,* the *disaffecteds,* and the *followers.* Upbeats are young, optimistic persons who have great faith in their country. They too are largely white. Their main political concerns are the budget deficit and other economic issues, and they lean toward Republican candidates in their voting. Disaffecteds also lean toward the Republican party. They are alienated, pessimistic, and skeptical of both big business and big government, but they are promilitary, support capital punishment, and oppose gun control. Followers usually lean toward Democratic candidates but sometimes support Republicans. They have little faith in their society, but tend also to be uncritical of either government or business.

The political rhetoric of the two-party system emphasizes the differences between the ideologies of the parties, as if there were no middle ground. Yet the American electorate is

FIGURE 14.6 *American Politics*

The makeup of American political parties is more diverse than one is generally led to believe. The Democratic Party, for example, is actually a coalition of several different groups. In 1984, the Reverend Jesse Jackson, the first black to run for president, represented several minority groups that favored government spending on social programs.

extremely diverse, and both parties unite people with important value differences. The election of a candidate from either party requires the support of a coalition of these different groups, and the wooing of the upbeats, disaffecteds, and followers is particularly important to both parties. So it can be argued that the political rhetoric of liberal versus conservative is an oversimplification of a more complex state of affairs. The centrist tendencies of both political parties may be seen best in the actual day-to day practice of American legislative politicians after their election, when mutual respect, compromise, bipartisan cooperation, and diplomatic statesmanship are commonly emphasized.

Power Relations

Just as Americans tend to deny the existence of ranked classes within their social structure, they tend to see the power of their society as being the property of the democratic majority. Their value system favors grass-roots political power, and they have tra-

TABLE 14.6   *Rates per 100,000 People of Serious Crimes Reported to Police in the United States and Canada, 1985*

Crimes Reported to Police	United States[a]	Canada[b]
Murder	8.9	2.8
Forcible Rape*	34.0	10.3
Robbery	205.3	85.9
Aggravated Assault*	289.0	513.0
Burglary	1,266.7	1,408.7
Larceny/Theft	2,901.2	3,245.6
Motor Vehicle Theft	504.5	324.7

Note. *Based on data for 1982, the most recent date for which information is available under current Canadian law.

Note. [a]From "Crime in the United States, Annual" by U.S. Federal Bureau of Investigation, cited in *Statistical Abstract of the United States: 1989* (109th edition) (pp. 168, 169) by U.S. Bureau of the Census, 1989, Washington, DC: U.S. Government Printing Office. Copyright 1988 by U.S. Bureau of the Census.

Note. [b]From *Canada Yearbook 1988* (Tables 20.1, 20.3) Ottawa: The Minister of Supply and Services, Canada. Copyright 1988.

ditionally viewed the federal government in negative terms. Politicians in general have been held in disdain as seekers after power; the expression "Politicians are all crooked" typifies this view. Political power is considered a necessary evil, and some political analysts claim that American voters most often cast their vote based on which candidate they oppose rather than on which they favor.

Americans view themselves as a peace-loving people who fight only when forced to. Nevertheless, the actual level of violence within the society is quite high. For instance, the homicide rate in the United States is among the highest in the world's industrialized nations. According to the annual *Uniform Crime Reports* of the FBI, the rate of murder and negligent homicide in the United States for 1987 was 83 per million people. This is about three times the rate among their culturally related Canadian neighbors to the north. In 1987, there were 20,100 murders in the United States. Other violent crimes also are frequent. For instance, there were 30,900 identified suicides in 1986, and it is estimated that there were 91,100 forcible rapes in the United States in 1987. Although Americans frequently complain that their judicial system is overly lenient with criminals, American courts convict a higher percentage of accused persons than do the courts of most other industrialized nations. Once convicted, American criminals are given and actually serve longer sentences than do their European counterparts. In 1987, there were 557,256 persons in American prisons.

Family

Americans often refer to the family as the basis of their society. In a society in which individuals must compete with one another for success, the family is one of the few relatively safe havens of close emotional ties and cooperation. However, the actual role of family in American society is minimal in contrast to the role of family in most other societies, and broken families are very common.

The limited role of the family.   The American family has lost most social functions beyond the basic socialization of children and the consumption of goods. Unlike families in peasant cultures, American families typically are not production units. With industrialization, home production declined, and the basic income of most Americans shifted to the non-domestic sphere.

The only economic function that most American families fulfill is that of consumption. In a sense, the American family could be defined as the group that eats together, but, since the rise of television, even this definition of the family might be invalid.

Even with industrialization, earlier American families often were held together by the presence of a mother whose work was home-centered. Before the development of effective contraceptive techniques, it was simply easier for the husband to seek employment outside the home than it was for the wife. Wives were likely to continue to bear children until about the age of 40, and most stayed home during their childbearing years. As the economic importance of domestic production declined, the American housewife was left in a dependent economic role. With increasingly effective birth control technology, the period of childbearing has declined from about 18 years in 1900 to about 6 years in 1980, and the average number of children born to a couple is now less than 2. Today, due to economic necessity, over half of American women are employed outside the home.

Since labor in America is extremely specialized, children are likely to enter occupations different from those of their parents. The family therefore has ceased to play any important educational role beyond the early socialization of children. After they learn the basic skills of language and acquire their society's basic values, ideas, and customs from their family, children receive most of their formal education in adult life skills through state and private educational organizations. However, although children often enter occupations requiring different skills from those of their parents, their occupations are not likely to differ greatly in rank. The occupational choices of children, therefore, are influenced by their parents' occupations, income, and social status as mediated by such other factors as their place of residence and the quality of the schools available.

The American family is not an autonomous spiritual center for its members; religious ritualism within the family, where it occurs, is practiced as an extension of the rituals of a larger religious body that unites members of many family groups on the basis of a common religious ideology. It is not a center of authority, either. A complex state-level government monopolizes the right to exercise all legal force, so the American family is lacking in all governmental authority outside the governing of the family itself.

Fragmentation of families.   Historically, the American family has been built around a norm of monogamous marriage—an exclusive, lifelong bond between one man and one woman. This ideal once fit into an extended family form, but industrialization has shrunk the family unit to the nuclear family, which is more readily adaptable to the demands of a highly mobile society. Different family members are not likely to find employment in the same place, and job changing has been frequent. Even the ideal of monogamous marriage has been influenced by the demands for social mobility. The increasing self-sufficiency of women has been paralleled by a rising divorce rate; the current average length of marriage is less than five years. Since 70 to 80 percent of divorced persons remarry, the American marriage system sometimes has been called serial monogamy, a form somewhere between strict monogamy and true polygamy.

THE LIFE CYCLE IN AMERICA

In every society, we pass through the same age-related stages: birth, childhood, adolescence, perhaps marriage, old age, and death. But how we experience each one is strongly molded by our culture. Even in the United States, where rites of passage are minimal and socialization diffuse, we tend to experience the life cycle in ways that are unique to our culture.

Pregnancy and Childbirth

Like those of many other societies, American culture includes several traditional pregnancy taboos and admonitions. One of these is the idea of marking. According to this belief, children may be influenced by things that are done by or that happen to their mothers. For instance, birthmarks might be attributed to the mother's having eaten too many strawberries, raspberries, or other red foods during the pregnancy. The most common expression of the concept of marking in the United States today is in admonitions to do things believed to influence the child in positive ways. For instance, a pregnant woman may hear that by spending time listening to classical music, reading good literature, and immersing herself in art she may predispose her child to similar pursuits. The concept of the marking of an unborn child by its mother parallels the idea that, after birth, mothers have the principal psychological influence on the development of the child and therefore usually receive greater credit or blame for what the child becomes.

Americans regard it as desirable for a woman to seek the services of a physician—most of whom are male in the United States—about two months into her pregnancy. This doctor will evaluate the health of the woman, check the progress of the pregnancy, and deliver the baby. Although some changes are occurring, for most Americans the preferred place for the delivery still is a hospital in the presence of the physician and one or more nurses. Only in recent decades have fathers been permitted in the delivery room. On entering the hospital, the woman spends several hours in a labor room. She is moved to a delivery room for the actual delivery and then to a hospital room for convalescence while the baby is cared for in a nursery. A few generations ago the convalescent period might have been several weeks long. Today it is usually no more than two days.

Due to the high costs of medical treatment and hospital costs, lower-income Americans do not follow the ideals outlined in the last paragraph with the same frequency as do members of the middle and upper classes. The last two decades also have seen an increasing return to the less expensive system of delivery at home with the aid of a nurse-midwife who offers more personalized care than does the hospital system. Many hospitals, in turn, are beginning to shift from the use of specialized labor and delivery rooms to the use of birthing rooms, which can save as much as half the hospital costs for a normal delivery. In this system the woman remains in the same room from labor through a convalescent period of up to 24 hours, and the child remains with the mother after the delivery.

Parents begin selecting a name for the child months before the birth. Most American families have no formal customary rules for selecting the name, such as a requirement to name the child after a particular relative, so the search for a name is largely a matter of the parents' agreeing on a name. To help them in this process, parents-to-be may even purchase a book of alphabetically arranged first names. Since the selection of the name is largely an aesthetic issue, the popularity of different names rises and falls over the generations much as do fashions in dress. Names like Blanche, Gertrude, Mildred, Helen, Edith, or Ada for girls and Edgar, Orville, Leonard, Albert, or Herbert for boys that were common among people born 80 years ago are uncommon today. Names are officially given without ceremony immediately after birth when the attending physician fills out a birth certificate to be filed in the county records. A religious naming ceremony may be conducted for the child a few weeks later.

Infancy and Childhood

After a period when breast-feeding was not common, it does appear to be increasing once again. Today 83 percent of mothers nurse their infants for at least six months, but not usually for much longer. Most American mothers stop nursing their children far short of the several years that is common in many of the world's nonindustrialized cultures.

Americans socialize their children differently depending on the sex of the child. Symbolically, the color pink is associated with girls and blue with boys as appropriate for clothing and decorations of the baby's crib. It has been noted that mothers speak more to girl babies than to boys, and fathers tend to play in a rougher, more jostling fashion with their male children. Before six months of age, male babies are touched more frequently by their mothers than are girls, but after six months of age the opposite is true. Boys are given less emotional support throughout the rest of their lives and learn rapidly that "big boys don't cry." Instead of emotional support from others, they are encouraged to obtain pleasure from success in competition and in demonstrating skill and physical coordination. Girls are encouraged to take care in making themselves pretty, and their clothing is often designed more for eye appeal than for practicality in play. By and large, differences in the socialization of children reflect a stereotype of sex differences that views males as strong, active, unemotional, logical, dominant, independent, aggressive, and competitive and females as weak, passive, emotional, intuitive, supportive, dependent, sociable, status-conscious, shy, patient, and vain. In the past 20 years, stereotypes such as these have changed tremendously among university students, but there is little evidence that this is the case for American society at large.

Adolescence and Courtship

At 5 years of age, children are enrolled in school. Schooling is typically required by most states until the age of 16, which also is a

FIGURE 14.7   *Romantic Love*

Romantic love as a basis for marriage is a highly regarded value in the United States, even though its ideal perpetuates the economic dependence of women on men.

common age for driving privileges to be obtained. There is no widespread practice of puberty rituals, and other adult rights and responsibilities, such as military service, voting rights, and the right to purchase alcoholic beverages, are acquired at different ages up to the age of 21. The absence of a clear-cut transition from childhood results in a great deal of uncertainty and turmoil about appropriate role behavior during adolescence.

During the teenage period, American adolescents explore their identities as social beings as they practice the skills necessary to achieve an independent adult status. Acceptance by their peers becomes extremely important, and adolescents begin to create a sense of independent functioning by adopting new values that are in harmony with their peer group and with the social milieu outside their family. This is a period of dating, in which adolescents begin to learn the skills of court-

ship and lay the foundations for their adult sexual identities. Although American ideals historically have required that both sex and pregnancy do not occur until after the marriage ceremony, the majority of both unmarried males and females experience sex by age 19. Tanfer and Horn (1985) found that in 1983, 82 percent of unmarried women aged 20 through 29 had experienced sexual intercourse. For 1977, there were 700,000 adolescent pregnancies (Byrne, 1977). Many teenage pregnancies are aborted, but there also are many births before marriage. For instance, in 1985 there were 259,477 children born out of wedlock to women from 15 through 19 years of age. This represented 49.2 percent of all births to women of this age in that year.

Marriage

Americans are marrying later today than they were a generation ago. In 1986, the median age of males marrying for the first time was 25.7 years, and for females it was 23.1 years. In the American view, the ideal reason for marriage is love. The ideal of romantic love as a basis for marriage is perhaps nowhere else in the world so strongly supported. As Ralph Linton (1936), an anthropologist noted for his interpretations of American culture, observed over half a century ago:

All societies recognize that there are occasional violent emotional attachments between persons of the opposite sex, but our present American culture is practically the only one which has attempted to capitalize on these and make them a basis for marriage. Most groups regard them as unfortunate and point out the victims of such attachments as horrible examples. Their rarity in most societies suggests they are psychological abnormalities to which our own culture has attached extraordinary value just as other cultures have attached extreme values to other abnormalities. The hero of the modern American movie is always a romantic lover just as the hero of the old Arab epic is always an epileptic. A cynic might suspect that in any ordinary population the percentage of people with a capacity for romantic love of the Hollywood type was about as large as that of persons able to throw genuine epileptic fits. However, given a little social encouragement either one can be adequately imitated without the performer admitting even to himself that the performance is not genuine. (p. 175)

Why is romantic love such an important ideal in the American courtship and marriage system? One factor, certainly, is the economic unimportance of the nuclear family as a unit of production in American society. As industrialization undermined the economic role of the extended family, the marital choices of children grew increasingly independent of parental authority. Emotional attraction has filled the void created by the declining role of parental decision making in the choice of mates. Romantic love as the basis of mate selection may be more prominent in the United States than elsewhere, but it certainly is not absent in other industrialized countries. Another factor in the maintenance of the ideal of romantic love between spouses appears to be the dependent economic status of women in countries where it is found. The romantic ideal stresses the role of women as objects of love, valued for their emotional, aesthetic, nurturing, and moral contributions to society rather than for their economic productivity and practical contributions to society outside the domestic sphere. Thus, the ideal of romantic love seems to play a role in perpetuating the economic dependence of women on men. This romanticism of women as love objects explains why, contrary to the popular American stereotype, it seems to be men who are the more romantic sex among Americans. Zick Rubin (1973) studied attitudes of dating couples at the University of Michigan and found that women were more likely than men to espouse practical issues over romantic considerations in spouse selection. The more pragmatic approach of women to marriage is not so surprising when one considers the higher income and broader economic participation in prestigious occupations that is enjoyed by men in the United States.

Just how does mate selection actually proceed? Several researchers suggest a model that involves a sequence of stages. First, proximity is an important factor. People are most likely to get together with those whom they are likely to encounter. Thus, in spite of their mobility, most Americans actually marry a partner who lives within a few miles of them. Ineichen (1979) found that almost 65 percent of a sample of 232 married couples lived in the same city

before they married, most of them coming from the same area or adjacent areas of the city.

Initial attraction is likely to be based on superficial, easily observable characteristics such as physical attractiveness, dress, and evidence of social power and prestige. After meeting one another, compatibility of values and attitudes is especially important. Agreement on values such as religious, sexual, familial, and political values is a good predictor of the development of a stable relationship (Kerkhoff, 1962). Burgess and Wallin (1953) found that engaged couples were remarkably similar in their physical attractiveness, physical health, mental health, social popularity, race, religion, parents' educational levels, parents' incomes, and the quality of their parents' marriages. Thus, similarity seems to be an important element in the attraction that leads to relationships.

The love ideal continues to shape relationships after marriage. Bean (1981) examined television soap operas for their portrayal of relationships within the family. Each weekday over 18 million Americans watch these dramatizations of human relationships even though the basic story lines are repeated over and over. According to Bean, "The triangle involving ties of love and marriage with various complications is the most frequently occurring plot" (p. 61). The American family is depicted in soap operas as composed of two sets of relationships: husband-wife and parent-child. Both are ideally composed of two and only two interacting units. That is, problems arise in either relationship if the interactions involve three persons, as when either husband or wife becomes involved with another person or when parents fail to relate to the child as a unit. Bean claims that according to the ideals held forth in soap operas,

Each dyadic relationship should contain three basic ingredients. A man and a woman should be united by love, marriage, and sex. Parents and child should be united by blood, love, and nurturing. Love is an element in both relationships, but the love between parent and child is different from the love between husband and wife. The former is parental or familial love derived from the blood tie between parent and child, and the nurturing of a child by its parent. It has a beginning but no end. To stop loving your child would be unnatural in the worst sense of the word. The love between husband and wife is romantic love, the source of which is mysterious so that it may begin and may end suddenly. It just happens to people (one falls, not jumps). The two kinds of love are sharply differentiated and people who share familial love are prohibited from sharing romantic love by the incest taboo. (p. 70)

Illness

Americans predominantly espouse a secular medical model of illness rather than a spiritual model. This feature corresponds to the existence of an extensive system of health care that is based on a scientific view of illness. Secular medicine has been successful enough in combating disease to make the status of physician one of the most prestigious and well-paid in the American social system. In 1985, the average net income (take-home pay after expenses such as taxes and malpractice insurance) of an American medical doctor was $106,300. As of 1986, there were 535,000 medical doctors practicing in the United States. This means that there was one physician for about every 459 Americans in that year. In the same year, there were approximately 1,406,000 active registered nurses and 631,000 practical nurses in the United States and over 3,000,000 auxiliary health workers such as nurse's aides, orderlies, attendants, and nonnursing health aides. As these figures suggest, health care is a major component of the American social and economic system. Without counting administrative personnel in hospitals, laboratory technicians, or paraprofessionals, nearly 1 in every 37 Americans is involved in the medical health care profession.

In 1986, there were about 7,000 hospitals and 25,646 nursing homes in the United States and approximately one and one third million hospital beds for patients. Given the large number of patients who must be dealt with in the hospital setting, it is understandable that hospital rules, regulations, and procedures generally are designed for the benefit of the hospital personnel—to make their work more efficient and easy to do. Although the standardization of hospital routine may have an overall effect of improved efficiency in patient care, one by-product of such standardization is a depersonalization of the patient as an individual. A person entering treatment in a hospital setting undergoes a status change, a loss of the usual prestige and access to decision-making power accorded normal members of society (Goffman, 1961). Patients are expected to give up their normal autonomy and to passively accept hospital routine and treatment procedures. Information about their own case is available to them only at the physician's discretion. Howard Leventhal (1975), who has studied patient reports of depersonalization, finds that American patients often experience themselves as objects or things rather than as people and that they feel psychologically isolated from other people.

Old Age and Death

In the United States, old age generally is thought of as beginning at 65 years, the traditional age of retirement from employment and the age of eligibility for old age social security benefits. With retirement comes a loss of many of the usual activities and social contacts that make life meaningful for the active person. This stage of the life cycle is the one most likely to be described as a time of loneliness and boredom. With retirement also comes a loss of the prestige and income associated with productive occupations. The low level of prestige and power associated with old age qualifies the aged in America for a minority status. Americans themselves are aware of the low rank of the aged and sometimes compare their own culture with other ways of life in which they believe the aged are accorded greater respect.

Death in America has been largely removed from the familial context by other social institutions that have taken over the management of the dying and the dead. Hospitals and nursing homes care for the terminally ill and insulate the surviving family members from much of the dying process. Americans are likely to die in either a hospital or a nursing home, often in isolation from their family members. Traditionally, doctors and nurses have tended to avoid telling terminal patients that they were dying. A specialized funeral industry exists to take care of the practical necessities preparatory to burial and to usher the survivors through the funeral and mourning process.

AMERICAN IDEOLOGY

Despite its social diversity, the United States has not only a rather standardized approach to the life cycle but also a recognizable pattern of beliefs. Those explored here are religious ideology and the framework of American values and drives.

Religion in America

Americans tend to view the universe in mechanistic terms, and, historically, a scientific world view has been held central to their approach to everyday problems. The government recognizes no official religion, for the Bill of Rights of the United States Constitution guarantees a separation between church and state. Nevertheless, the American government traditionally has fostered religion in general, granting tax-exempt status to churches and their properties, while Americans as a people tend to view membership in a church, synagogue, or equivalent religious organization to be evidence of full allegiance to one's community. In early days, the church was often the center of local community life, and Americans still tend to participate in religious activities more frequently, for instance, than do most Europeans. Nearly half of Americans are likely to attend religious services at least once a month.

Currently 68 percent of Americans hold formal membership in a religion, and 40 percent attend religious services in a typical week (the Gallup Report, 1985, p. 13). Most belong to Christian churches, Protestant denominations being the most common. Judaism is America's most visible non-Christian religion, but one also finds Buddhists and Moslems in most American communities as well as adherents of several other religions, especially indigenous varieties of Christianity. Native American religion and organized witchcraft are found throughout the country, but these have entered the mainstream consciousness less well than have the other organized religions. About 5 percent of Americans espouse no religious belief, and another 5 percent who do assert a belief in God or a Universal Spirit express no preference for a particular religion (the Gallup Report, 1985, pp. 13, 50). Interestingly, the American tendency to emphasize membership and participation in religious organizations over religious belief is also found among nonbelievers: For instance, the American Atheists have formed their own quasi-religious organization.

Bellah (1967), a Harvard sociologist who has specialized in the study of religion, has formulated a concept that the basic religious dimension of American life is a civil religion that coexists with the formally organized religions. The American civil religion is integrated into American social and political life and draws predominantly from Christianity and Judaism for its symbolism. Its God is the author of order, law, and morality and is actively involved in history, especially in American history, much as the God of ancient Israel. According to Bellah, the symbolism of American civil religion portrays America as the modern equivalent of the biblical Israel and the American Founding Fathers as the inspired prophets of American history. The Declaration of Independence, the Constitution, and Abraham Lincoln's Gettysburg Address are the three sacred documents of American civil religion. The first two grew out of the American Exodus from Europe, the symbolic Egypt from which God led people to the American Promised Land, which God set up as a light to all the world. Whereas Washington was the American Moses, Lincoln was the counterpart of Jesus, the wise and compassionate hero who counseled love of neighbor and whose life was taken by his enemies. Lincoln's Gettysburg Address, the New Testament of American sacred literature, is built around themes of death and rebirth such as "these honored dead," "conceived in liberty," and "a new birth of freedom." Bellah describes the sacred calendar of the American civil religion as consisting of Memorial Day, on which American communities honor their martyred dead, Thanksgiving Day, which integrates the family into the civil religion in a ceremonial feast of thanks to God for the bounties of American life, and the less overtly religious holidays of the Fourth of July, Veterans Day, and the birthdays of Washington and Lincoln. The recent addition of Martin Luther King's birthday to U.S. holidays to symbolize and encourage interracial respect may be viewed as an extension of the American sacred calendar since Bellah originally set forth his idea.

FIGURE 14.8 *Allegiance*

Allegiance as a conforming force in society can be either positive or negative. The other side of patriotism and loyalty is ethnocentrism and sexism.

American Drives and Values

As we saw in looking at the components of culture in general (chapter 2), every society holds certain concepts about how people should relate to each other and to the universe. But human behavior is characteristically symbolic and therefore subject to diverse interpretations. Scholars have commonly asserted that these value systems and the behavior they guide may coalesce into distinctive patterns (Kroeber, 1944). And in a society with as large a population as that of the United States, the broad generalizations that are necessary for the formulation of abstract values do not apply uniformly to all American subcultures, either past or present.

Nevertheless, there does seem to be a fair consensus in the writings of anthropologists and sociologists about the most important values that typify the dominant American way of life. These include emphasis on personal goal-directed effort, individualism, progress, freedom, equality, democracy, and an external conformity that is personally motivated by love of country, cooperation for the common welfare, a sense of personal morality and fair play, or the desire for social acceptance.

Although a great deal of agreement exists about the specific values that find their place in the American ideology, social scientists differ with one another in their efforts to find a pattern in American values. One attempt to reduce the complexity in the diverse list of values that have been ascribed to American culture is that of Henry (1963). Henry has suggested a distinction between what he calls drives and values. <u>Drives</u> are motives that people actually pursue, sometimes at great cost, rather than those to which they merely give lip service. Since it is in pursuit of their culture's drives that people invest their time and energy, drives represent the things that people value most strongly in the practical sense. They also are the source of stresses in life. What Henry calls <u>values</u> represent ideals that people long for but do not necessarily pursue. They are often opposites of drives, since they might give release from the stresses created by the pursuit of drives. Henry describes the roles of drives and values:

Drives are what urge us blindly into getting bigger, into going further into outer space and into destructive competition; values are

TABLE 14.7 *The Relationship Between Drives and Values in American Culture*

Social Traits Resulting from Industrialization and Role Specialization	Resulting Drives	Subtypes and Examples of Drives	Counter-Balancing Values	Examples of Values
Dependent status in employment ("self-alienation")	Conformity	*Allegiance* in-group sentiments; ethnocentrism; zenophobia; patriotism *Cooperation* obedience to authority; respect for law and office; opposition to boat-rocking and trouble-making *Equality* equality of opportunity; good citizenship; denial of class distinctions; mass education; democracy	Self-reliance	Freedom, autonomy, independence; the Marlborough Man; hero worship; preference for charismatic leaders; opposition to authority figures (politicians, etc.); desire for popularity; self-discovery; self-fulfilled meditation; favoring the underdog
Nonownership of products of own labor ("object alienation")	Work ethic (i.e., work is good in its own right, instead of in terms of its products)	*Optimism* future-orientation; desire for progress, improvement, getting ahead *Energy/Effort* effort-optimism; personal effort, vigor, and initiative; opposition to laziness and sensuality of youth *Purposefulness* purposeful recreation; pragmatic ingenuity; diligence; applied knowledge	Hedonism/ Pleasure/Aesthetics	Spontaneity and "nowism"; pleasure, relaxation, existentialism; veneration of wisdom and maturity; Santa Claus; nostalgia for carefree days of youth; desire for loss of control, "letting one's hair down," "getting crazy," and being taken care of; reckless abandon
Insecure status ("social alienation")	Competitiveness	*Competition* competition in recreation, scorekeeping; oneupmanship; status climbing and desire for upward mobility; free enterprise system; multiple party system in government *Materialism* material acquisitiveness; profit motive; quest for luxuries; high standard of living; conspicuous consumption; "keeping up with the Joneses" *Mobility* physical mobility; expansiveness; desirability for change and novelty; American restlessness; wanderlust	Personableness	Generosity, charity, kindness; relaxation of interpersonal relationships; love; openness; honesty; resentment of quota-busting over-achievement and those in high office; desire for physical security; desire for simplicity; idyllic pastoral existence; myth of the Noble Savage; American familialism; nostalgia for "good old days," roots; desire for security, stability

the sentiments that work in the opposite direction. Drives belong to the occupational world; values to the world of family and friendly intimacy. Drives animate the hurly-burly of business, the armed forces and all those parts of our culture where getting ahead, rising in social scale, outstripping others, and merely surviving in the struggle are the absorbing functions of life. When values appear in these areas, they act largely as brakes, on drivenness. (p. 14)

At the time of his writing early in the 1960s, Henry saw America as a culture driven by the needs for achievement, competition, profit, mobility, security, a higher standard of living, and expansiveness. American values—in effect, the things Americans long for as a result of being caught up by these drives—include such sentiments as love, kindness, quietness, contentment, fun, honesty, decency, relaxation, and simplicity.

Henry's drives may be understood as ideological reflections of the technologically and economically dictated means for achieving the necessities of life (see Table 14.7). Industrialization has created three prominent drives in American society: conformity, the work ethic, and competitiveness. These, colored by their counterbalancing values—self-reliance, fun, and personableness—can be seen as the basis of the distinctive pattern of American culture.

Conformity. All cultures impose a degree of conformity to socially determined norms, but all peoples do not value conformity to the same degree or become driven by their efforts to conform. The drive to conform is typical of large-scale industrialized societies because individuals in all walks of life are subordinated to rules, higher authorities, and powerful institutions whose goals often take precedence over the needs of individuals. Since most individuals in industrialized societies make their living by selling their labor as a commodity, income is partly contingent on conformity to the organizational and sometimes personal ideals by which supervisory personnel and management evaluate employees. Organizational efficiency is fostered by harmonious cooperation and "pulling together." Being "out of step," "rocking the boat," or "quota busting" are likely to be seen as forms of troublemaking precisely because they involve disruption of the routine of the group. One's economic security, personal prestige, and even status-linked rank are easily endangered by too much nonconformity.

The drive for conformity motivated by the need for greater security is manifest in several ways: allegiance to the nation, to one's occupation, religion, ethnic group, and race; cooperation for the common welfare; and support for equality. The Americans' allegiance to others seems largely motivated by the wish to avoid public criticism. It includes the positive sentiments of patriotism, loyalty, and love of country, but it is here that one also finds the darker side of American drives: ethnocentrism, antipathies toward outsiders or foreigners, racism, and sexism. Under the general label of cooperation fall the American stresses on cooperation for the common welfare, respect and deference to rank and obedience to authority, and antipathies toward "radicalism," nonconformity, and "boat-rocking." Americans also are driven to create greater equality for members of society. This aspect of their conformity drive stands in counterpoint to some of the frictions created by their in-group allegiances. The obligations of good citizenship include being a good neighbor and supporting equality of opportunity, participant democracy, and mass education.

CONFORMITY IN AMERICA, GERMANY, AND JAPAN

Although America shares a drive for conformity with other cultures, especially with other industrialized nations, the specific influence that this drive has is tempered by various other factors, such as how formally or informally it is taught and how other drives and values modify the manifestations of conformity. German and Japanese cultures also emphasize conformity. Both differ from American culture in teaching this drive more explicitly and formally.

The traditional German emphasis on the importance of order in social life, orderliness in private life, and respect for authority and obedience are all summed up in the common expression, *Ordnung muss sein!* ("There must be order!"). The typical heroes of traditional German literature were individuals who because of a personal flaw of character were unable to conform to the dictates of the social order and who were

FIGURE 14.9   *Conformity*

Some cultures value the ideal of conformity more than others. In military groups such as these Royal Canadian Mounted Police, A, conformity is obvious and necessary. Conformity may also be a more subtle value. These American teenagers, B, conform to a specific hairstyle while supporting the idea of independence.

tragically doomed because of this flaw. All this explicit emphasis on the subordination of individual needs to the society's need for order is likely to strike the American as too intolerant of individual differences and too restrictive of individual freedom to be palatable. Americans, too, conform, but they learn this drive more informally and are less conscious of their conformity to their society's rules for living. Although it is a fact of life, their drive for conformity is overshadowed by their continual praise of the value of self-reliance. American conformity is more a result of their search for friendship, respect, social power, and income or of avoiding rejection than it is a formal recognition of the importance of social order for its own sake. Americans are much more likely than are Germans to describe their conformity as a simple by-product of their personal and inner-regulated morality or their desire to be good neighbors rather than as evidence of respect for the authority of society as a whole over their lives as individuals.

The Japanese, whom Germans have called "the Germans of the East," have a similarly formal emphasis on the importance of conformity to the rules of social life, but they place greater emphasis on the necessity of orders being imposed from above. At the same time, they express more ambivalence about this state of affairs. Like Americans, the Japanese stress the importance of competition and success, but their emphasis is on competition between groups rather than individuals. Loyalty to the team counts more heavily than the individual's ability to excel. Whiting (1979) has compared the Japanese and American approaches to baseball and reports a consistent Japanese willingness to sacrifice outstanding individual team members when their lack of cooperative team spirit threatened the sense of *wa*, or group harmony. Whiting summarizes the different feelings about individualism and cooperation in the two cultures:

> The U.S. is a land where the stubborn individualist is honored and where "doing your own thing" is a motto of contemporary society. In Japan, *kojinshugi*, the term for individualism, is almost a dirty word. In place of "doing your own thing," the Japanese have a proverb: "The nail that sticks up shall be hammered down." It is practically a national slogan. (p. 60)

Self-reliance. The drives of conformity are counterbalanced by idealized values of self-reliance, expressed in praise of freedom, liberty, grass-roots government, and independence. The value placed on autonomy includes the worship of heroes such as Daniel Boone, John Wayne, James Bond, Luke Skywalker, and Indiana Jones who embody the traits of rugged individualism, self-motivation, and self-reliance. The well-known American distaste for politics and the commonly held view that "all politicians are crooks" are expressions of antipathy for "the Establishment," the system of authority that requires conformity. Americans prefer to follow the political leaders who show charisma in handling themselves, thereby "rising above the office." The desire for popularity is a more personal expression of this same value, as is rooting for the underdog and the covert admiration that Americans tend to feel for the individual who stands up against great odds or successfully "bucks the system" (as illustrated in films such as *Fun With Dick and Jane, Dog Day Afternoon, Rage,* and *Death Wish*). The overcoming of impossibly powerful adversaries by a hero with great personal skill is perhaps the most common theme in American literature, and the great popularity of the James Bond movies in the 1960s and the Rocky and Rambo movies in the 1980s illustrates how long-lived this value has been during a quarter century of great change.

Traditionally, the value of self-reliance has been especially emphasized for men. Women's status had less rank than did men's, and their roles as women were complementary to those of men. For instance, women featured in popular fiction generally have been adjuncts to men. Instead of seeking their own autonomy and independence, they usually have been portrayed as seeking love for and dependence on a man. There are increasing exceptions to this portrayal of women in the entertainment media, as women take an increasing role in American economic life. Similarly, a great deal of the feminist movement of the past two decades has been precisely focused on encouraging greater autonomy for women.

Francis Hsu (1961) believes that self-reliance in America is the central preoccupation from which all our other values arise. Hsu's self-reliance has as its primary psychological manifestation the fear of dependence. He contrasts Chinese and American society in respect to the ideal of self-reliance:

> A man in traditional China where self-reliance was not an ideal may have been unsuccessful in his life. But suppose in his old age his sons were able to provide for him generously. Such a person not only was happy and content about it; he was likely also to beat the drums before all and sundry to let the world know that he had good children who were supporting him in a style to which he had never been accustomed. On the other hand, an American parent who has not been successful in life may derive some benefit from the prosperity of his children, but he certainly will not want anybody to know about it. In fact, he will resent any reference to it. At the first opportunity when it is possible for him to become independent of his children, he will do so.
>
> Therefore, even though we may find many individuals in traditional China and elsewhere who were in fact self-sufficient, and even though we may find individuals in America who are in fact dependent upon others, the important thing is that where self-reliance is not an ideal, it is neither promoted nor a matter of pride, but where it is an ideal, it is both. In American society the fear of dependence is so great that an individual who is not self-reliant is a misfit. "Dependent character" is a highly derogatory term, and a person so described is thought to be in need of psychiatric help. (p. 250)

Hsu argues that self-reliance is actually an impossible goal to achieve. Human society is based on mutual dependence on our fellow human beings, and no one can meet his or her technological, social, intellectual, or emotional needs in isolation. Therefore, Hsu believes that the American ideal of self-reliance creates contradictions that lead to insecurity in the lives of individuals: Self-reliance means impermanence in relationships and competition for status, which in turn requires conformity to organizations or peer groups. "In other words," Hsu explains, "to live up to their core value orientation of self-reliance, Americans as a whole have to do much of its opposite. Expressed in the jargon of science, there is a direct relationship between self-reliance and individual freedom on the one hand and submission to organizations and conformity on the other" (p. 250).

The work ethic. An industrial technology leads to a high degree of labor specialization in which many individuals must work competitively to produce goods that they themselves do not own and that will be consumed by others. Under such circumstances, it is the labor itself that is rewarded, and work becomes a drive in its own right rather than simply the necessary means to create something of significant value to the worker. This work ethic may develop under other circumstances in societies with a nonindustrialized technology, but it would seem to be an inevitable drive wherever industrialization is prominent.

In normal day-to-day terms, it is work of a practical nature rather than work for work's sake that is likely to receive the greatest reward. Therefore, the work ethic is best understood as a drive that is more or less synonymous with a positive attitude toward

FIGURE 14.10 *Work Ethic*

The American concept of a work ethic involves the ability to accomplish purposeful goals, to put forth great effort to achieve these goals, and a belief in the positive accomplishments of progress.

pragmatic effort or accomplishment. The person who is well socialized for living in accordance with a work ethic will be optimistic, energetic, and purposeful. The specific evidences of a work ethic are manifestations of one of these three aspects.

Optimism is a positive expectation that the future is potentially better than the present state of affairs. In America one finds a traditional emphasis on progress, improvement, diligence, getting ahead, the expectation that children should grow up to be better and more successful than their parents, and the idea that, no matter how badly things are going, "Tomorrow is another day."

The emphasis placed on energy includes positive reactions to such traits as vigor, activity, personal effort, and initiative as well as negative responses to "laziness," passivity, and sensuality. In the opinion of Cora DuBois (1955) these traits form the underlying basis of the "cult of youthfulness" for which Americans are famous.

Where a work ethic is prominent, effort of any kind will be admired. But effort directed purposefully toward the achievement of specific ends will be more applauded than effort for which no clear purpose is evident. Purposefulness as an aspect of the work ethic is manifest in the national emphasis on pragmatism, ingenuity, inventiveness, and applied science and in the attitude that recreation, vacations, and other pleasurable activities should be undertaken because they are beneficial rather than for the sake of the pleasure itself. For instance, when I was a child, my father emphasized that meals should not be eaten for the pleasure of eating but because food is necessary so that one can work. He also insisted that the only good music is music with lyrics that convey a message. The value of purposefulness also was manifest in the attitude common among Americans of several generations ago that even sex should be for procreation and not merely for pleasure.

The idealized values that serve as brakes on these work ethic drives of future-oriented optimism, energetic effort, and purposefulness are nostalgia for the "good old days" (the presumably carefree, less hectic days of the

FIGURE 14.11 *Pleasure Seeking*

As a contrast to the work ethic of a generation ago, many people today value the existential philosophy of living for the moment and seeking pleasure in it.

past), relaxation, and fun. The latter is the value placed on spontaneity and the "Be here now" existential philosophy, the desire for enjoyment and pleasurable recreation, and the covert admiration for disaster-courting thrill-seekers.

Competitiveness. Along with conformity and the work ethic, competitiveness is the third major American drive. Like the others, its existence is inherent in an industrialized society. In such social systems, the products of labor usually are owned by someone other than the worker who produces them, and the working person generally is dependent on someone else for his or her livelihood. Since these conditions prevail in America, Americans must sell their labor as if it were a commodity. Economic statuses are insecure and dependent because they are organized around authority relationships and because holding them successfully is predicated on "selling oneself" effectively. It is the insecurity of American life that is the basis for the emphasis on the "spirit of competition."

Within the economic sphere, this drive manifests itself in the recurrent praise of the profit motive and the ideal of a free enterprise system, one in which economic competition is unhindered by noneconomic forces. Socially, the concept of enlightened self-interest is an attempt to reconcile the potential conflicts between drives of competition and drives of conformity, as noted by the French nobleman Alexis de Tocqueville (1969) over 100 years ago:

> In the United States there is hardly any talk of the beauty of virtue. But they maintain that virtue is useful and prove it every day. American moralists do not pretend that one must sacrifice himself for his fellows because it is a fine thing to do so. But they boldly assert that such sacrifice is as necessary for the man who makes it as for the beneficiaries. (p. 525)

Status climbing and upward social mobility are American drives that flow out of their competitive circumstances. The extreme emphasis on competition as a social good even carries over into the realm of relaxation and recreation. Even though Americans assert the idealized value that "it's not who wins the game that counts, but how you play the game," this statement is probably best understood as a

FIGURE 14.12   *Competition*

Competitiveness is a major drive in the American psyche manifesting itself in economic situations, social situations, and in sports.

wistful but unrealistic protestation against the practicalities of a way of life in which "nice guys finish last." Americans continue to teach their children to keep score when playing games, a practice that the traditional Zuñi of the American Southwest would have eschewed as abhorrent.

American material acquisitiveness also must be seen as a manifestation of competitiveness. In a society in which, by Old World standards, the majority has never suffered from a lack of physical security or even luxury, materialism is best understood not as physical need but as a manifestation of the competitive desire to "keep up with the Joneses," that is, as evidence of one's competitive success. Social movement often is accompanied by physical mobility—the expansiveness of American society and the "don't fence me in" restlessness of the American people that has been noticed so frequently by foreign observers and so often appears as a theme of American literature and song.

The idealized values that counter the implicit conflict and potential hostility in competition include relaxed interpersonal relations, friendliness, frankness, love, kindness, de-

FIGURE 14.13 *Relaxation*

Americans combine their love of competition and its counterpoint drive, relaxation, in the sports arena. These spectators are enjoying a college football game with the mascot of Brown University.

cency, openness, and good sportsmanship. Charity and generosity also are valued as contrasts to the drive to make a profit. Simplicity, idealization of the idyllic pastoral life, and the myth of the noble savage are the drives of material acquisitiveness. Praise of family as the foundation of American society, nostalgia, and reminiscence for the "good old days" (in the sense of a wistful desire for stability and roots) may be seen as growing out of the stresses inherent in a way of life that emphasizes mobility and being "on the go."

The Changing Context of American Values and Drives

The difference between American values and drives and those emphasized in other industrialized societies may reflect the evolutionary adaptation of American society to its unique social and physical environments. Historically, America was one of the first societies in which the benefits of industrialization could be obtained by building a society to fit the growing technological apparatus rather than by trying to fit an industrialized economy into a pre-existing social order. In America, factories could be built to house the new tools instead of trying to fit equipment into the buildings of a previous generation, as was done in Europe. Cities grew up in a frontier society, and their form could be guided by technological and economic needs as they arose. In Europe, centuries-old cities that had grown up reflecting the needs of a pre-industrial age were a factor with which the new technology had to cope. America's backwater frontier status was therefore an advantage that made it possible to obtain the greatest social benefits from its developing way of life.

Population patterns. The population of the United States has been growing at an accelerating rate throughout most of its history (see Fig. 14.14). One important implication of this growth was what appeared to be an ever-expanding consumer market. This social condition encouraged technological growth and economic expansion. In the early phase of industrialization, the amazing material output of this new mode of production encouraged rapid population growth, since consumers were needed to use the goods that were manufactured. Much of this growth was accomplished through a rapid influx of immigrant consumer/workers. Yet, there are limits on the number of people who can be supported by any mode of production. The closer the limit is approached, the more that members of the growing population must compete with one another to obtain both jobs and access to products. The growing competition results in increasing costs in obtaining the necessities of life.

FIGURE 14.14 *Population Growth in the United States from 1780–1965*

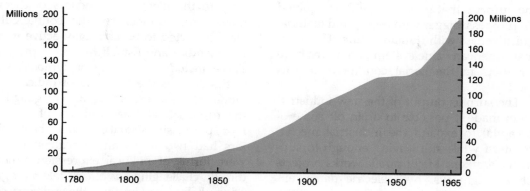

Note. From *Statistical Abstract of the United States: 1986* (106th ed.) [Table No. 1, p. 5] by U.S. Bureau of the Census, 1985, Washington, DC: U.S. Government Printing Office.

These increasing costs eventually must counterbalance the forces that induced the initial rapid population growth. At some point, the rate of growth begins to decelerate. In the United States, it took almost two centuries for this deceleration to begin. It was not until the early 1960s that the rate of American population growth stopped increasing. Since then, although it still is growing, it has been doing so at an ever-slowing rate. If this trend continues, it is estimated that the population of the United States will reach 310.8 million in 2080 (see Fig. 14.15). Most of the growth will occur by 2030 when the population will be about 304.8 million. After 2030 the growth rate will be relatively slow. If the growth rate were not to decelerate the competition for the goods produced would be so great that it would result in a decline in the standard of living of

the population as a whole. Thus, it is likely that the total population will finally level off. Given these past population changes, current patterns, and projected changes, it is possible to consider the implications of population growth rates on American ideology during three phases of population growth: the initial period of accelerating growth, the current period of decelerating growth, and the projected period of nongrowth in the population.

The period of growth. During the initial period of industrialization in the United States, the population was growing at a faster rate each decade. The internal consumer market seemed to offer unlimited potential for the expansion of sales. The same population growth represented a growing number of peo-

FIGURE 14.15 *Projected Population Growth in the United States from 1965–2080*

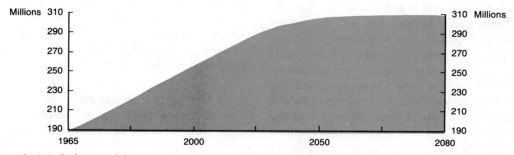

Note. From *Statistical Abstract of the United States: 1986* (106th ed.) [Table No. 1, p. 5] by U.S. Bureau of the Census, 1985, Washington, DC: U.S. Government Printing Office. Also from "Projections of the Population of the United States by Age, Sex and Race: 1983–2080" in *Current Population Reports: Population Estimates and Projections* (Series P - 25, No. 952) [Table 2, p. 30] by U.S. Bureau of the Census, 1984, Washington, DC: U.S. Government Printing Office.

ple in need of jobs, a further reason for expansion of industry. Under such circumstances it is no surprise that growth would be equated with progress, bigger with better, and material acquisitiveness with human nature. The traditional American value system and drives have their roots in the social conditions of this period.

The surplus output of the new industrial system made it possible to drain off some of the capital to expand the industrial mechanism itself while still leaving enough to support the workers. Major public works projects such as highways, hydroelectric dams, airports, and mass public educational facilities could be financed by creating bills that would have to be paid back by future citizens. Since the population was growing at an accelerating rate, this meant that the costs of growth would be spread out more and more thinly with each year.

The period of transition.   Since the 1960s, however, important changes in American values have been developing. In the early 1960s, the economics of American life were changing in ways that led to a decline in the fertility rate. The cost of living was growing rapidly, affecting childrearing expenses. As the fertility rate fell, population growth decelerated. Middle-class families were finding it increasingly difficult to maintain their standard of living unless both spouses were employed. The divorce rate continued to grow tremendously during this period. During the 1960s the United States also was becoming more and more heavily involved in an unpopular foreign war.

The initial ideological response to these changing social circumstances took form during the political and social turmoil of the student and minority protests of the 1960s. During this period, many people noted the discrepancy between traditional drives and values and the current social circumstances. They formulated a new ideology—called the counterculture—with its own system of values and drives as a part of their opposition to the established social order. These counterculture values largely took the form of opposites of the traditional system.

Born in a period of intense political activism, the central counterculture drive was one

that is necessary when people attempt to establish any new political movement: conformity to the ideas and practices of the new movement. Members of the counterculture were expected to be politically active in anti-war and "anti-Establishment" programs. These included a variety of symbolic shock tactics such as the adopting of radically new modes of dress, grooming, and language, and the espousal, at least verbally, of new and more permissive sexual customs. These behaviors had two important functions: (1) They were forms of political expression aimed at directly challenging customary, taken-for-granted symbols of conformity to the traditional social system; and (2) they simultaneously served as new symbols of group membership and cohesiveness. In the counterculture movement, failure to conform to the new group standards and failure to adopt an activist posture brought loss of esteem and personal distress.

As an offsetting value, the counterculture maintained the traditional American emphasis on self-reliance. But this established American value was spoken of in ways that contrasted with the usual ways of glorifying self-reliance. Counterculture self-reliance was described as noncompetitive individualism that rejected the traditional emphasis on acquisition of luxuries, rank within the established social order, and conformity to traditional morality.

Although the counterculture valued conformity and self-reliance, as did the mainstream culture, counterculture values did fundamentally diverge from those of the established value system in certain areas: (1) the rejection of materialism, monetary success, traditional education, pragmatic scientific rationality, efficiency, and cost-effectiveness as rationales for decisions, (2) an emphasis on sensory experiences and introspection as a source of knowledge in preference to abstract conceptual logic and objectivity, and (3) a quest for a return to harmony with nature as opposed to mastery over nature.

The period of stabilization.   The counterculture was the initial awakening to the fact that traditional American values no longer fit the new social conditions. Nevertheless, its ideology was largely a reaction against the contemporary political and economic conditions of its day and not a true adjustment to the social conditions that have prevailed since the rate of population growth began to decline. As such, it was doomed to fall by the wayside as the mainstream American system values and drives gradually were adjusted to the problems of life when a society approaches the upper limits of its social and economic growth.

Following the 1960s these new values and drives began to impress themselves on the public consciousness. The changes that reflect these new values and drives have been described commonly, if not completely accurately, as a return to political conservatism, a reawakening of religious fundamentalism, and a reassertion of a practical interest in job security. Perhaps the major change within the American system of drives and values has been a shift within the work ethic away from the optimism drives—such as the traditional emphasis on progress, getting ahead, and the future—toward a greater drive for achieving security in the present. Before the 1970s the word *progress* was equated with change of almost any kind. America was one of the few places where, instead of being encouraged to grow up to be just like their parents, children were expected to learn more and achieve a higher standard of living than their parents had. This is no longer so. Now the goal of young adults is the much less expansive one of achieving economic security or of simply "making ends meet."

Probably the two most fundamental changes in American ideology that have resulted from the economic pressures of the sixties and seventies have been changes in ideas about the roles of men and women and changes in attitudes toward sex. The pre-sixties idea that a married woman should be economically dependent on a working husband has ceased to be feasible. It is not surprising, then, that not only has it become acceptable for women to seek employment, but Americans also increasingly view an economically productive life as essential to a woman's self-fulfillment as a person.

Childrearing is now extremely costly. A study by Minge (Harris, 1981, p. 94) estimates that it now costs almost $200,000 to raise a child through four years of college. It is certainly not surprising, then, that the average couple now has fewer than two children. The

turn-of-the-century attitude that procreation was the only acceptable reason for sex is no longer tenable as the primary way in which Americans view their sexual lives. Increasingly, Americans are understanding sex primarily in the context of pleasure rather than reproduction. This change is well illustrated by a study by Lewis and Brissett (1967) of marriage counseling texts published from 1947 through 1965. They found that in that period, a good sex life typically was described as something a couple could achieve if they worked at it hard enough. One text (Eichenlaub, 1963) in their study is quoted as saying:

> An ardent spur-of-the-moment tumble sounds very romantic. . . . However, ineptly arranged intercourse leaves the clothes you had no chance to shed in a shambles, your plans for the evening shot, your birth control program incomplete, and your future sex play under considerable better-be-careful-or-we'll-wind-up-in-bed-again restraint. (pp. 34–35)

Today, in contrast, the emphasis in most publications about human sexuality is on sensuality, pleasure, and enjoyment, rather than on technique.

The desire for economic security has shown itself in enrollment trends in American universities. Enrollments have shifted in the past decade away from the humanities, arts, and social sciences toward applied fields that offer a more secure promise of employment. On the job, workers are changing jobs less frequently than they used to, even within companies. The desire for a greater sense of security also may be seen in trends toward more conservative political views, the rise of the yuppie attitude, and in a reawakening of religious interests. Not only is the percentage of Americans today who are members of a church greater than it was a generation ago, but also the 1970s saw a resurgence of religious fundamentalism. There also is growing emphasis on secular ways of finding personal security, such as the seeking of self-knowledge, self-realization, and fulfillment through therapy.

The second major change in American drives has been within the drive for the acquisition of material goods. Although this drive is still with us, the role of <u>conspicuous consump-</u>

tion—the acquisition and use of a surplus of goods as a way of competitively demonstrating one's success and prestige—is becoming less feasible for Americans. Instead, there is a growing emphasis on finding ways to conserve and extend the life of material goods. This trend is seen in such examples as the increasing popularity of smaller automobiles with greater gasoline mileage, the imposition of a 55-mile-an-hour maximum speed limit across the United States, the frequent discussion by the news media of ways in which conservation of energy and natural resources can be supported by citizens, the extension of tax credits for home insulation, the establishment of recycling centers in towns, and the passage of laws that require environmental impact studies before major building projects are undertaken.

If American population growth patterns continue, as has been predicted, stability rather than change will be the order of the day. Upward social mobility may be expected to become increasingly difficult as that stabilization is approached. The role of universities as a traditional means for upward mobility is likely to decline as the costs of a university education continue to grow beyond the means of more of the population. This process alone may ensure that the most prestigious occupations with the American economy will become more or less self-perpetuating across generations: Those who can afford to support their children through a university education will be those whose income is great enough to do so by virtue of their own university degrees. For reasons of political tradition, Americans may remain resistant to any official recognition of classes. Nevertheless, it is unlikely that we will remain as successful during the coming half century as we have been in the past at denying that there are differences in income, power, and prestige within our society.

It may be argued that many of our problems as a society have been intimately linked to the rapid pace of change in American life throughout most of our history and that with stability may come a lessening of many of these problems. At the same time, however, a greater awareness of the effects of social, cultural, and subcultural differences on our way of life—a major concern of the field of anthropology—is likely to be crucial if a harmonious

stability is to be achieved. Certainly, a more widespread recognition of the existence of social differences will make it more difficult to perpetuate the extremes of inequality that have long characterized U.S. society.

I will remind those of you who are not consoled by such thoughts that the very best of us these days are poor prophets, and the scenario of stability that I have sketched may not come to pass. The potentials embodied in new technologies such as computer communications and atomic or solar power—if they can be harnessed successfully for mass consumption—could bring about vast and beneficent changes in the lives of most Americans if they are ever developed to their full extent. Even more dramatic means for raising our standard of living as a society may yet be discovered. These as well as more tragic unpredictables, such as nuclear war, may circumvent the scenario that I have suggested as our most likely future. Yet, until those unpredictables become facts instead of mere possibilities, a course toward greater social stability appears to be the most likely continuing course of our internal social development in the coming half century.

External relations are another matter. As the effects of industrialization continue to spread around the world at the expense of technologically less complex ways of life, the cultures of the world are becoming more and more economically and politically interdependent. In this broader context, our future depends on what happens abroad as well as at home. Our relations with developing nations are likely to remain in a continuing state of flux as industrialization spreads and new power blocs and coalitions develop with the goal of ensuring the political and economic self-interest of developing nations. How we shall fare in this process will depend largely on a recognition that our own national self-interest is not likely to be furthered in the long run by a narrowly ethnocentric view of the other cultures with which we share the world.

SUMMARY

Despite Americans' belief that theirs is the best of all cultures, anthropological analysis of this society reveals areas of actual or potential problems. In contrast to the American ideal of a classless society with equality of opportunity, the reality is an unequal distribution of wealth and status that may stabilize or become more distinct in the near future. In contrast to the ideal of a peace-loving people, the United States has a high rate of crime. Families, assumed to be the core of society, have little power and often are broken by divorce.

Nor do Americans handle life cycle changes with wisdom and sensitivity. Birth is being treated more personally than in the past, but socialization of children perpetuates outdated stereotypes. Adolescents turn to their peer groups for socialization—and sex, with a high rate of teenage pregnancies. Marriages are occurring later—and breaking up sooner. Illness is treated according to a medical model, with the elderly placed in institutions to die.

In terms of ideology, the majority of Americans belong to some religious group or perhaps subscribe to the patriotic "civil religion." Driven by an emphasis on conformity, the work ethic, and competitiveness, Americans tend to balance these drives with contrasting values, such as love for fun, charity, and nostalgia for simpler times. These contrasting ideals developed as America's industrialization grew along with its population. But as the limits to growth are approached, the mainstream seems to be turning toward an emphasis on security and on conservative use of resources. During this period of stability, changes in other cultures will inevitably affect us all.

KEY TERMS
AND
CONCEPTS

unskilled laborers   323
pink collar   323
blue collar workers   324
white collar occupations   325
professionals   325
ethnic group   328
"protective" legislation   332
serial monogamy   336
marking   336
civil religion   341
drives   342

values   342
conformity   344
self-reliance   346
work ethic   347
optimism   348
energy   348
purposefulness   348
competitiveness   349
counterculture   352
conspicuous consumption   353

ANNOTATED
READINGS

De Toqueville, A. (1945). *Democracy in America*. New York: A. A. Knopf. Originally published in 1835, this classic description of American life was so insightful that it still rings true today.

Gorer, G. (1964). *The American people: A study in national character*. New York: W. W. Norton & Company. Revision of a classic description of the U.S.

Harris, M. (1981). *America now: The anthropology of a changing culture*. New York: Simon and Schuster. A provocative look at the effects of technological and economic change in American culture since World War II.

Hsu, F. L. K. (1983). *Rugged individualism reconsidered: Essays in psychological anthropology*. Knoxville, TN: University of Tennessee Press. Comparisons of traditional Chinese and American cultures by an anthropologist who was born in China.

Jorgensen, J. G., & Truzzi, M. (1974). *Anthropology and American life*. Englewood Cliffs, NJ: Prentice Hall. A useful collection of articles by anthropologists on American culture.

Schneider, D. M. (1968). *American kinship: A cultural account*. Englewood Cliffs, NJ: Prentice Hall. An examination of the role of kinship in the U.S.

Warner, W. L. (1953). *American life: Dream and reality*. Chicago: University of Chicago Press. An early study by an anthropologist of life in a U.S. city.

West, J. (1945). *Plainville, U.S.A.* New York: Columbia University Press. One of the first descriptions by an anthropologist of life in a small U.S. town.

Glossary

Page references indicate where term is first defined.

acculturation the process in which one culture adapts to the influence of another culture by borrowing many of its traits 276, 302

achieved statuses social positions that one acquires by demonstrating the necessary role-playing abilities 113

adaptation adjustment of an organism to a particular environment 52

affectlessness the complete control of emotion resulting in lethargy 251

agriculture the intensive working of land for food production through the use of tools and techniques such as the plow, irrigation, soil fertilization, and animal traction 64

alienation dissociation of workers from ownership of things they produce accompanied by feelings of powerlessness and boredom 297

allomorphs variants of a single morpheme that have the same meaning but different phonological structure 197

allophones phonetically variant forms of a single phoneme 196

altered state of consciousness a stress-induced trance state 251

ambilineal descent descent through parent of either sex, choosing only one parent for each link that connects a group of relatives 139

ambilineal descent group social group based on an ambilineal descent system 141

ambilocality residence for newly married couple may be in home of bride or groom 173

American Anthropological Association major professional organization for anthropologists in the United States 18

American Sign Language (ASL) a system of hand gesture symbols used by hearing-impaired persons for communicating. Although it is not a verbal system of symbols, ASL may be seen as a true nonverbal language, since it has its own grammar and vocabulary and is not simply a gestural copy of spoken language 193

amok a culture-specific hysterical disorder in which young men attack other people and destroy property 262

ancestral spirits souls of ancestors who remain interested and involved in affairs of their descendants 215

anger an emotional state during which another person is held responsible for one's own distress. Anger can substitute for anxiety, fear, guilt, grief, or shame in situations in which those emotions might otherwise be felt 251

animal-focused foraging fish and animal life provide basic food supply where plants are scarce 57

anorexia nervosa a culture-specific obsessive-compulsive disorder characterized by an unrealistic appraisal of one's own body as overweight and by self-starvation 266

anthropological linguists cultural anthropologists who specialize in the study of communication, human languages, and its role in human social life 7

anthropomorphism using human qualities to explain the nonhuman realm; interpreting or acting toward the nonhuman realm as if it were human, especially as if it were able to respond to symbolic communication 211

anxiety a distressful subjective awareness of stress; a general sense of powerlessness and foreboding without awareness of a specific danger 249

anxiety disorder a form of neurosis in which there is ritualistic expression of apprehension or panic without awareness of any specific danger 262

applied anthropology the attempt to use anthropological skills and insights to aid in the process of cultural development in nonindustrialized parts of the world or to aid in private and public policymaking 315

archaeologists cultural anthropologists who study the material remains of earlier societies in order to reconstruct their cultures 5

arctic hysteria *(amurakh)* a culture-specific hysterical disorder that is characterized by compulsive imitation of sounds and gestures 263

357

arid lands areas of low annual rainfall sparsely covered by low-growing desert shrubs 51

ascribed statuses social positions that one is assumed to occupy by virtue of the group into which one happens to be born—for instance, one's sex or race 113

association cortex the area of the cerebral cortex that coordinates information from various other parts of the brain 195

attitude a subjective reaction to an experience expressed in positive or negative terms 27

authority those to whom power is delegated 90

avunculocality the custom in which the newly married couple establishes residence with or near the groom's mother's brother 173

balanced reciprocity gift given with expectation of a return gift shortly 76

band a seminomadic, kinship-based society with no full-time government, economically based on a foraging subsistence technology 54, 90, 280

barter form of exchange of goods by trading 81

Basic Law of Cultural Evolution concept that increases in production of energy through technological change is the primary cause of cultural evolution 276

basic vocabulary words for basic things expressed in all languages. Because such words are learned early in life and used with high frequency, they are more resistant to change than are words from other parts of a vocabulary 202

behavioral superstructure those behaviors most closely linked to a culture's ideology, including art, ritual, recreation, philosophy, science 43

beliefs ideas people hold about what is factual or real 25

berdache female or male who adopts the sex role of his or her opposite sex 162

bifurcate merging derives its kinship terminology from contrast between maternal and paternal relatives and use of a small number of kin terms to refer to many different kin 147

big man economic entrepreneurs of horticulture societies who have power to demand cooperation of others 80

bilateral cross-cousin marriage (sister exchange) cross-cousin marriage in which a brother and sister marry cross cousins who are also brother and sister 167

bilateral descent tracing descent lines equally through males and females 139

bilocality (ambilocality) the custom in which a newly married couple may elect to set up residence with or near either the bride's or the groom's family 173

bint'amm patrilateral parallel-cousin marriage 168

biological and psychological needs the needs for nutrition, reproduction, bodily comforts, safety, relaxation, movement, and growth 40

biological anthropologist physical anthropologist 7

biological death measured by cessation of such organic functions as breathing, heartbeat, reaction to pain, or brain functioning 132

blue collar workers nonfarm manual laborers 324

bone-pointing a magical ritual for killing in which a sharp bone or stick is pointed at or ritually cast into the body of the intended victim 223

boreal forests heavily wooded regions dominated by coniferous trees 51

bound morphemes morphemes that can't stand as complete words 197

Brahmin the highest ranked Hindu caste, members of which are theoretically priests 115

brain stem the parts of the brain, except the cerebral hemispheres and cerebellum, that regulate involuntary processes such as breathing and heartbeat 194

bride price (progeny price) goods transferred from the groom's kin to the bride's to recompense them for her loss 169

bride service service performed by the groom for the family of the bride to recompense them for her loss 170

bride wealth compensation to the family for the loss of their daughter through marriage 169

Broca's area the part of the cerebral cortex involved in organizing words into grammatical sequences 195

carrying capacity ability of a species to survive on the available resources in a particular environment 52

caste a social class membership determined by birth, so that an individual cannot legitimately change class membership by acquiring a new status 114

cerebellum the part of the brain below and behind the cerebral hemispheres of the brain that functions in the coordination of muscular activity 194

cerebral cortex the surface layer of the two large hemispheres of the brain that functions in the analysis of sensory experiences and initiates conscious action 194

chief presiding political official of a chiefdom society or of a subdivision of a chiefdom society, whose legal authority extends in at least some areas over members of families other than his or her own 80

chiefdom a society, often of many villages, that has a government capable of coordinating social action within and between villages but in which governmental authority is balanced by the legal autonomy of families in many areas 92, 287

chiefdom (rank society) a partially kinship-based society with a government that exercises authority in some areas of law over all families which are ranked with respect to each other 258

chromosomes coiled, threadlike structures in plant and animal cells that are largely made up of the DNA responsible for inheritance 22

circumcision the surgical removal of the foreskin from the penis 127

city-states state-level societies in which each city is politically autonomous 228

civil religion a system of religious beliefs and values that is integrated into the broader, nonreligious aspects of society and is shared by its members regardless of their affiliation with formally organized religious organizations; in America, a system of largely Judeo-Christian religious symbolism within which the American political system is portrayed as divinely sanctioned and American society is viewed as God's modern chosen people. 341

civilization a culture characterized by a state government, large populations and economic specialists, social classes, draft labor and government-sponsored public works projects, markets and long-distance trade, an increased emphasis on residence location over family ties in determining social roles and usually, urban centers, writing, and mathematics 227

clan kinship group whose members believe themselves descended from a common ancestor far enough in the past that they cannot trace their specific genealogical ties to one another 137, 142

clan (sib) generations of lineage based on a common ancestor who might not be remembered 142

class a broad, ranked stratum within society made up of unrelated families that have more or less equal power and prestige 114

closure the tendency to treat conceptual systems as if they were more complete than the incoming perceptual data 180

cognatic (nonunilineal) descent descent bilaterally or ambilineally 139

cognatic clan (ambilineal clan) clan based on ambilineal descent 142

cognative lineage (ramage, sept) lineages formed using an ambilineal descent system 142

colonial peasants peasant societies that were politically and economically dependent on a foreign state that perpetuated its economic exploitation of the peasant area by military domination 309

commodities what is useful or valuable in a particular culture 70

communal foraging cooperative food gathering where fish and small game are meat resources and plants are easily collected 55

communal religions religions that include the performance of rituals by groups of lay practitioners, shamans or individuals 231

communication the transfer of information using objects and events to as signs or symbols transfer that information 183

communitas Turner's definition that emphasizes role of ritual in helping people achieve a sense of unity with each other 219

competitiveness a central drive in American culture—fostered by the need to sell one's labor as a commodity—that emphasizes excelling over others 349

complementary statuses a pair of statuses, each of which have roles that are different from but compatible with the roles of the other 112

concepts mental models of experienced things, built from percepts 180

conformity a central drive in American culture, motivated by the obligation to defer to the authority of others in many areas of life 344

conspicuous consumption the acquisition and use of a surplus of goods as a way of competitively demonstrating one's success and prestige 84, 353

consumer market where basic needs of consumers are met

by the system of production and there is no competition for sales 86

consumption final use by a society of goods and services

contagious magic ritual coercion of the supernatural realm by the use of the Law of Contagion 220

contextual cues culturally defined indicators such as setting, date, time of day, or the statuses of other persons present, that determine which roles are appropriate and which are inappropriate to play 116

Contrary Warrior a Cheyenne status that required the reversal of all normal behaviors, reserved for the bravest warriors 246

corporate group organizations such as ambilineal and unilineal descent groups that continue to exist when individual members change 141

corporation associations of employers and employees that are legally entitled to act as a single person that produce goods or provide services 85

counterculture a movement of the 1960s that, in response to the increasing cost of living and the perceived non-responsiveness of the established political environment to people's changing needs and goals, attempted to reformulate the American value system by inverting many traditional values 252

court formalized institution that asserts authority over parties in a dispute and over persons accused of violating the law 98

couvade a custom in which the husband acts as if he gives birth to his child 124

creationism the fundamentalist religious view that the Judeo-Christian scriptures are best interpreted from a highly literal point of view and as a valid source of scientific knowledge about the origins of the world and living things 235

creativity deviance that results in valuable new contributions to society 249

crime the harming of a person or personal property by another 103

cross-cultural comparison basing general conclusions about the nature of culture and its influence on society on the comparison of a diverse sample of cultures from many parts of the world, so that those conclusions will be generally valid for the human condition as a whole 14

cross-cultural research research that bases its conclusions from data drawn from many diverse ways of life rather than just one 4

cross cousins cousins who are related through parents who are brother and sister 167

Crow kinship terminology in matrilineal descent systems, where father's matrilineage are distinguished only by sex regardless of generation 148

cultural anthropologists anthropologists who specialize in the study of culture in general, or of specific cultures 5

cultural ecology the study of the ways in which cultures adapt to their specific habitats 41

cultural evolutionism the nineteenth-century emphasis on analyzing cultures in terms of their development through a series of stages from savagery to civilization 15

cultural materialism analyzes technological and social variables in explaining ideological facts of culture 43

cultural relativism principle that cultural traits are best understood in the context of the cultural system of which they are a part; the attempt to avoid the narrow bias of judging the value of a custom or entire culture on the basis of the values of one's own culture; the view that meanings of behaviors are best understood when interpreted in terms of the culture of the actors 17, 33

culture a learned system of beliefs, feelings, and rules for living around which a group of people organize their

lives; a way of life of a particular society 23

culture and personality the study of how a culture's childrearing patterns influence the mental characteristics and values of a people 18

culture areas geographical areas in which different societies share a complex of cultural traits due to similar adaptations to their environmental zone and to the effects of diffusion of cultural traits through those societies 17

culture of poverty an approach to life often found in situations of poverty in which actions are directed only to satisfying the needs of the present, by spending and consuming all income, because saving for the future seems futile 314

culture shock the loneliness and depression that is often experienced when one is in a foreign cultural setting 31

cultures ways of life, the rules for living that guide the customs of specific societies 5

depression a mental disorder characterized by overt expression of a sense of personal worthlessness, failure, and sadness. In terms of role-playing, depression involves failure to make status-appropriate demands for honor 262

descent the concept of kinship connections between a child and one or both of his or her parent's kin 138

descriptive kinship terminology Sudanese kinship 149

developed country an nation in which industrialization has become the primary basis of the economy 305

developing country underdeveloped nation undergoing industrialization 305

deviance behavior that differs enough from what society expects that they notice and react to it 249

deviant a person who has been labeled a rule violator by others for his or her role-playing errors 258

dialect a geographical or social subdivision of a language that differs systematically from other such subdivisions of the same language in its vocabulary, grammar, and phonology 205

diffusion the passage of a cultural traits such as customs, artifacts, and ideas from one society to another 17, 274

diffusionism the early twentieth-century approach to analyzing cultures that emphasized the historical reconstruction of the influences of one culture on another in contrast to the more general evolutionary perspective of earlier anthropologists 17

direct borrowing the adopting of a cultural trait by one society from another with relatively little change in form, as exemplified by traits acquired through trade or imitation 274

discovery the development of new insights and ideas 274

disease object an object such as a barbed stick or stone that is magically cast into the body of a victim to cause illness 222

distribution movement of resources or goods from where they are found or produced to where they will ultimately be used 75

divination the use of ritual to obtain answers to questions from supernatural sources 221

division of labor the rules that govern how the day-to-day work of life is divided among the holders of various statuses 113

domestic economy the reproductive, economic, and social behaviors that characterize life within the family or household 43

double descent (double unilineal descent) two separate sets of kin, one designated through mothers only and the other through fathers only 140

double unilineal descent double descent 140

dowry a payment from the family of a bride to the family of her husband to compensate them for their acceptance of the responsibility of her support 171

drives the ideals that people actively pursue, sometimes at great cost, rather than those to which they merely give lip service 342

dry land gardening planting in arid environments using several forms of irrigation 60

ecclesiastical religions religions that include not only individual, shamanic, and communal ritual practices but also a coordinating body of priests who perform rituals on behalf of congregations 232

economics system by which people obtain or produce, distribute, and consume material goods and services 70

emic analysis description of a culture as it would have meaning for an insider 35

emotion a pleasant or unpleasant subjective reaction to an experience, characterized by varying degrees of muscle tension and changes in respiration and heart rate 26

empiricism the viewpoint that conclusions should be based on careful observation and description, rather than on abstract theorizing 16

enculturation (socialization) the process by which children learn the customs, beliefs, and values of their culture 126

endogamy rule requiring marriage within specified kinship categories or other specified social or local groups to which one belongs 167

energy a positive American reaction—fostered by the work ethic—to such traits as vigor, activity, personal effort, initiative, and youthfulness 348

environmental values defines our relationship to the environment 94

Era of Incipient Agriculture the period in which the first sedentary tribal societies developed by supplementing the collection of wild foods with some food domestication 294

Era of Regional Florescence the initial period of state government in the early civilizations when the political system was theocratic 294

Eskimo kinship terminology bilateral kinship system in which terms for mother, father, brother, and sister are not used for relatives outside the nuclear family 147

ethnocentrism the attitude that one's own culture is the only good one and that other cultures are more inferior to one's own the more they differ from it 31

ethnocide the systematic destruction of a traditional way of life 302

ethnographers cultural anthropologists who spend prolonged periods living with and describing the cultures of specific peoples 5

ethnographies descriptions of customs, beliefs, and values of individual societies 5

ethnologists cultural anthropologists who formulate general laws of culture based on the study of the ethnographies of many diverse societies 5

ethnoscience (cognitive anthropology) systematically describes a culture by analyzing the linguistic categories used by informants to discuss their society 39

etic analysis description of a culture in categories based on universal principles 35

eureka experience a sense of intensified meaningfulness of experiences that sometimes occurs during an altered state of consciousness 252

excision surgical removal of all or part of the female clitoris 128

exogamy rule a rule forbidding an individual from marrying a member of the kinship, residential, or other specified group to which he or she belongs 166

extended family the form of family that includes two or more nuclear families and, often, their parents who reside together 172

external warfare warfare which is fought for prolonged periods in locations distant from the warriors' home with enemies who speak a foreign language and follow an alien way of life 100

face positive social value a person can contribute to a group; social standing 247

face-work interaction in which effort is directed to maintaining or returning behavior to roles considered appropriate for members of a group; efforts to maintain or reestablish face 248

family the group consisting of married persons, their children, and other relatives who reside with them 172

fear a distressful emotion characterized by concerns about inadequate power to protect oneself from specific danger 249

feelings subjective reactions to experiences as pleasant or unpleasant, good or bad. Feelings include emotions, attitudes, and values 25

female circumcision mutilation of female genitals, including infibulation and excision, to prevent intercourse; a symbol of male dominance in some societies 128

female infanticide the killing of female infants, a practice that is often associated with internal warfare 100

feudal peasants preindustrialized societies in which peasant food producers pay rent or perform service for the privilege of farming lands owned by local aristocratic officials who have obligations to provide police and military protection, judicial services, and care for the peasants in times of hardship 308

feuds armed conflicts between kinship groups initiated to avenge a wrong 99

fictive kinship kinship relationships created by societies but not otherwise considered relatives either by descent or marriage 150

fictive marriage legal marriage established for both partners to acquire social benefits 161

fieldwork the basic tool of anthropological research in which information is gathered from the context in which it naturally occurs 7

Fissure of Rolando a vertical fold in the surface of the brain that separates the motor areas which control conscious muscle movement from corresponding areas which receive sensory information from various parts of the body 195

foraging a subsistence technology based on gathering wild plant foods, hunting, and fishing 53

formal learning learning that proceeds by admonition and correction of the learner's errors with emotional emphasis on the importance of behaving acceptably 126

Formative Era the period in history in which chiefdoms arose in various parts of the world 294

fraternal groups groups of related males who work together and feel obliged to protect one another's common interests 100

fraternal polyandry the form of polyandry in which the husbands are brothers 158

free morphemes morphemes that can stand as complete words 197

frigophobia (*pa-ling*) a culture-specific obsessive-compulsive disorder characterized by fear of loss of body heat 265

frontier areas lands opened to settlement by national governments that do not recognize the claims of the indigenous population 311

function the contribution that any one cultural trait makes to perpetuating the unity, equilibrium, and adaptation of a way of life within its environment 18

functionalism the approach to analyzing cultures by examining the mechanics of society while it is in equilibrium, as opposed to the more historical emphasis of diffusionism or the developmental emphasis of evolutionism 17

funeral rite a rite of passage that formalizes the removal of an individual from the status of living member of the social group 133

ganzfeld phenomenon the inability to perceive when visual contrasts are not maintained 183

General Adaptation Syndrome the nonspecific changes that occur in the body as a result of stress, as it mobilizes itself to act against that stress 224

general evolution the process in which a culture becomes qualitatively more complex as it develops the technological means for harnessing new and greater amounts of energy 295

generalized reciprocity gift given with no expectation of immediate exchange 75

general-purpose money universal medium of exchange used to buy and sell any item 82

genocide the systematic extermination of a people 304

ghost marriages fictive marriage where a close male kinsman of a man or boy—married or unmarried—who died before he had any legal heirs, marries a woman in the name of the deceased 161

gift exchange reciprocal exchange of gifts between families who are party to a marriage 171

glossolalia behavior in religious ecstasy that may include groaning and uttering unintelligible sounds 218

glottochronology a technique for calculating the minimal length of time that two related languages have been diverging from a common ancestral language 203

grammar the analysis of the regular ways that the sounds of a language are combined to form meaningful utterances. Grammar includes morphology and syntax 197

grasslands grasses of different types that cover 26 percent of the earth's surface 51

grief a distressful emotion characterized by a sense of loss, failure, and personal worthlessness 251

group two or more individuals engaged in a common activity 112

group marriage the form of marriage in which two or more men are married to two or more women at the same time 159

guilt a distressful emotion characterized by remorse for having harmed another 249

hallucination a realistic-seeming experience—much like a vivid waking dream—that may include vision, hearing, the sense of touch, smell, and/or taste in the absence of external cause 252

Hawaiian kinship terminology simplest kinship designation, using terms parents, siblings, and children 146

hermeneutic anthropology examines the interaction between fieldworker and native informant 38

holistic emphasizing the full range of relations among parts of a system and the ways the operation of those parts helps to perpetuate the whole system 4

homophilic marriage same-sex marriage without transvestism or change in sex role by one of the partners 163

homosexual marriage marriage between members of the same sex 162

honor the ability to influence others without coercion or the threat of coercion 114

horticulture cultivation of crops using simple hand tools such as the hoe and digging stick and without fertilization of the soil, crop rotation, and often without irrigation 59

household a group of people who share a common residence 172

hsieh-ping a culture-specific hysterical disorder that is characterized by tremor, disorientation, clouding of consciousness, delirium, speaking in tongues, and hallucinations 263

Human Relations Area Files (HRAF) a research data pool containing information on over 1,000 cultures, each coded for the presence or absence of about 800 cultural and environmental traits 14

human soul the supernatural part of the human being that is believed to animate the human body during life or perpetuate the individual's memories or life-goals after death 215

hypochondriasis a form of neurosis in which the ritualistic expression of anxiety takes the form of preoccupation with physical health and the body or of unfounded beliefs that one is suffering from dire illnesses 262

hysteria a form of neurosis in which there is ritualistic avoidance of anxiety or ritualistic manipulation of others as a means of avoiding failure 262

ice-zone regions of permanent snow and ice 51

ideal culture the ways people perceive their own customs and behaviors, often more a reflection of their feelings and ideals about what it should be rather than an accurate assesment of what it is 28

ideological communication communication that reaffirms people's allegiance to their groups and creates a sense of community by asserting its ideology 24

ideology the consciously shared beliefs and feelings that members of a society consider characteristic of themselves 24, 276

image of limited good a fatalistic outlook common in situations of peasant poverty in which the drudgery of life is not believed to bring much reward, since the achievement of one person can only be accomplished at the expense of another 314

imitative magic attempted ritual coercion of the supernatural realm by use of the Law of Similarity 220

Imperial Era of Cyclical Conquests the period of expansionist state government that followed the theocratic states of early civilizations 294

imu an hysterical disorder found among the Ainu of northern Japan characterized by automatic obedience or negativism and uncontrollable imitation of sounds and gestures 263

incest taboo a rule that forbids sexual behaviors between designated kin, including but not limited to intercourse between parents and children and among siblings 166

indigenous people a people whose occupation of an area precedes the state political system that now controls that area and who have little or no influence within that political system 302

indirect dowry payment of goods made by the groom or his family to the bride either directly to her or indirectly through her father 171

individual foraging men and women gather their own plant foods; women provide for the children 55

industrialization the process of change from an economy based on home production of goods to one based on large-scale, mechanized factory production 304

industrialized agriculture the use of an industrialized technology and other techniques such as chemical soil fertilization to obtain high levels of food production per acre 65

industrialized state a society coordinated by a state form of political organization and economically supported by an industrialized system of food production 293

infibulation surgical closing of the female vulva over the vagina 128

informal learning learning by imitation 126

insanity process by which a person acquires and maintains deviant master status of residual rule breaker 259

intensive peasant smallholdings areas of small, individually owned peasant farms in impoverished rural settlements with population densities equivalent to urban areas 311

intergenerational marriage male mentorship 164

internal warfare where fighting is between peoples who share the same language and culture 100

International Phonetic Alphabet (IPA) a standard alphabet of nearly 100 sound symbols used by linguists throughout the world for writing phonetic transcriptions of languages 196

interpretive anthropology explains how each element of a culture relates meaningfully to its original context 38

intimate distance the distance from their bodies that people reserve for those with whom they are intimate enough to permit casual touching 188

intragenerational marriages pathic marriage 163

invention the act of combining preexisting cultural traits in new ways 274

Iroquois kinship terminology bifurcate merging system like the Crow and Omaha but where there is no merging of generations in the lineage that marries into ego's lineage 148

irrigated farmlands territories occupied and worked by peasants but owned by absentee landlords in which the productive land has sufficient water to make farming possible 310

jati an occupational subcaste in Hindu society 115

jokes humor that allows people to relieve tensions 242

kayak angst a culture-specific phobic disorder that is characterized by an inordinate fear of being at sea in a kayak 265

kindred a kinship group in a bilateral descent system that consists of the known relatives of an individual 144

kinesics the study of the body movements that accompany speech as a component of communication 190

kinship group the individuals related to one another by ties of descent or by ties of marriage 138

koro a culture-specific anxiety disorder characterized by

fear of death through loss of sexual essence 265

Kshatriya the second most important of the Hindu castes, members of which were the traditional warrior-rulers, nobles, and landowners of society 115

labor reserve (remittance economy) areas peasant areas that have been impoverished by a drain of working-age laborers who have emigrated to urban areas to find employment 311

language a system of rules that govern the production and interpretation of speech 191

large farm (estate) areas lands owned by foreign corporations or governments and worked by peasant wage laborers who live in housing provided by the corporate or governmental owners 310

latah a culture-specific hysterical disorder that is characterized by uncontrollable imitation of the actions and speech of others 263

law cultural rules that regulate human behavior and maintain order 95

Law of Contagion the principle that things that have been in contact remain supernaturally in contact or that contact between things can be used to transfer *mana* from one to the other 220

Law of Cultural Dominance the concept that the technological capacity to harness the energy available in an environment is the major determinant of which culture will become socially and politically dominant within that environment 276

Law of Evolutionary Potential the concept that a culture's capacity to move from one general evolutionary stage to another varies inversely with the degree of its specific evolutionary adaptation to its environment 295

Law of Local Discontinuity of Progress the idea that the successive stages of general evolutionary change are not likely to occur in the same locality 296

Law of Similarity the principle that things that are similar to one another are spiritually identical, and can be used in rituals to influence a desired outcome 220

learning changes in behavior that result from interaction with the environment 180

legal authority legitimate right to compel others to obey the law and to punish violators of it 95

legal rights and duties rules that define relationships between people by specifying the type of recompense an injured person should receive 96

legends stories about heroic characters involved in the creation of a society 217

levirate rule that requires kin of a deceased man to provide his widow with another husband, often one of the deceased man's brothers 161

life cycle the status changes from birth to death that are typical of a particular society 120

limbic system areas within the brain that deal with emotional experience 195

liminal period transition stage between the beginning and end of a ritual 219

lineage a kinship group whose members can trace their lines of descent to the same ancestor 142

linguistic relativity the idea that the characteristics of a language influence the way that its speakers think 198

magic the use of rituals that are believed to compel—as opposed to simply making requests of—the supernatural when performed correctly 220

maintenance system the parts of the economic and social structure of a society that determine its childrearing practices 241

male mentorships system whereby older male initiates a younger male into culture of a society where the male is socially dominant 164

male-ranked polygyny with related co-wives a more

descriptive term for sororal polygyny 158

male-stratified form of polygamy in which a small number of men of high rank and authority marry a larger number of wives 158

mana supernatural power or force 210

manic episode a period of exhilaration and high activity that sometimes occurs in depression. It involves unrealistically high estimates of one's own honor, skill, or self-worth 262

marginal and hill farming lands peasant farming areas in which only hand farming techniques are feasible due to isolation, lack of sufficient water for irrigation, or the steepness of the land 311

market a system of distribution for goods and services based primarily on the use of established locations for obtaining them 80

market economy a form of distribution in which established places are used for the direct exchange of goods and services 290

marking the idea that the behaviors of a woman during pregnancy may influence the physical or psychological characteristics of the unborn child 336

marriage a rite of passage that unites two or more individuals as spouses 154

marriage preference rules system that singles out certain kin as ideal marriage partners 167

Marxist anthropology the study of the effects of class conflict on social and cultural change 40

master status a social status that is noticed by others even when the contextual cues present do not call for the playing of its roles; a status that is its own contextual cue 116

matriclan clan based on matrilineal descent 142

matrilateral cross-cousin marriage marriage between a male and his mother's brother's daughter 168

matrilineage tracing descent lines through mothers 142

matrilineal descent descent defined through mother only 140

matrilocality uxorilocality 173

mediation negotiation between conflicting parties carried out by a neutral third party 97

meta-communication system a system of communication that includes the capacity to communicate about itself 191

minority status a low ranked master status, commonly but incorrectly called a "minority group" 117

mixed forests temperate climate with conifers and broadleaf trees 50

modal personality type the most common or typical pattern of personality traits in a particular society 240

mode of production the work practices by which people apply their subsistence technology within a particular environment 43

mode of reproduction the technology and practices operating within a particular social environment that influence the size of the society's population 43

moiety one of two basic complementary social subdivisions of a society 144

money standard medium of value that is itself not usually consumed 81

monogamous marriage form of marriage where one man and one woman are joined as husband and wife 157

monotheism the belief in a high god, a supreme being who either created the physical universe and other spiritual beings and rules over them or who at least maintains the order of the universe today 215

monotheistic religions ecclesiastical religions in which one god is supreme over all other gods or supernatural beings or in which all of the gods or supernatural beings are thought of as merely alternative manifestations of a single Supreme Being 232

mood disorders psychological problems of feeling 262

moral values rules that govern our relationships with our fellow human beings 94

morpheme the smallest meaningful sequence of sounds in a language 197

morphology the study of how phonemes are combined into the smallest meaningful units of a language 197

mountain lands a variety of environments, often within close distances of one another 50

myths beliefs usually told in stories about the origins of the supernatural realm, the universe, and humans 217

naming ceremony a rite of passage following birth at which the infant is declared a member of the human group by being given a name 125

natural selection the process whereby those members of a species that are better adapted to their environment contribute more offspring to succeeding generations than do other members so that the species gradually acquires those adapting traits that made some individuals more adapted than others 52

negative reciprocity one group or individual in a reciprocal exchange system attempts to get more than it gives 78

neocortex the evolutionarily younger surface portion of the human brain that controls the learning of conscious behaviors 180

neofunctionalism contemporary approach to studying functional processes of cultural systems, with emphasis on the ways in which conflict may be one of the mechanisms by which cultural stability is maintained 41

neolocality the custom in which the newly married couple sets up residence in a new location apart from either of their families 173

neuroses mental disorders characterized by, and rituals expressing anxiety about, inadequate social power. (*singular*, neurosis) 262

nonindustrialized (or traditional) agriculture intensive crop cultivation using simple tools such as hoes, shovels, and animal-drawn plows 65

nonindustrialized state a society coordinated by a state form of political organization and economically supported by a labor-intensive, non-mechanized system of food production 293

nonkinship associations groups formed from members drawn from all parts of a community based on criteria other than kinship, such as age category or common interest, for the purpose of fulfilling specific responsibilities that affect the community as a whole 285

nonscientific beliefs beliefs that grow out of people's feelings 26

nonsexual marriages marriages that fulfill economic, social, and kinship functions without sexual union between the partners 161

nonunilineal descent cognatic descent 139

nonverbal communication all transfer of information other than with words. Nonverbal communication includes such things as volume, pitch, tone of voice, and speed when speaking, as well as non-oral things such as gestures, posture, and use of space and time 186

nuclear family the form of family that consists only of married persons and their children 172

oaths ritual acts of swearing innocence on pain of punishment by deities 98

obsessive-compulsive neurosis a form of neurosis in which the ritualistic expression of anxiety about failure takes the form of make-work rituals 262

Olympian religions polytheistic eccclesiastical religions in which the gods or supernatural beings may be loosely ranked but in which no one of the supernatural beings is truly supreme over the others 232

Omaha kinship terminology in patrilineal descent systems, where mother's patrilineage are distinguished only by sex regardless of generation 147

optimal foraging theory asserts that foragers use food resources directly proportional to the caloric effort required to obtain them 57

optimism a positive American expectation—fostered by the work ethic—that the future is potentially better than the present 348

ordeals test of guilt or innocence by enduring dangerous or painful acts 98

ownership the right to use and the right to deny use rights to others temporarily 73

parallel cousins cousins whose parents are either two brothers or two sisters 168

participant observation the technique of cultural anthropology in which the researcher spends a prolonged period participating and observing subjects in their natural setting, as opposed to studying them in a laboratory setting 8

pastoral and ranching areas places occupied by low-density populations spread over large areas within which they make their living by the herding of livestock 310

pastoralism a subsistence technology based on animal husbandry 62

pathic same sex marriage involving a *berdache* 163

patriclan clan based on patrilineal descent 142

patrilateral cross-cousin marriage marriage between a male and his father's sister's daughter 167

patrilateral parallel-cousin marriage (*bint'amm*) marriage between a male and his father's brother's daughter 168

patrilineage tracing descent lines through fathers 142

patrilineal descent descent defined through father only 140

patrilocality place of residence for newly married couples in or near the husband's family 173

peasants people who use non-industrialized, labor-intensive techniques for producing food and who are politically and economically subordinate to a governing class of which they are not a part and with whom they have little influence 307

pederasty male mentorship 164

percepts the basic units of information about experienced things out of which concepts are built 180

peri-urban squatter settlements densely settled, legally unrecognized communities near rapidly growing cities occupied by peasants whose subsistence is based on extremely small farms, petty trading, casual work, gardening, and other services performed for citizens of the nearby cities 314

permissive societies tolerant of childhood sexual experimentation 127

personal distance the distance to which people adjust themselves when interacting with close friends 188

personality (psychological definition) a consistent pattern to an individual's behavior resulting from a more or less enduring set of inner forces; (anthropological definition) the pattern of an individual's behavior that results from the various social roles that an individual plays 240

personality (anthropological definition) consistent pattern of behavior related to external, cultural, and social pressures 240

phobia a form of neurosis in which there is ritualistic expression of fears of things not culturally defined as appropriate objects of fear 262

phone the smallest sound unit of a language 196

phoneme the smallest psychologically real unit of sound in a language 196

phonemic pertaining to the phonemes of a language. A phonemic transcription is a written record of speech that uses an alphabet composed of only one symbol for each phoneme of the language 196

phonetic pertaining to the smallest units of sound actually produced by speakers of a language. A phonetic transcription attempts to record all of the sounds consistently produced by the speakers of a language 196

phonology the study of the rules that govern the production and the organization of the sounds of a particular language 196

phratry group of clans thought to be related by kinship 144

physical (biological) anthropologists anthropologists who specialize in the study of the evolutionary origins of the human species, the relationships between the human species and other living primates, the physical variation within the human species today, and the relationships between human biology and our species's cultural capacities 7

pibloktoq a culture-specific hysterical disorder characterized by agitated attempts to flee the presence of other people 263

piety defines our relationship to the supernatural 94

pink collar occupations pertaining to service occupations that largely are held by women 323

plant-focused foraging plant resources are readily available, allowing hunting expeditions far from campsite 56

polar lands regions of cold climates near north and south poles 51

political economy the reproductive, economic, and social behaviors that are typical of life outside the family or household 43

politics manner in which power is achieved and used to create and implement public goals 89

polyandrous marriage the form of marriage in which one woman has more than one husband 158

polygamy form of marriage where a person is permitted to have more than one spouse at the same time 157

polygynous marriage form of marriage in which a man has more than one wife 157

polytheism the belief in superior (but not supreme) gods, each of whom controls or rules over some major aspect of the universe 215

potassium-argon dating an absolute dating technique for materials between 100,000 and 4.6 billion years old based on the known rate of decay of radioactive potassium 40 into argon 40 27

power the ability to exercise coercion 114

prairies areas with tall varieties of grass that tolerate wetter climates 51

Pre-Agricultural Era the period of foraging bands 294

pregnancy rituals religious rules such as taboos designed to protect the unborn child and the mother during pregnancy and childbirth or admonitions to engage in acts believed to be a positive influence on the developing child 123

priests religious practitioners who perform rituals for the benefit of groups. Often, priests are full-time religious practitioners whose emphasis is on preserving the established ritual forms, rather than on inspiration and innovation in the application of their rituals 232

primary institutions the parts of social life related to child-rearing, including the family and other primary care groups, feeding, weaning, care or neglect of children, sexual training, and subsistence patterns 241

Principle of Stabilization the concept that as a culture becomes efficient at harnessing energy for society, the more expensive and difficult it becomes to implement new means of increasing efficiency 295

professionals self-employed, college-educated service providers 325

progeny price bride wealth 169

"protective" legislation laws that are ostensibly intended to prevent the exploitation of women, but which in practice create social barriers against the full participation of women in social life outside the domestic sphere; for instance, many states in the U.S. have laws that prohibit the hiring of women into occupations that require the employee to lift more than 35 pounds 332

Proto-Germanic the ancestral language from which modern Germanic languages developed, including English, Dutch, German, Norwegian, Danish, and Swedish 201

Proto-Indo-European the ancestral language from which most of the contemporary languages of Europe, Iran, and India have developed 203

proverbs short statements, often inserted into conversations as admonitions, that embody the basic values of a culture 241

proxemics the study of how people structure the space around them when interacting with others 188

psychological death the process by which one subjectively prepares for impending biological death 132

puberty (adulthood) ritual a rite of passage that formalizes the change from the status of child to the status of adult 127

public distance the distance reserved for separating people whose interaction is not intended to perpetuate a social relationship 190

purposefulness a manifestation of the American work ethic that asserts the importance of goal-directed effort 348

racism the belief that differences in the expected roles of members of different racial groups are based on the hereditarily controlled behavioral predispositions of those groups 119

raids organized violence by one group against another to achieve economic benefit 100

ramage cognatic lineage 142

range management planning for effective use of land for raising livestock without depleting the environment 316

rank the relative importance of a status or group as measured by the amount of power and/or honor to which it is entitled 113

real culture culture portrayed in terms of the actually observable behaviors of a people 28

rebellion organized and violent opposition to the legitimacy of a society's current governing authority 106

reciprocity sharing of surpluses with the understanding that the party receiving the gift will respond in kind in the future but with no explicit agreement about when and with what 75

redistribution commodities are contributed by all members of a group to a common pool from which they will be distributed to where they will be used 79

reincarnation the belief that the soul of a human being may be repeatedly reborn into the human group to which it previously belonged or as an animal that may be symbolically associated with that group 215

religion beliefs concerning supernatural powers and beings and rituals designed to influence those beings and powers; a system through which people interpret the nonhuman realm as if it were human and seek to influence it through symbolic communication 210

reservations territories within a region controlled by a state political system that are set aside for the occupation of indigenous peoples 302

residual rules miscellaneous, normally unspoken rules that people are expected to follow to avoid violating the pattern or style of behavior that permeates the rest of the culture 258

restrictive societies societies that do not accept childhood sexual experimentation 127

retribution personal use of force to redress wrongs in simple societies with no centralized governmental authority 99

revolution organized use of force to alter the very form of government 106

riddles entertaining puzzles that describe common things in novel ways 242

rite of passage (life crisis rite) a ritual that formalizes a major change in social status 120

ritual behaviors, often performed in repetitive and stereotyped ways, that express people's anxieties by acting them out. May be an attempt to influence the supernatural realm to achieve greater control over the natural world 212, 255

role the skills, abilities, and ways of acting towards others that belong to each status of a society 113

role conflict emotional discomfort and confusion experienced in situations in which conflicting contextual cues indicate that an individual should play the roles of more than one of his or her statuses 116

sacred Durkheim's definition that included feelings of respect, awe, and reverence inspired by things set apart and forbidden 212

saka a culture-specific hysterical disorder that is characterized by repetition of actions or sounds believed to be a foreign language and loss of consciousness with body rigidity 263

sanction action taken by legal authorities responding to violations of law 96

savannas tall grasses and drought-resistant undergrowth found in tropical areas 51

scarification decorating the body by cutting designs in it and treating them with ashes or other material to ensure that they will produce raised scars 127

schizophrenia a mental disorder characterized by residual rule breaking caused by difficulty in communicating an acceptable social identity. Schizophrenia may include hallucinations and ideas about reality that are greatly at odds with mainstream ideas 261

scientific beliefs beliefs that are based on the desire to solve the practical day-to-day problems of living 26

scrub forests regions between coasts and mountains with mild, wet winters and hot, dry summers 50

secondary institutions the institutions in social life that satisfy the needs and tensions created by the primary institutions, including especially taboo systems, religion, rituals, folk tales, and techniques of thinking 241

sedentarism living in permanent or semipermanent settlements 59

self-reliance a value central to America that emphasizes the importance of independence, autonomy of the individual, and the primacy of the individual over the group 346

semirestrictive societies accepting of childhood sexual experimentation so long as those involved follow established rules of etiquette and discretion 127

sept cognatic lineage 142

serial monogamy a marriage pattern in which individuals of either sex may have only one spouse at a given time, but through divorce and remarriage may have several spouses during their lifetime 157, 336

serotonin a chemical produced in the brain during waking hours that inhibits the production of dreams or hallucinations 252

sexism the belief that differences in the sex roles of males and females are biologically determined 119

shamanic religions religions in which the only ritual specialist is the shaman and which contain only individual and shamanic ritual practices 228

shamans part-time religious practitioners who are believed to have access to supernatural power that may be used for the benefit of specific clients, as in healing or divining 225

shame (embarrassment) a distressful emotion characterized by a sense of personal ineptness resulting in damage to one's reputation 251

shifting cultivation slash and burn horticulture 60

sib clan 142

sign an object or event that represents another object or event because of a similarity between them or a tendency for the two to occur together in nature 183

signalized behavior normally symbolic behavior (especially speech) that has become more expressive of feelings and less indicative of the factual information it usually conveys 256

sin a form of taboo violation in which the rule breaker is thought of as morally responsible for the act 223

sister exchange form of cross-cousin marriage in which a brother and sister marry cross cousins who are also sister and brother to each other 167

slash and burn cultivation a form of farming in which the land is prepared by cutting and burning the natural growth and in which several plots, in various stages of soil depletion, are worked in a cycle 60

sleep crawling a Samoan sexual practice in which an uninvited youth would enter a young woman's house with the intent of seduction 129

social anthropology Radcliffe-Brown's idea that social interactions are important in determining customs of a culture 39

social death the point at which people respond to a person with the behaviors appropriate to one who is biologically dead 132

social distance the distance to which people adjust themselves when interacting in impersonal situations such as business transactions 190

social organization the relationships between the groups, statuses, and division of labor that structure the interaction of people within society 112, 276

social structure the part of social organization made up of groups and their relationships with each other 39, 112

socialization the process of learning a culture and the role-playing skills necessary for social life 93

sociobiology emphasis on role of natural selection on genetic predispositions for specific behaviors 42

sodality volunteer associations whose members are drawn from several tribal families 91

sorcerers practitioners of magical rituals that are done to harm others 227

sorcery the learned use of rituals to magically control the supernatural realm to achieve human goals 215

sororal polygyny the form of polygyny in which the wives are sisters 158

sororate a rule that requires the kin of a deceased woman to provide her widower with another wife, often one of the deceased woman's sisters 161

soul loss in primitive societies, the belief that the departure of the soul from the body, usually caused by a sudden fright, causes the body to weaken and die 222

special-purpose money medium of exchange restricted to the buying and selling of a single commodity 81

specific evolution the process in which a culture becomes better adapted to its specific environment by using the available energy more efficiently 295

speech an audible sequence of verbal symbols 191

speech motor area the part of the cerebral cortex that controls the production of speech sounds 195

spirit possession trance a trance in which individuals feel as if their behavior is under the control of one or more spirits that have entered their bodies 223, 254

spirit travel trance a trance in which individuals experience

themselves as leaving their bodies 254

spiritual values defines our relationship to the supernatural 94

states societies with centralized governments that monopolize the legal authority to use force 93, 290

status a culturally defined relationship that one individual may have with one or more other individuals; the position within a group that each member holds 112

status income goods produced over and above subsistence needs 84

status pair two statuses that together form one of the relationships that may exist between people in a particular culture 112

status-appropriate roles the ways of behaving that are culturally defined as expected of an individual who holds a particular social status 247

steppes short, hardy variety of grass that covers stretches of southeastern Europe and Asia 51

stigma loss of rank that accompanies the social rejection of persons who have violated accepted role behavior 249

stimulus diffusion the borrowing of the idea for a cultural trait by one society from another, with the implementation of that idea being more or less determined within the borrowing culture 274

stress a physiological response to any demand characterized by the body's preparing itself for action 251

structural-functionalism determining customs of a culture by the analytical method of social anthropology 39

structuralism Lévi-Strauss's concept of underlying unity of all cultures to think in dualities 36

subsistence how people obtain the necessities of life, particularly food, from the environment 53

subsistence economy when people consume most of what they produce 83

subsistence income each family produces goods for its own consumption 83

subsistence technology the tools and techniques by which people obtain food 53

Sudanese kinship (descriptive kinship) terminology occurring mostly in North Africa, this system distinguishes maternal and paternal relatives by separate terms 149

Sudra the lowest of the Hindu castes, made up of farm artisans, servants, farmers, and laborers 115

supernatural that which transcends the natural, observable world 211

supernatural sanctions for violations of moral rules punishments for immoral acts by spiritual agencies as opposed to human agencies. In most societies, the enforcement of morality is a strictly human responsibility, rather than a religious preoccupation 215

survivals remnants of earlier social customs and ideas that can be used for reconstructing the evolutionary past of societies 16

susto (espanto, pasmo) culture-specific anxiety disorder with depressive features interpreted by the victim as caused by soul loss 265

swidden horticulture slash and burn horticulture 60

symbol an object or event that represents another object or event only because of the agreement between people that it will 24, 184

symbolic marriages those marriages not establishing economic and social ties between kinship groups 160

symmetrical statuses a pair of statuses each of which has the same roles to play in respect to the other 112

syntax the study of the rules for combining morphemes into complete and meaningful sentences 197

Systema Naturae the book in which Carolus Linnaeus classified plants and animals into a hierarchical system based on their degree of similarity to one another 15

taboo a rule forbidding contact with sacred things, those containing *mana* 211

taboo violation the breaking of a supernatural rule, whether intentional or not. Taboo violations are often believed to be a cause of illness 223

taiga swampy coniferous forests of the northern lands south of the tundras 51

technical learning learning that occurs when the logical rationales for specific ways of doing things—rather than emotional pressure to behave in that way—are given to the learner 126

technology tools and techniques through which human beings harness the energy available in their environment 40, 276

teknonymy the custom of referring to a person as the parent of their child rather than by their birth name 130

tenant or refugee farms farms worked by laborers who were dispossessed when the traditional system of mutual obligations between landowners and the tenant farmers was replaced by a system in which the farming is simply a paid labor 313

trance (altered state of consciousness) subjective states of mind where experiences are not interpreted in terms of normal symbolic categories of one's culture 251

transhumance migratory way of life in pastoralism 62

transvestism gender-mixed or cross-sex dressing 163

tribe a semisedentary kinship-based society without a full-time government. Most tribal societies are economically based on a simple food do-mestication subsistence technology, either horticulture or pastoralism 91, 284

tropical forests regions with warm climates and abundant rainfall, plants, and animal life 50

tundra level treeless plains in the arctic and subarctic regions of North America, Asia, and Scandinavia 51

underdeveloped country nation with a largely nonindustrialized economy 305

unilineal descent descent through a single sex line rather than both parents equally 139

unilineal descent group social groups based on a matrilineal or patrilineal descent system 141

universal application principle that legal authority should apply uniformly in similar situations 96

unskilled laborers low-paid workers, including part-time or seasonal workers, who usually are paid by the hour or for the quantity of goods they produce 323

Untouchables the lowest status members of Hindu society who belonged to none of the traditional castes and who performed the ritually polluted tasks of life 115

uxorilocality (matrilocality) the custom in which a newly married couple is expected to set up residence with or near the bride's family 173

Vaisya the third Hindu caste, comprised of commoners 115

value a subjective reaction to experiences expressed in terms of good or bad, moral or immoral; the ideals that people long for but do not necessarily pursue. Values are often opposites of drives 27, 94, 342

virilocality (patrilocality) custom where a newly married couple is expected to set up their residence with or near the groom's family 173

voodoo death (magical death) death that occurs following a magical ritual performed to kill 223

war organized, armed conflict between political communities 100

wealth-increasing polygyny male-stratified polygyny 158

Wernicke's area the part of the cerebral cortex involved in processing speech sounds 195

white collar occupations pertaining to service-providing occupations such as clerical, sales, managerial, and administrative jobs 325

witchcraft the innate ability to influence supernatural forces to operate usually in ways that are harmful to others without the necessity of using rituals 216

witches persons believed to have the innate supernatural ability to harm others without the use of ritual 228

women exchange rather than exchange of gifts between families, they exchange women, losing a daughter but gaining a daughter-in-law 172

work ethic a central drive of American culture in which work is felt to be good in and of itself—a feeling fostered by an economic system in which individuals must work competitively to produce goods that they themselves do not own and that will be consumed by others 347

Bibliography

Abd Allah, M. M. (1917). Siwan customs. *Harvard African Studies, 1, 7.*

Aberle, D. F. (1961). 'Arctic hysteria' and latah in Mongolia. In Y. A. Cohen (Ed.), *Social structure and personality: A casebook* (pp. 471–475). New York: Holt, Rinehart & Winston.

Adam, B. D. (1981). *Christianity, social tolerance and homosexuality: A symposium.* Paper presented at the Society for the Study of Social Problems, Ontario, Canada.

Adam, B. D. (1986). Age, structure, and sexuality: Reflections on the anthropological evidence on homosexual relations, *Journal of Homosexuality, 11*(3/4), 19–33.

Agar, M. H. (1980). *The professional stranger: An informal introduction to ethnography.* New York: Academic Press.

Altman, S. A. (1973). Primate communication. In G. A. Miller (Ed.), *Communication, language and meaning: Psychological perspectives* (pp. 84–94). New York: Basic Books, Inc.

Angeloni, E. (Ed.). (1987). *Annual Editions: Anthropology.* Guilford, CT: The Dushkin Publishing Group.

Baal, J. van. (1966). *Dema.* The Hague: Martinus Nijhoff.

Barker-Banfield, G. J. (1983). The spermatic economy: A nineteenth century view of sexuality. In Dr. T. Altherr (Ed.), *Procreation or pleasure: Sexual attitudes in American history* (pp. 47–70). Malabar, FL: Robert E. Krieger Publishing.

Barnes, G. H., & Dummond, D. W. (Eds.). (1934). *Letters of Theodore Dwight Weld, Angelina Grimké Weld and Sarah Grimké: 1822–1844* (Vol. 1). New York: Appleton-Century.

Barnouw, V. (1985). *Culture and personality.* (4th ed.). Homewood, IL: Dorsey.

Barry, H., III, Child, I. L., & Bacon, M. K. (1959). Relation of child training to subsistence economy. *American Anthropologist, 61,* 51–63.

Barth, F. (1954). Father's brother's daughter marriage in Kurdistan. *Southwestern Journal of Anthropology, 10*(1), 164–171.

Basedow, H. (1925). *The Australian aboriginal.* Adelaide: F. W. Preece and Sons.

Bateson, G. (1936). *Naven: A survey of the problems suggested by a composite picture of the culture of a New Guinea tribe drawn from three points of view.* Cambridge, MA: Cambridge University Press.

Beals, A. M. (1974). *Village life in south India.* Chicago: Aldine.

Beals, A. M. (1980). *Gopalpur.* New York: Holt, Rinehart & Winston.

Bean, S. S. (1981). Soap operas: Sagas of American kinship. In S. Montague & W. Arens (Eds.), *The American dimension: Cultural myths and social realities* (pp. 61–75). Sherman Oaks, CA: Alfred Publishing Co.

Beattie, J. (1964). *Other cultures: Aims, methods, and achievements in social anthropology.* New York: Free Press.

Becker, H. S. (1963). *Outsiders: Studies in the sociology of deviance.* NY: Free Press.

Behnam, D. (1985). The Tunis conference. *Current Anthropology, 26,* 555–556.

Bellah, R. (1967). Civil religion in America. *Daedelus.* Winter, 1–21.

Benedict, R. B. (1932). Configurations of culture in North America. *American Anthropologist, 34,* 1–27.

Benedict, R. F. (1934). *Patterns of culture.* Boston, MA: Houghton Mifflin.

Bernard, H. R., & Pelto, P. J. (Eds.). (1972). *Technology and social change.* New York: Macmillan.

Binford, L. R. (1968). Post-Pleistocene adaptations. In L. R. Binford & S. R. Binford (Eds.), *New perspective in archaeology* (pp. 22–49). Chicago: Aldine.

Bird, C. (1973). *Born female: The high cost of keeping women down.* New York: David McKay.

Birdwhistell, R. L. (1970). *Kinesics and context: Essays on body motion communication.* Philadelphia, PA: University of Pennsylvania Press.

Black, D. (1976). *The behavior of law.* New York: Academic Press.

Bloomfield, L. (1933). Dialect geography. In H. Hoijer (Ed.), *Language history* (pp. 321–345). New York: Holt, Rinehart & Winston, Inc.

Blount, B. G. (1974). *Language, culture and society: A book of readings.* Cambridge, MA: Winthrop.

Blumenbach, J. (1775). *De Generis Humani Varietate Nativa*. Göttingen. Translated by T. Yshe as *On the natural history of mankind* (1865) in The Anthropological Treatises of Blumenbach and Hunter (p. 145–276). London: Anthropological Society.

Boas, F. (1888). *The central Eskimo*. (Annual Report, 6). Washington, D.C.: Bureau of American Ethnology.

Boas, F. (1911). Handbook of American Indian languages. Smithsonian Institution, Bureau of American Ethnology, Bulletin 40. Washington, DC: Government Printing Office.

Bodley, J. H. (1975). *Victims of progress*. Menlo Park, CA: Cummings.

Bogoras, W. (1907). *The Chukchee—religion*. (Memoirs of the American Museum of Natural History, No. 11, Part 2). New York: American Museum of Natural History.

Bohannan, P. (1955). Some principles of exchange and investment among the Tiv. *American Anthropologist, 57*, 60–70.

Bohannan, P. (1963). *Social anthropology*. New York: Holt, Rinehart & Winston.

Bohannan, P., & Glazer, M. (Eds.). (1973). *High points in anthropology*. New York: Alfred A. Knopf.

Bohannan, P., & Middleton, J. (Eds.). (1968). *Marriage, family, and residence*. New York: Natural History Press.

Bonwick, J. (1884). *The lost Tasmanian race*. London: S. Low, Marston, Searle, & Rivington.

Boserup, E. (1965). *The condition of agricultural growth: The economics of agrarian change under population pressures*. Chicago: Aldine-Atherton.

Boswell, J. (1980). *Christianity, social tolerance and homosexuality: Gay people in western Europe from the beginning of the Christian era to the fourteenth century*. Chicago: University of Chicago Press.

Bourguignon, E. (1974). Culture and the varieties of consciousness. *Addison-Wesley Module in Anthropology* (No. 47). Reading, MA: Addison-Wesley Publishing.

Bourguignon, E., & Greenberg, L. (1973). *Homogeneity and diversity in world societies*. New Haven, CT: Human Relations Area Files.

Briggs, J. (1980). "Kapluna daughter: Adopted by the Eskimo." In Spradley & D. McCurdy (Eds.), *Conformity and Conflict* (4th ed., pp. 44–62). Boston: Little, Brown & Company.

Brown, J. (1963). A cross-cultural study of female initiation rites. *American Anthropologist, 656*, 837–853.

Buchsbaum, M. S. (1979). Tuning in an hemispheric dialogue. *Psychology Today, 12*(8), 100.

Bunzel, R. (1952). *Chichicastenango: A Guatemalan village* (Monographs of the American Ethnological Society, 22). New York: J. J. Augustin.

Burch, E. S., Jr. (1970). Marriage and divorce among the north Alaska Eskimos. In P. Bohannan (Ed.), *Divorce and after*. Garden City, NY: Doubleday.

Burch, E. S., Jr. (1975). *Eskimo kinsmen: Changing family relationships in northwest Alaska*. American

Ethnological Society Monograph 59. St. Paul: West.

Burgess, F. W., & Wallin, P. (1953). Homogamy in social characteristics. *American Journal of Sociology, 49*, 109–124.

Burling, R. (1970). *Man's many voices: Language in the cultural context*. New York: Holt, Rinehart & Winston.

Byrne, D. (1977), A pregnant pause in the sexual revolution. *Psychology Today, 11*(2), 67–68.

Calder, J. E. (1874). Some accounts of the wars of extermination, and habits of the native tribes of Tasmania. *Journal of the Anthropological Institute of Britain and Ireland, 3*.

Callender, C., & Kochems, L. (1983). The North American berdache. *Current Anthropology, 23*(4), 443–456.

Campbell, S. (1983). Kula in Vakuta: The mechanics of *keda*. In J. Leach & E. Leach (Eds.), *The kula: New perspectives on Massim exchange*. Cambridge: Cambridge University Press.

Cannon, W. B. (1942). Voodoo death. *American Anthropologist, 44*, 169–181.

Carniero, R. (1970). A theory of the origin of the state. *Science, 169*, 733–738.

Carniero, R. (1978). Political expansion as an expression of a principle of competitive exclusion. In R. Cohen & E. Service (Eds.), *Origins of the state* (pp. 205–233). Philadelphia, PA: ISHI.

Carroll, J. B. (1956). *Language, thought and reality: Selected writings of Benjamin Lee Whorf*. Cambridge, MA: M.I.T. Press.

Casagrande, J. B. (Ed.). (1960). *In the company of man: Twenty portraits by anthropologists*. New York: Harper & Row.

Cassirer, E. (1944). *An essay on man: An introduction to a philosophy of human culture*. New Haven, CT: Yale University Press.

Chagnon, N. A. (1968). *Yąnomamö: The fierce people*. New York: Holt, Rinehart & Winston.

Chagnon, N. A. (1974). *Studying the Yąnomamö*. New York: Holt, Rinehart & Winston.

Chagnon, N.A. (1977). *Yąnomamö: The fierce people* (2nd ed.). New York: Holt, Rinehart & Winston.

Chomsky, N. (1965). *Aspects of the theory of syntax*. Cambridge, MA: The M.I.T. Press.

Chomsky, N. (1971). Language acquisition. In J. P. B. Allen & P. Van Buren (Eds.), *Chomsky: Selected readings* (pp. 127–148). London: Oxford University Press.

Clements, F. E. (1932). *Primitive concepts of disease*. (Publications in American Archaeology and Ethnology, 32[2]). Berkeley, CA: University of California Press.

Cline, W. (1936). Notes on the people of Siwah and El Garah in the Libyan desert. *General Series in Anthropology*. Menasha: Banta.

Codere, H. (1950). *Fighting with property*. (Monographs of the American Ethnological Society, 18). New York: J. J. Augustin.

Coe, R. (1970). *The sociology of medicine*. New York: McGraw-Hill.

Cohen, W. (1957). Spatial and textural characteristics of the ganzfield. *American Journal of Psychology, 70,* 403–410.

Cohen, Y. A. (1964). *The transition from childhood to adolescence: Cross cultural studies in initiation ceremonies, legal systems, and incest taboos.* Chicago: Aldine.

Cohen, Y. A., (Ed.) 1974. *Man in adaptation: The cultural present.* Chicago: Aldine.

Cohn, W. (1967). "Religion" in non-western culture? *American Anthropologist, 69,* 73–76.

Conklin, H. C. (1956). Hanunóo color categories. *Southwestern Journal of Anthropology, 11,* 339–344.

Cooper, J. M. (1946). The Yahgan. In J. H. Steward (Ed.), *Handbook of South American Indians* (Vol. 1, pp. 97–98). Washington, DC: Smithsonian Institution, Bureau of American Ethnology. Bulletin 143.

Coult, A. D., & Habenstein, R. W. (1965). *Cross tabulations of Murdock's world ethnographic sample.* Columbia, MO: University of Missouri Press.

Council of State Governments, The. (1986). State elective officials & the legislature: 1985–86. Lexington, KY: Author.

Crane, J., & Angrosino, M. V. (1974). *Field projects in anthropology: A student handbook.* Morristown, NJ: General Learning Press.

Crapo, Richley H. (1987). Sexuality and kinship: Factors in the cross-cultural patterning of homosexuality. Paper presented at the annual meetings of the American Anthropological Association, Chicago.

Critchfield, R. (1981). *Villages.* Garden City, NY: Doubleday Anchor Press.

Culbert, S. S. (Ed.). (1982). *The world almanac and book of facts.* New York: Newspaper Enterprise Association.

Czaplicka, M. A. (1914). *Aboriginal Siberia: A study in social anthropology.* Oxford, CT: Clarendon.

Dahlberg, F. (Ed.). (1981). *Woman the gatherer.* New Haven, CT: Yale University Press.

Dalby, L. (1985). *Geisha.* New York: Random House, Vintage Books.

Dalton, G. (1969). Theoretical issues in economic anthropology. *Current Anthropology, 10,* 63–102.

D'Andrade, R. (1961). The anthropological study of dreams. In F. L. K. Hsu (Ed.), *Psychological anthropology* (pp. 296–332). Homewood, IL: Dorsey.

Darwin, C. (1857). *On the origin of species.* New York: Atheneum.

Deacon, A. (1934). *Malekula: A vanishing people in the New Hebrides.* London: Routledge.

Dentan, R. K. (1968). *The Semi: A nonviolent people of Malaya.* New York: Holt, Rinehart & Winston.

Dentan, R. K. (1988). Rejoinder to Nanda. *American Anthropologist, 90*(2), 423.

De Toqueville, A. (1969). *Democracy in America.* New York: Knopf. Originally published as *De la démocratie en Amérique* (1835). London: Saunders & Otley.

Devale, W. T., & Harris, M. (1976). Population, warfare and the male supremacist complex. *American Anthropologist, 78,* 521–538.

DeVore, P. (1965). Language and communication. In P. L. Devore (Ed.), *The origin of man* (pp. 77–77a). New York: The Wenner-Gren Foundation for Anthropological Research.

Dibble, C. E., & Anderson, A. J. O. (Trans.). (1950–1969). *Florentine codex: General History of the things of New Spain* (Vols. 1-12). Salt Lake City, UT: The School for American Research and the University of Utah.

Divale, W. (1972). Systematic population control in the middle and upper Paleolethic: Inferences based on contemporary hunters and gatherers. *World Archaeology, 4,* 222–243.

Divale, W., Chambaris, F., & Gangloff, D. (1976). War, peace and marital residence in pre-industrial societies. *Journal of Conflict Resolution, 20,* 57–78.

Divale, W., & Harris, M. (1976). Population, warfare and the male supremacist complex. *American Anthropologist, 78,* 521–538.

Douglas, M. (1966). *Purity and danger: An analysis of conflicts of pollution and taboo.* New York: Praeger and London: Routledge & Kegan Paul.

Douglas, M., & Isherwood, B. (1979). *The world of goods: Toward an anthropology of consumption.* New York: W. W. Norton.

Dover, K. J. (1978). *Greek homosexuality.* New York: Vintage Books.

Downie, D. C., & Hally, D. J. (1961). A cross-cultural study of male transvestism and sex-role differentiation. Unpublished manuscript. Dartmouth College.

DuBois, C. (1944). *People of Alor: A social psychological study of an East Indian island* (Vols. 1-2). Minneapolis, MN: University of Minnesota Press.

DuBois, C. (1955). The dominant value profile of American culture. *American Anthropologist, 57,* 1232–1239.

Duff-Cooper, A. (1985). Notes about some Balinese ideas and practices connected with sex from western Lombok. *Anthropos, 80*(4/6), 403–419.

Dumont, J. P. (1978). *The headman and I: Ambiguity and ambivalence in the fieldwork experience.* Austin: University of Texas Press.

Dumont, L. (1970). *Homo heirarchicus.* Chicago: University of Chicago Press.

Durkheim, E. (1915). *The elementary forms of the religious life.* J. W. Swain (Trans.). London: Allen & Unwin. (Original work published 1912)

Eastwell, H. D. (1982). Voodoo death and the mechanism for dispatch of the dying in East Arnhem, Australia. *American Anthropologist, 84,* 5–18.

Edgerton, R. B. (1976). *Deviance: A cross-cultural perspective.* Menlo Park, CA: Cummings.

Eichenlaub, J. E. (1963). *The marriage art.* New York: Dial Press.

Eliade, M. (1964). *Shamanism: Archaic techniques of ecstasy.* Princeton, NJ: Princeton University Press.

Ella, S. (1895). The ancient Samoan government. *Australasian Association for the Advancement of Science, 5.* Brisbane, Australia.

Ember, M. (1982). Statistical evidence for an ecological explanation of warfare. *American Anthropologist, 84,* 645–649.

Ember, M., & Ember, C. R. (1983). *Marriage, family, and kinship: Comparative studies of social organization.* New Haven, CT: HRAF.

Emerson, O. (1923). *A Middle English reader.* New York: Macmillan.

Erikson, K. T. (1962). Notes on the sociology of deviance, *Social Problems, 9,* 307–314.

Evans-Pritchard, E. E. (1937). *Witchcraft, oracles and magic among the Azande.* Oxford: Clarendon.

Evans-Pritchard, E. E. (1940). *The Nuer: A description of the mode of livelihood and political institutions of a Nilotic people.* London: Oxford University Press.

Evans-Pritchard, E. E. (1951). *Kinship and marriage among the Nuer.* New York: Oxford University Press.

Evans-Pritchard, E. E. (1956). *Nuer religion.* Oxford: Clarendon.

Evans-Pritchard, E. E. (1970). Sexual inversion among the Azande, *American Anthropologist,* 72(6), 1430.

Evans-Pritchard, E. E. (1971). *The Azande.* Oxford: Clarendon.

Faron, L. C. (1961). *Mapuche social structure: Reintegration in a patrilineal society of central Chile.* Urbana, IL: University of Illinois Press.

Faron, L. C. (1964). *Hawks of the sun: Mapuche mortality and its ritual attributes.* Pittsburgh, PA: University of Pittsburgh Press.

Faron, L. C. (1968). *The Mapuche Indians of Chile.* New York: Holt, Rinehart & Winston.

Fillmore, R. (1989). Ph.D. survey results: 1988 doctor rate update. *Anthropology Newsletter,* 30(3), 30–32.

Fischer, J. (1961). Art styles as cultural cognitive maps. *American Anthropologist, 63,* 80–84.

Fischer, J. (1972). Why do prospects fail to come up to expectations? *CENTO Seminar on Agricultural Planning* (pp. 106–113). Ankara, Turkey: Public Relations Division, Central Treaty Organization.

Flannery, K. V. (1971). The origins and ecological effects of early domestication in Iran and the Near East. In S. Struever (Ed.), *Prehistoric agriculture* (pp. 50–79). Garden City, NY: Natural History Press. (Original work published in P. J. Ucko & G. W. Dimbleby, *The domestication and exploration of plants and animals.* (1969). Chicago: Aldine)

Ford, C. S., & Beach, F. A. (1951). *Patterns of sexual behavior.* New York: Harper & Row.

Fortune, R. (1932). Incest. *Encyclopedia of the Social Sciences, 7,* 620–622.

Fortune, R. F. (1963). *Sorcerers of Dobu: The social anthropology of the Dobu Islands of the Western Pacific.* New York: E. P. Dutton. (Original work published 1932)

Foster, G. (1965). Peasant society and the image of limited good. *American Anthropologist, 67,* 293–315.

Foulks, E. F. (1972). *The arctic hysterias of the north Eskimo* (No. 10). In Maybury-Lewis, (Ed.), *An-thropological Studies* Washington, DC: American Anthropological Association.

Fouts, R. S., Fouts, D. H., & Schoenfeld, D. (1984). Cultural transmission of a human language in a chimpanzee mother-infant relation. *Sign Language Studies,* 42 (Spring), 1–17.

Fox, R. (1967). *Kinship and marriage: An anthropological perspective.* Baltimore, MD: Penguin.

Frake, C. O. (1961). The diagnosis of disease among the Subanum of Mindanao. *American Anthropologist, 63,* 113–132.

Frake, C. O. (1964). A structural description of Subanum religious behavior. In W. Goodenough (Ed.), *Explorations in cultural anthropology* (pp. 111–129). New York: McGraw-Hill.

Frayser, S. G. (1985). *Varieties of sexual experience: An anthropological perspective on human sexuality.* New Haven, CT: HRAF.

Frazer, J. (1910). *Totemism and exogamy* (Vols. 1-4). London: Macmillan.

Frazer, J. (1922). *The golden bough: A study in magic and religion* (Vols. 1-12). New York: Macmillan. (Originally printed in 12 vols., London: Macmillan)

Freeman, D. (1983). *Margaret Mead in Somoa: The making and unmaking of an anthropological myth.* Cambridge, MA: Harvard University Press.

Freuchen, P. (1935). *Arctic adventure.* New York: Farrar & Rinehart.

Fried, M. H. (1967). *The evolution of political society: An essay in political anthropology.* New York: Random House.

Friedl, E. (1975). *Women and men: An anthropologist's view.* New York: Holt, Rinehart & Winston.

Frisch, R. (1975). Critical weights, a critical body composition, menarche and the maintenance of menstrual cycles. In E. Watts, F. Johnston, & G. Lasker (Eds.), *Biosocial interrelations in population adaptation* (pp. 309–318). The Hague: Mouton.

Frisch, R., & McArthur, J. (1974). Menstrual cycles: Fatness as a determinant of minimum weight for height necessary for their maintenance or onset. *Science, 185,* 949–951.

Furst, P. T. (Ed.). (1972). *Flesh of the gods: The ritual use of hallucinations.* New York: Praeger.

Gallup Report, The. (1985). *Religion in America, 50 years: 1935-1985.* Reprint No. 236 (May).

Gardner, B. T., & Gardner, R. A. (1969). Teaching sign language to a chimpanzee. *Science, 165,* 664–672.

Gardner, B. T., & Gardner, R. A. (1985). Signs of intelligence in cross-fostered chimpanzees, *Philosophical Transactions of the Royal Society of London,* B308, 150–176.

Geertz, C. (1963). *Agricultural involution: The processes of ecological change in Indonesia.* Berkeley, CA: University of California Press.

Geertz, C. (1966). Religion as a cultural system. In M. Banton (Ed.), *Anthropological approaches to the study of religion.* London: Tavistock.

Geertz, C. (Ed.). (1971). *Myth, symbol, and culture.* New York: W. W. Norton.

Geertz, C. (1972). Deep play: Notes on the Balinese cockfight. *Daedalus, 101,* 1–37.

Geertz, C. (1973). *The interpretation of cultures*. New York: Basic Books.

Gibbs, J. L. (Ed.). (1965). *Peoples of Africa*. New York: Holt, Rinehart & Winston.

Gloucester, R. of. (1905). *Robert of Gloucester's chronicle—how the Normans came to England*. In O. F. Emerson, *A Middle English Reader* (pp. 203–210). New York: Macmillan.

Goffman, E. (1955). On face-work: An analysis of ritual elements in social interaction. *Psychiatry, 18*, 213–231.

Goffman, E. (1961). *Asylums*. New York: Anchor.

Goffman, E. (1967). *Interaction ritual: Essay on face-to-face behavior*. Garden City, NY: Doubleday.

Goldman, I. (1972). *The Cubeo: Indians of the northwest Amazon*. Urbana, IL: The Illinois University Press.

Goldman, M. F. (1986). The Soviet Union: Striving for the ideal. In M. F. Goldman (Ed.), *Global Studies: The Soviet Union and Eastern Europe*, Guilford, CT: The Dushkin Publishing Group, Inc.

Goleman, D. (1978). Why the brain blocks daytime dreams. *Psychology Today, 9*(10), 69–70.

Gona, D. (Ed.). (1987). *State elective officials and the legislature: 1987–1988*. Lexington, KY: Council for State Governments.

Goode, W. J. (1963). *World revolution and family patterns*. New York: Free Press.

Goodenough, W. H. (1956). Componential analysis and the study of meaning. *Language, 32*, 195–216.

Goody, J. (1970). Cousin terms. *Southwestern Journal of Anthropology, 26*, 125–142.

Goody, J. (1973). Bridewealth and dowry in Africa and Eurasia. In J. Goody & S. J. Tambiah (Eds.), *Bridewealth and Dowry*. Cambridge: University of Cambridge Press.

Gordon, E. (1981). An analysis of the impact of labour migration on the lives of women in Lesotho. *Journal of Development Studies, 17*(3), 59–76.

Gorer, G. (1964). *The American people: A study in national character*. New York: W. W. Norton.

Gorer, G. (1966). *The danger of equality*. London: Cresset.

Gough, K. (1959). The Nayars and the definition of marriage. *Journal of the Royal Anthropological Institute, 89*, 23–34.

Gough, K. (1961). Nayar: Central Kerala. In D. Schneider & K. Gough (Eds.), *Matrilineal Societies*. Berkeley: University of California Press.

Graburn, N. (1971). *Readings in kinship and social structure*. New York: Harper & Row.

Greenberg, J. H. (1968). *Anthropological linguistics: An introduction*. New York: Random House.

Gregerson. E. (1983). *Sexual practices: The story of human sexuality*. New York: Watts.

Gregor, T. (1983). Dark dreams about the white man. *Natural History, 92*(1), pp. 8–14.

Grinnell, G. B. (1961). *The Cheyenne Indians: Their history and ways of life* (Vol. 2). New York: Cooper Square Publishers.

Gudschinsky, S. C. (1956). The ABC's of lexicostatistics (glotto-chronology). *Word, 12*, 175–210.

Gussow, Z. (1960). Pibloktoq (hysteria) among the polar Eskimo: An ethnopsychiatric study. In W. Muensterberger & S. Axelrad (Eds.), *The psychoanalytic studies of society* (Vol. 1). New York: International University Press.

Gussow, Z. (1963). A preliminary report of kayak-angst among the Eskimo of West Greenland: A study in sensory deprivation. *International Journal of Social Psychiatry, 9*, 18–26.

Guthrie, S. (1980). A cognitive theory of religion. *Current Anthropology, 2*, 181–203.

Hall, E. T. (1959). *The silent language*. Greenwich, CT: Fawcett Publications.

Harding, T. G. (1960). Adaptation and stability. In M. D. Sahlens & E. R. Service (Eds.), *Evolution and culture* (pp. 45–68). Ann Arbor, MI: University of Michigan Press.

Harner, M. (1977). The ecological basis of Aztec cannibalism. *American Ethnologist, 4*(1), 117–135.

Harré, R. (1984). *Personal being*. Cambridge, MA: Harvard University Press.

Harris, G. (1957). Possession 'hysteria' in a Kenya tribe. *American Anthropologist, 59*, 1046–1066.

Harris, M. (1968). *The rise of anthropological theory: A history of theories of culture*. New York: Crowell.

Harris, M. (1974). *Cows, pigs, wars and witches: The riddle of culture*. New York: Random House.

Harris, M. (1979). *Cultural materialism*. New York: Thomas Y. Crowell.

Harris, M. (1979). *Cultural materialism: The struggle for a science of culture*. New York: Random House.

Harris, M. (1981). *America now: The anthropology of a changing culture*. New York: Simon & Schuster.

Harris, M. (1986). *Good to eat*. New York: Harper & Row.

Haub, C., & Kent, M. (1988). *1988 world population data sheet*. Washington, DC: Population Reference Bureau.

Hayami, Y., & Kikuchi, M. (1981). *Asian village economy at the crossroads: An economic approach to institutional change*. Tokyo: University of Tokyo Press and Baltimore, MD: The Johns Hopkins University Press.

Hayes, K. J., & Nissen, C. H. (1971). Higher mental functions of a home-raised chimpanzee. In A. M. Schrier & F. Stollnitz (Eds.), *Behavior of non-human primates*. (Vol. 4, pp. 59–115). New York: Academic Press.

Heeren, J., Lindsay, D. B., & Mason, M. (1984). The Mormon concept of mother in heaven. *Journal for the Scientific Study of Religion, 23*(4), 396–411.

Herdt, G. (1984). *Ritualized homosexuality in Melanesia*. Berkeley: University of California Press. (Originally published 1982, Mitchell Beazley Publishers, London)

Herskovits, M. J. (1940). *The economic life of primitive peoples*. New York: Knopf.

Hill, J. (1978). Apes and language. *Annual Review of Anthropology, 7*, 89–112.

Hoebel, E. A. (1949). *Man in the primitive world*. New York: McGraw-Hill.

Hoebel, E. A. (1954). *The law of primitive man: A study in comparative legal dynamics*. Cambridge, MA: Harvard University Press.

Hoijer, H. (1964). Cultural implications of some Navaho linguistic categories. In D. Hymes (Ed.), *Language in culture and society: A reader in linguistics and anthropology* (pp. 142–153). New York: Harper & Row.

Hollingshead, A. B., & Redlich, F. C. (1953). Social stratification and psychiatric disorders. *American Sociological Review, 18,* 163–169.

Holmberg, A. R. (1950). *Nomads of the long bow: The Sirionó of eastern Bolivia.* Institute of Social Anthropology Publication No. 10. Washington, D.C.: Smithsonian Institution.

Honigmann, J. J., & Honigmann, I. (1965). *Eskimo townsmen.* Ottawa: University of Ottawa.

Hosken, F. P. (1980). Women and health: Genital and sexual mutilation of women. *International Journal of Women's Studies,* 3(1–3), 300–316.

Hsien, R. (1963). A consideration on Chinese concepts of illness and case illustrations. *Transcultural Psychiatry Research, 15,* 23–30.

Hsien, R. (1965). A study of the aetiology of koro in respect to the Chinese concept of illness. *International Journal of Social Psychiatry, 11,* 7–13.

Hsu, F. L. K. (1961). *Chinese and Americans: A study of two cultures.* New York: Henry Schuman.

Hsu, F. L. K. (Ed.). (1972). *Psychological anthropology: Approaches to culture and personality.* Morriston, NJ: Schenkman.

Hsu, F. L. K. (1983). *Rugged individualism reconsidered: Essays in psychological anthropology.* Knoxville, TN: University of Tennessee Press.

Hugh-Jones, S. (1979). *The Palm and the Pleiades.* New York: Cambridge University Press.

Hymes, D. (1964). *Language in culture and society: A reader in linguistics and anthropology.* New York: Harper & Row.

Hymes, D. (1967). Models of interaction of language and social setting. *Journal of Social Issues,* 23(2), 8–28.

Ihara, S. (1972). *Comrade loves of the Samurai.* Rutland: Tuttle.

Ineichen, B. (1979). The social geography of marriage. In M. Cook & G. Wilson (Eds.), *Love and attraction.* New York: Pergamon.

Jacobs, B. L. (1978). Serotonin, the crucial substance that turns off dreams. *Psychology Today,* 9(10), 70–71.

James, P. E. (with collaboration by Kline, H. V. B., Jr.). (1959). *A geography of man.* Boston: Ginn.

Jenness, D. (1922). *The Life of the Copper Eskimo,* Report of the Canadian Arctic Expedition 1913–1918, Vol. 12. Ontario, Canada: The National Museum of Canada.

Johnson, P. (1979). *The civilization of ancient Egypt.* London: Weidenfeld & Nicholson.

Joint Economic Committee, Congress of the United States. (1986). Concentration of wealth in the U.S.: Trends in the distribution of wealth among American families. Washington, DC: U.S. Government Printing Office.

Jorgensen, J. G., & Truzzi, M. (1974). *Anthropology and American life.* Englewood Cliffs, NJ: Prentice Hall.

Kaplan, D. (1960). The law of cultural dominance. In M. D. Sahlins & E. R. Service (Eds.), *Evolution and culture* (pp. 69–92). Ann Arbor, MI: University of Michigan Press.

Kaplan, D., & Manners, R. A. (1972). *Culture theory.* Englewood Cliffs, NJ: Prentice Hall.

Kardiner, A. (1946). *The individual and his society.* New York: Golden Press.

Katz, J. J. (1972). *Semantic theory.* New York: Harper & Row.

Keesing, R. M. (1975). *Kin groups and social structure.* New York: Holt, Rinehart & Winston.

Keller, H. (1954). *The story of my life.* Garden City, NY: Doubleday and Company.

Kellog, W. N. (1968). Communication and language in the home-raised chimpanzee. *Science* 162, 423–427.

Kelly, R. (1976). Witchcraft and sexual relations. In P. Brown & G. Buchbinder (Eds.), *Man and woman in the New Guinea highlands.* Washington: American Anthropological Association.

Kemper, T. D. (1978). *A social interactional theory of emotions.* New York: John Wiley & Sons.

Kent, M. M., & Haub, C. (1985). *World population data sheet.* In E. M. Murphy *World population: Toward the next century.* Washington, DC: Population Reference Bureau.

Kenyatta, J. (1968). *Facing Mount Kenya: The tribal life of the Gikuyu.* New York: Random House.

Kerkhoff, A. C., & Davis, K. E. (1962). Values consensus and need complementary in mate selection. *American Sociological Review, 27,* 295–303.

Kiev, A. (1972). *Transcultural psychology.* New York: Macmillan.

Kispert, R. J. (1971). *Old English: An introduction.* New York: Holt, Rinehart & Winston.

Kluckhohn, C. (1944). *Navaho witchcraft.* Papers of the Peabody Museum of American Archeology and Ethnology, Harvard University, 22(2). Cambridge, MA: Harvard University Press.

Kluckhohn, C. (1965). Recurrent themes in myth and myth-making. In A. Dundes (Ed.), *The study of folklore* (pp. 158–168). Englewood Cliffs, NJ: Prentice Hall.

Kluckhohn, C., & Leighton, D. (1962). *The Navaho.* Garden City, NY: Doubleday. (Originally published 1946 by the President and Fellows of Harvard University)

Koestler, A. (1964). *The act of creation.* New York: Macmillan.

Kolanda, P. (1978). *Castes in contemporary India.* Menlo Park, CA: Cummings.

Kolata, G. B. (1974). !Kung hunter-gatherers: Feminism, diet and birth control. *Science, 185,* 932–934.

Kramer, S. N. (1959). *History begins at Sumer.* Garden City, NY: Doubleday.

Kroeber, A. L. (1939). Cultural and natural areas of native North America. *American Archaeology and Ethnology, 38.*

Kroeber, A. L. (1944). *Configurations of culture growth.* Berkeley, CA: University of California Press.

Kroeber, A. L., & Kluckhohn, C. (1952). *Culture: A critical review of concepts and definitions.* Papers of the *Peabody Museum of American Archaeology and Ethnology, 47,* (November 1). (Reprinted by Random House, n. d.)

Krupke, D. F., & Lavie, P. (1975). Ultradian rhythms: The 90-minute clock inside us. *Psychology Today, 8*(11), 54–57.

Kübler-Ross, E. (1969). *On death and dying.* New York: Macmillan.

Lancaster, J. B. (1968). Primate communication systems and the emergence of human language. In P. C. Jay (Ed.), *Primates: Studies in adaptation and variability* (pp. 447–454). New York: Holt, Rinehart & Winston.

Langness, L. L. (1965). Hysterical psychosis in the New Guinea highlands: A Bena Bena example. *Psychiatry, 28,* 258–277.

Lappé, F. M., & Collins, J. (1977). *Food first: Beyond the myth of scarcity.* New York: Random House.

Lawless, R., Sutlive, V. H., Jr., & Zamora, M. D. (1983). *Fieldwork: The human experience.* New York: Gordon & Breach.

Leach, E. (1969). Virgin birth. In E. Leach, *Genesis as myth and other essays.* London: Jonathan Cape.

Leaf, M. (1971). Baking and roasting: A compact demonstration of a cultural code. *American Anthropologist, 73,* 267–268.

Lee, G. R., & Kezis, M. (1968). Family structure and the status of the elderly. *Journal of Comparative Family Studies, 10,* 429–443.

Lee, R. B. (1972). *The Dobe !Kung.* New York: Holt, Rinehart & Winston.

Lee, R. B. (1979). *The !Kung San: Men, women and work in a foraging society.* Cambridge: Cambridge University Press.

Lee, R. B. & DeVore, I. (Eds.). (1968). *Man the hunter.* Chicago: Aldine.

Lee, R. B. & DeVore, I. (1968). Population growth and the beginnings of sedentary life among the !Kung Bushmen. In B. Spooner (Ed.), *Population growth: Anthropological implications* (pp. 329–342). Cambridge, MA: MIT Press.

Lehmann, A. C., & Myers, J. E. (1985). *Magic, witchcraft, and religion: An anthropological study of the supernatural.* Palo Alto, CA: Mayfield.

Lehmann, H. E. (1975). Schizophrenia: Clinical features. In A. M. Freedman, H. I. Kaplan, & B. J. Sadock (Eds.), *Comprehensive textbook of psychiatry-II* (Vol. 1, pp. 890–923). Baltimore, MD: Williams & Wilkins.

Lenneberg, E. H. (1967). *The biological foundations of language.* New York: Wiley.

Lessa, W. A., & Vogt, E. Z. (Eds.). (1979). *Reader in comparative religion.* (4th ed.). New York: Harper & Row.

Leventhal, H. (1975). The consequences of depersonalization during illness and treatment: An information-processing model. In J. Howard & A. Strauss (Eds.), *Humanizing health care* (pp. 119–162). New York: Wiley-Interscience.

Lévi-Strauss, C. (1950). *Structural anthropology.* C. Jacobson & B. G. Schoepf (Trans.). New York: Basic Books. Reprint, 1963.

Lévi-Strauss, C. (1955). The structural study of myth. *Journal of American Folklore, 67,* 428–444.

LeVine, R. A. (1973). *Culture, behavior and personality.* Chicago: Aldine.

LeVine, R. A. (Ed.). (1974). *Culture and personality: Contemporary readings.* Chicago: Aldine.

Lewis, I. M. (1971). *Ecstatic religion.* Baltimore: Penguin Books.

Lewis, O. (1966). Culture of poverty. *Scientific American, 215,* 19–25.

Lewis, L. S., & Brissett, D. (1967). Sex as work: A study of avocational counseling. *Social Problems, 15*(1) 8–18.

Li, An-che. (1937). Zuñi: Some observations and queries. *American Anthropologist, 39,* 62–77.

Linden, E. (1974). *Apes, men and language.* New York: Penguin.

Linnaeus, C. (1735). *Systema naturae per regna tria naturae secondum classes, ordines, species cum characteribus, differentiis, synonymis, locis.* Stockholm: Laurentii Salvii. (1956 photographic facsimile of the First Volume of the Tenth Edition. London: British Museum [Natural History])

Linton, R. (1936). *The study of man: An introduction.* New York: Appleton-Century-Crofts.

Llewellyn, K. N., & Hoebel, E. A. (1941). *The Cheyenne way.* Norman, OK: University of Oklahoma Press.

Lomax, A. (1968). *Folk song style and culture* (Publication No. 88). Washington, DC: American Association for the Advancement of Science.

Lomax, A., & Arensberg, C. M. (1977). A worldwide evolutionary classification of cultures by subsistence systems. *American Anthropologist, 18,* 659–708.

Lowie, R. H. (1937). *The history of ethnological theory.* New York: Holt, Rinehart & Winston.

Ludwig, A. M. (1972). Altered state of consciousness. In C. T. Tart (Ed.), *Altered states of consciousness* (pp. 11–24). Garden City, NY: Doubleday. (Original work published 1966, *Archives of General Psychiatry, 15,* 215–234)

Lustig-Arecco, V. (1975). *Technology: Strategies for Survival.* New York: Holt, Rinehart & Winston.

Maine, H.S. (1879). *Ancient law: Its connection with the early history of ideas, and its relation to modern ideas.* London: J. Murray.

Malinowski, B. (1922). *Argonauts of the western Pacific.* New York: Dutton.

Malinowski, B. (1926). *Crime and custom in savage society.* London: Rutledge & Kegan Paul.

Malinowski, B. (1929). *The sexual life of savages in northwestern Melanesia: An ethnographic account of courtship, marriage and family life among the natives of the Trobriand Islands, British New Guinea.* New York: Harcourt, Brace & World.

Malinowski, B. (1939). The group and the individual in functional analysis. *American Journal of Sociology, 44,* 938–964.

Mandelbaum, D. G. (1968). *Selected writings of Edward Sapir in language, culture and personality.* Berkeley, CA: University of California Press.

Mandelbaum, D. G. (1972). *Society in India.* Berkeley, CA: University of California Press.

Marett, R. R. (1909). *The threshold of religion.* London: Methuen.

Marriage: A garment of society. (1984). *Mahjubah*, 3(3), 16–19.

Marsella, A. J., DeVos, G., & Hsu, F. L. K. (Eds.). (1985). *Culture and self: Asian and western perspectives*. New York: Tavistock Publications.

Martin, M. K., & Voorhies, B. (1975). *Female of the species*. New York: Columbia University Press.

Marx, K. (1961). *Economic and philosophic manuscripts of 1844*. Moscow: Foreign Language Publishing House.

Mathews, R. H. (1900). Native tribes of western Australia. *Proceedings of the American Philosophical Society*, 39(161), 125.

McCarley, R. W. (1978). Where dreams come from: A new theory. *Psychology Today*, 12(7), 15–20.

Mead, M. (1928). *Coming of age in Samoa*. New York: Morrow.

Mead, M. (1950). *Sex and treatment in three primitive societies*. New York: Mentor.

Miller, S. N. (1974). The playful, the crazy and the nature of pretense. In E. Norbeck (Ed.), *The anthropological study of human play* (Rice University Studies 60[3]), 31–52. Houston, TX: William Rice University.

Minister of Supply and Services, The. (1988). *Canada yearbook: 1988*. Ottawa: The Minister of Supply and Services.

Minturn, L., & Lambert, W. W. (1964). *Mothers of six cultures: Antecedents of child rearing*. New York: Wiley.

Montagu, A. (1974). *Man's most dangerous myth: The fallacy of race*. Fair Lawn: Oxford University Press.

Montagu, A. (Ed.). (1980). *Sociobiology examined*. New York: Oxford University Press.

Morgan, L. H. (1851). *League of the ho-de-no-sau-nee or Iroquois*. Rochester, NY: Sage & Brothers.

Morgan, L. H. (1877). *Ancient society*. New York: World.

Moris, J. (1981). *Managing induced rural development*. Bloomington, IN: International Development Institute.

Mounin, G. (1976). Language, communication, chimpanzees. *Current Anthropology*, 17, 1–21.

Mueller, M. B. (1977). *Women and men in rural Lesotho: The periphery of the periphery*. Waltham, MA: Brandeis University.

Munroe, R. L., & Munroe, R. H. (1977). Male transvestism and subsistence economy, *The Journal of Social Psychology*, 103, 307–308.

Munroe, R. L., Munroe, R. H., & Whiting, J. (1973). The couvade: A psychological analysis. *Ethos*, 1(1), 30–74.

Munroe, R. L., Whiting, J. W. M., & Hally, D. J. (1969). Institutionalized male transvestism and sex distinctions, *American Anthropologist*, 71(1), 87–91.

Murdock, G. P. (1934). *Our primitive contemporaries*. New York: Macmillan.

Murdock, G. P. (1950). Family stability in non-European cultures. *Annals of the American Academy*, 272, 195–201.

Murdock, G. P. (1957). World ethnographic sample. *American Anthropologist*, 59, 664–487.

Murdock, G. P. (1967). *Ethnographic atlas*. Pittsburgh: The University of Pittsburgh Press.

Murdock, G. P., Ford, C. S., Hudson, A. E., Kennedy, R., Simmons, L. W., & Whiting, J. W. (1981). *Outline of cultural materials* (5th ed.). New Haven, CT: Human Relations Area Files.

Murphy, J. M. (1976). Psychiatric labeling in cross-cultural perspective. *Science*, 191(4230), 1019–1028.

Murphy, R. F., & Kasdan, L. (1959). The structure of parallel cousin marriage. *American Anthropologist*, 61, 17–29.

Musil, A. (1928). *Manners and customs of the Rwala Bedouins*. New York: The American Geographical Society.

Nader, L. (Ed.) (1965). The ethnography of law. *American Anthropologist* (special supplement to Vol. 67, pp. 3–32).

Nader, L., & Todd, H. F., Jr. (1978). *The disputing process: Law in ten societies*. New York: Columbia University Press.

Nanda, S. (1988). More dialogue on the 'bloodthirsty' Semai. *American Anthropologist*, 90(2), 422–423.

Naroll, R. (1966). Does military deterrence deter? *Trans-Action*, 3(2), 14–20.

Naroll, R. (1973). Holocultural theory tests. In R. Naroll & F. Naroll (Eds.), *Main currents in cultural anthropology* (pp. 309–384). New York: Appleton-Century-Crofts.

Nash, M. (1966). *Primitive and peasant economic systems*. San Francisco: Chandler.

Nassehi-Behnam, V. (1985). Change and the Iranian family. *Current Anthropology*, 26, 557–562.

National Center for Health Statistics, Vital and Health Statistics. (1963). *Divorce statistics analysis United States* (Series 21, No. 13, Table C). Washington, DC: U.S. Government Printing Office.

Neale, W. C. (1976). *Monies in societies*. San Francisco: Chandler & Sharp.

Needham, R. (Ed.). (1972). *Rethinking kinship and marriage*. London: Tavistock.

Nemiah, J. C. (1975). Phobic neurosis. In A. M. Freedman, H. I. Kaplan, & B. J. Sadock (Eds.), *Comprehensive textbook of psychiatry-II* (Vol. 2, pp. 1247–1255). Baltimore, MD: Williams and Wilkins.

Neusner, J. (1979). *The Talmud as anthropology*. NY: The Jewish Theological Seminary of America.

Newman, P. L. (1964). Wild man behavior in a New Guinea highlands community. *American Anthropologist*, 66, 1–19.

Noll, R. (1985). Mental imagery cultivation as a cultural phenomenon: The role of visions in shamanism. *Current Anthropology*, 26, 443–461.

O'Kelley, C. G. (1980). *Women and men in society*. New York: Van Nostrand.

Otterbein, K. F. (1970). *The evolution of war*. New Haven: HRAF.

Otto, R. (1923). *The idea of the holy: An inquiry into the non-rational factor in the idea of the divine and its relation to the rational*. J. W. Harvey (Trans.). London: Oxford University Press.

Palmer, I. (1985). *The impact of male out-migration on women in farming*. West Hartford, CT: Kumarian Press.

Parker, S. (1962). Eskimo psychopathology in the context of Eskimo personality and culture. *American Anthropologist, 64*, 76–96.

Pasternak, B. (1976). *Introduction to kinship and social organization.* Englewood Cliffs, NJ: Prentice Hall.

Patterson, F. (1978). Conversations with a gorilla. *National Geographic, 154*(4), 438–465.

Paul, R. A. (1978). Instinctive aggression in man: The Semai case. *Journal of Anthropology, 1*(1), 65–79.

Pelto, P. J., & Pelto, G. H. (1978). *Anthropological research: The structure of inquiry* (2nd ed.). New York: Cambridge University Press.

Peters, L. G., & Price-Williams, D. R. (1980). Towards an experiential analysis of shamanism. *American Ethnologist, 7*, 397–418.

Phillips. D. L. (1963). Rejection: A possible consequence of seeking help for mental disorders. *American Sociological Review, 28*, 963–972.

Pike, K. (1954). *Language in relation to a unified theory of the structure of human behavior,* Vol 1. Glendale: Summer Institute of Linguistics.

Popkin, S. L. (1979). *The rational peasant: The political economy of rural society in Vietnam.* Berkeley: University of California Press.

Popov, A. A. (1936). *Tavgytsy: Matgerialy po ethnografi avamskikh i vedeyevskikh tavgytzevi.* Moscow and Leningrad: AN, Trudy Instituta Anthropologii i Ethnografii I, 5.

Pospisil, L. (1971). *Anthropology of law: A comparative theory.* New York: Harper & Row.

Pospisil, L. (1972). *The ethnology of law.* (Module 12). Reading, MA: Addison-Wesley Modular Publications.

Poussaint, A. F. (1967, August 20). A Negro psychiatrist explains the Negro psyche. *New York Times,* Section 6, pp. 52–80.

Powell, B., & Jacobs, J. A. (1983). Sex and consensus in occupational prestige ratings. *Sociology and Social Research 67*(4), 392–404.

Premack, A. J., & Premack, D. (1972). Teaching language to an ape. *Scientific American, 227*, 92–99.

Price-Williams, D. R. (1975). *Explorations in cross-cultural psychology.* San Francisco, CA: Chandler & Sharp.

Price-Williams, D. R. (1985). On mental imagery and shamanism. *Current Anthropology, 26*(5), 656.

Price-Williams, D. R. (n.d.). The waking dream in ethnographic perspective. In B. Tedlock (Ed.), *Dreaming: The anthropology and psychology of the imaginal.* Albuquerque, NM: University of New Mexico Press.

Rabinow, P. (1977). *Reflections on fieldwork in Morocco.* Berkeley: University of California.

Radcliffe-Brown, A. R. (1952). *Structure and function in primitive society.* London: Oxford University Press.

Radcliffe-Brown, A. R. (1958). Taboo. In W. A. Lessa & E. Z. Vogt (Eds.), *Reader in comparative religion: An anthropological approach* (pp. 45–68). Evanston, IL: Row, Peterson.

Radin, P. (1937). *Primitive religion.* New York: Dover.

Rappaport, R. A. (1967). Ritual regulation of environmental relations among a New Guinea people. *Ethnology, 6*, 17–30

Rappaport, R. A. (1968). *Pigs for the ancestors: Ritual in the ecology of a Papua New Guinea people.* New Haven, CT: Yale University Press.

Rassmussen, K. (1922). *Grønlandsagen.* Berlin: Gyldendal'scher Verlag.

Rattray, R. S. (1923). *Ashanti.* London: Oxford University Press.

Rattray, R. S. (1929). *Ashanti law and constitution.* London: Clarendon Press.

Redfield, R., & Rojas, A. V. (1934). *Chan Kom, A Maya village.* Carnegie Institution Publication 448. Washington, DC: The Carnegie Institution.

Reiss, I. L. (1986). *Journey into sexuality: An exploratory voyage.* Englewood Cliffs, NJ: Prentice Hall.

Ribiero, D. (1971). *The Americas and civilization.* New York: Dutton.

Riley, P. J. (1989). *The effect of newly introduced technology on women agriculturalists in Lesotho.* Final Report, USAID Lesotho Consultancy.

Rivers, W. H. R. (1906). *The Todas.* New York: Macmillan.

Rivers, W. H. R. (1914). *The history of Melanesian society.* Cambridge, MA: Cambridge University Press.

Robarcheck, C. A. (1987). Blood drunkenness and the bloodthirsty Semai: Unmaking another anthropological myth. *American Anthropologist, 89*(2), 356–365.

Robarcheck, C. A., & Dentan, R. K. (1979). Conflict, emotion, and abreaction: Resolution of conflict among the Semai Senoi. *Ethos, 7*, 104–123.

Roberts, J., Arth, M. J., & Bush, R. R. (1959). Games in culture. *American Anthropologist, 61*, 597–605.

Roberts, J., & Sutton-Smith, B. (1962). Child training and game involvement. *Ethnology, 1*, 166–185.

Roberts, S. (1979). *Order and dispute: An introduction to legal anthropology.* New York: St. Martin's.

Robinson, J. T. (1972). *Early hominid posture and locomotion.* Chicago: University of Chicago Press.

Rodney, W. (1972). *How Europe underdeveloped Africa.* London: Bogle-L'Ouverture Publications.

Rosaldo, M. Z., & Lamphere, L. (Eds.). (1974). *Woman, culture, and society.* Stanford, CA: Stanford University Press.

Rosenhahn, D. L. (1973). On being sane in insane places. *Science, 179*, 250–258.

Roth, W. E. (1903). Superstition, magic and medicine. *North Queensland Ethnographic Bulletin 5.* Brisbane: G. A. Vaughn, Government Printer, Home Secretary's Department.

Rubel, A. J. (1960). Concepts of disease in Mexican-American culture. *American Anthropologist, 62*, 795–814.

Rubin, Z. (1973). *Liking and loving: An invitation to social pyschology.* New York: Holt, Rinehart & Winston.

Ruby J. (Ed.). (1982). *A crack in the mirror: Reflexive perspectives in anthropology.* Philadelphia: University of Pennsylvania Press.

Rumbaugh, D. M. (1977). *Language learning by a*

chimpanzee: The Lana project. New York: Academic Press.

Rumbaugh, D. M., von Glasersfeld, E. C., Warner, H., et al. (1977). A computer-controlled language training system for investigating the language skills of young apes. *Biological Research Methods and Instruments, 5,* 355–362.

Safilios-Rothschild, C. (1985). The persistence of women's invisibility in agriculture: Theoretical and policy lessons from Lesotho and Sierra Leone. *Economic Development and Cultural Change, 33*(1), 299–317.

Sahlins, M. D. (1960). The origins of society. *Scientific American, 203,* 76–89.

Sahlins, M. D. (1962). *Primitive social organization: An evolutionary perspective.* New York: Random House.

Sahlins, M. D. (1968). *Tribesmen.* Englewood Cliffs, NJ: Prentice Hall.

Sahlins, M. D. (1972). *Stone age economics.* New York: Aldine.

Sahlins, M. D. (1976). *Cultural and practical reason.* Chicago: University of Chicago Press.

Sahlins, M. D., & Service, E. R. (1960). *Evolution and culture.* Ann Arbor, MI: University of Michigan Press.

Sanday, P. R. (1981). *Female power and male dominance: On the origins of sexual inequality.* New York: Cambridge University Press.

Sapir, E. (1924). Culture, genuine and spurious. *American Journal of Sociology, 29,* 401–429.

Sapir, E. (1949). *Language: An introduction to the study of speech.* New York: Harcourt, Brace & World.

Sapir, E. (1970). Language. In D. G. Mandelbaum (Ed.), *Edward Sapir: Culture, language, and personality* (pp. 1–44). Berkeley, CA: University of California Press.

Saussure, F. de. (1959). *Course in modern linguistics* (W. Baskin, Trans.). New York: The Philosophical Library.

Savage-Rumbaugh, E. S., Pate, J. L., Lawson, J, Smith, S. T., & Rosenbaum, S. (1983). Can a chimpanzee make a statement? *Journal of Experimental Psychology: General, 112*(4), 457–492.

Savage-Rumbaugh, E. S., Rumbaugh, D. M., & Boysen, S. L. (1980). *American Scientist, 68,* 49–61.

Scheff, T. (1966). *Being mentally ill: A sociological theory* Chicago: Aldine.

Scheff, T. (1977). The distancing of emotion in ritual. *Current Anthropology, 18*(3), 483–506.

Schlegel, A., & Barry, H., III. (1986). The cultural consequences of female contribution to subsistence. *American Anthropologist, 88,* 144–150.

Schlegel, A., & Eloul, R. (1988). Marriage transactions: Labor, property, status. *American Anthropologist, 90*(2), 291–309.

Schneider, D. M. (1968). *American kinship: A cultural account.* Englewood Cliffs, NJ: Prentice Hall.

Schneider, D. M. (1980). *American kinship: A cultural account.* (2nd Ed.). Chicago: University of Chicago Press.

Schneider, D. M., & Gough, K. (Eds.). (1961).

Matrilineal kinship. Berkeley: University of California Press.

Schusky, E. L. (1971). *Manual for kinship analysis* (2nd ed.). New York: Holt, Rinehart & Winston.

Schusky, E. L. (1975). *Variation in kinship.* New York: Holt, Rinehart & Winston.

Scoditti, G. (1983). Kula on Kitava. In J. Leach & E. Leach (Eds.), *The Kula: New perspectives in Massim exchange.* New York: Cambridge University Press.

Scott, J. C. (1976). *The moral economy of the peasant: Rebellion and subsistence in Southeast Asia.* New Haven, CT: Yale University Press.

Scott, R. (1969). *The making of blind men.* New York: Russell Sage Foundation.

Scull, A. (1979). *Museums of madness: The social organizations of insanity in nineteenth century England.* New York: St. Martin's Press.

Segall, M. H., Campbell, D. T., & Herskovits, M. J. (1966). *The influence of culture on visual perception.* Indianapolis, IN: Bobbs-Merrill.

Selye, H. (1976). *The stress of life.* New York: McGraw-Hill.

Service, E. R. (1962). *Primitive social organization: An evolutionary perspective.* New York: Random House.

Service, E. R. (1971). *Cultural evolutionism: Theory in practice.* New York: Holt, Rinehart & Winston.

Service, E. R. (1975). *The origins of the state and civilization: The process of cultural evolution.* New York: W. W. Norton.

Service, E. R. (1978). *Profiles in ethnology.* New York: Harper & Row.

Service, E. R. (1979). *The hunters* (2nd ed.). Englewood Cliffs, NJ: Prentice Hall.

Sharon, D. (1978). *Wizard of the four winds: A shaman's story.* New York: Macmillan.

Sharp, L. (1952). Steel axes for stone age Australians. In E. H. Spicer (Ed.), *Human problems in technological change* (pp. 69–90). New York: Russell Sage Foundation.

Shepherd, G., & Shepherd, G. (1984). *A kingdom transformed: Rhetorical patterns with institutionalization of Mormonism.* Salt Lake City, UT: University of Utah Press.

Shostak, M. (1982). *Nisa: The life and words of a !Kung woman.* New York: Random House.

Sihler, A. L. (1973). Baking and roasting. *American Anthropologist, 75,* 1721–1725.

Simmons, L. W. (Ed.). (1942). *Sun Chief: The autobiography of a Hopi Indian.* New Haven, CT: Yale University Press.

Simons, R. C., & Hughes, C. C. (1985). *The culture-bound syndromes: Folk illnesses of psychiatric and anthropological interest.* Boston: D. Reidel

Spindler, G. D. (Ed.). (1970). *Being an anthropologist: Fieldwork in eleven cultures.* New York: Holt, Rinehart & Winston.

Spradley, J. F. (1980). *Participant observation.* New York: Holt, Rinehart & Winston.

Stephens, W. N. (1963). *The family in cross-cultural perspective.* New York: Holt, Rinehart & Winston.

Steward, J. H. (1938). Great-Basin sociopolitical groups. *Bureau of American Ethnology Bulletin 120.*

Washington, DC: U.S. Government Printing Office.

Steward, J. H. (1949). Cultural causality and law: A trial formulation of the development of early civilizations. *American Anthropologist, 51,* 1–27.

Steward, J. H. (1955). *The theory of cultural change: The methodology of multilinear evolution.* Urbana, IL: University of Illinois press.

Stockwell, E. G., & Laidlaw, K. A. (1981a). *Third world: Problems and prospects.* Chicago: Nelson-Hall.

Stockwell, E. G., & Laidlaw, K. A. (1981b). *Third world development.* Chicago: Nelson-Hall.

Stow, G. W. (1905). *The native races of South Africa: A history of the intrusion of the Hottentots and Bantu into the hunting grounds of the Bushmen, the aborigines of the country.* London: S. Sonnenschein.

Sussman, R. (1972). Child transport, family size and the increase in human population size during the neolithic. *Current Anthropology, 13,* 258–267.

Swanson, G. E. (1960). *The birth of the gods: The origin of primitive beliefs.* Ann Arbor, MI: University of Michigan Press.

Swartz, M. J., Turner, V. W., & Tuden, A. (Eds). (1966). *Political Anthropology.* Chicago: Aldine.

Szasz, T. (1970). *Ideology and insanity: Essays on the dehumanization of man.* Garden City, NY: Doubleday.

Tanaka, J. (1977). Subsistence ecology of the Central Kalahari !Kung. In R. B. Lee & I. Devore (Eds.), *Kalahari hunter gatherers* (pp. 99–119). Cambridge, MA: Harvard University Press.

Tanfer, K., & Horn, M. (1985). Contraceptive use, pregnancy and fertility patterns among single American women in their 20's. *Family Planning Perspective, 17*(1), 10–19.

Terrace, H. S. (1979). *Nim.* New York: Knopf.

Terrace, H. S., Pettito, L. A., Sanders, R. V., & Bever, T. G. (1979). Can an ape create a sentence? *Science, 206,* 891–902.

Terrace, H. S., Pettito, L., Sanders, R. J. & Bever, T. G. (1980). On the grammatical capacity of apes. In *Children's language* (Vol. 2., pp. 371–495). New York: Garner Press.

Thomas, E. M. (1959). *The harmless people.* New York: Knopf.

Tien, H. Y. (1983). China: Demographic billionaire. *Population Bulletin, 38*(2). Washington, DC: Population Reference Bureau.

Times Mirror. (1987). The people, press & politics. Reading, MA: Addison Wesley.

Toelkin, B. (1979). *The dynamics of folklore.* Boston: Houghton Mifflin.

Tonkinson, R. (1974). *The Jigalong mob: Aboriginal victors of the desert crusade.* Menlo Park, CA: Cummings.

Toth, E. L. (1986). *The velvet ghetto.* Research Report, San Francisco: International Association of Business Consultants Foundation.

Toth, E. L. (1989). *Beyond the velvet ghetto.* Research Report, San Francisco: International Association of Business Consultants Foundation.

Turnbull, C. M. (1961). *The forest people: A study of the pygmies of the Congo.* New York: Simon & Schuster.

Turnbull, C. M. (1965). The Mbuti pygmy of the Congo. In J. L. Gibbs, Jr. (Ed.), *Peoples of Africa* (pp. 279–317). New York: Holt, Rinehart & Winston.

Tyler, E. B. (1871). *Primitive culture: Researches into the development of mythology, philosophy, religion, language, art and custom.* London: J. Murray.

Uberoi, J. P. S. (1962). *The politics of the Kula ring: An analysis of the findings of Bronislaw Malinowski.* Manchester: University of Manchester Press.

United Nations. (1989). The prospects of world urbanization as of 1984–1985. NY: United Nations.

U.S. Bureau of the Census. (1984). Projections of the population of the United States by age, sex and race: 1985–2080. In *Current population reports: Population estimates and projections* (Series P-25, No. 952). (Table 2, p. 30). Washington, DC: U.S. Government Printing Office.

U.S. Bureau of the Census. (1985). *Statistical abstract of the United States: 1986* (106th ed.). Washington, DC: U.S. Government Printing Office.

U.S. Bureau of the Census (1989). *Statistical abstract of the United States: 1989* (109th ed.). Washington, DC: U.S. Government Printing Office.

U.S. Department of Labor, Employment and Training Administration. (1977). *Dictionary of occupational titles.* Washington, DC: U.S. Government Printing Office.

U.S. Federal Bureau of Investigation. (1985). *Uniform Crime Reports.* Washington, DC: U.S. Government Printing Office.

U.S. National Commission on the Causes and Prevention of Violence. (1969). *Justice: To establish justice, to ensure domestic tranquility.* Final Report. Washington, DC: U.S. Government Printing Office.

Van Gennep, A. (1960). *The rites of passage.* S. T. Kimball (Trans.). Chicago: University of Chicago Press. (Originally published 1908)

Van Loon, F. H. G. (1926). Amok and latah. *Journal of Abnormal and Social Psychology, 21,* 434–444.

Vayda, A. P. (Ed.). (1969). *Environment and cultural behavior: Ecological studies in cultural anthropology.* New York: Natural History Press.

Vayda, A. P. (1976). *War in ecological perspective.* New York: Plenum.

Vayda, A. P., & Rappaport, R. A. (1968). Ecology: Cultural and noncultural. In J. H. Clifton (Ed.), *Introduction to cultural anthropology.* Boston: Houghton Mifflin.

Vetter, B. M., & Babco, E. L. (1986). *Professional women and minorities: A manpower resource data service.* Washington, DC: Commission on Professionals in Science and Technology.

Walker, E. (1972). *The emergent Native Americans.* Boston, MA: Little, Brown.

Wallace, A. F. C. (1961). *Culture and personality.* New York: Random House.

Wallace, A. F. C. (1966). *Religion: An anthropological view.* New York: Random House.

Wallace, A. F. C. (1972, New edition). Mental illness, biology, and culture. In F. L. K. Hsu (Ed.), *Psychological anthropology* (pp. 363–402). Cambridge, MA: Schenkman.

Warner, W. L. (1953). *American life: Dream and reality.* Chicago: University of Chicago Press.

Watzlawick, P., Beavin, J. H., & Jackson, D. (1962). *Pragmatics of human communication: A study of interactional patterns, pathologies, and paradoxes.* New York: W. W. Norton.

Weis, J. (1974). The Gemblakan: Kept boys among the Javanese of Ponorogo. Paper presented at the American Anthropological Association meetings, Mexico City.

Wertheimer, M. (1938). Laws of organization in perceptual forms. In W. D. Ellis, *A sourcebook of Gestalt psychology* (pp. 73–88). New York: Farrar, Straus & Giroux.

West, J. (1945). *Plainville, U.S.A.* New York: Columbia University Press.

White, D. R. (1987). *Cultural diversity data base.* La Jolla, CA: National Collegiate Software Clearinghouse.

White, D. R. (1988). Causes of polygyny: Ecology, economy, kinship, and warfare. *American Anthropologist, 90*(4) 871–887.

White D. R. (1988). Rethinking polygyny: Cowives, codes, and cultural systems. *Current Anthropology, 29*(4), 529–572.

White, L. A. (1939). A problem in kinship terminology, *American Anthropologist, 41,* 569–570.

White, L. A. (1949). *The science of culture: A study of man and civilization.* New York: Grove Press.

White, L. A. (1959). *The evolution of culture.* New York: McGraw-Hill.

White, L. A. (1971). *The science of culture: A study of man and culture.* New York: Farrar, Straus & Giroux.

Whiting, B. (1950). *Paiute sorcery (No. 15).* New York: Viking Fund Publications in Anthropology.

Whiting, J. W. M. (1959). Cultural and sociological influences on development. In *Growth and development of the child in his setting* (pp. 3–9). Baltimore, MD: Maryland Child Growth and Development Institute.

Whiting, J. W. M. (1964). Effects of climate on certain cultural practices. In W. H. Goodenough (Ed.), *Explorations in cultural anthropology: Essays in honor of George Peter Murdock* (pp. 175–195). New York: McGraw-Hill.

Whiting, J. W. M., & Child, I. L. (1953). *Child training and personality: A cross-cultural study.* New Haven, CT: Yale University Press.

Whiting, J. W. M., Kluckhohn, R., & Anthony, A. S. (1958). The function of male initiation ceremonies at puberty. In E. E. Maccoby, T. M. Newcomb, & E. L. Hartley, *Readings in social psychology* (pp. 359–370). New York: Holt, Rinehart & Winston.

Whiting, R. (1979, September 25). You've gotta have 'Wa.' *Sports Illustrated,* pp. 60–71.

Whorf, B. L. (1971a). Languages and logic. In J. B. Carroll (Ed.), *Language, thought and reality: Selected writings of Benjamin Lee Whorf* (pp. 233–245). Cambridge, MA: The MIT Press.

Whorf, B. L. (1971b). The relation of habitual thought and behavior to language. In J. B. Carroll (Ed.), *Language, thought, and reality: Selected writings of Benjamin Lee Whorf* (pp. 134–159). Cambridge, MA: The MIT Press.

Williams, F. E. (1936). *Papuans of the Trans-Fly.* London: Oxford University Press.

Wilson, B. (1980). Kut: Catharsis, ritual healing or redressive strategy? Paper presented at the Conference on Korean Religion and Society. Mackinac Island, MI.

Wilson, E. O. (1975). *Sociobiology: The new synthesis.* Cambridge, MA: Harvard University Press.

Wilson, E. O. (1978). *Human nature.* Cambridge, MA: Harvard University Press.

Wilson, M. H. (1951). Witch beliefs and social structure. *American Journal of Sociology, 56,* 307–313.

Winiarz, W., & Wielawski, J. (1936). Imu—A psychoneurosis occuring among Ainus. *Psychoanalytic Review, 23,* 181–186.

Witherspoon, G. (1977). *Language and art in the Navajo universe.* Ann Arbor, MI: University of Michigan Press.

Wittfogel, K. (1957). *Oriental despotism: A comparative study of total power.* New Haven, CT: Yale University Press.

Wittkower, E., & Fried, J. (1957). A cross-cultural approach to mental health problems. *American Journal of Psychiatry, 116,* 423–428.

Wolf, E. R. (1964). *Anthropology.* Englewood Cliffs, NJ: Prentice Hall.

Wolf, E. R. (1966). *Peasants.* Englewood Cliffs, NJ: Prentice Hall.

Wolf, E. R. (1969). *Peasant wars of the twentieth century.* New York: Harper and Row.

Worsley, P. (1957). *The trumpet shall sound: A study of "cargo" cults in Melanesia.* London: MacGibbon & Kee.

Wright, G. D. (1954). Projection and displacement: A cross-cultural study of folk-tale aggression. *Journal of Abnormal and Social Psychology, 49,* 523–528.

Yap, P. M. (1951). Mental illness peculiar to certain cultures: A survey of comparative psychiatry. *Journal of Mental Science, 97,* 313–327.

Yap, P. M. (1963). Koro or suk-yeong—An atypical culture-bound psychogenic disorder found in southern Chinese. *Transcultural Psychiatric Research, 1,* 36–38.

Yap, P. M. (1965). Koro: A culture-bound depersonalization syndrome. *British Journal of Psychiatry, 111,* 43–50.

Zelnick, M., & Kantner, J. (1977). Sexual and contraceptive experiences of young unmarried women in the United States, 1976 and 1971. *Family Planning Perspectives, 9,* 55–71.

Zetterberg, P. (Ed.). *Conference on Evolution and Public Education: Resources and References.* St. Paul, MN: University of Minnesota Center for Educational Development.

Index

Page references in **bold** indicate glossed terms.

Staff

Editor   M. Marcuss Oslander
Production Manager   Brenda S. Filley
Designers   Harry Rinehart and Charles Vitelli
Art Editor   Pamela Carley Petersen
Typesetting Supervisor   Libra Ann Cusack
Typesetter   Juliana Arbo
Systems Coordinator   Richard Tietjen
Editoral Assistant   Diane Barker

Kinship charts by Rex Doane.
Cover design by Harry Rinehart. Photo of Masai children by
Marc and Evelyne Bernheim—Woodfin Camp.